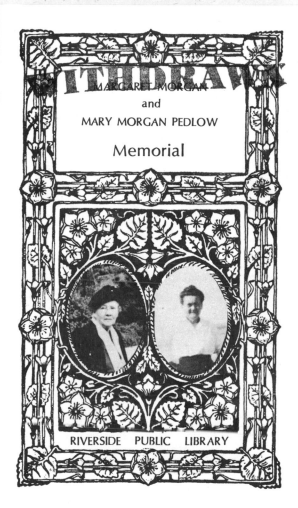

WITHDRAWN

MARGARET MORGAN
and
MARY MORGAN PEDLOW

Memorial

RIVERSIDE PUBLIC LIBRARY

The New York Times

CENTURY
-*of*-
BUSINESS

The New York Times

CENTURY
-*of*-
BUSINESS

Floyd Norris

and

Christine Bockelmann

Foreword by

Paul A. Volcker

McGraw-Hill

New York San Francisco Washington, D.C. Auckland Bogotá
Caracas Lisbon London Madrid Mexico City Milan
Montreal New Delhi San Juan Singapore
Sydney Tokyo Toronto

To our son, John
—F.N. & C.B.

McGraw-Hill
A Division of The **McGraw·Hill** *Companies*

1 2 3 4 5 6 7 8 9 0   COU/COU   9 0 9 8 7 6 5 4 3 2 1 0 9

ISBN 0–07–135589–8

Book design by Tina Thompson

This book was set in Minion and Interstate by Tina Thompson.

Printed and bound by Courier.

McGraw-Hill books are available at special quantity discounts to
use as premiums and sales promotions, or for use in corporate
training programs. For more information, please write to Director of
Special Sales, McGraw-Hill, 11 West 19th Street, New York, NY 10011.
Or contact your local bookstore.

Contents

Sources and Acknowledgments   vii

Foreword by Paul A. Volcker   ix

INTRODUCTION by Floyd Norris   1

CHAPTER ONE: 1900–1909
Roosevelt vs. Morgan   10

CHAPTER TWO: 1910–1919
World Unity, World War   34

CHAPTER THREE: 1920–1929
Prosperity—Then Ruin   60

CHAPTER FOUR: 1930–1939
Battling the Great Depression   82

CHAPTER FIVE: 1940–1949
From Devastation to Innovation   114

CHAPTER SIX: 1950–1959
What's Good for General Motors . . .   138

CHAPTER SEVEN: 1960–1969
A Long Boom   168

CHAPTER EIGHT: 1970–1979
Doubts and Deregulation   206

CHAPTER NINE: 1980–1989
The Great Turnaround   244

CHAPTER TEN: 1990–1999
The American Decade   284

Index   320

Sources and Acknowledgments

The principal source for this book is The New York Times. The articles chosen tell some of the most important and interesting business, financial and economic stories of the 20th century.

Each chapter covers a decade and opens with an overview and a timeline that highlights business events covered in the chapter. The primary article for each section is accompanied by an introduction and a reproduction of the page on which it appeared in The New York Times. In many cases, related articles and photos are printed to provide additional perspective. Along the top of the articles in each chapter is a stream of "headlines" covering other business events of the decade.

Many of the articles have been edited for length, and in some cases typographical errors have been corrected. But the articles have not been rewritten, allowing the reader to see how the style of The Times has evolved through the years.

In addition to back issues of The Times, a number of other sources were consulted in the preparation of this book. A particularly useful book in identifying subjects that might need to be covered was the "Chronology of Twentieth-Century History: Business and Commerce," edited by Frank N. Magill (Chicago, Fitzroy Dearborn, 1996). "The People's Chronology," by James Trager (New York, Henry Holt, 1992), and "The Timetables of History," by Bernard Grun (New York, Simon and Schuster, 1979), were very useful in compiling lists of events, as were various issues of The New York Times Almanac and the World Almanac.

"Morgan," by Jean Strouse (New York, Random House, 1999), was consulted for several sections regarding J. P. Morgan, and "Titan," by Ron Chernow (New York, Random House, 1998), was consulted regarding Standard Oil. "America in the Twenties," by Geoffrey Perrett (New York, Simon and Schuster, 1982), and "Germany in the Twentieth Century," by Edmond Vermeil (New York, Praeger, 1956), were consulted for the chapter on the 1920's. "Once in Golconda," by John Brooks (Harper & Row, 1969), provided insights into the 1920's and 1930's. "Willow Run," by Lowell J. Carr and James E. Stermer (New York, Harper, 1952), was helpful in the 1940's. Insights on takeover battles, particularly in the 1950's, were provided by "The White Sharks of Wall Street: Thomas Mellon Evans and the Original Corporate Raiders," by Diana Henriques (New York, Scribner, forthcoming). "The Go-Go Years," by John Brooks (New York, Weybright and Talley, 1973), was consulted for the 1960's, as were "Dangerous Dreamers," by Robert Sobel (New York, Wiley, 1993), and "A Piece of the Action: How the Middle Class Joined the Money Class," by Joseph Nocera (New York, Simon and Schuster, 1994).

We have numerous people to thank for their help. The book was conceived by Nancy Mikhail, executive editor of McGraw-Hill's business and general reference group, and Mitchel Levitas, editorial director of book development for The Times, who together provided invaluable guidance and assistance. Chris Fortunato and Tina Thompson designed the various elements of this book and kept us on schedule. Donna Anderson, Marilyn Annan, Lora Korbut and John Motyka of the library and research staffs of The New York Times assisted in obtaining books and information. Jim Mones and Dennis Laurie diligently searched The New York Times Photo Archives to find the appropriate historical photographs, and Paul Hacker reproduced, and skillfully refined, as necessary, the old photos and the pages from The Times. The staff of The New York Times Morgue—Louis Ferrer, Jeffrey Roth and Charles Pate, assisted by Michael Ryan Murphy, Christopher Krantz, Marietta Hoferer and Neil Azevedo—provided much-needed support during the research and microfilming process. Dylan McClain researched and produced the graphics.

New York Times colleagues who were generous with their time and insights include Brent Bowers, Jim Cobb, Alison Cowan, Kurt Eichenwald, Stuart Elliott, Jonathan Fuerbringer, Diana Henriques and Glenn Kramon.

Last but not least, we thank our young son, John, for being a very good sport throughout this project.

Floyd Norris and
Christine Bockelmann

Foreword

By PAUL A. VOLCKER

One hundred years may be but a blink of an eyelash in the perspective of eons of earthly existence, but the 20th century has surely been without parallel in all of human history. Nowhere have the changes been so remarkable as in the American economy.

As the new millennium approaches, the United States is enjoying a sustained period of strong growth, low unemployment, rising productivity and relative price stability. It is a combination beyond expectations—in truth, beyond imagination—of all but a very few economists only a decade ago.

We are in the midst of transforming technological change, the full implications of which we can only dimly foresee. What we can see here and now is a truly enormous generation of wealth, wealth that at least as we record the dollar values far exceeds anything in the past.

The new entrepreneurs of the "information age"—the masters of the laptop and the Internet and those who finance them—in a matter of a few years have amassed fortunes that surpass our comprehension. The benefits have been spread far more widely among Americans. In the first six months of 1999 alone, the increase in household net worth in the United States was roughly equal to the total annual income of the 2.5 billion people living in China, India, Russia and Brazil.

Amazing. Without precedent. Enough to make many of us at least a bit uneasy about how it can go on. But, interestingly, not so unlike the American economic scene at the beginning of the century.

Of course, the numbers are quite different. But consider the very first sentences of the first chapter in this remarkable compendium of business and economic news straight from the archives of The New York Times:

"As the century began, business was growing at a pace so remarkable it alarmed many. John D. Rockefeller had formed the Standard Oil trust that dominated an industry that would soon expand dramatically as the automobile—still deemed an oddity—conquered America. J. P. Morgan, the commanding investment banker of the era, was putting together trusts in other industries as well. . . ."

Substitute in those sentences Bill Gates for Rockefeller, the Internet for the automobile, Goldman Sachs/Morgan Stanley/Merrill Lynch for J. P. Morgan, "mergers" for "trusts"—and it all could come out of yesterday's New York Times.

There are some important differences. The boom a hundred years ago was characterized by mass: steel, machinery, bridges, big ships—heavy things. Things that took brawn to build and transport, and things whose workings, once invented, seemed more or less self-evident.

In contrast, progress today is driven by tiny chips with minute etchings, by exploitation of invisible electronic impulses, by things that put a premium on brains to understand and operate rather than on muscle.

But as much as or more than those differences, what jumps out from the old headlines and text of old articles are recurring themes of business and finance—I am tempted to say of human nature itself.

There are fascinating stories of the builders and heroes set against the titillating tales of those whose foibles and frailties became part of our social history. More broadly, there is the recurrent conflict between the drive of ambitious businessmen to control and consolidate and the Federal "trust busters," a tug of war as old as the breakup of Standard Oil in 1911 and as up-to-date as the Microsoft trial of 1999.

Then there are the landmarks of constructive legislation—the Federal Reserve Act and the liberal Underwood-Simmons Tariff Act of 1913, the New Deal legislation a generation later, the Bretton Woods agreements after World War II—interspersed with policy debacles: the Versailles Treaty, the Smoot-Hawley Tariff Act, Roosevelt's experiments with national planning and the inflation of the 1970's.

Most of all, we are reminded that, for all of the stupendous economic success of the 20th century, that progress has been marked by recurrent crises and severe economic distress. Financial crises seem about as common today as a century ago—and if the United States has escaped the worst of it since World War II, much of the world has not. The fact that many Americans—and very large parts of an integrating world—have not shared fully in our success raises important questions.

This old central banker could not read without a twinge of concern the words of one old New York Times editorial. Written in October 1929, it described the early stages of the stock market crash as the "inevitable sequel" to an "orgy of speculation," forecasting that "we shall hear considerably less in the future of those newly invented conceptions of finance which revised the principles of political economy with a view solely to fitting the stock market vagaries."

Rereading history may never substitute fully for personal experience in shaping our behavior. But there is something to the admonition of one of the 20th century's leading philosophers, George Santayana, about the importance of understanding the past. And this book surely brings our economic history alive.

Paul A. Volcker was chairman of the Federal Reserve Board from 1979 to 1987.

Introduction

By FLOYD NORRIS

The time is the turn of the century. One man stands astride American business, his vision and power altering the economic landscape. His many critics see in almost everything he does an effort to squash competition and thereby increase his monopoly profits no matter how much that hurts consumers.

His own view is far different. He believes he is operating in the national interest. Indeed, he regards himself as vital to that interest and cannot understand why others would see any distinction between the two.

The Government has great admiration for his accomplishments, but it nonetheless takes him to court in the most important antitrust suit of the era.

At the start of the 20th century, it was John Pierpont Morgan who stood accused. As the 21st century nears, it is William Henry Gates 3d.

To be sure, Gates controls a business very different from that ruled by Morgan. But in each era, their businesses have been crucial for the growth of the American economy.

Morgan was the dominant financier at a time when access to capital was essential for an emerging economy that needed foreign investment if it was to develop and grow. Because he was trusted by British investors and allied with major American banks and insurance companies, he could decide what enterprises would be funded. He despised inefficiency and believed it was far more productive to have most of an industry controlled by one company. Companies simultaneously vied for his favor and resented his power.

Gates founded and rules Microsoft, the dominant technology company at a time when computers are changing the economic landscape. Like Morgan, he despises inefficiency, and he has tried to make computers—and, potentially, many other products—more efficient by having them controlled through the operating system designed by his company. He, too, is both resented and admired.

Both men gained their power at a very young age, giving them the potential to play a major role for many decades. And just as the accomplishments of Morgan—and the way the Government dealt with his power—constituted the most important story of the first decade of the 20th century, so too may the actions, and regulation, of Gates dominate the next decade.

One can envision that the eventual result will also be the same. Morgan's enterprises did not suffer crushing defeats, and Microsoft is also unlikely to see its predominance evaporate overnight. But economic reality is that monopoly power inevitably erodes, with or without effective government action. The companies Morgan sponsored, such as U.S. Steel, saw competitors arise and chip away at their domination. Morgan's own bank could not maintain its supreme influence as other financial institutions emerged. Microsoft will be similarly challenged, although it is impossible to forecast with assurance just who will challenge it effectively, or with what tactics and technology.

This book tells a part of the stories of Morgan and Gates—and of a host of other figures and companies—as those stories were seen and written at the time in the pages of The New York Times. As such, the work is inevitably episodic, but there are themes that stand out as one reviews how the world has changed in the past century.

The American capitalist system, for instance, has evolved in ways that have made it more likely capital will be used efficiently—even though that sometimes now means firing both workers and bosses. Capital markets have expanded as savers became investors. The role of the Government has grown, but the power of business has also grown as major companies became international players. And technology, which has revolutionized whole industries and ways of life, holds the promise of changing the face of the economy even more, even though history has taught some lessons about just how long it takes to absorb change and how often the unexpected can happen.

THE CONTROL OF CAPITAL

Capital is not the only thing necessary for a successful business, but no business can get started or survive long without it.

Steven Jobs and Stephen Wozniak may have been able to build the Apple 1 personal computer in a garage with just $1,500 that they got by selling an old Volkswagen van, but most businesses need far more than that.

When Morgan rose to power in the late 19th century, America needed to import capital, much as emerging economies now do. That meant courting foreign—largely British—money.

Foreign investors who saw the United States as a growth story had been burned time and again as American railroads were built and then went bankrupt, often with evidence that insiders had stolen assets and signed sweetheart deals that helped themselves while damaging the interests of the overseas sources of capital.

J. P. Morgan was set up in business by his father, Junius Morgan, an American who ran an investment banking firm in Britain, and he succeeded in large part because the British investors who provided the capital trusted Junius and came to trust his son.

Morgan was smart, and he was honest with his clients. He believed that it was in America's interests for corporations to prosper and that cooperation was far better than cutthroat competition.

> "A man I do not trust could not get money from me on all the bonds in Christendom."
>
> J. P. MORGAN [Chapter 2]

In 1901, when Edward H. Harriman tried to take control of the Northern Pacific Railroad away from Morgan's ally, James J. Hill, Morgan fought back and won the battle. But once things calmed down, his instincts were to seek harmony. Speculators who had suffered as a result of the battle were allowed to get out with far less financial loss than Morgan could have exacted. Harriman was given a seat on the Northern Pacific board of directors, and an arrangement was reached to create the Northern Securities Company, which would control all the major rail lines of the Pacific Northwest.

That was good for investors, but not necessarily for customers of the railroads, and the Government filed the first major antitrust suit of the century.

When Morgan testified in that trial, he asserted that the motive for creating the umbrella company had not been to suppress competition but merely to assure that no one could take the Northern Pacific away from management by mounting a raid. "The capital of the Northern Securities Company was so large," at $400 million, he said, that he believed no one would be able to buy control, as Harriman had almost done at the Northern Pacific, without Morgan's approval.

Whether or not we accept Morgan's statement as to motive, he was certainly right that in 1902 $400 million was a huge amount of money. Only a handful of companies or individuals could conceivably have tried to take over such a company, and none of them would have been likely to succeed over Morgan's opposition.

Nearly a century later, no one would make such a statement, and not just because $400 million is not what it used to be. (Adjusted for inflation, $400 million then equals about $7.6 billion now.) The capital markets have expanded, and many companies could finance such a deal today either by borrowing money or by issuing stock, whether or not the management of the company being acquired liked the deal.

That takeovers—even hostile ones—are now possible is one of the most important aspects of modern American capitalism, and one of the advantages the United States has over the other major economies of Europe and Japan, where tradition and corporate ownership structures have made hostile takeovers virtually impossible.

There is never any guarantee that a new management will be better able to oversee a company than an old one—and there have been plenty of cases where the opposite proved to be the case—but the possibility of change serves as a spur to existing management to perform for the shareholders.

The change from dominance by Morgan to a wider shareholder democracy was one that took many decades. In the Northern Pacific fight in 1901, public shareholders were little more than uninformed spectators. Some did well by selling

> "If Bill [Gates] succeeds in his strategy, in my opinion he'll become the wealthiest, most powerful person in the history of mankind."
> PAUL GRAYSON, chairman of Micrografx [Chapter 9]

into the rising market; others were hurt when they sold shares short—that is, sold shares they did not own in expectation of a decline in price—but most learned what Harriman and Morgan had been up to only after the battle was over.

By the 1950's, when Robert Young waged a proxy fight for the control of the New York Central, the role of the public shareholder had been completely changed. Even then, it was taken for granted that no one would actually try to buy a huge company such as the Central, and certainly not without management approval.

Banks would have been horrified at the suggestion that they should lend money to a corporate raider with the loan to be secured by the assets of the company being acquired. Instead, Young and his allies bought a substantial number of shares and mounted a proxy fight.

That proxy fight was conducted like a political campaign, complete with newspaper ads and television interviews. Young assailed the incumbent managers for letting the railroad's profits fall, and he promised that he would pay higher dividends if his side won. Young emerged victorious, but proved unable to stem the Central's decline.

That period was probably the peak in terms of the influence of individual shareholders. Institutional investors were becoming a more significant force, and, more important, capital markets were expanding. By the age of the conglomerates, in the late 1960's, the way to take control of another company was to buy it. Shareholders did not need to be persuaded that the raider was a better manager, only that he was willing to pay enough for the stock.

Moreover, a company with a hot stock could in effect print its own money. It could issue stock to make an acquisition, or it could issue other securities convertible into common stock. That latter course was especially attractive in the 1960's because the accounting rule makers had not yet figured out what was going on. Companies that issued convertible securities to make acquisitions could inflate their earnings per share because shares that would be issued on conversion of the securities were not counted in the calculation. That made the companies look more profitable than they were and thus drove up their stock prices, which made more acquisitions possible.

The end of the conglomerate era coincided with a major decline in the stock market, the bear market of 1973–74. Some conglomerates went broke, having paid too much for diverse operations or simply having been unable to operate them well, but even the more successful ones found it difficult to continue expanding once their shares had dropped in price.

Over the next several years, stocks simply went out of fashion. Many believed that America's economy was in a long-term decline. Wealth, it was said, would flow to those who owned natural resources, most particularly oil but also other commodities that would hold their value as inflation eroded the value of paper money.

It was in that atmosphere that the leveraged buyout was born. In such an arrangement, a company is acquired with virtually all borrowed money, with the loans secured by the assets of the company being bought.

The takeover of Gibson Greeting Cards was not the first such deal, but it was the one that caught Wall Street's attention. Gibson was sold by RCA, which had concluded that the company was a diversification it did not need, to a group led by William Simon, who had been Treasury Secretary under President Nixon. Simon put up so little cash that the company had a debt-to-equity ratio of 113-to-1 when the deal was done. (In a normal company, 2-to-1 is deemed highly leveraged.)

"If you expect to get anything out of a man nowadays, you must pay him well."

HENRY FORD [Chapter 2]

But the banks financed it anyway, and with good reason. The company was sold for so little that cash flow was more than twice the amount needed to pay interest on the loans. In the spring of 1983, a little more than a year after the buyout, Gibson sold stock to the public for 80 times what Simon's group had paid.

Eventually, leveraged buyouts ran into two problems that reduced the volume of deals being done. First, the booming stock market made many companies too expensive by the late 1980's. The biggest leveraged buyout of all time—the purchase of RJR Nabisco for $24.88 billion in 1988 by Kohlberg, Kravis, Roberts—cost too much for investors to make decent profits. But the financiers of that deal did far better than those who put money into some other deals, notably the acquisitions by Robert Campeau of the Allied and Federated department store chains, which ended in bankruptcy.

The second factor could be called the rebellion of the bosses. Managements circled the wagons, devising a variety of tools to keep shareholders from deciding whether to sell their companies, and persuaded legislatures in most states to pass laws to make hostile takeovers more difficult. At a minimum, these measures gave the target company time to plot defense strategy and find a more congenial merger partner. Even so, a determined, well-capitalized bidder still has a good chance to prevail eventually if management cannot persuade the shareholders that they should not sell.

The result at the end of the 20th century is that capital is more widely available for business than ever before, whether to create new enterprises or to take over existing ones.

THE PATTERN OF INVESTING

The story of investing in this century has been one of changing technologies and of changing institutions. In the end, the markets have been democratized, in the sense that a larger proportion of Americans has a stake in stocks and bonds than ever before.

The 1920's marked the first experience in stocks for many Americans, as brokerage firms expanded and sought out customers in large cities and small towns. As the market rose through that decade, there were warnings from older investors who remembered that the 19th century had seen panics more or less every 20 years. But as the dire forecasts did not prove accurate, those who made them were largely discredited.

This volume contains what looks like a prescient warning of the crash that was to follow. Written by Alexander Dana Noyes, the financial editor of The Times, it catalogued all the signs of rising speculation. Unfortunately, the article appeared in 1925, at a time when stock prices were less than half the level they would reach in 1929.

During that rise, it became fashionable to use leverage to increase profits. One could buy stocks with only 10 percent down, but even that does not capture the extent of available leverage. Closed-end funds became popular. People borrowed money to buy shares in the funds, and the funds borrowed money to buy stocks. All that leverage meant that when the crash came, the losses for many investors were far greater than would be indicated by the simple decline in share prices, although those declines were bad enough. The Dow Jones industrial average plunged 89 percent from its 1929 peak to its 1932 low.

For a generation of Americans, the crash became the defining fact about stock market investing. For more than two decades, a diversified portfolio of common stocks would pay dividends that were greater than the interest income that could be earned on a bond portfolio. That made perfect sense to investors at the time. Obviously those who bought stocks deserved to be compensated for the risk they were taking that stock prices would decline. When, in the 1950's, the yield on stocks fell below that of bonds, many saw that as a sign of dangerous speculation.

One way to deal with such speculation was to make it harder to gamble. In 1933, when stocks

"We are coming out with our heads high, knowing that we have achieved victory."

"BUD" SIMON, sit-down strike leader [Chapter 4]

were cheap and speculation nonexistent, Congress ordered the Federal Reserve Board to set limits on the amount of money that could be borrowed to buy stocks. In the 1950's, when many feared speculation was getting too great, the Fed pushed the required margin up to 90 percent. That meant that to buy stock worth $100, an investor would have to put down at least $90—the exact reverse of the practice in 1929.

There was no collapse in the 1950's, and speculation increased in the 1960's. By 1972, the so-called "Nifty Fifty"—also known as "one-decision stocks" because it was thought they could be bought and held forever as the companies continued to grow—were all the rage. Then came the 1973–74 bear market, with the Dow falling 45 percent as oil prices

soared and Americans waited in gas lines. That was followed by a prolonged period in which stocks went up and down but never did anything for long. A generation learned that to make money in the stock market, one needed to know when to sell as well as when to buy.

The 1980's and 1990's changed that. The bull market that began in 1982 was unprecedented, and gradually more and more investors joined in. The 1987 crash, which seemed epochal at the time, was not followed by a recession, and within a few years was recalled primarily as a great buying opportunity. Dividends went out of fashion, since the big profits were obviously in capital gains, which also got preferential tax treatment. Microsoft, now the most valuable company in the world, has never paid a dividend.

"My father always told me that all business men were sons-of-bitches, but I never believed it until now."

PRESIDENT KENNEDY [Chapter 7]

Leverage also grew in the 1990's. While the margin rate was a relatively high 50 percent, it was no longer a hindrance to someone with a desire to take larger risks. The rule covered only loans taken out to buy stocks and secured by those stocks. If you borrowed money with other collateral—or with no collateral—there were no margin limits. Moreover, stock index futures and options made it possible to place large bets with very little money down.

Public participation in the stock market was encouraged by other factors. In the late 1970's and early 1980's, Americans grew accustomed to high interest rates, and many had their first experience of putting savings to work anywhere other than a bank, as they bought bonds or money market mutual funds. When interest rates came down, they wanted more than the banks would pay, and stocks began to look more attractive—especially as they performed well year after year.

At the same time, changes in America's pension system forced many to consider the stock market for the first time. In the 1970's, when the stock market seemed to be going nowhere, concerns grew over corporate pension plans that appeared to be underfunded. Congress passed legislation to force companies to honor their pension promises, and accountants changed rules to make companies do a better job of estimating the costs. Companies shifted to "defined-contribution" plans—widely known as 401(k)'s, after a section of law that authorized them—which left it up to the employee to make investment choices. Companies were relieved because it would be the worker's problem, not the company's, if the value of the investments declined. Instead, the value of the investments soared, to the joy of the workers.

Many of those investments were in mutual funds, which enjoyed growing popularity. One reason for that was that it had become cheaper to buy a fund with a diversified portfolio of stocks than it was to buy the stocks individually. After the end of fixed brokerage commissions in 1975, individuals paid much higher commissions—on a per-share basis—than did institutions that placed big orders. The commission savings could more than offset the fees charged by fund managers.

The growth of mutual funds also encouraged "momentum investing," the purchase of stocks simply because they are rising, not because they appear to be a good value. Funds that were doing well got more money from investors and put it in more of the shares they already owned. That drove up the value of those stocks—and the value of the fund—and brought in still more money.

In 1999, there are tentative signs that the mutual fund boom is slowing as less money has come in. Funds are still the predominant way to invest for retirement, but the rise of the Internet has made it possible to buy and sell individual stocks on line with minimal commissions, and more investors seem to be willing to do so.

THE ROLE OF GOVERNMENT

For much of the 20th century, the role of government in regulating and controlling business has been an important issue. In interesting ways, both sides gained power during the decades.

Certainly government did. There is a maze of regulatory agencies now that were not even dreamed of as the century began, ranging from the Securities and Exchange Commission to the Consumer Product Safety Commission. The income tax—which dates from 1913—gives the Government the right to pry into a company's finances, while environmental and safety regulations make it possible for the Government to order a company to change the way it operates.

But the idea that government economic planning works best is now as unpopular as it has ever been. It was tried in this country, most notably in the 1930's with the Works Progress Administration, and was used with apparent—although temporary—success in Japan in the 1970's and 1980's. But Japan's planning did not cope well with the problems of the 1990's, in part because governments are likely to be overly influenced by the powerful established business order just at the time when new ideas are needed.

In addition, corporations have become adept at playing off one government against another. That technique was perfected in the United States, where companies could and did move operations from one state to another in search of lower costs. Now, with corporations having become multinational, the same tactics are used with national governments around the world. In 1999, the finance minister of Germany tried to raise taxes on German businesses, only to hear major German companies threaten to move operations out of the country. Not long after, it was the finance minister, not the companies, that departed.

Meanwhile, the power over money—that is, over its value—has come to be divided in interesting ways. A century ago, everyone knew that gold was money, and that national currencies had value to the extent they were convertible into the metal.

> "I am not an Abraham Lincoln signing the Emancipation Proclamation. . . . This decision does not destroy baseball."
> PETER SEITZ, arbitrator [Chapter 8]

But the gold standard made needed economic adjustments impossible in the Depression and was pushed out of the way. At Bretton Woods during World War II, a new monetary standard was devised, with the dollar tied to gold and every other currency tied to the dollar. That system collapsed in 1971 after the dollar became hopelessly overvalued, bringing on the era of floating exchange rates.

Currencies now have little if any connection to gold, whose price is being depressed as central banks sell the metal. Wise central banks—not gold in vaults—are relied upon today to maintain the value of a nation's currency. In that sense, the power of government over money has never been greater.

And yet that power is in other ways weaker than it has ever been. Markets now set the value of dollars against euros or yen every day, and countries that have tried to fix the value of their currencies have found it difficult. The foreign exchange markets have become a way for the private sector to express opinions on—and sometimes force changes in—the economic policies pursued by governments. That happened in the late 1970's, when a weak dollar was one reason the Federal Reserve drastically tightened monetary policy, and it happened in 1997 when collapsing Asian currencies brought down governments.

THE FUTURE

As the century ends, the promise of technology has never seemed greater. The miniaturization of electronics makes it possible to make many products much smarter, whether in rockets or toys, with the products doing what computer programs tell them to do. Many fear that the control over those systems will be accomplished using Microsoft programs, greatly expanding the company's already formidable power.

There are other areas where the hope of technology is great. Animals have been cloned; genes have been mapped. Biotechnology has made it possible to grow more crops and to produce crops with pesticides built in. The Internet is already changing the face of retailing and has the potential to change many other industries as well. Telecommunications companies are investing huge sums to make it easier and cheaper to send data from place to place.

And yet history teaches several lessons about technology. One is that innovation finds its own time and place. Long periods can elapse between invention and impact. Only when a new technology is shaped and refined and meets a ready public does it become an overnight success. Willis Carrier installed his first air-conditioning system in 1902, for example, but it was not until the 1950's that air-conditioning spread to millions of homes as part of a new suburban life style. The Wright Brothers were long dead when airlines drove the railroads out of the passenger travel business. Computers were demonstrated in the 1940's—big, lumbering ones, to be sure—but it was not until the 1990's that they became standard in middle-class homes and seemed ready to revolutionize the economy through the Internet.

"There is time for work. And time for love. That leaves no other time!"

COCO CHANEL [Chapter 3]

Another lesson in the development of any great technology is that there will undoubtedly be major disappointments. Some innovations do not develop quite as expected. (In the 1950's, there were forecasts that by now most families would own helicopters. In the 1960's, computers were expected to have produced paperless offices by now.) Or pioneers may fail to keep up. (Sony's Betamax videocassette recorder lost the battle to the VHS system pushed by other companies. Bowmar had the first successful pocket calculator, and Osborne's personal computer was a market leader.) Or a new product can draw a lot of customers, only to see them lose interest after the novelty wears off. (Polaroid's instant photography is still a viable business, but it is nowhere nearly as successful as seemed likely 30 years ago.)

History also teaches a clear lesson about power: Fortunes change, for better or for worse. Thirty years ago, it was I.B.M. that was the undisputed heavyweight of computer technology and the subject of a Justice Department antitrust suit; by 1993, it was bringing in new management in a desperate effort to regain its luster. In 1930 and again in 1980, American capitalism appeared to be in very bad condition; in each case, America was triumphant two decades later. Ten years ago, Japan had the world's most successful economy; now its system no longer works and the country is edging toward emulation of the American system.

In all probability, the current dominance of America in the world economic system will be challenged. Some technologies being pursued here may not work out as expected. Other countries may find ways to exploit innovations better than the United States does, as Japan appeared to be doing in computer chips in the 1980's. As the society deals with technological advances, we may be surprised to find that big changes still take longer than expected to affect the world. Investors who are so enthusiastic now about the Internet may become disillusioned and start to focus on the risks, rather than the possible rewards, associated with young companies that have more plans than profits.

It is a paradox of modern economic life that the winners of one economic era can be the ones who get into the worst trouble when times change. In the 1970's, when oil prices rose to the sky, Mexico was among the largest beneficiaries in the Western Hemisphere. Yet when commodity prices fell, it was Mexico that set off the Latin American debt crisis in 1982.

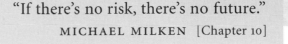

"If there's no risk, there's no future."
MICHAEL MILKEN [Chapter 10]

Why? Those who feel like winners tend to spend like winners, and to spend more than they have. Credit is readily available, and it is used. If the good times end, the erstwhile winners can be worse off than before, with a mountain of debt that was incurred when prospects seemed bright.

It may be that something like that is going on now. The savings rate in the United States has fallen dramatically in the late 1990's, and consumer credit has risen rapidly, but Americans feel—and are—much richer because an ever-increasing percentage of personal wealth has gone into the stock market, which has risen so far. The United States is running a record trade deficit, but that has not created problems for the value of the dollar because foreigners collecting dollars for their exports are eager to invest them in this country. A change of heart could cause a sudden fall in both the dollar and America's self-confidence.

For now, however, such worries are on the horizon, not in the foreground. The American economic system is the envy of many in the world. The articles that follow tell the story of how it rose to that position.

CHAPTER ONE

1900—1909

Workers on the Singer Building in 1908. Elevators helped cities reach new heights. The Brady Building is at rear.

Roosevelt vs. Morgan

As the century began, business was growing at a pace so remarkable it alarmed many. John D. Rockefeller had formed the Standard Oil trust that dominated an industry that would soon expand dramatically as the automobile—still deemed an oddity—conquered America. J. P. Morgan, the commanding investment banker of the era, was putting together trusts in other industries as well, and pressure was growing on the Federal Government to reduce the concentration of economic power.

The country was coming together thanks to the railroads that had straddled the nation in the late 19th century and thanks to such innovations as the electric light that were making large-scale industrialization possible. The first decade saw another amazing technological stride—the airplane—although it would be many years before air travel became important to the economy.

The face of cities was also changing with the advent of the elevator. Being on a high floor no longer meant lower rents for landlords because of all those stairs. Building a skyscraper—preferably the tallest in the world—was a way for companies to proclaim their success.

The country's financial system remained far less centralized than it would become. The panics of the decade, in 1901 and 1907, would lead to major changes, both involving Morgan. The first one was set off by a battle for control of the Northern Pacific Railroad—a battle in which Morgan's side was overconfident and almost lost control of a line he had believed to be locked up.

The Panic of 1907 was far more serious, and it ended only because Morgan organized banks in New York to stop it. The fact the Government appeared to be helpless and dependent on the actions of an investment banker to save the situation led to a growing consensus that the power of the Government had to be increased, although it was not until 1913 that the Federal Reserve System was created.

There have been 18 Presidents in the 20th century, but by far the two most influential in terms of establishing the Government's relationship with business shared the same last name: Roosevelt. It was Theodore in this decade who determined how the antitrust laws would be enforced. His adoption of a middle road, going after some trusts while cooperating with Morgan when that was needed, set the pace for an uneasy cooperation between Government and business.

Two Supreme Court decisions in the decade set the pace for the century. One, involving a Federal law barring the interstate sale of lottery tickets, established the Federal dominance of interstate commerce. If that 5–4 decision had gone the other way, it is hard to see how the economy could have grown as it did. The high court's other decision, throwing out a New York State law that limited working hours, set the stage for a series of anti-labor decisions that would not be reversed until the other Roosevelt occupied the White House.

1900 — Hawaii and Puerto Rico become U.S. territories.

1901 — Queen Victoria dies. President McKinley is assassinated, and Theodore Roosevelt is sworn in.

1902 — President Roosevelt helps mediate the Pennsylvania coal strike.

1903 — Orville and Wilbur Wright conduct the first powered flight.

1904 — Work begins on the Panama Canal.

1905 — The Supreme Court strikes down limits on the length of the working day.

1906 — Earthquake devastates San Francisco; hundreds die and great buildings collapse or burn.

1907 — Panic prompts a run on banks and a crash on Wall Street; J. P. Morgan engineers a rescue.

1908 — Ford's Model T goes on sale. The F.B.I. is established.

1909 — Robert E. Peary reaches the North Pole.

Disaster and Ruin in Falling Market
PANIC WITHOUT A PARALLEL IN WALL STREET

For Americans worried about the power of big financiers, the saga that unfolded in May 1901 provided ample evidence that something had to be done. James J. Hill controlled the Northern Pacific Railroad and the Great Northern Railroad, the two great lines of the Pacific Northwest, and was an ally of J. P. Morgan. Edward H. Harriman controlled the Union Pacific but had lost a battle with Hill and Morgan for control of the Chicago, Burlington & Quincy line, which he thought he needed for access to Chicago. He hadn't given up the fight, however. If he could gain control of the Northern Pacific, he decided, then perhaps he could force Hill to let him have the C.B.&Q.

In April, with Morgan in Europe for his annual vacation, Harriman began buying up Northern Pacific stock. By the time Morgan's partners realized what was going on, it was almost too late. As both sides tried to buy enough shares to take control, the price of Northern Pacific hit the stratosphere. In the end, Morgan's side prevailed, but barely.

In the stock market, it is possible to sell stock that you do not own—that is, to sell stock short. A substantial number of investors did just that as the price of Northern Pacific soared to levels completely unjustified by the railroad's profits. Those investors thought they would profit when the share price fell back. Instead, they fell into a "corner," which The Times described next to its lead front-page story.

Between them, Morgan and Harriman's camps had bought more shares of Northern Pacific than existed. That meant they could force the short-sellers to pay them any price they wanted to close out the short positions. The realization that that had happened produced panic on Wall Street.

In the aftermath, Morgan engineered an alliance that bound together Hill and Harriman in Northern Securities, a company that controlled all three lines, the Great Northern, the Northern Pacific and the C.B.&Q. Peace reigned, along with high freight rates. That combination would lead to the first great antitrust case the next year.

The greatest general panic that Wall Street has ever known came upon the stock market yesterday, with the result that before it was checked many fortunes, the accumulation in some cases of years, had been completely swept away.

The collapse, merely a logical sequence to the incipient panic of the previous day, growing out of a continuation of the disturbing conditions which had shattered confidence then, was so sudden and so terrible once it got fairly started, that it gave neither time nor opportunity for speculators to save themselves. Prices fairly crumbled away—went down in some cases 10 and 20 points between sales. It was a veritable slaughtering of prices and sellers.

Panic-stricken, holders of stocks, forgetful or perhaps heedless of the fact that the tape was some ten minutes behind time, and that prices might be far below what the ticker was recording, rushed excitedly to their brokers with instructions to sell "at the market," only to find some time later, when the transactions were reported, that they had obtained for their securities prices perhaps a dozen or more points below what they hoped and expected. In many cases this meant but one thing to the sellers—ruin, pitiless, desperate ruin. On the day previous many of these men had counted their money, not by the thousands, but by the hundreds of thousands of dollars. Almost in the time that it takes to tell it, their wealth had gone from them as though it had never been.

And hence it is that Wall Street, which these recent months had been in the sunshine of prosperity, was at the close of business last night in many parts plunged into the deepest gloom. And in many homes far removed in point of distance from the "Street" there was gloom also. Members of those homes had been in the market and had lost heavily, for throughout the entire country men, women, and children alike had been tempted into the whirl of speculation by the promises of fortunes to be made over night. To them the day's developments were in keeping with the weather—cheerless and without comfort.

Such a record had never before been approached. It was more than a panic; it was a wholesale sacrifice of prices and of people—a sacrifice, it is generally agreed, if not to the greed, at least to the stupidity and vaulting ambition of men, leaders in the financial and railroad world, who in their efforts to secure control of a great railroad property sacrificed all things else.

Not till the damage was done, not till prices had crashed as they had not crashed even on Black Friday, did these men apparently awake to a realizing sense of the gravity of the situation, of the wreck of financial values they had made.

Then, when innocents—speculators and investors alike—had suffered greater loss than speculators and investors at any other time in Wall Street had ever suffered, the warring forces came to an agreement, deciding upon a plan of action calculated to give relief to a distressing and unfortunate situation.

This plan is nothing more nor

J. P. Morgan, financier.

THE NORTHERN PACIFIC "CORNER" NOW BROKEN

UNPARALLELED IN HISTORY OF SUCH MOVEMENTS—MIGHTY FIGHT FOR CONTROL—MEASURES OF RELIEF

A "corner" more complete and more disastrous in its results than any that Wall Street has ever before known came to its culmination yesterday. All eyes for the past three days have been fixed upon the course of Northern Pacific, the "corner" in which was daily seen to be working out the ruin of many unfortunate speculators who had been caught in this unlooked for whirlpool.

The "corner" was one radically different from any of the others that Wall Street has experienced—it was neither planned nor desired. The fact is that a gigantic struggle has been going on for control of the property, and in the efforts of the opposing forces to secure a majority of the stock, each side had made contracts with sellers to a larger amount than there was stock actually in existence. The enormous purchases made recently by the Harriman syndicate and by the Hill-Morgan syndicate had completely cleared the market of all floating stock, so that the "shorts" were placed in the position of having to deliver stock that they did not own, and which they could neither buy nor borrow.

From the opening of the market yesterday it was evident that there had been no foundation for the hope that the Northern Pacific "corner" had been broken by private settlement made overnight. The first sale of Northern Pacific common was at 170, an advance of ten points over the previous day's final transaction. Then by tremendous strides, jumping sometimes as much as 200 or 300 points between sales, the stock rose to 1000, many sales being made cash for yesterday's delivery.

At this point a little help came to the panic-stricken "shorts" in the form of an announcement by J. P. Morgan & Co. and Kuhn, Loeb & Co. to the effect that they would not at once demand delivery of the stock due them yesterday. This announcement was soon followed by similar announcements from several brokerage firms who have been prominently identified in the recent trading in the stock, including Street & Norton, who within the last few days have been the largest buyers of Northern Pacific common.

The effect of these announcements was immediate and marked. The next sale after the one made at 1000 was made at 600, a decline of 400 points. Three hundred shares sold at this price; then there was a sale of 700 shares at 500, and this was followed by a sale of 100 at 450. Then came another jump in the stock which carried it to 700, but the price soon fell off again 200 points, and from that time on the quotation worked its way to a lower level. The last sale of the day was made at 325.

During all this disastrous trading in Northern Pacific, the statements that a settlement of some kind would be

reached as a result of the conferences being held were afloat. The fact was that the whole day was given over to these conferences.

At the conference held at Mr. Harriman's office during the morning there were present, besides Mr. Harriman, George J. Gould, William Rockefeller, Jacob Schiff of Kuhn, Loeb & Co.; Robert Bacon of the firm of J. P. Morgan & Co., and James Stillman, President of the National City Bank. Many of these gentlemen later attended the conferences held during the afternoon at the office of Kuhn, Loeb & Co., where H. McK. Twombly, representing the Vanderbilt interest, joined the conferences.

Latest of all the meetings was that held at the office of J. P. Morgan & Co. late in the afternoon and which was attended by James J. Hill, Daniel Lamont, H. McK. Twombly, Jacob Schiff, and George F. Baker. It was after the conclusion of this conference that it was announced that a plan had been agreed upon for the settlement of the short contracts in Northern Pacific.

Upon the return of Mr. Schiff to his office it was announced there that Kuhn, Loeb & Co. would notify all those who owed Northern Pacific stock that they would settle with them at 150. This meant that the "corner" in the stock would be broken.

The fact remains that the agreement to settle with the shorts at 150, although relieving the market of a most perilous element, does not settle the question as to supremacy in Northern Pacific.

It may be that the announcement of the plan may indicate that mutual concessions have been made, and that each side, while not securing all the advantages it sought, found it preferable to accept a modification of its demands rather than continue a situation that was working ruin on all sides.

The one thing certain is that the market is not again likely to be disturbed by an unmanageable short interest in Northern Pacific.　　　　　　　　　　　　　　　　[May 10, 1901]

The attempt to take over the Northern Pacific Railroad—shown here during a spike-driving ceremony in 1883—sent shock waves through Wall Street in 1901.

1900–1909

DIES IN VAT OF HOT BEER

TROY, N.Y., May 9—The body of Samuel Bolton, Jr., a prominent brewer and business man of this city, was found to-day in a vat of hot beer. Mr. Bolton had but a short time before returned from a pleasure drive, and chatted pleasantly with friends. About noon his hat was seen beside the vat of boiling beer and an investigation brought to light his body in the steaming liquid. Doctors were called, who gave their belief that death was instantaneous.

Besides Mr. Bolton's hat, his coat, watch, and pocketbook were found near the vat, and the general belief is that it was a case of suicide. It is said that Mr. Bolton had lost heavily in stocks lately.

[May 10, 1901]

Edward H. Harriman, railroad baron.

less than the breaking of the Northern Pacific "corner"—a corner that yesterday forced the price of that stock up to $1,000 a share, an advance within the week of nearly $900 a share. To-day the "shorts" in the stock will be allowed to settle at $150, and no further sacrifices of other stocks will needs be made by those caught short of Northern Pacific.

Had only this decision to break the corner been arrived at twenty-four hours earlier there would never have been chronicled as a record for May 9, 1901, the distressing story of crumbling prices and the sweeping away not of millions of dollars, but of tens and hundreds of millions of dollars, in little more than an hour. That this is so will appear the more clearly when it is stated that once a semi-official suggestion was made of a break in the "corner," the intention along those lines being evidenced by a break in the price of the stock from $1,000 to $325, the general market at once began to recover, almost by leaps and bounds.

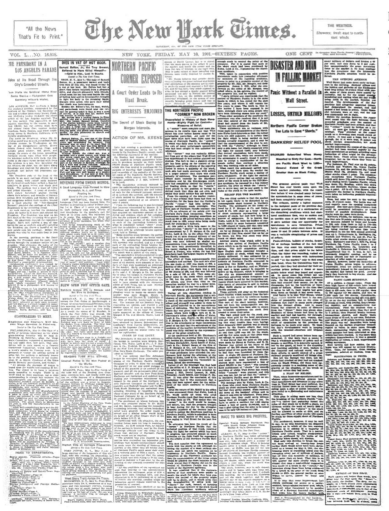

While the panic lasted there were some fortunate people who, not being in it, could afford to smile, for it offered them one of the greatest opportunities for bargains Wall Street has ever seen. As a result of the mad, unreasoning rush to sell, many stocks broke far below what is recognized as their real value. Hence it was that bargain hunters and rich men pounced upon these stocks and snapped them up with avidity, this buying contributing not a little to the market's rise. These men, buying at or near the low figures of the day, were able in a few short hours to make fortunes. And at their elbows, gathered around the tickers, were men who had just lost fortunes. It is almost incomprehensible, but it is true. That is Wall Street.

The strongest banks in the financial district took a hand in the stock market panic when it was most turbulent yesterday, and by forming a pool had soon collected $19,500,000 to loan to approved borrowers in Wall Street at the market rate. Frederick D. Tappen of the Gallatin National Bank headed the syndicate. This action was resorted to for the purpose of checking the panic rise in money, which jumped up as high as 60 per cent, during the trading.

It took Mr. Tappen just fifteen minutes to raise $15,000,000. The rest came to him by telephone after he had taken his seat at his desk again, after his little spurt of activity. It had jumped to the $19,500,000 figure before he had left the Gallatin Bank, and others willing to join the pool were still being heard from at the close of the day's business. [May 10, 1901]

Coal Strike Ends; Arbitrators Named
TO RESUME WORK AT ONCE

WASHINGTON, Oct. 16—The great anthracite coal strike is settled. A commission of six persons, with a seventh, Carroll D. Wright, as recorder, will adjust the differences between the operators and the miners. President Mitchell of the Miners' Union will take the necessary measures to call the strike off.

The President will urge the immediate resumption of mining, and operations will, it is expected, begin next week.

The following official statement announcing the close of the strike was issued at the White House at 2:20 A.M.:

"After a conference with Mr. Mitchell and some further conference with representatives of the coal operators, the President has appointed the members of the commission to inquire into, consider, and pass upon all questions at issue between the operators and miners in the anthracite coal fields.

"Brig. Gen. John M. Wilson, United States Army, retired, [late Chief of Engineers, United States Army,] Washington, D. C., as an officer of the Engineer Corps of either the military or naval service of the United States.

"Mr. E. W. Parker, Washington, D. C., as an expert mining engineer. Mr. Parker is chief statistician of the coal division of the United States Geological Survey and the editor of The Engineering and Mining Journal of New York.

"Hon. George Gray, Wilmington, Del., as a Judge of a United States Court.

"Mr. E. E. Clark, Cedar Rapids, Iowa, Grand Chief of the Order of Railway Conductors, as a sociologist, the President assuming that for the purpose of such a commission the term sociologist means a man who has thought and studied deeply on social questions and has practically applied his knowledge.

"Mr. Thomas H. Watkins, Scranton, Penn., as a man practically acquainted with the mining and selling of coal.

"Bishop John L. Spalding of Peoria, Ill. The President has added Bishop Spalding's name to the commission.

"The Hon. Carroll D. Wright has been appointed Recorder of the commission."

The operators' proposition was for a commission of five, but the miners insisted on the enlargement of the commission. They are reported to have suggested seven, but if so Mr. Mitchell's objections have been so far overcome that he now consents to six.

Most significant in the list of appointments is that of E. E. Clark as a "sociologist." It has been rumored here that the objection of the miners to the selection of a commission suggested by the operators would be obviated by the assurance of the President that at least one of those appointed should be a man who would not be accused of prejudice against unionism.

This, with the addition of a sixth member of the commission, would give the miners the fair chance which the critics of the operators' proposal have denied was intended.

[Oct. 16, 1902]

The first great labor confrontation of the 20th century broke out in 1902 in the coal fields of Pennsylvania, where miners went on strike seeking a raise—the first one in 20 years—plus an eight-hour day and union recognition. The strike drove up the price of coal, causing great hardship for many who relied on it for heat, but President Roosevelt refused to send in troops to force the miners back to work. George F. Baer, the president of the Reading Railroad, which owned coal fields, aroused widespread resentment when, in response to a letter appealing for a settlement, he asserted that the rights of working men could best be protected "not by labor agitators," but by the Christian men who were entrusted with running the coal fields.

The strike was finally settled when Roosevelt appointed an arbitration panel that both sides agreed to respect. It was the first time the Federal Government appeared to be neutral, not pro-management, in a large labor dispute.

1900–1909

SYNOPSIS OF COAL STRIKE

The anthracite mine workers, after eighteen months of uncertainty as to action, voted to strike May 15, when in convention at Hazleton, Penn. It was then assumed that 145,000 men would be in conflict with the operators. The strike was voted for, by 461¼ yeas to 349¾ nays. At the convention President John Mitchell plainly and forcefully advocated peace. The strike once declared, he zealously supported the action of the convention and planned to have a special National convention of United Mine Workers, so as to have the bituminous coal workers involved in the struggle and 450,000 men out, with the idea of forcing a compromise, as the railroads and business of the entire country could be tied up. Before the strike was declared, hard coal in New York was $5.35 a ton on an average daily consumption in the city of 13,000 tons. In a few days the price advanced $1 a ton. Soft coal advanced 50 cents a ton within a week.

LEWIS HINE / LIBRARY OF CONGRESS

Young driver at a coal mine.

When the strike was declared, the wages of miners netted from $60 to $100 a month for from four to six hours' work daily. He blasted out the coal, which was picked up by laborers paid by him, he paying for powder and other requirements. He averaged six cars a day at $1 each. The laborers worked eight to ten hours daily, each receiving $2 a day from the miner. Engineers and breaker boys who were called out received, respectively, $60 to $80 a month and 75 cents a day.

The strike demands were 20 per cent increase to miners and an eight-hour work day for men paid by the day, such as engineers, pumpmen, and breaker boys, and that 2,240 pounds and not 2,750 pounds shall constitute a ton. The plight of the laborers was ignored. For them there was no demand made for increase of wages or shorter hours.

The strike's importance was gradually evidenced in various ways, until the situation dominated all factors in business and financial interests. Phases of it were conferences at all points, including this city, between President Mitchell and others identified with the strikers and those identified with the operators. Views on the subject were expressed by laymen, clergy, and leading economists, including Abram S. Hewitt. In the mining district were scenes of riot, incendiarism, mine flooding, a state of siege where mines were operated or attempts made to this end, lives were lost in riot, murders were committed, and scores of persons were injured. After attempts to deter the strikers with paid police had failed, appeals for protection were made vainly to Gov. Stone of Pennsylvania.

President Baer of the Philadelphia and Reading Railroad went down in history early in August in replying to an appeal, asking him as a Christian to settle the strike, by replying:

The rights and interests of the laboring man will be protected and cared for not by the labor agitators, but by the Christian men to whom God in His infinite wisdom has given control of the property interests of the country.

President Mitchell Sept. 20 set forth the claims and cause of the miners at Madison Square Garden. The situation had grown more tense and serious when, Oct. 1, President Roosevelt in his desire to mediate asked President Mitchell and the leading anthracite coal operators to come to Washington and confer with him. Naught came of this, as on Oct. 4 the operators rejected the offer of the miners to arbitrate and to mine coal pending a decision. Affairs in Pennsylvania were at their worst Oct. 6 when Gov. Stone yielded and ordered on duty the entire National Guard of the State, putting 9,000 militiamen in the disturbed districts.

Anthracite coal, domestic grades, had then in New York City reached famine prices, dealers demanding from even old customers from $20 to $25 a ton, and were unwilling to dispose of more than half a ton to one person. The price of soft coal had risen to $10 a ton. More than 300,000 tons of anthracite had been ordered in Europe.

During the next few days the President exerted his influence to induce the miners to go back to work, and several conferences were held between Mitchell and Senators Quay and Penrose. Gov. Odell on Oct. 11 issued an appeal to the operators to make concessions, but they would not yield their ground. At this time the Erie Railroad asked the striking miners to resume work, and guaranteed them protection. A proposition to abolish the tariff of 67 cents a ton on coal was also discussed. The final and eventually successful negotiations for a settlement began on Oct. 11, when Secretary of War Root paid a visit to J. P. Morgan, then on his yacht, lying in the North River. Two days later, at nearly midnight, Mr. Morgan laid before the President the statement of the coal operators, in which they agreed to leave the matter to be adjusted by arbitration, and, pending arbitration, to work the mines on the condition that the union men did not interfere with the workers.

The President, after a consultation with Mr. Mitchell, appointed as arbitrators Gen. John M. Wilson, E. W. Parker, Judge George Gray, Bishop John L. Spalding, E. E. Clark, and Thomas H. Watkins. On the following day, Oct. 17, the strike was practically ended by the acceptance of the commission by the miners' Executive Committee.

The cost of the strike, figured at Wilkes-Barre last night, was:

Loss to operators in price of coal	$55,100,000
Loss to strikers in wages	29,700,000
Loss to employes other than strikers	6,900,000
Loss to railroads in earnings	13,400,000
Loss to business men in the region	16,800,000
Loss to business men outside the region	10,300,000
Cost of maintaining coal and iron police	2,300,000
Cost of maintaining non-union men	650,000
Cost of maintaining troops in the region	850,000
Damage to mines and machinery	6,500,000
Total	$142,500,000

Items overlooked in the computation of losses and outlays would swell the total to about $147,000,000.   [Oct. 19, 1902]

Government Upheld in the Lottery Suit

SUPREME COURT SAYS CONGRESS HAS POWER TO PROHIBIT TRAFFIC

WASHINGTON, Feb. 23—The Supreme Court this morning handed down its decisions in the so-called lottery cases and affirmed the power of Congress to prohibit the sending of lottery tickets from one State to another by other means than the United States mails. The question arose in connection with two cases, that of Champion vs. Ames and that of Francis vs. the United States, and in both cases the constitutionality of the act of Congress of 1895 prohibiting the transmission of lottery tickets from one State to another by express or otherwise was challenged.

The question as to the constitutionality of the act of Congress was disposed of in the opinion in the case of Champion vs. Ames, in which the Supreme Court, by a majority of one, decided in favor of the Government and held that the act was constitutional. The opinion of the majority was delivered by Justice Harlan, and Justices Brown, White, McKenna, and Holmes concurred with him. A vigorous dissenting opinion was filed by the Chief Justice, and concurred in by Justices Brewer, Peckham, and Shiras. The opinions fully discuss the constitutional questions which were discussed in the argument, and the opinion of the majority of the court fully sustains the contention of the Government.

In the Francis case, Justice Holmes spoke for the court, holding that the offense alleged did not come within the scope of the law in question. From this conclusion Justice Harlan dissented.

The cases conclude a prolonged legal contest over the power of the Federal Government to prohibit the transmission, by means other than the mails, of lottery matter.

The lottery and express companies were represented by ex-Senator George F. Edmunds, ex-Secretary John G. Carlisle, James C. Carter, and William D. Guthrie of the New York bar. Assistant Attorney General James M. Beck represented the Government.

Champion at the time of his arrest was in Chicago, representing what was known as the Pan-American Lottery of Paraguay. The particular charge against him was that of delivering a box of lottery tickets to the Walls-Fargo Express Company in Texas for shipment to California. He was arrested in Chicago to be taken to Texas, and immediately sued out a writ of habeas corpus, which the Federal Circuit Court sitting in Chicago refused to grant. He appealed from that adverse decision to the Supreme Court, and it is this appeal which was decided to-day, the decision being adverse to him.

Francis operated in Cincinnati, Ohio, and was charged with conducting "a policy shop." The "numbers" were selected by players in Newport, just across the Ohio River in Kentucky and brought to the main office in Cincinnati by ferry or over a bridge by carriers. This, it was charged, was a violation of the statute of 1895, and Francis was arrested and found guilty. His sentence was affirmed by the Circuit Court of Appeals for the Sixth Circuit and the case then removed to the Supreme Court. The effect of Justice Holmes's decision reversing the lower court's is to send the case back for a new trial.

The principal contention of counsel for the lottery men was that the suppression of lotteries belongs exclusively to the police power of the several States, and is not a Federal function, and that consequently the law of 1895 is in derogation of the Tenth Amendment of the Constitution, which provides that "the powers not delegated to the United States by the Constitution, nor prohibited by it to the States, are reserved to the States respectively or to the people." They also contend that the sending of lottery tickets or policy slips from one State to another does not constitute an act of inter-State commerce.

Under the Constitution, Congress has the power to regulate interstate commerce, but it was unclear just how broad a power that was until 1903 when the Supreme Court ruled, 5-4, that the Government could stop the transportation of lottery tickets from one state to another. To the dissenting justices, it was up to the states to decide whether or not to prohibit lotteries, and the law in question amounted to a Federal seizure of police powers reserved by the state. The decision made possible a national economic system regulated from Washington—including, as The Times noted in an editorial the same day, the Federal regulation of securities—by providing a broad definition of commerce.

1900–1909

THE MAJORITY OPINION. The following is the opinion of the majority of the court in the case of Champion vs. Ames:

"The questions presented by these opposing contentions are of great moment and are entitled to receive, as they have received, the most careful consideration.

"We are of opinion that lottery tickets, being subjects of traffic, are subjects of commerce, and the regulation of the carriage of such tickets from State to State, at least by independent carriers, is a regulation of commerce among the several States.

"But it is said that the statute in question does not regulate the carrying of lottery tickets from State to State, but by punishing those who cause them to be so carried Congress in effect prohibits such carrying; that in respect of the carrying from one State to another of articles or things that are, in fact, or according to usage in business, the subjects of commerce, the authority given Congress was not to prohibit but only to regulate. This view was earnestly pressed at the bar by learned counsel, and must be examined.

"It is to be remarked that the Constitution does not define what is to be deemed a legitimate regulation of inter-State commerce. In Gibbons vs. Ogden it was said that the power to regulate such commerce is the power to prescribe the rule by which it is to be governed. But this general observation leaves it to be determined, when the question comes before the court, whether Congress in prescribing a particular rule has exceeded its power under the Constitution. While our Government must be 'acknowledged by all to be one of enumerated powers,' the Constitution does not attempt to set forth all the means by which such powers may be carried into execution. It leaves to Congress a large discretion as to the means that may be employed in executing a given power. The sound construction of the Constitution, this court has said, 'must allow to the National Legislature that discretion, with respect to the means by which the powers it confers are to be carried into execution, which will enable that body to perform the high duties assigned to it, in the manner most beneficial to the people.' Let the end be legitimate, let it be within the scope of the Constitution, and all means which are appropriate, which are plainly adapted to that end, which are not prohibited, but consist with the letter and spirit of the Constitution, are constitutional.

"In legislating upon the subject of traffic in lottery tickets, as carried on through inter-State commerce, Congress only supplemented the action of those States—perhaps all of them—which for the protection of the public morals prohibit the drawing of lotteries, as well as the sale or circulation of lottery tickets, within their respective limits. It said, in effect, that it would not permit the declared policy of the States, which sought to protect their people against the mischiefs of the lottery business, to be overthrown or disregarded by the agency of inter-State commerce. We should hesitate long before adjudging that an evil of such appalling character, carried on through inter-State commerce, cannot be met and crushed by the only power competent to that end.

"We say competent to that end, because Congress alone has the power to occupy, by legislation, the whole field of inter-State commerce. What was said by this court upon a former occasion may well be here repeated: 'The framers of the Constitution never intended that the legislative power of the Nation should find itself incapable of disposing of a subject matter specifically committed to its charge.' If the carrying of lottery tickets from one State to another is inter-State commerce, and if Congress is of opinion that an effective regulation for the suppression of lotteries, carried on through such commerce, is to make it a criminal offense to cause lottery tickets to be carried from one State to another, we know of no authority in the courts to hold that the means thus devised are not appropriate and necessary to protect the country at large against a species of inter-State commerce which, although in general use and somewhat favored in both National and State legislation in the early history of the country, has grown in disrepute and become offensive to the entire people of the Nation. It is a kind of traffic which no one can be entitled to pursue as of right.

THE DISSENTING OPINION. The following is a synopsis of the dissenting opinion delivered by Chief Justice Fuller:

"Is the carriage of lottery tickets from one State to another commercial intercourse?

"The lottery ticket purports to create contractual relations and to furnish the means of enforcing a contract right. This is true of insurance policies, and both are contingent in their nature. Yet this court has held that the issuing of fire, marine, and life insurance policies in one State, and sending them to another, to be there delivered to the insured on payment of premium, is not inter-State commerce.

"Does the grant to Congress of the power to regulate inter-state commerce impart the absolute power to prohibit it? It was said in Gibbons vs. Ogden that the right of intercourse between State and State was derived from 'those laws whose authority is acknowledged by civilized man throughout the world,' but under the articles of confederation the States might have interdicted interstate trade, yet when they surrendered the power to deal with commerce as between themselves to the general Government it was undoubtedly in order to form a more perfect union by freeing such commerce from State discrimination and not to transfer the power of restriction.

"It will not do to say—a suggestion which has heretofore been made in this case—that State laws have been found to be ineffective for the suppression of lotteries, and therefore Congress should interfere. The scope of the commerce clause of the Constitution cannot be enlarged because of present views of public interest.

"I regard this decision as inconsistent with the views of the framers of the Constitution and of Marshall, its great expounder. Our form of government may remain notwithstanding legislation or decision, but, as long observed, it is with Governments as with religion, the form may survive the substance of the faith."

[Feb. 24, 1903]

THE LOTTERY CASE DECISIONS

The decisions of the Supreme Court in the lottery cases are, as Mr. Justice Harlan, who delivered the opinion of the majority of the court, well said, "of great moment." Their least important but not unimportant aspect is that they mark the termination of a prolonged legal contest over the power of the Federal Government to prohibit, in the interests of public morals, the transmission of lottery matter. Excluded from the mails since 1899, the lotteries had recourse to the transportation companies as a means of carriage, and these companies transmitted lottery matter, notwithstanding the fact that every State and Federal Government had put this traffic under a legal ban. The cases derive their greatest importance from the important constitutional question which they presented to the Supreme Court. Once again that tribunal, as if to disprove that law is an exact science, has divided almost equally upon an important public question.

The lottery cases seem to establish several propositions of great importance. The first is that any article is the subject of commerce which can be bought or sold, even if it be only a piece of paper having a contractual character and no intrinsic value. Counsel for the lottery companies had cited the so-called insurance cases, which had held that insurance policies were not the subjects of commerce, but in the cases just decided an informal lottery ticket, containing little more than the promise upon a future and remote contingency to pay a given sum, is held to be an article of commerce. If this be so, it must follow that certificates of stock, bonds, promissory notes, bills of lading, assignable contracts, and all other commercial instruments which may be bought and sold are also articles of commerce and subject to Federal regulation. If the cases had decided nothing more their far-reaching importance could not well be underestimated. The Supreme Court further decides, however, that it is in the power of the legislative branch of the Government to declare that a given article of commerce is prejudicial to the public health or morals and that such conclusion cannot be reviewed by the courts.

A still more important question is expressly decided, whether the right to "regulate" includes the right to prohibit commerce in articles deemed prejudicial to the public health or morals. As to this the court says: "Are we prepared to say that a provision which is in effect a prohibition of the carriage of such articles from State to State is not a fit or appropriate mode of regulation of the particular kind of commerce?" The decision appears to confirm the right to prohibit and sustains the contention of the Government.

Its significance is recognized by the Chief Justice in the dissenting opinion, when he says that the act of Congress under discussion cannot be held valid "unless the power to regulate inter-State commerce includes the absolute and exclusive power to prohibit the transportation of anything or anybody from one state to another." Given a plenary power to prohibit, there must exist a lesser power to permit subject to conditions. If, therefore, Congress has the power to prohibit such inter-State traffic as either in its nature or in its methods it deems prejudicial to the public morals, then it has also the right to permit this traffic to exist, provided those who conduct it subject themselves to conditions which Congress may, in its assumed wisdom, prescribe. [EDITORIAL, Feb. 24, 1903]

1900–1909

Supreme Court Wrecks Merger
NORTHERN SECURITIES COMPANY AN UNLAWFUL COMBINATION

President Theodore Roosevelt, responding to popular suspicion of the trusts, ordered his attorney general, Philander Knox, to sue to break up Northern Securities early in 1902 under the Sherman Antitrust Act of 1890. That prompted a visit to the President and Attorney General from J. P. Morgan, the financier who had engineered the deal and who demanded to know why he had not been warned so that a way could be found to "fix it up." To which Knox replied, according to Roosevelt's memoirs: "We don't want to fix it up, we want to stop it."

In 1904, the Supreme Court did just that.

The Times deemed the ruling "almost inevitable" because of the language of the law; then it excoriated the law as being "crude" and "destructive" and pressed that it be changed.

WASHINGTON, March 14—The United States Supreme Court today handed down an opinion in the merger case of the United States versus the Northern Securities Company sustaining the contention of the Government that the railroad merger was illegal and affirming the judgment of the United States Circuit Court of Appeals.

The decision was reached only by the narrowest possible margin, the alignment of the Justices being five to four. Justices Harlan, Brewer, Brown, McKenna, and Day formed the majority, while Chief Justice Fuller and Justices Holmes, White, and Peckham dissented. The narrowness of the Government's victory is accentuated by the fact that though Justice Brewer assents to the judgment of the majority, he reaches his conclusion by a different course of argument and writes a separate opinion to explain his views.

The prevailing opinion was written by Justice Harlan and proceeded on the theory that Congress has a right under the Constitution to control inter-State commerce, no matter how conducted.

Justice Harlan holds that the evidence shows the Northern Securities Company to constitute such restraint of inter-State commerce as violates the Anti-Trust Act and that the original purpose of the merger was to prevent competition between its constituent companies.

"The mere existence of such a combination," says Justice Harlan, "constitutes a menace" to the freedom of commerce which the public is entitled to have protected.

Justice Harlan goes on to hold that the Anti-Trust Act is not limited to application in unreasonable restraints on trade and commerce, but applies to all such restraints, reasonable or unreasonable, and declares that an act of Congress, constitutionally passed, "is binding upon all as much as if it were included in terms in the Constitution itself."

It is held that the court, having found an unlawful combination, has the power to end its existence.

Justice Brewer in his separate opinion expresses the view that recent antitrust decisions have gone too far and holds that the Anti-Trust Act should not be interpreted as applying to reasonable restraints on commerce, but only to unreasonable ones. He is, however, persuaded that the formation of the Northern Securities Company constitutes such an unreasonable restraint.

Justice Holmes, in behalf of the minority, protested against the decision on the ground that it interfered with the exercise of powers incidental to the ownership of property. He declared that such a doctrine might be extended so that "the advice or mere existence of one man might be a crime."

Justice White declared that mere ownership of stock in a State corporation could in no sense be held to be an interference with traffic between States. Such a doctrine, he asserted, would give power to Congress to control the organization of all railroads doing an inter-State business, and to abrogate every charter and every consolidation of such lines. Such power might even extend to the prevention of organization of labor associations.

"Indeed," he said, " the doctrine must in reason lead to a concession of the right in Congress to regulate concerning the aptitude, the character and capacity of persons."

The decree of the Circuit Court which was affirmed "enjoined the Securities Company, its officers and stockholders:

"From acquiring or attempting to acquire any more of such stock.

"From exercising or attempting to exercise any control, direction, supervision or influence on the acts of either railway company by virtue of its holding of stock therein.

"From paying any dividends on such stock to the Securities Company.

"From permitting the Securities Company or its officers, &c., to exercise any control over the corporate acts of such railway companies."

An effort was made by the court to prevent knowledge of the fact that the opinion was to be rendered today from getting to the public, but when the members of the court filed into the chamber at noon they were awaited by an expectant crowd which filled every seat.

Attorney General Knox and Secretary Taft and an unusual number of Senators and members of the House of Representatives were present when Justice Harlan began the delivery of the opinion.

All told, the court consumed two hours and three-quarters in disposing of the case. The fact was noted by several persons that the argument in the case was begun Dec. 14, just three months previous to the decision.

The case decided was originally brought by the United States against the Northern Securities Company, a corporation of New Jersey; the Great Northern Railway Company, a corporation of Minnesota; the Northern Pacific Railway Company, a corporation of Wisconsin; James J. Hill, a citizen of Minnesota, and William P. Clough, D. Willis James, John S. Kennedy, J. Pierpont Morgan, Robert Bacon, George F. Baker, and Daniel Lamont, citizens of New York.   [March 15, 1904]

President Theodore Roosevelt, in 1903.

1900–1909

UNLAWFUL RESTRAINT OF TRADE

The Supreme Court, expressing its opinion by the pen of Justice Harlan in the Northern Securities case, makes a fetish of competition and in effect declares that the strong arm of the Federal Government should be stretched forth to interpose the shield of the law wherever a community finds itself "at the mercy" of a single railroad corporation which has obtained an uncontested supremacy in the inter-State commerce of that region. The States and cities which lie "at the mercy" of the railroads brought into one system by the Northern Securities merger, are growing rich and prosperous. Such restraints of trade as have been imposed upon them by this railroad system have by an astonishing paradox augmented their commercial exchanges and fostered their industries, while at the same time organizing and constituting a great highway of trade between the vast fields of production in the heart of this continent and the markets of the distant East. Unrestricted competition, with the evils it engenders of the secret rebate and the rate war, would have hampered the creation of this avenue of commerce and would measurably have hindered the development of the rich and productive but comparatively new States through which run the railroads that Mr. Hill, Mr. Morgan, and their associates have unlawfully attempted to weld into one system.

In other great commercial countries, the policy of promoting competition among railroads has long since been abandoned. It has been recognized that within its legitimate field a railroad must enjoy a reasonable monopoly of traffic if it is to continue in profitable operation; and other methods have been found and successfully applied to protect the public against extortionate charges. In the process of our economic evolution, we have not yet come to that stage.

This decision was expected; we may say that it was almost inevitable. The language of the law and previous decisions of the court left practically no room for doubt about the nature of the decision. Yet is it not true that under the anti-trust law of 1890 rigorously applied to every form of inter-State commerce, whether reasonable or unreasonable, as the Supreme Court says it may and must be applied, ancient rights hitherto held to be incontestable are abridged, industrial tendencies that promote the increase of National wealth are suddenly checked, business is thrown into intolerable confusion in the channels it has chosen, and men who have supposed they were conducting lawful affairs in a lawful manner find themselves in peril of prosecution, fine, and imprisonment?

Congress has given to the country this crude, ill-considered, harsh, destructive, and dangerous statute; it is to Congress the country must look for a remedy.   [EDITORIAL, March 15, 1904]

New York 10-Hour Law Is Unconstitutional

The efforts of state governments to put limits on the power of employers were dealt a severe setback in 1905 when the Supreme Court overturned a New York State law limiting the hours of bakers to 10 hours a day. In a victory for laissez-faire capitalism, the court ruled the law violated the right of workers to enter into a contract to work longer hours. The ruling set the tone for most court decisions in the area until the 1930's. The day after the ruling, The Times featured a front-page profile of the man who, as a journeyman baker, pressed to have the 10-hour law passed and then, as the lawyer for the master bakers, succeeded in having it overturned.

WASHINGTON, April 17—In an opinion by Justice Peckham the Supreme Court of the United States today held to be unconstitutional the New York State law making 10 hours a day's work and 60 hours a week's work in bakeries in that State. Justices Harlan, White, Day and Holmes dissented, and Justice Harlan declared that no more important decision had been rendered in the last century.

The decision was based on the ground that the law interferes with the free exercise of the rights of contract between individuals.

The case that gave rise to it was that of Lochner vs. The State of New York. Lochner is a baker in the city of Utica and was found guilty of permitting an employe to work in his bakery more than 60 hours a week and fined $50.

The Court of Appeals of the State upheld the law and affirmed the judgment of the trial court finding Lochner guilty. Judge Parker wrote the opinion, holding that the measure was within the police power of the State for the protection of the public health from improper conditions surrounding the preparation of food.

Today's opinion dealt entirely with the constitutional question involved. Justice Peckham said that the law was not an act merely fixing the number of hours which should constitute a legal day's work, but an absolute prohibition on the employer permitting under any circumstances more than 10 hours' work to be done in his establishment. He continued:

"The employe may desire to earn the extra money which would arise from his working more than the prescribed time, but this statute forbids the employer from permitting the employe to earn it. It necessarily interferes with the right of contract between the employer and employes concerning the number of hours in which the latter may labor in the bakery of the employer.

"The general rights to make a contract in relation to his business is part of the liberty of the individual protected by the Fourteenth Amendment to the Federal Constitution. Under that provision no State can deprive any person of life, liberty or property without due process of law. The right to purchase or to sell labor is part of the liberty protected by this amendment unless there are circumstances which exclude the right."

Justices Holmes and Harlan delivered dissenting opinions and Justices White and Day concurred in the views of Justice Harlan, who said in part:

"I do not stop to consider whether any particular view of this economic question presents the sounder theory. The question is one about which there is room for debate and for an honest difference of opinion. No one can doubt that there are many reasons, based upon the experience of mankind, in support of the theory that, all things considered, more than 10 hours steady work each day, from week to week, in a bakery or confectionery establishment, may endanger the health, impair the usefulness, and shorten the lives of the workmen.

"Our duty then is to sustain the statute as not being in conflict with the Federal Constitution, for the reason—and such is an all-sufficient reason—it is not shown to be plainly and palpably inconsistent with that instrument.

ONEIDA HISTORICAL SOCIETY

Lochner's bakery in Utica, N.Y., figured in a 1905 U.S. Supreme Court landmark decision that struck down the 10-hour day.

"Let the State alone in the management of its purely domestic affairs, so long as it does not appear beyond all question that it has violated the Federal Constitution. This view necessarily results from the principle that the health and safety of the people of a State are primarily for the State to guard and protect, and is not a matter ordinarily of concern to the National Government."

The decision of the United States Supreme Court declaring the bakers' 10-hour law unconstitutional will be followed by a strike of 85,000 bakers throughout the United States if the threats of the union men are carried out.

International Secretary Frank H. Harzbecker of the Journeymen Bakers' and Confectioners' International Union said yesterday that there would be "a fight all along the line" if the bakers' 10-hour day demand was refused on May 1.

Business Manager George Krebs of Bakers' Union No. 164 said the unions would continue to fight for the 10-hour day in spite of all opposition by the employing bakers or the courts. "The Supreme Court decisions will be no setback to us," he said.

[April 18, 1905]

1900–1909

MADE THE 10-HOUR LAW, THEN HAD IT UNMADE

The New York State law making ten hours a day's work and sixty hours a week's work in bakeries was declared unconstitutional by the Supreme Court of the United States as the result of arguments advanced by Henry Weismann, counsel for the master bakers of the State of New York.

This same law was passed by reason of the labors of Henry Weismann, International Secretary of the Journeyman Bakers' Union of America.

Henry Weismann, counsel of the master bakers, and Henry Weismann, International Secretary of the Journeyman Bakers' Union of America, are one and the same man.

"When I was young–a journeyman baker and Secretary of their National organization–I thought labor was right in all things," said Mr. Weismann yesterday afternoon. "I was fiery and full of ideals. Later I become a master baker, and, undergoing an intellectual rev-

olution, saw where the law which I had succeeded as a journeyman baker in having passed was unjust to the employers. I withdrew from labor circles because I was unwilling to keep on saying 'Yes' and 'Amen' to measures which were manifestly wrong.

"The fight which the master bakers have won against an arbitrary ten-hour day does not mean that they are opposed to ten hours as a working day. It means that they wish to preserve inviolate the principle of the freedom of contract, and that they object to the criminal feature which was injected into the enforcement of the law when, in 1898, it was codified as a labor law. As the legal representative of the master bakers I am free to say that if the journeymen bakers would go before the Legislature and ask for the creation of a ten-hour day by law, eliminating the criminal provisions of the measure, we would not oppose the amendment which would achieve such an end."   [April 19, 1905]

Tallest Skyscraper to Stand in Broadway
SINGER COMPANY'S TOWER WILL BE THE HIGHEST BY 200 FEET

With the advent of modern construction techniques—and, most important, the elevator—buildings could rise taller than ever before. That started a race between companies to build the world's tallest building as a measure of great success. Singer, the maker of sewing machines, was the first to claim the honor, but Metropolitan Life quickly followed and then Equitable Life announced its plans for a skyscraper. Before it was built, however, F.W. Woolworth erected a 60-story building that opened in 1913 and was to remain the tallest until 1931.

The Singer Manufacturing Company filed plans yesterday for a structure which will be higher than all existing skyscrapers by from 200 to 300 feet, and will be about 40 feet higher than the Washington Monument.

In connection with the improvement of the property which it already owns adjoining its present building at the northwest corner of Broadway and Liberty Street, the company will erect over the central part of the enlarged structure a tower of forty stories, which will rise to the height of 593 feet 10⅔ inches.

The tower will be sixty-five feet square for thirty-six stories, and will be surmounted by a dome containing four additional stories, above which will be a cupola and—if that isn't high enough—a flagstaff. The façades of the tower will be of ornamental brick and limestone with four rows of windows on each side. It will contain more than 150,000 square feet of floor space and will be fitted with a group of four elevators.

Borings have been taken over the area to be covered by the tower, and it has been found that there will be no difficulty in reaching a sufficiently firm foundation on bedrock to carry the enormous weight. All engineering problems in connection with the project, it is said, have been satisfactorily worked out.

With the exception of the Eiffel Tower the Singer Building will be the loftiest structure in the world. It will be nearly 60 feet higher than the Philadelphia City Hall, more than 200 feet higher than the Park Row Building or THE TIMES Building, and over 100 feet higher than any of the famous spires of Europe, with the exception of those of the Cologne Cathedral, which rise 512 feet above ground.

[Feb. 22, 1906]

The Singer Tower Soon to Be in Second Place

So swiftly do the wheels of progress revolve in New York that one great achievement may not be finished before another and a more wonderful improvement is under way. It is so with the two tallest skyscrapers ever erected, and which are in course of construction here.

One is the Singer tower. It has been more than a seven-day wonder. For as many months people on lower Broadway have been twisting their necks to see the graceful structure soar 612 feet in air. Yet before the Singer tower is finished the steel skeleton of the Metropolitan Life tower, a larger, higher, and in some ways an even more remarkable building, is rearing its stately bulk on Madison Square.

For the first time last week a reporter climbed up into the steel skeleton of the Metropolitan Life tower, very much as he had done a few months before into the Singer Building. He did not care so much for the builders' and architects' technicalities as for the facts about it which would bring the giant structure home to the mind of the average New Yorker. From the wind-swept summit he and a photographer looked down upon a new and a strange New York. The steel, the cement and marble were spread out on the ground, so to speak, and reconstructed into blocks of dwellings. The sweep of the wind suggested odd facts regarding precautions for safety. The deeper the inquiry, the more interesting this newest wonder of the metropolis became.

The first question was of height. Those who have seen the plans of the Metropolitan Life tower say at once that it suggests the famous Campanile, which for centuries dominated the skyline of Venice. There are so many suggestions of the old Campanile in the new skyscraper, indeed, that they might be called twin sisters. There is this vital difference: Two Venetian Campaniles might be placed one on top of the other, yet they would not be as high as the Metropolitan Life tower. The same fact is true of the tower of Madison Square Garden. The Metropolitan Life skyscraper is as high now as the Diana on the Garden. The steel frame is just about half done.

The Metropolitan Life tower will overtop the Singer Building in all of its measurements. The Singer tower is 674 feet high, measuring from the basement to the top of the flagstaff; the Metropolitan building will be 680 feet from the cellar floor to the top. Measuring from the sidewalk, the new skyscraper on Madison Square will be 658 feet; the Singer tower is 612 feet to the roof of the topmost lantern, not including the flagstaff. The Singer tower has forty-seven stories; the Metropolitan structure, forty-eight above the sidewalk.

Already the marble walls of the tower, repeating the design of the larger Metropolitan Life structure, of which it will be a part, have reached the cornice of the older building, ten stories above the ground. With nothing but this marble used for the outer walls, there will be enough stone in the tower to build nearly three blocks of four-story dwellings.

Up through the unfinished skyscraper, past floor after floor where 500 masons, concrete workers, and bridgemen were at work, the reporter reached the twenty-fifth story, 335 feet above the sidewalk and not quite one-half the final height of the tower. For eighteen floors the visitors soared upward in a builder's elevator so swift that it seemed to defy the laws of gravitation and made the surrounding skeleton a mottled blur. The elevator was rigged in one of the shafts up which a year hence New Yorkers will soar skyward in the longest lifts in the world.

There will be six elevators in the centre of the tower. They will be of the electric traction type, the cables being wrapped on two drums which receive the ropes and pay them out at the same time, balancing the car with counterweights. There is no known limit in the height of such lifts.

The view from the top was of a new New York. No other skyscrapers obstructed the vista in either direction. Passing the green roof of the Flatiron Building, the gaze literally spanned the Jersey City Heights and rested on Newark and towns on the Orange Mountains, fifteen miles away.

To the southward the skyscrapers bulked large like a range of hills in steel and mortar, the Singer tower rising in the midst, a solitary watch tower on a peak. This hid the harbor, but to the left beyond the bridges, reduced at this height to gray cobwebs, the eye caught the sunlight on the sea—a long strip of shimmering silver beyond Coney Island and the Rockaways.

An early Otis elevator car.

1900–1909

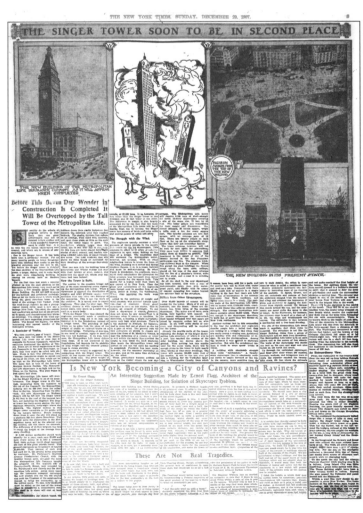

In the foreground the Bowery and lower east side offered the most curious spectacle of all. The roofs, all about the same height, might have been a pool of steaming lava. For the sun on the skylights reflected a thousand little tips of flame; the smoke from scores of chimneys covered it with an obscuring haze.

To the north the city had the curious flatness observed while soaring over it in a balloon. Long Island City was little more than a green table spread with dice. The Times Building might have been a lofty volume bound in vellum. Beyond, the gaze passed the Palisades and penetrated into the Highlands.

Within a year this view should be accessible to every New Yorker.

[THE NEW YORK TIMES MAGAZINE, Dec. 29, 1907]

909-Foot Skyscraper to Tower Above All
ARCHITECTS FILE PLANS FOR NEW EQUITABLE LIFE BUILDING HERE 62 STORIES HIGH

If plans which were filed yesterday with Building Superintendent Murphy are approved and permission to build is granted, the towering Singer Building and the Metropolitan Life tower will be put in the shade by the projected new building, planned to stand on the block bounded by Broadway, Nassau, Pine, and Cedar Streets, the site of the present building of the Equitable Life Assurance Society. The cost of the new building is estimated at $10,000,000.

This new building is to be 909 feet above the curb, exclusive of the flagstaff, which will be 150 feet higher to its tip. D. H. Burnham & Co., Chicago architects, acting for the Equitable Life, filed the plans which provide for a building sixty-two stories in height.

With its 909 feet the new building will tower nearly 300 feet over the 612 feet 1 inch of height of the Singer Building, and the Metropolitan's 637 feet 5 inches will seem also to be comparatively stunted. The Washington Monument, only 555 feet 5⅛ inches in height, will measure scarcely more than half the height of this new skyscraper, and the famous Pyramid of Cheops, now only 451 feet high, will be actually less than half as high.

Only one structure erected by man will exceed the new building in height. That is the Eiffel tower at Paris, which towers 984 feet above the ground, and if the flagpole of the new skyscraper be included in measuring its height, even the Eiffel tower will have to take second place, for from curb to flagpole tip there will be a stretch of 1,059 feet.

The main building will be thirty-four stories, or 480 feet high, with a frontage of 167.1 feet on Broadway, 152.3 feet on Nassau Street, and 304.2 feet and 312.3 feet respectively on Pine and Cedar Streets. Above the main building will be a square tower of twenty-eight stories, capped with a cupola, the tower and cupola being 420 feet high.

The building is to be equipped with a group of thirty-eight passenger elevators built in two rows in a great elevator corridor finished in ornamental bronze. Eight of these elevators will run to the top of the tower extension. In addition to these, there will be several elevators exclusively for freight.

[June 30, 1908]

Meat Inspection Bill Passes the Senate
ITS ADOPTION UNEXPECTED

WASHINGTON, May 25—The Senate to-day furnished another surprise in the line of radical legislation by passing the Beveridge Meat Inspection bill. Fifteen minutes before it was passed not a Senator would have admitted that the bill had a ghost of a chance to become a law—certainly not this session. Its passage is the direct consequence of the disclosures made in Upton Sinclair's novel, "The Jungle."

The Indiana Senator only introduced the bill three days ago, and it had been referred to the committee on Agriculture without any notion that it would ever see the light of day again. But Beveridge saw his chance to put it on the Agricultural bill as an amendment, and he offered it in his abrupt and incisive way just as the bill was about to be put on its passage. Proctor, who was in charge of the measure, expressed surprise, but in courtesy he could hardly object to the reading of his bill, which was a long one.

The reading had not gone far before it was apparent that the amendment had been drawn with care and was a good piece of work. There were possibly twenty Senators present when the amendment was offered, but in the number were three or four to whom the President had said within the last few days that he would send to Congress and make public the special report by the Commissioner of the Labor Bureau, Charles P. Neill, and Assistant Secretary of the Treasury James B. Reynolds, on the condition of things in Chicago unless something were done to correct the evils complained of in the conduct of the packing business.

When the reading clerk had finished the bill the vote was put at once without debate. There was no call for division. The amendment was adopted.

The amendment provides for the inspection at every packing house in the United States in a post mortem examination of all cattle, sheep, swine, and goats slaughtered for human consumption. Every carcass thus prepared at any packing house must bear a tag showing the date and place where it was slaughtered. All carcasses or parts of carcasses found to be unfit to eat are to be destroyed and the penalty for violation or evasion of the law is a fine of $10,000 and imprisonment for two years. The cost of inspection is to be paid by the packing houses. All meat foods found to have been dyed or colored artificially in any manner so as to be unfit for food are also to be destroyed.

The law applies to canned meats and all forms of prepared meats as well as to fresh meat shipped in cold storage.

After Jan. 1, 1907, packers who claim the right under State law to deny the Government inspectors access to their packing houses will be barred from inter-State or foreign commerce. No packer or business firm can alter or fail to use any mark, stamp, or tag used in the inspection on the meats by Government officials. The inspection is to be carried on in the night time as well as day time.

The Secretary of Agriculture authorized to arrange the fees for inspection, which must be uniform throughout the country. No vessel having a cargo of meat for foreign ports shall be allowed to clear until satisfactory evidence is given

Rarely has an exposé resulted so quickly in legislation than did the publication of Upton Sinclair's novel "The Jungle," decrying the unsanitary practices of the meatpacking industry. It sickened Americans and created a demand for legislation that even a powerful industry could not stop. The bill to inspect meat was passed by the Senate three days after it was introduced in 1906, to the surprise of almost everyone. It took longer for the House to act, and the eventual bill included some compromises, but the course of Federal regulation was set.

The meatpackers angrily denied that Sinclair's book was accurate, but their claims only brought scorn from the public, including a New York Times Magazine article fantasizing on how "The Jungle" would have read if the industry had written it.

1900–1909

Upton Sinclair prompted reform with his novel "The Jungle."

the port officers that the cargo has been duly inspected and the proper tags and certificates have been given showing that the meat is sound and wholesome.

The disclosures made in Upton Sinclair's novel, "The Jungle," which led to the passage of the measure, astounded President Roosevelt when he read the book. He could not believe they had any foundation of truth. He put Sinclair in the muck-rake class, and it was some time before he was persuaded to regard his book as having any basis. He then sent Mr. Sinclair an invitation to come to Washington and tell him how he got his information.

The author became the President's guest and told him how he had gone and lived in Packingtown with his family, had joined the Socialist societies there, and had got acquainted with men who saw and had a part in the horrible things described in "The Jungle." He told how diseased hogs and cattle were slaughtered at night and the Government Inspectors baffled in tracing the carcasses. He described how the men were unclean in their habits, and took no pains to keep clean in their handling of meats, and how the packing houses were overrun with rats, that were sometimes caught and shoveled into the hoppers to be converted into canned meats.

The President saw that he was dealing with a man who knew what he was talking about, and he told Labor Commissioner Neill and Assistant Secretary of the Treasury Reynolds to go to Chicago and make an investigation. They did so, and it is said that they found Sinclair had not exaggerated the actual conditions. Their report in a preliminary form has been in the hands of the President for several days and would have been sent to Congress had not the Beveridge bill been passed.

Several Western Senators at the request of certain packers and livestock men asked the President not to make public the Neill report. To one Senator who so urged him, the President wrote a letter saying that if the Beveridge bill were passed there would be no occasion to make the report public.   [May 26, 1906]

EXTRACTS FROM "THE JUNGLE" AS THE PACKERS WOULD HAVE WRITTEN IT

Promptly at the hour appointed Jurgis presented himself at the gate leading to the packing houses.

"Have you been thoroughly sterilized?" asked the gateman.

Jurgis showed his doctor's certificate of sterilization.

"Come along, then," said the gateman. He led Jurgis to the Superintendent's office. The Superintendent eyed Jurgis with approval. The germ-free condition of the young Lithuanian was quite apparent.

"I'll give you a job," he said.

Jurgis was overjoyed. At last he had found work. It was high time. A large part of his money had been spent by him on getting sterilized. Unscrupulous doctors, who often reaped a harvest from the ignorant foreigners who sought work at the stockyards had not failed to fleece poor Jurgis. For a week they had kept him in a glass case and watched him through a gigantic microscope. It had been very expensive.

"You can start right away," said the Superintendent; "report to the foreman of the Fan Room, in the Potted Ham Department."

The Potted Ham Department! Jurgis could hardly believe his ears. He, Jurgis Rawcuss, unskilled, uneducated, and but recently sterilized, was to help make the most carefully prepared, the purest, the most delicious food known to mankind! Impossible! He had never in his most sanguine moments dreamed of such a piece of good luck. What would his wife, patient little Blona, say when he told her that he was to assist in the making of the food of Kings and the inspiration of poets? How pleasant it would be to return home, put his anti-bacteria glove in her little disinfected hand, and shout the glad news through the hygienic speaking tube running through the vacuum tank and the chloride basin, to her ear. The Potted Ham Department!

In a daze, Jurgis inquired his way until he found himself in the Fan Room. It was a beautiful, spacious room. The walls were papered with pink. A myriad of electric globes shed a soft, dim light. Dreamy music sounded from a raised gallery at the further end of the room. Along the walls were a number of pens, in which sleek pigs were slumbering or lurching contentedly about. Before each pen sat a sterilized man with a large fan, which he moved rhythmically.

Jurgis was told to wait by the door for the foreman. While doing so, he turned to the nearest man and asked the object of the dim light, the music, and the fanning.

"Potted ham must be made from calm pigs," said the man, "otherwise it ain't good enough for the American public, and we have to ship it to Europe."

Here the foreman of the Fan Room came up and handed Jurgis a large fan.

"You must fan rhythmically and slowly," he told the young Lithuanian; "nothing sudden or violent, you know. The pigs arrive here in a very nervous state and they must be soothed before they are fit to be killed. Do you understand?"

Jurgis nodded.

"I'll assign you to 348," continued the foreman; "you're a greenhorn and ought to have an easy job to start with. Three-forty-eight is a calm pig—very calm pig, indeed. He don't need an expert soother."

After a few months of work in the Fan Room, where he fanned rhythmically and well, and always kept himself carefully disinfected, in accordance with the strict rules of the place, Jurgis was delighted one day at getting a germ-proof note, inclosed in a celluloid envelope, and written in ink fatal to animal life, telling him that his salary had been raised, and directing him to report on the next day to the foreman of the Spotting Room.

He did so, and, with twenty-four other men, entered a room filled with the most delicious air that he had ever breathed in his life. Jurgis and his companions then sat on chairs that were arranged in a circle. In front of each was fixed a telescope, connected with an X-ray apparatus, and fitted with magnifying lenses of tremendous power. The twenty-five telescopes all pointed at a small space in the middle of the floor, upon which a little platform revolved slowly. On this platform a ham dropped presently from an opening in the ceiling of the room. Jurgis and his twenty-four fellow-spotters immediately turned on the X-rays, glued their eyes to their telescopes, and minutely examined the ham as it slowly revolved before their gaze. At the end of five minutes of the closest possible scrutiny not one of the spotters had been able to detect the slightest impurity in the ham. It was therefore tipped off the platform and shot through a trap-door to the potting department below. Then the trap-door shut, the opening in the ceiling opened again, and another ham dropped on the revolving platform.

This went on all day. Whenever one of the spotters detected something wrong with a ham, he shouted "Spotted!" at the top of his lungs, whereupon the Head Spotter would immediately scoop up the ham and shunt it down a slide to the European Export Department.

A month in the Spotting Room deeply impressed Jurgis. He began to appreciate the worth of a country that could have such cleanliness in its food-producing plants. His love for the green forests and smiling fields of his native Lithuania began to wane. At last he went before a Magistrate one day and took out naturalization papers. He swelled with pride as he walked homeward. He was one of the Americans!

"They produced George Washington," he said in his simple Lithuanian way, "and they make potted ham."

[THE NEW YORK TIMES MAGAZINE, July 8, 1906]

A Chicago meatpacking plant, circa 1900.

CHICAGO HISTORICAL SOCIETY

1900–1909

Knickerbocker Will Not Open
EIGHT MILLIONS WITHDRAWN

The Panic of 1907 ended a boom with the collapse of a number of New York trust companies, banks that in many cases had made risky real estate loans. A series of runs against these institutions began in late October on news that a big copper speculator who controlled a chain of banks had failed. The panic that seized the financial institutions and Wall Street was halted by collusion among banks that agreed to keep the Trust Company of America afloat, although a competitor, the Knickerbocker Trust Company, was not rescued.

In effect, J. P. Morgan became the lender of last resort, a role that was needed because there was no central bank. That led to the establishment, in the next decade, of the Federal Reserve System.

After the conference of bankers last night it was learned that the Knickerbocker Trust Company, which shut its doors yesterday afternoon after the withdrawal of $8,000,000 by depositors, was regarded by those at the conference as insolvent, and that no aid was to be extended to that institution.

It was the opinion of all the bankers at the conference that the general banking situation, not only as far as it concerned the banks, but the trust companies as well, has been very much strengthened, and no further trouble is apprehended. Such trust companies as may deserve assistance, it was learned, will receive it.

Early this morning a Knickerbocker Trust Company Director said to a TIMES reporter:

"There is no chance that the Knickerbocker Trust Company will reopen in its old form. I can say nothing more, now."

It was stated authoritatively after the conference that the reason the Knickerbocker Trust Company was not aided by the Clearing House Association and Mr. Morgan and his associates was that the company's capital and surplus were impaired, and that Mr. Morgan did not care to assume the responsibilities of previous poor management.

The closing of the bank, which some Directors still hoped up to a late hour last night was only temporary, although such hopes were entirely abandoned by other Directors, led to complete demoralization upon the Stock Exchange, where Mayer & Co. went down and prices crumbled without resistance under an avalanche of selling orders. It necessitated the formation of a big money pool by the leading Clearing House banks, helped out by the loaning of $6,000,000 of Government money, brought Secretary of the Treasury Cortelyou hurriedly to this city, and led at once to conferences of Knickerbocker officers and the leading bankers of New York at Morgan & Co.'s offices, with Mr. Morgan presiding. The sole aim was to devise immediate plans to meet the situation thus created.

When Mr. Morgan left his office late in the evening at the close of this gathering he made this statement to the waiting reporters:

"We are doing everything we can, as fast as we can, but nothing has yet crystallized."

Asked whether any outside efforts were being made to enable the Knickerbocker Trust Company to resume Mr. Morgan said:

"I don't know anything about that; I am not talking about that." [Oct. 23, 1907]

Aid Trust Co. of America
J. P. MORGAN IS TO HELP

At a conference between Secretary Cortelyou, who came on from Washington in response to a hurry call, and the chief bankers of the city, headed by J. P. Morgan, at the Hotel Manhattan last night, it was formally decided that the point needing buttressing now is the Trust Company of America, the third largest institution of its kind in the city, and of which Oakleigh Thorne is President.

The Panic of 1907 on Wall Street was far worse than the one six years earlier.

Earnest attention was given to this new problem, and the result was the formation of a powerful syndicate to stand by the company at its opening to-day.

This determination was announced at 1 A.M. in the following official statement, after Mr. Perkins and President Thorne had been in conference at the Union League Club subsequent to the Hotel Manhattan gathering:

"The chief sore point is the Trust Company of America. The conferees feel that the situation there is such that the company is sound. Provision has been made to supply all the cash needed this morning. The conferees feel sure the company will be able to pull through. The company has twelve million dollars cash and as much more as needed has been pledged for this purpose. It is safe to assume that J. P. Morgan & Co. will be leaders in this movement to furnish funds.

"A committee has been named, including a representative of Morgan & Co. and others, to look over the accounts of the Trust Company of America, with the idea of definitely determining its position.

"The guarantees of cash made last night are for the purpose of meeting any demands upon the Trust Company of America, pending the completion of this examination."

After the close of the Manhattan conference one of the chief conferees, a Clearing House committeeman, said:

"I think it safe to say now that no other financial institution of the least importance will have to undergo the experiences of the Knickerbocker Trust Company. I feel optimistic for the first time since these troubles began."

It was also said there was no thought that the Trust Company of America was in anything like the position of the Knickerbocker Trust Company, but these steps were taken with the intention of making an authoritative statement before noon to-day that the Trust Company will be taken care of in any eventuality, providing conditions are found as sound as there is every reason to believe them to be.

That these interests have agreed, pending final examination of its accounts, to supply the Trust Company of America with any cash needed was pointed to as proving the confidence of all interests in the soundness of the company.

Those who were at the Hotel Manhattan conference with Mr. Cortelyou were J. P. Morgan, George F. Baker, George W. Perkins, Frank A. Vanderlip, A. B. Hepburn of the Chase National Bank, President Stillman of the City National Bank, J. G. Cannon, Vice President of the Fourth National Bank, and State Controller Glynn.

Most of them stayed an hour or more, and Mr. Perkins was the last to leave, not getting away until nearly 12 o'clock.

While the financial community was busy yesterday in watching closely the efforts which were being made to rehabilitate the affairs of the Knickerbocker Trust Company, if possible, the State Banking companies were giving close attention to the affairs of other institutions. State Bank Examiner Albert C. Judson, it was learned last night, made an examination yesterday of all of the loans of the Trust Company of America.

Mr. Judson was asked if his examination revealed any loans by the Trust Company of America to its President Oakleigh Thorne. Mr. Judson said Mr. Thorne had not a single loan with the Trust Company of America. [Oct. 23, 1907]

1900–1909

A Harvard Business Course
CORPORATION FINANCE AND INDUSTRIAL ORGANIZATION TO BE TAUGHT

The idea that one could teach management in a classroom was still experimental when Harvard University announced in 1908 that it was starting a graduate business school. It felt constrained to emphasize that it would accept only highly qualified students, in contrast to the low standards of early law and medical schools.

The Times reported on the plan when it was announced in August 1908 and editorialized on it in October, when courses began at the Harvard Graduate School of Business Administration.

CAMBRIDGE, Mass., Aug. 19— The Official Register of Harvard University, in its issue of this week, contains the first detailed announcement of the Graduate School of Business Administration, which will be opened to students on Oct. 1, under the direction of Dean Edwin F. Gay. The feature of the school is that, unlike other professional schools of law or medicine, which started with low requirements for admission and graduation and gradually raised their standards, the new school starts with the requirement of a college degree for admission. Upon that foundation of liberal education it rests a severe two years' course, partly prescribed and partly elective, leading to the

Frederick W. Taylor, efficiency engineer.

degree of Master in Business Administration and representing work in the following special fields: Banking and finance, accounting and auditing, insurance, industrial organization, transportation, commercial law, economic resources, and public service.

Two of the most important courses to be offered will be entitled "Corporation Finance" and "Industrial Organization." Each of these courses will consist almost wholly of lectures given on various aspects of the subject by a number of practical business men of high standing in the community. Among those who have been engaged to lecture on corporation finance are Herbert Knox Smith, Commissioner of Corporations in the United States Department of Commerce and Labor; Frederick P. Fish, Prof. Edwin S. Meade of the University of Pennsylvania; James F. Jackson, ex-Chairman of the Massachusetts Railroad Commission; C. C. Burlingham of New York, receiver of the Westinghouse Company; Judge C. M. Hough of the United States District Court for the Southern District of New York; F. A. Cleveland of the New York Bureau of Municipal Research, and G. W. Wickersham, the New York lawyer.

Among those who have been engaged to lecture on industrial organization are Frederick W. Taylor, ex-President of the American Society of Mechanical Engineers and the leading authority on factory organization; J. O. Fagan, a signalman employed by the Boston & Main Railroad, the author of the recent articles in The Atlantic Monthly entitled "Confessions of a Signalman," and Russell Robb of the firm of Stone & Webster of Boston.   [Aug. 20, 1908]

HARVARD'S SCHOOL OF BUSINESS

Duke Karl August of Weimar nearly lost the services of his austere Councilor Fritsch, who saw with disgust, after twenty-two years of faithful service in managing the business of the kingdom, a twenty-seven-year-old poet named Goethe elevated to a seat beside him. The Duke was firm, however. He declared that such a man as Goethe "would not endure the tedious and mechanical labor of working up from the bottom." With difficulty Fritsch was persuaded to withdraw his proffered resignation. But within three years the despised poet had proved his business worth, and in ten years he had set Weimar in such order as had never been seen in a European Government. Goethe's biographer, Prof. Bielschowsky, thus describes his activities in 1779:

He studies the regulations of the excise and of the pawn-shop and the rules governing the manufacture of cloth, devises new rules for the Fire Department, dictates reflections on a new bankrupt law, levies recruits, carries on a correspondence about the leather breeches of a Hussar, issues orders concerning the posts on the Weimar promenade, is busy with the construction of roads and canals, reformation of poorhouses, division of estates, irrigation of meadows, reopening of old mines and quarries, appointing of professors in the University of Jena, equipping of scientific institutions, prevention of damage to farms by game, balancing of finances, and a thousand other things.

Harvard University opened on Wednesday its school for young men who have already received a college training, to fit them to occupy advanced positions in the business world. These men are not geniuses, but liberally educated. Goethe's biographer says that

he had qualified himself for his job by early "objective and penetrative observation":

Even when, as a boy, he was sent by his father to the craftsmen, he did not merely watch them at their work, but looked into their business and social conditions and sought to form general ideas of the mutual influences of occupation and life. This was his method everywhere and at all times.

Similarly, the Harvard school thus announces its method:

The school does not pretend to graduate men who will begin at the top or high up in their several lines of business. It does aim to teach them how to work and how to apply powers of observation, analysis, and invention to practical business problems.

The students will each Summer do practical work in factories and in business houses, and they will be brought in contact with the men with whom their lifework will be done. These business men may be persuaded that a judicious combination of theory and practice is better, at the start, for young men who already know how to use their brains. Yet an investigation recently made by Harper's Weekly showed that 90 per cent of living "captains of industry" started at the lowest rung of the business ladder, and on the day the new Harvard school was opened a son of the president of the United States, just graduated from Harvard, donned a millhand's overalls and began sorting wool at $8 a week for a carpet company.

[EDITORIAL, Oct. 2, 1908]

1900–1909

HARVARD GRADUATE SCHOOL OF BUSINESS ADMINISTRATION

A 1910 portrait of students and faculty at the Harvard Graduate School of Business Administration, which was founded two years earlier.

1910–1919

At the Ford plant assembly line in Highland Park, Mich., circa 1913, auto bodies are lowered onto chassis.

World Unity, World War

THE WORLD BECAME a much smaller place in the second decade of the century as radio dispatches made it possible for newspapers to learn what had happened across the ocean on the same day rather than days or weeks later, after a ship arrived. The Panama Canal also opened, in 1914, drastically shortening the time needed to ship goods between the Atlantic and the Pacific.

The automobile was on the way to becoming the standard mode of transportation, with Henry Ford relentlessly driving down the price of his Model T and making profits that were hard to believe in the process. The idea of sharing those profits with workers was not an easy one for many businesses to accept, and Ford was subjected to plenty of criticism when he shocked other auto makers by announcing in 1914 that, based on their share of the profits, all adult workers would now receive a minimum of $5 a day, around twice the going pay. He also cut the work-day to eight hours from nine and was rewarded with a flood of job applicants.

But lucky were the ones who got such high-paying jobs. Thousands of people, many of them immigrants, toiled in sweatshops in New York for minimal wages. The country was shocked by a fire that broke out in one such garment factory, killing more than 100 people. The fire sparked reforms in fire laws, but, while sweatshops eventually moved overseas, they would not disappear during the century.

The Government was growing, meanwhile, taking more responsibility for the economy and broadening its sources of revenue at the same time. For the first time since the Civil War, Americans began paying an income tax. At the start it was small and affected only those with very high incomes. That was destined to change.

President Woodrow Wilson, the first Democratic President of the century, was elected largely because the Republicans were split between President William Howard Taft and former President Theodore Roosevelt. But that did not stop the new President from pushing through a bold economic program that included establishing a central bank—albeit a decentralized one meant to reassure farmers that Wall Street would not be in control—and a plan to slash tariffs.

It was the decade that saw the breakup of the Standard Oil Company on terms that made John D. Rockefeller richer and that paradoxically established that big business was not necessarily bad. And it was the decade that witnessed the passing of J. P. Morgan, who died a few months after astonishing the country with his assertion to Congressional investigators that he neither sought nor had power.

When war broke out in Europe, the United States tried to stay out. But in the end President Wilson joined the conflict, tipping the balance and providing the men and resources needed to defeat Germany. As the decade ended, the United States was more prosperous than ever before.

1910	Halley's comet is observed.
	The Boy Scouts of America is founded.
1911	Roald Amundsen reaches the South Pole.
	Marie Curie wins the Nobel Prize for Chemistry.
1912	The *Titanic* sinks and more than 1,500 passengers die.
	Woodrow Wilson is elected President.
1913	The U.S. Federal income tax is introduced by the 16th Amendment.
	The U.S. Federal Reserve System is established.
1914	World War I begins; the U.S. declares neutrality.
	Henry Ford sets an 8-hour day and raises pay.
	The Panama Canal opens.
1915	Albert Einstein postulates his General Theory of Relativity.
	Telephone service begins between New York and San Francisco.
1916	Margaret Sanger opens the first birth-control clinic in the U.S.
	The U.S. National Park Service is created.
1917	The U.S. joins the war against Germany and Austria-Hungary.
1918	World War I ends.
	The Supreme Court strikes down child-labor laws.
1919	President Wilson wins the Nobel Peace Prize.

141 Men and Girls Die in Waist Factory Fire; Trapped High Up in Washington Place Building; Street Strewn with Bodies; Piles of Dead Inside

Few fires have shocked America more than the 1911 fire at the Triangle Waist Company plant in lower Manhattan, where men and women were employed sewing shirtwaists. The building itself withstood the fire well, but, because there were no exterior fire escapes and no sprinklers, the people inside the building were trapped and confronted with the choice of burning to death or leaping from the windows of the factory, which was on the eighth through tenth floors of the building. Most of the workers were young immigrant women, many of them able to speak little or no English.

The disaster sparked new fire laws at the same time as it horrified Americans who had not known of the conditions in the textile factories—soon to be known as sweatshops—that had sprung up to produce clothing. It was an issue that would endure for the rest of the century. Even in the 1990's, companies that made clothing were facing charges that they treated their employees badly. By then, however, most of the businesses had long since fled the United States, and the worst conditions were in developing countries.

Three stories of a ten-floor building at the corner of Greene Street and Washington Place were burned yesterday, and while the fire was going on 141 young men and women—at least 125 of them mere girls—were burned to death or killed by jumping to the pavement below.

The building was fireproof. It shows now hardly any signs of the disaster that overtook it. The walls are as good as ever; so are the floors; nothing is the worse for the fire except the furniture and 141 of the 600 men and girls that were employed in its upper three stories.

Most of the victims were suffocated or burned to death within the building, but some who fought their way to the windows and leaped met death as surely, but perhaps more quickly, on the pavements below.

Nothing like it has been seen in New York since the burning of the General Slocum. The fire was practically all over in half an hour. It was confined to three floors—the eighth, ninth, and tenth of the building. But it was the most murderous fire that New York has seen in many years.

The victims who are now lying at the Morgue waiting for some one to identify them by a tooth or the remains of a burned shoe were mostly girls of from 16 to 23 years of age. They were employed at making shirtwaists by the Triangle Waist Company, the principal owners of which are Isaac Harris and Max Blanck. Most of them could barely speak English. Many of them came from Brooklyn. Almost all were the main support of their hard-working families.

There is just one fire escape in the building. That one is an interior fire escape. In Greene Street, where the terrified unfortunates crowded before they began to make their mad leaps to death, the whole big front of the building is guiltless of one. Nor is there a fire escape in the back.

The building was fireproof and the owners had put their trust in that. In fact, after the flames had done their worst last night, the building hardly showed a sign. Only the stock within it and the girl employes were burned.

A heap of corpses lay on the

The Triangle Waist Company fire in New York City in 1911.

ASSOCIATED PRESS

sidewalk for more than an hour. The firemen were too busy dealing with the fire to pay any attention to people whom they supposed beyond their aid. When the excitement had subsided to such an extent that some of the firemen and policemen could pay attention to this mass of the supposedly dead they found, about half way down in the pack, a girl who was still breathing. She died two minutes after she was found.

The Triangle Waist Company was the only sufferer by the disaster. There are other concerns in the building, but it was Saturday and the other companies had let their people go home. Messrs. Harris and Blanck, however, were busy and their girls—and some men—stayed.

At 4:40 o'clock, nearly five hours after the employes in the rest of the building had gone home, the fire broke out. The one little fire escape in the interior was never resorted to by any of the doomed victims. Some of them escaped by running down the stairs, but in a moment or two this avenue was cut off by flame. The girls rushed to the windows and looked down at Greene Street, 100 feet below them. Then one poor, little creature jumped. There was a plate glass protection over part of the sidewalk, but she crashed through it, wrecking it and breaking her body into a thousand pieces.

Then they all began to drop. The crowd yelled "Don't jump!" but it was jump or be burned—the proof of which is found in the fact that fifty burned bodies were taken from the ninth floor alone.

They jumped, they crashed through broken glass, they crushed themselves to death on the sidewalk. Of those who stayed behind it is better to say nothing—except what a veteran policeman said as he gazed at a headless and charred trunk on the Greene Street sidewalk hours after the worst cases had been taken out:

"I saw the Slocum disaster, but it was nothing to this."

"Is it a man or a woman?" asked the reporter.

"It's human, that's all you can tell," answered the policeman.

It was just a mass of ashes, with blood congealed on what had probably been the neck.

Messrs. Harris and Blanck were in the building, but they escaped. They carried with them Mr. Blanck's children and a governess, and they fled over the roofs. Their employes did not know the way, because they had been in the habit of using the two freight elevators, and one of these elevators was not in service when the fire broke out.

Chief Croker said it was an outrage. He spoke bitterly of the way in which the Manufacturers' Association had called a meeting in Wall Street to take measures against his proposal for enforcing better methods of protection for employes in cases of fire.

The Triangle Waist Company employed about 600 women and less than 100 men. One of the saddest features of the thing is the fact that they had almost finished for the day. In five minutes more, if the fire had started then, probably not a life would have been lost.

Last night District Attorney Whitman started an investigation—not of this disaster alone but of the whole condition which makes it possible for a firetrap of such a kind to exist. Mr. Whitman's intention is to find out if the present laws cover such cases, and if they do not to frame laws that will.

[March 26, 1911]

The Burning Building at 23 Washington Place.

1910–1919

Standard Oil Company Must Dissolve in 6 Months; Only Unreasonable Restraint of Trade Forbidden

The breakup of the Standard Oil Company of New Jersey was perhaps the high-water mark for antitrust law early in the century, but the result was correctly recognized at the time as a victory for big business because the Supreme Court concluded that only "unreasonable" restraints of trade were illegal.

In fact, although it was not recognized at the time, the breakup may also have been a victory for John D. Rockefeller, the man who dominated Standard Oil. He ended up with large stakes in the companies spun off from Standard Oil, and his wealth grew enormously.

Nonetheless, the decision in 1911 wrapped up a long effort to bring Standard Oil under control. The company had survived legislation intended to end its preferential status in rail shipping rates, and it had survived litigation in Ohio that had ruled the Standard Oil "Trust" illegal, whereupon Rockefeller created the Standard Oil "Company." The suit that the Supreme Court ruled on had been filed in 1906, at the order of President Roosevelt.

Two weeks after the Standard Oil ruling, the Supreme Court issued a similar decision breaking up the American Tobacco Company. That created a group of competing companies that began introducing new brands of cigarettes and stepped up advertising expenditures.

WASHINGTON, May 15—Final decision was returned late this afternoon by the Supreme Court of the United States in one of the two great trust cases which have been before it for so long—that of the Standard Oil Company. The decree of the Circuit Court for the Eighth Circuit directing the dissolution of the Oil Trust was affirmed, with minor modifications in two particulars. So far as the judgment of the court is concerned the action was unanimous, but Justice Harlan dissented from the argument on which the judgment was based.

The two modifications of the decree of the Circuit Court are that the period for execution of the decree is extended from thirty days to six months, and the injunction against engaging in Inter-State commerce on petroleum and its products pending the execution of the decree is vacated. This latter modification is made distinctly in consideration of the serious injury to the public which might result from the absolute cessation of that business for such a time.

Broadly speaking, the court determines against the Standard Oil Company on the ground that it is a combination in unreasonable restraint of Inter-State commerce. For the first time since it has been construing the Sherman Anti-Trust act the court takes that position, and thus definitely reads the word "unreasonable" into the law. It was on this ground that Justice Harlan dissented. This decision, therefore, is a practical reversal of the position taken by the court in the trans-Missouri case, one of the first cases under the Sherman law.

In that case Justice White joined with the late Justice Brewer in a dissenting opinion, while Justice Harlan was with the majority of the court. That decision held, as Justice Harlan now holds regarding the Standard Oil Company, that the combination complained of was in restraint of Inter-State commerce and therefore under the inhibition of the statute. Justices White and Brewer then held that the combination complained of was an "unreasonable" restraint of commerce, and so brought itself under the ban of the law.

Justice Harlan sharply criticised the majority of the court for taking this position. He declared it to be a menace to the institutions of the country. He said it was amending the Constitution by judicial interpretation, and was unjustified. And he asserted that one of the greatest dangers to the country was the willingness of the courts to take such action.

The decision was received with varying emotion by the crowd in the little court room. Attorney General Wickersham hailed it as a victory for the Administration. Frank B. Kellogg, the Assistant "Trust Buster," who has had the chief management of the case from the Government from its inception, was of similar opinion. Progressive Senators like LaFollette openly expressed distrust of the effect of the decision, and Senator Kenyon, who only a few weeks ago left the Department of Justice to enter the upper house of Congress, spoke of it as a "dangerous decision."

While in the Department of Justice, Mr. Kenyon was in charge of the prosecution of the Beef Trust, the members of which will be indicted individually on the criminal count. The department hopes to bring these cases to trial in the near future.

Trust lawyers who were in court did not display any willingness to comment on the decision. But among the lawyers who heard the Chief Justice deliver his epitome of the opinion, which he did without referring to the printed text of the decision, and who were not connected with the case, the opinion prevailed that the decision was distinctly favorable to "big business." For a long time there has been open expression of the hope on the part of "big business" that when the decision in the oil and

HISTORY OF THE OIL TRUST

The Standard Oil Company was incorporated in August, 1882, and reincorporated on June 14, 1899, under the laws of New Jersey. At that time its capital stock was increased from $10,000,000 to $100,000,000 of common and $10,000,000 preferred. The latter has all been retired. The present outstanding stock is $98,338,300. There are no bonds against the company.

The origin of the oil industry in the United States dates from the drilling of what is known as Drake's well, on Aug. 28, 1850. Among the first men to realize that the industry would eventually become an important one was John D. Rockefeller. While running a small refinery in Cleveland in 1865, he saw that unless he combined his capital and energy with other men in the same business all of them were likely to fail. Accordingly, he united in one firm the four refineries controlled by himself, William Rockefeller, Mr. Andrews, S. V. Harkness, and H. M. Flagler.

From this combination of men there was formed in 1870 the Standard Oil Company of Ohio, with a capital of $1,000,000. These four refineries in Cleveland thus started what is the Standard Oil Company of New Jersey to-day. At the same time that Rockefeller and his associates were developing the business in the West, W. C. Warden was doing the same in Philadelphia, Lockhart in Pittsburg, and Charles Pratt in Brooklyn. In 1872 these men combined forces with the Rockefeller combine and formed what was known as the Standard Oil "Alliance," which ten years later was made the basis for the Standard Oil Trust.

The difficulties besetting refiners in 1865 were chiefly such as could be cured by an increase in capital. In 1861 the best wells were thirty miles from the railroads, and owing to difficulties of transportation, petroleum had fallen from $20 a barrel to almost nothing. Two years later boats had begun carrying the crude oil and small pipe lines and branch railways had been built. In 1866 a more efficient refining method was invented, and the tank car began to replace the old flat car, with its wooden tubs. These changes called for much more capital than any of the oil men could command unassisted, and resulted in Mr. Rockefeller's determination to organize the leading producers into a union.

The years from 1865 to 1870 determined the most efficient unit of production, while the next seven years brought lower costs of transportation. Large refineries soon began to manufacture their own barrels, cases, and materials used in their manufacturing processes. In 1875 a method had been found for utilizing a great deal of the waste product.

By an act of the Pennsylvania Legislature, the South Improvement Company was created in 1871. Of the two thousand shares, 900 were owned by H. M. Flagler, O. H. Payne, William Rockefeller, J. H. Bostwick, and J. D. Rockefeller. This company soon effected favorable contracts with the Pennsylvania, New York Central, and Erie Railroads, under which the oil company got rebates, while outsiders paid regular rates. Knowledge of this aroused great indignation throughout the oil region and before the South Improvement Company had an opportunity to enjoy the benefits of its arrangement the Pennsylvania Legislature summarily destroyed its charter.

In 1870 the Standard Oil Company controlled 4 per cent of the production of the oil regions. Two years later the capital of the Standard Oil Company of Ohio had been increased to $3,500,000, and the control of the "Alliance" had been extended over more than half the refining industry. From 1874 to 1877 the company devoted itself to acquiring control of pipe lines. These became involved in a war with rival railroads, with the result that in 1874 freight charges from Chicago to the seaboard fell from $1 to 10 cents. New York Central and Erie lost millions, while the Baltimore & Ohio and Pennsylvania ceased paying dividends. On Oct. 17, 1877, the Pennsylvania abandoned the struggle and signed a contract giving the Standard Oil Company a practical monopoly of the production and transportation of oil in the United States. In 1878 and 1879 the Oil Trust owned or controlled by contract every transporting agent in the oil regions.

The Inter-State Commerce Act in 1887 forbade discriminations by railroads, and the Standard's special rates were abolished. In spite of that the company's growth and prosperity continued. Property of the various companies which entered the trust in 1887 was valued at $75,000,000. In 1892 the value was estimated at $122,000,000, and 50 per cent of the increase had come from profits invested. Dividends rose from 5¼ per cent in 1882 to 12 per cent in 1891.

In 1891 the State of Ohio began an action to oust the Standard Oil Company on the ground that it had become a party to an agreement against public policy. The court's decision in the following year made it necessary to dissolve the company. The trust dissolved in its constituent companies, and the Standard Oil Company of New Jersey was organized in 1899.   [May 16, 1911]

John D. Rockefeller grew wealthier after Standard Oil was broken up in 1911.

The New York Times.

STANDARD OIL COMPANY MUST DISSOLVE IN 6 MONTHS; ONLY UNREASONABLE RESTRAINT OF TRADE FORBIDDEN

tobacco cases did finally come down, they would at least point a way under which the big corporations could continue to do business.

President Taft himself, in messages to Congress and in public speeches, has declared himself earnestly in favor of retaining the economy and efficiency of combinations and of destroying merely those practices which unduly restrained Inter-State commerce and stifled competition. There was a time when the President was in favor of some amendment to the Sherman law in the effort to reach this situation. But he finally came to the conclusion that it was impracticable to write the word "unreasonable" into the law, and pointed out that more and more the Supreme Court was tending toward the point where its decisions in trust cases would be based on that construction of the statute.

Now it seems to have been done, and the forceful personality of Chief Justice White has so impressed itself upon the court that he has carried seven of the other Justices with him. Representatives of "big business" who heard him this afternoon did not hesitate to declare emphatically that the decision was all that the big corporations could ask. They regarded with especial favor the establishment of the proposition that a combination must be in "unreasonable" restraint of commerce to be unlawful.

This they believe points out the way by which the big corporations in the country can continue to exist. They recalled with satisfaction the fact that President Taft has specifically declared that it is not mere size which puts a corporation or combination under the ban of the law; it is not the breadth or scope of its operations or the amount of its capitalization, but whether or not it does two things: fixes prices and controls output.

The representatives of corporations here to-day find in Chief Justice White's decision a practical agreement with the position of President Taft. They have been satisfied with that position and have realized for a long time that business must conform to such standards. Now they find relief in the decision of the highest court in the country, and some of them expressed the opinion this evening that the effect on the general business situation would be good.

Long before noon there was a long line of waiting men and women in the corridor before the door of the courtroom, a line that extended clear across the rotunda of the Capitol. And despite the oppressive atmosphere of the courtroom very few of those who managed to get in left and made room for others.

The Chief Justice did not read the long opinion, but, speaking extemporaneously, delivered a synopsis of the decision. He spoke, as usual, rapidly and with great variation in volume of voice, so that at times his words were distinctly audible. In every part of the room and at other times even the stenographers directly in front of him were unable to catch a syllable. Several times Justice McKenna, who sits at his left hand, leaned over and suggested that he raise his voice so that he could be heard. Once or twice on such suggestions the Chief Justice repeated what he had said, and then for a time would speak forcibly, so that all could hear.

Always with earnestness and conviction the Chief Justice spoke, often accompanying his words with a gesture. When he discussed the motive of the men who enacted the Sherman law his voice rang through the courtroom as he said:

"The writers of that law were legislating for freedom."   [May 16, 1911]

Money Monopoly an Impossibility, Morgan Asserts

FINANCIER TELLS PUJO COMMITTEE HE DOESN'T KNOW HE HAS VAST POWER AND DOESN'T SEEK IT; LIKES 'A LITTLE COMPETITION'

WASHINGTON, Dec. 19—Alert and refreshed after a good night's rest, J. Pierpont Morgan, the most influential factor in the American financial world, to-day resumed and completed his testimony before the Pujo Money Trust investigation committee. The marble committee hall was packed with several hundred spectators, most of whom had to stand throughout the long examination of the financier. Immediately after the session Mr. Morgan and party went direct to the Union Station and left for New York on a special train.

Mr. Morgan's testimony was of a most absorbing character. Whether stating his personal views respecting control of credit, when he insisted that "money is gold, and nothing else," or ridiculing the idea of there being a money trust and telling Mr. Untermyer "You can control business, but you cannot control money," or asserting that he had many times drawn his check for a million dollars to men who did not have a cent, but who had character, Mr. Morgan always riveted the attention of those who heard him testify.

Interwoven with such striking phrases as these, the story of Mr. Morgan reached its climax this afternoon when he told how he acquired personal ownership and control of the stock of the Equitable Life Assurance Society with its present assets of more than $504,000,000 from Thomas F. Ryan. Mr. Untermyer plied Mr. Morgan hard and steadily with pointed questions, in an effort to discover what motive actuated Mr. Morgan when he paid about $3,000,000 for this stock, although its par value was $51,000, and the transactions yielded him a return of only about one-eighth of one percent annually.

The question was put in many different forms, but Mr. Morgan steadily replied that he thought "it was the thing to do," to make this purchase.

Some Congressmen in the audience fairly gasped when Mr. Morgan told of the reluctance of Mr. Ryan to part with his Equitable stock, and said Mr. Ryan hesitated, but finally consented to sell when Mr. Morgan insisted that he wanted to buy. Previously Mr. Morgan had disclaimed any realization of his power.

Apropos of this Equitable transaction Mr. Morgan made his only appeal of the day to counsel for advice. Mr. Untermyer wanted to know whether James Stillman, ex-President of the National City Bank and George F. Baker, President of the First National Bank, were associated with Mr. Morgan in the purchase of the control of the Equitable from Ryan and Harriman. Mr. Morgan paused and consulted several minutes with his counsel, De Lancey Nicoll and Richard V. Lindabury, and Henry P. Davison, one of the leading partners of J. P. Morgan & Co.

The throng waited intently while these four men had their heads together, expecting a clash between Mr. Morgan and the committee, since he had stated that he considered this private business that he could not disclose. Mr. Morgan disappointed his audience in this regard by answering the question, but did so in a way that gave ample compensation when he disclosed an interesting financial secret, stating that neither Mr. Baker nor Mr. Stillman had any interest in his purchase of the Equitable, but he had a written agreement under which Messrs. Baker and Stillman were to take half of his stock interest in the Equitable any time he "wished" them to do so.

The vigor and alertness of Mr. Morgan to-day was in striking contrast with his tired expression of yesterday. He seemed to enjoy every minute of the day, and several times toward the end of the morning testimony, after he had been on the stand two hours, when the committee expressed a willingness to take a recess, Mr. Morgan

J. P. Morgan was an intensely private man, and much of America was fascinated when, as an elderly man, he was forced to testify before a Congressional committee that was investigating the concentration of economic power in America and that had compiled evidence showing a hub of interlocking directorships centered at J.P. Morgan & Company. The companies in that web controlled 25 billion in resources—equal to about two-thirds of the United States' gross national product at the time.

The glimpse of the man who had been the most powerful financier in the country for decades fascinated Americans, but few were persuaded by his claim that he neither had nor sought power. They were amazed that, in response to a question regarding whether he had a large interest in a certain bank, he could respond: "Not very large. About a million dollars." Questioned by Samuel Untermyer, the committee counsel, he insisted that it was character, not collateral, that determined whether a man would receive a loan from his firm, adding that "a man I do not trust could not get money from me on all the bonds in Christendom." Morgan was 75 years old when the hearing took place in late 1912. He would die a few months later.

1910–1919

J. P. Morgan told Congress in 1912: "I want to control nothing."

replied that he was ready to continue. At another time Mr. Untermyer wanted to know whether he was going too fast for the witness and Mr. Morgan replied:

"Not in the least. I can keep up with you."

Frequently, however, Mr. Morgan dropped his jaw and opened his mouth as if gasping for breath. It was learned later that this was due to a slight cold he had contracted. Again, during the course of the afternoon, Mr. Morgan's cold bobbed up and made it difficult for him to hear Mr. Untermyer's questions.

At his request, Mr. Morgan was allowed to take another chair, this time at the long table on a raised dais, where the committee sat, and this brought Mr. Morgan within arm's reach of Mr. Untermyer during the most absorbing part of his testimony. After making this change Mr. Morgan seemed to be able to hear very distinctly, and the questioning of the witness became as rapid as a fusillade.

Mr. Morgan insisted very positively that he did not dominate anything and that he wanted "to control nothing"—that he was not even in control of the firm of J. P. Morgan & Co.

Among other notable statements that he made in explaining his views were these:

That there was no way in which one man could obtain a money monopoly. That the control of money in this country at least was based on personality. That he would rather have combination than competition, but did not mind competition, and, in fact, would like to have a little of it. That credit cannot be bought. That "all the money in Christendom cannot control credit."

Nor did Mr. Morgan think it unwise or dangerous to control vast concentrations of wealth in various institutions by means of so-called interlocking Directorates. While he would not prohibit the practice, Mr. Morgan unhesitatingly asserted that he was opposed to "manipulation" of stocks, but not to legitimate "speculation." He had never considered whether the Stock Exchange should be placed under some sort of Governmental control, but was not inclined "off-hand" to favor such regulation. He had never done any "short" selling in his life; did not like the practice, but would not criticise it because he did not see how it could be avoided.

[Following are excerpts from Morgan's testimony, as printed in The Times:]

Q.—You have a large interest in the National Bank of Commerce, have you not? A.—I do not remember. Not very large. About a million dollars. You have the statement there.

Q.—You have $1,686,000. A.—How much is down there for me?

Q.—The firm as a firm and the individual members have $1,686,000. The firm has one million and the individual members $686,000.

. . .

Q.—You are an advocate of combination and co-operation, as against competition, are you not? A.—Yes. Co-operation I should favor. I do not object to competition, either. I like a little competition.

Q.—You like a little, if it does not hurt you? Competition that hurts you you do not believe in? A.—I do not mind it. Now, another point. This may be a sensitive subject. I do not want to talk of it. This is probably the only chance I will have to speak of it.

Q.—You mean the subject of combination and concentration? A.—Yes, the question of control. Without you have control, you cannot do anything.

Q.—Well, I guess that is right. Is that the reason you want to control everything? A.—I want to control nothing.

Q.—What is the point, Mr. Morgan, you want to make, because I do not quite gather it? A.—What I say is this, that control is a thing, particularly in money, and you are talking about a money control—now, there is nothing in the world that you can make a trust on money.

Q.—What you mean is that there is no way one man can get it all? A.—Or any of it, or control of it.

Q.—He can make a try of it? A.—No, Sir; he cannot. He may have all the money in Christendom, but he cannot do it.

Q.—Suppose you owned all the banks and trust companies, or controlled them, and somebody wanted to start up in the steel business, you understand, against the United States Steel Corporation. You would be under a duty, would you not, to the United States Steel Corporation to see that it was not subjected to ruinous competition? A.—No, Sir. It has nothing to do with it.

Q.—You would welcome competition? A.—I would welcome competition.

Q.—The more of it the better? A.—Yes.

Q.—Your idea is that when a man has got a vast power, such as you have—you admit you have, do you not? A.—I do not know it, Sir.

Q.—You admit you have, do you not? A.—I do not think I have.

A.—You do not feel it, at all? A.—No, I do not feel it at all.

Q.—Your idea is that when a man abuses his power he loses it? A.—Yes, and he never gets it back again, either.

Q.—Do you think that a competitive condition in the banks and trust companies of New York is more or less preferable than a concentrated control over those banks? A.—I would rather have competition.

Q.—You know every big thing is run by one or two men? A.—No, I do not know that.

Q.—Your firm is run by you, is it not? A.—No, Sir.

Q.—You are the final authority, are you not? A.—No, Sir.

. . .

Q.—Is it not a fact that in this country there has not been in the last ten years, any railroad construction of parallel or competing lines to any great system existing here? A.—I understand that to be so; yes.

Q.—And is it not the fact that in this country there has been a consistent and continuous and increasing, cementing and concentration and consolidation of the great systems? A.—I think that is true.

Q.—Do you attribute the absence of competing railroad building to the fact that in this comparatively new and growing country there is not any need for any more railroads? A.—I do not.

Q.—Do you attribute it to the difficulty of getting new capital? A.—I do. I think it is owing in large measure to the fact of the want of protection against railroads that has been current in this country for the last ten years.

Q.—You mean the want of protection to the railroads? A.—To the railroads; yes. Nobody wants to put money into a new railroad in these times.

Samuel Untermyer, Congressional committee counsel.

Q.—The railroads are doing pretty well, are they not? A.—Some of them are. The old ones are. Yes.

Q.—Take for instance, the Reading road. You and Mr. Baker dominate the anthracite coal road situation, do you not, together? A.—No, we do not. At least, if we do, I do not know it.

Q.—Your power in any direction is entirely unconscious to you, is it not? A.—It is, Sir, if that is the case.

. . .

Q.—You do not think you have any power in any department of industry in this country, do you? A.—I do not.

Q.—Not the slightest? A.—Not the slightest.

Q.—And you are not looking for any? A.—I am not seeking it, either.

Q.—This consolidation and amalgamation of systems and industries and banks does not look to any concentration, does it? A.—No, sir.

Q.—It looks, I suppose to a dispersal of interests rather than to a concentration? A.—Oh, no; it deals with things as they exist.

Q.—It is for the purpose of concentrating the interests that you do amalgamate, is it not? A.—If it is desirable, yes. If it is good business for the interests of the country to do it, I do it.

. . .

Q.—Is not the credit based upon the money? A.—No, Sir.

Q.—It has no relation? A.—No, Sir; none whatever.

Q.—So that the banks of New York City would have the same credit, and if you owned them you would have the same control of credit as if you had the money, would you not? A.—I know lots of men, business men, too, who can borrow any amount, whose credit is unquestioned.

Q.—Is that not so because it is believed that they have the money back of them? A.—No, Sir. It is because people believe in the man.

Q.—And he might not be worth anything? A.—He might not have anything. I have known men to come into my office, and I have given them a check for a million dollars when I knew they had not a cent in the world.

Q.—There are not many of them? A.—Yes, a good many.

Q.—That is not business? A.—Yes, unfortunately it is. I do not think it is good business, though.

Q.—Is not commercial credit based primarily upon money or property? A.—No, sir; the first thing is character.

Q.—Before money or property? A.—Before money or anything else. Money cannot buy it.

Q.—So that a man with character, without anything at all behind it, can get all the credit he wants, and a man with the property cannot get it? A.—That is very often the case.

Q.—That is the rule of business? A.—That is the rule of business, Sir.

Q.—If that is the rule of business, Mr. Morgan, why do the banks demand, the first thing they ask, a statement of what the man has got, before they extend him credit? A.—That is what they go into; but the first thing they ask is "I want to see your record."

Q.—For instance, if he has got Government bonds, or railroad bonds, and goes in to get credit, he gets it, and on the security of those bonds, does he not? He does not get it on his face or his character, does he? A.—Yes, he gets it on his character.

Q.—I see; then he might as well take the bonds home, had he not? A.—Because a man I do not trust could not get money from me on all the bonds in Christendom.

[Dec. 20, 1912]

Wilson Signs New Tariff Law

CALLS IT ONLY FIRST STEP TOWARD FREEING THE NATION OF MONOPOLY

WASHINGTON, Saturday, Oct. 4—The Underwood-Simmons Tariff bill is now a law. President Wilson signed the measure at 9:10 o'clock last night, and it went into effect one minute after midnight. It is the first tariff law placed on the statute books by the Democratic Party in nearly twenty years.

The signing of the measure was made the occasion of considerable ceremony. Although the bill had reached the White House from the Capitol with the signatures of Speaker Clark and Vice President Marshall attached early in the afternoon, its approval by the President was purposely postponed until 9 o'clock at night. President Wilson had said that he would sign the bill the minute he received it. But he explained to the assembled crowd of interested onlookers that in deferring immediate action he had followed the advice of Attorney General McReynolds that it would be well not to take any chances of putting the law in operation until all the Custom Houses of the country had been closed for the day.

"I have delayed signing the bill," he said, "until this hour on the advice of the Attorney General, who thought it might interfere with business to sign it sooner, as most of the provisions go into effect immediately. I understand that it is now after five o'clock in San Francisco, and I presume the ordinary business transactions of the day have been closed."

Then the President sat down at his desk and took up one of two gold penholders that he had purchased for the occasion.

Taking his watch from his waistcoat pocket, the President glanced at it quickly and, after replacing it, began writing the indorsement that made the new Tariff bill the law of the land. With one pen he wrote "Approved," and the date and hour, and the name "Woodrow." Then he took up the other pen and wrote "Wilson."

Rising quickly, the President handed one of the pens to Mr. Underwood, who smilingly accepted it and murmured, with a choke in his voice:

"I thank you very much, Mr. President, for this souvenir."

What Mr. Simmons said as he took his particular pen from the President's hand could not be heard in the room, but it was apparent that Mr. Simmons was very happy.

The President went back to his desk and in an easy conversational way began a little speech that lasted nine minutes. In it he told of his gratification over signing the bill and said that "something like this" had been in his heart ever since he was a boy. He spoke of regarding the accomplishment of his tariff legislation as an event that would set the country free from monopolistic conditions, but he insisted that the journey had been only half completed and declared that currency legislation was now necessary. He expressed the utmost confidence that the Senate would pass the currency measure sooner than some pessimistic individuals believed.

A brief summary of the new

The United States had an income tax during the Civil War, but it was later ruled unconstitutional, and not until the Constitution was amended did a new income tax become possible. It was enacted as a major part of President Wilson's economic program, with the revenue from the tax enabling the Government to reduce the tariffs on imported goods that had been the Government's major source of revenue—and that had both protected domestic industries and raised the prices of many goods for Americans.

When the bill was passed in 1913, The Times reported in great detail on the tariff provisions, but gave little attention to the income tax. It was covered more thoroughly on Nov. 1, the date the law took effect, although it covered income earned since March 1. The tax rate was 1 percent, and because the minimum income level at which it took effect was so high— 2,500 for a single person—the tax was expected to be paid by fewer than half a million well-off people. Those who did have to file faced a three-page form with an additional page of instructions.

Few forecasts ever made in The Times have proven to be as inaccurate as one made in an editorial on Nov. 9: "That the institution of the income tax will tend to silence all boasting about wealth may therefore be regarded as one blessing associated with it; we know at present of no others."

1910–1919

MINNEAPOLIS JOURNAL

President Wilson led resistant Democrats to currency and tariff reform.

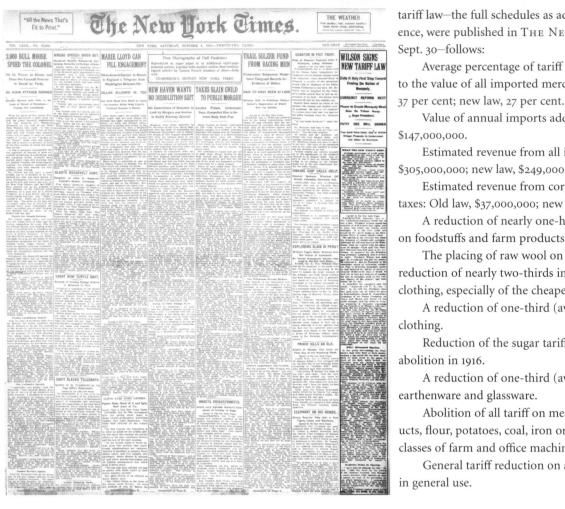

tariff law—the full schedules as adopted by the conference, were published in THE NEW YORK TIMES on Sept. 30—follows:

Average percentage of tariff rates, as compared to the value of all imported merchandise: Old law, 37 per cent; new law, 27 per cent.

Value of annual imports added to the free list, $147,000,000.

Estimated revenue from all import rates: Old law, $305,000,000; new law, $249,000,000.

Estimated revenue from corporation and income taxes: Old law, $37,000,000; new law, $122,000,000.

A reduction of nearly one-half in the average tariff on foodstuffs and farm products.

The placing of raw wool on the free list, and a reduction of nearly two-thirds in the tariff on woolen clothing, especially of the cheaper grades.

A reduction of one-third (average) on cotton clothing.

Reduction of the sugar tariff and its ultimate abolition in 1916.

A reduction of one-third (average) in the tariff on earthenware and glassware.

Abolition of all tariff on meats, fish, dairy products, flour, potatoes, coal, iron ore, lumber, and many classes of farm and office machinery.

General tariff reduction on all important articles in general use. [Oct. 4, 1913]

Income Tax Law in Effect To-Day

TREASURY DEPARTMENT ISSUES REGULATIONS SHOWING HOW IT IS TO BE WITHHELD AND PAID; SOME CONFUSION IS CERTAIN

WASHINGTON, Oct. 31—The income tax starts to-morrow, and the Treasury Department to-night made public new regulations concerning the requirements of the law with relation to the collection of the 1 per cent normal tax on the incomes of individuals at the source of such incomes.

The regulations require that the amount of the tax shall be deducted from salaries and other sources of income by the persons of concerns that pay these incomes. One of the interesting features of the new regulations is that a tenant who pays a rental of more than $3,000 is made responsible for deducting the normal tax from this income of his landlord and turning the amount of the tax over to the Internal Revenue Collector for the district in which he lives.

The man in the street who knows he makes more than $3,000 a year, and is personally responsible for his share of the tax, does not need to begin worrying about his payment for the present. The operation of the law to-morrow affects only banks, corporations and others responsible for payment on bonds, mortgages, salaries, etc. For such part as they are bound by the law they must withhold "at the source." The amounts so withheld are not payable immediately to the Treasury and the money from the tax will not begin flowing into the Treasury vaults for many months.

A BRIGHT SIDE, AFTER ALL

The announcement in THE TIMES on Saturday that on the salaries of actors, too, who receive more than $500 weekly the income tax must be collected at the source was accompanied by the pleasing assurance that we shall hear less in the future of the supposedly enormous wages of actors. Many intelligent persons have often wondered why the world is kept so well informed as to the earnings of the persons of the stage when men and women of other professions, who may have labored to so good purpose that their names are well known to the multitude, are not accustomed to advertise their incomes. That the actors will now talk less about their earnings proves that there is a bright side, even to an income tax.

There are others, many others, besides the actors who have been indiscreet in the persistent proclamation of their alleged market value to whom the enforcement of the income tax will teach the value of silence on such purely personal matters as their earnings and investments. Hereafter the only persons who will feel that they can afford to brag about their wealth will be those who really possess wealth, and it has often been noted by students of human nature that persons who have the most are apt to talk the least about their property. Ordinarily, few of us who are not downright busybodies care to know how much our neighbors own; we are willing to take their solvency for granted unless they are our debtors; and we are willing, also, that they should assume that we have money enough to pay our own way and not bother about our incomes. That the institution of the income tax will tend to silence all boasting about wealth may therefore be regarded as one blessing associated with it; we know at present of no others.   [EDITORIAL, Nov. 9, 1913]

The tax for 1913 is to be collected from March 1, shortly after the Constitutional amendment was ratified, until Dec. 31. Withholding agents, however, must begin deducting the normal tax of 1 per cent at the source to-morrow, withholding it for November and December, with certain exceptions. The exemptions for 1913 are $2,500 for a single man and $3,333.55 for a married man, and the normal tax is not to be withheld until the total income for the year exceeds such amount. The individual reporting upon his own income of more than $3,000 a year makes his return to the collector of Internal Revenue in his district next March.

Ever since President Wilson signed the tariff bill with its income tax provision early in the present month, the machinery of the Treasury Department has been at work upon the regulations that are to govern the collection of the tax. It has been a task that has kept Assistant Secretary Williams, Deputy Commissioner of Internal Revenue Speer, and other officials constantly at work, and the end is not in sight.

Mr. Williams said to-night that the regulations of the department were not difficult to understand, but some of the other officials in the department do not agree. Thousands of letters and telegrams bringing up for settlement points in the new law have poured into the department. They have come from every conceivable source and have greatly added to the labor of making regulations.   [Nov. 1, 1913]

Money Bill Goes to Wilson To-Day

Special to The New York Times

WASHINGTON, Dec. 22—By the overwhelming vote of 298 to 60 the House of Representatives shortly before 11 o'clock to-night adopted the conference agreement on the Currency bill. The Senate remained in session until the conference report was received from the House and then adjourned until to-morrow morning under an arrangement to vote on the bill as agreed to by the conferees not later than 2:30 o'clock to-morrow afternoon.

It now appears to be certain that the currency measure will become a law by President Wilson's signature to-morrow night.

The new law will go into effect immediately upon approval, but it will not become operative until after an organization committee, consisting of the Secretary of the Treasury, the Secretary of Agriculture, and the Controller of the Currency, have drafted and promulgated a plan of procedure. That it may be months before this plan is inaugurated is indicated by the extension of the Aldrich-Vreeland emergency currency law for one year beyond the date fixed for its expiration June 30, 1914.

The House adopted the conference report without change, and the Senate is expected to take the same action by a good majority. In the House only two Democrats—Calloway of Texas and Witherspoon of Mississippi—voted against the adoption of the conference agreement, while forty-nine Republicans and progressives voted for it.

It was not until the small hours of this morning, after an all-night session, that the Democratic Senators and Representatives of the Conference Committee harmonized their differences and drafted the bill in its final shape. Later in the day the Republican conferees were called in and went through the experience of having the Democratic steamroller flatten out their objections.

The perfected conference report did not get before the House until this evening, and after a debate lasting two hours and forty minutes the agreement of the conferees was confirmed and sent post-haste to the Senate, which had previously agreed merely to receive it and then adjourn until to-morrow.

In the concluding hours of the conference the provision for the guarantee of bank deposits was dropped and a provision adopted for the retirement of the 2 per cent bonds at the rate of not more than $25,000,000 a year, half that amount of bonds to be exchanged annually for one-year 3 per cent gold notes renewable for twenty years, and the other half for 3 per cent gold bonds maturing in thirty years.

The Controller of the Currency was retained as a member of the Federal Reserve Board, with a salary of $12,000 a year, and the board will consist of the Secretary of the Treasury, the Controller, and five members to be appointed by the President for terms of ten years.

Another important agreement was the elimination of the provisions permitting Federal reserve notes to be used as reserves in individual banks. Net earnings of the new banks are to be applied to the gold redemption fund or to reducing the bonded indebtedness of the Government. Five dollars will be the minimum denomination of the new circulating notes. There are to be not less than eight nor more than twelve Federal reserve banks. The gold reserve is to be 40 per cent, with a tax of 1 per cent on all amounts between 40 and 35 per cent.

Several of the Republicans who afterward voted for the conference agreement spoke vigorously in favor of its provisions and showered praise upon the Democrats for their ability to bring the measure successfully to the point of actual enactment.

Chairman Glass opened the debate with a twenty-minute explanation of the differences between the Senate and House forms of the bill and the adjustment of

---

In 1913, the Congress passed a Currency Act that made possible the issuance of more currency and—most important to posterity—established the Federal Reserve system. It had taken six years for the lessons of the Panic of 1907 to produce legislation, and it would be many more years before the Federal Reserve became an efficient central bank.

Because the public continued to fear the concentration of wealth, the Federal Reserve was divided into regional banks, which for many years had considerable autonomy from the Washington headquarters. Even with that limitation, however, the establishment of the Federal Reserve gave the country a national financial institution for the first time since Andrew Jackson prevented the renewal of the charter of the Second Bank of the United States in 1832.

The need for a central bank had become clear in the Panic of 1907, which the Government had been unable to do much to stem and was instead stopped by bankers organized by J. P. Morgan, who died a few months before the Federal Reserve was established. The Aldrich-Vreeland bill, which provided a cumbersome means of increasing currency in circulation in an emergency, was passed in 1908 but was never used and was widely considered inadequate. But there had been no consensus on what to do, in part because many feared the power of a national central bank, until President Wilson pushed the Currency Act through Congress. One provision that did not make it into the final bill was a guarantee of deposits. That would not be enacted until the Great Depression.

these differences by the conferees. Mr. Glass voiced gratification over the elimination of the Senate provision for the guarantee of bank deposits.

"The House conferees," asserted Mr. Glass, "opposed this proposition as a mere pretense of a deposit guarantee and were successful in forcing it out of the bill." The House conferees insisted that the retention of the Senate guarantee of bank deposits provision would have delayed, if not defeated, a real guarantee of deposits.

Representative Hayes of California, the ranking Republican conferee of the House, criticised the conference agreement, and voted against its adoption. He said that the conferees had not seen fit to remove the provision that makes the Government primarily liable for the Federal reserve notes to be issued.

"The people of the country," said Mr. Hayes, "suppose that these are to be banknotes. In reality they are to be Government and not banknotes. The people will hold the Democratic Party to account for this sort of a currency. It is unsound. It will rise to plague the Democratic Party hereafter as the free silver idea once did. Having lent the credit of the Government to the bankers for their purposes, how will the Democrats now be able to resist the demand of the farmers

PAUL THOMPSON

President Woodrow Wilson with his predecessor, William Howard Taft, in 1913.

CURRENCY BILL CONFERENCE REPORT

WASHINGTON, Dec. 22–The new bill affecting the currency, banking, and finances of the country is one of the most far-reaching measures relating to finance that has been enacted in many years.

Generally speaking, the first steps to be taken to bring into operation the nation's new financial system will be through an organization committee of the Secretary of the Treasury, Secretary of Agriculture, and Controller of the Currency. Banks have sixty days within which to file their applications for membership in the new system, and one year's time is allowed before the Government will compel the dissolution of any national bank that refuses to join.

The new law will make little direct change in the operation of the present national banks, except to allow them to loan a certain amount of their funds upon farm mortgages. Its chief purpose is to add a new piece of machinery to the banking system that will "take up the slack" during the changing business conditions of each year; that will give the banks a place to convert quickly their assets into cash in time of need; and that will bring out new Federal currency when it is needed, and retire it when money becomes cheap.

Banks are now required to keep a certain percentage of their deposits as reserves, part in cash in their own vaults and parts redeposited in the banks of New York, Chicago, St. Louis, and other designated cities. In times of sudden financial demands, when banks have loaned up to the full limit of their resources, these reserves furnish little relief, because if they are paid out to meet demands the banks are left in a precarious condition.

The basic principle of the new law is to get these reserve funds out into circulation when necessary, without lessening the safety of any bank and to provide a place to which local banks may rush in a crisis and get cash for the prime commercial paper they hold in their vaults.

This is to be accomplished through a chain of regional reserve banks, or "reservoirs of reserves," in which all banks shall deposit a stated part of the money they are required to hold as reserves. Under the new system, when a financial flurry comes, the banks can take commercial paper, such as notes, drafts, and bills of exchange, to these "reservoirs," and secure the use of their own reserves, or if necessary even the reserves of other banks, by depositing this security.

The new regional banks will receive about one-half of the bank reserves of the country. They, in turn, will be permitted to loan back to the banks all but 55 per cent of these reserves, so that in case of emergency millions of cash can be brought out into circulation quickly. The banks will have to pay for these loans, however, as individuals have to pay for a loan from any local bank, and this charge is expected to prevent the too free use of the reserves held by the regional banks.

A new form of paper currency is also provided for, to come out in case of emergency, and is expected to go back into the hands of the Government when times are normal. These "Treasury notes" will be printed by the Government and issued through each regional reserve bank, and will bear the guarantee both of the regional bank and the Government.

If the demand for currency in any section of the country exceeds the supply of circulating money, a regional bank can secure this new money from the Government and put it into circulation; but a gold reserve of 40 per cent and commercial paper equal to the full value of the note must be held as a reserve behind each note so issued. This provision is expected to be the influence that will drive the new money back into retirement when it is no longer needed.   [Dec. 23, 1913]

and cotton growers that they be granted the right to borrow on the credit of the Federal Government to enable them to market their products? I deny that the Republicans are responsible for any of this. If I had my way I would provide for the redemption of these notes by the banks. The burden of redeeming them ought to rest on the banks."

Several Republicans wanted to know from Mr. Hayes whether the Republican conferees had participated in the conference. Mr. Hayes answered that the Republican managers for the House had been freely consulted by the Democratic managers for the House before the joint session of the conference was held. He said the Republican conferees were not admitted to yesterday's all-day and all-night session, at which the agreement on the bill was reached, but were called in this afternoon after the Democrats had adjusted the bill to their own sweet will.

Representative Carter Glass.

PAUL THOMPSON

Mr. Glass interrupted to say that after the Republicans had been called in they, of their own volition this afternoon, had walked out of the conference before it was over.

"The members of the minority," said Mr. Hayes, "felt that they had not only been spit upon by the Democrats but that the latter had rubbed it in. After they had written their conference report they asked us in. It was a mere farce."

Representative Lenroot of Wisconsin, a Republican, announced his intention to vote for the bill.

"I think the conference bill an improvement over both the House and Senate bills. I shall vote for it because it establishes national control over the finances of the country, like the control of the Interstate Commerce Commission over railroad rates and practices; also because it removes the reserves of banks throughout the country, that have been piled up in New York City and used for speculation, and distributes them back to the sections of the United States from which they came. I am for the bill because those reserves cannot under this measure be used for speculation but for commercial purposes.

"The bill will provide elasticity and does provide substantials for the farmers in farm loans. It will insure and be a guarantee against financial panics like that of 1907. It will not prevent industrial panics, but so far as the manipulation of finance is concerned, it certainly will prevent panics." [Dec. 23, 1913]

Henry Ford Explains Why He Gives Away $10,000,000

A sixteen-year-old lad decided one day that he was "through" with farm work. He wanted to be a machinist. He walked eight miles to Detroit and applied at one of the biggest machine shops for a job. He got it.

Some years later the youngster went to a bottling establishment and saw for the first time a gasoline engine at work. He had been experimenting for years on an idea that a road vehicle ought to be made to propel itself, but the weight of a steam furnace and boiler seemed an insurmountable obstacle.

He saw the boilerless stationary engine doing the same kind of work as a small steam engine, and an idea came to him: Why not put a similar engine on wheels?

He did it. Two years of hard labor in spare times it cost him, for he had to fashion every part of the thing himself.

But another inventor, he learned afterward, had obtained what many people seemed to think a blanket patent for a gasoline engine. Most of the others who started in to develop the automobile were frightened into acknowledging the monopoly of the idea, and for years paid tribute to that monopoly in the shape of a royalty on every machine they made.

Not so with Henry Ford. He knew his engine was different from the type covered by the Selden patent, and he determined to fight. At first he had allies. When the lower courts decided against him these fell away, but he continued his contest single handed. He won.

Within ten years from the time he started his present business he built up the biggest automobile manufacturing plant in the world. He dumfounded foreign manufacturers by a demonstration that he could turn out cars that could go, and stand hard service as well, at a fifth or a sixth or less of the price at which they could afford to sell them, and his factory grew so fast that he came to turn out completed automobiles in less time than rivals could manufacture some parts.

Last year, so successful was his business, his company, on a capital of $2,000,000, made profits of $25,000,000. It is asserted that no other industry of the present time, where money has been legitimately invested and where work is actually done—not mere high financing—can show a like result.

Such is a brief history of Henry Ford.

On Tuesday the whole world was startled by the announcement in the newspapers that this same Henry Ford or the company of which he is the biggest owner had adopted a scheme of sharing equally its profits with its employes. Fifty per cent of its net profits, it was told, the company would take. The other 50 per cent, estimated for the year 1914 at $10,000,000, would be distributed among the men working for the Ford company on a new plan. It would be given in the regular pay envelopes handed out every week, in proportion to the daily wage now received.

Of such importance was this dividend that in some cases it was more than equal to the wage a man actually received for his work. The lowest paid employe, the sweepers, who receive $2.34 a day for work which in New York City may claim $1 to $1.50, was to receive $5. That sum, it was announced, was to be the least given to anybody in the establishment over twenty-two years of age.

In the open-mouthed wonder resulting from this announcement the public has hardly had time to realize what this means. While the course of Mr. Ford and his associates has been generally approved, the very novelty of the plan has provoked doubt as to its practicability. That Mr. Ford, by this unprecedented generosity, has made it difficult for those employers of labor who have to figure on very small profits, and who, therefore, cannot increase wages without wrecking their business, has been pointed out. The scheme has been pronounced Utopian, or, at least,

The automobile was in the process of revolutionizing America, and Henry Ford's company had become the most successful of auto makers when, in early 1914, the Ford Motor Company announced it was going to share profits with workers, who would be paid at least 5 a day. The company would also employ three shifts of eight hours, instead of two nine-hour shifts, to produce the Model T cars, whose prices were declining each year.

On the Sunday after the developments were reported on Jan. 6, The Times featured a long Magazine piece in which Henry Ford was interviewed on what he was up to. In that piece, the reporter marveled at the efficiency of Ford's manufacturing process—the assembly line the company had recently introduced.

The extent to which Ford's actions on wages and work hours horrified other companies can be grasped in an excerpt from an editorial in The Times that ran the day after the Ford announcement and was titled "An Industrial Utopia." It warned that these developments would bring labor unrest at other companies because "the manufacturing industries of the country cannot follow an example which requires an eight-hour day" and wages that were "approximately double the prevailing rate."

1910–1919

extremely altruistic, and some critics have pronounced it fore-doomed to failure.

A special correspondent of THE TIMES went out to Detroit to see what manner of man this was that seemed to be shoveling out money by the million to men who were already said to be better paid than any other workmen in the automobile industry, and just why he was doing it—if, perhaps, there was any reason that had not been made known.

Mr. Ford is a tall, slim, keen-eyed, alert man, who is apparently never too much occupied to see anybody that actually has something to talk over with him; a man who is just fifty, in perfect health, and as active as any of his young employees; a man who speaks in millions with no more effort than many of us think in single dollars. Mere money-getting and the spending of it do not seem to have absorbed Henry Ford. He still spends half the day in his factory, much of the time in going through it, exchanging a word here and there, or making a suggestion.

Then, his actual workday done, he gets into his own car and heads, not for his fine house in the city, but to his place in the country, the farm on which he was born. For he is a man with a hobby, and that hobby is farming and the care and conservation of wild creatures, particularly birds.

If you look about Detroit for a sign of the Ford Motor Company you will find in the outskirts a huge concrete structure bearing the company's name. But this is only a warehouse. To find the place where much of the prosperity of the city has its origin you have to board a trolley car for a six-mile journey into the country to a fashionable suburb.

For the manufacturing plant of the company is at Highland Park. To be more definite, it is on a spot where people used to throw away money on race horses. The great office building stands on what used to be the race track, and now, where the cries of the bookmakers and the cheers of winners used to resound, the roar of acres of machinery is continuous.

When one learns that Henry Ford has a son, a young man, one's first thought is—is he the familiar type of son of the usual unusually successful man? Should not the father, one cynically asks, be hoarding up money so that his successor may make ducks and drakes of it? If you suggest that to Mr. Ford he smiles.

"My son," he says proudly, "is in the business. When he finished the high school last year I had him come right into the factory. All the bodies of our cars he designs himself, and I have no fear that he will not be able to take care of himself. My son is a worker."

On Tuesday, following the announcement that had appeared in the morning papers, a crowd of something like 10,000 men flocked to the gates of the factory, at Highland Park, besides the 15,000 men that went there to their regular work. It had been announced that the company was going to take on another 5,000 men in addition to its present force. The idea of making $5 a day or more made a strong appeal. At many factories workmen reported late that day. The police had to appear in strong force, and while the crowd was told that nobody would be engaged at the works many persisted in lingering. To disperse them a show had to be made of bringing up a fire hose.

Wednesday morning, one who rode out to Highland Park about 9 o'clock found the car packed, and policemen were busy at the entrance of the big factory keeping away such as had no errand there. At the same time, Ford agents were stationed at various points in the town taking on men who seemed to meet the requirements.

Highland Park is not a workingman's colony. It is a fashionable residential place. A few of the workmen live near by, but the great number live in the city and come out on the cars. Under the new three-shift plan which will be installed men will keep coming and going all the time. In fact, shifts begin work each of the first six hours of the eight. This solves the transportation problem and makes it possible for the street car company to handle the workingmen without difficulty.

In the vast lobby of the big office building a crowd of men were sitting, waiting to see various officials of the company. A clear-eyed, clear-headed young woman commanded the scene from behind a desk on a raised platform.

Mr. Ford was found on the second floor in a big office at the left-hand corner of the front. In discussing his excellent health, he said:

"The only boiler that bursts is one which has too much fuel. No man need be sick, in my opinion, if he exercises a moderate care in the food he consumes."

When he guided the visitor through the vast building where the automobiles that bear his name are made one was able to discover one secret of the success of the business. That is specialization. A glance through the vast forest of machinery, with its veritable jungle of presses and stamps and furnaces, the overhead railway, with its regular service, maintained by a manager and a force of eighty men, gave an impression of bustle and confusion. But if one picked out a single workman and regarded him for a minute, one found that as a rule that workman's duty was to make four or five motions—nothing more. The machine he was operating required a stroke of this lever or that, and, presto! out came the finished product.

Indeed, when you watched closely, nobody seemed to be hurrying. He performed the few motions his work required him to make, and that was all. There was no haste. It was all just—clockwork!

Once back in his office, Mr. Ford introduced his son, Edsel B. Ford, a youth of twenty, who seemed to be on friendly terms with everybody, and who was waiting to make a report, and then he gave himself up to be interviewed.

"Our capital," Mr. Ford said in answer to a question, "is $2,000,000, but our assets now are about $35,000,000. We have no stock in the market. There are only seven stockholders in the company, and of these Mr. James Couzens and I hold the majority. My own holdings are 58½ per cent.

"This idea of the distribution of part of our profits with our employes, Mr. Couzens, our Vice President and treasurer, and I have been working on for some years," said Mr. Ford.

"It is not, I may emphasize, an increase in wages. It is a system of profit sharing which we have carefully worked out and which, we believe, will be successful in operation.

"Our scheme is to distribute among our employes about one-half of the year's profits. Our men have been efficient and faithful, and we believe they should share in what this means to us.

"At the same time, mind you, we have always paid good

Ford workers on an assembly line in 1913 in Highland Park, Mich.

FORD MOTOR COMPANY

1910–1919

AN INDUSTRIAL UTOPIA

The theory of the management of the Ford Company is distinctly utopian and runs dead against all experience. The movement for the bettering of society need not be universal; in their opinion, "we think that one concern can make a start and create an example for other employers. That is our chief object." They make the pace hard for "other employers," for there are mighty few industries in the country that can make up a payroll upon the basis of $5 a day as a minimum wage. The manufacturing industries of the country cannot follow an example which requires an eight-hour day and a standard of wages that from the scant outlines of the Ford Motor Company's plan seems to be approximately double the prevailing rate.

Under the operation of general laws trade seeks its level almost as certainly as water. The exceptions, the "peaks" here and there, are rare, artifically maintained, and the invariable tendency is toward their disappearance. The natural operation of this law was seen yesterday when 10,000 men struggled or actually fought around the works of the Ford Company at Detroit, clamoring for jobs. The man who offers extravagant prices for goods gets all the goods, at least more than he can take. Serious disturbances in the automobile industry labor market will, of course, follow. The Ford Company cannot hire all the men, yet there will be unrest and dissatisfaction in the shops of other companies. Strikes are likely enough, and conditions of peace cannot be looked for until the equilibrium is somehow restored.

The theory of the company as to its own favored employes is tinged with the utopian quality. The men are to receive their share of the profits in semi-monthly payments but efficiency is to be insisted upon and the "sociological department" of the company will keep an eye on the men, and "any who are found using the extra money in a way considered improper for right living will be eliminated as beneficiaries under the plan." Perhaps it is at this point that the plan will break down. Elimination will be resisted, for the injury to one will as certainly be the concern of all in this fortunate body of men as it is in organized labor unions. Profit-sharing does not change human nature.

[EDITORIAL (excerpt), Jan. 7, 1914]

wages. Our lowest wage at present is $2.34 per day. The lowest we pay girls who work in our factory is $12.50 a week. The work they do is mostly making magnets—all light work.

"We have never had any difficulty in getting plenty of labor, and we have never had any labor trouble.

"But how do you figure that you will be able this year to give your employes $10,000,000 as half of your profits?" Mr. Ford was asked.

"On the basis of last year's profits," he replied. "We made last year $25,000,000. We figure that this year one-half of our profits will be fully $10,000,000 to $12,000,000, and that sum we shall distribute to our employes. "

"What do you expect to result from this distribution?"

"For one thing, we shall get increased efficiency. Bear in mind that we are shortening the length of a day from nine to eight hours. I am positive the men will feel a keener interest in their work. Under the terms of the plan, it is not a stated sum that is to be distributed. The figures we name—$10,000,000 to $12,000,000—are approximate. The men will get half the profits. Is it not to their interest to increase their output and thus increase their share of the profits?"

"But what do you think will be the effect of your example on other automobile manufacturers?" Mr. Ford was asked. "Will they not find it difficult to keep their workmen, not feeling, perhaps, that they can afford to pay wages on a scale that yours, joined with the profit sharing, will amount to?"

"We cannot give employment to all the men in the automobile industry," was the reply. "Let me tell you something: There is no factory that is big enough to make two models of automobiles. The secret of successful modern business is concentration. Let automobile manufacturers concentrate."

"But some call your scheme Utopian," was suggested.

Mr. Ford smiled. "If you remember, there were many 'practical' people, so called, who solemnly warned us, several years ago, that it was impossible to make a car for $500 that would carry anybody anywhere.

"If you expect to get anything out of a man nowadays you must pay him well. If you want the best there is in him, you must make it really worth his while. You must give him something to live for.

"I do not believe in prolonging the conditions which ever since the civil war have been developing into a curse upon the country, and which in these last few years have caused the Federal Government to step in and make war upon big corporations. You know what I mean—the conditions which have built up a few millionaires and actually pauperized millions or kept them poor. They are out of date."

"The suggestion has been made that you might let the public in on this by putting a lower price on your cars."

"We shall continue to make our cars better and cheaper, and we shall cut the price regularly every Fall. With increased economy in manufacture we shall be able to lower the price next Fall by fully $30—perhaps by more. If we have to lay off men on account of overproduction, or for any other reason, we shall do this during the summer, in time for them to go to the farms and help in the harvesting.

"Let me tell you one of our business principles which may explain a lot to some of those who are painfully distressed over the impracticability of our distribution scheme," Mr. Ford continued. "We don't borrow money.

"When we first started business we decided we would be our own bankers. Now, we started last Fall with between $15,000,000 and $20,000,000 of our own money to keep us going through the Winter. And I may tell you that so far we haven't had to draw much on that fund."

[THE NEW YORK TIMES MAGAZINE, Jan. 11, 1914]

Governors Close Stock Exchange

OTHER EXCHANGES ALSO SHUT TO CHECK EUROPE'S DUMPING OF SECURITIES HERE

The financial developments in the United States yesterday growing out of the European war situation were the closing of the New York Stock Exchange, followed by the suspension of trading on the other Stock Exchanges of the country, the closing of the Cotton and Coffee Exchanges here, and the adoption of measures here and at Washington to provide for additional national bank circulation to meet the conditions created by the continued withdrawal of gold by Europe. For this purpose the machinery provided in the Federal Reserve Bank act, which re-enacted the Aldrich-Vreeland law, is to be set in motion.

The Senate yesterday adopted an amendment to this law, the effect of which is to extend to all national banks the right to put out additional circulation. Under the law as it now stands, only banks having bond-secured circulation to the extent of 40 percent of their capital are entitled to issue the additional notes provided for by this act. Secretary of the Treasury McAdoo pointed out yesterday that under the law a total of $500,000,000 of this additional circulation can be put out. Details of the steps taken at Washington to facilitate the issue of additional bank notes will be found in the Washington dispatches to THE TIMES.

A few minutes before the time for the opening of the New York Stock Exchange yesterday, when the most tumultuous session in its history was expected, members of the Governing Committee began gathering in the office of the President, H. G. S. Noble, on the sixth floor.

There had been no call for a meeting, and the understanding was that the Exchange would open as usual, but the successive shocks of the advance in the English bank rate to 8 per cent, the discovery that the market was loaded down with big selling orders, and almost bare of buying orders, and the news of the beginning of runs on banks in London and Berlin alarmed the brokers so much that they hurried upstairs to urge a reconsideration of the decision to remain open. Besides the pressure brought to bear on Mr. Noble from this source telegrams were pouring in on him from out-of-town banks and Exchanges calling on the New York market to remain closed.

New arrivals reported that suspension of the British Bank act was imminent, and that Germany practically had declared war. By the time the Acting Chairman of the Exchange had mounted his little balcony to wait for the stroke of 10 o'clock, thirty-seven members of the Governing Board had gathered in the President's office. There was an insistent demand for a vote.

At ten minutes before the hour Mr. Noble hurried his associates across the hall to the Governors' room. An instant later and the crowd had voted almost unanimously to close the Exchange. At once word went out that for the third time in history the Stock Exchange had been compelled to close to protect the solvency of hundreds of firms. [Aug. 1, 1914]

The outbreak of war in Europe in 1914 was initially viewed as a disaster for American business and investors, and the New York Stock Exchange and other exchanges were closed on July 31, 1914, not to reopen until December, amid fears that stock prices would collapse.

It was not the first time, nor would it be the last, that Wall Street misread the situation. War in Europe enhanced demand for American goods at the same time that competitive suppliers were out of business.

By November, a Times editorial saluted the "brightening financial skies" as exchanges began to reopen and took pleasure in the decline in anti-business sentiment. When the New York market reopened, prices moved sharply higher and prosperity was rising. Never again would the stock market be closed for such a long period of time.

1910–1919

BRIGHTENING FINANCIAL SKIES

The news from London yesterday told the same story about the dreaded Stock Exchange settlement there that was told about the opening of our Cotton Exchange. It had been feared that there would be failures for millions. The fact was that there were only a few minor embarrassments due to the inability to make foreign collections, and assistance was forthcoming in those cases, so that the trouble was merely of personal significance. Each fresh step toward the revival of business promises to have the same encouraging results as in these two cases, and for the same reason. There is a new spirit of co-operation abroad, to use the President's word. The business world is passing through troubles thrust upon it, not springing from faults of its own. It is a common calamity which would be irretrievable if met with spears which knew no brothers. But in all lands there is instead a helping hand to every one who deserves it.

These unprecedented trials have been borne without panic and ruin. The astonishment is not that the situation is so bad, but that it is so good, and with such promise of improvement. Conditions prove beyond doubt that we are leaving our troubles behind us. Comparison with the rest of the world is even more encouraging than comparison with ourselves of the recent past. Peace and plenty and a general spirit of hope are among the most enviable of our possessions. It would be easy to figure fabulous losses on paper. On another piece of paper it could be shown that those losses have been retrieved by the new spirit of thrift and industry such as has been characteristic of our most productive periods. We have learned that our exuberant periods are those which threaten our national welfare, and that it is in our sober seasons that we thrive in both spirit and estate.

There is no land where wealth accumulates at such a rate as in the United States when it is in its present mood, just as there is no land where there is such prodigality when the restraints are removed. When workers are willing to work there is hope of dividends. When there are dividends it is sure that wages have preceded them. With dividends and wages, with unprecedented crop values, and with natural resources hardly touched or even appreciated, it is not possible to think of anything but temporary embarrassment for the United States.

For these conditions we have in some measure to thank the war. It is the storm which has cleared the air and brought the country to stop its foolishness and get down to business. That is the meaning of the election, the result of which was a bomb among the politicians. There will be less of such legislation as has afflicted the country, and the prosecutors of prosperity will have a rest. On the whole, the credits of the situation are stronger than the undeniable debits. The future belongs to the courageous, and they deserve it. [EDITORIAL, Nov. 20, 1914]

German soldiers in 1914 marched off to World War I, which was a boon to the U.S. economy.

Exchange to Trade in All Stocks Now
STRONG UPWARD SWING CAUSES DECISION TO RESCIND WARTIME RESTRICTIONS

The Committee of Five at the Stock Exchange decided yesterday to throw the market open for general trading in stocks without any restriction except the minimum prices. Beginning today, therefore, business will be conducted practically as it was before the war caused the closing of the security markets on July 31. Yesterday's forward swing of prices carried the quotations for most shares so far above the minimum level established last week that the continuance even of the minimum price restriction seemed necessary only as a guard against extraordinary happenings in international finance.

The committee's decision was unexpected. The Street had thought that the 145 stocks left in the Clearing House last Saturday would be transferred gradually as the public interest called for additions to the trading list, but early in the afternoon the buying movement showed that the time had come to concentrate dealings on the board.

Wall Street found much satisfaction and a great deal of significance in the ruling. As members of the Stock Exchange, many Governors among them, had thought the admission to public quotation of such prominent stocks as Union Pacific, Steel, Canadian Pacific, and Southern Pacific would not be allowed for some time, the transfer of Clearing House issues to the board in a lump on the first trading day after the resumption of business was considered the most important reflection of stock market soundness that had yet been seen.

A collateral occurrence that attracted much attention was the calling of a special meeting of the Governing Committee for this afternoon. The purpose was not announced, but it was learned that the Committee of Five desired the Governors formally to legislate them out of office and return the management of the board to its normal control.

The Committee of Five has been in absolute charge of the Exchange since it closed on July 31. The desire of its members to relinquish this control was interpreted as evidence that the war emergency had passed in so far as the leaders of the Stock Exchange and the bankers could estimate the situation.

The chief factor in the elimination of Clearing House dealings was the strong demand for stocks on the Exchange. Following Saturday's substantial rise, buyers appeared in force, causing a steady advance for most shares dealt in.

The course of prices in Clearing House transactions was more significant, if anything, than the progress on the Exchange. Steel, which in October sold in the New Street market at 38½, rose for the first time above the minimum price established for it, and at 55 was 5 points higher than it sold in the unofficial market last Friday.

The Clearing House Committee reported early in the day to the Committee of Five that the volume of business was getting beyond them. It was when this report, practically a call for relief, came from the Clearing House that the Committee of Five canvassed the situation afresh and decided that the time had come for general trading in the open.   [Dec. 15, 1914]

1910–1919

Peace Finds Business and Financial Structure Firm

By the end of World War I, the United States knew it was the world's preeminent economic power, but it did not want the responsibilities that came with that power and soon retreated into political isolationism by refusing to join the League of Nations. Throughout the 19th century, the United States had been a major importer of capital, but by the end of the war it was running a large trade surplus and was in a position to invest abroad. The confidence born of the improved trade position was reflected in an economic analysis published in early 1919, less than two months after the end of the war.

Standing at the threshold of the new year, the people of the United States have reason to contemplate with satisfaction the testing of internal powers and resources which occurred in 1918. The transcendent fact for retrospective survey is the winning of the world war and the great part which the nation took in the struggle, but interwoven with the threads of hard-fought campaigns and gallant deeds on the field were the strong cords of co-operation between industry and Government and between Government and the individual. The nation has learned that the process of subjugating private interest to the general good can be carried out with speed and with the practical elimination of selfish desires. It has proved, so that all the world may see, that the American habit of thought is not centered solely around the pursuit of wealth and the expansion of business. The process has cost something, but not so much in contrast with our resources as the burden assumed by the allied countries. There has been a wrenching and strain of the industrial and financial structure which can be repaired only through the exercise of careful thought, patience, and sacrifice. Yet no one may look back on the vast result attained without counting as slight the temporary unsettlement of our normal activities and mode of living.

A year ago few thought that the Teutonic menace could be subjugated within twelve months. The country then was only beginning to gather its strength together for the actual participation in the world war. After the start was made, however, it was little short of amazing how rapid progress was. The public entered 1918 with the full knowledge that the country had become the keystone of hope for the allied nations, but it was not completely realized how great would be the demands upon us. The plans then being laid by the national leaders for the conservation of food, credit, labor, materials, although fairly well worked out before the beginning of 1918, were measured only in broad terms by the people. True, two vast war loans had been raised, to a total of $6,800,000,000, and the certainty that further tremendous calls would be made upon savings was evident to every one, but the first loans were floated with a relatively small outlay of effort and the patriotic impulse colored the future in a fashion to lessen the true consideration of the task ahead.

It was a fortunate thing in many ways that during the months when the Government was drawing upon the people for its initial supply of funds and while terms of the tax law were being completed the security markets were reacting from their previous high levels. The result of this process was that when the nation entered 1918 a great deal of the war-brought enthusiasm for speculation had been eliminated and the groundwork was laid for the concentration of credit upon the great undertaking across the sea. The railroads had been stripped for action, so to speak, and through Government control were being prepared when the year opened to concentrate their facilities on the transportation of war materials and foodstuffs to the Eastern seaboard. The wisdom of this procedure was displayed time and again during the succeeding months.

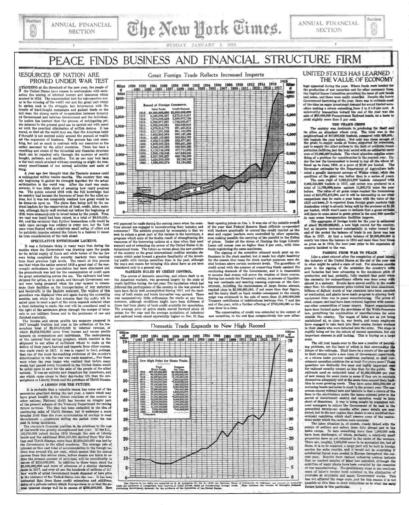

The income and excess profits tax measure prepared in 1917 brought fruition last year in the collection of the tremendous total of $3,694,619,000 in internal revenue, of which $2,838,900,000 came from income and excess profits imposts on corporations and individuals. The underpinning of the national food saving program, which results in the shipment to our allies of sufficient wheat to make up the deficit of their year's harvest and imports from other sources, was made ready in 1917. It was in regard to food, perhaps, that one of the most far-reaching evidences of the country's determination to win the war was made manifest. Few there were when the year began who realized that before many weeks had passed every household in the United States

Huge loads of ore are removed at the docks of U.S. Steel in Conneaut, Ohio, in 1919.

would be called upon to save for the sake of the people of the allied nations. It was an entirely new departure for Americans, and one which came closer to their day-to-day life than the subscriptions to Liberty Bonds and the purchase of Thrift Stamps.

It is probable that a valuable lesson has come out of the economies practiced during the last year, a lesson which may have great benefit in the future relations of the country to other nations. National thrift has become an integral part of the present scheme of the Treasury Department for raising future revenue. The plan has been embodied in the idea of continuing sales of Thrift Stamps, but it embraces a much broader field than the mere accumulation of savings to meet Government expenditures during the period when the war cost is being liquidated.

The country's financial position in its relations to the rest of the world was greatly strengthened last year. Of the $11,100,000,000 raised during 1918 through the sale of Liberty Bonds and the additional $950,000,000 derived from War Savings and Thrift Stamps, more than $5,000,000,000 was lent by the Government to the allied countries. The average rate of interest on this vast total of accommodation to the foreign nations was around 4¾ per cent, which means that the annual income from this source alone, before means are taken to reduce the present amount of principal, will be considerably in excess of $200,000,000. In addition to these loans stand the $3,000,000,000 and more of advances of a similar character made in 1917, and over all are the hundreds of millions of dollars' worth of allied Government bonds disposed of here prior to the entrance of the United States into the war. It has been estimated that from these credit extensions and additional debts of a private nature which Europe owes to us that the annual interest charge will be in excess of $500,000,000. How will payment be made during the coming years when the countries abroad are engaged in reconstructing their industry and commerce? The solution proposed by economists is that we seek to reloan a great part of this income to the borrowers, a program which aims at the double result of strengthening the resources of the borrowing nations at a time when they need support and of extending the power of the United States in international trade. The future as woven about the new position of the country as the great international creditor contains elements which point toward a greater familiarity of the investing public with foreign securities than in the past, although the ways and means for bringing this about have as yet been considered only in a general way.

[ANNUAL FINANCIAL SECTION, Jan. 5, 1919]

1910–1919

1920–1929

"A street of vanished hopes." Nervous spectators outside the New York Stock Exchange on Oct. 29, 1929.

Prosperity—Then Ruin

A CONFIDENT AMERICA ENTERED THE 1920's with an industrial capability that had not been damaged by World War I. Europe, however, was still torn by the hatreds of the war, and the peace treaty, requiring massive reparations from Germany, seems in retrospect to have been destined to create disaster. A prescient warning of that, from John Maynard Keynes, was received with hostility, but in due course Germany's currency collapsed in the worst inflation ever seen in a major country.

A great new industry was born with the decade, as a radio station began broadcasting in Pittsburgh, stimulating the sale of receivers. Soon there were stations in other cities, and, while it was initially not clear who would pay for broadcasting, it soon evolved into a commercial medium, with advertisers buying time to promote themselves. The decade also saw the first talking motion picture, and it witnessed the first demonstration of television, featuring a speech by a politician and jokes by a comedian, although it would be many years before television became the country's dominant entertainment industry.

Other industries were changing as well. The liquor industry was legislated out of (legal) existence as the decade began. Farmers suffered during the decade as crop prices failed to keep up with those of industrial goods, and by the end of the decade the Government tried to help. The trend to convenience in preparing food advanced greatly when Clarence Birdseye perfected a technique for freezing food products. General Motors surpassed Ford as the nation's largest car company because it recognized that people wanted cars that were different from those of their neighbors and because it was willing to extend credit. Ford briefly regained the lead, but in the next decade G.M. would become the world's largest car company and hold that position for the rest of the century.

The decade began with the Supreme Court throwing out an antitrust case against the U.S. Steel Corporation in a decision that assured antitrust law would be dead for many years, and for most of the decade big business grew amid general public acclaim. "The chief business of the American people is business," President Calvin Coolidge asserted in 1925.

In that climate, the stock market rose, and rose some more, with those who counseled caution shown to be foolish. The public began investing in stocks to a greater extent than ever before, with many taking advantage of easy credit—it was possible to borrow 90 percent of the purchase price when buying stocks—to amass paper fortunes. So much money was being used by Wall Street, in fact, that companies in the hinterland complained that interest rates were being driven so high they could not afford to borrow money for productive purposes. Then, in the fall of 1929, came the crash. The next decade was to be far different.

1920 Prohibition begins.

Women get the right to vote in the United States.

1921 Warren G. Harding is inaugurated President.

Ireland becomes a free state within the British empire.

1922 India arrests Gandhi on charge of sedition.

Coco Chanel introduces Chanel No. 5 perfume.

1923 President Harding dies and Calvin Coolidge becomes President.

King Tutankhamen's tomb is opened in Egypt.

1924 V. I. Lenin dies and a triumvirate led by Josef Stalin takes over in Russia.

1925 Hitler publishes the first volume of "Mein Kampf," completing it in 1927.

John T. Scopes is tried for teaching evolution in a Tennessee school.

1926 The first motion picture with sound is demonstrated.

Robert H. Goddard launches the first liquid-fuel rocket.

1927 Charles Lindbergh flies from New York to Paris in the first nonstop solo transatlantic flight.

1928 Herbert Hoover is elected President.

1929 The stock market collapses, ushering in the Great Depression.

Faults and Weaknesses of Mr. Keynes's Attack on Treaty

EXPERT ANALYSIS OF HIS CRITICISM OF WHAT THE ALLIED LEADERS DID AT THE PARIS PEACE CONFERENCE SHOWS THE STRONG AND SIGNIFICANT BIAS OF HIS BOOK ON "THE ECONOMIC CONSEQUENCES OF THE PEACE"

It is a rare decade that begins with a prominent book that correctly predicts what will shortly go very wrong and bring the world into misery. But the 1920's began with just such a book: "The Economic Consequences of the Peace," by John Maynard Keynes, the British economist who had resigned in disgust from the British delegation to the Versailles peace conference.

To Keynes, who was to become the most famous economist of the century, the Versailles Treaty was a recipe for disaster because it required Germany to pay reparations that it could not hope to pay, which he thought would lead to despair and revolution that would destroy Germany and other countries. He also denounced the provisions requiring the allies to repay debts to each other, the principal beneficiary of which was to be the United States.

The book caused quite an uproar, with a discussion of it topping the front page of The Times about a month after a very angry history professor, reviewing the book for The Times book review, ripped into it for being too friendly to Germany and seemingly oblivious to the horrible crimes Germany had committed in the war.

In the discussion of the book featured on the front page, Keynes's defender was Paul D. Cravath, a lawyer and founder of Cravath, Swaine & Moore, which remains one of New York's leading law firms.

Few books have gained more attention than did this one, or been proven to be more correct. But the message was not heeded by the political leaders of the era.

By CHARLES DOWNER HAZEN, Professor of History at Columbia University

The Economic Consequences of the Peace. By John Maynard Keynes. New York: Harcourt, Brace & Howe

Mr. Keynes, an English economist, and a financial adviser to the British mission at Paris, has written a book on "The Economic Consequences of the Peace." Let no one think that, because written by an economist, it must be dry and dull. It is anything but that. It is a very angry book. Mr. Keynes resigned his position in Paris when he saw that the treaty about to be signed was not to his liking, and ignored his advice. Paris, he says, "was a nightmare and every one there was morbid." Ordinarily any one who has just experienced five months of nightmare is in no condition to write a calm and balanced book. Mr. Keynes's book is written with passion, and it has this peculiarity, that all the passion is directed against the Allies, who dictated an abominable peace to the Germans, a "Carthaginian peace" as he calls it, thus striking at the outset a high rhetorical note, and evidently not fearing that the great, classically educated American democracy would be able to detect some quite important differences between that and the Peace of Versailles.

Who were the architects of the great crime of Paris? They were three men, Clemenceau, Lloyd George and Wilson. Orlando evidently did not count, for he is mentioned only once and is then lost to view. It is Mr. Keynes's vivid and confident portraits of these three that are giving great pleasure to all those who dislike any one or all of the individuals concerned. In this revolting melodrama of our days Clemenceau is the heavy villain, Lloyd George the mountebank and weathercock, and Wilson the Simple Simon, for whom the tolls were nicely spread, and who was easily snared, or to stick closely to the language of our author, an "old Presbyterian" whom it was easier to "bamboozle" than to "debamboozle."

What did the three blunderers do, since a Carthaginian Peace is surely worse than a crime? They made a solemn promise to the Germans that they should have a peace in accordance with the terms "laid down in the Fourteen Points and the subsequent addresses of the President," and they then gave them the negation of all this. Mr. Keynes admits in one place that the celebrated points were, in part, ambiguous; in another that there were many questions to which they gave no clear answer. Yet he is positive that the treaty departs from those points, in spirit altogether, and literally in many sections, and he sums up the matter in these words:

> The German commentators had little difficulty in showing that the draft treaty constituted a breach of engagements and of international morality comparable with their own offense in the invasion of Belgium.

This amazing statement accurately presents the tone that pervades the book from cover to cover. From this passage, as from many others, the reader can form his own idea of the sobriety of judgment, the restraint of language, the intellectual discrimination of the author. The world outside Central Europe long ago formed a very definite idea of the morality involved in the invasion of Belgium. Mr. Keynes places the treaty alongside as a fit and adequate companion piece. He is entitled to all the repute he may get as a fair thinker from that phrase. At any rate he gives us a clear revelation of his critical standards.

One of the ways in which the "points" were flouted was in the financial clauses of the treaty. Mr. Keynes estimates that the treaty exacts $40,000,000,000 from the Germans, that the sum is not only immoral but preposterous, that the Germans could not possibly pay it even if they desired to, that to try to exact it or to hang it over them is more than likely to breed a revolution of despair which will not only ruin Germany but other countries as well, very likely undermining the hitherto existing economic system and social order of the world. It would be impossible in any review that seeks to allude to all the aspects of this book to summarize Mr. Keynes's evidence on this matter, evidence which fills a hundred pages packed with statistics, tables, estimates. All the author's technical information, and it is very great, is marshaled to establish his point. The discussion is close but not dull, as all through it is spiced with the denunciatory epithets and the charges of bad faith with which we have become familiar. One

John Maynard Keynes, the most influential economist of his era.

may well agree with Mr. Keynes that Germany should not be "ruined," should not be "destroyed," terms which he constantly uses, without being convinced that the framers of the treaty intended to accomplish any such thing or will try to accomplish it. Concerning the actual amount of reparations due there is doubt. Concerning the power of the Reparation Commission to remit or modify a considerable part there is no question and to assume that it never will remit or modify, should it be wise and expedient to do so, is gratuitous until some proof can be brought forward as to the exceptional ignorance of malevolence of that Commission.

Another remedy urged by Mr. Keynes for the betterment of the world is that the Allies should cancel all the debts they owe each other, debts incurred for the purposes of the war. This proposal "is one which I believe to be absolutely essential to the future prosperity of the world. It would be an act of far-seeing statesmanship for the United Kingdom and the United States, the two powers chiefly concerned, to adopt it."

As far as the United States is concerned, this means about $10,000,000,000 wiped off. Mr. Keynes's method of argumentation is peculiar and somewhat invidious. If the Allies do not do this, what will happen? They will be exacting intolerable "indemnities" from each other. In the case of "victorious" France "she must pay her friends and allies more than four times the indemnity which in the defeat of 1870 she paid Germany. The hand of Bismarck was light compared with that of an Ally or an Associate."

We doubt if any Frenchman has had this brilliant thought that the hand of the Ally lies more heavily upon him than Bismarck's. It does not require an exceptionally acute mind to see some differences between borrowing from a friend for the purpose of saving your country and having an enemy extort an indemnity from you and also take some of your provinces. Whether indemnity is the happy word to use in both cases is questionable, but Mr. Keynes has a more or less discreet way of throwing out words that fester, and apparently for the purpose that they should fester.

Unless these Inter-Allied loans are cancelled he expects that the allied nations will try to evade payment and that the demand for repudiation will arise, and this demand he apparently approves if necessary. "In short, I do not believe that any of these trib-

CORBIS/UPI

1920–1929

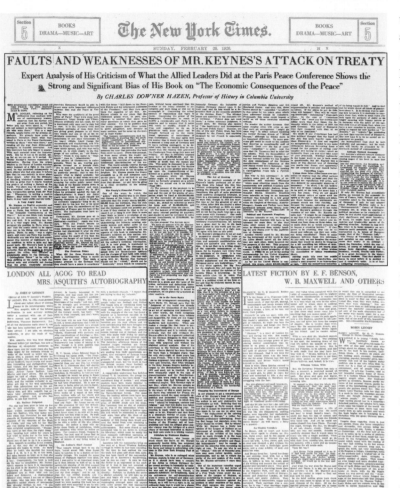

utes will continue to be paid, at the best, for more than a very few years. *They do not square with human nature or agree with the spirit of the age.*" The italics are mine, put there because the sentiments expressed struck me very forcibly, and because the reader, reflecting on them, may get additional light as to the value of Mr. Keynes's guidance through the troubles of our times. Mr. Keynes admits that "it might be an exaggeration to say that it is impossible for the European Allies to pay the capital and interest due from them on these debts, but to make them do so would certainly be to impose a crushing burden." If they prove to be crushing, they can be reduced and relieved, can they not, without being repudiated? There is some distance between these two extremes. At any rate, we can imagine the enthusiasm that would be shown in Congress for a bill cancelling ten billions of debt. Moreover, we have not yet heard from any Government that it either wishes the cancellation or thinks repudiation likely.

The Treaty of Versailles is imperfect and satisfies no one entirely, but because that treaty is an attempt to clinch the liberation, which the war effected, of scores of millions of human beings from degrading subjection to Germany, Austria, Russia and Turkey, it is a great document in the history of human freedom. That fact should be borne in mind before it is decided to cast it completely aside. It is at least a mitigating circumstance.   [BOOKS SECTION, Feb. 29, 1920]

CRAVATH ADVISES TREATY REVISION

DECLARES GERMANY'S BURDEN MUST BE LIGHTENED FOR BENEFIT OF ALLIES; WARNS OF ECONOMIC CHAOS

At the luncheon of the League of Free Nations Association at the Commodore yesterday Paul D. Cravath, who was legal adviser to the United States Treasury Finance Commission in Europe, declared that in the interests of France, Italy and Great Britain, as well as Germany, the Versailles Treaty should be revised and the payment of indemnity be kept well within Germany's capacity to pay.

Referring to the Reparations Commission, Mr. Cravath asked whether any machinery that could be devised was more calculated to drive Germany to despair and revolution. The prompt revision of the treaty, he continued, is the most important single factor in the world today. He urged that the United States should be a party to the treaty and the League of Nations and have membership on the Reparations Commission, so that it could bring pressure to bear to "accomplish this great reform."

The speakers discussed J. M. Keynes's book, "The Economic Consequences of the Peace." Those who took part were David Hunter Miller, legal adviser of the United States Commission to Negotiate Peace; Professor Allyn A. Young, economic adviser of

the commission, and Alvin Johnson, an editor of The New Republic.

Although the meeting was not scheduled as a debate it soon proved to be a contest between Mr. Cravath and Mr. Miller. Mr. Cravath supported, in the main, the conclusions of Mr. Keynes, and Mr. Miller asserted that the book "would substitute reaction for progress, injustice for justice and tyranny for freedom."

The economic sections of the treaty did not comply with the Fourteen Points of President Wilson, asserted Mr. Cravath, and unless the economic terms of the treaty were revised nothing could stop Europe from going headlong into chaos.

The statesmen at Paris who framed the treaty differed from those who drew up the Treaty of Vienna, said Professor Young, because they were not endowed with absolute power, but were leaders and servants of public opinion. With all its weaknesses the treaty was an accurate index of public opinion in the four countries. The failure of the treaty was the failure of democracy. The provisions of the commercial clauses were not likely to have a serious effect on Germany's economic life, he added. [March 28, 1920]

Supreme Court Holds U.S. Steel Legal; Public Interest Declared Paramount; May Affect Many Other Anti-Trust Suits

Special to The New York Times

WASHINGTON, March 1—In one of the most important opinions ever handed down by that body, the United States Supreme Court today held that the United States Steel Corporation is not a trust within the meaning of the Sherman anti-trust law.

The decision, opposite in effect to those of the court in the Standard Oil and American Tobacco Company cases, was concurred in by only four of the nine members of the court. Three dissented and two took no part in the consideration of the case or the decision.

The opinion was read by Justice McKenna and was concurred in by Chief Justice White and Justices Holmes and Vandevanter. Justice Day read the dissenting opinion, in which he was joined by Justices Clarke and Pitney. Justices McReynolds and Brandeis did not have any part in the case.

The majority opinion held, in effect, that the Steel Corporation had committed no overt acts violative of the Sherman law since the Government's suit was filed; that although by its size and its control of equipment and resources in the steel business the corporation was in a position to dominate the trade, the mere fact that it was able to do so should not be taken as indicating that it did, in the absence of any evidence; and finally, that to order the dissolution of the corporation would involve the risk of great disturbance in the financial, commercial and economic structure, and thus would menace the public interest, which in this case the court held to be of paramount importance.

In a vigorous dissenting opinion, Justice Day said that he could find no reason for the court's failure to apply in this case the same policy as was followed with respect to the Standard Oil and American Tobacco Company cases. The failure to follow that rule, he said, constituted an annulment of the Sherman act, making necessary some action by Congress indicating anew just what limitations were to be put upon trade combinations.

Justice Day said that he knew of no public interest that sanctioned the violation of law and no disturbance of foreign or domestic commerce that would justify the abrogation of statutes.

The dissenting opinion concerning the nullification of the Sherman law by reason of the alleged setting aside in this case of the precedents of the Standard and Tobacco cases caused a great stir. The majority opinion justifies this setting aside of the heretofore usual rule in cases under the Sherman act, on the ground that in this case there was no proof, as in the other two, that the corporation had from its inception been a law-breaker.

That the decision of the Supreme Court in the Steel Corporation litigation may have a far-reaching effect upon other anti-trust cases now pending or

The Supreme Court sounded the death knell for the early-20th-century wave of antitrust prosecutions by ruling that U.S. Steel, the company put together in 1901 by J. P. Morgan to dominate the American steel business, was legal because, while it had the power to control the steel trade, it had not exercised that power. In addition, said the court, the public interest could be harmed by the disturbance of such a large company.

The ruling meant that for the rest of the decade American business could operate largely unfettered by Government regulation or oversight. That would not change until the 1930's, after the arrival of the Great Depression.

1920–1929

Workers filling molds at a U.S. Steel plant.

U.S. STEEL

which may have been contemplated was the belief expressed tonight by more than one official. Attorney General Palmer and C. B. Ames, his assistant in charge of the anti-trust cases, withheld comment but it was admitted that many vital points of law involved in other cases pending were dealt with in the court's findings.

Mr. Ames at once began a study of the decision and the minority report of the court and will make a statement to the Attorney General. In the meantime the status of other litigation must remain in doubt. The fact that the decision in favor of the Steel Corporation was rendered by a minority of the whole court may have some effect upon the program of the Department of Justice, but the intimation tonight was that a change of policy would not be surprising.

One expert, who has reviewed other anti-trust cases, expressed the belief that if the decision in regard to United States Steel remained effective a precedent would be established that would seem to settle in favor of the corporate interests several methods of attack adopted by the Department of Justice.

For instance, the suit against the American Sugar Refining Company et al. was postponed "awaiting the decisions of the Supreme Court in the Harvester and Steel cases," according to the Attorney General's annual report. In the event, for example, that prosecution of the American Sugar case were to be continued, it would appear that the Attorney General would have to attempt to overthrow findings made by the Supreme Court in the Steel case in order to hope for success.

The circumstances surrounding the decision in the case of United States Steel may result in the whole program of anti-trust prosecutions being brought to the attention of President Wilson.

Advocates of methods, other than the employment of anti-trust legislation to control the corporations, were using today's decision as an argument in favor of their contentions. The declaration of the minority of the court that the Sherman act is made void by the decision is likely to revive agitation for legislation looking to Federal chartering or Federal licensing systems.

The Federal licensing system has been urged upon Congress by President Wilson. Attorney General Palmer has looked with favor upon this plan. The Trade Commission is also a supporter of Federal charters for great corporations, along the lines suggested to the Roosevelt administrations by the then Commissioner of Corporations James R. Garfield, whose views were indorsed by Roosevelt.

Had Justices McReynolds and Brandeis taken part in the case and voted for dissolution, the court would have stood five to four in favor of dissolution, instead of four to three against it. It was under the regime of Justice McReynolds as Attorney General of the United States that the Government's dissolution suit was instituted.

Justice Brandeis, prior to his appointment to the Supreme bench, set forth his belief as to the status of the Steel Corporation under the Sherman Anti-Trust act when he appeared in 1911 as "counsel for the people" before a committee of the Senate, of which Senator Clapp was chairman, directed to investigate the whole subject of trusts. At that time Mr. Brandeis expressed an opinion to the effect that the Steel Corporation was in fact a trust. [March 2, 1920]

It Was Twelve Years Ago

THAT KDKA THE PIONEER WENT ON THE AIR AND THE RADIO GOLD RUSH BEGAN— HOW BROADCASTING HAS CHANGED SINCE 1920

Broadcasting celebrates its twelfth anniversary on Wednesday. It was on Nov. 2, 1920, that the pioneer Station KDKA went on the air at Pittsburgh to send out Harding-Cox election bulletins. The audience consisted of wireless amateurs with homemade receivers designed to pick up code messages.

A visionary Pittsburgh department store advertised radio parts for sale. A fine business resulted. Electrical manufacturers caught on to the idea and began to build the various devices, coils, headphones and crystal detectors needed to intercept the broadcasts. The demand in the Pittsburgh area was surprising. Other broadcasting stations were established, and wherever they reached the demand for receiving sets increased.

KDKA had the air to itself that Winter, but in 1921 radio pushed ahead at a hectic pace and KDKA had plenty of company.

The Dempsey-Carpentier fight was broadcast from Boyle's Thirty Acres at Jersey City on the sweltering July 2. There was no station in the vicinity, so a temporary transmitter was hooked up at Hoboken.

The excited announcer's voice, heard through the metropolitan area, revealed new possibilities for radio and stirred up a demand for receiving sets. And since that day the ringside scenes have been near the top of popular events on the air.

Station WBZ, Springfield, Mass., began to broadcast on Sept. 27, 1921. WJZ officially opened at Newark, N.J., on Oct. 1, 1921, as the first regular broadcaster in the New York area. It was located in a small room in a factory building, extremely humble when compared to the elaborate studios of 1932 and those now under construction in Radio City. WJZ's initial program featured world series bulletins.

The burial of the unknown soldier at Arlington, including an address by President Harding, was broadcast on Nov. 11, 1921. Station KYW, Chicago, made its appearance on that day.

The year 1922 saw radio hitting a rapid stride. WGY made its debut at Schenectady on Washington's Birthday. The broadcasting business was growing more or less wildly, so Herbert Hoover, then Secretary of Commerce, who had jurisdiction over radio, called a conference to avert chaos in the ether.

Station WBAY, which had been operated by the American Telephone and Telegraph Company as an experimental unit, was abandoned on July 25, 1922, and on Aug. 16 WEAF made its appearance atop the Western Electric Building on West Street. By this time the broadcasters were wondering who was going to pay for broadcasting.

The 1920's saw the introduction of two new entertainment technologies that revolutionized America and a demonstration of one that would do even more to change the country, albeit not for another quarter century.

In 1920, KDKA in Pittsburgh became the first station to go on the air. No one knew what radio was to become, and so no stories memorialized the event until years later. But by 1932 it was clear what radio had wrought, and The Times published a retrospective noting that it took some time for anyone to figure out how to pay for the broadcasts. A realty company became the first sponsor of a broadcast. Before the 1920's were through, CBS and NBC had been formed, and the Radio Corporation of America, which owned NBC and made radio receivers, had become the hottest stock in the great bull market of the era.

In 1926, Warner Brothers announced a system to allow movies to talk, and the next year "The Jazz Singer," starring Al Jolson, amazed the country.

In 1927, a front-page article in The Times reported on a demonstration of television in which Herbert Hoover, then the Secretary of Commerce, made a speech in Washington that was seen and heard in New York on a screen that measured two by three inches.

In that same demonstration, a vaudeville comedian told some jokes, and The Times passed along a quite accurate, if carefully qualified, forecast: "The commercial future of television, if it has one, is thought to be largely in public entertainment."

1920–1929

WESTINGHOUSE

The radio industry, born in Pittsburgh, spread from coast to coast.

They began to realize it was expensive business, especially if they were to keep pace with progress.

The Western Electric Company, receiving numerous demands for transmitters, finally asked those desirous of going on the air, "Why not rent the facilities of WEAF?" So, the first commercially sponsored program filtered through space on Sept. 7, 1922. A realty organization paid the bill.

Many of the other broadcasters were aghast. They contended advertising contaminated the air and was not the correct answer to "Who will pay for broadcasting?" It was not long, however, before the majority did the same thing. And so broadcasting changed.

Now there was money for the entertainers, many of whom up to that time had refused to broadcast. But when the sponsors crossed their palms with silver, those who frowned upon the microphones as a menace to artistry smiled at the mute device, blessed the invisible audience and told them how delighted they were to sing and to play for so many millions.

Each year since 1920 has witnessed remarkable progress. Millions of dollars' worth of quickly antiquated equipment has been scrapped as inventive geniuses pushed something new onto the world-wide stage. And most of the improvement is attributed to the magic of the vacuum tube, which even today seems unlimited in its possibilities.

[SPECIAL FEATURES SECTION, Oct. 30, 1932]

CLOCK TRADE HURT BY RADIO TIME BROADCASTING

BRUSSELS, June 6–An old-established clock and watch maker says that his trade is being ruined by the radio. Before its introduction people were forced to have clocks that kept accurate time and chronometers were the fashion in the business world. Nowadays, with the correct time broadcast from various countries several times a day, clock hands are put right as often as may be necessary.

Before the coming of the radio numbers of clockmakers were employed in paying periodical visits to houses to wind big clocks and keep them in order. People now do the winding themselves. This has thrown a large number of men out of work.

[EDITORIAL SECTION, June 18, 1933]

Far-Off Speakers Seen as Well as Heard Here in a Test of Television

THE FIRST TIME IN HISTORY; COMMERCIAL USE IN DOUBT

Herbert Hoover made a speech in Washington yesterday afternoon. An audience in New York heard him and saw him.

More than 200 miles of space intervening between the speaker and his audience was annihilated by the television apparatus developed by the Bell Laboratories of the American Telephone and Telegraph Company and demonstrated publicly for the first time yesterday.

The apparatus shot images of Mr. Hoover by wire from Washington to New York at the rate of eighteen a second. These were thrown on a screen as motion pictures, while the loudspeaker reproduced the speech. As each syllable was heard, the motion of the speaker's lips and his changes of expression were flashed on the screen in the demonstration room of the Bell Telephone Laboratories at 55 Bethune Street.

When the television pictures were thrown on a screen two by three inches, the likeness was excellent. It was as if a photograph had suddenly come to life and begun to talk, smile, nod its head and look this way and that. When the screen was enlarged to two by three feet, the results were not so good.

At times the face of the Secretary could not be clearly distinguished. He looked down, as he read his speech, and held the telephone receiver up, so that it covered most of the lower part of his countenance. There was too much illumination also in the background of the screen. When he moved his face, his features became clearly distinguishable. Near the close of his talk he turned his head to one side, and in profile his features became clear and full of detail.

On the smaller screen the face and action were reproduced with perfect fidelity.

After Mr. Hoover had spoken, Vice President J. J. Carty of the American Telephone and Telegraph Company and others in the demonstration room at Washington took his place and conversed one at a time with men in New York. The speaker on the New York end looked the Washington man in the eye, as he talked to him. On the small screen before him appeared the living face of the man to whom he was talking.

Time as well as space was eliminated. Secretary Hoover's New York hearers and spectators were something like a thousandth part of a second later than the persons at his side in hearing him and in seeing changes of countenance.

The faces and voices were projected from Washington by wire. It was shown a few minutes later, however, that radio does just as well.

In the second part of the program the group in New York saw and heard performances in the Whippany studio of the American Telephone and Telegraph Company by wireless. The first face flashed on the screen from Whippany, N.J., was that of E. L. Nelson, an engineer, who gave a technical description of what was taking place. Mr. Nelson had a good television face. He screened well as he talked.

Next came a vaudeville act by radio from Whippany. A. Dolan, a comedian, first appeared before the audience as a stage Irishman, with side whiskers and a broken pipe, and did a monologue in brogue. Then he made a quick change and came back in blackface with a new line of quips in negro dialect. The loudspeaker part went over very well. It was the first vaudeville act that ever went on the air as a talking picture and in its possibilities it may be compared with the Fred Ott sneeze of more than thirty years ago, the first piece of comedy ever recorded in motion pictures. For the commercial future of television, if it has one, is thought to be largely in public entertainment—super-news reels flashed before audiences at the moment of occurrence, together with dramatic and musical acts shot on the ether waves in sound and picture at the instant they are taking place in the studio.

A coincidence is that "Metropolis," the German film now showing what purports to be the New York of a century or centuries hence, has a make-believe screen in connection with the telephone—a case of a prophecy being fulfilled about as soon as it started.

The demonstration of combined telephone and television, in fact, is one that outruns the imagination of all the wizards of prophecy. It is one of the few things that Leonardo da Vinci, Roger Bacon, Jules Verne and other masters of forecasting failed utterly to anticipate. Even interpreters of the Bible are having trouble in finding a passage which forecast television. H. G. Wells did not rise to it in his earlier crystal-gazing. It is only within the last few years that prophets have been busy in this field. Science has moved ahead so rapidly in this particular line that one of the men, who played a major part in developing the television apparatus shown yesterday, was of

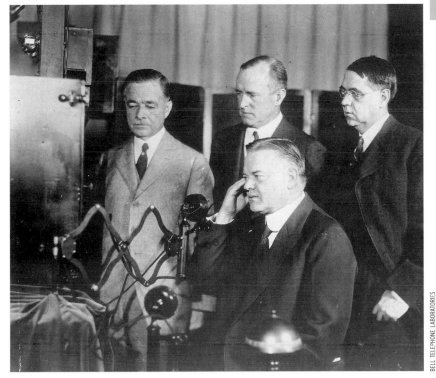

Herbert Hoover, then the Secretary of Commerce, made television history in 1927.

BELL TELEPHONE LABORATORIES

1920–1929

The New York Times.

"All the News That's Fit to Print."

THE WEATHER

FAR-OFF SPEAKERS SEEN AS WELL AS HEARD HERE IN A TEST OF TELEVISION

LIKE A PHOTO COME TO LIFE

Hoover's Face Plainly Imaged as He Speaks in Washington.

THE FIRST TIME IN HISTORY

Pictures Are Flashed by Wire and Radio Synchronizing With Speaker's Voice.

COMMERCIAL USE IN DOUBT

But A.T.&T. Head Sees a New Step in Conquest of Nature After Years of Research.

the opinion four years ago that research on this subject was hopeless. More than twenty years ago, however, Dr. Alexander Graham Bell, the inventor of the telephone, predicted at a gathering in the tower of the Times Building that the day would come when the man at the telephone would be able to see the distant person to whom he was speaking.

The demonstration began yesterday afternoon at 2:15 with General Carty at the television apparatus in Washington.

Mr. Hoover was then called on to take a seat before the light which divides the sitter into 45,000 squares a second. A few seconds later, the voice of Secretary Hoover was heard over the loudspeaker, as his face appeared on the large screen.

The illuminated transparent screen seemed somewhat corrugated. This is due to the fact that the squares which make up the picture are arranged in fifty rows, one on top of the other. In the centre of the screen appeared a white glare, surrounded by darker markings.

As the eye became accustomed to looking at the screen in the darkened room, the larger luminous patch took shape as the forehead of Secretary Hoover. He was leaning forward in such a way that the forehead was taking up too much of the picture, while his mouth and chin were blotted out behind the telephone transmitter. When he moved, however, the picture became clearer.

The face looked up from the manuscript, the lips began to move and the first television-telephone speech started as follows:

"It is a matter of just pride to have a part in this historic occasion.

"We have long been familiar with the electrical transmission of sound. Today we have, in a sense, the transmission of sight, for the first time in the world's history.

"Human genius has now destroyed the impediment of distance in a new respect, and in a manner hitherto unknown. What its uses may finally be no one can tell, any more than man could foresee in past years the modern developments of the telegraph or the telephone. All we can say today is that there has been created a marvelous agency for whatever use the future may find, with the full realization that every great and fundamental discovery of the past has been followed by use far beyond the vision of its creator.

"Every school child is aware of the dramatic beginnings of the telegraph, the telephone and the radio, and this evolution in electrical communications has perhaps an importance as vital as any of these.

"This invention again emphasizes a new era in approach to important scientific discovery, of which we have already within the last two months seen another great exhibit—the transatlantic telephone. It is the result of organized, planned and definitely directed scientific research, magnificently coordinated in a cumulative group of highly skilled scientists, loyally supported by a great corporation, devoted to the advancement of the art. The intricate processes of this invention could never have been developed under any conditions of isolated individual effort."

The process by which yesterday's results were achieved appears infinitely complicated and difficult on first encounter, but becomes fairly simple when traced step by step.

The thing that chiefly staggers the mind is that all that traveled over the wire from Washington to New York or over the ether from Whippany to New York is a series of electrical impulses.

Speed and exactitude are the tremendous achievements in the process. Dots of light are put together at the rate of 45,000 a second to form the motion pictures. Each dot has to be in its exact place. The mosaic of squares would be a jumble—the picture would be completely "pied"—if there was an error of one ninety-thousandth part of a second in the synchronization between the sending apparatus in Washington and the receiving apparatus in New York.   [April 8, 1927]

Perfect Automatic Music for Movies

Special to The New York Times

ATLANTIC CITY, N.J., April 25—Perfection of a new apparatus which makes possible the release of music and reproduction of the human voice in their natural tones, to be used in connection with motion pictures, has been attained, according to announcement made here today. The American Telephone and Telegraph Company, the Western Electric Company and the Bell Laboratories cooperated in the development of the new apparatus and rights for exclusive use of it have been purchased by the Warner Brothers, motion-picture producers and exhibitors.

Albert Warner, spending the week end at the Ritz-Carlton, told reporters today that "this mechanical development, combining the practical and the artistic, will revolutionize the motion-picture industry." "It means," he went on, "that even in the most modest motion picture theatre patrons will obtain the best music available, perfectly synchronized with the film."

John McCormick had already signed through the Victor Company to sing special ballad numbers for motion-picture scenes of sentimental appeal and Rudolph Frimol was already working on music to be released in connection with John Barrymore's new picture, "Don Juan," Mr. Warner said.

The new apparatus was not an experiment, but a practical device which had been tried out in the Warner Studios.

"Psychologically, we are not unaware of the subtle influence that pervades an audience when music in key and theme with the action of the picture is played," said Mr. Warner. "At a phenomenally small cost, the unquestionably planned and perfected radio music program will begin a new era for moving-picture patrons throughout the country.

"The paths of development in the musical field have been spanned by the larger moving-picture houses, but because of lack of funds and equipment have been hardly ventured upon by smaller houses. We plan to introduce this method of musical dissemination to all. Artistically, this will provide another outlet for the creative mind of this country also."   [April 26, 1926]

THE NEW YORK TIMES CENTURY OF BUSINESS • 71

Chanel: The Fashion Spirit of the 20th Century

Gabrielle Chanel, known to all as Coco, became a fashion industry phenomenon who created a business empire based partly on fashion and partly on the unusual perfume that she introduced in 1922 and to which she attached her name and favorite number: Chanel No. 5.

Chanel dominated the Paris fashion world of the 1920's and at the height of her career was running four enterprises—a fashion business, a textile business, perfume laboratories and a workshop for costume jewelry—with a total of 3,500 employees.

While she was perhaps the most prominent woman in business of her generation, her career was not one of uninterrupted success. Her perfume company was controlled by men with whom she eventually had a falling-out, and she was ousted as president of the perfume company in the 1930's.

The story of her rise, fall and rise again was told in The Times in her obituary when she died in 1971, at the age of 87, in her apartment at the Ritz Hotel in Paris.

By ENID NEMY

An intense woman with a scalding tongue, hair-trigger wit, unbounded immodesty and ineffable charm, Gabrielle Chanel was, throughout her life, a free spirit who used fashion as her pulpit. Her message was carried to millions through the medium of the Paris haute couture, a world over which she reigned, with arrogant self-assurance, for long stretches of almost six decades.

The darling of French society, a good friend of dukes and dandies, a confidante of the rich and famous, she was impatient of pretense, intolerant of restrictions, incapable of self-deception.

"There is no time for cut-and-dried monotony," she once said. "There is time for work. And time for love. That leaves no other time!"

Chanel was the fashion spirit of the 20th century, a Pied Piper who led women away from complicated, uncomfortable clothes to a bone-simple, uncluttered, and casual look that eventually became synonymous with her name.

Without marching in a parade or campaigning for right, she emancipated her sex from the tyrannies of fashion. Her strong convictions and independent opinions, her unswerving belief in simplicity and elegance, freed women of unnecessary constrictions and what she called "ludicrous trimmings and fussy bits and pieces."

Among her innovations, most of them considered revolutionary at the time, were jersey dresses and suits, tweed suits with jersey blouses, bell-bottom trousers, trenchcoats, pea jackets, turtleneck sweaters, sailor hats, bobbed hair, costume jewelry and the little black dress, often collared and cuffed in white.

The omnipresent Chanel suit, with its collarless, braid-trimmed cardigan jacket and graceful skirt, has probably been copied more, in all price ranges, than any other single garment designed by a couturier.

Chanel's handbag—soft, quilted leather, with a chain handle—was copied so widely that it became one of the most universal accessories of the nineteen-sixties. Other widespread Chanelisms were ropelike necklaces, sling-back pumps in her special colors—beige and black—and large, flat, tailored hair bows.

The copying of her designs never disturbed her. "Let them copy," she said. "My ideas belong to everyone. I refuse no one."

Perhaps the strongest tribute to her genius was that women of wealth, who took pride in exclusivity of design, did not mind being seen in the same clothes as working girls. Both groups wanted, and were willing to pay for, in varying degrees, the Chanel look.

The customers who went to the House of Chanel, a six-story building at 31 rue Cambon in Paris, included, at one time or another, Marlene Dietrich, Romy Schneider, Juliette Greco, Elsa Martinelli, Anouk Aimée, Bettina, Suzy Parker, François Sagan, Colette, Mrs. Georges Pompidou, Princess Paola, wife of the younger brother of King Baudouin of the Belgians; Mrs. Hélène Gordon-Lazaroff, editor of the French fashion magazine Elle; Mrs. Diana Vreeland, editor in chief of Vogue; the Rothschild baronesses and countless American socialites.

Chanel, despite her own taste for luxury and her patrician friends, was the constant democratizer of fashion. Her friend Picasso once said, "She is the most sensible woman in Europe," and her own definition of true luxe as "clothes they [women] can wear for years" confirmed the artist's description.

For Chanel, the great changes in fashion stemmed from significant changes in the manner and requirements of daily life. She explained her philosophy in 1957 when she traveled to the United States to receive, from Neiman-Marcus in Dallas, an award as the most significant designer of the last 50 years.

She told a reporter from The New Yorker that she inspired women to take off their bone corsets and to cut their hair, in 1925, because they were just beginning to work in offices.

"Women drive autos, and this you cannot do with a crinoline skirt," she said.

"But the grand problem," she added, "the most important problem, is to rejuvenate women, to make women look young. Then their outlook on life changes. They feel more joyous."

In Chanel's 87th year, on Dec. 18, 1969, the name that illuminated fashion went up in lights on Broadway. Coco (Little Pet), the nickname bestowed on the couturier by her father, became the title of a musical show based on her life. Starring Katharine Hepburn, it was produced by Frederick Brisson, a longtime friend of Chanel's.

During her lifetime, Chanel created an empire. In the twenties, at a time when she employed 2,400 people in her workrooms, her personal fortune was rumored to be $15 million.

The financial basis of the empire was Chanel No. 5, a perfume that she introduced in 1922 and named after her lucky number. Created by a chemist on the Riviera, it was an unorthodox blend of fragrances and soon became the most familiar perfume in the world.

"Women are not flowers," she once said, commenting on the scent. "Why should they want to smell like flowers?"

In 1924, Chanel founded Les Parfums Chanel with Pierre and Paul Wertheimer, owners of the Bourjois perfume interests. They became the majority stockholders in the new company.

By 1934, Chanel had been removed as president and the next year the company, in which she had a 10 per cent interest, began to cede its rights to subsidiaries and to Bourjois.

Les Parfums Chanel became the parent company of a large perfume empire that operated in France, Britain and the United States.

In 1946, Chanel sued Les Parfums Chanel, charging that it had produced merchandise of an inferior quality. The suit asked that the French parent concern be ordered to cease manufacturing and selling all products and restore to her the ownership and sole rights over products, formulas and manufacturing processes.

The suit was unsuccessful, but the feud apparently healed because when Chanel returned to the fashion world in 1954, after an absence of about 15 years, she exchanged her substantial stock ownership for another system of compensation that involved royalties and commissions.

The career that was to make her name began in the summer of 1913 in Deauville. She opened a tiny hat boutique. It was the heyday of elaborate and grotesque hats and she detested them.

"How can the brain function under those things?" she asked, and went on to provide millinery that offered nothing but simplicity and line. She took a fancy to turtleneck sweaters worn by English sailors in port, and sold a few of them.

The next year she returned to Paris and opened a shop at 31 rue Cambon, where she sold hats, then sweaters and a few clothes. Within five years she was a force to be reckoned with in the world of fashion.

She began to impress wealthy, influential women with her originality. She was the first designer to use ordinary jersey for clothes; the September, 1917, issue of Vogue magazine referred to the Maison Chanel as "the jersey house." A little later, she started the "poor-girl look," and rich women playfully wore clothes based on the garments of the humble.

In the mid-twenties, Chanel's name grew luminous. By 1924, well-dressed women on both sides of the Atlantic were taken with a Chanel costume of a beige jersey blouse

1920–1929

TIMES WIDE WORLD PHOTOS

Coco Chanel created a fashion empire.

worn with a single strand of pearls, and a tweed suit with a cardigan jacket. It is possible to appreciate the revolution she wrought only if one studies the ornate creations of the House of Worth and the pictures of pre–World War I Edwardian elegance.

Chanel's first period of professional pre-eminence, from the mid-twenties to the late thirties, coincided, in part, with her most famous alliance, with Hugh Richard Arthur Grosvenor, the second Duke of Westminster, one of Europe's wealthiest men, who was married four times and divorced three times.

The Duke's devotion to Chanel was expressed in gifts of remarkably valuable jewels. She often had the gifts copied in fake stones.

"I couldn't wear my own real pearls without being stared at in the street, so I started the vogue of wearing false ones," she said.

Although there was considerable speculation, both in Europe and the United States, that Chanel might marry the Duke, the volatile high priestess of couture preferred to retain her own identity.

"Everyone marries the Duke of Westminster," she reportedly said. "There are a lot of duchesses but only one Coco Chanel."

In the late thirties, when the fashionable world deserted Chanel for Elsa Schiaparelli, the Italian designer, and World War II broke out, Chanel shut her couture house and went across the street to hibernate at the Ritz. The Nazis later took many rooms there but they never commandeered the hotel. Chanel remained there, then went on to Vichy and to Switzerland, but the record of her life for 15 years is more blurred than usual.

Chanel's comeback, on Feb. 5, 1954, was a major turning point in the fashion world although hardly anyone realized it.

She showed a suit in heavy navy jersey with two patch pockets, worn with a white tucked muslin blouse and a sailor hat. The critics' reaction was civil but not ecstatic; however, women bought it. It was the forerunner of a style that evolved year after year with increasing success.

The reception was equally lukewarm after her second collection in October of that year. Chanel had always been considered a rebel and people expected shocks. Instead, Chanel, as always, was simply extending and developing the shapes that satisfied her.

The suit that was in every city in America by 1964 was an evolution of the navy design of a decade earlier. Her own favorite was a beige tweed trimmed with red and dark-blue braid, with the patch pockets used as purses.

The last years of her life were relatively quiet, dedicated to the couture house (which was often operated at a loss, the deficit paid cheerfully by the parent company because the publicity helped the sales of every other Chanel product) and to acerbic comments and racing horses. Her stables in Chantilly included a well-known mare, Romantica.

Chanel outlived many of her closest friends and felt separated from others. She had never married, not because she preferred solitude but, according to one quotation, because she "never wanted to weigh more heavily on a man than a bird."

Her weight on fashion was immeasurable.   [Jan. 11, 1971]

German Hope Sinks; Mark 7,000,000 to $1
POINCARE'S SPEECH AND REICHSBANK STATEMENT PLUNGE BERLIN IN GLOOM

By CYRIL BROWN

By Wireless to The New York Times

BERLIN, Aug. 27—Today witnessed another slump in German finance and German morale.

Like that American invention, the "switchback" or scenic railway, after making up-grade for the past two weeks, Germany suddenly has started on another breath-taking downward plunge, and may continue "roller-coasting" for weeks, possibly months. But the sum total of Germany's direction, like gravitation, is downward.

Today's features were:

First, Poincaré's Sunday speech scattered Germany's newly born foreign political hopes.

Secondly, the Boerse experienced a new record-breaking "catastrophe boom," stocks gaining up to 30,000,000 points.

Thirdly, the mark tobogganed to 7,000,000 to the dollar by evening.

As Germany struggled to make reparation payments required by the Versailles Treaty, its printing presses turned out ever more marks and its inflation problem grew worse and worse. In 1923, Britain suggested easing the reparations requirement but France would have none of it. A statement by French Premier Raymond Poincaré rejecting the demands for a reduction and saying France would continue to occupy the Ruhr area of Germany until the payments arrived caused another plunge for the mark, which was reported on the front page of The Times. Poincaré had ignored a speech by the new German chancellor, Gustav Stresemann, calling on Germans to sacrifice but saying Germany could not afford the reparations demanded by France.

A few months later, The Times highlighted a short story reporting on the dining experience of an American tourist who had visited a Berlin restaurant and asked for all the food a dollar could buy. Course after course was served. Then, when the diner thought he was through, more food arrived—with the explanation that the mark had just been devalued again.

The depreciation of the currency continued until April 1924, when it ended with a dollar worth 4.2 trillion marks. The mark's value had fallen by 99.99999995 percent since the spring of 1923, just a year earlier, when the dollar had sold for 2,000 marks. A new mark, effectively tied to gold, was established in April 1924 and exchanged for old ones at the rate of 1 trillion to one. The German economy stabilized with the aid of foreign loans until 1929, when the Depression came, followed by the rise of Adolf Hitler.

1920–1929

BILDER DIENST SÜDDEUTSCHER VERLAG

Worthless German bank notes were baled into wastepaper in the 1920s.

Fourth, the Reichsbank, several days overdue, published the most disastrous weekly statement to date.

Little comment is heard on Poincaré's speech. There is little for Germans to say. Political and financial circles were painfully affected by the fact that Poincaré, in their opinion, indulged exclusively in old-style polemics and made not the slightest gesture of even conditional willingness to grasp Stresemann's olive branch, and seemingly completely ignored Stresemann's speech, according to advanced bulletins from Paris. The full text of Poincaré's address has not arrived in Berlin as yet.

But Germans saw one faint ray of satisfaction in Poincaré's reported remarks about the Washington Institute of Economics in that they are hoping Poincaré committed a faux pas which will alienate various distinguished Americans whose names are associated with the Institute, whose report was received with approval throughout Germany. But here optimism ended.

The paper mark stampeded weirdly today. After a weak intervention by the Reichsbank at 1 o'clock, which set the rate officially at 5,600,000 to the dollar, it dropped so rapidly that at the close of the day it was somewhere around 7,000,000.

In addition to Poincaré's speech, Reichsbank President Havenstein's defense oration, wherein he spoke of "fantastic circulation figures" and intimated that inflation must continue as there was no way of checking it, and Sunday's figure showing that Germany's floating debt trebled in ten days, were important factors in sending the mark down.

A more important factor, however, was the Reichsbank statement for the week ended Aug. 15. The fact that this, long overdue, was not made until after Havenstein's apologia was launched was in itself ominous. But its bare figures fully justified the most pessimistic prognostications for the future.

During that week Germany's paper circulation was more than doubled by the emission of 54 trillions of paper marks, to a grand total of 116 trillions.

[Aug. 28, 1923]

BERLIN FEAST ON YANKEE CASH; DOLLAR RISES, DINNER GROWS

BERLIN, Oct. 29–"Give me all the food an American dollar will buy," was the order of a prosperous looking stranger in one of the lesser restaurants of Berlin. Such lavish orders are unusual in these days of bad exchange, but the waiter recovered from his astonishment and began to serve the guest.

Soup, several meat dishes, fruit and coffee were served. While the guest was smoking his cigar the waiter brought another plate of soup, and later another meat dish.

"What does this mean?" the astonished and satisfied guest asked.

The waiter bowed politely and replied: "The dollar has gone up again."

[Oct. 30, 1923]

Even a bank note for 50 million marks became worthless during Germany's spiraling inflation.

Stocks Collapse in 16,410,030-Share Day, But Rally at Close Cheers Brokers; Bankers Optimistic, to Continue Aid

Stock prices virtually collapsed yesterday, swept downward with gigantic losses in the most disastrous trading day in the stock market's history. Billions of dollars in open market value were wiped out as prices crumbled under the pressure of liquidation of securities which had to be sold at any price.

There was an impressive rally just at the close, which brought many leading stocks back from 4 to 14 points from their lowest points of the day.

Trading on the New York Stock Exchange aggregated 16,410,030 shares; on the Curb, 7,096,300 shares were dealt in. Both totals far exceeded any previous day's dealings.

From every point of view, in the extent of losses sustained, in total turnover, in the number of speculators wiped out, the day was the most disastrous in Wall Street's history. Hysteria swept the country and stocks went overboard for just what they would bring at forced sale.

Efforts to estimate yesterday's market losses in dollars are futile because of the vast number of securities quoted over the counter and on out-of-town exchanges on which no calculations are possible. However, it was estimated that 880 issues, on the New York Stock Exchange, lost between $8,000,000,000 and $9,000,000,000 yesterday. Added to that loss is to be reckoned the depreciation on issues on the Curb Market, in the over the counter market and on other exchanges.

There were two cheerful notes, however, which sounded throughout the pall of gloom which overhung the financial centres of the country. One was the brisk rally of stocks at the close, on tremendous buying by those who believe that prices have sunk too low. The other was that the liquidation has been so violent, as well as widespread, that many bankers, brokers and industrial leaders expressed the belief last night that it now has run its course.

A further note of optimism in the soundness of fundamentals was sounded by the directors of the United States Steel Corporation and the American Can Company, each of which declared an extra dividend of $1 a share at their late afternoon meetings.

Banking support, which would have been impressive and successful under ordinary circumstances, was swept violently aside, as block after block of stock, tremendous in proportions, deluged the market. Bid prices placed by bankers and brokers trying to halt the decline were crashed through violently, their orders were filled, and quotations plunged downward in a day of disorganization, confusion and financial impotence.

That there will be a change today seemed likely from statements made last night by financial and business leaders. Organized support will be accorded to the market from the start, it is believed, but those who are staking their all on the country's leading securities are placing a great deal of confidence, too, in the expectation that there will be an overnight change in sentiment; that the counsel of cool heads will prevail and that the mob psychology which has been so largely responsible for the market's debacle will be broken.

The fact that the leading stocks were able to rally in the final fifteen minutes of trading yesterday was considered a good omen, especially as the weakest period of the day had developed just prior to that time and the minimum prices for the day had then been established. It was a quick run-up which followed the announcement that the American Can directors had declared an extra dividend of $1. The advances in leading stocks in this last fifteen minutes represented a measurable snapback from the lows. American Can gained 10; United States Steel common, 7½; General Electric, 12; New York Central, 14½; Anaconda Copper, 9½; Chrysler Motors, 5¼; Montgomery

There had never been a bull market like the one produced in the 1920's. That market was based on the optimism of the decade and on the clear technological progress symbolized by radio. For those who recalled earlier market moves, however, the advance seemed far too great, and by late 1925, Alexander D. Noyes, the financial editor of The Times, was warning—albeit prematurely—of a possible collapse.

In February of 1929, the Federal Reserve Board, nervous about the speculation, told banks to stop borrowing money from the Fed and then lending it to stock speculators. In late March, the stock market cracked as interest rates soared and banks refused to lend more money for stocks. Then Charles Mitchell, president of the National City Bank in New York (a predecessor of Citibank), announced that his bank was prepared to lend money anyway. The bull market was on again.

In October, the real crash came. After the first very bad day, The Times printed an editorial—later reported to have been written by Noyes, who by then had moved to the editorial page—that described the crash as an "inevitable sequel" to an "orgy of speculation."

The worst days were Thursday, Oct. 24, Monday, Oct. 28, and Tuesday, Oct. 29, when waves of selling led to unprecedented volume and price breaks. Many small investors, who had borrowed as much as 90 percent of the price of the shares they bought, saw their stocks sold for less than they owed and wound up in debt to their brokers.

The Times reported the falls completely, but tried to avoid adding to the panic. Each main headline during the crash included something that could be seen as encouraging, but any optimism was misplaced. By the time the Dow Jones industrial average hit bottom in 1932, at 41.22, it was down 89 percent from the 1929 peak of 381.17. That level would not be reached again until 1954.

1920–1929

WALL STREET PULSATES TO ANOTHER BOOM

BASIS OF THE SEASON'S SPECULATIVE MANIA EXAMINED

By ALEXANDER D. NOYES

For the first time in six years the attention of the whole community has been directed to a speculative craze of immense proportions in Wall Street, with what the Stock Exchange calls the "outside public" visibly and on the largest scale infected with the speculative mania.

"Bull markets" and "bear markets," meaning a gradual and irregular rise or fall in prices as the country's business outlook seems to Wall Street to be growing better or worse, are of frequent occurrence, but the periodical movements of that sort are looked upon only as the orderly ebb and flow of the financial tide. At widely separated intervals, however, there are times when the rise in prices, beginning deliberately like the others, gathers such support from an excited speculative public that eventually the market becomes uncontrollable; that prices of stocks lose all relation to earnings and dividends and the business outlook; that the speculative army buys with borrowed money for a further rise, merely because prices have risen so far already; that no end to the advance seems possible; and that even Wall Street asserts that there is nothing which can stop an indefinitely continuing upward movement.

Such an outburst of speculation is always ascribed to some special causes. In the present case Wall Street has attributed the episode to the large bank reserves, to the consequent easy credit, to the increase in the country's wealth and prosperity as a result of the great crops of 1924 and, more particularly, to the remarkably large sales by motor-car manufacturing companies, with resultant unexpectedly large earnings.

Probably the speculation in motor-car shares, which has been the focus of this particular Stock Exchange speculation, was really started when $146,000,000 cash was paid by a bankers' syndicate for the Dodge Brothers automobile property. That appealed to the speculative imagination last April; the excitement reached its climax when some of the companies reported earnings almost double those of the same period a year ago. It was further stimulated by the familiar Wall Street rumors of "amalgamation," "mergers," "buying for control."

In some stocks of the motor-car group, the subsequent advances ranged from 100 up to 145 points; but the speculation spread, as it always does on such occasions, to shares of all other more or less experimental industrial companies and to the general market. The statisticians who compute the "averages" of the prices of representative stocks have lately reported the figure to have reached the highest average price on record, nearly 80 per cent above the high point of 1924.

As in the present instance, every past outburst of wild speculation by the public on the New York Stock Exchange has similarly had its own particular focus of interest, from which the buying spread to the entire list—in 1919, shares of industrial companies with a large accumulated surplus, out of which impending "stock dividends" were rumored; in 1915 and 1916, shares of manufacturing companies whose machinery had been converted into the turning out of unlimited war orders; in 1901, shares of railways for possession of which other railways were imagined to be bidding against one another.

No market of the kind was ever created without some such direct appeal to the speculative imagination. But behind this speculative influence there has always been a larger influence, arising partly from the condition of the country but largely from the financial condition of the outside public itself, from whom the speculative buying orders poured into the stock market. In order to create such a market, this public must have not only the requisite spirit of confidence but the actual personal resources. Therefore movements of the kind usually occur not only when business is reviving and the financial outlook improving but when business at large is actually making and accumulating money by increased personal earnings or by close economies.

Money burns in the pockets of great masses of men under such circumstances, as it is apt to do in the pocket of a single fortunate individual. It is very human to wish to invest such a surplus in "something that is going up." When that something is a stock which continues to advance uninterruptedly, the gambling appetite is stirred. Tips on the winning stock of the day are given out as industriously in Wall Street as tips on the winning horse in the racing columns of the sporting pages. If the rise in prices continues long enough, and especially if it results in sudden forward leaps of 10 to 20 points in an hour in the price of one or another speculative stock—an occurrence brought about both through the manipulation by professional operators and the inrush of outside speculators to attract whose buying orders the stock had been bid up—the outcome eventually will be a kind of frenzy on the part of the speculating public.

Commission houses on Wall Street, whose customers' room would at ordinary times be only half filled with clients listlessly watching the blackboard or the tape, find every inch of space occupied by eager speculators who will not trust to telephoning their orders but who crowd into offices where they can "see the market move" and need lose no time in "getting aboard." At the climax of the great Wall Street speculation of 1901 the volume of outside buying orders grew so overwhelmingly large that on one or two days it was impossible for the ticker to report all sales.

Nobody knows what the total Stock Exchange business was on April 30, 1901. Brokers' clerks worked over their books that week until 2 or 3 o'clock in the morning and slept at the old Astor House or in the other far downtown hotels of that day, all of which were crowded to the limit with Wall Street guests. At one time in April, 1901, the Stock Exchange actually decreed a special holiday, the real purpose of which was known to be to give the physically exhausted "floor brokers" a day of rest and sleep and to make it possible for commission houses to catch up on their books.

In its earlier stages, what the Stock Exchanges call a "big bull movement" has always been explainable by financial causes which have operated legitimately to change intrinsic values on an investment market. Even with what are classified as the celebrated speculative illusions of the past, this statement will hold good. The "Mississippi Bubble," usually referred to as the maddest exploit in speculative history, was actually based on the obtaining for French investors, through a company with a capital stock originally of 100,000,000 livres, or about $20,000,000, the exclusive privilege of trading on the Mississippi and Ohio Rivers. The "South Sea Bubble" of 1720, almost equally celebrated in London's financial history, undertook to care for the British national debt of £10,000,000, in exchange for which service the company obtained a monopoly of trade in the South Sea region which now contains the British territories of Australia and New Zealand.

The purpose of both undertakings was obviously a century or so ahead of time. But the glamour which surrounded the picture of opportunities for lucrative trade appealed strongly to the speculative imagination, and the French and British public of the day, which happened to be well supplied with surplus savings, rushed into the market for the shares with complete absence of restraint. The same substratum of reason existed even in the strangest of all episodes in the history of speculation, the Dutch "tulip mania" of the seventeenth century, when the bull movement and the rise of prices reached such proportions that groups of speculators would be formed to take shares in a single bulb of a description favored by the excited market and quoted at a hundred or a thousand times its original price. Nothing could nowadays seem more foolish. Yet the export of bulbs is today one of the important branches of Holland's foreign trade. The Dutch market sold $4,900,000 worth of them to the United States even in 1924, when all the rest of the world sold us only $2,100,000.

During the last quarter century there have been only four of what Wall Street calls its "major bull movements" and what the general public calls a speculative mania. Frequently a movement of the kind in this period, with speculation rising to huge proportions, would be interrupted by violent downward reaction, after which the speculation would be renewed on an even more extensive scale.

The four occasions have been the after-war Wall Street "boom" of 1919, which had two stages, one in the Spring of that year and another in the Autumn, with a two months' break in prices between them; the war boom itself, which lasted from the Spring of 1915 well into December, 1916, similarly with extensive intervals of reacting prices; the persistent bull market of 1905 and 1906, occurring between the so-called "rich men's panic" of 1903 and the great financial crisis of 1907; and the most spectacular craze of all, which reached its real climax in the Spring of 1901, but which really included the prolonged speculation for the rise in 1899 and the series of wild and spasmodic advances in the Stock Exchange of 1902.

Speaking generally, it may be said that the speculative mania of 1901, despite its extravagances, really foreshadowed the immense expansion of American resources and prosperity of the next half-dozen years. But on the other hand, the war market reflected only the present and not at all the future, while the violent bull market of 1905, like the similar market of 1919, was based on a mistaken view of the immediate situation and belonged in the class of economic illusions. Exactly what the speculative mania of 1925 will turn out to have foreshadowed in our industrial and financial history we must wait for the facts to show. [SPECIAL FEATURES SECTION, Nov. 15, 1925]

Ward, 4¼; and Johns Manville, 8. Even with these recoveries the losses of these particular stocks, and practically all others, were staggering.

Yesterday's market crash was one which largely affected rich men, institutions, investment trusts and others who participate in the stock market on a broad and intelligent scale. It was not the margin trailers who were caught in the rush to sell, but the rich men of the country who are able to swing blocks of 5,000, 10,000, up to 100,000 shares of high-priced stocks. They went overboard with no more consideration than the little trader who was swept out on the first day of the market's upheaval, whose prices, even at their lowest of last Thursday, now look high in comparison.

The market on the rampage is no respecter of persons. It washed fortune after fortune away yesterday and financially crippled thousands of individuals in all parts of the world. It was not until after the market had closed that the financial district began to realize that a good-sized rally had taken place and that there was a stopping place on the downgrade for good stocks.

The market has now passed through three days of collapse, and so violent has it been that most authorities believe that the end is not far away. It started last Thursday, when 12,800,000 shares were dealt in on the Exchange, and holders of stocks

AFTER THE FALL IN STOCKS

The fall in prices on the Stock Exchange, which on Thursday reached such proportions as to bring Wall Street momentarily almost to the verge of panic, will undoubtedly be recognized in future financial discussions as the inevitable sequel to what the Chancellor of the British Exchequer lately described as a prolonged "orgy of speculation." Readjustment of such scope and character never leaves the speculative mentality what it was before. We shall hear considerably less in the future of those newly invented conceptions of finance which revised the principles of political economy with a view solely to fitting the stock market vagaries. It will not be easy, after this week's occurrences, to dismiss contemptuously the teachings of past financial experience. Wall Street itself will now be ready to confess that, however surrounding circumstances may change from one era to another, the great underlying influences which go to make sound or unsound finance, reasoned prosperity or inflation and subsequent disaster are precisely the same today as in the all-but-forgotten "pre-war period."

[EDITORIAL, Oct. 26, 1929]

commenced to learn just what a decline in the market means. This was followed by a moderate rally on Friday and entirely normal conditions on Saturday, with fluctuations on a comparatively narrow scale and with the efforts of the leading bankers to stabilize the market evidently successful. But the storm broke anew on Monday, with prices slaughtered in every direction, to be followed by yesterday's tremendous trading of 16,410,030 shares.

Sentiment had been generally unsettled since the first of September. Market prices had then reached peak levels, and, try as they would, pool operators and other friends of the market could not get them higher. It was a gradual downward sag, gaining momentum as it went on, then to break out into an open market smash in which the good, the bad and indifferent stocks went down alike. Thousands of traders were able to weather the first storm and answered their margin calls; thousands fell by the wayside Monday and again yesterday, unable to meet the demands of their brokers that their accounts be protected.

There was no quibbling at all between customer and broker yesterday. In any case where margin became thin a peremptory call went out. If there was no immediate answer the stock was sold out "at the market" for just what it would bring. Thousands, sold out on the decline and amid the confusion, found themselves in debt to their brokers last night.

Three factors stood out most prominently last night after the market's close. They were:

Wall Street has been able to weather the storm with but a single Curb failure, small in size, and no member of the New York Stock Exchange has announced himself unable to meet commitments.

The smashing decline has brought stocks down to a level where, in the opinion of leading bankers and industrialists, they are a buy on their merits and prospects, and bankers have so advised their customers.

The very violence of the liquidation, which has cleaned up many hundreds of sore spots which honeycombed the market, and the expected ability of the market to right itself, since millions of shares of stock have passed to strong hands from weak ones.

ASSOCIATED PRESS

Tense crowds across from the New York Stock Exchange on "Black Thursday," Oct. 24, 1929, as the market began to unravel.

One of the factors which Wall Street failed to take into consideration throughout the entire debacle was that the banking consortium has no idea of putting stocks up or to save any individual from loss, but that its sole purpose was to alleviate the wave of financial hysteria sweeping the country and provide bids, at some price, where needed. It was pointed out in many quarters that no broad liquidating movement in the stock market has ever been stopped by so-called good buying. This is helpful, of course, but it never stops an avalanche of liquidation, as was this one.

There is only one factor, it was pointed out, which can and always does stop a down swing—that is, the actual cessation of forced liquidation. It is usually the case, too, that when the last of the forced selling has been completed the stock market always faces a wide-open gap in which there are practically no offerings of securities at all. When that point is reached, buying springs up from everywhere and always accounts for a sharp, almost perpendicular recovery in the best stocks. The opinion was widely expressed in Wall Street last night that that point has been reached, or at least very nearly reached.

The opening bell on the Stock Exchange released such a flood of selling as has never before been witnessed in this country. The failure of the market to rally consistently on the previous day, the tremendous shrinkage of open market values and the wave of hysteria which appeared to sweep the country brought an avalanche of stock to the market to be sold at whatever price it would bring.

From the very first quotation until thirty minutes after 10 o'clock it was evident that the day's market would be an unprecedented one. In that first thirty minutes of trading stocks were poured out in 5,000, 10,000, 20,000 and 50,000 share blocks at tremendous sacrifices as compared with the previous closing. The declines ranged from a point or so to as much as 29½ points, and the reports of opening prices brought selling into the market in confused volume that has never before been equaled.

In this first half hour of trading on the Stock Exchange a total of 3,259,800 shares were dealt in. The volume of the first twenty-six blocks of stock dealt in at the opening totaled more than 630,000 shares.

There was simply no near-by demand for even the country's leading industrial and railroad shares, and many millions of dollars in values were lost in the first quotations tapped out. All considerations other than to get rid of the stock at any price were brushed aside.

Wall Street was a street of vanished hopes, of curiously silent apprehension and of a sort of paralyzed hypnosis yesterday. Men and women crowded the brokerage offices, even those who have been long since wiped out, and followed the figures on the tape. Little groups gathered here and there to discuss the falling prices in hushed and awed tones. They were participating in the making of financial history. It was the consensus of bankers and brokers alike that no such scenes ever again will be witnessed by this generation. To most of those who have been in the market it is all the more awe-inspiring because their financial history is limited to bull markets.

[Oct. 30, 1929]

1920–1929

1930–1939

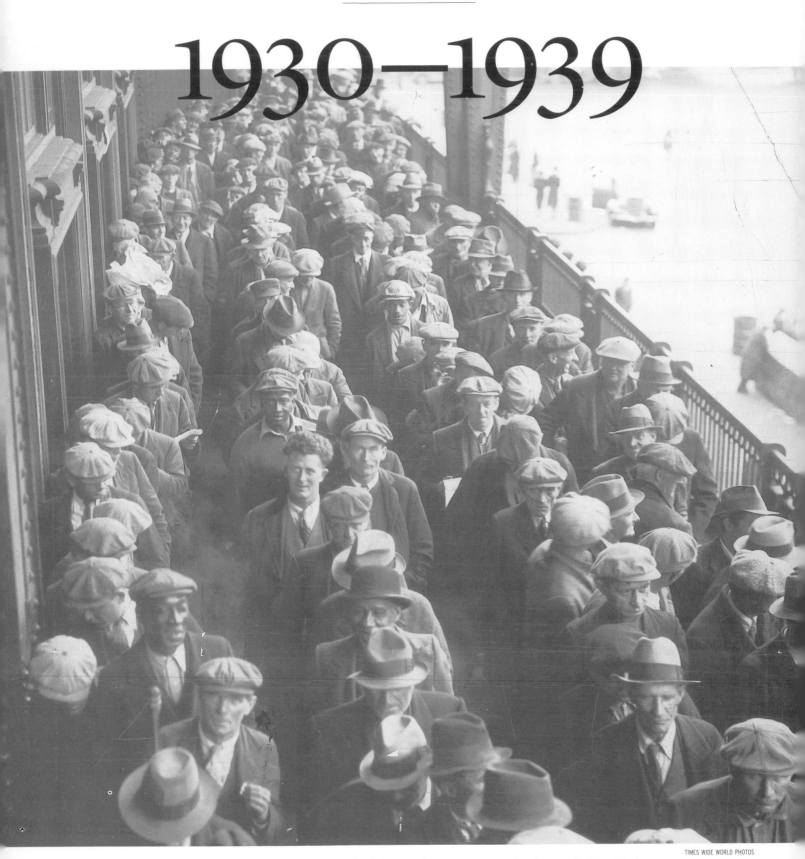

Unemployed men line up for food during the Great Depression in 1935 in New York.

Battling the Great Depression

NEVER BEFORE, OR SINCE, has the Federal Government moved so quickly and decisively to deal with economic problems as it did in the first 100 days of the Administration of Franklin D. Roosevelt. When he was inaugurated on March 4, 1933, the need for action to deal with the long Depression—made worse by a banking panic—was clear, and the newly elected Democratic Congress was willing to do whatever Roosevelt wanted.

Legislation passed then set the tone for much of the relations between Government and business during the remainder of the century. When Roosevelt was elected, veterans' benefits were by far the largest expenditure of the Federal Government. By the end of the decade, Government spending had risen sharply to cover a vast array of programs, many of them still around 60 years later. Bank deposits were guaranteed, the elderly were promised Social Security benefits and the Government established a minimum wage for workers.

Roosevelt was elected after Republicans were unable to deal with the Depression. There were tentative relief efforts in the Hoover Administration, but they were undone by a disastrous decision to raise tariffs in 1930 and by the fiscal orthodoxy of the day, which called for Governments to balance budgets to restore business confidence when fiscal stimulus might have better helped the country. That orthodoxy was not challenged in the 1932 election, as both candidates vowed to practice fiscal conservatism. Rarely has a President so completely repudiated the economic platform on which he ran.

Farmers suffered greatly in this decade. As incomes fell, they tried to increase production. The damage that did to the land was shown when drought affected much of the central part of the country in the mid-1930's. With trees sparse and much of the grasslands overgrazed, huge dust storms arose. Roosevelt's efforts to help farmers set the trend for agricultural programs during the rest of the century that subsidized farmers while trying to limit production.

Despite the economic doldrums—the United States economy would not grow larger than it was in 1929 until 1937, and then a recession arrived in 1938—the decade also saw a succession of innovations, among them nylon, which became known as a miracle fabric, and the growth of passenger aviation. The first television sets were sold to the public in 1939, but that technology was more than a decade from revolutionizing American life. The 1930's saw Americans regain the right to legally drink liquor, and lose the right to own gold coins or bullion.

Obsessed with their own problems, Americans were not inclined to get involved overseas, and the rise of Adolf Hitler—whose party gained the most seats in Germany's parliament in an election held just as President Roosevelt's first term was beginning—was not the focus of attention it might have been. As the decade ended, however, America was beginning to build up its military might in order to fight Hitler.

1930	President Hoover signs the Smoot-Hawley Tariff Act.
	The ninth planet is discovered and named Pluto.
1931	The Empire State Building, the world's tallest, opens in New York.
1932	Franklin D. Roosevelt is elected President.
	The Dow Industrials average hits bottom at 41.22 on July 8.
1933	President Roosevelt declares a national bank holiday and pushes his New Deal through Congress in his first 100 days.
	Prohibition is repealed.
1934	Hitler assumes the title of Führer on the death of German President Paul von Hindenburg.
1935	President Roosevelt signs the Social Security Act.
	Dust storms devastate Western states.
1936	Edward VIII abdicates the British throne to marry Wallis Simpson; his brother succeeds him as George VI.
1937	The German dirigible *Hindenburg* explodes in Lakehurst, N.J.
1938	Howard Hughes sets record for a round-the-world flight in less than four days.
1939	Pan Am begins regularly scheduled commercial flights across the Atlantic.
	"Gone With the Wind" wins the Academy Award as Best Picture.

Hoover Says He Will Sign Tariff Bill; Hails Flexible Clause as Giving Power to Correct Faults, End Foreign Protests

The first effort by the Federal Government to aid businesses damaged by the Great Depression came in 1930 when Congress voted to raise tariffs on most industrial and agricultural commodities. The bill was a controversial one, pitting rural interests, who wanted heavy farm tariffs but did not like industrial tariffs, against manufacturing ones, who wanted the reverse. Consumers were not especially powerful, but they opposed both, arguing that raising prices was no way to help them make ends meet. The compromise raised all tariffs, but increased those of industrial goods more.

There were voices warning that other nations would retaliate by raising their own tariffs, and President Hoover, in announcing he would sign the bill, said the Tariff Commission could respond if American tariffs proved to be too high. To Hoover, the point was that the Republican Party, in its 1928 platform, had promised to raise tariffs and promises must be kept.

In supporting the bill, Nicholas Longworth, the speaker of the House of Representatives, sounded the same arguments that would be heard for much of the rest of the century when industries sought protection. The increased tariffs were needed, he said, to support United States corporations that had to compete with foreign companies paying low wages. He also forecast that the bill would help to restore depressed industries.

The Smoot-Hawley Tariff Act, as it was called after its Congressional sponsors (although The Times said it would be known as Hawley-Smoot), came to be viewed as one of the most misguided pieces of legislation in history. The resulting trade wars, coupled with competitive currency devaluations, became known as "beggar thy neighbor" policies and served to prolong the Depression in the United States and other countries.

By RICHARD V. OULAHAN

Special to The New York Times

WASHINGTON, June 15—"I shall approve the tariff bill," said President Hoover in a statement handed to newspaper representatives at the White House offices this afternoon.

The statement does not express any opinion as to whether the prospective law is good or bad, although the President makes clear his belief that "no tariff bill has ever been enacted or ever will be enacted under the present system that will be perfect."

Standing out in the President's declarations, however, is an unmistakable intention to use the new Tariff Commission machinery to remedy inequalities in the rates fixed by Congress.

At last, he says in effect, we have a scientific and businesslike way of correcting tariff injustices. Judging by his assertions, the President intends to make his own revision as far as the authority vested in himself and the Tariff Commission, which is to be recognized with increased powers, will permit.

The unusual course of the President in making an advance announcement that he would approve the tariff measure was designed to put an end to uncertainty in the business world and in the securities market.

Apparently a fear prevailed in administration quarters that if the President's action on the bill was delayed there would be a continuance of the nervousness manifested in the stock market while the measure was in its final legislative stages, and might result in a bad reaction.

The measure, which was signed by Speaker Longworth in the presence of the House yesterday, will be sent to the Senate tomorrow to be attested by Vice President Curtis, who must sign while the Senate is sitting. It will reach the White House tomorrow afternoon. Its approval by the President on Tuesday will mean that the rates in the bill will go into effect on Wednesday, a matter of great consequence to importers.

There is more vigor of expression in the President's statement than in any of his recent utterances. With obvious reference to the bill which is to become law through his promised approval, he says that any tariff bill is bound to contain "some inequalities and inequitable compromises." Some items will be found to be too high and some too low, he concedes. Surrounded by "lobbies, log-rolling and the activities of group interests," any tariff bill is certain, in the President's expressed conclusion, to disturb business and public confidence.

The President makes known that he looks to the exercise of the joint authority vested in him and the Tariff Commission to provide an orderly readjustment of inequalities in rates and through that means end agitation over the tariff. "Nothing would contribute to retard business recovery more than this continued agitation," he says.

"If the power vested in him to raise or lower a rate proves unsatisfactory, he will ask Congress for 'further authority.'"

The widespread criticism of the new tariff measure on the score that it will result in reprisals by foreign governments and business interests against American trade and commerce is not overlooked by the President. In a brief paragraph he holds out the promise that if the duties complained of are found to be unduly high they can be remedied by "proper application to the Tariff Commission."

The statement of the President, a document of about 1,800 words, reflects the satisfaction he feels over the retention of his flexible tariff authority.

Under the tariff law now in force, the Fordney-McCumber act of 1922, the Executive has the right to raise or lower a rate 50 per cent, or to prescribe a rate within that limitation, after the Tariff Commission has made an investigation and reported the facts concerning the effect of the particular rate.

Under the bill which the President has promised to make into law through signature, which will be known as the Hawley-Smoot tariff act of 1930, his authority to increase or decrease a rate is continued with the restriction that he must make the increase or decrease a flat 50 per cent without the right to fix any intermediate figure.

Using the commission's figures, the President sets forth that the average level of the bill is 16 per cent of the value of all imports, both free and dutiable, and compares this with a range from 13.83 per cent in the present law and to 25.8 per cent in the Dingley act, the highest percentage of any of the seven tariff structures mentioned. With reference to the Underwood, or Democratic, tariff act of 1913, he says that "the amounts were disturbed by war conditions, varying 6 per cent to 14.8 per cent."

The proportion of imports that will be admitted free of duty under the new law, the President, also using the Tariff Commission figures, estimates at from 61 to 63 per cent, as compared with 83.8 per cent in the present law. The proportion is higher in both cases than the free list percentages of the McKinley, Wilson, Dingley and Payne-Aldrich acts. Special mention is made of the Underwood law to the effect that "disturbed conditions varied the free list from 60 per cent to 73 per cent, averaging 66.3 per cent."

The course of the Republican Administration and the Republican Congress in undertaking tariff revision is justified by the President by reference to the tariff plank of the party's national platform adopted by the Kansas City convention in 1928.

Senator Robinson of Arkansas, Democratic floor leader, made this comment tonight on President Hoover's declaration.

"I express the hope, but not with great confidence, that the Executive's dream of a scientific tariff, uninfluenced by political considerations, may be realized through the efforts of the Tariff Commission as approved by the Executive. The promise by the President that complaints from foreign countries that duties have been fixed unduly high will be remedied by the Tariff Commission is likely to unsettle conditions and disturb the peace of mind of those who believe they have won a victory in the passage of the bill.

"The complaints from foreign countries involve many rates, and if the commission is to open the whole question of the tariff upon applications inspired by foreign governments or peoples it is difficult to see how the anxiety and uncertainty which has embarrassed business during the last fifteen months can be escaped or terminated.

"Of course, one must admit it would have required great courage to veto the tariff bill."

[June 16, 1930]

Roosevelt Orders 4-Day Bank Holiday, Puts Embargo on Gold, Calls Congress

As the inauguration of President Franklin D. Roosevelt approached in 1933, the United States financial system was growing more endangered by the day. Fear that Roosevelt would devalue the currency led speculators to exchange dollars for gold, causing the Treasury to lose gold at a rapid rate. More and more people tried to withdraw money from banks, leading some to close and accelerating withdrawals from others. By the inauguration on Saturday, March 4, all but 10 states had declared bank holidays. It was clear that drastic action was needed.

Late Sunday night, March 5, Roosevelt ordered a national bank holiday, closing all banks while Congress decided what to do. He also suspended the payment of gold for dollars and ordered Americans to turn in their gold coins.

Within days, Congress was passing bills as asked by Roosevelt. It was the most massive Government intervention in the history of the economy. The dollar was effectively devalued, farmers were to get assistance, bank deposits were to be guaranteed and commercial banking separated from investment banking. The National Recovery Administration was to set up boards by which different industries would cut production.

In the end, many of the programs did not work and were dropped, either by Congress or by the Supreme Court, which eventually found some of the laws, including the one establishing the N.R.A., illegal. But those that did survive—among them banking reform, Federal regulation of the securities industry, agricultural programs and public works plans to stimulate the economy—became the essential elements of Government intervention in the economy for the rest of the century.

On June 17, The Times reported on the President approving some of the most important legislation. An appraisal of the actions appeared the next day.

It would be two years before the N.R.A. was ruled unconstitutional, but it took less than two months for it to become clear that the Government's effort to "voluntarily" restructure every American industry was a difficult, if not impossible, task. On Aug. 20, The Times reported on the problems Roosevelt faced getting the coal and oil industries to agree to their codes.

Special to The New York Times

WASHINGTON, March 5—To prevent the export, hoarding or earmarking of gold or silver, coin or bullion or currency, President Roosevelt issued a proclamation at 11 o'clock tonight, in which he ordered a bank holiday from tomorrow through Thursday, March 9. Earlier in the day he had summoned a special session of Congress to meet on Thursday.

This sweeping action was taken after a day of conferences among officials and bankers, the President taking recourse to war powers granted under the trading-with-the-enemy act.

As a result of the proclamation all banking activities will be suspended during the holiday, except as permitted by regulations of the Secretary of the Treasury, thus taking this country technically off the gold standard until the four-day period expires.

In order that there may not be a complete suspension of all banking and exchange operations, the proclamation authorizes the issuance of Clearing House certificates, which may be used as currency until the banks return to more normal functioning.

The main points in the proclamation are:

1. A national banking holiday from March 6 to March 9 inclusive.

2. An embargo on the withdrawal of gold and silver for export or domestic use during that period, except with permission of the Secretary of the Treasury.

3. The issuance of Clearing House certificates or other evidence of claims against the assets of banking institutions to permit business to carry on.

4. Authorization to banking institutions under regulations of the Secretary of the Treasury to receive new deposits and make them subject to withdrawal on demand without any restrictions or limitations.

Friends of the President said he had a definite three-point program for the solution of the banking problem and that tonight's action included two of them. The first, they said, was a protection of the currency against unreasonable withdrawal. The second was to furnish a temporary currency. The third is permanent reorganization of the whole banking system, which, they predicted, would be proposed to the special session of Congress meeting here Thursday.

The Federal Reserve Board and Secretary Woodin, with the advice of former Secretary Ogden L. Mills, acted immediately after the issuance of the proclamation to make it effective.

The proclamation was issued at 11 o'clock, bringing to an end a series of conferences held by Treasury officials and the new Cabinet throughout the day.

This exercise of Presidential power, the most drastic ever taken in peacetime to safeguard the nation, climaxed the nation-wide sweep of State banking holidays which had reached into practically every State of the Union on the day that President Roosevelt was inaugurated.

The banking situation on March 4 overshadowed every other feature of the inauguration of the new Administration and during the following twenty-four hours reached a point where the President and his advisers were forced to agree that national leadership was required.

In diplomatic circles it was expected that France would follow suit and restrict the exporting of gold.

Even while President Roosevelt was reviewing the inaugural parade, two hours after he had taken the oath of office, members of his Cabinet and other close advisers were holding conferences in the rear of the reviewing stand.

During the four-day bank holiday, personal checks were accepted in place of cash.

Many of the measures embraced in the President's proclamation tonight were advanced in tentative form at such informal conferences. Secretary of the Treasury Woodin, after consulting with Secretary of State Hull and other officials, left the scene and summoned by telegraph and telephone governors of Federal Reserve Banks and leading bankers to join with them today in perfecting the provisions of the forthcoming Presidential proclamation.

The atmosphere of official Washington was tense throughout inauguration day, and even more so this morning when Federal Reserve officials and leading bankers assembled early at the Treasury Building to study measures to prevent a complete banking collapse.

President Roosevelt, after an all-day conference of Federal Reserve officials and bankers and a special meeting of the Cabinet, issued a proclamation this evening calling Congress into special session next Thursday at noon to deal, during the opening days, entirely with the banking crisis.

This action was followed by a statement in which the President declared that he would be ready to present a program to Congress when it assembled to relieve the banking crisis.

Republican leaders said tonight that they would cooperate in every way to expedite the reorganization so that Congress could get to work at once on the remedial legislation. They said that the responsibility for the program was with the Democrats but that no dilatory tactics would be countenanced on their side.

Senator Glass of Virginia urged President Roosevelt to include in his message to Congress a recommendation for the prompt enactment of the Glass banking bill, which would permit branch banking, by national banks, set up a liquidating corporation to aid in the freeing of assets of closed banks and divorce national banks from their security affiliates.

[March 6, 1933]

1930–1939

The New York Times

ROOSEVELT ORDERS 4-DAY BANK HOLIDAY, PUTS EMBARGO ON GOLD, CALLS CONGRESS

President Starts Recovery Program, Signs Bank, Rail and Industry Bills

Special to The New York Times

WASHINGTON, June 16—Assuming unprecedented peacetime control over the nation's economic life, President Roosevelt placed in operation today his sweeping program for recovery from the depression.

Within two hours he signed acts of Congress giving him control over industry, power to coordinate the railroads, and authority to start work on a $3,300,000,000 public works program, and then began the active administration of these and other major measures.

In signing the National Industrial Recovery Act the President declared that it was "the most important and far-reaching legislation ever enacted by the American Congress," and said that it "represents a supreme effort to stabilize for all time the many factors which make for the prosperity of the nation and the preservation of American standards."

The Glass-Steagall Banking Reform Act, which the President described as "the second most important banking legislation enacted in the history of the country"; the long-disputed Independent Offices Act, including the veterans legislation; the Deficiency Act, the Taxation Act, and the Farm Credits Act received the President's signature during the day.

Turning to the administrative side of the industrial recovery program, the President appointed General Hugh S. Johnson, former soldier and manufacturer, as administrator of industry; made available $400,000,000 under the public works title for State roads, and allotted $238,000,000 to the Navy Department for laying down thirty-two new war vessels under the terms of the London treaty.

A special recovery board was named by Mr. Roosevelt to work with General Johnson. It consists of Secretary of Commerce Roper, chairman; Attorney General Cummings, Secretaries Wallace, Perkins and Ickes, Budget Director Douglas and Chairman March of the Federal Trade Commission.

General Johnson also will have an advisory council of business and labor leaders, the personnel of which has not yet been announced. Among those reported under consideration, however, are Myron C. Taylor, Alfred P. Sloan, Walter C. Teagle, Gerard Swope and Will Vereen.

Colonel Donald H. Sawyer was named temporary administrator of public works and was directed, with a special Cabinet board consisting of Secretary Ickes, chairman; Secretaries Wallace, Roper and Perkins, Assistant Secretary of the Treasury Robert, Colonel George R. Spaulding, and Budget Director Douglas, to submit to the President without delay the works on which construction can be undertaken promptly and to outline a program for future work.

Joseph B. Eastman, a member of the Interstate Commerce Commission, was appointed coordinator of railroads and was directed to begin his work at once. His most important immediate concern will be the railway wage scale negotiations, following which, savings by the reduction of duplicating facilities will be undertaken.

General Johnson conferred with the President late today and then left by airplane for Chicago to meet with leaders of the bituminous coal industry. He said that he would return late tomorrow night, and that he hoped to name a large group of men to aid him in perfecting trade codes. Most of the ten major industries, he said, had made rapid progress in this respect, and he hoped to see final agreements reached by the big trade associations within a very short time.

Expressing hope that unemployment would be decreased by at least 1,000,000 men by Oct. 1, President Roosevelt took an optimistic view of the industrial situation in a long statement on the Industrial Recovery Act. He called upon industry to cooperate by hiring more men to do existing work, at shortened working hours and a living wage.

President Franklin D. Roosevelt addressing the nation in March 1933.

The President said that the act was a challenge to industry and labor, and pledged the protection of the government to both against unfair practices, if they would assist in raising price levels, increasing wages and reducing work hours. He promised that "this is not a law to foment discord, and it will not be administered as such."

While the anti-trust laws will be relaxed by the new legislation, the public will be protected against the abuses which led to their enactment, the President promised in his statement. He said that they would still be enforced against "monopolies that restrain trade and price fixing which allows inordinate profits or unfairly high prices."

The whole spirit of the act, he declared, would be to protect industry that cooperates completely and endeavors to raise prices justly, and at the same time keeps up wages and shortens the working hours so as to increase employment.

Mr. Roosevelt appeared to be in a happy frame of mind this morning as he affixed his signature to the new measures. The first he signed during the day was the Banking Reform Act, which was carried through perseveringly by Senator Glass of Virginia in the face of many obstacles.

As Senator Glass, accompanied by Senator Bulkley, Representative Steagall and others, appeared in the circular office of the President to be photographed during the ceremonies the President addressed Mr. Glass affectionately, saying:

"You old warrior! If it had not been for the veterans, Congress would have adjourned last Saturday and you would not have had your pet measure on the statute books."

Describing the measure as having had more lives than a cat, he declared it had been killed "fourteen times in this session," to be revived in the final days.

Senators Wagner and Robinson of Arkansas and Representatives Doughton and Ragon were present at the signing of the Industrial Recovery Act. President Roosevelt's statement follows:

> History probably will record the National Industrial Recovery Act as the most important and far-reaching legislation ever enacted by the American Congress. It represents a supreme effort to stabilize for all time the many factors which make for the prosperity of the nation and the preservation of American standards.

1930–1939

FAR-REACHING SCOPE OF THE "NEW DEAL"

By BERNHARD OSTROLENK

With the passage of the Industrial Recovery Bill the administration has rounded out its economic program. That program includes supervision of industry, a large program of public works, and regulation of agriculture, banks and railways. Although the government has had a long experience in the regulation of railroads, utilities and, to some extent, of banking, the regulation of industry and agriculture on the scale contemplated is entirely new in the United States.

Some of these measures are regarded as of a temporary character only, designed to meet the emergency of depression. Thus, provision is made in the Industrial Recovery Act that its operations are to be limited to a period of only two years and that they may be terminated sooner if the emergency has passed. The act providing for limitation of farm production is also subject to termination by Presidential proclamation.

It is the purpose of this article to discuss not only these but the other measures enlarging the government's field of supervision.

Through the Industrial Recovery Act it is planned to have the government regulate industry by compelling industry to regulate itself. The government will deal with each industry through a trade association, which the industry must organize. Trade associations are not a new idea, but hitherto membership in them has not been compulsory, and their objectives have been limited by the Federal Trade Commission.

Under the new law, membership in the trade association of an industry virtually becomes mandatory; non-members will be licensed under conditions that will force them to adopt the code of the association. In some degree the anti-trust laws are suspended. Though price fixing itself continues to be forbidden, the association may limit production, which is tantamount to price fixing. But in return for this privilege, the codes which the trade associations must adopt, subject to acceptance by the government, must provide for the right of employees to bargain through representatives of their own choosing, must not require an employee to join company labor unions, and must specify the hours of labor, rates of pay and other working conditions. There must be provisions also to protect the small business man.

President Roosevelt's own description of the National Industrial Recovery Act is that it provides for "a great cooperative movement throughout all industry in order (1) to obtain wide re-employment; (2) to shorten the working week; (3) to pay decent wages for the shorter week; (4) to prevent unfair competition, and (5) to prevent disastrous overproduction."

The $3,300,000,000 public works and construction program included in the recovery act has in it features that will further extend governmental control over labor and industry. The money may be expended on public highways, public buildings, conservation and development of natural resources, utilization and purification of water, development of water power, transmission of electrical energy, construction of river and harbor improvements, low-cost housing and slum-clearing projects, and any other public or semi-public enterprises which the President may approve. This vast construction program is to be financed by loans from the Federal Government to States, municipalities or other public or semi-public bodies which may include public schools, colleges, railroads and others.

Under a separate act there is created the Tennessee Valley Authority with power to maintain and operate the Muscle Shoals property acquired by the government during the World War and developed at a cost of $500,000,000. This bill empowers the government to develop the valley for agricultural and industrial purposes, to build dams, power houses, reservoirs and navigation projects, and to manufacture electricity, fertilizers, explosives. The Authority is permitted to sell $50,000,000 worth of bonds to carry out these provisions.

The Agricultural Adjustment Act, recently passed by Congress, provides not only for further drastic extension of governmental control over marketing, but also for control over production. By means of the voluntary-allotment plan, the cotton-option plan, the land-leasing plan, and other devices, the President has the authority to limit and to regulate the production of our 6,500,000 farmers, now cultivating an area of 1,903,000,000 acres and producing crops with an annual value, in normal times, of more than $10,000,000,000.

After March 4, 1933, by Executive order and through legislation, the banks of the country were virtually put under a licensing system and permitted to conduct business only after satisfying the Treasury of their solvency and liquidity. Recent legislation permits a government agency, the Reconstruction Finance Corporation, to invest government funds in preferred stock of closed banks, with temporary control privileges, in order to supply banking services to communities deprived of them.

The Glass-Steagall Bill, passed by Congress last week, further extends this governmental control and supervision in many fields of banking operations. By its most important provisions it prohibits commercial banks from having investment affiliates; compels a limited insurance of deposits from a fund to which all member banks of the Federal Reserve System must contribute; limits group banking; brings savings banks into the Federal Reserve System; definitely regulates bank loans, investments, interest rates and call loans, and gives permission for a limited amount of branch banking.

In the case of the railroads the history of government control goes back almost half a century. After some attempts at State regulation, the Federal Government in 1887 passed the Interstate Commerce Act, which was intended to protect the public from such abuses as discrimination and rebates. Later, regulations were extended to prevent pooling and merging of competitive lines, and to fix rates. Finally, such phases of railroad activity as labor disputes and security emissions were placed under governmental control.

By 1920, however, the fallacy of attempting to promote competition among railroads was evident, and the Interstate Commerce Commission was empowered to draw up plans for the consolidation of the roads into not less than twenty or more than thirty-five systems.

According to one important railroad executive, the waste in railroading, because of competition, is prodigious. Every hour a train runs on each of the two lines connecting New York with Philadelphia. Few of these trains are filled. The railroad legislation now enacted provides for railroad combinations and coordination, under a Federal administrator, to link the railroads together, enable them to use one another's terminals, jointly adjust schedule and services, and to bring about savings to investors and to shippers.   [SPECIAL FEATURES SECTION, June 18, 1933]

Its goal is the assurance of a reasonable profit to industry and living wages for labor, with the elimination of the piratical methods and practices which have not only harassed honest business but also contributed to the ills of labor.

While we are engaged in establishing new foundations for business which ultimately should open a return to work for large numbers of men, it is our hope through the so-called public works section of the law to speedily initiate a program of public construction that should early reemploy additional hundreds of thousands of men.

Obviously, if this project is to succeed, it demands the wholehearted cooperation of industry, labor and every citizen of the nation.

Late in the afternoon, before calling his last conference with the press prior to going on his vacation, the President signed the Independent Offices Appropriation Bill containing the veterans' allotment plan which caused the controversy in the closing days of the session of Congress, the Deficiency Bill with its appropriation for the public works section of the Recovery Act and several other measures. Among the acts signed to wipe the slate clean were those on taxes and farm credits.

The Taxation Act continues for an additional year the current levies on gasoline and on electric current, but provides that after Sept. 1 the electric power tax will be levied on power companies instead of consumers. Total revenue from this act is expected to be $165,000,000.

The Farm Credit Act establishes a new organization for the purpose of centralizing farm credit extensions. The amount of money to be at the disposal of this agency is indefinite, as into it is to be paid the remainder of the revolving fund of the Federal Farm Board. Its resources are estimated at $175,000,000.

The men who had sponsored the bills that became law today were happy, although most of them seemed tired and nerve-wracked by the turmoil through which they had passed in the closing days of Congress.

Senator Glass, who was co-author of the Federal Reserve Act, admitted that he had almost sent himself to the hospital in behalf of the banking reform legislation. He said that he would do it again, and declared he experienced a great thrill when the President signed it.

"The bank reforms provided in the act," Senator Glass said, "are almost as important to the banks and the public as the Federal Reserve Act itself. It supplements and strengthens the Federal Reserve Law."

The Glass-Steagall Act is directed toward a unified banking system, provides a limited deposit guarantee, requires divorcement of security affiliates from banks under government supervision, compels private bankers to give up either the deposit or security business, and requires stricter regulation of national banks.

Senator Wagner of New York, who helped frame the Industrial Recovery Act and direct its passage, hailed that law as the greatest achievement of the administration in an economic and industrial way.

"It will bring us on the road to recovery," he said. "Ultimately, if it is intelligently administered, as I know it will be, it will bring this country out of the depression."

The most far-reaching of the administration's legislation, the Recovery Act gives the President, through administrators, wide power to promote the self-regulation of industry under Federal supervision as a means of curtailing overproduction, improving wages, shortening hours of labor and, thereby, increasing prices and employment. A bond issue of $3,300,000,000 is authorized to finance the construction of Federal, State and local public projects. [June 17, 1933]

1930–1939

'Big Stick' Is Wielded by Another Roosevelt

By TURNER CATLEDGE

WASHINGTON, Aug. 19—Another President—another Roosevelt—has taken in hand that problem child of American business, the bituminous coal industry.

When President Roosevelt last Thursday reached the limit of his forbearance and called in the soft coal operators and told them to get down to business on their fair competition code under the NRA, he was but fulfilling that part of the fate of Presidents for nearly forty years. All of them have had difficulties with this trouble-maker in the economic family, but this Roosevelt felt it all the more incumbent upon him to take the incorrigible by the ear to keep him from upsetting the table just when it seemed that the household was about to sit down to its first real meal in four years.

There is no question in Washington that President Roosevelt regards a satisfactory solution of the soft coal muddle as possibly the greatest single blessing that could come from NRA. The economic aspects involved, the social and humane side of it and the possibility for evolving a new cure that may be applied in the future to similarly ailing industries have appealed to Mr. Roosevelt as they could appeal only to a man with his intimate knowledge of the problem.

Coal men who sat around the desk in the circular office of the President last Thursday were startled to find him with such an understanding of the coal situation as he displayed. Technical terms, shop names and economic maxims rolled off his tongue at times as if he were an operator himself, at other times as if he were a miner with the dust on his face and signs of fatigue in his eye, and at still other times as if he were a social reformer—even a labor agitator—telling them that if they did not set their house in order communism would wreck what is left of a "diminishing" industry.

Moreover, these coal men saw that "big stick" of which they had heard their anthracite brethren speak more than thirty years ago. It was in the hands of another Roosevelt then—one who told the miners and operators to mine that coal or the government would mine it for them. But it apparently was the same weapon.

Mr. Roosevelt's determination to have a showdown on the coal problem came as only a part, however, of the show of force on his national industrial recovery program. While the operators were listening to his cool, clear demands—he smiled little at the conference—General Hugh S. Johnson, his ex-cavalry officer recovery administrator, was virtually "reading the riot act" to that other problem child, the oil industry, on its fair competition code.

After weeks of wrangling and arguing in private conferences in and out of Washington, General Johnson summoned the oil operators to an open session at the Chamber of Commerce of the United States and there he presented a code draft with the old ultimatum, "Take it or leave it," amended by striking out the "or leave it." He told them if they had anything to say about it, "say it in writing, and before 10 A.M. the next day."

And the oil men said a few things. More than a score of "sets" of objections were on the administrator's desk before the appointed hour of 10. How many specific objections were in each "set" not even he could tell accurately at that hour.

The administrator's action with the oil men, which in effect was giving them a dose of their own product, was little more harsh than certain sections of the code itself. One of its main proposals would make the President or his designated agent a virtual czar over the industry, particularly as to production and price-fixing. The President said the next day that he proposed to exercise that power in person.

The intense, at times desperate, efforts of the President and his recovery administrator to pull the coal, oil and steel industries into line for NRA held the centre of the stage in domestic activities for the week. It was obvious in Washington that they believed that the crisis in the great recovery experiment actually had arrived.

They started out on June 16 to codify the bulk of American industry by Labor Day. They surely expected to have the unidentified "big ten" under satisfactory fair practice codes by that time. They expected that this would place more than 70 per cent of the employing power of the entire country directly behind the recovery program.

When Aug. 16 came around, however, it was found that only one of the "big ten" had been enlisted. This was the cotton textile industry. They redoubled their efforts.

It was not only necessary that the purchasing power of these industries should be added to that which already had been restored, but it was most desirable that hundreds of thousands of small enterprises might be assured that they were being helped to carry the extra load which they saddled upon themselves.

The move for speed on the part of the administration made it appear that the whole program was in another jam. In fact, it was. Some within the official family of President Roosevelt thought for a time last week that the recovery program either would have to be compromised or modified.

Not so with General Johnson, however. As for him, "These guys have got to come under," and that is the spirit that has reassured President Roosevelt on more than one occasion when men with names that used to sound like ominous thunder tried to tell him that his experiment would not and could not work.

The week saw the President more prominent in the front lines of the industrial recovery campaign than at any time since it was begun. He even went on sort of exploratory missions of his own to see what was holding up the basic codes for the basic industries.

As early as Sunday he called in the deputy adminis-trator who was handling the coal, oil and steel codes to find out just what or who was causing the trouble. After a study of only one day of the difficulties as represented to him, the President indicated he was ready to act, if necessary, to break the growing jam. When, later in the week, he actually stepped out with the "big stick" he made good on that warning.

Then it appeared that the steel people were about to get together on their code. These tidings came soon after Myron Taylor and Charles M. Schwab, the mentors of the industry, had spent an hour with President Roosevelt. Did they, too, see the big stick?

Whatever they saw, the results were achieved, and President Green of the American Federation of Labor and other labor leaders serving the govern-ment joined in the satisfaction that the keystone of American industry had decided to take its place in the recovery program.

Unmistakable indications developed during the week that capital and labor are nearing a test on some of their most persistent issues. The old-time "open shop" ques-tion is literally leaping to the front. Part of the backward-ness of some industries to fall in immediately with their codes is said to arise from the fear that the government, under the present administration, soon will find itself, either intentionally or otherwise, in the labor unionizing movement. [EDITORIAL SECTION, Aug. 20, 1933]

1930–1939

Chase Stock Sold Short by Wiggin Before 1929 Crash

The Securities Act passed during the first 100 days of the Roosevelt Administration required companies to disclose information when selling securities but did nothing to regulate the trading of securities, particularly on the New York Stock Exchange. That omission reflected the power of the N.Y.S.E. and its president, Richard Whitney, who deemed the exchange to be a perfect institution.

Senate hearings on the exchange in late 1933 helped to mobilize public pressure for such regulation, particularly by exposing the activities of Albert H. Wiggin who, as president of Chase National Bank, made huge profits in the 1920's through side deals with the bank's securities arm and who was shown to have personally sold Chase stock short—that is, sold shares he did not own in the hope of buying them back for less after they fell—just before and during the 1929 crash. Given that the president of a company owed a duty to shareholders to make the company as successful as possible, that seemed to be a clear conflict of interest, but not an illegal one.

The Securities Exchange Act passed by Congress in 1934 specifically made it illegal for a corporate officer to short his own company's stock, but it left many other issues to be decided by the S.E.C. itself. While the stock exchange was forced to register with the commission, no specific changes in the way the exchange was run were required. Limits were placed on the ability of speculators to borrow money to buy stock, but they were made flexible, with changes to be made by the Federal Reserve Board.

The first two chairmen of the S.E.C., Joseph P. Kennedy, himself a Wall Street speculator (and father of a future President, John F. Kennedy), and James M. Landis, a former Harvard law professor, chose to go slow in regulating the exchange, and it continued to operate largely under the control of the brokers that had always dominated it. The third chairman, William O. Douglas, the future Supreme Court justice, thought the exchange was too much of a private club and set out to force reforms. But he did not succeed until fate brought an end to the power of Whitney in 1938.

Special to The New York Times

WASHINGTON, Oct. 31—Albert H. Wiggin admitted before the Senate Banking and Currency Committee today that he began to "sell short" in stock of the Chase National Bank a month before the market crash of 1929.

This was done, the former head of the bank testified, through his personally owned Shermar and Murlyn corporations, which developed a short position of 42,506 shares and were forced to borrow $6,588,430 from the Chase bank to cover that position.

Mr. Wiggin's testimony relative to these short sales, into which the committee will delve deeper tomorrow, came after he had disclosed that he had formed six Wiggin family corporations, three of them in Canada, to cut down the payment of income taxes in the United States.

It likewise followed the disclosure of a trading account in Sinclair Consolidated Oil Company common managed by Arthur Cutten, Chicago market operator, in 1929, in which the participants were Mr. Cutten, Harry F. Sinclair, Blair & Co., the Chase Securities Corporation and the Shermar Corporation, with total profits of $12,200,109.41.

Under an examination by Ferdinand Pecora, counsel to the committee, which at times made the witness wince, Mr. Wiggin named nine other officers or directors of the bank who were directors of his personally owned Shermar Corporation.

Among them was Gates W. McGarrah, then chairman of the board of the New York Federal Reserve Bank and at the same time of the Bank for International Settlements. To a number of them the Shermar Corporation made loans which were used for "investment" in Chase National and other shares.

"These loans were all subsequently repaid in full," he said. "They were always secured by collateral by ample margin."

Between Nov. 8, 1929, and Dec. 11, 1929, Mr. Wiggin continued, the Shermar Corporation had borrowed $5,000,000 and the Murlyn Corporation $3,000,000 from the Chase National.

"Then this short position commenced about a month before the more or less famous market crash of Oct. 26, 1929?" Mr. Pecora pressed.

Albert H. Wiggin, former president of Chase National Bank.

"It began; yes," the witness replied.

"I suppose you made them because you read the financial skies," said Mr. Pecora, "and concluded that the trend was going to be downward in the value of the Chase bank stock?"

"I do not think I was wise enough for that," the witness countered.

Q.—You did sell it short commencing with September? A.—Yes, and I did think that the bank stock market was high and I did want a buying power for that bank stock.

Q.—And you developed that buying power through the operations of your own private corporation at what proved to be eventually a substantial profit to your corporation? A.—On that transaction, yes, sir.

Mr. Pecora asked if Mr. Wiggin considered that "an ethical practice for the head of a bank to engage in."

The witness replied:

"I think it is commendable to provide a buying power for your own stock. Incidentally, as I have stated, at the end of 1932 we still had practically 200,000 shares that dropped from those very high prices to $40. At the time of that short sale of 42,000 shares there were 116,000 shares owned by myself and my family."

"How much of the stock do you and your family now hold?" Senator Gore asked.

"I cannot tell you at the moment," Mr. Wiggin answered, "but at the end of the 1932 period it was 194,000 shares." [Nov. 1, 1933]

Exchange Bill Agreement Provides New 5-Man Board, Flexible Curb on Margins

Special to The New York Times

WASHINGTON, May 26—Complete agreement on the Stock Exchange Regulation Bill was reached by conferees today after a long and bitter controversy. Formal signing of the conference report was deferred until Tuesday.

Under its terms, which Senate and House are expected to accept promptly, stock market regulation will be concentrated in a new agency to be known as the "Securities and Exchange Commission," consisting of five members to be appointed by the President. This provision was a part of the Senate bill.

The House conferees agreed to surrender not only their contention for administration by the Federal Trade Commission, but also to accept the Senate provision transferring supervision of the Securities Act of 1933 to the new agency. The Securities Act is modified to a minor extent by the compromise bill.

The conferees agreed to the House limitation on marginal trading, which would put control of credit for this type of market operations in the hands of the Federal Reserve Board, but under the additional stipulation that marginal traders be required to carry 45 per cent of the value of any security traded in. The Reserve Board would have discretion to raise or lower this marginal requirement should circumstances warrant.

The penalty provisions were modified by the conferees to differentiate between violations of the law and violations of regulations made by the commission under authority of the act.

For unintentional violations of any regulation the compromise bill provides that there shall be no prison sentence, but a fine not to exceed $10,000; but for willful violation of regulations or infractions of the act itself the prison sentence of not to exceed two years or a fine of not more than $10,000 or both are retained.

President Roosevelt, who advocated the Federal Trade Commission as the agency for administration, is understood to have acceded to the new commission to speed Congress's adjournment.

The conferees agreed that the act should become operative July 1 with regard to the registration of securities and Oct. 1 with regard to marginal requirements. The Reserve Board must set before Oct. 1 the amount of margin required.

Members of the new commission will receive salaries of $10,000 a year. One member will be appointed for a year, one for two years, one for three, one for four and one for five years, so as to provide constant change in the membership of the body. Successive appointments are to be for five years each.

It was reported that Chairman James M. Landis of the Federal Trade Commission might be transferred to head the new commission and that Ferdinand Pecora, who conducted the stock market investigation, might also be a member.

Conferees praised the terms of the agreement. Chairman Fletcher of the Senate Banking and Currency Committee said that "all the modifications were liberalizing."

Chairman Rayburn of the House committee expressed his belief that the measure would be approved.

Mr. Pecora thought that it was "a very happy compromise."

"I think that the stock market bill will purge the securities market of the evil practices shown to have existed in the past," he added.

"Under its terms there is made available to investors more complete and reliable data with regard to the value of securities than hitherto have been obtained by them. It will thereby give greater confidence to the investors.

"The power given to the Federal Reserve Board over margins puts in the hands of the board a brake which will enable it to check undue or excessive speculation and gives it a firmer control over the use of bank credits for stock market transactions.

"Among the outstanding evils which can be curbed by the wise use of the powers conferred by the act upon both the commission and the Federal Reserve Board is the inflation of security prices which has always attended excessive speculation.

"The bill spells the end of the manipulator, jiggler and pool operator."

Mr. Pecora held that the legislation would do no injury to brokers and dealers, and that they would in fact end by blessing it.

"The restrictions and requirements imposed by the act upon brokers, dealers, and corporations having listed securities are in my opinion entirely reasonable and readily workable," he said. "They should experience no difficulty in adjusting themselves to these restrictions and requirements." [May 27, 1934]

Court Backs Government on Gold; 5-4 for Bond Payment in New Dollar; Business Surges Forward, Stocks Rise

By ARTHUR KROCK

Special to The New York Times

WASHINGTON, Feb. 18—Headed by the Chief Justice of the United States, a majority of five members of the Supreme Court today overrode their four colleagues in the cases growing out of the repeal of the gold-payment clause in public and private contracts by the Seventy-third Congress, involving more than 100 billions, and held in effect that government and private creditors must accept, in depreciated currency, dollar for dollar on interest and principal sums named in the contracts.

The majority and the minority agreed only on one point—that the gold-clause repeal in government contracts was unconstitutional. But the majority offered no redress to the litigating contract-holders, on the ground that no damage had been shown, while the four dissenters insisted that the damage was demonstrable as the precise difference of 69 cents in the value of the "old dollar" containing 25.8 grains of gold nine-tenths fine and the "new" dollar containing 15.5–21 grains.

Since there is no practical effect of the majority's one agreement with the minority, the government's victory was materially complete in all respects. Bond-holders may not sue for nominal damages in the Court of Claims. Some lawyers hold, however, that if, at some future time, the dollar is revalued to a point where it can be shown in the Court of Claims that it will purchase less than the dollar did when a citizen bought a government security, containing the gold clause, he can recover the proved difference under the majority opinion.

Joining with the Chief Justice in affirming the lower court judgment that sustained government action throughout were Justices Brandeis, Roberts, Cardozo and Stone. The dissenting four, whose views were orally expounded in a remarkable address by Mr. Justice McReynolds, were himself, Justices Van Devanter, Butler and Sutherland.

In announcing its rulings, the nation's highest court broke one precedent and badly shattered another. The Chief Justice read a brief summary of the findings before he began reading the text, an unprecedented action. Mr. Justice McReynolds, putting aside the dissenting text, interposed for nearly half an hour heated and extemporaneous remarks in which he confessed "shame and humiliation" over the majority decision.

In open court he said: "The Constitution is gone!"

The cases decided were those of citizens suing to recover the currency equivalent of the former gold value of the dollar on railroad bonds and of gold or its currency equivalent on Liberty bonds and gold certificates.

Government officials, from the President down, greeted the decision with elation. In a statement issued early in the afternoon the President expressed himself as gratified.

From Capitol Hill the comment was generally favorable. On all sides it was asserted that the decision established the complete power of Congress over the monetary system and its power in law, if not in morals, to alter any contract, public or private, in terms of the currency. Inflationists prepared to press their campaign for further devaluation of the dollar to 50 or 40 cents, but there was no indication that any such step would be successful.

In the first opinion, Norman v. the Baltimore & Ohio Railroad and others, which dealt with the 75 billions in private contracts, the Chief Justice described the steps by which the administration met the banking crisis of 1933 when it assumed office, and progressed to a description of the erection of the new monetary system by Congress and the President on the authority of Congress.

In the first year of the Roosevelt Administration, a series of actions by the President and Congress first suspended the payment of gold coins and then devalued the dollar against gold, raising the gold price from 20.67 an ounce to 35. It was the end of legal ownership of gold coins or bullion by Americans for a generation. Not until the 1970's, after the dollar was completely severed from gold, would Americans again be able to buy the precious metal.

The devaluation raised legal questions because Government and corporate bonds specifically said that no devaluation was possible, assuring holders that they would get dollars valued at gold's old rate of 20.67. Gold was then viewed as the ultimate money, and most countries were on the gold standard, tying the value of their currencies to the metal. If those contracts were enforceable after the devaluation, however, then a company that had borrowed 1 million would have to repay 1.67 million. Many companies already in trouble because of the Depression would be sure to fail if that extra burden were added.

On a 5-4 vote, the Supreme Court upheld the gold action. It conceded that the Government's repudiation of the gold clause in its own bonds was illegal but said that there was nothing that could be done about it. It said that Congress had the power to alter corporate bond contracts.

It was one of the most bitter splits ever on the court. Justice James C. McReynolds compared the actions of Congress to those of the Roman emperor Nero and complained that the Constitution was "gone."

1930–1939

CONSTITUTION GONE, SAYS M'REYNOLDS

WASHINGTON, Feb. 18–In an extemporaneous speech bristling with scorn and indignation, Justice McReynolds, delivering the opinion of the minority in the gold clause cases, startled spectators in the Supreme Court chamber today with a blistering attack on New Deal currency policies.

There were gasps as the 73-year old Tennessean, scarcely glancing at his manuscript, declared that Nero undertook to use a debased currency, asserted that the Constitution had "gone" and expressed the "shame and humiliation" of the minority consisting of himself and Justices Vandevanter, Sutherland and Butler.

At the very outset he said that to share the view of the majority would mean a "repudiation of national obligations," and "these things are abhorrent" to himself and the three other associate justices.

He scoffed at the idea that the framers of the Constitution would for a moment sanction repudiation of the "solemn pledges" of the gold clauses, which Congress had "swept away with a word." He remarked that "millions of dollars" had been invested with these "solemn pledges" as an assurance to investors.   [Feb. 19, 1935]

"We are not concerned here," he said, "with the wisdom of these steps. We are concerned with power, not with policy."

The question in the Norman case was, should the bondholder receive $22.50 interest in the devalued currency, or $38.10, the equivalent of the former gold dollar? The court agreed with the Attorney General's argument that the monetary acts formed a continuous chain and revealed a fixed intention by Congress to exercise its constitutional authority to regulate the value of the currency. The gold clauses in these private contracts interfered with the exercise of that power. Nothing in the Legal Tender or any previous cases bore on the situation—it was new.

If the gold clause in the private contracts were enforceable, said the court, States, municipalities, railroads and other corporations would be in the position of receiving payment for services at the rate of $1 and meeting their obligations at the rate of $1.69. It would require no "profound economy," said the court, to recognize the impossibility of such an arrangement.

Gold clauses, the court continued, were to be found in a large part of the outstanding obligations of these debtors.

"We are not concerned with consequences," read the Chief Justice, "in the sense that consequences, however serious, may excuse an invasion of constitutional rights. We are concerned with the constitutional power of the Congress over the monetary system of the country and its attempted frustration * * *. In the light of abundant experience, Congress was entitled to choose such a uniform monetary system and to reject a dual system with respect to all obligations within the range of its constitutional authority."

Finding that the gold clauses interfered with its authority to fix a new monetary policy, Congress, said the court, had abolished them not "capriciously or arbitrarily." There was "a congenital infirmity" in contracts which deal with subject matter within the control of Congress. The plaintiffs had no case.

The Chief Justice then turned to the "gold certificates case," brought by F. Eugene Nortz to receive gold coin as nominated in the bond.

The court held that, despite any words of the Secretary of the Treasury, the $106,300 in gold certificates held by the plaintiff were not "warehouse receipts" for bullion, that they called for dollars and not bullion, and, as for gold coin, this had been withdrawn from circulation by the uncontested power of the government and therefore the plaintiff would not have been permitted to keep or use the coin if he got it. The plaintiff was restrained by law from resorting to free gold markets abroad, and there was none in this country. Having suffered no damages, he was not entitled to receive gold coin or its currency equivalent, and had no standing in the Court of Claims.

[Feb. 19, 1935]

Mickey Mouse Emerges as Economist

CITIZEN OF THE WORLD, UNEXPLAINED PHENOMENON, HE WINS VICTORIES IN THE FIELD OF BUSINESS MAN AND BANKER

By L. H. ROBBINS

New applause is heard for Mickey Mouse rising high above the general acclaim for him that already rings throughout the earth. The fresh cheering is for Mickey the Big Business Man, the world's super-salesman. He finds work for jobless folk. He lifts corporations out of bankruptcy. Wherever he scampers, here or overseas, the sun of prosperity breaks through the clouds.

Cutting up on the screen in every clime, entertaining a million audiences a year in eighty-eight countries, Mickey Mouse is the best-known and most-popular international figure of his day. One touch of Mickey makes the whole world grin in a very dark hour. But he does not stop with entertaining.

He rolls up his sleeves and grapples with the world's economic problem. He puts his shoulder to the stalled wheel of trade, and the wheel that won't budge for the statesmen and the international bankers turns for the small and mighty Mickey.

Assisted by faithful Minnie, he pumps a key-winding handcar around a track of tin and pulls a two-million-dollar toy-making concern out of a receivership. Then by himself he restores a famous but limping watch-making company to health—after eight weeks of his treatment the company throws away its crutches, adds 2,700 workers to its payroll and proceeds to sell 2,000,000 watches.

Again, through three lean years he keeps a knitting mill busy making sweatshirts with his portrait in color on them—a million shirts a year, and one-third of the population of the mill town assured of three meals a day from the overtime work alone.

Mickey Mouse has his commercial headquarters in the United Artists Building in Seventh Avenue, just off Times Square. He lives in Hollywood, of course, pursuing there the fine art of the funny films with his creator, Walt Disney. Their art yields by-products worth millions to business men, hence Mickey's New York office, with his name on the directory board downstairs and also in the telephone book.

A neat sign on the door says: "Kay Kamen: The Walt Disney Enterprises." Mickey himself, portrayed in bright hues and heroic size, greets you from the wall of the pleasantly appointed reception room. Beyond are showrooms where Disney commodities fill glass cases with color and humor; also workrooms where Disney artists, trained in the technique of the Hollywood studio, draw the countless pictures used in Mickey's commercial undertakings.

The office controls the by-products of the Disney art. If you wish to manufacture a Mickey Mouse roller-skate or a Mickey Mouse electric refrigerator, you come here for Mickey's permission, and Mr. Kamen, his merchandising representative, grants you a license, provided no one else is making the article you desire to make, and provided you convince him that your wares will measure up to the quality standard of the Disney animated cartoons.

It is a busy place. While you wait, an official of a national metal institute is phoning about Mickey Mouse book-ends, and a maker of optical instruments comes in to discuss Mickey Mouse thermometers. The first concession went to a doll maker in 1930. Now there are eighty licensees in the United States, fifteen in Canada, forty in England, eighty on the Continent and fifteen in Australia. There are branch offices in Chicago, Toronto, London, Paris, Copenhagen, Milan, Barcelona, Lisbon and Sydney.

Mickey Mouse whistled his way into the hearts of America and beyond when the cartoon "Steamboat Willie" was released by Walt Disney in 1928 with the then-novel technique of synchronized sound.

By 1935, Mickey Mouse was a merchandising icon, as The Times chronicled in a Magazine article entitled "Mickey Mouse Emerges as Economist." This came about notwithstanding the fact that Disney had yet to make a major motion picture, having established his fame with nine-minute cartoons.

In 1937, Disney released his first full-length animated film, "Snow White and the Seven Dwarfs." Many had questioned whether "Snow White," which cost nearly 2 million to make, could possibly make money. But it became one of the most successful movies of all time. It also became such a merchandising success that The Times, in an editorial, discussed it as a means of overcoming the 1938 recession.

When Disney died in 1966, an appraisal of his life by Bosley Crowther, the film critic of The New York Times from 1940 to 1967, celebrated, among his many contributions, that "place of delight for millions" that he created, Disneyland.

1930–1939

© DISNEY ENTERPRISES, INC.

Mickey Mouse made his film debut in "Steamboat Willie."

The licensees make thousands of merchandise items—the latest in England is Mickey Mouse marmalade. Their royalties help to nurture the Hollywood art, which is laborious and expensive. An ideal arrangement it is and highly suggestive of perpetual motion; for the better the art of the Disney studio, the better the by-products sell, and the better they sell, the better the art again. It is something novel in business cycles; it never gets worse. With commodity sales boomed periodically by the fame of new films, the Mickey Mouse fad goes on as if forever—and Mr. Disney is still young.

Conservative business houses join in the rush to employ Mickey Mouse and his friends, the Three Little Pigs, the Wolf, the Grasshopper, Horace Horsecollar and Pluto, the dog. Among them are leading makers of pencils and of paper. The world's largest food-products company hires Mickey to sell a breakfast food and spends a million and a half to proclaim the tie-up. The manufacturer of half of the table silver sold in the United States dispenses Mickey Mouse cutlery in all grades, including sterling, and Fifth Avenue offers Mickey Mouse charms and bracelets in gold and platinum set with diamonds, retailing up to $1,200.

Mickey is such a literary lion, he has to have four publishers; one of his books last year sold 2,400, 000 copies. His school notebooks and tablets go by the million. So do his neckties and handkerchiefs—the kerchief trade is keen for the cotton print that shows Pluto writing, on the sidewalk, "Mickey loves Minnie." Department stores by the hundreds, here and abroad, go Mickey Mouse, even to the length of spending $25,000 on a single window display, and a great rubber company pauses in making Zeppelins to turn out fifty-foot Mickeys for their street parades.

Undeniably, and appallingly, it is Mickey Mouse's day. Shoppers carry Mickey Mouse satchels and briefcases bursting with Mickey Mouse soap, candy, playing-cards, bridge favors, hairbrushes, chinaware, alarm clocks and hot-water bottles, wrapped in Mickey Mouse paper, tied with Mickey Mouse ribbon and paid for out of Mickey Mouse purses with savings hoarded in Mickey Mouse banks.

At the lunch counter—Mickey Mouse table covers and napkins—they consume Mickey Mouse biscuits and dairy products while listening to Mickey Mouse music from Mickey Mouse phonographs and radios. Then, glancing at their Mickey Mouse wrist-watches, they dash away to buy Mickey Mouse toothbrushes that will make oral sanitation attractive to little Michael and Minerva.

And the children live in a Mickey Mouse world. They wear Mickey Mouse caps, waists, socks, shoes, slippers, garters, mittens, aprons, bibs and underthings, and beneath Mickey Mouse rain-capes and umbrellas they go to school, where Mickey Mouse desk outfits turn lessons into pleasure.

They play with Mickey Mouse velocipedes, footballs, baseballs, bounce-balls, bats, catching gloves, boxing gloves, doll houses, doll dishes, tops, blocks, drums, puzzles, games—

Paint sets, sewing sets, drawing sets, stamping sets, jack sets, bubble sets, pull toys, push toys, animated toys, tents, camp stools, sand pails, masks, blackboards and balloons—

Until day is done, when they sup from Mickey Mouse cups, porringers and baby plates and lie down to sleep in Mickey Mouse pajamas between Mickey Mouse crib sheets, to waken in the morn smiling at Mickey Mouse pictures on

---

8 — THE NEW YORK TIMES MAGAZINE, MARCH 10, 1935.

MICKEY MOUSE EMERGES AS ECONOMIST

Citizen of the World, Unexplained Phenomenon, He Wins Victories in the Field of Business Man and Banker

By L. H. ROBBINS

The Mouse That Brings Forth a Mountain of Fan Mail—And His Creator, Walt Disney.

the nursery walls. In time, no doubt, there will be Mickey Mouse wallpaper for them.

After all, these material and tangible creations of the factories are only shadows of the real thing; manifestations, as it were, of a spirit; physical effigies of a vital reality who is but a shadow himself and has no material existence, no tangibility at all. They merely reflect, they don't explain the excitement over Mickey Mouse.

What is the secret of his appeal? How has an imaginary creature only 6 years old, going on 7, captured the interest of almost every tribe on this terrestrial ball? Why is it that university presidents praise him, the League of Nations recommends him, Who's Who and the Encyclopaedia Britannica give him paragraphs, learned academies hang medals on him, art galleries turn from Picasso and Epstein to hold exhibitions of his monkey-shines, and the King of England won't go to the movies unless Mickey is on the bill?

Crowds of ambitious folk looking for ideas and fortune would like to know, to say nothing of people trying to interpret day-by-day phenomena for the press, psychologists who must somehow account for human behavior, and historians who will have to record this age for posterity's eye. Mickey Mouse is Public Question No. 1 to a lot of people.

Sages in great argument try to explain Mickey Mouse, and, in the fashion of the blind men of Hindustan who went to see the elephant, they reason variously, each according to his feeling. To the timid among us, Mickey represents mankind beset by grim circumstances and escaping whole and right-side up through luck. To them he is

PROSPERITY OUT OF FANTASY

1930–1939

It is said that what America needs to swing it out of the present economic tailspin is a new industry. Many things just over the horizon, such as television, air-conditioning in the home and flivver airplanes, have been suggested. But none of them seems yet to have materialized in terms of wages and heavy sales. Would it be ridiculous to suggest that industrialized fantasy may prove to be the answer?

Industrialized fantasy sounds like something extremely complex. Yet it is quite simple. Walt Disney's picture-play "Snow White and the Seven Dwarfs" is an excellent example. Here is something manufactured out of practically nothing except some paint pots and a few tons of imagination. In this country imagination is supposed to be a commodity produced in unlimited quantities. If it can be turned out as an article of commerce which the public will readily buy, then prosperity should be—well, just around the corner, anyway.

The Disney picture cost about $2,000,000 to produce. To be sure, it gave employment to no flesh-and-blood actors, human attributes being confined to voices on the sound tracks. But it kept a small army of artists, animators and gag men busy for many months. And from all reports it will not only return more than this investment to Mr. Disney, but is showering fortune on every playhouse that shows it. Dopey, Grumpy and their fellow-dwarfs, despite the fact that they get no wages themselves, have been the most valiant miners and sappers against recession whom the moving picture magnates have hired this year. No matter what business may have been in most theatres, the exhibitors of "Snow White" have not had to lay off a single dwarf.

Moreover, the picture has virtually developed a new industry from its by-products. Figments of Disney's imagination have already sold more than $2,000,000 worth of toys since the first

of the year. Since January, says Kay Kamen, Mr. Disney's representative here, 117 toy manufacturers have been licensed to use characters from "Snow White." The only thing in the picture that the public doesn't seem to crave is poisoned apples.

One factory in Akron, Ohio, which makes little rubber dwarfs, has been running twenty-four hours a day, while many of the other rubber factories are closed. Dopey and Grumpy are putting men to work in paint shops, box factories, silica mines, stone quarries and mills all over the map. Wherever they turn up, prosperity begins to radiate. "Snow White" is Disney's first full-length picture. What is going to happen when he really gets into his stride? Industrialized fantasy? It should be industrially fantastic.   [EDITORIAL, TOPICS OF THE TIMES, May 2, 1938]

Disney's "Snow White and the Seven Dwarfs."

THE DREAM MERCHANT

By BOSLEY CROWTHER

"Snow White and the Seven Dwarfs" . . . was the Continental Divide in Mr. Disney's creative career. It marked his fateful migration into a new and less personal fantasy realm. He began working with the stories of other people—old familiar ones mostly—and he took to a kind of representational animation that was not esthetically felicitous. Not to him.

He was now moving in the area of the big producer, the Hollywood tycoon, and this was a role that he managed with more pretension than with comfort and ease. More work was delegated to others. His associates, whom he credited, did the things that he himself formerly executed. The Disney plant was a factory.

In this situation, which was inevitable, you might say, and pressed by economic circumstances that were discouraging to the making of cartoons, it might well have been that Mr. Disney would have quietly withdrawn into a shell, committed his business to his brother, and lived happily ever after on television residuals. And, indeed, I recall an occasion of a visit to him at his studio back in the early nineteen-fifties when I got the distinct impression that something of this sort was going on.

He seemed totally disinterested in movies and wholly, almost weirdly, concerned with the building of a miniature railroad engine and a string of cars in the workshops of the studio. All of his zest for invention, for creating fantasies, seemed to be going into this plaything. I came away feeling sad.

I needn't have been. Mr. Disney, the cinema artist and tycoon, was even then joyously gestating another Mouse. It was born as Disneyland. This great amusement park may be a symbol of mass commercialism in our day. It may be an entertainment supermarket. It may be many things that high-brow citizens frown on. But it is tasteful, wholesome and clean. It is a place of delight for millions, who escape into its massive fantasies.

It and "Mary Poppins," which he produced and in which he took a hand, were the final achievements of Mr. Disney, the most persistent and successful fantasist of our age. He managed to come out very nicely for an artist in Hollywood.

[AN APPRAISAL (excerpt), Dec. 16, 1966]

that dearest figure in fiction, the ill-used, defenseless, well-deserving Cinderella in disguise. To the aggressive and the predatory among us, on the other hand, he symbolizes cleverness and resource. He is "little, but oh my!" He outsmarts even Behemoth.

Again, world-weary philosophers find in Mickey's antics "a release from the tyranny of things." He declares a nine-minute moratorium on the debt we owe to the iron facts of life. He suspends the rules of common sense and correct deportment and all the other carping, conventional laws, including the law of gravity, that hold us down and circumscribe our existence and cramp our style.

These observers tell us there is in human nature's streak of rebellion, a yearning to cut loose, to be free to overleap the moon if we like, even at the cost of a headache and an unpleasant taste in the cold gray dawn of the morning after. This craving of ours Mickey, with his absurdities, his defiance of reason and his accomplishment of the impossible, gratifies for us vicariously.

It sounds a bit highbrow to those who have most to do with Mickey Mouse's career. So does the explanation of educators who recall that folk tales have always been popular and fables of talking animals beloved; who cite the instances of Reynard the Fox and Brer Rabbit, and conclude that Mickey's creator has merely applied the old, tested method of Aesop.

There would seem to be more to Mickey Mouse than that, and besides, he is not an animal; he is a personality, along with Uncle Sam, John Bull, Mr. Dooley and the Tammany Tiger. He is not a mouse at all; he is Mickey Mouse. In one way or another, since there is a bit of Mickey's helplessness, shrewdness, madness and mischief in the best of us, he is an approach, the nearest one in our day, to that mythical and ubiquitous fellow, Everyman.

All these piecemeal explanations help in explaining Mickey Mouse, but they ignore the two obvious ones—that Mickey is superlatively funny, and that he is simple. The world, in all its continents and islands, wants to laugh, and never more than now. Mickey makes it laugh till the roof shakes. Moreover, the occasion of the laughter is always harmless, and the world likes decency.

The world wants also to understand, and Mickey is so simple that anybody of any age in any stage of the rather spotty civilization extant on this planet can understand him. His simplicity makes him so nearly universal that any land can take him for its own. Wherefore he is at once hot stuff in Chile, a smash in China, "it" in Italy, cheered in Algiers, pined for in the Philippines and a wow all over the map. Wherefore, also, he has many an alias—Michel Souris, Michael Maus, Miguel Ratonocito, Michele Jopolino, Miki Kuchi, according to the locality.

Add to all this that his nine minutes on the screen contain as many plot situations and surprises and as much pathos and comedy as three hours of spoken drama; and that because all these are present the public is satisfied, yet because the thing is over so soon the public is left hungry for more.

Last, and most important of all, consider that Disney, as a dramatist and a producer, is a genius whose work the scholarly of the world hail as an immortal contribution to literature. Disney, who is modest, would probably offer the further explanation of Mickey Mouse's success that his distributers have excellent connections abroad.

After these reasons have been recited, Mickey's professional friends confide that the real, final secret of Mickey's appeal is still a secret to them and to Disney himself.

If the reason for the public response were surely known, Disney could make pictures to fit the response. He could have a formula and follow it. But he has still to discover the magic formula. He still adventures in the dark and mysterious terra incognita of popular taste, as he did in 1928, when he and Mickey Mouse, unhonored and unsung, came to town to seek their fortune.

[THE NEW YORK TIMES MAGAZINE, March 10, 1935]

Strikers Quit Auto Plants; Operations Resume Monday; $25,000,000 Rise in Wages

By LOUIS STARK

Special to The New York Times

DETROIT, Feb. 11—The nation's first major labor dispute in the automobile industry ended at noon today when representatives of General Motors Corporation and the International Union, United Automobile Workers of America, signed an agreement terminating the forty-four-day strike which had crippled the production of automobiles by the corporation.

While the signatures were being affixed to the document in Judge George Murphy's court, with Governor Frank Murphy, his brother, the focus of Kleig lights and newsreel cameras, Alfred P. Sloan Jr., president of General Motors, in New York, announced a $25,000,000 wage increase to General Motors employes.

A mile from the court room where an excited crowd applauded the speeches of the principals on both sides, John L. Lewis, strike generalissimo and chairman of the Committee for Industrial Organization, smiled happily as the radio carried the news to him in the hotel room where he has been confined with influenza for two days.

Late today three General Motors plants in Flint were evacuated by sit-down strikers, who embraced each other with joy as they were told by their leaders that their union had been recognized by the company.

To members of the C. I. O. in the steel and rubber industries, as well as those in the automobile industry, the agreement, they felt, was the first major offensive won by them in their program of unionizing the nation's basic industries.

A crowd formed an eager circle around the signers of the agreement in the high vaulted court room. In seats arranged for them and flanked by two court officers, were James F. Dewey, Federal conciliator; W. S. Knudsen, vice president of General Motors; Governor Murphy and Wyndham Mortimer, vice president of the union. Behind them stood John Thomas Smith and Donaldson Brown, vice presidents of the company, and Lee Pressman, general counsel of the C. I. O. On the judge's dais behind these participants were other union officers and reporters.

"Let us have peace and make automobiles," said Mr. Knudsen with a smile and the crowd laughed and cheered.

General Motors executives were relieved that the long and costly strike was at an end and that negotiations for the remainder of the union's demands would begin here on Tuesday. They said that today's agreement covered the extent of recognition that their corporation would extend to the union.

From President Roosevelt and Secretary Perkins the Governor of Michigan received the highest praise, while many others telegraphed congratulations and commented on his tenacity in keeping the conferees together until an agreement was reached.

Above all other praise of Governor Murphy was the comment from many who called him, praising his handling of the tense situation in Flint, where he sent the National Guard to protect strikers as well as non-strikers and successfully averted a "vigilante" outbreak.

Restoration of production at the struck plants of the corporation was ordered at once by Mr. Knudsen. Some employes will report tomorrow but most of the idle workers, some 115,000, will begin their former tasks on Monday or Tuesday. Mr. Knudsen said he expected that a peak output of 225,000 cars would be accomplished in March.

Under the agreement the corporation recognizes the union as the bargaining

By 1936, it appeared the country was coming out of the Great Depression. Auto sales were the highest that year for any year since 1929, and General Motors, the largest car company, announced pay increases totaling 20 million for its workers—an average of about 100 a worker. At the same time, the auto maker announced a 62.3 million dividend for its shareholders, which The Times noted was "the largest single dividend in the history of the corporation."

A few weeks later, on Dec. 18, John L. Lewis, the leader of the Committee for Industrial Organization, the C.I.O., announced that the United Auto Workers would try to organize workers at General Motors. The first strike began on Dec. 28 using a new strategy for organized labor, a "sit-down" strike that effectively shut down a G.M. factory in Cleveland. The strike spread to G.M.'s most important plants in Flint, Mich., on Dec. 30. G.M. denounced the strike as an illegal trespass and got a court order requiring the workers to leave the premises, but the workers defied that order.

On Jan. 11, violence broke out in a pitched battle between strikers and police in Flint, leaving at least 24 people injured but the strikers still in control of the buildings despite the use of tear gas by the police. The violence could have grown much worse, but on Jan. 14, with thousands of National Guardsmen gathering outside the plant, the company and the union agreed to a truce while talks went on.

On Feb. 11, the strike was settled, with the company agreeing to an additional pay increase and to union recognition. The workers marched out of the plants, singing the song "Solidarity Forever." It was a turning point in the efforts of organized labor to gain representation of workers in basic industry, and made the C.I.O., soon to be renamed the Congress of Industrial Organizations, into a major power in the labor movement.

1930–1939

Auto workers during their sit-down strike in Flint, Mich., in 1937.

ASSOCIATED PRESS

agency for its members, agrees not to interfere with anybody's right to join the union, and promises not to interfere, coerce, restrain or discriminate against an employe because of union membership.

The union agreed to terminate the strike and to evacuate the plants, to refrain from calling strikes pending negotiations on other points, and not to strike during the existence of the contemplated agreement.

The corporation agreed to consent to the dismissal of the drastic injunction which would have banned picketing and other strike activities had it been effectively carried out, or obeyed by the strikers.

The corporation further agreed to take back all strikers and to discriminate against none because of strike activity or union affiliation.

The much-debated "sole-bargaining agency" demand of the union is covered in a letter from Mr. Knudsen to Governor Murphy. In this letter Mr. Knudsen said that the union feared that "without protection of some kind" the corporation "might deliberately proceed to bargain with other groups for the purpose of undermining" the union.

"We have said that we have no such intention," Mr. Knudsen declared.

"On the other hand, we cannot enter into any agreement with any one which can have the effect of denying to any group of our employes the rights of collective bargaining to which it is entitled and which fails to protect them in the exercise of these rights."

Therefore, he said, the corporation undertook "not to seek nor to inspire such activities on the part of other groups for the purpose of weakening this particular union."

As an evidence of its intention and on condition that the union refrain from "coercion and intimidation inside and outside the shop in its efforts to increase its membership," the corporation agreed that for six months it would not bargain or make agreements with any other union or representative of any of the struck plants without first submitting the facts of the situation to the Governor. The latter would then be empowered to "sanction any such contemplated equity or justice toward the group of employes so represented."

This provision, on its face, would reserve to the corporation the right to deal with any group in the struck plants only if the Governor agreed that

Striking General Motors workers celebrate victory on Feb. 11, 1937, days earlier than they had predicted.

such an arrangement did not run counter to the automobile agreement for a period of six months.

The working-out of this provision in practice will answer the question as to whether the corporation has agreed to have the union act as sole bargaining agent in the struck plants. On their side the union officials feel that the Governor will not permit the status quo to be changed for six months. This period would permit the union to consolidate its position, build up its membership further and work out its program in other ways.

In his statement Mr. Sloan emphasized that he wanted it understood that there could be no charge of bad faith against General Motors Corporation, since it had written a statement of its position to Governor Murphy explaining that it had no desire to undermine the automobile workers' union.

"There is no crowing on either side," said Mr. Knudsen. "I hope not. What we think is most important is to get people back to work and get the plants running again, because you know that when a big machine is stopped you have to monkey with the flywheel a bit before you get it going again. That flywheel has got to be tolerance. There must be a desire for peace and no animosity on either side."

Mr. Lewis said:

"Another milestone on labor's march.

"The settlement establishes collective bargaining and security for the union. It institutes for the first time a rational relationship in the automobile industry.

"Automobile workers can rejoice in their achievement. The efficiency and precision of their strike has been magnificent.

"Their devotion and self sacrifice has been rewarded. They can now perfect their union and go forward.

"Governor Murphy has contributed greatly to the settlement. The nation is the beneficiary of his statesmanship."   [Feb. 12, 1937]

1930–1939

STRIKERS AT FLINT MARCH AS VICTORS

LEAVE PLANTS, HEADS HIGH, SINGING 'SOLIDARITY' AND GREETING FAMILIES
PEACE HAILED BY CITY
PAYROLL PROSPECT IS CHEERING AFTER LONG TRADE TIE-UP–TROOPS STILL ON HAND

By RUSSELL B. PORTER
Special to The New York Times

FLINT, Mich., Feb. 11–The sit-down strikers who stalled the General Motors production machine and paralyzed the economic life of this city of 165,000 persons evacuated the three occupied plants late this afternoon and tonight.

About 400 men left Fisher Body Plant No. 1, 125 quit Fisher 2, and 200 to 300 walked out of Chevrolet 4 engine plant. The sit-downers had held possession of the two Fisher plants for forty-four days and the Chevrolet plant for ten days.

During the last ten days the occupants of Fisher 2 and Chevrolet 4 have been held virtually incommunicado as voluntary prisoners in those plants, which were surrounded by National Guard troops after the rioting a week ago Monday.

The 3,500 troops are still on duty here. They continue to hold an eighty-acre military zone around the Fisher 2-Chevrolet plants, although they withdrew their sentries and patrols from Chevrolet Avenue tonight while the sit-downers evacuated the plants.

Military headquarters said no orders for demobilization had been received.

More than 35,000 General Motors workmen who have been forced off the payroll by the strike will return to work during the next week or ten days.

The city was overjoyed at the prospect of $250,000 to $300,000 daily in wages being paid out again and of the end of potential civil warfare. While the strikers celebrated their "victory" in mass demonstrations in front of the evacuated plants and in an automobile parade through the center of the city, the rest of the town celebrated the coming return to work.

Before the evacuation the sit-downers in the plants voted to accept the peace settlement and leave the plants. They questioned the first clause, in which the union was recognized as the bargaining agency for its own members only, and not as the exclusive bargaining agency for all G. M. employes.

Some of them accepted this with reluctance after a union official read the letter from William S. Knudsen to Governor Murphy, in which the company agreed not to bargain with or enter into agreements with any other representatives of the plants on strike during six months after the resumption of work, except with the Governor's sanction.

The evacuation of Fisher 1 took place at 5:30 after the sit-downers had been addressed by Homer S. Martin, president of the United Automobile Workers, who spoke from a sound truck outside the plant.

A large banner proclaiming that "victory is ours," in red letters on a white background, was strung for fifty feet along the front of the plant. Another banner read: "United we stand."

A crowd of 1,500 to 2,000 waited outside the plant to see the evacuation. Among them were wives, children, relatives, friends and sympathizers of the strikers.

"We are coming out with our heads high, knowing that we have achieved victory," said "Bud" Simon, chairman of the plant strike committee: "the battle has just begun to build up the union."

"We will march out as a victorious army, in a glorious crusade for a better life," declared Roy Reuther, union organizer.

"We have held our forces for forty-four days," he went on. "And we are about to evacuate this plant under the victorious banner of the auto union, and not because the Sheriff showed us a piece of paper and told us to get out.

"The eyes of the country are on Flint at this moment. Now let us march down Saginaw Street (Flint's Broadway) in the greatest demonstration this city has ever seen."

The sound car started part of the crowd singing "Solidarity Forever" as the men started out to the north gate, while relatives and friends in the crowd cheered and called to the strikers.

The men walked out two by two. A color bearer carried a large American flag at the head of the procession, and almost every striker carried or wore a small one.

One woman edged into the line of march and walked to the street beside her husband. Another wife had handed her baby in through a window, and her husband came out carrying the infant in his arms.

Wives and friends of strikers belonging to the "Women's Emergency Brigade" marched in the parade, wearing red or green berets and arm bands.

A dozen or more of the men were heavily bearded, having sworn some days ago not to shave until the strike was settled.

After the sit-downers had paraded on foot in front of the plant, all were loaded into automobiles, and scores of cars, all tooting their horns continuously, drove several miles through town in a "victory parade" to the Fisher 2-Chevrolet sector.

Here another crowd had gathered in front of the two plants, which are on opposite sides of Chevrolet Avenue.

It was now dark and huge flares for the movie cameras cast a weird light over the scene.

The sit-downers there were lined up inside the gates or on the roofs, waiting for the automobile caravan. A banner reading "One Hundred Per Cent Sit-Down" hung from the Chevrolet plant.

Neither Buick nor Chevrolet can start final assembly lines and produce complete cars again until the Fisher plants are reopened. It was estimated tonight that it would take at least a week and possibly two weeks to recondition the body plants.

Although the sit-downers did not injure the valuable dies and machinery, so far as known, they damaged car seats and cushions, and used much company property, such as bodies, wrenches, bars, bolts, fire hose, leather and rubber to make weapons and set up barricades and other defenses. It is expected that it will take several days to make an inventory.

[Feb. 12, 1937]

Whitney Receives 5 to 10 Year Term; Court Berates Him

Richard Whitney spent last night in a cell in the Tombs prison and will be taken in handcuffs to Sing Sing by train today in the company of two extortioners who used to be lawyers, a gunman and a man convicted of rape.

Immediately after he had been sentenced yesterday by Judge Owen W. Bohan to serve from five to ten years, he vetoed the suggestion made to the court by his counsel, Charles H. Tuttle, that he might at least be sent to prison alone.

He said he wanted no favors, and thereby won the approval of Deputy Sheriff Matthew Larkin, who took him from the court room in General Session to lodge him in the Tombs for the night. The deputy sheriff would otherwise have had to make a special trip with him to Sing Sing.

It was learned this was the opening of Whitney's attempt to win good-behavior marks, after Mr. Tuttle explained to him that his sentence could thereby be shortened to three years and four months of actual servitude, if the Parole Board is satisfied he will not revert to crime.

He had already eliminated himself for life from the security business before he appeared for sentence yesterday morning, by signing consent to a permanent injunction by Attorney General John J. Bennett, Jr.

It was on this injunctive farewell to the business in which he had once ruled as president of the New York Stock Exchange and on a final appeal by Mr. Tuttle to Judge Bohan that Whitney depended to the last for leniency. He had staked everything in the security business until he was caught, and then he had thrown his hand in, staking everything once more on complete confession.

He stood with his feet planted, hands behind his back, listening attentively while Mr. Tuttle reminded the judge of this and added that Whitney had "neither avoided the law nor chosen the coward's course of flight from the country or from life."

"He still has courage," said Mr. Tuttle. "He still has character. Though his former prominence made confession inexpressibly hard and an unspeakable punishment in itself, nevertheless he has confessed. He has faced his friends, which perhaps is the hardest task of all. The strengthening and redemptive power of confession is a spiritual truth taught by every religion and all human experience.

"Fortunately the losses which his wrongdoing has caused have not fallen upon many persons and certainly upon none of slender means. Nor has there been claim that his acts were with any purpose of permanent spoliation. The spectacle of his fall constitutes in itself a deterrent which no one in like station will soon have the hardihood to defy; and the process of reconstitution and the material for it are already manifest.

"Save for his counsel, he stands here alone. He has chosen to drain this bitter cup by himself, without even the presence of those persons who sought the opportunity to intercede and who expressed the wish to be with him today.

"Even his own brother (George Whitney, partner of J. P. Morgan & Co.), who desired most earnestly permission to stand by him at this bar today, shoulder to shoulder, is at Mr. Whitney's own imperative wish now with the loyal wife and two daughters upon whom the shadow of grief and desolation today falls."

Mr. Tuttle spoke for half an hour and left no indication where, between a suspended sentence and the maximum of twenty years, he thought justice would be served.

Whitney's head advanced perceptibly as Judge Bohan addressed him directly, and he turned his right ear slightly, the better to hear. It was several minutes before he realized that the judge was reading, not talking, and that Mr. Tuttle's impassioned plea had fallen on a prepared manuscript. His face seemed to sag for a moment. Then he pulled himself back to the same impassive front.

Until his fall, Richard Whitney seemed to embody the best the Eastern Establishment could offer. He had been captain of the baseball team at Groton, a leading prep school, and a member of the varsity crew at Harvard. His brother was a partner in the firm of J. P. Morgan, the most prestigious firm on Wall Street, while Whitney ran his own firm, Richard Whitney & Company, which dealt mainly in bonds.

A member of the stock exchange since 1912, he had been its vice president during the 1929 crash and, with the president out of town, gained a public reputation as a Wall Street strongman for his widely publicized efforts to halt the crash through loud bids to buy U.S. Steel shares on behalf of a consortium of bankers. In 1930, he became president of the exchange, a job he held until 1935. Even after stepping aside as president, though, he continued to dominate the exchange as chairman of important committees.

But for the entire decade he was a crook. He stole from his customers and he looted an exchange fund to aid widows and orphans of members. He began doing that after he suffered large losses in the 1929 crash resulting from stock speculations—losses that he managed to hide for years.

The scandal became public on March 8, 1938, when it was announced that his firm was insolvent and had been suspended from the exchange. In fact, there had been signs of trouble for years. Numerous exchange members and officials had known he was in financial distress, borrowing money from anyone he could, but either had not thought it possible that Whitney was a crook or had simply covered up for a powerful friend.

Whitney pleaded guilty to theft charges. He was sentenced to five to ten years in prison and entered Sing Sing on April 12, 1938. His brother eventually repaid all the money Whitney had borrowed or stolen, and Whitney was paroled in 1941.

Whitney's conviction broke the back of N.Y.S.E. resistance to reform, and within months the S.E.C. was able to impose stiff new rules on the exchange.

1930–1939

"The Court has carefully read the memorandum filed by the District Attorney (Thomas E. Dewey), the Probation Report and the Psychiatric Report," said the prepared judgment which the Court thereafter released. "Were you the ordinary type of cashier or other faithless employe, the Court might be disposed to temper justice with mercy. It is apparent, however, from the memorandum filed by the District Attorney, that your criminal conduct has extended over a period of six years.

"To cover up your thefts and your insolvency, you resorted to larcenies, frauds, misrepresentations and falsifications of books and financial statements causing losses of several millions of dollars. As a result of your misconduct you were caught, to use your own works, 'like a rat in a trap.'

"Your acts have been deliberate and intentional and were committed with an unusually full opportunity for understanding their effect upon others and the consequences to yourself. You have enjoyed the advantage of the best education in America; you had the fruits of business and financial success; you had bestowed upon you the confidence and trust of testamentary benefactors and were repeatedly chosen as spokesman of one of the largest financial markets in the world. All these you have betrayed.

"I can find nothing in your record to mitigate the sentence which I am about to pronounce."

Whitney barely waited to hear the judge declare the indeterminate sentence of five to ten years would cover both of his pleas of guilty, one for the theft of $109,000 in securities from the New York Yacht Club and the other for the theft of $105,000 in securities from the estate of George R. Sheldon, his father-in-law.

He picked up his blue topcoat and gray felt hat and grimly faced left, holding up one elbow slightly as if he expected it to be taken. It was. He was marched into the pen behind the court room.

He sat there almost an hour, with counsel, while his commitment papers were drawn up. During this interval his counsel explained the sentence to him and he made his first declination of a prisoner's favor.

Mr. Tuttle, however, obtained authorization later for counsel to travel to Sing Sing with Whitney today to consult en route about the disposition of what remains of his personal affairs.

By noontime he had first felt handcuffs, when Deputy Sheriff Larkin handcuffed him in order to lead him across the Bridge of Sighs from the Criminal Court Building into the Tombs. Thereafter he sat motionless on the cot of the cell in which he was locked, alone. The prison lunch of frankfurters and sauerkraut went untouched.

After four solitary hours Warden William A. Adams of the Tombs went into his cell and talked to him awhile. Once more Whitney won prison approval. "He's taking it like a man," said the warden.

When the prison supper of spaghetti with meat sauce was served at 4:40 P.M., the last meal of the day, Whitney ate all of it.

Even in this last public appearance Whitney behaved in complete accordance with the analysis of his character and habits furnished to the court by the psychiatric board and the probation officers of General

Sessions. Dr. Walter Bromberg, head of the psychiatric clinic, even appeared in the court room to verify the board's conclusion that Whitney's psychologic reactions are "urbane and sportsmanlike."

The Bromberg report gave Whitney an "intelligence rating which could not be equalled by more than 1 per cent of the American population," but it adds: "He was sometimes stubborn and at no time did he believe he would run afoul of the law."

A further appraisal of Whitney's character in the report of Irving W. Halpern, chief probation officer, declared that "contributing factors in his delinquency are pride, obstinacy, unshakable belief in his own financial judgment and a gambling instinct."

The probation report revealed Whitney's own unpublished explanation that his financial troubles really began when he lost $2,000,000 in the market crash of 1929. Thereafter, the report says, "he went on with an invincible belief in his own financial judgment notwithstanding the unsuccessful outcome of his various enterprises."

Richard Whitney, hat in hand, in court after pleading guilty.

The report called attention to the fact that Whitney, as president of the New York Stock Exchange until 1935, was a rigid disciplinarian within the Exchange and a public maker of speeches stressing the necessity of personal and business honesty among brokers. At the very same time, the report pointed out, he was appropriating securities belonging to an estate for the purpose of borrowing on them without authority.

The sentence was pronounced in the presence of District Attorney Dewey and of Assistant Attorney General Ambrose V. McCall, the prosecutors who obtained the two independent grand larceny indictments to which Whitney pleaded guilty. The judge did not call upon them, however.

They indicated that there would be no further criminal indictments in the Whitney case.

The total losses involved in the collapse of Richard Whitney & Co. were still unrevealed yesterday, although Whitney had signed the completed bankruptcy schedules. They are to be filed today when the signatures of his other partners have been obtained.

In Washington today the Securities and Exchange Commission will continue its inquiry into the supervisory problems raised by the Whitney failure.

From Sing Sing came word last night that Warden Lewis E. Lawes intended to put Whitney through the usual prison routine.

When he arrives there today, therefore, he will doff the double-breasted blue flannel suit of yacht club style which he wore when imprisoned and will get into gray shoddy. Richard Whitney will become a number.

He will be assigned to a cell with solid stone sides like a tomb, ventilated only through a grated door. For ten days of reception, or quarantine, he will not be allowed to associate with the other prisoners.

Then he will be put to outdoor labor, rising eventually to clerical work. His prison salary will be 5 cents a day which may be supplemented from the outside for luxuries up to $3 a week. In five months of good behavior he may earn permission to have a radio in his cell.

He will get out of his stone cell into better quarters in a new cell block by "seniority," as prisoners longest there are released and make way for him.   [April 12, 1938]

1930–1939

Du Pont Discloses New Yarn Details
NYLON IS NAME GIVEN TO FIBER MADE FROM COAL, AIR AND WATER

"New and improved" sometimes seemed like a slogan for business in the century, but most of the time the claims were exaggerated, at best. There were, however, some advances that proved to be of great benefit to customers and companies alike.

One such was nylon, a fiber invented by E.I. du Pont de Nemours & Company in 1930 and developed at a cost of 27 million over the next eight years. After it was announced in 1938, The Times worried in an editorial that fashion-concious women might not want stockings that were "as strong as steel." But when nylons went on sale a year later, The Times reported on the crush of customers to buy them.

The real boom for nylon, however, was to come a few years later. With silk supplies drastically reduced during World War II, nylon replaced it in parachutes and also appeared in flyers' flak jackets and in tires for military vehicles. What little nylon was released for the civilian market was in great demand, and nylon stockings sold—surreptitiously, given price controls—at premium prices.

The huge success of nylon eventually aroused the interest of antitrust regulators. While du Pont licensed a second company to make the material in 1951, that was deemed insufficient and the Government sued to make the company grant royalty-free licenses. That effort was rejected by the courts.

The first ad for nylon.

Coal, air and water were revealed yesterday as the basic source of the material from which E. I. du Pont de Nemours & Co. will produce its new textile yarn, known until now simply as "Yarn 65." The yarn will be produced from a material developed by du Pont chemists, which has been given the generic name "Nylon," and has hundreds of potential uses, according to an announcement issued from the concern's Wilmington office.

The material is the outgrowth of research covering the last ten years, which was regarded as an effort in the direction of economic nationalism. The concern announced that the objective of the research was "the synthesis from readily available native raw materials of a wholly new group of chemical compounds capable of meeting definite deficiencies in many existing industrial materials that in the main are now imported." The development's most immediate effect in this direction will be toward making the United States relatively independent of Japanese raw silk as a material for fine, sheer hosiery.

"Nylon" is a generic name, coined by the du Pont chemists, to designate all materials defined scientifically as "synthetic fiber-forming polymeric amides having a protein-like chemical structure; derivable from coal, air and water, or other substances, and characterized by extreme toughness and strength and the peculiar ability to be formed into fibers and into various shapes, such as bristles and sheets."

Details of the yarn were explained yesterday by Dr. Charles M. A. Stine, vice

TIME-DEFYING HOSIERY

Industry now promises the women of America a new hosiery fiber as strong as steel. The question arises whether this isn't a good deal more than the women want. It must be fine to have a synthetic silk stocking immune to the runs that flesh-colored hosiery is heir to. But there should be a middle ground between silk stockings that tear at the slightest opportunity and stockings that never wear out. Tradition says that men like to keep on wearing their clothes, but women suffer dreadfully from wearing the same old thing forever, as the phrase goes.

The real boon of stockings as strong as steel is obviously for the parents of small boys and mothers who mend and fathers who buy. They constitute a very large class of people who never get tired of seeing the children wear the same old thing all the time.

[EDITORIAL, TOPICS OF THE TIMES, Oct. 29, 1938]

Nylon: "Strong as steel."

president of du Pont, in an address on the work of industrial laboratories before the fifth session of The New York Herald Tribune forum, in the Business Systems Building at the World's Fair. His description of the yarn as one which is run-resistant in hosiery drew vigorous applause.

For several months a pilot plant has been operating near Wilmington to produce small commercial quantities of nylon yarn and Exton toothbrush bristles made from nylon. Exton is the trade name for the first product to reach the market commercially. It was advertised for the first time this week in a center-spread in The Saturday Evening Post by Weco Products Company, producers of Dr. West's toothbrushes, which are promoted as the first toothbrushes made without animal bristles.

Nylon will not be widely available until completion of a plant projected at Seaford, Del., on which construction will start next month.

Like natural silk, du Pont announced, nylon is a polymide having a protein-like structure. Filaments of extreme fineness can be spun, much finer than the filaments of either silk or rayon. The dyeing of nylon presents no particular difficulty. In general, it will take dyes used for silk, wool, acetate and certain of the direct dyes used for cotton or rayon.

One of the more important uses to which nylon will be put is the manufacture of fine hosiery from high-twist nylon year. Hosiery made of the new product possesses extreme sheerness, high elasticity, high strength and improved resistance to runs, according to du Pont.

Other uses are sewing thread, knit goods, brush bristles, racquet strings, fishing lines and leaders, narrow fabrics, woven dress goods, velvets, knitted and woven underwear, transparent wrapping film, plastic compositions, textile finishing agents and coated fabrics.

[Oct. 28, 1938]

1930–1939

FIRST OFFERING OF NYLON HOSIERY SOLD OUT; OUT-OF-TOWN BUYERS SWAMP WILMINGTON

WILMINGTON, Del., Oct. 24–Nylon hosiery produced by half a dozen unidentified manufacturers from the new yarn of E. I. du Pont de Nemours & Co. went on sale for the first time today and was given a clamorous reception by Wilmington women.

Stocks laid in by the six stores taking part in the experimental sale scheduled to continue until the stockings are in full production about Jan. 1 were sold out by 1 P.M., and a special force of the du Pont Company was kept busy filling new orders from the stores.

Customers were lined three deep at the counters most of the day. Many of them were men and many were from out-of-town, although the sale was limited to three pairs per customers and supposedly to Delaware residents.

All the stockings, labeled merely "Nylon" or "Miss Nylon," were of slightly sheerer texture than what is customarily known as "two-thread," the sheerest silk hosiery, but orders were taken on the basis of "gauge," or the number of needles per square inch sewed in their manufacture. There were three qualities and three prices, 45-gauge at $1.15; 48-gauge at $1.25, and 51-gauge at $1.35. The most expensive of the three was the most popular.

Du Pont Company officials estimated that 4,000 pairs were sold at six stores, all of which were better quality women's apparel shops. This number was several times the normal daily sale of silk stockings for these stores.

[Oct. 25, 1939]

Ocean Air Service Begun by Clipper

Only 12 years after Charles Lindbergh became a national hero by flying solo and nonstop across the Atlantic, it became possible to fly to Europe by simply buying a ticket. The inaugural flight was in a pontoon plane, which took off on June 28, 1939, from Port Washington, a Long Island suburb of New York, and then flew to the Azores before proceeding to Lisbon and then Marseilles. The flight was scheduled for only 22 hours, which was deemed an amazing time, and a ticket cost 375 each way.

The carrier was Pan American Airways, which became the most famous international carrier but neglected over the decades to build a solid base of domestic routes. By the end of the century, airplanes would be the dominant means of passenger travel, but by then Pan Am was long since bankrupt and out of business.

Although it was deemed safer at the time of that first scheduled Pan Am flight across the ocean to make the trip in a pontoon plane, the DC-3 was already being made by Douglas Aircraft and helping to increase significantly the volume of passenger traffic within the United States. It would become the workhorse of passenger travel, and a modified cargo version, the C-47, became the primary cargo plane for World War II.

But, as in airlines, the first success did not preordain dominance. Douglas was the major maker of passenger planes until the jet era arrived in the late 1950's, but it then lost its dominance to Boeing, which eventually took over the company in the 1990's.

Air transport entered a new era yesterday afternoon when twenty-two men and women filed casually abroad Pan American Airways' Dixie Clipper at Port Washington, L.I., and settled back in their seats for a twenty-two hour flight to Europe.

At 3 P.M., the scheduled time, the 41½-ton craft started to move away from the floating dock, and twelve minutes later it was in the air on the first regularly scheduled commercial passenger flight by airplane over the North Atlantic.

At 1 o'clock this morning the ship was reported 1,397 miles out from Port Washington and 1,000 miles from the Azores.

The fanfare and excitement that might naturally have been expected at the take-off were entirely absent. In spite of the fact that this was the first paid passenger airplane flight between this country and Europe, neither the passengers nor the crew of eleven under Captain R. O. D. Sullivan, displayed any sign of excitement, nervousness or tension.

Not even among the several thousand persons who had crowded into the airport to see the plane off was there anything like the flurry that marks the sailing of an ocean liner. However, a feeling of amazement, even awe, was noticeable at the thought that one could now purchase a ticket for $375, board a plane at Port Washington and less than a day later step off in Lisbon.

Just before 2 P.M. several coaches carrying the passengers and newspaper reporters and photographers arrived at the city limits of Port Washington, from where a police escort led them to the airport. The town had declared a "semi-holiday" and had decorated the main street.

The twice national champion high school band of Port Washington was at the airport to greet the passengers and crew. In blue and white uniforms, eighty-five musicians lined up on the airport apron and saluted the travelers with several selections.

Inside the administration building there was the usual scene before any take-off; passengers were checking reservations, being weighed and having their luggage weighed, only this time newspaper photographers were flashing bulbs at a prodigious rate. Passengers laughingly posed for them and then answered questions of reporters.

Most of them declared they were highly pleased to be on the first flight, but nearly all of them declared it was "just another flight" otherwise. All were seasoned

A Pan American Airways clipper prepares for takeoff to Bermuda from Port Washington, N.Y., in March, 1939. Three months later Pan Am started scheduled flights to Europe.

air travelers, many having flown over the Pacific and the Caribbean on Pan American planes.

At 2:30 a bell sounded and the crew left an office in the building and started for the plane. On the apron of the hangar they were surrounded by photographers and newsreel men and were kept there ten minutes posing for pictures. Finally they got aboard the plane and at 2:44 P.M. started to warm up the four 1,500-horsepower Wright Cyclone engines.

Soon afterward 408 pounds of mail were put aboard and then the passengers left the ticket office. They, too, posed for photographers while the band played.

After a brief benediction pronounced by the Rev. William J. Woon of Port Washington, Captain John J. Floherty of the Port Washington Chamber of Commerce handed to Captain Sullivan three scrolls to be delivered to the Mayors of Horta, Lisbon and Marseille. Each scroll said:

"The people of the Town of Port Washington, on Long Island, in the State of New York, have honored us with the mission of extending to you their cordial greetings on this momentous occasion, at which regular passenger service commences between your famous city and ours.

"Like the Port of [Marseille, Horta and Lisbon inserted], this town has its own and ancient history as one of the oldest ports of this country. Now both our cities share the honor of being among the newest airports of the world.

"Permit us, my dear sir, to extend to you and your city our fervent wishes for prosperity and peace."

The scrolls were signed by Dorothy Grant Ford, W. Davis Hegemen and Jack Champlain.

Last good-byes were exchanged and the passengers moved toward the big plane.

"Write me a letter," a young girl called to her mother, who was waving as she went down the boardwalk.

"I'll be back before the letter," her mother laughed.

Manhasset Bay was crowded with sailing craft and motor boats decorated in bunting and flying pennants. The sky was almost cloudless and there was a fresh breeze out of the south as the plane taxied out in the bay for the take-off run.

It went out of sight around a point, then soon there was the hum of the engines and the craft appeared over the trees lining the point. Slowly it circled, came over the port and pointed its nose toward the Azores.

It will follow the southern Great Circle route, over which Pan American craft have already made fourteen flights. The first stop on the 4,650-mile trip that ends in Marseille tomorrow afternoon will be Horta. The clipper is expected to arrive there about 7 A.M. today. Some of the passengers plan to come back on the return trip of the Dixie Clipper next Sunday, but others will return later by air or by boat.

[June 29, 1939]

1930–1939

1940–1949

Industry turned to war production in the 40's. Boeing marked a B-29 milestone at its plant in Wichita, Kan., in 1945.

NEW YORK, SUNDAY, OCTOBER 4, 1942.

From Devastation to Innovation

When the 1940's began, most people in the United States hoped the country would be able to stay out of the war then engulfing Europe, and isolationism, in business as well as politics, was strong. By the end of the decade, America stood astride the globe financially and was the leader of one of two great military and political alliances whose struggles would dominate world news for the next 40 years.

Less noticed at the time, but perhaps more important, the 1940's were a period of technological innovation in America. Those innovations would become hugely important in later years, revolutionizing many aspects of ordinary life and by the end of the century enabling an America that had stumbled to reassert its economic leadership. It was a decade that witnessed the first public demonstrations of electronic computers, transistors, instant cameras and of a new technology called xerography.

To a significant extent, it was the industrial might of the United States that won World War II. Auto plants stopped making cars and started making tanks. Bomber plants were built in areas that had been empty only months before. There were inevitable production problems—and complaints of war profiteering—but within a surprisingly short period of time the factories were producing weapons that were often technologically superior to the best that could be produced in Germany and Japan.

The decade also saw the country struggle with inflation for the first time since World War I. Wage and price controls were introduced during World War II and worked reasonably well. But they were quickly abandoned after the war, producing a spurt of inflation that led unions to seek protection against rising prices. Because there was little available to buy during the war, as industrial production was shifted to war needs, Americans ended the war with extensive savings and buying power that helped to avert the postwar recession that was widely forecast. The war also saw millions of women take jobs out of the home for the first time, but the vast majority of them did as expected and returned home after the soldiers returned to work.

Unions, which had seemed like underdogs fighting for impoverished workers, took on a more ominous air to many Americans, particularly after a nationwide rail strike briefly paralyzed the country in 1946. A law reining in union power was passed the following year. Even before the war ended, the postwar economic system was designed at Bretton Woods, N.H. Centered on the dollar, it provided relative stability for more than two decades.

1940 President Roosevelt is re-elected to a third term.

Winston Churchill becomes prime minister of Britain.

1941 Japanese planes bomb Pearl Harbor; the United States enters World War II.

1942 First nuclear chain reaction takes place in Chicago.

President Roosevelt freezes wages and prices to forestall inflation.

1943 General Dwight D. Eisenhower is named the Supreme Commander of the Allied forces in Europe.

1944 The Allied forces land at Normandy.

The musical play "Oklahoma!" wins a special Pulitzer Prize.

1945 President Roosevelt dies at the start of his fourth term; Harry S. Truman succeeds him.

The war in Europe and Japan ends.

1946 An "electronic brain" called Eniac is demonstrated at the University of Pennsylvania.

1947 Congress passes the Taft-Hartley Act, curbing labor, over President Truman's veto.

1948 President Truman wins re-election in a close race with Thomas E. Dewey of New York.

Gandhi is assassinated in India.

1949 Mao Tse-tung declares China the Communist People's Republic.

FCC Orders NBC to Drop Network in Opening Chains to Competition

As the radio industry developed in the 1930's, two companies, NBC and CBS, gained major power over the industry. CBS, run by William S. Paley, had one radio network and NBC, headed by David Sarnoff, had two, known as the Red and Blue networks. Stations that affiliated with the networks gave up control over their programming and were forced to sign long-term contracts. The Mutual Broadcasting System was a lesser force, and it sought Government action to restrain the power of the giants.

In 1941, the Federal Communications Commission ordered NBC to sell one of its networks and issued rules that reduced the power of the networks relative to their affiliated stations. NBC appealed the case to the Supreme Court, but lost. It sold its Blue Network, which eventually became ABC. The rules adopted for radio set the stage for the development of the television industry, which for decades was dominated by networks run by the same companies. CBS and NBC were the strongest, with ABC, the weakest of the radio networks, remaining the No. 3 television network for many years.

Special to The New York Times

WASHINGTON, May 3—Far-reaching regulations designed to prevent the development of monopoly in the radio broadcasting industry were adopted today by the Federal Communications Commission by a 5-to-2 vote. The regulations are intended to open the field to new chains in order to foster and strengthen network broadcasting by free competition, the commission said.

The rules, which were denounced by the commission's minority as tending toward "anarchy" and by spokesmen for the large networks as Federal "usurpation" of program control, would force the National Broadcasting Company to divest itself of one of its two networks by sale, transfer or dissolution and would restrict the relations between the large networks and their local outlets.

Since the new regulations would cause readjustments throughout the industry, changes which one broadcaster asserted would convert the major chains into "mere catch-as-catch-can, fly-by-night sellers of programs," it was expected that the commission's decision would be appealed to the courts. The spokesmen for the larger of the major chains indicated that a court test would be undertaken.

An investigation begun three years ago convinced the commission majority, it said in the report, that contract and other practices by the networks had the effect of creating or tending toward the creation of a monopoly in radio, which already was naturally restricted by the limited range of the broadcast band. This enriched a few to the detriment of the public, the majority held.

The report sharply criticized "monopolistic practices" of the National Broadcasting Company in its operation of the NBC Red and Blue networks and it also hit at the single-network operations of the Columbia Broadcasting System and the Mutual Broadcasting System. The operation of two networks, it said, gave NBC a

Top trio of CBS in 1946: Chairman William S. Paley with Edward R. Murrow, left, who shaped the network's role in broadcast journalism, and Frank Stanton, right, president.

decided advantage over the others, and it charged that NBC used the Blue network to forestall competition with the Red one.

Chief among the regulations are those which will put an end to the five-year contracts often demanded of stations, and which will do away with contract clauses demanding exclusive use of network programs.

These restrictions and restraints, the commission found, have impaired the "ability of stations to render service in the public interest" by denying them a wide latitude in obtaining programs particularly desirable under varying local conditions.

Three alternatives face the broadcasting industry, the commission found. These were listed as free competition, government ownership and rigid regulation such as is now applied to railroads and telephone companies. This is the conclusion:

"Competition, after a fair test, will best protect the public interest. That is the American system."

Conceding that the network system of program distribution is in the public interest, the commission held that the regulations, by assuring competition, not only would stimulate existing networks, but also would encourage the formation of competitive systems.

The contention of those who appeared at hearings that more open competition "would result in the destruction of the national program service" was rejected, as was the plea that any change in the status quo would induce advertisers to desert radio in favor of newspapers, magazines or billboards.

James Lawrence Fly, chairman of the commission, declared that the regulations might properly be called a "magna charta for American broadcasting stations."

The report states that the regulations have been drawn so as not to interfere with the major functions of a network, that is, the sale of time to advertisers, the presentation of commercial and sustaining programs and distributing programs to stations.

The commission, in reaching its conclusions, was particularly concerned with maintaining the freedom of stations to change their regular network affiliations, to broadcast programs from networks with which they are not regularly affiliated and to maintain freedom to use independent judgment in rejecting network programs not suitable to their own fields.

Remarking that existing networks have left many communities in the West and Middle West entirely without network service, the commission then charged "failure to render service on a truly national basis" and thus justified ending the exclusion of new networks from the industry.

The "exclusivity clause" in existing contracts was condemned, since it prevents a station affiliated with one network from carrying a program of any other network. The regulations put an end to this practice.

"Territorial exclusivity" also must cease. This is the contract system under which a network is bound not to send a program to any other station in an area served by its affiliated station, even though the affiliate rejects the program. This practice was compared to drowning out a program by electrical interference.

David Sarnoff, left, with Guglielmo Marconi, inventor of wireless telegraphy, in 1933.

Another of the regulations limits affiliation contracts to one year on the ground that no business need has been shown for longer contracts and that stations would serve the public interest better if they were free to change their affiliations every twelve months.

The "network optional time" practice also will be abolished. This system has forced stations to cancel any programs offered during periods when the affiliated network offers a program, and, according to the commission, has restricted the freedom of stations to offer advertising and program material.

Clauses in affiliation contracts which restrict the right of a station to reject network programs are to be terminated, and stations may hereafter choose programs which are considered of greatest national or local importance or interest.

The report was concurred in by Chairman Fly and by Commissioners Paul A. Walker, George H. Payne, Frederick A. Thompson and Ray C. Wakefield.

A dissenting report was made by Commissioners Norman S. Case and T. A. H. Craven, who wrote:

"The minority disagrees with the proposals which the majority has adopted as a method of securing improvements. We fear that the proposals of the majority will result inevitably in impaired efficiency of the existing broadcast system of the country."

The regulations are effective immediately, except that those which are concerned with existing contracts become effective in ninety days.

Neville Miller, president of the National Association of Broadcasters, has called a special meeting of the association's executive committee for Wednesday in New York City.

Mr. Miller termed the regulations "usurpation of power which has no justification in law and which menaces the freedom of the American system of broadcasting."

The directors of the association declared on March 18 that the philosophy of broadcasting, as expressed in decisions of the Supreme Court and all applicable statutes, "envisages control of programs, of business management and of policy in the broadcaster, and not subject to the supervisory control of the government."

An indication that the new FCC rules would meet a last-ditch fight in the courts was given yesterday by William S. Paley, president of the Columbia Broadcasting System. Mutual, which has repeatedly alleged before the FCC that the NBC and CBS constituted a monopoly, indicated that the report met with its satisfaction.

If the commission succeeds in enforcing its regulations, Mr. Paley said, "the first paralyzing blow will have been struck at freedom of the air, because a commission which can exercise such drastic powers without even going to Congress for authority to exercise them will have reduced the networks and stations to impotent vassals."

He also hit at "opportunistic elements in the industry who will see in a sudden upset of the whole broadcasting structure a chance to gain temporary commercial advantage."

Declaring that the competition in broadcasting existed now and that the principal limitation on it was imposed by physical capacity of existing facilities, he said the commission was making "a fetish of competition" which he believed that neither the President nor Congress would countenance.

[May 4, 1941]

Willow Run Plant a Wonder of War

By SIDNEY M. SHALETT

Special to The New York Times

DETROIT, May 21—There she stood—one of the seven wonders of the world of war; vast enough to swallow up an entire city; awesome enough to reduce man, her creator, to a lost speck in a jungle of giant machines.

The name is Willow Run. Mark it. If America's coming offensive depends on her power to blast, and blast hard, from the air, the news learned here yesterday may presage one of the turning points of the battle of production. For Willow Run, the big bomber factory which "Charlie" Sorensen described as "the invitation for Hitler to commit suicide," is "just about on the edge of turning over and becoming a real plant."

Newspaper correspondents on the "Production for Victory" tour arranged by the National Association of Manufacturers yesterday visited the Willow Run plant in the Detroit area and saw the first bomber that has made a test run of an assembly line unparalleled in the history of airplane manufacture. It was a monster Consolidated B-24-E, a bomber in the size-class of the Boeing Flying Fortresses.

They also heard Edsel Ford, president, and Charles E. Sorensen, vice president, of the Ford Motor Company, which will operate the plant for the government, explain how their stupendous dies and presses will stamp out the big bombers almost as easily as Model T's once were produced.

The survey of the Detroit production arsenal also took in visits to several General Motors converted war plants in the Detroit and Flint areas, and O. E. Hunt, vice president and executive assistant to the president of the corporation, gave the group an overall picture of what the ninety-odd, far-flung units in thirty-two cities and thirteen States are doing. Touching on many phases of war production, it added up to a tremendous total, which, Mr. Hunt predicted, might be doubled before the peak is reached.

Bombers are not the only things on the crowded schedule in Henry Ford's industrial empire. There are at least fourteen major jobs, including the Army's new model medium tanks which Mr. Sorensen considers much better powered than the German tanks: a Pratt & Whitney airplane engine (the 2,000th of which was completed recently); another aviation engine; various types of armored cars, precision aircraft parts and high precision fire-control instruments. Then there is a new tank engine of the liquid-cooled V-8 type.

As Mr. Sorensen put it, "Ford is ninety-nine and nine-tenths converted to war industry," and, as Edsel Ford announced, its employment today is as large as it was in peacetime and probably will be doubled by the end of the year.

But it was the Willow Run plant that made the executives leave their desks and ride a bus across the Michigan countryside to show it off. Financed by the government and operated by Mr. Ford, the huge factory stands on a site that was a farm field covered with soy-bean stubble only thirteen months ago. Mr. Sorenson—his colleagues call him Charlie—pointed out pridefully that even now the machine-installation crews were pushing the still-working contractors out of the last incompleted stretch. Edsel Ford, a quiet son of a famous father, fiddled in his pocket as the bus neared the war plant and said: "I guess I'd better get out my badge."

Henry Ford, too, walking with a springy step despite his nearly eighty years, was waiting to greet the visitors. The elder Ford smiled warmly as he shook hands, and the son, looking at his father affectionately, said: "He put a lot of his own ideas into this place. He's quite proud of it."

It loomed there, an unbelievable symbol of the machine and bomb age. Great doors, which one day will spit out the big bombers, yawned open. A mammoth air field and concrete apron made a crisscrossed lap for the giant.

As World War II engulfed Europe, American business leaders went out of their way to avoid appearing to promote American involvement. Some were genuinely opposed to entering the conflict, but others feared being viewed as eager for war profits. "American industry is fundamentally opposed to war," said H. W. Prentis Jr., the president of the National Association of Manufacturers, in a speech reported on the front page of The Times a year before Pearl Harbor.

When war did come, however, the pressure was on for business to switch as rapidly as possible to war production. In Detroit, cars were replaced by jeeps on assembly lines. Ford built a new bomber plant in a rural area known as Willow Run, 27 miles west of Detroit. That plant was to become a symbol of all the problems—and the successes—involved in the war production effort. It was built rapidly and began producing bombers in May 1942, only a few months after the United States entered the war. In that month, a Times feature article called the plant "a wonder of war," and in the 43 months it operated Willow Run produced 8,524 B-24's. But it was slow to get up to speed, provoking Congressional hearings, and the huge work force that arrived overwhelmed the local community. Housing conditions for many of the workers were deplorable. The War Production Board ran into difficulties in getting needed parts and supplies to plants on a schedule that would keep them operating efficiently.

Willow Run also came to symbolize the hiring of women—or girls, as the newspapers often called them. The Times reported on Feb. 19, 1942, that women would be hired at Willow Run, saying they would do relatively light work and would receive lower pay than men but better than women had previously received.

1940–1949

The newspaper men on the "Production for Victory" tour have been cooperating with Army and Navy censors in observing regulations against printing anything that would give aid and comfort to the enemy. Mr. Sorensen, the Danish-born mechanic who teamed up with Henry Ford at the beginning of the Dearborn days and rose through the years to the vice presidency of the company, felt "cramped" by some of the rulings. Making a sweeping gesture within the incredible confines of the factory, he said in a voice that had a bite in it:

"Bring the Germans and Japs in to see it—hell, they'd blow their brains out."

Then he began explaining some of the things that will make Willow Run the great producer it is destined to become. In normal times, airplanes were made pretty much by limited assembly line operations, involving relatively inexpensive dies. Mr. Sorensen, again in the voice with the bite, observed that the auto industry really looked on the plane-makers as little custom tailors.

There has been a lot of talk from aviation men about the inability of auto-makers to produce planes properly, because they (1) go in for expensive, permanent dies that do not allow for quick changes in design, and (2) because, in mass-producing parts, they do not stamp them out accurately enough for the exacting needs of aerodynamics. The latest views on these subjects came from J. H. Kindelberger, president of North American Aviation, Inc., at Kansas City last Monday. Mr. Sorensen struck out at both points.

On the accuracy charge, Mr. Sorensen stated that Willow Run's dies—great, solid, steel things, firmly imbedded into concrete foundations—were so immovably set up and scaled to the fraction of an inch that they could turn out thousands upon thousands of parts without variation. Parts from Willow Run's machines, he said, would be as interchangeable between bombers as parts between "flivvers," and that would be a great help to the mechanics who would have to service the giant Consolidated on the battlefield. On the expense and "no change" point, he gave an emphatic reply.

"What if we do spend $40,000,000 on dies?" he asked, explaining that all the figures he was giving were hypothetical and had no bearing on actual costs or prospective production figures. "Once we get them set up, we could run out 4,000 ships. What would such an investment amount to in our four thousand $250,000 planes? Why, I could write off the whole cost of the dies.

"It is our understanding that the country wants planes, wants a lot of them and wants them fast. That's why we set up this plant this way."

He also pointed out that the "permanent" dies actually were adjustable. Willow Run figured on changes coming up in bomber design and constructed its dies with that in mind, he said. They allow for a good deal of latitude in design changes, he added.

One of the principal features of the Willow Run assembly line is that parts such as wings will be put together on vertical fixtures with elevator platforms, rather than by the customary horizontal operation, permitting the workman great speed and convenience of operation. Some of the figures cited by Mr. Sorensen on time and

DETROIT'S PLANTS TAKING ON WOMEN

Special to The New York Times

DETROIT, Feb. 18—Blue denim dungarees are displacing afternoon dresses and tea cups are giving way to riveting hammers in the hands of Detroit women who, in increasing numbers, are taking their places in war production work.

Detroit's automobile plants have always found employment for women, usually in specialized jobs such as upholstery work. Now, however, in the switchover from automobile to armament manufacturing, women are to assume a more important role. Shortage of manpower has opened new fields for women.

The War Department has just ordered the Ford Motor Company to employ 12,000 to 15,000 women in the huge new Willow Run bomber plant, where total employment within a year is expected to reach a peak of 125,000.

The order called on the company to survey its personnel problems to determine just where the women could fit into the production scheme. The company previously had stated that it would employ 12,000 to 15,000 women at the plant, so no revision of personnel plans was required, a company spokesman said. There are twenty-eight women working there now.

The women will be used on light construction work at which they are said to be faster and more efficient than men.

Ernest C. Kanzler, chief of the automotive division of the War Production Board, stated recently that thousands of women would find jobs in the automobile plants. They are the only untapped source of needed labor, he said. Estimates have placed the ultimate number of jobs for women in the Detroit area as high as 100,000.

At present the number of women working in defense plants in Detroit is estimated at 4,000 to 5,000. Because of the change-over in the type of manufacturing, with its attendant general unemployment, women workers will not be called to their new jobs until the general trend turns upward. It may be a year before the peak employment is reached.

Comparatively few women are working now in the large plants. Most of those who are employed have jobs in the smaller plants.

The Murray Corporation and Turnstedt Manufacturing Company are already using women on bomber assemblies. At the Kelsey-Hayes Wheel Company plant they are helping turn out anti-aircraft guns. Several hundred women are employed on gas-mask production by the Eureka Vacuum Cleaner Company.

The women's work consists largely of machine operation in the lighter production processes. They are working punch presses and drills. They are used extensively in inspection and blueprint reading. As one executive stated, there will be a place for women in any operation demanding manual dexterity.

Women are finding a place also in the extensive industrial-training program that is being conducted by the various factories and the Detroit public schools.

Although these courses have been confined largely to men, plans are being made to expand technical training for women as soon as the surplus of men has been absorbed. However, in one class, thirty women are receiving six to eight weeks' instruction in machine-tool operations; twenty-five are learning to weld stainless steel, twenty-five are studying blue-print reading and inspection, and 120 are learning airplane riveting. These courses require about thirty hours a week and last six to eight weeks.

The women workers of Detroit are neither asking nor receiving favors. They are working the night shifts; they are putting in overtime, and are carrying their lunch pails the same as the men.

The absorption of women into defense work is creating some problems. Local labor unions are looking on their employment with no favor until the men, with their seniority, all have been put to work. In general, the women are receiving lower wages than men, although their rates are higher than they previously received. In some plants they are getting as much as 80 cents an hour. [Feb. 19, 1942]

BOEING AIRCRAFT COMPANY

Millions of women, like these at a Boeing plant, joined the wartime work force.

money savings made his listeners whistle in amazement. For instance, one fixture, which performs ten boring operations at once on a wing panel, saved $1,000 per ship and cut a day's work to two hours, Mr. Sorensen said.

After the plane parts, stamped out by the huge presses and put together on the maze of assembly lines, are finally sub-assembled into large parts, they move to another ingenious fixture, which, employing conveyors and elevators, fastens center wings, nose and tail onto the body. Then a big crane picks up the bomber as if it were a tin prize from a candy package and sets it down on a large area where the wing tips are attached.

"Then she's ready to fly, wherever they want her," Mr. Sorensen said.

This is only the sketchiest description of the way the planes will come off at Willow Run, but it may be said that the system looked convincing, and the parts being run through sections of the line yesterday seemed extremely well-fashioned. The place suggested tremendously exciting possibilities in the turning out of sky-commanding bombers along automobile mass-production lines, and it was easy to catch the enthusiasm that Mr. Sorensen, Mr. Ford and the other officials displayed. Once it gets to moving, it should be the most amazing sight in plane manufacture anywhere in the world.

Peak production, however, Mr. Sorensen warned the public, was not just around the corner.

The two-day visit to the Detroit and Flint areas has been an inspiring, if exhausting, experience. The correspondents, after seeing Willow Run, were whirled through several of the General Motors plants and saw places that once ground out spark plugs, speedometers, auto bodies and other accessories of that vanishing luxury, the automobile, now turning out tanks, machine guns, anti-aircraft guns and other tools of war.

One of the Fisher plants, once known as the largest auto body factory in the world, was turning out the new model medium tanks—all welded, not riveted. Production still was a trickle, but a projected landslide output is in store. The Fisher operation was especially impressive since it really was a post-Pearl Harbor development. They were just talking about making tanks there last December, but they turned out the first one in forty-seven days. Production now is seven months ahead of schedule.

Some of the car and body plants looked extremely lonesome in some of the still unused sections, where unconvertible machinery, decommissioned "for the duration," stood in idle rows, the various parts of which looked for all the world like so many tombstones.

The picture of General Motors' total operation on war work, presented last night by Mr. Hunt, was another encouraging factor in the production picture. The idea of a gigantic corporation, capable in peacetime of producing $2,000,000,000 worth of goods, going 100 per cent into war work and already converting more than 65 per cent of its old tools, as well as acquiring many thousands of new ones, was an impression that carried tremendous significance.

Mr. Hunt rolled off the list of products that General Motors now is making—airplanes and aircraft parts, engines, armored vehicles, tanks, guns, ammunition from small caliber to artillery shells, vital machine tools, all of them backed by the corporation's vast research facilities which are constantly developing improved methods of making things, and it sounded good.

Even though Paul Garrett, vice president in charge of public relations, warned that "we're not over the hump yet," there was a distinct impression conveyed that such a massive weight of production, once it achieved full momentum, could not help but swamp the Axis eventually. [May 22, 1942]

ASSOCIATED PRESS

Willys-Overland Motors produced an army of military vehicles in Toledo, Ohio, in 1942.

Roosevelt Freezes Wages, Rents, Farm Prices

By C. P. TRUSSELL

Special to The New York Times

WASHINGTON, Oct. 3—President Roosevelt appointed Associate Justice James F. Byrnes of the Supreme Court today to be Director of Economic Stabilization, clothed him with sweeping authority to control civilian purchasing power, created a board to help him coordinate and command the war upon inflationary living costs, and ordered the immediate stabilization of farm prices, urban and rural rents, wages and salaries paid in industry.

Justice Byrnes resigned his court post to assume the task in which he is charged with formulating and developing, with Presidential approval, a comprehensive national policy covering not only prices, pay and rentals, but profits, rationing, government subsidies and all related matters.

On White House order, Leon Henderson, Price Administrator, put sixty-day emergency ceilings, effective Monday, over the prices of sufficient foods to increase from 60 to 90 per cent the OPA control over the commodities which go into the household market basket.

Acting twenty-nine days before the November date set only last night by the Congress, President Roosevelt put the statutory directives of Congress into motion before noon today, stating:

"The Congress has done its part in helping substantially to stabilize the cost of living. The new legislation removes the exemption of certain foods, agricultural commodities and related products from the price controls of the Emergency Price Control Act, with the result that I have today taken action to stabilize 90 per cent of the country's food bill.

"It leaves the parity principle unimpaired. It reaffirms the powers of the Executive over wages and salaries. It establishes a floor for wages and for farm prices.

"I am certain that from now on this substantial stabilization of the cost of living will assist greatly in bringing the war to a successful conclusion, will make the transition to peace conditions easier after the war and will receive the wholehearted approval of farmers, workers and housewives in every part of the country."

The President's prompt and decisive action and his selection of Justice Byrnes, a former member first of the House and later of the Senate, as the head of civilian economy received a favorable reaction in Congress.

Representative McCormack, House Majority Leader, expressed belief that the President had chosen "the best-equipped man in the nation" for the post. Representative Martin, the Minority Leader, called upon Mr. Byrnes and the administrative agencies he would direct to act "quickly, decisively and completely" to halt inflation.

For the new director the President established an Office of Economic Stabilization to function as a part of the Office of Emergency Management, and to advise and consult him the President created an economic stabilization board of which Mr. Byrnes is chairman. This board includes the Secretaries of the Treasury, Agriculture, Commerce and Labor; the chairman of the board of governors of the Federal Reserve System; the director of the Bureau of the Budget; Price Administrator Henderson and William H. Davis, chairman of the National War Labor Board. Still to be named to the board are two representatives each of labor, management and the farmers.

In charting his new anti-inflation program, Mr. Roosevelt followed closely the Congressional directives and took full advantage of the authorizations contained in the bill which the Congress rushed to him last night, one day after the expiration of the deadline which he had set in his "you-do-it-or-I-will" message of Sept. 7.

On the salary question the President carried into practice, though in a form less

For most of the 1930's, inflation was anything but a problem. Deflation was the issue, as prices and wages fell. But with the arrival of war, people feared a return to the high inflation levels of World War I. They had good reason for such worries. The sharp increase in employment brought on by the war meant that incomes would grow. But far fewer consumer goods would be produced. More money chasing fewer goods is the classic recipe for inflation. Wage and price controls were introduced in January 1942 and then intensified 10 months later, as The Times reported on Oct. 4, 1942. Virtually all food prices were controlled, as were the prices of most other things along with wages and rents. Rationing coupons were issued to assure that what food was available was made available to all.

The controls brought distortions to the economy and were often violated. Posters urged consumers to "pay no more than ceiling prices." But the controls did keep inflation far lower than it had been during World War I. After the war would be a different story.

1940–1949

rigid and sweeping than many here had believed he had in mind, his repeatedly recommended limitation of individual income to $25,000 a year net. He applied the principle only to salaries, under an authorization which had been sponsored by Senator Overton of Louisiana and written into the anti-inflation bill. It permits reductions, under certain circumstances, of annual salaries of $5,000 or more.

To correct "gross inequities" and to provide for "greater equality in contributing to the war effort," the President authorized the director to take the necessary action and issue appropriate regulations so that, in so far as was practicable, no salary should be authorized to the extent that it exceeded $25,000 after payment of taxes allocable to the sum in excess of that amount.

However, he added, the regulations should provide for the payment of life-insurance premiums on policies now in force and for required payments on fixed obligations incurred prior to the issuance of the order. Provision also must be made, the Chief Executive said, to prevent undue hardship.

One of the White House secretaries, William D. Hassett, said that the President's salary of $75,000 a year "surely" would be adjusted to conform with the limitation.

Policies to be established by the Director of Economic Stabilization, the President directed, must be shaped to the mission of preventing avoidable increases in the cost of living, of cooperating in minimizing the unnecessary migration of labor from one business, industry or area to another, and to facilitating the prosecution of the war. These policies, he ordered, should be carried out by all Federal department and agencies concerned.

Jurisdiction of the War Labor Board was extended to cover all industries and all employes. Until now the WLB could act only in instances where employers and workers were in dispute over wages or working conditions or both.

Former Justice Byrnes went to the White House this afternoon, to discuss the post to which the President had assigned him. After their conference Mr. Byrnes said that he would have an office in the new Executive wing at the White House.

"It is the left wing," he said, "but there is no political or economic significance in my assignment there. On Monday morning I expect to leave my office in the court to come down here and go to work.

"Until I have had an opportunity to study the Executive Order I would not want to make an interpretation of it. The President conferred upon me the power to determine a policy to bring about stabilization, to bring about the accomplishments of the objectives of this legislation.

"That power to determine policy does not mean that I would be called upon to administer it. The control of prices necessarily involves many departments, and, necessarily, conflicts will arise. My duty would be to hear the differences, resolve the conflicts and relieve the President of that determination.

"In time of peace I would not resign from the Supreme Court to accept any office. In the situation now confronting the nation, I could not decline to serve wherever the Commander in Chief requests."   [Oct. 4, 1942]

World Bank Urged by Keynes as Vital

By RUSSELL PORTER

Special to The New York Times

BRETTON WOODS, N. H., July 3—Lord Keynes, chairman of the British delegation to the United Nations Monetary and Financial Conference, described for the first time today the broad outlines of the plan for setting up of a $10,000,000,000 international bank for reconstruction and development to "guarantee" international loans somewhat after the fashion of the Reconstruction Finance Corporation in domestic loans.

Speaking at an afternoon meeting of the bank commission, which will draw up proposals for approval by the conference as a whole, Lord Keynes, who is economic adviser to the British Treasury, said that the plan originated in the United States Treasury.

He called it a sound, fundamental contribution to the post-war task of rebuilding the world for a new age of peace and progress and declared that it would promote "expansion" and not "inflation."

The World Bank program is entirely separate from the currency stabilization goals of the proposals for an international monetary fund, also being considered here, but both plans are closely related, not only to one another, but also to the whole broad United Nations program of international cooperation to lay the eco-

M. S. Stepanov, head of the U.S.S.R. delegation, with John Maynard Keynes at Bretton Woods.

Even before World War II was over, the major countries met at a New Hampshire resort to map the postwar economic system. The result was the creation of two new international agencies, the International Monetary Fund and the World Bank, to provide assistance to countries that needed it. It was the establishment of these two institutions that occupied most of the conferees for more than three weeks, with the final arguments coming over the Soviet Union's successful push to qualify for a larger share of aid. In the end, that proved irrelevant because after the war the Communist bloc countries stayed out of the system.

The Times covered the conference extensively, including an early address by John Maynard Keynes, by then the most famous economist in the world, pleading for a World Bank to help in reconstruction. Getting such a bank proved to be the hardest part of the conference, but in the end it was approved, albeit with a smaller capitalization than Lord Keynes had sought.

To history, the most important result of the Bretton Woods conference, however, was the exchange rate system that was created. Since that was also the least controversial at the time, it received little coverage. Under it, the United States dollar was linked to gold, and other currencies were linked to the dollar. It was a system of fixed rates that could be adjusted from time to time.

For many years, the system worked well. But the seeds of its destruction were being sowed even then. In the years after World War II, there was much talk of a "dollar shortage" internationally. The United States, unique among major countries in having had its industrial might undamaged by the war, inevitably ran trade surpluses. Just finding dollars to pay for imports was a major challenge for many countries.

But as other countries rebuilt their industries, the United States began running trade deficits. That did not seem to matter for many years, given the huge demand for dollars. But by the late 1960's the dollar was severely overvalued. It alone among nations was not supposed to be able to devalue its currency, which was tied to gold. Finally, in 1971, President Richard Nixon ended the Bretton Woods system, and an era of floating exchange rates was ushered in.

CORBIS/UPI

nomic foundation for the post-war world. The bank and the fund are intended to be permanent institutions.

Lord Keynes urged the delegates and their technical advisers, who had not given as much attention to the bank as to the fund, since they have considered the fund to be the more urgent problem, to speed their consideration of the bank proposals.

He asserted that the bank should be ready by the end of the war, so that the liberated countries would know immediately what credit resources they could rely on and thus proceed with their reconstruction programs, get back into production and resume their role in world trade as quickly as possible. Any time lag, he warned, would prevent the establishment of good government and good order and might postpone return of Allied soldiers to their homelands.

He said that the "novelty" of the bank proposals lay in their guarantee feature, which points up the "international character" of the proposed institution. Under this plan, he added, post-war foreign loans would come mainly from the United States, the world's largest creditor nation, but the risks would not fall exclusively on the Government or investors of this country, being spread rather over all the bank's member countries in proportion to their capacity.

Guarantees would be "joint and several," he stated, up to the limit of any member's subscription and the guaranteed bonds to be issued would be of the first order, because they would be backed by the full resources of the bank in gold or free exchange, would be safeguarded against waste and extravagance, and would have the guarantee of the borrowing country.

There would be a guarantee for the annual servicing of interest and amortization, he added, so that the debt would not fall due suddenly as a lump sum obligation. A 1 per cent annual commission would be paid by the borrower on long-term loans, a provision which he characterized as a mutual pool of credit insurance.

Lord Keynes' statement was regarded as designed largely to counteract criticism from orthodox American banking circles, which have expressed skepticism of his post-war ideas because of his longtime advocacy of deficit financing, and from others who have declared both the fund and bank proposals to be of British origin cleverly designed to entrap the United States into playing the "Santa Claus" role after this war, although in a form other than after the last war.

His emphasis on the soundness of the bank plan, its American origin and its safeguards for American investors was viewed as an appeal to American sentiment, as was his linking of prompt acceptance of the plan to quick return of the troops.

Although reconstruction would mainly occupy the bank in its early days, he declared, it would later have another primary duty—"to develop the resources and productive capacity of the world, with special attention to the less developed countries, to raise the standard of life and the conditions of labor everywhere, to make the resources of the world more fully available to all mankind and so to order its operations as to promote and maintain equilibrium in the international balance of payments of all member countries."

[July 4, 1944]

Electronic Computer Flashes Answers, May Speed Engineering

By T. R. KENNEDY JR.

Special to The New York Times

PHILADELPHIA, Feb. 14 One of the war's top secrets, an amazing machine which applies electronic speeds for the first time to mathematical tasks hitherto too difficult and cumbersome for solution, was announced here tonight by the War Department. Leaders who saw the device in action for the first time heralded it as a tool with which to begin to rebuild scientific affairs on new foundations.

Such instruments, it was said, could revolutionize modern engineering, bring on a new epoch of industrial design, and eventually eliminate much slow and costly trial-and-error development work now deemed necessary in the fashioning of intricate machines. Heretofore, sheer mathematical difficulties have often forced designers to accept inferior solutions of their problems with higher costs and slower progress.

The "Eniac," as the new electronic speed marvel is known, virtually eliminates time in doing such jobs. Its inventors say it computes a mathematical problem 1,000 times faster than it has ever been done before.

The machine is being used on a problem in nuclear physics.

The Eniac, known more formally as "the electronic numerical integrator and computer," has not a single moving mechanical part. Nothing inside its 18,000 vacuum tubes and several miles of wiring moves except the tiniest elements of matter-electrons. There are, however, mechanical devices associated with it which translate or "interpret" the mathematical language of man to terms understood by the Eniac, and vice versa.

Ceremonies dedicating the machine will be held tomorrow night at a dinner given for a group of Government and scientific men at the University of Pennsylvania, after which they will witness the Eniac in action at the Moore School of Electrical Engineering, where it was built with the assistance of the Army Ordnance Department.

The Eniac was invented and perfected by two young scientists of the school, Dr. John William Mauchly, 38, a physicist and amateur meteorologist, and his associate, J. Presper Eckert Jr., 26, chief engineer of the project. Assistance also was given by many others at the school.

Army ordnance men had been on the lookout for a machine with which to prepare a large volume of ballistic data, which in turn was needed to break a threatened bottleneck in the production of firing and bombing tables for new offensive weapons going overseas. Without the tables the guns could not be used effectively.

Capt. H. H. Goldstine, Army ordnance mathematician, then at the school, heard of Dr. Mauchly's ideas, told Col. Paul N. Gillon of the Aberdeen (Md.) Proving Ground, enlisted his enthusiastic support, and the project went forward with Government aid. Thirty months to the day later it was finished and operating, doing easily what had been done laboriously by many trained men. The Eniac soon will be permanently installed at Aberdeen.

A very difficult wartime problem was sent through its intricate circuits soon after it was compiled. The Eniac completed the task in two hours. Had it not been available the job would have kept busy 200 trained men for a whole year. So clever is the device that its creators have given up trying to find problems so long that they cannot be solved.

This resolver of difficult problems is what computing experts call a "digital" counter. Basically, it does nothing more than add, subtract, multiply and divide. It does this by generating very accurately timed electrical impulses at a speed of 100,000 per second, and can do one operation every twentieth pulse, thereby adding, for instance, at the rate of 5,000 per second.

Since all mathematical tasks, no matter how abstruse or involved, can be resolved to basic arithmetic if enough time is available, the Eniac can reverse the process,

---

The dawn of the computer age came in 1946 when a machine called Eniac, developed in secret during World War II, was unveiled. It had 18,000 vacuum tubes and almost filled a room measuring 30 feet by 60 feet. It could, The Times reported, multiply 97,367 by itself 5,000 times, and do it "in less than the wink of an eye." The article said computers could "revolutionize modern engineering."

That forecast would prove true within two decades, but not while computers needed thousands of vacuum tubes, miles of wiring and extensive cooling systems. The solution to that problem appeared a couple of years later, when the Bell Telephone Laboratories reported developing what The Times described, in a brief report on the radio page, as "a device called a transistor." Many more advances would be needed, but computers were on their way to changing from hugely expensive and delicate pieces of machinery into ubiquitous devices found, by century's end, in everything from cars to toys.

1940–1949

Eniac, the world's first electronic computer, in operation at the University of Pennsylvania.

NEWS OF RADIO

A device called a transistor, which has several applications in radio where a vacuum tube ordinarily is employed, was demonstrated for the first time yesterday at Bell Telephone Laboratories, 463 West Street, where it was invented.

The device was demonstrated in a radio receiver, which contained none of the conventional tubes. It also was shown in a telephone system and in a television unit controlled by a receiver on a lower floor. In each case the transistor was employed as an amplifier, although it is claimed that it also can be used as an oscillator in that it will create and send radio waves.

In the shape of a small metal cylinder about a half-inch long, the transistor contains no vacuum, grid, plate or glass envelope to keep the air away.

The working parts of the device consist solely of two fine wires that run down to a pinhead of solid semi-conductive material soldered to a metal base. The substance on the metal base amplifies the current carried to it by one wire and the other wire carries away the amplified current.   [July 1, 1948]

eliminate time, and arrive at an answer to virtually any problem. So say its inventors.

The machine, however, can do much more. It has the human faculty of "memory," four kinds of it, to perform certain tasks in the proper sequence. It also has "control" elements, and can, up to a point, dictate its own action. It can, for instance, compare two numbers and, depending on which one is larger, choose one of two possible courses.

First, it gets its original numbers from a series of cards in which holes are punched to indicate the "initial and boundary conditions" of the problem. One of the Eniac "minds" performs this job.

When the problem is punched on the cards they are dropped into a slot in a "reader." The man who wants the answers may then sit down and await results. He seldom has to wait long; the Eniac does most of its tasks in seconds.

A unit called "a master programmer" oversees the whole computation and makes sure it is carried out.

The Eniac has some 40 panels nine feet high, which bristle with control and indicating material. Pink neon lights blink on several panels as buttons are pressed. Numbers are printed beside the lights.

Those who witnessed the demonstration entered a 30-by-60-foot room. The computer took up most of the space.

Dr. Arthur W. Burks of the Moore School explained that the basic arithmetical operations, if made to take place rapidly enough, might in time solve almost any problem.

"Watch closely, you may miss it," he asked, as a button was pressed to multiply 97,367 by itself 5,000 times. Most of the onlookers missed it—the operation took place in less than the wink of an eye.

To demonstrate the Eniac's extreme speed, Dr. Burks next slowed down the action by a factor of 1,000 and did the same problem. Had the visitors then been content to wait 16⅔ minutes they could have observed the answer in neon light. The next was multiplication—13,975 by 13,975. In a flash the quotient appeared—195,300,625. A table of squares and cubes of numbers was generated in one-tenth of a second. Next, a similar one of sines and cosines. The job was finished and printed on a large sheet before most of the visitors could go from one room to another.

The Eniac was then told to solve a difficult problem that would have required several weeks' work by a trained man. The Eniac did it in exactly fifteen seconds.

All problems must first be resolved to their essentials, punched on cards and run through an International Business Machines unit called a "reader." The reader translates the mathematical language to that of the Eniac, and vice versa. When this is done the machine is ready to operate. Numerical values covering a wide range of scientific "constants" are interjected as and when they are needed. There are four kinds of "memory" in the Eniac to accomplish this. Constant adjustments are made in advance for each type of problem.

Normally the Eniac handles ten-digit numbers—a billion, for instance—but it can handle twenty-digit numbers just as easily, resulting in numbers running to astronomical size.

More than 200,000 man-hours went into the building of the machine. It contains more than half a million soldered joints, and cost about $400,000. Three times as much electricity is required to operate it as for one of our largest broadcasters—150 kilowatts.

Little more than three years ago the Eniac was only an idea; today it is perhaps the greatest marvel of electronic ingenuity. Dr. Mauchly joined the Moore School staff in 1941, hoping he might be able to realize his ambition to revolutionize the art of dealing with huge numbers in complex form. He believed, for instance, that something could be done about long-range weather predicting.

In the field of peacetime activities Dr. Mauchly foresees not only better weather-predicting—months ahead—but also better airplanes, gas turbines, microwave radio tubes, television, prime movers, projectiles operating at supersonic speeds carrying cargoes in peace and even more and better accuracies in studying the movement of the planets."

According to Colonel Goldstine, "mountainous" computational burdens have been carried by scientists in the past, which will be largely removed by electronic computers. He pointed out that the solution of equations of motion has been a hindrance in the past and that studies of shell flight, high-speed planes, rockets and bombs are "a few of the fields that will benefit hugely through electronic computing."

Mr. Eckert predicted an era in which, with electronic speeds available, problems that have been thought impossible because they might require a lifetime will be readily resolved for man's use.

"The old era is going, the new one of electronic speed is on the way, when we can begin all over again to tackle scientific problems with new understanding," he told reporters. [Feb. 15, 1946]

One-Step Camera Is Demonstrated
PROCESS THAT MAKES FINISHED PICTURE IN MINUTE IS WORK OF POLAROID COMPANY HEAD

The Eastman Kodak Company dominated the photography business for most of the century, having introduced its Brownie camera in 1900. While other companies prospered selling film or cameras that competed with Kodak using the same basic process, it faced only two fundamental technical challenges that threatened to revolutionize the photography industry during the century. The second of those, digital photography, is still a young technology late in the century, one that has made only limited inroads into the mass consumer market. The first such challenge came from the Polaroid Corporation and its founder, Edwin H. Land. In 1947, he announced a camera that could take instant photographs, which developed in the camera rather than in a lab. The Times reported on the announcement and, on the same day, ran an editorial hailing it.

The announcement created a sensation, and demand for the camera was great when it went on sale in 1948. Polaroid improved the technology in coming decades, and eventually Kodak came out with its own models, only to face, and eventually lose, a patent infringement suit from Polaroid. But while Polaroid cameras continued to sell throughout the rest of the century, their popularity faded as the quality of conventional photographs exceeded those available instantly.

By WILLIAM L. LAURENCE

A revolutionary new camera, which turns out a finished picture one minute after the shutter is snapped, was demonstrated last night in the Hotel Pennsylvania at the winter meeting of the Optical Society of America by its inventor, Edwin H. Land, president and director of research of the Polaroid Corporation.

The new camera is described in the published program of the Optical Society as "a new kind of photography as revolutionary as the transition from wet plates to daylight-loading film," more than half a century ago.

The camera accomplishes in a single step all the processing operations of ordinary photography. The turn of a knob produces a positive print in permanent form. The camera contains no tanks; the picture comes out dry and requires no further processing. Thus snapshots can be seen at once, while technical pictures could be put to immediate use.

The one-step camera, Mr. Land said, can be manufactured in the same variety of sizes and shapes as conventional cameras, not only for popular snapshot use but also for X-ray and other technical applications. It will be several months, however, before the Polaroid company will be ready to announce when these cameras will become available and what they will cost.

With the new camera, Mr. Land pointed out, it will be possible for the amateur to take a snapshot and compare it with the scene before he leaves the spot. If he is not satisfied with the exposure he can retake it immediately and correct the fault. The new cameras, he added, "will make it possible for anyone to take pictures anywhere, without special equipment for developing and printing and without waiting for his films to be processed."

One type of camera described and demonstrated by Mr. Land contains a pair of small rollers and a place for a roll of special paper in addition to the usual roll of film. Otherwise it is like an ordinary folding roll-film camera. After a picture is snapped, a turn of a knob on the side of the camera advances the film and paper out of the camera, through the rollers. Film and paper are pressed together into a temporary sandwich by the pressure of the rollers. When they are peeled apart, a minute later, the paper has become the finished picture.

When the sandwich passes through the rollers, the pressure breaks a tiny pod or sealed container attached to the special paper. The pod releases a few drops of a viscous chemical mixture that spreads in a moist layer between film and paper. The chemicals instantly start their work. They develop the negative and simultaneously form the positive print during the brief time the film and paper are in contact.

Each pod has exactly enough chemicals to produce one picture. The opaque outer surfaces of the film and paper prevent the negative from being fogged by light when it is pulled out of the camera.

The most important materials in the tiny

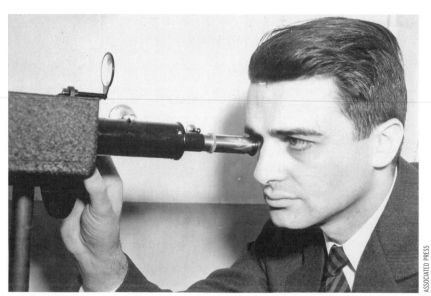

Edwin H. Land, founder of the Polaroid Corporation, in 1940.

ASSOCIATED PRESS

pod on the special paper are the standard photographic developer, hydroquinine, and the conventional fixing chemical, sodium thiosulfate or hypo. These chemicals together form the positive image from the silver in the unexposed areas of the negative, which is discarded in ordinary photography.

The pictures, Mr. Land showed, can be black-and-white, like conventional snapshots, or various shades of sepia, or brown, like rotogravure printing. The new processes, however, "are also inherently adaptable," he disclosed, "for making pictures in color and for making motion pictures." Several one-step processes have been developed by him, he added.

In some of the processes, Mr. Land told the meeting, the negative can be used to print additional pictures by the conventional method. All the processes, however, permit additional prints of a scene to be made conveniently by photographing the original print as many times as desired. New positives can also be made by re-photographing the first positive as many times as desired.

The film used with the new one-step processes, he said, can be any of the conventional types. Combinations of different films and different formulas for the chemicals carried by the special paper provides, he added, "a wide range of speeds, contrasts and other photographic characteristics."

Mr. Land, not yet 38, invented Polaroid light-polarizing plastics at the age of 21. He first became interested in quick photography as a hobby. He found time for some of his work on the new processes even during the war, when he was leading a number of Polaroid research teams formed to develop new weapons and war materials and directing a Navy plant for the development and manufacture of guided missiles.

[Feb. 22, 1947]

1940–1949

THE CAMERA DOES THE REST

As early as 1890 George Eastman was selling his Kodak by telling the world, "You press the button, we do the rest." Since then "the rest" has come to mean some shop to which the film is taken for transmission to a developing and fixing establishment. It was the taking and not the making of pictures in the chemical sense that Eastman so greatly improved. Now comes Edwin H. Land with the startling announcement that he has invented a camera which not only takes but develops and fixes pictures a minute after the button or bulb is pressed. Dr. Vannevar Bush, who sighed two years ago in The Atlantic Monthly for a way of snapping pictures and looking at them immediately, has been heard.

When the motion picture was invented and it became possible to project news events on the screen, the need for quick developing and fixing was urgent. The steps necessary to shorten the process were reduced. Hot chemicals and ingenious darkroom mechanical devices have made it possible to present a picture in a minute and less after exposure. Blueprints have been produced

with almost instantaneous rapidity, and mechanical processes have made it possible for visitors to Coney Island to see pictures of themselves a few minutes after they have posed in a dummy automobile or a fishing boat. But all this is crude compared with what Mr. Land has done. He simply presses the exposed film and a strip of paper into a sandwich. The "ham" in the sandwich is a sticky yet almost dry mixture of developer and fixer which is squeezed out of a capsule. A turn of a knob and out comes the picture–a permanent positive.

All this seems so simple that, as usual, we wonder why it was not done before. Though the chemicals are the familiar ones used in darkrooms, the process is really new. In ordinary developing and fixing, silver in the unexposed areas is lost–washed away. This very silver now forms a positive which pops out of the camera when the knob is turned. There is nothing like this in the history of photography. The method is not simple, but it is new.

[EDITORIAL, Feb. 22, 1947]

Bill Curbing Labor Becomes Law as Senate Overrides Veto, 68-25

In the years after World War II, there were some large and bitter strikes, most notably a national rail strike in 1946 that took place despite President Truman seizing the railroads and ordering the workers not to strike. The strike ended only after the President threatened to run the rails with soldiers. There was widespread agreement that some changes were needed in labor laws, but Republicans in Congress insisted on going further. The result was the Taft-Hartley Act, passed by Congress over President Truman's veto in 1947.

The bill revised the Wagner Act, which had established the National Labor Relations Board in 1945. It outlawed the closed shop, in which only union members could be employed, although it allowed union shops, in which all workers had to pay dues even if they did not belong to the union. It also barred certain types of boycotts by unions and said that unions, like employers, could be sued for unfair labor practices. It barred Communists from holding union offices.

As the bill became law, it appeared that a new conservative era was dawning in the country. President Truman was unpopular and viewed as unlikely to win election in 1948. It even seemed symbolic that Sen. Robert Wagner, Democrat of New York, was ill and unable to vote to sustain the veto of the bill written by two Republicans, Representative Fred A. Hartley and Senator Robert A. Taft.

In fact, in the greatest political surprise of the century, Truman won in 1948 and swept in a Democratic Congress, thanks in part to vigorous campaigning by unions. Even so, the most important parts of Taft-Hartley were never repealed.

On June 24, 1947, The Times reported that the Senate had overridden the President's veto, making the law effective. It also printed a detailed analysis of the new law's likely effect.

By WILLIAM S. WHITE

Special to The New York Times

WASHINGTON, June 23—The Senate by 68 to 25, or six votes more than the necessary two-thirds, overrode President Truman's veto of the Taft-Hartley Labor Bill today, and at 3:17 P.M., Eastern daylight time, made it the law of this country.

It automatically went on the statute books at that moment as the Senate's presiding officer announced the result of the ballot because the House had voted to override last Friday by 331 to 83.

The Senate cast aside one brief and final appeal from Mr. Truman as, in a warm, hushed and crowded chamber, it took the last decision to turn away from much of the labor policy of the Roosevelt and Truman Administrations. The measure it approved represented the first peacetime Federal restraint on the power of labor unions in half a generation.

In a letter to Senator Alben W. Barkley of Kentucky, minority leader, Mr. Truman made his third and final effort to sustain his veto, but it caused little change in Senate sentiment as it had been established in previous tests on the bill.

However, two Democrats who had not heretofore been with him voted today to uphold him. They were Senator Scott W. Lucas of Illinois, the party whip, and John J. Sparkman of Alabama, who had for some days been counted with the anti-veto forces.

Twenty Democrats joined forty-eight Republicans in voting to override. Twenty-two Democrats voting to sustain the head of their party were aided by three Republicans, who were Senators William Langer of North Dakota, George W. Malone of Nevada and Wayne Morse of Oregon.

Where Mr. Truman had been unsparing in his denunciation of the bill in his veto message last Friday and his speech to the country that night, he was more restrained today in his letter to Mr. Barkley, who read it to the Senate just before the vote was taken.

The text of the President's letter was as follows:

"Dear Senator Barkley:

"I feel so strongly about the labor bill which the Senate will vote on this after-

Representative Fred A. Hartley and Senator Robert A. Taft, sponsors of the 1947 labor bill.

noon that I wish to reaffirm my sincere belief that it will do serious harm to our country.

"This is a critical period in our history, and any measure which will adversely affect our national unity will render a distinct disservice not only to this nation but to the world.

"I am convinced that such would be the result if the veto of this bill should be overridden.

"I commend you and your associates who have fought so earnestly against this dangerous legislation.

"I want you to know you have my unqualified support, and it is my fervent hope, for the good of the country, that you and your colleagues will be successful in your efforts to keep this bill from becoming law."

Another written communication was received from Senator Robert F. Wagner, Democrat of New York, whose National Labor Relations Act would be considerably altered for the first time in the twelve years of its existence by the new law.

A statement issued through the office of the Senator, who is ill, said that he believed that the Taft-Hartley bill would "destroy what he has so long labored to develop—industrial peace through democracy."

Senator Wagner, it was added, had made every effort, supported by "every facility at the disposal of the city of New York," to come here to stand with the minority, but had been forbidden not only by his two physicians but by the Commissioner of Hospitals of New York, Dr. Edward M. Bernecker.

It was apparent this morning, from the maneuvering before the Senate met, that the President's supporters were in positions that would be taken in the first assault and overrun. The counter-attack was plainly hopeless from the start.

Nevertheless, counter-attacks were put in as the Senate convened, and Senator Robert A. Taft, Republican, of Ohio, co-author of the bill, took command of the majority debate.

The Senate, after many days of debate in the past, had, by agreement, only three more hours of discussion when it assembled at noon.

Mr. Taft's forces moved with massive bi-partisan strength into the struggle, while Senator Claude Pepper, Democrat, of Florida, carried the titular leadership for the opposition, in the sense of controlling the time of that side. The regular Democratic leader, Senator Barkley, was reserved to close for the Administration.

Senator Pepper told his colleagues that "this is not the first time that a mighty storm of reaction has burst over this nation and its people, but I am comforted by the testimony of history that victories of reaction have never been permanent ones."

Closing for the majority, Senator Taft reiterated the assertion that where employers at one time had "all the advantage" in dealing with workers, Federal policy had so altered the balance that now "the labor leaders have every advantage." The one purpose of the bill, he added, is to "swing the balance back to where the two sides can deal equally with each other." [June 24, 1947]

ANALYSIS OF THE LABOR ACT SHOWS CHANGED ERA AT HAND FOR INDUSTRY

By LOUIS STARK

Special to The New York Times

WASHINGTON, June 23—The "Labor Management Relations Act, 1947" is the first amendment to the National Labor Relations (Wagner) Act of 1935. It adds a new story and a new façade to the earlier law in an effort to "equalize the relations between employers and employes."

By removing most of the administrative work of the National Labor Relations Board and vesting it in a new statutory general counsel, the act turns the board into a labor court.

In order to cope with the backing of cases which continue to mount, the act increases the NLRB from three to five members. Their salaries are increased from $10,000 to $12,000 a year.

The provisions applying to the NLRB, the general counsel and unfair labor practices by employes become effective within sixty days. Also deferred for that period are the provisions outlawing the closed shop, regulating the union shop, requiring registration of data by unions, depriving unions with Communist officers of their rights under the law and forbidding foremen a recognition by law.

The other sections become effective at once. They include the following subjects:

Creation of a new statutory Federal mediation service to replace the present Conciliation Service in the Department of Labor; emergency machinery for handling "national-paralysis" disputes or strikes which "imperil the national health or safety"; stability of unions; regulation of welfare funds and check-off; banning of strikes by government workers; appointment of a joint Congressional committee to study labor-management relations and to observe the workings of the new law.

In shifting administrative responsibilities from the new NLRB's shoulders elsewhere, the law abolished the review section, comprising about fifty lawyers. This section had "predigested" all records for NLRB members but had been attacked as unduly "influencing" its chiefs.

The closed shop-union shop section affects some 7,000,000 employes.

The closed shop (in which an employe must be a union member to obtain a job) is outlawed, while the union shop (in which an individual may be employed even if he is not a union member but must become one after a trial period) is hedged about with certain restrictions.

In order to qualify for the union shop a labor organization must be the representative of the majority of the employes. It must also be certified by the NLRB that the employes, by a majority of those eligible, have signified their desire to have the union shop. Then the union may ask for it.

But if the employer agrees to this request the union will be unable to dismiss anybody for any reason other than for failure to keep up dues payments.

Thus, in the eyes of the bill's opponents, the usual reasons for the union shop (the union's right to discipline recalcitrants, "spies," provocateurs, etc.) would be excluded.

This section was framed for the frank purpose of depriving union leaders of their prerogatives regarding the disciplining of union members, on the ground that the leaders had abused this power in many instances and had unduly deprived employes of jobs.

One of the most important sections of the law deals with unfair labor practices by employes. This is a new provision which evoked heated debate during the consideration of the bill.

In addition to retaining the old Wagner Act sections prohibiting employers from discriminating against employes because of union activity, the law now provides for the following six "unfair" labor practices by labor organizations:

1. Restraining or coercing employes in the exercise of their guaranteed rights or employers in the selection of their bargaining agency; (intended to prevent unionization by force and to stop unions from compelling employers to bargain either as individuals or as members of larger units);

2. Persuading or attempting to persuade employers to discriminate against an employe, unless in accordance with the law; (the limited union-shop action);

3. Refusing to bargain collectively; (to stop unions from serving ultimata on employers);

4. Conducting strikes or boycotts for various purposes which are stated in some length; (aimed to lessen jurisdictional disputes and secondary boycotts and strikes against NLRB certification);

5. Requiring initiation fees which the NLRB finds "excessive or discriminatory"; (to meet the charge that unions keep out qualified workers by excessive charges);

6. Causing or attempting to cause an employer to pay money for services which "are not performed or are not to be performed"; (to offset "featherbedding" practices).

These labor practices furnish the "heart" of the first section of the new law and may change the entire course of industrial relations.

The NLRB would be empowered to obtain injunctions against jurisdictional strikes and secondary boycotts. The board itself would also have the power to decide which employes should do the task over which they are fighting. The board, however, would not be permitted to name an arbitrator to take this problem off its hands.

Unions would also be subject to suits for unfair labor practices and the courts may now provide damages against them resulting from jurisdictional strikes and secondary boycotts.

Employers receive more leeway in a "free-speech" section which states that expression of any views "shall not constitute or be evidence of an unfair labor practice if such expression contains no threat of reprisal or force or promise of benefit."

The NLRB is not permitted to investigate any union complaint unless there is on file with the NLRB an affidavit by each labor union official stating "that he is not a member of the Communist party" or affiliated therewith, "and that he does not believe in and is not a member of or supports any organization that believes in or teaches the overthrow of the United States Government by force or by any illegal or unconstitutional methods."

The foregoing would deprive all members of a union of their rights under the act if their officers failed to sign the anti-Communist affidavits.

Another section permits Communists or others to be employed under union-shop contracts so long as they pay dues.

[June 24, 1947]

Inkless Process in Printing Hailed

By HARTLEY W. BARCLAY

A revolutionary process of inkless printing has been developed that might completely change all the operations of the printing and publishing industry. This was announced yesterday by Joseph C. Wilson, president of the Haloid Company, Rochester, and officials of the Batelle Memorial Institute, Columbus, Ohio.

Invented by Chester F. Carlson, a New York lawyer, and known as "Xerography," this basic addition to the graphic arts reproduces pictures and text at a speed of 1,200 feet a minute, on any kind of a surface, within forty-five seconds after exposure of the photographed subject. It uses only dry powders, and no wet chemicals or ink in the process.

Earlier in the week, at a demonstration of the process in a preview at the Waldorf-Astoria Hotel, Dr. R. M. Schaffert, a Batelle scientist, predicted that, "when fully developed, it can be incorporated into a portable Xero-camera, in which finished printed pictures can be made within seconds after snapping a camera shutter."

During the demonstration, inkless printed copies of drawings and letters were made, and a protrait of a living subject was reproduced, while observers timed the work at exactly forty-five seconds.

Yesterday, at a second demonstration before a technical society in Detroit, officials reported by telephone that the later public test had been timed at thirty-eight seconds from exposure to printed results. The material that substitutes for ink is a fine iron powder, mixed with a dry plastic substance that makes a permanent mark when heated.

The new principle of science used in the process, to displace all need for a chemical reaction or any wet mixtures, is called "electrostatic" effect, or the same thing that causes "static" electricity to appear when dry silks are rubbed together.

Numerous large companies missed out on the opportunity to revolutionize the way offices work by declining to develop a technology called xerography. The Haloid Company, a small company based in Rochester, N.Y., took the chance.

Within a few decades after the process was disclosed by Haloid—later renamed the Xerox Corporation—in 1948, carbon paper had disappeared from offices, and secretaries who were told to make a copy were expected to use a Xerox machine, not to sit down at a typewriter.

The Times gave prominent coverage to the process when it was announced in 1948, but the story discussed it as an improvement in printing and as a type of camera. The possibility of a copying machine to be used for documents was not emphasized.

Nor would such machines arrive quickly. It took many years to advance the process to the point where a machine could be sold. While it had sold expensive machines for some specialized uses in the late 1950's, it was not until 1960 that the Xerox 914 went on the market as a general-purpose office copier.

That introduction was not as smooth as it might have been. The machine was so prone to catching on fire that Xerox put a fire extinguisher on it. Since it broke down so often, companies were reluctant to buy it. But they wanted it because the copies that were produced when it worked were vastly superior to anything else available. The solution was for Xerox to lease the machine on a per-copy basis. That enabled the company to promise customers that if the machine did not work it would cost them nothing. It also meant that Xerox ended up getting far more for each copier than it ever would have made if they had worked well enough to persuade customers to buy them. Xerox became a giant company.

Xerox was, however, destined to stumble in the 1970's, as Japanese companies took away market share. In 1982, as a new chief executive took over, The Times reviewed the company's history and prospects.

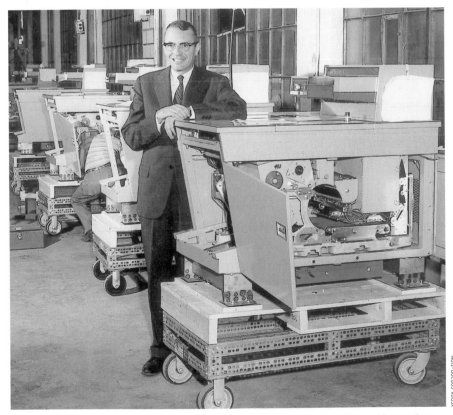

Joseph C. Wilson, president of Haloid, with the 914, the first general purpose office copier.

The only difference is that a system has been discovered to make the static electricity appear only on parts of materials on which printed words or figures are desired.

Compared to older printing methods, this process now makes it possible to use lighter machinery, without any need for heavy frames and plates of type or metals, because the dry iron powder that substitutes for ink actually jumps into place to form needed words or pictures.

Costs of printing can now be reduced to a fraction of former expenditures, Mr. Wilson asserted in an interview. He said that the Xerographic method is so simple that the speed of printing can be increased, because no heavy pressures are required to make impressions of type on printed paper.

Among typical publishing operations eliminated by the process are many steps now ordinarily required in engraving electroplates, by wet development processes. Here hours of development time may be consumed before older types of engravings can be reproduced in printed results. Even an unskilled person can make good Xerographic prints easily by following an established routine, Mr. Wilson continued.

Mr. Carlson, the inventor, discovered the method while trying to find an inexpensive way to print his own manuscripts. However, the development work required to convert the process to a commercial system was carried on by Batelle Memorial Institute researchers. This 19-year-old non-profit scientific organization is continuing research on this process under the sponsorship of the Signal Corps, Engineering Laboratories, in addition to The Haloid Company's contracts.

The heart of the process is a plate made with a metal backing that will conduct electricity. This is coated with another material that will conduct electricity only when exposed to light. This coated plate is then sensitized for use by spraying it with electrons in a simple device. The electrically charged surface that is produced retains this charge only at points on which light does not fall when exposed.

In the second step of the process dry iron powder is dusted over the plate, which now holds an "image pattern," duplicating the dark areas on which light did not fall. These darker areas are the type, pictures, or drawings, which appear in the final printed result.

A sheet of almost any kind of material or paper is then placed over the plate and both plate and paper are passed under a wire that discharges a "corona," or an electric static discharge. This causes the iron powder to adhere to the paper, and after a final step of momentary heating, the permanent image remains on the printed sheet.

During this last step the plate is electrically recharged for repeating this process and each successive printing merely duplicates this simple cycle step by step.

Because aluminum plates are used, even the plates now required for the process are extremely light in weight. They also can be used in a thinner form. Mr. Wilson said they could be stored or reused indefinitely, without further expense after original uses had been completed.

[Oct. 23, 1948]

XEROX: NEW CHIEF'S CHALLENGE

By ANDREW POLLACK

When C. Peter McColough steps down as chief executive officer of the Xerox Corporation on Thursday, the company will lose one of the last links to its glorious past and one of the major architects of its troubled present.

Mr. McColough, who will turn 60 this year and will remain as chairman, joined the company in 1954, when it was still a small supplier of photographic paper known as the Haloid Company.

He played a vital role in the 1960's as the company gave birth to a new industry that turned Xerox into a corporate giant and a household word in a dizzying few years.

But he also presided over the company in the 1970's as it failed in new ventures and gave way to competitors in the copier business. Thus his successor as chief executive, David T. Kearns, Xerox's president, will inherit a far different company than the one Mr. McColough inherited in 1968 and will face the stiff challenge of restoring Xerox's former luster.

"The Xerox machine was really the last great thing the company did," said Eugene G. Glazer, who follows the company for Dean Witter Reynolds Inc. "The company has been in a decline for a decade, and that time was McColough's. Much of it was inevitable. Nevertheless, he was running the company when it happened."

Competition, particularly from Japanese companies, reduced Xerox's share of the American copier market to 42 percent in 1981. Forays into new businesses have foundered. The company's growth rate has slowed and profit margins have shrunk. Last year, revenues and earnings grew at 6 percent, to $8.7 billion and $598 million, respectively, but pretax profits actually fell 8 percent.

The after-tax profit margin fell to 6.9 percent last year from 12.9 percent in 1968. And Xerox stock, once the darling of Wall Street, is now selling for 5 times earnings, compared to as much as 88 times in the 1960's.

Mr. Kearns, 51, said in a telephone interview last week that his main tasks would be to fend off the Japanese in the copier business and make Xerox successful in selling word processors, computers and other office automation equipment.

The work has already begun. "I think the major changes organizationally were made in the last year," said Mr. Kearns, a former International Business Machines Corporation executive, who joined Xerox in 1971 and has been president and chief operating officer since 1977. "I don't see any major organizational changes coming," he added.

Since mid-1981, some 3,300 of Xerox's 120,000 employees have been dismissed or induced to elect early retirement as part of an effort to reduce overhead and make Xerox more competitive. The company has divided its copier business into what it calls smaller "strategic business units," to quicken new product development.

One thing Xerox still needs to do, Mr. McColough said in a separate telephone interview, is to combine its copier sales force with its office products sales force so that a single salesman can handle all the needs of a large corporate client. I.B.M. undertook such a reorganization last year.

But such reorganizational efforts are bound to put further pressure on Xerox's short-term performance. Mr. Kearns said that "1982 and 1983 will not be easy profit years for Xerox." Nor is it clear how quickly such efforts will bear fruit. Mr. Kearns said he did not expect the office automation business to become profitable until 1984, a year or two later than some previous forecasts made by Xerox officials.

Mr. Kearns, who received a degree in business administration from the University of Rochester and rose to be vice president of I.B.M.'s data processing division before joining Xerox, is said to be similar in many ways to Mr. McColough. Both have a marketing orientation and are said by associates to have agreed on most decisions. Both are polite and eloquent.

"In terms of policies and philosophies, I would find it hard to separate the two," said a former Xerox executive. Mr. McColough, however, is described as being more prone to stand back and take a broad view of the company, while Mr. Kearns is described as an aggressive "race horse" type who likes to get directly involved in daily activities.

When the next history of Xerox is written, Mr. McColough's role is likely to be a controversial one. Clearly he has had more influence on the company than anyone, with the possible exceptions of Chester Carlson, the patent attorney who invented the process he called xerography in a makeshift Queens laboratory in 1938, and of Joseph C. Wilson, Mr. McColough's predecessor, who risked his company on Mr. Carlson's process.

During Mr. McColough's tenure as chief executive, the company grew from $900 million in revenues in 1968 to $8.7 billion last year. Its net income has increased year by year, except for 1975. The fact that growth has slowed is to be expected as Xerox has become larger, yet Wall Street still is seen as having unrealistic expectations. "The company would announce record earnings and the stock would drop two points," said Kenneth R. Andrews, a Harvard business professor, editor in chief of the Harvard Business Review and a Xerox director.

Mr. McColough is credited with establishing Xerox's sales force, which propelled its rapid growth. He is also credited with realizing early that Xerox would have to go into electronic information processing because the use of paper would gradually give way to the use of computer terminals in the so-called office of the future.

But while his vision might have been good, the implementation was poor. In 1969, Xerox paid nearly $1 billion to acquire Scientific Data Systems, a computer company, only to have to abandon the effort and take an $84 million write-off in 1975. Its word processors fared poorly. Last year, Xerox abandoned an idea for a telecommunications service after a $30 million investment in it.

Still, Xerox has also come forth with some innovative and competitive products and is expected to eventually prove successful in office automation. "When I'm asked about Scientific Data Systems, I have usually said, 'Yeah, that was a mistake,'" Mr. McColough said. "I think, as a matter of fact, that we got tremendous value out of S.D.S. I don't think we'd be anywhere near where we are today if we hadn't acquired the company."

It is harder for Mr. McColough to be apologetic about the company's failure to notice the Japanese move into the copier business in the mid-1970's. "There were signal flags then and they weren't heeded at all for quite a while," said one retired Xerox executive.

Reflecting on the struggles of Haloid, the dizzying explosion of Xerox, its subsequent fall from grace and now, perhaps, its rebuilding, Mr. McColough said, "I feel I've worked for five different companies; it's been a mad scramble from the beginning."

[May 17, 1982]

1940–1949

CHAPTER SIX

1950–1959

Postwar suburbia: 17,000 homes were built on former potato fields, creating Levittown, N.Y.

What's Good for General Motors . . .

IN 1953, CHARLES E. WILSON, the president of General Motors, was selected by President Dwight D. Eisenhower to be Secretary of Defense, and he promptly ran into a buzz-saw of criticism. He saw no reason why he should have to sell his G.M. stock to take the post and could not understand why anyone would see a potential conflict of interest.

"I cannot conceive of one," he told a Senate hearing, "because for years I thought that what was good for our country was good for General Motors, and vice versa. The difference did not exist. Our company is too big. It goes with the welfare of the country."

Mr. Wilson was forced to sell his stock, but his attitude summed up the prevailing wisdom for much of the decade. Business was back in the good graces of the American public and politicians. The economic planning of the 1930's and 1940's was dropped. President Harry S. Truman's seizure of the steel mills in 1952 marked the last major government-business confrontation of the decade.

It was, in fact, a glorious decade for much of American business. With Europe and Japan slowly rebuilding after the destruction of World War II, there was demand for American products but relatively little international competition. In that era, the big industrial companies could raise prices to pass on rising costs, and labor unions were able to get good raises in basic industries. The power of organized labor also hit its highest level in American history.

The stock market boomed, with the Dow Jones industrial average finally surpassing its 1929 high of 381.17 in 1954 and ending that year with a 44 percent gain. The rising market brought profits but also unease to a generation whose memories of the 1929 crash and ensuing Depression were still vivid. A Senate commitee, after investigating the stock market, warned that speculation might be reaching a dangerous level.

Shareholders began to be heard from as a constituency that could throw out managers who did not perform well enough. The owners of the New York Central Railroad elected insurgents in the first proxy fight to draw widespread attention. But new management could not reverse the decline of the railroads as cars, trucks and planes came to dominate the transportation system.

The postwar prosperity led to the development of suburbs, increasing the demand for cars and providing profits for those merchants who followed their customers into areas that had recently been fields. Montgomery Ward, one of the great retailers, delayed the move for years because its chairman, Sewell Avery, was sure a depression was coming. By the time he stepped down under pressure, it was too late for Ward's to catch its big rival, Sears, Roebuck & Company.

Television rose from curiosity to necessity during the decade, and gained color. Many homes installed air-conditioning, and computers began to have an impact on business. But by the end of the decade, signs of problems were appearing. A host of European auto makers were establishing a market in small cars, something the big American companies did not want to make. When they finally did, as the decade ended, they did it badly.

1950	North Korean forces invade South Korea.
1951	Julius and Ethel Rosenberg are sentenced to death for spying against the U.S.
1952	King George VI dies and Elizabeth II becomes queen of England.
	President Truman seizes steel mills to prevent a strike.
1953	Gen. Dwight D. Eisenhower is inaugurated President after a landslide win.
	The Korean War ends.
1954	The Supreme Court bans school segregation.
	Robert R. Young wins proxy fight for the New York Central Railroad.
1955	The A.F.L. and C.I.O. merge.
	The Salk polio vaccine proves a success.
1956	Egypt nationalizes the Suez Canal.
	President Eisenhower is re-elected in another landslide.
1957	The Soviet Sputnik I becomes the first satellite to orbit Earth.
	The first underground atomic test is conducted in Nevada.
1958	Gen. Charles de Gaulle becomes premier of France.
	Pope Pius XII dies and is succeeded by John XXIII.
1959	Fidel Castro takes over Cuba.
	Alaska becomes the 49th state, and Hawaii the 50th.

Supreme Court Voids Steel Seizure, 6 to 3; Holds Truman Usurped Powers of Congress; Workers Again Strike as Mills Are Returned

After the beginning of the Korean War, wage and price controls were again imposed to hold down inflation, with a Wage Stabilization Board able to recommend fair wage increases if disputes were referred to it. In early 1952, the board recommended a wage increase for steelworkers that was rejected by the steel companies out of fear they would not be able to recoup the costs in higher prices. To prevent a steel strike that he said would harm the war effort, President Truman seized the steel mills in April that year and had the Government operate them using the same workers and managers.

When a lower court judge ruled the seizure illegal, the strike began, but the workers returned when that order was stayed pending Supreme Court review. They walked out again, however, as soon as the Supreme Court ruled against Truman in a decision that set limits on the extension of Presidential power over business. The strike lasted 53 days, ending with an agreement that gave the workers less than the wage board had recommended but more than the companies wanted to pay. At the same time, the steel companies were authorized to raise prices.

By JOSEPH A. LOFTUS

Special to The New York Times

WASHINGTON, June 2—The Supreme Court of the United States ruled, 6 to 3, today that President Truman's seizure of the steel industry to avert a strike violated the Constitution by usurping the legislative powers reserved to Congress.

The President bowed promptly by directing Secretary of Commerce Charles Sawyer to release the properties to their private owners, and the United Steelworkers of America, C. I. O., went on strike.

As a result of the walkout the Government ordered a halt in deliveries of steel from retail warehouses to consumer goods producers in an effort to conserve steel for defense needs.

Authorities said the action was directed at preventing a drain on warehouses by buyers who usually got their steel at the mills. Manufacturers who ordinarily receive steel from warehouses will continue to do so, they added. No order was issued against steel exports.

The Supreme Court justices who voted to uphold District Judge David A. Pine's order dispossessing the Government were: Hugo L. Black, Felix Frankfurter, William O. Douglas, Robert H. Jackson, Harold H. Burton and Tom C. Clark.

Dissenting were: Chief Justice Fred M. Vinson and Justices Stanley F. Reed and Sherman Minton.

The court ruled in effect that when the President seized the steel mills he seized the lawmaking power, because only Congress could authorize the taking of private property for public use.

"The Constitution did not subject this law-making power of Congress to Presidential or military supervision or control," said the opinion of the court, written by Justice Black.

"The founders of this nation entrusted the lawmaking power to the Congress alone in both good times and in bad times," it added. "It would do no good to recall the historical events, the fears of power and the hopes for freedom that lay behind their choice. Such a review would but confirm our holding that this seizure order cannot stand."

Chief Justice Vinson, writing a vigorous dissent, declared that the President's action to keep steel flowing was warranted by the world emergency.

"History bears out the genius of the founding fathers, who created a Government subject to law but not left subject to inertia when vigor and initiative are required," the Chief Justice wrote.

"As the district judge stated, this is no time for 'timorous' judicial action," he declared. "But neither is this a time for timorous executive action."

Chief Justice Vinson said the majority of the court, not the minority, was seeking to amend the Constitution. He declared:

"The broad Executive power granted by Article II to an officer on duty 365 days a year cannot, it is said, be invoked to avert disaster.

"Instead, the President must confine himself to sending a message to Congress recommending action. Under this messenger-boy concept of the office, the President cannot even act to preserve legislative programs from destruction so that Congress will have something left to act upon."

The court, contrary to a widely held exception among lawyers, grasped the Constitutional issue firmly and interpreted it without equivocal language. It might have disposed of the case without reaching the ultimate question; indeed, it is the practice of the judiciary to do so whenever possible.

The court acted with unusual speed. Legal controversies often take years in their course through the three levels of the Federal judiciary. This decision came less than eight weeks after the President seized the steel mills.

The seizure took effect on April 9. The district court granted the steel companies' injunction against seizure on April 29. The Circuit Court of Appeals stayed the injunction the next day. The Supreme Court accepted the case the same week and heard oral arguments on May 12.

In the three-week interval since the argument was heard, the justices wrote more than 50,000 words in opinions in the steel case alone. Each of the six justices in the majority wrote concurring opinions. Only Justices Reed and Minton refrained from writing.

The history-making case hereafter will be known to law students and lawyers as Youngstown Co. v. Sawyer.

Delivery of the opinions took two hours and thirty-five minutes. The court convened at noon and Chief Justice Vinson announced that, contrary to custom, the admissions of attorneys to practice before the Supreme Court would be deferred until later. Usually that is the first order of business.

Justice Black started reading the opinion of the court at 12:01. It was comparatively brief, and he finished about 12:15. Justice Frankfurter followed with his concurring opinion. He spoke for thirty minutes and scarcely referred to the printed page, except near the end of his opinion.

Chief Justice Vinson cited the positions taken by Justices Jackson and Clark with respect to the President's powers when they were Attorneys General. Referring extemporaneously to Justice Jackson in what was taken to be friendly sarcasm, the Chief Justice remarked that changing one's mind is "evidence of strength."

At that point Justice Black turned and caught Justice Jackson's eye two seats away and grinned at him. Justice Jackson reciprocated.

The Chief Justice continued to refer to Justice Jackson's position as Attorney General in the seizure of the North American plant in June, 1941, when Mr. Jackson was Attorney General. He said that Mr. Jackson stated his opinion in support of seizure then as vigorously and as forcefully "as he ordinarily does now." The lawyers caught the inflection on "ordinarily" and there was a spontaneous burst of laughter. Justice Jackson joined in it.

The differences among the six opinions were mainly differences in emphasis, except Justice Clark's. He said he concurred in the judgment, but not the opinion, of the court. He used a different approach to the same conclusion, declaring that the President's reservoir of nonstatutory powers was not available to him when Congress had provided statutory procedures.

Justice Jackson saw a tendency of Congress to abdicate its powers. He wrote:

"But I have no illusion that any decision by this court can keep power in the hands of Congress if it is

not wise and timely in meeting its problems. A crisis that challenges the President equally, or perhaps primarily, challenges Congress.

"If not good law, there is worldly wisdom in the maxim attributed to Napoleon that 'the tools belong to the man who can use them.' We may say that power to legislate for emergencies belongs in the hands of Congress, but only Congress itself can prevent power from slipping through its fingers."

Here and there in the opinions reversing the President there were friendly expressions directed to Mr. Truman, the man, and the justices seemed to be saying that this was a decision for the ages and must be viewed impersonally.

Justice Frankfurter, for example, said: "It is absurd to see a dictator in a representative product of the sturdy democratic traditions of the Mississippi Valley. The accretion of dangerous power does not come in a day. It does come, however slowly, from the generative forces of unchecked disregard of the restrictions that fence in even the most disinterested assertion of authority."

Justice Douglas remarked: "We pay a price for our system of checks and balances, for the distribution of power among the three branches of government. It is a price that today may seem exorbitant to many. Today a kindly President uses seizure power to effect a wage increase and to keep the steel furnaces in production. Yet tomorrow another President might use the same power to prevent a wage increase, to curb trade unionists, to regiment labor as oppressively as industry thinks it has been regimented by this seizure."

Chief Justice Vinson stressed the emergency aspect of the seizure. "One is not here called upon even to consider the possibility of Executive seizure of a farm, a corner grocery store or even a single industrial plant," he said. "Such considerations arise only when one ignores the central fact of this case—that the nation's entire basic steel production would have shut down completely if there had been no Government seizure." [June 3, 1952]

Picketing steelworkers at a South Chicago mill in May 1952.

Debut of the World's Smallest Radio Fails to Excite Phlegmatic Times Sq.

By JACK GOULD

The world's smallest regular radio—small enough to fit in the palm of the hand—was demonstrated yesterday afternoon in Times Square. The populace took the coming of the "Dick Tracy Age" with disconcerting calmness.

Walking along the street with a radio blaring full blast from an inside pocket may mark the final death knell of the rugged individualist; now he, too, can be wired for sound—and for commercials. At least it seemed so yesterday.

The six-volt radio set is an experimental model made by the Radio Corporation of America. It probably will not be in commercial production for at least a couple of years, which means that the national sanity still has a little time to go.

The set weighs one pound and is about the size of two packages of cigarettes laid side by side. The receiver measures 5⅛ inches long, 2¾ inches wide and 1⅜ inches deep. It employs the new transistors, which do the work of vacuum tubes at a fraction of the power. The receiving circuit is a standard superhetrodyne and covers everything on the dial from WMCA to WQXR.

Yesterday afternoon the receiver with its built-in antenna was slipped into the breast pocket of a man's coat jacket. The receiver was completely hidden by a trench coat. Unsuspecting passers-by merely knew that the chatter of disk jockeys and commentators came from within the wireless wanderer.

Three young ladies out for a stroll on West Forty-third Street turned their heads in amazement as the gentleman walked by, giving forth the tune "Ebb Tide." It was probably the first time the cry of sea gulls have come out of a trench coat. The women looked again and again. They giggled.

A policeman at Forty-third Street and the Avenue of the Americas turned, looked casually in the direction of the sound's origin and then turned away. One male pedestrian trailed the receiver for several steps, looked searchingly to see where it was and then turned away. A salesman in a candy store, hearing news bulletins come from a customer who had asked for peppermints, said: "Hey, you've got something there."

The transistor makes unnecessary the bulky "B" battery common to present portable receivers. With four mercury cells, the set shown yesterday would run fifty hours, giving ample volume for listening in a good-sized room.

The transistors are smaller than a grain of wheat, but at this stage in their development they are expensive. The eight transistors in the demonstration set would probably cost $80. With ultimate mass production, the cost of transistors may drop to a comparatively few cents.

The set seems to work satisfactorily in a taxicab, but subway riders may be cheered to hear that the device is not expected to work well below the earth's surface. If the New York City Transit Authority can guarantee the town's only refuge from pitchmen and giveaways, the 15-cent fare on the subway may prove quite a bargain.   [Dec. 15, 1953]

The era of transistors and semiconductors meant that electronic items could shrink ever smaller. In 1953, a Times reporter ventured out into Times Square with what was described as the world's smallest radio tucked in a coat pocket and tested the reactions of passersby.

The radio was made by RCA, but that company said it would be a couple of years before it was available commercially. Such delays in commercializing inventions eventually opened up great opportunities for Japanese companies, particularly Sony.

1950–1959

TV Makers Differ Sharply on Color in 1954 or Later

By the early 1950's, television was replacing radio as the nation's preeminent broadcasting medium, and color television was on the horizon. In setting out how to move to color, however, the Federal Communications Commission botched the decision. It first chose a system developed by CBS that would not have been compatible with the existing black-and-white sets. Then it reversed itself and chose a system pushed by RCA, which both made televisions and owned the NBC network.

When all that was done, the television industry confronted a chicken-and-egg problem. The set makers saw no reason to try to sell expensive color sets if few color programs were available, and the networks saw no reason to spend extra money for color broadcasting if few sets were available. That left the market to RCA, which stood to profit from both ends of the business. It was the first to make color sets and for many years dominated the field, much as it had done in radio, guided still by the aggressively pioneering David Sarnoff.

By JACK GOULD

Disagreement over when color television should be introduced to the public has split the set-manufacturing industry.

On one side is the Radio Corporation of America, which on Friday plans to begin its "big push" in color TV and, if necessary, to invest another $30,000,000 to get the new medium off the ground.

On the other side are virtually all the other set makers, who do not believe that it is either technically or economically feasible to begin color for some time. They contend that public interest in color has subsided because of the high retail cost of initial sets—more than $1,000 for twelve-inch pictures—and that the "immediacy" of tinted TV now can be discounted.

Last week, it became known yesterday, a number of manufacturers canceled orders for various color TV parts. Earlier, the General Electric Company and Sylvania had suspended plans to commit themselves to volume production of color picture tubes.

One factor behind the Columbia Broadcasting System's decision of two weeks ago not to expand its color programs was an informal survey that showed the number of color TV sets in use this year would be far below many enthusiastic estimates.

Several manufacturers confirmed that most companies apart from R. C. A. were not tooling up as yet for color and that each would make only a trickle of receivers, perhaps a hundred or so for laboratory and promotional purposes, by the end of this year.

David Sarnoff, chairman of the board of R. C. A., acknowledging the differences in the industry attitude towards color TV's future, said that his concern's position would be explained in detail on Friday at a meeting of manufacturers' representatives at the R. C. A. plant in Bloomington, Ill.

There the company will reveal its manufacturing methods and the color programing intentions of its subsidiary, the National Broadcasting Company.

Mr. Sarnoff noted, however, that he believed the rest of the industry was waiting for R. C. A. to carry the ball on color TV and this would be a repetition of the history of radio.

He added that he felt increasing enthusiasm for color and that his company already had invested $30,000,000 in the medium. A like amount would be forthcoming, if required, to put color on its feet, he said. To start network radio cost R. C. A. $50,000,000, he added.

Mr. Sarnoff said that he always had held 1954 would be only "an introductory year" for color television.

Seventy-five thousand color sets could be manufactured this year, Mr. Sarnoff said, with conceivably a million next year.

Other manufacturers, not all of whom subscribe to Mr. Sarnoff's estimates, said that

RCA technicians adjust test patterns on new color television sets.

even under such a schedule color on a mass basis could not be a reality until 1957 or 1958, by which time the economics and techniques of the industry might have changed materially. Black-and-white TV is nearing the 30,000,000-set mark.

Dr. W. R. G. Baker, chairman of the National Television System Committee and vice-president of General Electric, it was learned, is scheduled to give the views of other manufacturers in a talk early next month in California. Other industry leaders also plan to discuss the situation publicly.

Differences in the industry have been brewing for some months, but apparently they came to a head with the imminence of the R. C. A. meeting and today's opening of the convention of the Institute of Radio Engineers at the Kingsbridge Armory in the Bronx and at the Waldorf-Astoria Hotel. The engineers' sessions attract thousands of electronic specialists from all parts of the country and many of them are doing color TV research. Manufacturing companies also exhibit their new products at the convention.

Indicative of the over-all confusion and tension in the color TV industry was the disclosure yesterday that one project was supposedly so secret that it was discussed by some executives only under the code word "apple." In a way, it is agreed, "apple" is symbolic of perhaps the major point of controversy confronting color TV.

"Apple" is one of several prototypes of color picture tubes designed to simplify the task of projecting the electronic primary colors of red, blue and green on the home screen. It is being developed by a group of manufacturers reportedly anxious not to be dependent on R. C. A. for color tubes.

Existing color tubes employ three guns—one for each color—to direct the primary hues on the face of the tube. Their major drawback is that they are relatively delicate and the three colors must be made to converge with meticulous accuracy.

"Apple," on the other hand, employs a single gun for the three colors and, theoretically, minimizes or does away with convergence difficulties. Other companies, including R. C. A., are working on single gun tubes. "Apple" is said to reproduce a brilliant color picture but to require complicated circuits.

Similarly, the matter of size of color pictures is at issue. The thinking of many manufacturers thus far has revolved around a fifteen-inch, three-gun tube, giving the equivalent of about a twelve-inch picture in black and white. However, R. C. A. has promised for this year a nineteen-inch, three-gun tube. Other manufacturers, including the Chromatic Television Laboratories, are working on still larger sizes. For practical purposes the fifteen-inch color tube is now obsolete. R. C. A. is making only a limited run of fifteen-inch sets, perhaps 5,000 in all.

Some manufacturers fear that if they start with a nineteen-inch screen, a twenty-one-inch tube might come soon thereafter.

Apart from uncertainties about the size and internal structure of tubes that a viewer watches directly, research also is being done on projection color receivers. These would throw a picture on a screen on a wall. The Hazeltine Corporation,

1950–1959

North American Philips and R. C. A. are working on projection color, which would give far larger pictures than direct-view tubes. The loss of light that handicaps projection receivers in black and white is said to be much less severe in color.

The economic problems of color TV may exceed the technical for the immediate future. The set giving a twelve-inch picture now costs $1,000. Larger screens will cost more. Manufacturers who are cool to color maintain that such devices fall into the class of luxury items. No one can afford to make a luxury item if it might soon be out of date for reasons of size or quality, they noted.

There was general agreement that color sets would be harder to sell than the early black and white. Monochrome TV constituted a brand-new and novel service, it was observed, whereas color is an improvement on an old service. Today a potential viewer has two choices of sets—an expensive color receiver or inexpensive black and white set. Previously there was only one way to see TV.

Linked to the selling problem is the fate of the market for current black and white sets. Partly because of color and partly because of the general economic conditions, monochrome sets have been subjected to strong price cutting, discounts and "dumping" of some lines.

A number of set makers argued that lessened income from black and white sales was an added reason not to gamble on interim color TV sets until uncertainty over public reaction was minimized. The R. C. A. philosophy is that color TV will pep up the set market and the only practical course is to shorten, not protract, the transitional period.   [March 22, 1954]

R.C.A. SET SALES RECORD IN '59; COLOR TV IN BLACK FOR FIRST TIME

The Radio Corporation of America will make a profit on its sales of color television sets this year, David Sarnoff, chairman, declared yesterday. He said that 1959 will be the first year in which color receivers have been profitable since their introduction in 1955.

In a year-end statement Radio Corporation's chief executive officer predicted that sales will set a record this year and added that earnings will increase 29 per cent from those in 1958 on a 17 per cent volume gain.

Sales, Mr. Sarnoff said, will reach $1,375,000,000 for its hundreds of consumer, industrial and military electronic products. Last year, overall volume reached $1,176,000,000 and was $1,176,277,000 in 1955, the previous record year.

Profits this year, Mr. Sarnoff predicted, will reach $40,000,000 compared with $30,900,000 in 1958. The net will be equal to $2.65 a common share, against $2.01 in 1958. The record year for earnings was 1955, when profits were $47,525,000, or $3.16 a share.

Mr. Sarnoff did not say how much the profit was on color television but estimated that sales this year will finish 30 per cent ahead of 1958.

"As sales volume continues to increase, so will the profits," the chairman said.

Improvements in earnings, according to Mr. Sarnoff, will "reflect increases in virtually all of the company's major operating units, and the cumulative effects of a corporate-wide cost-reduction program."

Mr. Sarnoff predicted that R.C.A. would have continued increases in sales and earnings next year and double its volume in five years.

Terming the next ten years the "dynamic decade" in electronics, he predicted the following developments in this period:

¶ Super computers—smarter, smaller and speedier by as much as a thousand times to take over more and more factory and office chores.

¶ Global television in full color, relayed by orbiting satellites.

¶ Electronic systems with no moving parts that will heat and cool homes more efficiently and electroluminescent panels in walls that will replace bulky electrical fixtures and cumbersome cords.

¶ New homes and apartments fully equipped with electronic sight and sound systems for communications and entertainment.

¶ Accurate long-range weather forecasts by means of electronic observation of cloud formations by satellites.

¶ Electronic safety devices for highways and automobiles that will take much of the danger out of driving.

¶ An "avalanche" of new electronic tools in the continuing war on disease.

¶ "Commonplace" classes of 100,000 or more students with one instructor by means of educational television and other electronic educational aids.

¶ An effective anti-missile missile guided by electronics.

¶ Greatly advanced systems for defense and space exploration achieved through improved basic circuitry—components and materials that will amplify, direct and control electronic impulses.   [Dec. 30, 1959]

Young Wins Fight for the Central; Margin Is 1,062,000

By ROBERT E. BEDINGFIELD

Robert R. Young has won control of the New York Central Railroad Company.

Neither Central nor Young spokesmen would confirm or deny this officially yesterday, but unofficially they agreed it was a fact.

The certificate that the election inspectors will deliver will show that Mr. Young's slate of directors won by a margin of 1,062,000 votes. The three judges of the proxy count will report to the thrice-recessed annual meeting of the railroad's stockholders when it reconvenes in Albany at 10 A. M., Monday.

Mr. Young is chairman of the board of the Alleghany Corporation, a railroad holding company.

Word of his victory leaked out late yesterday afternoon. The report came as the election inspectors were finishing their tally of the more than 5,800,000 votes of 40,979 shareholders cast at the initial session of the annual meeting in Albany on May 26.

Neither Mr. Young, who left for his summer home in Newport, R. I., last night, nor William White, Central president, would comment on the reports of the election results.

Meanwhile, Alfred E. Perlman, executive vice president of the Denver and Rio Grande Western Railroad, arrived in New York yesterday morning with his wife. Mr. Perlman is Mr. Young's "twenty-to-one" favorite for the presidency of the Central. It is expected that Mr. Perlman will be elected to that office on Monday when Mr. Young holds the organization meeting of his board.

At that meeting Mr. Young will be named the Central's $1-a-year board chairman, a post that he has sought since 1947.

Mr. Young was confident of victory from the start of his proxy fight and he became more confident as the contest progressed. On Thursday he alerted the thirteen men and the woman who will be directors of the road under his chairmanship to come to New York for their first board meeting.

He expects this group to gather at his offices on the forty-fifth floor of the Chrysler Building to wait for the official announcement of their election from Albany. Then the group is to walk over with him to the Central's board room on the thirty-second floor of the railroad's executive offices at 230 Park Avenue and to hold the meeting that will officially elect him chairman.

Two other proposals will be presented to the group.

Robert R. Young, financier.

ASSOCIATED PRESS

The fight for control of the New York Central Railroad in 1954 was the first proxy battle to capture the attention of mainstream America. The battle pitted the incumbent management led by William White, the president of the line, against Robert R. Young, who had run other railroads and claimed that with better management the New York Central could make more money and pay higher dividends. The battle raged for months, with newspaper ads and court fights over whether certain shares could be voted. On the Sunday before the vote, Young and White appeared on NBC's "Meet The Press" to state their case to the thousands of individual shareholders.

Corporate America was not used to proxy fights, and it took weeks after the May 26 vote to count the ballots. But on June 12, The Times reported that Young had won a convincing victory. It also reported on the difficulties he would confront in running a heavily indebted railroad that was losing money on passenger travel and faced increased competition from trucks.

As promised, Young did raise the dividend, to 2 a year. In May 1957, he told shareholders that he believed the Central could one day pay a dividend of 8 a year "unless the country goes crazy and turns its transportation system over to the highways and airways." But the economy slowed; the Central stock price sagged, and by the end of that year Young was forced to sell most of his stock to meet margin calls from brokers who had lent him money to buy the stock. On Jan. 20, 1958, the New York Central directors, meeting in Young's Palm Beach mansion, voted to stop paying dividends. Five days later, in the billiard room of that home, Young used a shotgun to commit suicide.

The New York Central went on to merge with the Pennsylvania Railroad in 1968 to form the Penn Central. In 1970, that

1950–1959

They are: the acceptance of Mr. White's resignation as president and the selection of Mr. Perlman as his successor with the additional title of chief executive officer, and the induction of a corporate secretary.

Central's new directors, in addition to Mr. Young, will include:

Allan P. Kirby, president of the Alleghany Corporation. Mr. Kirby, an heir to the F. W. Woolworth chain store chain fortune, was Mr. Young's principal backer when he acquired control of Alleghany during the Nineteen Thirties. When Mr. Young first made his demand on the Central management earlier this year for the board chairmanship for himself, he asked that Mr. Kirby also be made a director.

Clint W. Murchison and Sid W. Richardson, owners of 800,000 shares of Central stock. These two prominent Texas oil men paid $20,000,000 for the stock to the Chesapeake and Ohio Railway to insure Mr. Young's victory, although he himself, early in the fight, predicted he would win "even without the 800,000 shares."

Others on the board will be: Earl E. T. Smith, a member of the New York Stock Exchange, who was once married to the former Consuelo Vanderbilt, a great-great-granddaughter of Commodore Cornelius Vanderbilt. Commodore Vanderbilt is the man who nearly a century ago successfully fought Daniel Drew for control of the Central.

Dr. R. Walter Graham of Baltimore, a physician; William E. Landers, a retired New York Central engineer; D. E. Taylor, president of the West India Fruit and Steamship Company of Norfolk, Va.; Frederick Lewisohn, member of the New York Stock Exchange; Richard M. Moss, president of Clinton Foods Inc.; Eugene C. Pulliam, publisher of The Indianapolis Star and The Indianapolis News.

Also, Orville Taylor, Chicago attorney and member of the law firm Taylor, Miller, Busch & Wagner; Andrew Van Pelt of Philadelphia, a director of the Alleghany Corporation and a former director of the Chesapeake and Ohio Railway; William P. Feeley, president of the Great Lakes Dredge and Dock Company, and Lila Bell Acheson Wallace, co-editor and co-owner of the Reader's Digest.

Mr. Young said for years that if he ever won his fight for the Central he would nominate a woman director. When he first opened his proxy battle he announced that his opposition board would include at least one woman, adding, "We need a woman's touch on the railroads."

Mrs. Wallace, in accepting the nomination, said, "I agree. I think that everything needs a woman's touch."

The new directors own or control 1,118,880 shares of the Central's 6,447,410 shares of stock, or 17.4 per cent.

The Central board that Mr. Young has defeated owned or controlled only 106,122 shares, a mere 1.6 per cent.

Estimates are that costs of the advertisements of the two sides finally reached hundreds of thousands of dollars. The cost of mailing reprints of the advertisements and other proxy-soliciting material amounted to more than $50,000 for stamps alone.

[June 12, 1954]

PROXY VICTOR GETS BIG ROAD, BIG WOES

The prize that financier Robert R. Young won at Albany is a century-old railroad with assets of more than $2,600,000,000 and a fine reputation for public service.

Only the Pennsylvania Railroad is bigger. Although its route mileage is slightly less (it operated 10,066 miles of track last year), the Pennsylvania has the largest total trackage, the biggest investment in road and equipment, the greatest traffic and the largest operating revenues.

The New York Central, as the nation's second largest rail system, operates 10,713 miles of track in eleven states and two provinces of Canada. It owns some of the world's most valuable real estate.

But the financial troubles of the Central are impressive, too. The road is one of the most heavily mortgaged carriers in America. It has a net bonded debt of more than $527,947,000 and a total funded debt exceeding $800,000,000. Well over $113,000,000 of its debt obligations will mature within the next ten years.

Many times since the Great Depression, Wall Street analysts have thought the road would not be able to avoid reorganization. As recently as 1946 there was considerable doubt about the system's solvency when its operating ratio (the percentage of operating revenue consumed by operating expenses) climbed above 90 per cent. That ratio last year was still high at 82.8 per cent—the average for all major roads was around 76 per cent.

The Central has been known for generations as a first-rate passenger carrier. Yet, financially speaking, its passenger business has been a millstone around its neck. For years, except during a World War II interval when troop movements were heavy, the road has lost money on passenger traffic. This drain has been particularly severe since the war because of sharply higher labor and passenger terminal costs and a steep falling off in passenger revenues.

Last year the Central's net revenue from railway freight operations amounted to about $177,500,000 after operating expenses while its passenger operations resulted in a revenue deficit of about $37,000,000. Its total operating revenue was at a record high of $825,348,776, and its net income was the best since 1944 at $34,002,039.

Although the New York Central officially came into existence on July 7, 1853, when ten small railroads in mid-state New York were consolidated, its first predecessor company received a charter in 1826. This was the seventeen-mile Mohawk and Hudson Rail Road, linking Albany and Schenectady. Its first train started service in 1831 and was hauled by one of the first locomotives in America, the DeWitt Clinton.

The ten railroads that united in 1853 had for some time been advertising themselves as "the central route" across the state and this is believed to have been the origin of the Central name. The new company was capitalized at $23,000,000—a sensational figure at the time—and boasted 154 wood-burning steam locomotives.

In 1869 Commodore Cornelius Vanderbilt, who had acquired control of the Hudson River Railroad connecting New York and Albany, effected its merger with the Central and became president of the combined line, renamed the New York Central and Hudson River Railroad.

The same year, three railroads between Buffalo and Chicago were consolidated into the Lake Shore and Michigan Southern Railroad. Commodore Vanderbilt obtained control of this line by 1873 and was elected president—and the New York-Chicago through route that became the Central's main line was established.

In 1914 the name was changed back to the New York Central Railroad Company when the Central, the Lake Shore and Michigan Southern and nine subsidiaries were consolidated.

[June 12, 1954]

1950–1959

The proxy battle over the New York Central Railroad in 1954 gained national attention.

A.F.L. and C.I.O Will Merge, Ending 20-Year Labor Split; Meany Will Head New Body

15 MILLION UNITING

The power of organized labor rose sharply in the 1930's and then again after World War II. Large unions that represented workers in major industries, particularly coal, steel and autos, had the power to severely damage the companies in the industry and to hurt the American economy.

In 1955, with the merger of the two largest labor organizations–the American Federation of Labor and the Congress of Industrial Organizations–it appeared that the power of labor was destined to grow even more. But in fact, it was peaking, and labor's power declined in coming decades.

In part, that was because organized labor came under attack politically, with investigations of corruption and a Congressional bid to strengthen the Taft-Hartley Law that had been passed over Truman's veto. In 1957, the newly unified labor movement was forced to split again, as the corruption-ridden Teamsters were kicked out of the A.F.L.-C.I.O. And in 1959, Congress passed the Landrum-Griffin Act, named for the two Republicans who sponsored it in the House, which imposed new reporting requirements on unions and tried to guarantee that union leaders were regularly subjected to elections among their members.

But the more important issues in the decline of labor power were less obvious. The large industrial companies that had the strongest unions–autos, steel and coal–were gradually becoming less important in the rapidly growing economy. Moreover, as the 1950's progressed and Europe and Japan rebuilt their industrial capacity, the threat of overseas competition grew. By the end of the century, that competition would force many unions to make concessions they never would have considered in the 1950's.

The coming decline was not apparent, however, when The Times reported plans for the merger and offered a profile of George Meany, the man who would be the main leader of organized labor for many years to come.

By A. H. RASKIN

Special to The New York Times

MIAMI BEACH, Feb. 9—A detailed formula for labor unity was approved today after twenty years of civil war.

The pact made it certain that the 15,000,000 members of the American Federation of Labor and the Congress of Industrial Organizations would come under one banner by the end of this year.

Every problem that could block a merger was overcome in the unity plan. Even the question of who would head the pooled organization was settled. He will be George Meany, now president of the A. F. L.

His opposite number in the C. I. O., Walter P. Reuther, announced that he would be happy to step aside in Mr. Meany's favor. William F. Schnitzler, secretary-treasurer of the A. F. L., will occupy the same post in the new group.

There was no formal name given as yet to the merged organizations. But the thirty-four unions now in the C. I. O. will go into it as a special department to be known as a Council of Industrial Organizations.

This will enable the group to preserve the initials that were used in the unionization of steel, automobile, rubber and other mass production industries in the early years of the split.

The ticklish issue of interunion raiding was settled through adoption of a joint declaration that the integrity of every A. F. L. and C. I. O. union would be preserved after the merger.

The new organization's constitution will contain a specific declaration that affiliated unions are to respect the established bargaining relationship of sister unions. It will call on all unions to avoid stealing members from one another.

The precise machinery for enforcing this anti-raiding provision was not specified. However, both sides agreed that "appropriate machinery" was to be established. Its nature was left to the committees charged with drafting a constitution.

In the meantime both groups will seek to get more unions to subscribe on a voluntary basis to the existing no-raid agreements between the A. F. L. and C. I. O. Seventy-seven of the 111 unions in the federation already have bound themselves to eschew poaching. On the C. I. O. side thirty out of thirty-four have signed.

These pacts are scheduled to expire at the end of this year. Part of the merger understanding is that the voluntary ban on raiding would be extended for two years. This would provide more time for implementation of the constitutional declaration against raids.

The A. F. L. will control the executive council of the merged organization by a margin of nearly two to one. In addition to the two chief officers, it will have seventeen vice presidents in the new body. The C. I. O. will have ten vice presidents.

The ratio roughly reflects the present membership strength of the two existing bodies. The A. F. L. claims 10,300,000 members. The C. I. O. reports membership fluctuating between 4,500,000 and 5,000,000.

The Federation, which now has fifteen vice presidents, will have to choose two more to fill its unity quota. The C. I. O. now has nine vice presidents, plus its president and secretary-treasurer. It is expected that Mr. Reuther and James B. Carey, secretary-treasurer of the C. I. O., will serve as vice presidents of the merged group, along with all but one of the present C. I. O. vice presidents.

Much of the authority now exercised by the A. F. L. Executive Council will pass to a nearly completed executive committee. This will consist of Mr. Meany, Mr. Schnitzler and six vice presidents—three from the A. F. L. and three from the C. I. O. Conventions of the new organization will be held every two years.

Twenty A. F. L. and C. I. O. executives signed the unity agreement at the Roney Plaza Hotel here this afternoon. They said its ratification would "materially benefit the entire nation" and add to the strength and effectiveness of the labor movement.

MEANY'S DREAM REALIZED

The dream of labor unity with himself as top man has been fulfilled for the Bronx unionist known as "The Honest Plumber."

George Meany wears the American Federation of Labor leadership mantle of Sam Gompers, the cigar maker, and William Green, the coal miner. He comes to his new command after a long union career. That career began here thirty-three years ago when he won election as business agent for Plumbers Local Union No. 463.

Titles do not impress Mr. Meany, but his sobriquet indicates the respect he has won among unionists and management groups.

He has no patience with double-dealing. A boss of a building trades union made an agreement with a struck Long Island plant to limit the number of pickets at each entrance. He then arranged to mobilize 2,000 strong-arm pickets for the next day's demonstration. Next he raced to Mr. Meany to tell him about the clever trick.

Mr. Meany, a smooth orator, lapsed into Bronx-isms like "dese" and "poissonally" (which he does when he gets excited), injected a few unprintables and has not talked to the local boss since that day.

The President of the United States, then Harry S. Truman, got a taste of Mr. Meany's determined manner, too, in 1951, when the White House called labor leaders for a conference. The purpose was to discuss labor's "strike" against defense agencies. Union officials felt they had been stripped of any real voice in preparedness. The President urged the unionists to rely on him to see to it that they got adequate representation.

Polite assents from the labor delegation greeted Mr. Truman's request. But Mr. Meany spoke up. "That doesn't take care of it, Mr. President." By the time the delegation left all issues had been spelled out, and nobody was upset.

Mr. Meany, born at 125th Street and Madison Avenue on Aug. 16, 1894, followed his father's footsteps as a plumber. Early in his life the family moved to the Bronx. At 16 young Meany decided that he had had enough full-time schooling and became an apprentice plumber. Five years later he became a journeyman and a full-fledged union member.

Mr. Meany rejected the stand maintained by his predecessor, Mr. Green, that it was up to the C. I. O. to "return to labor's house." He favored a mutual approach.

He is a maverick in the ranks of current-style labor bosses. These are inclined to favor the notion that they should act like business executives with chauffeur-driven limousines and big suites at fashionable hotels. Where some labor chiefs tend to be gaudy, Mr. Meany is serious and laconic. He is subdued even in his dress. He does favor, occasionally, pearl-grey vests and sometimes a bright tie.   [Feb. 10, 1955]

THE NEW YORK TIMES

George Meany, architect of labor unity.

1950–1959

The A. F. L. Executive Council is scheduled to give its blessing to the pact here tomorrow. The C. I. O. executive board will take similar action at a board meeting in Washington Feb. 24.

After this clearance, the same unity committees that drafted today's peace plan will work out full constitutional language. When the proposed constitution has been approved by the leaders on both sides, it will be submitted to separate conventions of each group. Then a joint convention will be held to finalize the merger.

No convention timetable was fixed. However, it was believed probable that both groups would seek to have all arrangements complete for a joint convention in the latter part of September.

The A. F. L. is scheduled to hold its regular convention in Chicago Sept. 15. The C. I. O., now set to meet in Buffalo Oct. 17, may shift its plans to mesh with those of the Federation on both city and date. This would make it easy to hold a joint ratification session without the expense of special conventions for both groups.

The amalgamation plan would protect the jobs of all persons now on the headquarters and field staffs of the two organizations. Overlapping state and city central bodies would be merged on a gradual basis over a two-year period.

The same gradualness would characterize the merging of individual unions now having similar jurisdictions. The pact provided that there was to be no compulsion on unions to get together. Where conflicts between unions exist, the new parent body would encourage—but not force—an effort to try to work out merger arrangements.

The charter recognized that industrial and craft unions were "appropriate, equal and necessary as methods of trade union organization."

It was this issue that touched off the original division in 1935. At that time the A. F. L. was dedicated to the protection of craft rights. Now the principle of industrial organization has gained such wide acceptance within the federation that this presented no real hurdle in the unity negotiations.

An industrial union is often described as a vertical union. Its members are in one industry from top to bottom. In this sense a craft union is described as horizontal. Its members are in the same skill stratum extending through several kinds of industry.

The new industrial department will have the right to maintain a separate treasury to finance organizing drives in such industries as chemicals. However, the bulk of the funds now held by the C. I. O. will be turned over to the merged group as part of a common central treasury.

The A. F. L. comes into the merger with $3,500,000 in cash, bonds and real estate. The C. I. O. is to put up roughly half as much, in recognition of its smaller membership. This will take virtually all of the $1,800,000 now held by the C. I. O.

However, the industrial group will have an opportunity to pile up additional funds for organizing by continuing to collect a per capita tax of ten cents a month. Under the merger, the central organization will get a payment of four cents a month for each member. This is the present A. F. L. rate. The difference between this and ten cents would stay with the industrial department.   [Feb. 10, 1955]

Avery Overcomes Drive by Wolfson to Control Ward

By ROBERT E. BEDINGFIELD

CHICAGO, April 22—Louis E. Wolfson conceded today he had lost the battle for control of Montgomery Ward & Co. to its chairman, 81-year-old Sewell Avery.

Before the counting of ballots began, he said his forces would get only three of the nine Ward directorships. Mr. Avery's group would thus win six.

The Florida financier made his estimate as the annual meeting of Ward shareholders got under way here at 10:30 A. M. in Medinah Temple, 600 North Wabash Street. He had earlier claimed voting strength sufficient to gain at least four places on Ward's board.

Mr. Avery, chairman since 1931, did not concede that the opposition would elect any directors. He declined to estimate his own voting strength.

Within the last year there have been more than thirty proxy contests for control of American corporations. Six of them were won by the insurgent groups, including the 1954 fights for the New York Central Railroad Company, the New York, New Haven and Hartford Railroad and the Minneapolis and St. Louis Railway Company.

The Wolfson forces' defeat in the Ward's contest marks the first time in 1955 that a major corporation has succeeded in turning back a bid for control.

Mr. Wolfson explained his sudden concession in this way: "We had expected four seats at least, right up until late last night. Then we were double-crossed. Some big foreign holders who had pledged their proxies to us washed out.

"But we are going to put three in," he added. "I bought 38,000 additional shares myself yesterday."

Three election inspectors, aided by proxy-counting clerks of the Corporation Trust Company of New York, will begin today a count of ballots that is expected to last three weeks.

The shareholders' meeting was the climax of one of the fiercest proxy contests in the history of corporate finance. The battle had raged since last Aug. 26. At that time Mr. Wolfson called reporters to his Madison Avenue offices in New York to confirm that he had been buying Ward's stock since early in 1954 with the aim of wresting control from Mr. Avery, Ward's unchallenged chairman since 1931.

Although today's session lasted for more than six hours and was attended by some 2,500 of Ward's 68,000-odd shareholders, it was a surprisingly quiet affair most of the time.

Mr. Avery received a long, warm ovation when he stepped to the rostrum of Medinah Temple's vast stage, which is used as a circus ring each March by the Shriners in their fundraising campaign for crippled children.

Mr. Avery opened the meeting but turned over the chair to Ward's vice president and secretary, John A. Barr, who also is a director. This action brought strong protests from the Wolfson supporters until Mr. Wolfson rose and said:

"Without showing or intending to show any disrespect of Mr. Avery, it seems clear that the chairman is not able to conduct this meeting. I would appreciate it if any of my supporters would accept Mr. Barr as the chairman."

Mr. Avery returned to the dais several times to address stockholders and to answer their questions. But he appeared to have considerable difficulty in forming his words and expressing his thoughts. He excused himself time and again, saying:

"I can't hear. Everything they are saying is a jumble. I am utterly confused by our friend who has a very hungry eye for Montgomery Ward."

Despite Mr. Wolfson's admonishment to his supporters, stockholders on several occasions addressed questions directly to Mr. Avery. One question, which proved

---

Sewell Avery was a very cautious man. That caution helped him save Montgomery Ward, one of the nation's largest retailers, during the Depression. It also led him to damage the company severely after World War II.

By 1955, the 81-year-old Avery was one of the best-known businessmen in America. In 1944, he had defied Federal Government orders to recognize unions at Ward's, and a photograph of him being carried out of the Montgomery Ward building in Chicago in a chair held by two soldiers ran in virtually every newspaper in America. He won that fight.

After the war, Avery expected a depression to arrive, and he husbanded the company's cash while his main competitor, Sears, Roebuck, expanded by building stores in the growing suburbs. Ward's executives who suggested doing the same were fired.

In 1955, Louis Wolfson, a Florida financier, mounted a proxy campaign to oust Avery. Avery fought bitterly, and won. Under the voting system being used, Wolfson could elect three of the nine directors, not enough to take control.

But to win, Avery had had to lose much of what he stood for. The Teamsters, who were trying to organize Ward's truck drivers, owned a large block of stock in union pension funds. Ward's recognized the Teamsters, and they voted their shares for Avery. There were unconfirmed rumors that in order to get support from some institutions, Avery promised to step down after winning. He did so within three weeks of his victory. His hand-picked successor did adopt expansion plans, but they were too little and too late. Ward's never did recover its former glory.

When The Times reported on Avery's victory, it also traced his history and his continuing fear that economic disaster was just around the corner.

1950–1959

highly unpopular with the meeting, was: "Mr. Avery, do you intend to resign as Ward's chairman?"

Mr. Avery replied: "If I am undesirable I'll step down very readily. I am vigorous physically, although during the last year I have been having difficulties with a medical attachment."

Mr. Avery reviewed his stewardship at Ward's over the last twenty-four years, recalling the "sad plight" in which he had found the company when he took it over in 1931. He emphasized his willingness to retire if need be, saying: "If I am unworthy of the job, I will cheerfully resign, but I can't sit down or back."

Mr. Barr called for nominations within a half an hour after the meeting began.

After nominations were closed, Albert M. Sheppherd, a stockholder, requested that the chair invite Mr. Wolfson to address the meeting. Mr. Wolfson spoke from the floor. He read a prepared statement in which he said his primary aim during the last several months had been to defeat the Ward's staggered system of electing directors.

"This is not a Wolfson nor an Avery company," he said.

He added that as a Ward director he would attempt to carry out all of his campaign promises by putting them in the form of a motion to the board. "I won't say that I'll do the greatest job, but no man will be willing to try harder than I shall."

At about 3:30 P. M., Mr. Barr announced that the polls would close within an hour and that it was planned to recess the meeting until 10:30 A. M., Friday, May 13. At that point both the management and the Wolfson proxy committees cast their ballots.

After the meeting Mr. Avery issued a statement thanking the stockholders for their expressions of confidence. He said: "We have over and over assured the stockholders, the press and the public that the contest would resolve itself, as it has, with the management retaining control. Outside of the holdings of his own group Mr. Wolfson received only a small minority vote."

Mr. Wolfson issued a statement tonight in which he asserted that he had not suffered a defeat but could actually "claim a tremendous victory."

"I have eliminated the stagger system," he said. "I have elected a minimum of three and possibly four to the board of directors of Montgomery Ward's private club of directors."

The impact of these results, he said, "will be felt in publicly owned companies across the country.

"As the significance of this victory becomes understood," he continued, "shareholders will recognize that they are not voiceless and directors and executives will become aware of the power of the investor to hold management to account for their stewardship."

"I am sorry," Mr. Wolfson said, "that Mr. Avery was subjected to this terrible trial. I wish it could have been avoided. It seems to me that it would have been only charitable, only proper respect for a great name in American industry, if those who surround Mr. Avery had had the decency to have spared him this."

[April 23, 1955]

Louis E. Wolfson, proxy warrior.

ASSOCIATED PRESS

CRISES AND CRITICS DON'T FAZE AVERY

In the depression year of 1894, a young man from Saginaw, Mich., received a law degree at the University of Michigan. He never practiced.

The story is that the young man, Sewell Lee Avery, chose law because he was weak in mathematics. Somewhere along the line, to judge from the balance sheet of Montgomery Ward & Co., he overcame this weakness.

Mr. Avery has been Ward's chief executive since Nov. 1, 1931. In March, 1932, just three months after assuming the chairmanship, Sewell Avery signalized his complete control by taking over the presidency as well.

By the time he had been president three years, earnings of the Chicago mail order house had leaped from a $9,000,000 deficit to a $9,000,000 profit.

But even before going to Ward, Mr. Avery was a successful business man.

When the United States Gypsum Company was formed at the turn of the century, one of its constituent concerns was the Alabaster Company, a gypsum-producing concern of Alabaster, Mich. With the Alabaster Company, United States Gypsum obtained the services of the concern's secretary, Sewell Avery.

Mr. Avery served initially as Eastern sales manager for the budding enterprise. In 1902, when the company's offices were established in Chicago, he returned to the Midwest. Three years later he was elected president—then a $6,000-a-year job. He held the post until a few years ago, and is still a board member.

Under Mr. Avery's direction, United States Gypsum prospered. It also prepared for adversity. A month before the 1929 stock market crash the company laid off 2,000 men. It went into the troubled Thirties with a $35,000,000 surplus.

Ward's was an old and a big business—in its way a national institution—in 1931 when J. P. Morgan and Co. offered Sewell Avery $100,000 a year, plus an option to buy 100,000 shares of Ward common at $11 a share, to take over.

At the time, the option did not look like any windfall. Wall Street greeted the change in management at Ward by letting the stock fall to $3.50 a share. The option, however was good until 1936. By then Ward common was selling at $68. Mr. Avery bought more than 60,000 shares.

The Avery charm, drive and ability soon were producing results. Occasionally a top official would depart from the company, but that was hardly unusual for an enterprise as big as Ward. One of the first to leave was Walter Hoving, vice president and general sales manager. He is now president of the Hoving Corporation, which owns Bonwit Teller, Inc., one of New York's most successful women's specialty stores.

By 1939, however, when three vice presidents departed at various times during the year, there were rumblings that Ward was gradually becoming a one-man operation. The whisperings of friction between Sewell Avery and his executive assistants grew louder during World War II.

They were fully confirmed in 1948 when the president, Wilbur H. Norton, and all the vice presidents threatened to resign in a body unless they were permitted to exercise the normal functions of their offices without interference.

Mr. Avery let them go.

Mr. Avery never has been a man to compromise his convictions, and by stubbornly being himself he has supplied his enemies with plenty of ammunition. During the New Deal era he expressed himself freely concerning the Administration. During the war he defied War Labor Board attempts to force recognition of a union.

In 1944, when Ward was seized by order of President Roosevelt, Mr. Avery had to be carried bodily out of his office, cradled in the arms of two soldiers. It did nothing to improve his opinion of New Deal policies and of some of his business contemporaries who, he believed, had compromised themselves to "play ball" with Washington.

A defiant Sewell Avery in 1944.

Mr. Avery is as well known for his abiding fear of depressions as he is for his inability to get along with his subordinates who don't share his views. After World War II he made it company policy to conserve cash in anticipation of a collapse in the general economy.

Mr. Avery is a great believer in charts. He has been greatly influenced by one in particular, prepared by a Ward economist. It traced the course of commodity prices for the years 1805 to 1945 and with stress on four war periods: the Napoleonic War of 1812, the Civil War and World Wars I and II.

The chart indicated, contrary to popular impression, that there had been no long uptrend of commodity prices. Just prior to World Wars I and II, for example, they were substantially lower than in 1805-07 or 1855-57. In each past war period, prices soared, only to plunge when peace returned. There was a remarkable continuity to the pattern. "Who am I," Mr. Avery asks, "to argue with history?" [April 23, 1955]

1950–1959

Ford Stock to Go on Sale to the Public in January, Ending Family's Sole Rule

Among the great industrialists of American history, none was as hostile to bankers as Henry Ford. In the early days, his company did have minority shareholders, but after a suit by some shareholders forced him to distribute profits to them in 1919, he bought back their stock. The Ford Motor Company remained private, although the family donated a large amount of non-voting stock to the Ford Foundation, a charitable institution.

Not until 1955, eight years after the death of the founder, was Ford Motor willing to sell shares to the public. It was reorganized to allow shares sold by the foundation to vote, and the foundation sold 10.2 million shares in early 1956, raising 642.6 million for itself while underwriters—including nearly every major firm on Wall Street—shared in 15.3 million in underwriting fees. It was by far the largest initial public offering of stock up to that point.

When Henry Ford II, the founder's grandson, announced the plans to go public, The Times covered the announcement and, in an editorial the next day, described Ford's move as "in the American tradition." It also recalled how the first Henry Ford had felt about doing business with Wall Street: "Stockholders, to my way of thinking," Mr. Ford had declared, "ought to be only those who are active in the business and who will regard the company as an instrument of service rather than as a machine for making money."

By A. H. RASKIN

Common stock of the Ford Motor Company, the world's largest family-owned industrial empire, will go on public sale in January for the first time.

The way was cleared for the biggest stock offering in financial history by an announcement yesterday that the Ford family would relinquish majority control over the company founded by Henry Ford fifty-two years ago.

Sixty per cent of the voting power will go to holders of the new common stock; 40 per cent will stay with the family. The decision to let the public share the wheel with the Ford heirs means that industry's richest and most tightly held "closed corporation" will have to lift the blinds that have concealed its profits from outside scrutiny. How much the company earned always has been closely guarded.

The initial sale of 6,952,293 Ford shares is expected to bring in $400,000,000 to $500,000,000. This would indicate a price of $60 to $70 a share, although no official determination has yet been made.

The stock will not be offered by the company but by the Ford Foundation, which made the announcement. This is the giant philanthropic trust the family set up in 1936 to make grants for the promotion of human welfare in a broad area of national and world affairs.

The foundation owns 88 per cent of all Ford stock, but none of it has voting power. Under the present stock arrangement, full voting power resides in 172,645 shares of family-owned stock. The stock-sale plan involves an intricate shift in the whole financial base of the company. The total number of shares will rise from 3,495,040 to 53,461,470, and the family will surrender three-fifths of its control.

The desire of the foundation trustees to diversify their investment portfolio was a major factor in the decision of the Ford family to permit the sale of the Ford stock.

Henry Ford, seated in a Quadricycle, with his grandson Henry Ford II in October 1946.

The family shared the trustees' belief that it was unsound for the foundation to put all its eggs in one basket.

After the initial stock distribution, Ford will join General Motors, Chrysler and 1,100 other corporations whose securities are listed on the New York Stock Exchange. Keith Funston, president of the exchange, hailed the Ford decision as "a landmark in the history of public ownership" of American business.

Ford, with 193,000 employes and assets that a year ago totaled more than $2,000,000,000, is operating at a profit rate that exceeds the company's total earnings for all the twenty-one years preceding World War II. It expects to produce 2,500,000 automobiles and trucks this year, more than one-quarter of the national total.

The decision to let the public share in the company's ownership and control reversed a policy its founder set when he and eleven associates started the enterprise in 1903 with an actual cash investment of only $28,000.

Sixteen years later, after some of his fellow stockholders had questioned the wisdom of his expansion plans, Mr. Ford and his son, Edsel, bought the others out and full control passed into the hands of the family.

The policy shift in favor of public sale was made by agreement of the Ford heirs and the foundation trustees after more than two years of negotiation. Charles E. Wilson, former president of the General Electric Company, chairman of the foundation's finance committee, and Sidney J. Weinberg, banker and director in a dozen large corporations, were reported principally responsible for persuading the family to let the public share the driver's seat.

The plan calls for basic recapitalization of the company. At present, the family holds all 172,645 shares of voting stock. In addition, there are 3,322,395 shares of Ford stock with no voting rights.

The refinancing program calls for splitting the 3,322,395 shares of nonvoting stock on a fifteen-for-one basis. The family-owned voting stock would be split on a twenty-one for one basis. The difference was intended to compensate the family for its willingness to give up its sole right to vote on management affairs.

Wall Street experts noted that effective control of the company was virtually certain to remain with the family, even after the transfer of 60 per cent of the voting rights to outsiders. In practice, the holders of 5 to 10 per cent of the stock usually are able to exert a controlling voice in the affairs of a corporation that has large numbers of stockholders.

One unusual aspect of the Ford stock program is that all the money to be realized from sales to the public will go for charitable purposes. None will be used to help pay for the company's expansion program or to provide working capital.

It was believed likely that as many as 500 brokerage houses would be involved in the Ford sale. The demand for shares is likely to be so strong that many Wall Street analysts predicted that an allocation system would have to be devised to guarantee that the distribution would be handled equitably. Some said they were sure that the issue would be oversubscribed on the first day.   [Nov. 7, 1955]

1950–1959

Climate Control Finds Big Market

By JOHN A. BRADLEY

There is probably no better example of how long it can take for an invention to move into broad use than the case of air-conditioning.

The air-conditioner was invented in 1902 by Willis H. Carrier, and by the 1920's movie theaters were cooled. But it was not until 1951 that the Carrier Corporation's profits took off as homeowners began to buy the machines. By the mid-1950's, home builders had discovered that air-conditioners, especially central air-conditioners, were a big selling point, and new subdivisions began to get them routinely.

Air-conditioners also meant that developers did not need to worry about air circulation in designing windows for homes. One result was that suburban homes could be designed with less regard for the sites upon which they would be built. That helped to create the uniformity that would later come to characterize the 1950's.

Rapid gains are forecast for this year in the sale of central air-conditioning units for dwellings. There has been a steady rise in the past three years in the use of the central systems as opposed to the use of single units in individual rooms. The increase is expected to continue this year and some predictions here have been made that it may nearly double that of 1955.

Efforts are being made by some manufacturers to have home builders include the air-conditioning equipment in the price of the dwelling. Some of the leaders in the field believe that it will not be long before the air-conditioners are included as standard equipment in new dwellings along with the range, refrigerator and other kitchen installations.

This trend was believed to have been foreshadowed last week when Levitt & Sons, Inc., signed a contract for the purchase of 702 central air-conditioning units to be installed in dwellings in Levittown, Pa. The contract was signed by William J. Levitt, president of the building concern, and Cloud Wampler, chairman and president of the Carrier Corporation.

The conditioners will be included in dwellings to be completed this year in the Country Club section of the Pennsylvania development. The houses are to be priced at $18,990. The buildings will have three bedrooms, two baths and two-car garages.

This model without air-conditioning has been priced at $17,500. The difference in price, it was explained, does not represent the cost of the air-conditioning equipment. Changes also have been made in the style of refrigerator and other kitchen equipment, it was said, which are included in the new price.

The Levitt purchase was described by Mr. Wampler as the largest single transaction in the home air-conditioning field. Estimating that the industry will have a total retail volume of about $3,200,000,000 in 1956, Mr. Wampler said the biggest gain will be in home installations. The industry's retail sales for 1955 are estimated at $2,900,000,000.

Central systems which air-condition the entire home have also gained in popularity. Mr. Wampler said about 200,000 of these systems will be installed in dwellings during the next twelve months. There were 50,000 such installations in 1953, 75,000 in 1954 and 125,000 in 1955.

Improvements in design have increased the efficiency of air-conditioning equip-

Shoppers look over new air-conditioners in 1955.

ARTHUR BROWER/THE NEW YORK TIMES

ment and mass production has brought down the cost. Research development by the Institute of Boiler and Radiator Manufacturers has opened up a new field for air-conditioning in houses heated by a hot water system.

The work has been carried out in cooperation with the University of Illinois at a six-room test house in Urbana, Ill., under the direction and supervision of university staff members. Warren S. Harris, research professor who directed the study, reported that centralized summer cooling with chilled water is now economical for any house heated by hot water.

Professor Harris reported that the system used in the research house produced satisfactory room air temperature humidity control with no compromise as far as winter heating performance was concerned. As to the operating costs, he said they were comparable to those of other successful systems.

Although air-conditioning for the home is expected to show the greatest gain for this year, the industry is prepared for increased business to supply the needs of stores, offices and factories. With the trend toward complete home weather control there are expected to be changes in the residential heating business.

Builders also will be alert to the changes. After a few developments have offered new dwellings complete with air-conditioning, other builders will have to meet the competition.

The condition also will have an effect on the sale of "used" homes. The older dwellings will be less desirable unless central air-conditioning units are installed.

[Jan. 8, 1956]

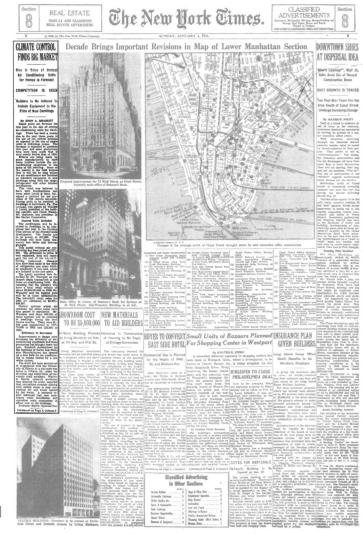

1950–1959

AIR-CONDITIONING, A HOT EXPORT, IS COOLING OFF TROPICAL CLIMES

By BRENDAN M. JONES

A sheikh's palace, a Hong Kong theatre, a Pakistani naval station or even a Borneo native hut may all have something in common these days—American air-conditioning. An increasing variety of places abroad are being cooled with this distinctly American "institution." As a result, exports of American air-conditioning units are rising sharply.

Their value last year, by conservative estimate, was a record exceeding $60,000,000. They have increased during the last year or two at a rate of 35 per cent. Demand is vigorous, and the industry cheerfully regards the trend as still in the beginning stage.

Moreover, the recent rate of increase is expected to be maintained through the next several years. About two-thirds of exports are self-contained units, the balance are central systems. This country has about 90 per cent of world markets in the self-contained category, about 75 per cent in other kinds.

Economic progress producing higher living standards in many lands, and sales promotions are obvious factors in the boom.

Air-conditioning abroad cannot be compared with its much more advanced development in this country. But it has made notable gains in just the last few years.

Although coolness is the chief benefit sought, working efficiency, health and prestige also motivate foreign purchases. A fully automatic telephone exchange in Malaya, for instance, has been equipped with air-conditioner and electrostatic equipment to protect the mechanism from dust and tropical mold.

Air-conditioning has become a "must" in modern tourist facilities burgeoning in tropical and other areas. It also is becoming more common in government and professional offices and in homes.

Air-conditioning abroad turns up in unexpected places, for instance, that native-hut job. The order was handled by a Carrier Corporation branch in British North Borneo.

An oil company's night shift drillers, working at Brunei, found that daytime sleep in their hut was next to impossible because of the heat and noise. Carrier sent a conditioner by helicopter, the hut was sealed up and presently it resounded to air-cooled snores.

Air-conditioning abroad may indeed become one of the "great levelers" as its popularity grows. Meanwhile, it illustrates how new products can sustain United States exports.   [May 26, 1957]

Do Giant Computers Pay Off? For Big Concerns, Anyhow, Yes

The computer revolution was slow to conquer the world, let alone the United States.

In 1958, 12 years after the Eniac computer was first exhibited, The Times reported that some large companies were saving money by using them but that smaller companies had hesitated to take the plunge. Computers were, to say the least, still a specialty item.

Three years later, in 1961, a survey reported in The Times found that 5,371 computers had been installed since the Eniac machine was built.

By ALFRED R. ZIPSER

Huge electronic computers are more than earning their keep in large corporations. Dollars-and-cents operational savings as well as incalculable improvements in efficiency in all types of business organizations were reported last week. It appears the Big Business is sold on computers.

The recession has made small and medium size companies take a long look at the data processing devices before ordering them. Only a year ago these companies were determined to install them as were larger concerns.

High purchase or rental charges as well as installation expenses are causing the small and medium size companies to consider carefully the replacement of clerical and other systems by computers, even when they know the long-range savings are assured. The devices sell for $35,000 to $3,000,000. Rental charges run from $1,000 to $60,000 a month.

Installation, which includes a site and providing essential temperature and humidity control for the machines, costs from $75,000 to $100,000 more. Programming, or arranging data on production, inventory engineering and other functions to be processed, takes another $100,000 to $400,000.

All these costs make the computers less and less attractive to small concerns, hard pressed by falling sales, earnings and working capital. They do not worry the large companies, and these are making the computer makers richer.

Increases in orders from big companies were reported by the principal computer producers. These are International Business Machines Corporation, the Remington-Rand division of the Sperry Rand Corporation, the computer division of the Bendix Aviation Corporation, the Datatron division of the Burroughs Corporation, the Radio Corporation of America, the National Cash Register Corporation and the Datamatic Corporation, a subsidiary of the Minneapolis-Honeywell Regulator Corporation.

An example of savings achieved and the attitude toward computers by top managements of big companies was offered last week at an American Management Association's computer conference. It was set forth by R. B. Curry, controller of the Southern Railway Company, other railroads and several enterprises that serve fourteen states.

Mr. Curry's organization began operation of an I.B.M. 705 giant computer in January, 1957. The computer has saved the company $850,000 in clerical costs in its year of operation. Mr. Curry said he believed this annual savings rate would reach $1,250,000 to $1,500,000 in another year.

The computer rents for $50,000 a month. Mr. Curry, after giving a description of its functions and the savings effected, quoted H. A. De Butts, president of the Southern Railway. Asked if the computer really would save the system money at the time of its installation, Mr. De Butts said:

"Well, they tell me it will more than save its cost when it gets going—and it had better get going or I'll save

I.B.M. technicians working on descendants of Eniac in 1958.

it at a lot faster rate by eliminating the salaries of the officers who recommended it."

Apparently Mr. De Butts now is satisfied.

Another cost savings testament for the I. B. M. 705 was supplied by John S. Woodbridge, controller of Pan American World Airways, Inc. He said the device was paying for itself a few weeks after it was installed in 1954.

"Right off the bat, " Mr. Woodbridge added, "we picked up $350,000 a year in interest by our ability to process bills for the airline clearing houses in two days instead of two weeks."

The General Electric Company has one of the most ambitious computer networks in the country. Eleven giant computers, one Remington Rand-Univac and ten I. B. M. "700 series" machines, are in plants in this country and Canada. In addition, twenty-nine so-called medium capacity computers made by I. B. M. and Datatron have been installed. If bought outright, the network would have cost more than $25,000,000.

James W. Pontius, General Electric electronic data processing development consultant, said that all machines were rented. He declined to give the total monthly charges, but said the system, installed in October, 1954, was paying for itself and achieving savings in two to four years.

Mr. Pontius said General Electric had on order three additional large computer systems and at least fifteen medium capacity ones for delivery in a year or so.

A Remington-Rand Univac, installed at the East Pittsburgh plant of the Westinghouse Electric Company at a yearly rental of $400,000, paid for itself in the first eight months. It has been saving substantial sums ever since at the plant, which turns out electric motors, turbines and generators.

J. Stanley Hill, second vice-president and actuary of the Minnesota Mutual Life Insurance Company, said a Burroughs Datatron computer installed last August would be paid off in four years by operational savings. The computer cost $400,000.

"In addition," Mr. Hill said: "We are certain that once the original investment is paid off we are in for a net savings of $1,000,000 over a ten-year period." [March 9, 1958]

I.B.M. CORPORATION

1950–1959

Plot Thickening in an Auto Drama
STAGE SET FOR 3-WAY FIGHT FOR SMALL-CAR MARKET

By the mid-1950's, the automobile industry seemed to be getting more and more like the fashion industry, with new styles each year that Americans were expected to line up to buy. But while the Big Three companies—General Motors, Ford and Chrysler—were happily competing on style and offering the larger cars that had good profit margins, a significant opportunity was being opened for European makers and for the two remaining smaller American companies, American Motors and Studebaker. They offered small cars that cost less and had better fuel economy, and their sales began to rise.

In 1959, the three American makers began selling their own small cars, for the 1960 model year. The Ford Falcon, Chevrolet Corvair and Plymouth Valiant initially cut into the sales of imports and damaged American Motors, which was destined to be acquired by Chrysler many years later, and Studebaker, which stopped making cars in 1963. But the quality of the American brands soon became suspect, and while most European makers saw American sales drop, there was another competitor. In the fall of 1958, The Times carried a wire story reporting that Toyota and Nissan had shipped a total of 500 cars to the United States, and that Toyota hoped to ship as many as 200 a month, "if there is a demand for that many." There was.

The Corvair became a huge embarrassment for General Motors after a young lawyer named Ralph Nader wrote a book titled "Unsafe at Any Speed" that was published in 1965 and claimed the car had a badly designed suspension system that could cause the driver to lose control during turns. Hoping to discredit the book, G.M. hired detectives to try to find dirt on Nader. G.M. was forced to apologize, making Nader a celebrity and providing both the launching pad for a consumer movement and the impetus for enactment of Federal auto safety legislation in 1966.

The Times reported on the surge of imports and the response of the American makers on Oct. 16, 1959. More than a year earlier, a Times Magazine article had detailed the increased reliance that auto makers were putting on "flash and fire power" to lift sales and pointed out the risks that that entailed.

By RICHARD RUTTER

The stage has been set for the automotive battle of the year—and of many years. It's a three-sided contest, involving the American industry's "Big Three" manufacturers, independent domestic producers and foreign manufacturers. The prize is the rapidly growing small-car market.

In the opinion of some observers, the upshot could be a stand-off with all parties involved hitting a golden jackpot of sales in 1960.

The conflict became inevitable when the Big Three—General Motors Corporation, Ford Motor Company and Chrysler Corporation—decided to bring out their own compact, lower-price models. These are, respectively, G.M.'s Corvair, Ford's Falcon and Chrysler's Valiant.

The decision of the auto industry giants to enter the small-car field came only after long deliberation and careful planning. In a sense, it was a forced decision, imposed by the spectacular success of the compact models. This phenomenon actually dates back several years to the beginning of imports of foreign cars in volume. That volume has swollen to the point where it may exceed 600,000 cars this year.

There are now more than 15,000 dealers handling eighty-one foreign makes. These now account for about 10 per cent of all sales in the United States. More than 1,000,000 cars made overseas are now rolling along American highways. More than half are 1958 and 1959 models, reflecting the recent upsurge in sales.

If one single factor had to be cited for the public acceptance of foreign models it would undoubtedly be price. Gasoline economy, ease of handling, style and just plain novelty also have been attractions. But a lower-than-American price has furnished the major impetus to the expansion of the imported-car market. Automotive News, the trade publication, estimates that some seventy foreign models retail here for $1,800 or less.

Beetle invasion: By 1958, Volkswagen was producing a car a minute.

The two domestic companies that so far have offered the most direct competition to foreign models are American Motors Corporation and Studebaker-Packard Corporation. For them the battle of the small car may well be the most critical of all, involving their very survival. Both companies have concentrated on compact models with notable results.

The story of American Motors with its now-famous Rambler is certainly one of the most striking in America's recent industrial history. Only a few years ago, when it was still turning out the Nash and Hudson lines, the company was deep in the red. Then it switched to the compact Rambler—and zoomed to success. Earnings last year were $26,085,134.

The profits for nine months ended June 30 came to $49,509,962 against $14,583,416 in the 1958 period. The company sold 351,000 cars in the past model year and expects sales of 500,000 this year. The main problem has been meeting demand.

How does American Motors regard the coming competition from the Big Three with their prestige, vast promotional and dealer resources? George Romney, ebullient president of the company, is not daunted.

He commented:

"We look at the Big Three entry into the Rambler field as one of the biggest product endorsements any car has ever received. It is now becoming generally evident that the Rambler success formula is going to revolutionize the American automobile market.

"One big question about the compact market at this minute is the speed with which the compact car will dominate the total car market.

"Rambler has the advantage of leadership in the basic compact car concept, in the single-unit aircraft construction concept, in sales and in public approval for sparking this revolution in consumer benefit. On top of this, we've got their present programs surrounded with not one, but with three different compact models. We also have them surrounded price-wise. The Rambler American costs less and the Rambler economy six just slightly more.

"The Big Three entry is a threat not principally to us but to their own big cars. The Big Three have joined us in annihilating the big-American-car myth and the compact car rush is now on."

Studebaker-Packard also has gone from red to black ink since bringing out its compact Lark. Earnings in the first half of this year were $12,073,281. In the 1958 period this company lost $13,314,164. In 1956, the deficit was $43,318,257.

Here, too, there is confidence about the possible Big Three threat. Studebaker sold about 140,000 cars in the model year just ended and expects a 33 per cent increase next year to 175,000 or 180,000 units.

In a recent press conference, Harold Churchill, president, called the Big Three entry a "plus" factor for his company. He said:

"All the promotion that is now getting under way is going to increase greatly the desire of the American car buyers for sensible automobiles." Mr. Churchill has remarked that compact cars offer the only growth market. He observes that their

1950–1959

DETROIT'S BILLION-DOLLAR GAMBLE

By JOSEPH C. INGRAHAM

Within ninety days the automobile industry will gamble more than a billion dollars on its new cars–the 1961 models that will not appear in dealers' showrooms until twenty-seven months from now.

This calculated risk, representing cost of design, retooling, dies, and so on, is not to Detroit's liking but it has no choice, for one of the hard facts of automobile life is that buyers' preferences must be gauged eighteen to thirty months before cars are ready for market. From the industry's point of view, the 1959 models are history, at least as far as style, shape and power plant go. Even the 1960 models are well under way, with only costly crash redesigning possible at this late stage.

Whether the 1959 cars–keyed to flash and fire power–will lift the industry out of its depressed state is something that only time will determine. At the moment, with sales down to the lowest point in six years, an increasingly vocal section of the public has been complaining that the familiar Detroit product is not what it wants, or will buy.

In self-defense, the auto makers point out that, bad as 1958 may be, they expect to sell 4,200,000 American-built cars this year, and that the plushiest cars with the fanciest trim and the extra-cost power and gadgets are the leaders in each line. But there is no doubt that if the 1959 models fail to win a big audience, and if inexpensive foreign models keep cutting into profits, Detroit will start building its own "compact" cars in another year or two. The tentative plans are there, the machinery is available, but the industry is unable to gear itself to faster change in response to shifts in public taste.

An automobile is an assembled product of more than 13,000 parts. The forces that shape it are just as diverse, and, like the car itself, must be welded into a cohesive pattern two or three years ahead of introduction. Before the public, which is a key force in the whole business, gets a peek at a car, the engineers, the sales force, the stylists, the color artists, the body design experts, the production managers and the top factory management all have had their say–and at length.

But the public is in the act from the start, too. Designing a new model begins with trying every kind of market research technique to find out what the prospective customer says he wants. Microphones are planted in showroom displays to eavesdrop as he looks over current offerings; elaborate "dream cars" are displayed at auto shows; opinions are sought by door-to-door canvass; and 6,000,000 lengthy questionnaires are sent out each year.

About 2,000,000 replies to these questionnaires come back. The information gleaned from them is classified, for competitive reasons, but it serves as the main springboard for designers' and engineers' future thinking. The industry concedes that the method is not infallible, for many persons answer one way and want the opposite. One of the big makers supplemented the standard questionnaire–asking the customer to check his preferences in order of importance–by asking, "What kind of car does your neighbor want?" For himself the customer said he wanted economy, durability and simple conservative styling. His neighbor wanted a powerful, flashy-looking vehicle. The company built the "neighbor's" car–and had highly successful sales.

Once consumer preferences are established, Detroit is ready to crystallize its new car designs. While the survey teams have been busy, so have the engineers and the advanced stylists. All work in a cloak-and-dagger atmosphere for the automobile business is a high-investment, high-risk enterprise.

The car must be vigorously competitive. The basic package must be set. How big or how small, how high or how wide is the new car to be? Performance (Detroit's new cover word for "horsepower," which the industry has agreed not to mention in the interest of public safety) is discussed.

The paper program for the future model is put into a book crammed with infinite detail. The company now knows everything about the new car except how it will look.

Now it is time for the stylists and the sales force to move in. They have replaced the engineers as kingpins of the industry, for it is eye appeal that sells cars, says Detroit. "Everyone takes mechanical function for granted."

By definition, the stylist is a man (women, so far, specialize only in colors and interiors) who is dissatisfied with everything and restless for the arrival of the future. Styling means building cars out of ideas. But form must follow function and once the package is set changes can be costly. Thus, the stylist and the engineer are constantly at war.

The stylists may personally cringe at chrome but they put it on lavishly. The public wants it, they say, and to prove their point they note that the 1958 leader in the medium-priced field is the metal-decked Oldsmobile, known throughout the country as the "king of chrome." Of course, chrome–jewelry to the stylists–does not always sell cars. Buick, for example, which is almost as heavily chromed as Oldsmobile, is having its second poor year in a row. But the industry sticks to its precept that "$10 worth of chrome does more for sales than $100 worth of engineering."

The stylist's role is so dominant that he often can compel engineering changes to gain eye appeal. Safety engineers, who naturally would like every piece of the car to be as safe as possible, fight a losing battle, too. They speak out against bomb-shaped bumper guards and sharp metal headlamp visors that can cause injuries, but so far, the stylist has been soundly supported by top management, which makes the final decision.

In a sense, however, car designing is a form of perpetual motion, and when a company is caught out on a sales limb with a drab model it must move fast to recoup. Chrysler managed the trick, in part, with hurriedly restyled 1955 models after its comfortable 1954 cars "flopped" because they were high and short, while longer and lower rivals enjoyed a sales boom. Then Chrysler took one of the industry's most sensational gambles and brought out its 1958 models a year ahead of schedule.

The result was the sweeping fins that made its 1957's a hit. Chrysler, as well as its competitors, believed the "forward look" would survive a second year. But sales this year are down and Detroit, with hindsight, now finds in Chrysler's experience confirmation of its belief that the public demands dramatic annual change.

Auto life was much simpler in the days of the Model T Ford. For fifteen years it was the market leader–and unchanged. Styling to Henry Ford was about as easy as the decision he made–and stuck to–when an assistant (there were no stylists in those days) asked how much floor space should be put between the back and the front seats. "Just leave enough room for the farmer's milk cans," said Henry.

[June 29, 1958]

high resale value, rather than the traditionally planned obsolescence of the auto industry, will stimulate public interest in the compact lines.

And what do foreign makers think about the Big Three competition? For the record at least, they are taking it in stride with no qualms about being "shut out" of the American market. A typical comment comes from Dr. Heinz Nordhuff, head of Volkswagen, which leads all imported makes in sales here. He finds:

"The coming of the compact car in the United States is a sound and sensible development from an engineering point of view as well as economically. I am quite convinced that these cars will be successful.

"It is my conviction, however, that these cars, still big by European standards and approximately 25 per cent higher in price than the Volkswagen, will not affect the sale of our cars in America. In the final analysis, price and value will be the deciding factors.

"In my opinion, 1960 will be the most interesting year in American automobile history and I sincerely admire the skill and the courage of the American auto engineers."

Renault is the second-ranking imported car in volume. The feeling among top officials at the American headquarters of Renault, Inc., is that the Big Three compact car will "not directly compete" with Renault's Dauphine or 4CV.

Simca, another leading import, is confident it will continue to get a sizable market share of the economy market and calls attention to the fact that its most popular models are priced well below the American-built economy cars.

All the leading foreign makers have increased their 1960 budgets for advertising in this country. Renault, for instance, leads the parade with a rise from $1,000,000 to $5,000,000.

It is noteworthy that, almost without exception, foreign makers stress lower prices as sort of an ace in the hole. Only American Motors, among the domestic producers, has attempted to meet this challenge directly. The company cut prices on some of the 1960 models by $40 to bring them below $1,800.

So there it is. Both domestic and foreign auto makers have openly welcomed the introduction of the Big Three models. Is this so much whistling in the dark? The outcome should be fairly clear, one way or the other, by this time next year. It shapes up, indeed, as a most interesting twelve months for the auto industry.

[Oct. 16, 1959]

To compete in the growing small-car market, General Motors introduced the Corvair . . .

1950–1959

. . . and Ford rolled out the Falcon.

1960–1969

A huge oil field was discovered in northern Alaska in 1968.

A Long Boom

THE 1960'S BEGAN WITH A YOUNG and handsome Presidential candidate vowing to get the country moving again. It was a promise that was kept. A recession in 1960 played a role in the election of that candidate, John F. Kennedy, and the economy proceeded to grow throughout his Administration and that of his successor, Lyndon B. Johnson. It was the longest expansion in American history.

With that expansion came a confidence that, within a few years, would look like hubris. By January 1969, as the Johnson Administration was preparing to leave office, the Economic Report of the President celebrated "prosperity without parallel in our history" and attributed that glorious state to the decision to cut taxes in 1964.

The economic boom allowed the bull market to continue to roar. As trading volume soared, Wall Street was unprepared to deal with it, however, and a paperwork crisis led to the New York Stock Exchange being forced to close on Wednesdays for much of 1968 to give back-office workers time to clear all the paper that was being generated. To cope with changes, brokerage firms needed to computerize and they needed more capital. To get it, they would turn to their own customers by going public in the 1970's.

The bull market also made possible a new kind of takeover. Conglomerates—companies that operated in numerous industries—became popular with investors.

The early part of the decade was a contentious time for many large companies. The Eisenhower Administration had brought price-fixing charges against virtually every company in the electrical equipment industry. And in 1962 President Kennedy angrily forced U.S. Steel to roll back a price increase (raising a ruckus in the process by blasting businessmen—he later explained he only meant steel executives—with a term of derision not used in polite company).

McDonald's gained national attention in the 1960's, making fast food increasingly available around the country, and bank credit cards began to proliferate, making credit easily available to millions whenever they wanted it. Jet planes began to fly passengers faster and in larger numbers than ever before. The railroads, meanwhile, were in deep trouble, although it was not yet clear just how severe the problems were.

On the oil front, there were two events whose importance stretched into the next decade and beyond. In 1960, after the major oil companies reduced the price they would pay to foreign countries for their oil, the countries banded together as the Organization of Petroleum Exporting Countries in an effort to push up prices. In 1968, a huge oil discovery was made at Prudhoe Bay in Alaska.

The most important stories of the decade were the civil rights movement, which had little immediate impact on business, and the Vietnam War, whose economic impact would become clear only later. Spending on the war stimulated the American economy and helped inflation to accelerate.

1960 John F. Kennedy is elected President in a narrow victory over Richard M. Nixon.

OPEC is formed.

1961 Alan B. Shephard Jr. becomes the first American in space in the Freedom 7 Mercury rocket.

East Germany builds the Berlin Wall.

1962 President Kennedy persuades the steel companies to rescind a price increase.

1963 President Kennedy is assassinated in Dallas, and Lyndon B. Johnson becomes President.

1964 Congress passes the Civil Rights and Economic Opportunity acts.

1965 Congress approves the Medicare program.

A power failure blacks out New York City and parts of nine Northeast states.

1966 Cesar Chavez leads farm workers in a strike and boycott against California's grape growers.

Congress enacts automobile safety standards.

1967 Thurgood Marshall becomes the first black Supreme Court justice.

Christiaan Barnard performs the first heart transplant.

1968 Martin Luther King is murdered in Memphis, Tenn.; Robert F. Kennedy is killed in Los Angeles.

A major oil field is discovered in northern Alaska.

1969 Richard M. Nixon is inaugurated President.

Neil Armstrong and Buzz Aldrin walk on the moon.

5 Big Electrical Concerns Charged With Bid Rigging

In his economic classic "The Wealth of Nations," Adam Smith observed: "People of the same trade seldom meet together, even for merriment and diversion, but the conversation ends in a conspiracy against the public, or in some contrivance to raise prices." That is most likely to happen in relatively stable businesses where competition is based less on innovation than on pricing and where there is a widespread perception that one supplier's product is no better than another's.

In the early 1960's, Justice Department investigations led to charges being filed against pharmacists in Northern California, milk suppliers in Baltimore, household movers and makers of asphalt. All were accused of fixing prices.

The most prominent cases involved the electrical equipment industry, whose major companies were named in a series of indictments that began with charges against five companies and 18 of their officers. The indictments laid out a well-organized conspiracy to allocate business among the companies and assure that prices were kept at acceptably high levels. More indictments followed, and eventually 29 companies and 45 of their executives pleaded guilty or no contest to charges of price-fixing, paying 1.9 million in fines. Seven of their executives served 30-day prison sentences.

To some, sending executives to jail sent a powerful message. But the brief jail terms—given only to policy-makers, not to those the judge thought were following orders—also seemed to indicate that fixing prices was far less serious than, say, burglary, even if it did cost victims far more money than any burglar could hope to realize. The lawyer for one executive pleaded with the judge not to put his client in jail "with common criminals who have been convicted of embezzlement and other serious crimes."

There is no way to ascertain just how large a deterrent effect such prosecutions have. But it is clearly not a permanent one. There would be more prosecutions of elaborate price-fixing conspiracies in the 1990's, in markets ranging from food additives to common stocks traded on the Nasdaq market.

By ANTHONY LEWIS

Special to The New York Times

WASHINGTON, Feb. 16—The country's five principal manufacturers of heavy electrical equipment and eighteen of their officers were indicted today on charges of rigged and collusive bidding in sales to Government and private industry.

A Federal grand jury in Philadelphia brought criminal antitrust charges against the General Electric Company, Westinghouse Electric Corporation, Allis-Chalmers Manufacturing Company, I-T-E Circuit Breaker Company and Federal Pacific Electric Company.

The indictments were the first results of a year-long investigation of the electrical industry, and the Justice Department hinted that there would be more soon. Its announcement called the cases "the first in a series of proceedings."

The Justice Department regards the cases as among the most important it has brought in recent years. Those filed today involve annual sales of more than $200,000,000, and the total under inquiry by the grand jury is between $1,000,000,000 and $2,000,000,000 in annual sales.

The indictments alleged a conspiracy among executives of the companies. These were some of the highlights in the charges:

¶ The companies allocated among themselves the percentage of Government business each would get on specific products—42 per cent for G. E., for example, and 38 per cent for Westinghouse on one item.

¶ Since the Government buys by sealed bids, the companies get their agreed percentage of business by arranging who would submit the low bid each time.

¶ On sales to private utilities and manufacturers, the companies agreed on a formula under which they took turns in submitting low bids. They called the formula "phase of the moon."

¶ The executives met dozens of times in cities all around the country to arrange their prices and bids, and they used code names in communicating with each other.

¶ On some items the companies agreed to raise prices simultaneously.

The maximum penalty for a violation of the Sherman Antitrust Act is a fine of $50,000 and, in the case of individuals, a year in prison.

The seriousness of the cases has been indicated by the board chairman of General Electric, Ralph J. Cordiner.

In an extraordinary statement last month, Mr. Cordiner said he had learned from the Philadelphia investigation—for the first time—that certain G. E. officials had violated the company's policy of strict compliance with the antitrust laws.

These officials' legal punishment "could be most severe," he said. But because the company had its own responsibility, he added, he had demoted the offenders and removed them from positions of responsibility in G. E.

A General Electric vice president, George E. Burens, and four general managers of G. E. divisions were among the individuals indicted.

Those named from G. E., aside from Mr. Burens, were R. W. Ayres Jr., Lewis J. Burger, Clarence E. Burke, Royce C. Crawford, G. R. Fink, N. F. Hentschel, Houston Jones, William H. Schick and Frank E. Stehlik.

The Westinghouse officials indicted were Landon Fuller, A. W. Payne, W. T. Pyle, J. W. Stirling and J. T. Thompson.

The three other individual defendants were from Allis-Chalmers—L. W. Long, Frank M. Nolan and David W. Webb.

The products involved in today's indictments are power switchgear assemblies and two kinds of circuit breakers. All are large items used in the generation and transmission of electricity.

An example of the conspiratorial activities charged by the grand jury can be spelled out from the indictment relating to the switchgear assemblies.

During the year 1956, the indictment charges, representatives of all the defendant companies except Federal Pacific met numerous times to allocate their sales to Federal, state and local governments.

At that time, it is charged, G. E. was given 42 percent of the business, Westinghouse 38, Allis-Chalmers 11 and I-T-E 9 per cent. The indictment continues:

"Particular bid invitations were discussed and one of the manufacturers was designated to submit the lowest bid for each invitation and thus secure that particular sale."

In 1958, it is charged, Federal Pacific got into the act. At a meeting on Nov. 9, 1958, at the Traymore Hotel in Atlantic City, the allocations were shifted to the following: G. E. 39 per cent, Westinghouse 35, I-T-E 11, Allis-Chalmers 8 and Federal Pacific 7 per cent.

From November, 1958, to October, 1959, the indictment says, the company representatives held "at least thirty-five" meetings in New York, Philadelphia, Chicago, Pittsburgh, Detroit, Newark, Louisville, Milwaukee and Cherry Hill, N.J.

"At these periodic meetings," the indictment says, "a cumulative list of sealed bid business secured by all the defendant manufacturers was . . . circulated and the representatives present would compare the relative standing of each company."

The meetings were also used, the indictment charges, to set the operation "phase of the moon" for sales to private industry.

The way this worked, according to the indictment, was that on each job one company would quote the low price, one an intermediate price and one the high. They rotated regularly, and the prices were fixed at percentages below or above known "book" or list prices.

Finally, the switchgear assembly indictment charges that at a meeting in September, 1959, the conspirators agreed to change the prices of certain products and to try to eliminate competition from some smaller companies not in the conspiracy.

One of the other two indictments charges a similar pattern of rigged bidding. The third deals only with alleged price-fixing and price increases arranged by the conspirators in one type of circuit breaker.

The three indictments charge that, as a result of the conspiracy, numerous Government agencies have been "forced to pay high, artificially fixed prices" for electrical products. Among the agencies named are the Tennessee Valley Authority and the armed services.

The Government also brought today companion civil cases seeking injunctions to prevent future activities of the kind alleged in the indictments.

The suits ask that the companies be made to issue new price lists drawn up independently, and that in the future they file affidavits along with any Government bids swearing that there has been no collusion in the bids.

Robert A. Bicks, acting chief of the Justice Department's Antitrust Division, was in general charge of the cases.

1960–1969

Both General Electric and Westinghouse asserted yesterday that they were opposed in policy to collusive actions restricting competition. They took pains to point out that all their employes had been told of this policy.

Mr. Cordiner said that regardless of what action may be taken by enforcement officials, General Electric would continue to refuse sanction to restrictive or collusive practices contrary to antitrust laws.

"Even if this were not a matter of law and business ethics, sound business judgment would argue against actions that restrict competition," he said.

"Nothing could be more self-defeating than to artificially impose a limitation on the business results of leadership by engaging in price restrictions."

Dale McFeatters, vice president of Westinghouse, said the actions charged to employes of his company were contrary to long-established policies.

"It is the objective of Westinghouse to comply fully with antitrust, marketing and trade regulation laws," he said. "No employe is authorized to participate in joint activity with competitors regarding prices."

He declared that the indictments mentioned products that had been declining, not rising, in price since 1957. If the unlawful acts did occur, he said, they did not benefit the company or hurt customers.

Harold S. Silver, general attorney for Allis-Chalmers Manufacturing Company, said at West Allis, Wis., that his company had fully cooperated with the Federal grand jury and had urged employes to do so.

Spokesmen for the I-T-E Circuit Breaker and Federal Pacific Electric reserved comment until they had received copies of the indictment.

The indictment of the electrical manufacturers by a Federal Grand jury brought this comment from James B. Carey, president of the International Union of Electrical, Radio and the Machine Workers:

"We who bargain collectively with General Electric for more than 100,000 of its employees find particularly ironic the fact that while this $1,000,000,000 corporation sanctimoniously lectures the trade union movement on moral and ethical responsibilities, G. E. itself displays increasing evidence of moral and ethical bankruptcy.

"G. E.'s hypocrisy is nowhere better manifested than in its announcement that it will resist any wage increase in 1960 because it might be inflationary, while at the same time profiteering extravagantly and outrageously at the expense of the Government and the American taxpayers." [Feb. 17, 1960]

A Westinghouse plant in East Pittsburgh, Pa. The company was one of many charged with price fixing.

World Oil Cartel May Take Shape

By J. H. CARMICAL

The formation of an international oil cartel may be in the offing. Sponsored by the governments of the oil-producing countries of Venezuela and the Middle East, such a cartel would control at the start some 85 per cent of the oil moving in international trade.

Discussed unofficially for more than a year, the drive by the major oil exporting nations for concerted action to control prices and limit exports received new impetus when Middle East crude oil prices were reduced by the major companies in August. A conference of these countries and Venezuela was called for Sept. 10 in Baghdad, Iraq, and a permanent organization of the participating countries was formed.

The conference ended on Sept. 15, with unanimous agreement for the formation of a coordinating organization to include four Middle East states and Venezuela, which would work for stable oil prices free from all unnecessary fluctuations and use all means to restore prices to the level existing before the recent reductions.

Further, the representatives of the conference pledged that their governments would join in a study of measures to maintain price stability, including schemes for limitation of production.

Iraq, Venezuela, Kuwait, Iran and Saudi Arabia were the founding members of the organization, but membership will be open to other important exporters if the charter members concur. The organization is to have a permanent secretariat. The next meeting is scheduled for Jan. 15, at Caracas, Venezuela.

Qatar, a sheikdom on the Persian Gulf, attended the Baghdad meeting as an observer and is expected to go along with the permanent organization.

Indications are that efforts will be made to get the Soviet Union, which is exporting some 360,000 barrels of oil a day to free world countries, to cooperate with the new organization.

Recently, President Betancourt of Venezuela was reported ready to send a delegation to the Soviet Union to discuss that country's undercutting of petroleum prices. Before the Baghdad meeting, Alfonos Pérez, Venezuelan Minister of Mines and Hydrocarbons, said he would sound out the Soviet Union with respect to what its attitude would be if a production-price control plan should be adopted.

What the Soviet attitude will be is anybody's guess. If the Kremlin thought that its cooperation with the group would further its political position abroad, the chances are that it would not hesitate to aid, if not join. Or Russia might agree to stay out of certain markets, if it were permitted a relatively free hand in some of the markets in which it is now selling oil.

As a result of the present excessive oil-producing capacity, any plan for price stabilization naturally takes on an added appeal to any oil exporting nation. Largely for that reason, some of the small exporting countries such as Colombia, Trinidad and Indonesia might join in the movement.

In the 1950's and 1960's, the world oil market was firmly under the control of the international oil companies. In 1960, angered by a decision by the oil companies to reduce the price being paid, countries that exported oil got together to attempt to form a cartel to push up the price of oil.

The Times reported on the move in an article that correctly analyzed the challenges the cartel was likely to face. In fact, the Organization of Petroleum Exporting Countries drew little attention in the United States until the aftermath of the 1973 Arab-Israeli war, when Arab oil producers embargoed oil sales to the United States and discovered that they had the power to set prices that they had dreamed of in 1960.

1960–1969

An oil well in Saudi Arabia, which helped form OPEC in 1960.

Generally, the oil companies are opposed to any such government cartel arrangement on international oil sales. They consider it impossible to establish a fair and workable program and they fear that the result, in the long run, would be a withering away of the market outlets, now enjoyed by the oil-producing countries that participated.

Even if the participating countries should include all now exporting oil in the free world, including the Soviet Union—and this is an assumption almost impossible to accept—it would be only a question of time before oil from new producing areas, substitutes such as oil from shale, and other forms of energy would come on the market in growing volume.

Prorating to market demand was instituted in Texas in the Nineteen Thirties because of overproduction and sagging prices. This has resulted in steadily rising prices, but Texas has lost ground in United States production because oil is produced in other states under less restrictive conditions. At present, the Texas wells are permitted to produce only eight days a month and their percentage of United States production last year was 38.2 per cent, against 44.7 per cent in 1948.

Exclusive of the Soviet Union and its satellites, there are forty-three countries producing oil in some volume. Of these, fifteen fall in the group of net exporters and they produce roughly 50 per cent of the free world's output.

For a production control program to be completely effective, all the fifteen major exporting areas would have to cooperate fully. Depending upon the basis of the prorating scheme, it is quite likely that some would have to hold exports at least to the present level, which would mean a static revenue from oil. To further their economy, most of the exporting nations must have a rising trend in exports.

It has been suggested that the basic factor in prorating oil production should be the proved oil reserves of each country. If that yardstick should be used exclusively, the Middle East countries, with their huge reserves, would be able to hold their position in the market. On the other hand, Venezuela's reserves are relatively small in proportion to present production and that country probably would have to cut back sharply.

The allocation of exports according to reserves also would produce disparities among the Middle East countries. Kuwait has the largest reserves of any of these countries and a formula based on reserves entirely would tend to increase Kuwait's dominant position further. With a population of only 250,000, Kuwait does not need any additional revenue from oil operations to carry out its program.

The position of Kuwait also has brought up the question of whether population should be considered in any allocation of exports. If not, it is argued that part of the revenue received by the relatively small sheikdom should be distributed among more heavily populated countries in the area.

Another problem connected with the attempt to base exports on reserves involves the difficulty of determining just what the reserves may be. The determination of the amount of oil underground is subject to many variables, and competent engineers nearly always reach different figures in making estimates.

Middle East oil prices now have been established by all companies at 4 to 10 cents a barrel below those prevailing on Aug. 9, when the price adjustments started. At first some of the companies cut deeper than that, but subsequently rescinded part of their cuts to make Middle East prices uniform. Despite the adjustments, the revenues accruing this year to the Middle East governments from oil operations will be some $100,000,000 greater than in 1959 when they amounted to $1,250,000,000. The increase will result from higher production.   [Sept. 25, 1960]

'Silent Spring' Is Now Noisy Summer
PESTICIDES INDUSTRY UP IN ARMS OVER A NEW BOOK

By JOHN M. LEE

The $300,000,000 pesticides industry has been highly irritated by a quiet woman author whose previous works on science have been praised for the beauty and precision of the writing.

The author is Rachel Carson, whose "The Sea Around Us" and "The Edge of the Sea" were best sellers in 1951 and 1955. Miss Carson, trained as a marine biologist, wrote gracefully of sea and shore life.

In her latest work, however, Miss Carson is not so gentle. More pointed than poetic, she argues that the widespread use of pesticides is dangerously tilting the so-called balance of nature. Pesticides poison not only pests, she says, but also humans, wildlife, the soil, food and water.

The men who make the pesticides are crying foul. "Crass commercialism or idealistic flag waving," scoffs one industrial toxicologist. "We are aghast," says another. "Our members are raising hell," reports a trade association.

Some agricultural chemicals concerns have set their scientists to analyzing Miss Carson's work, line by line. Other companies are preparing briefs defending the use of their products. Meetings have been held in Washington and New York. Statements are being drafted and counter-attacks plotted.

A drowsy midsummer has suddenly been enlivened by the greatest uproar in the pesticides industry since the cranberry scare of 1959.

Miss Carson's new book is entitled "Silent Spring." The title is derived from an idealized situation in which Miss Carson envisions an imaginary town where chemical pollution has silenced "the voices of spring."

The book is to be published in October by the Houghton Mifflin Company and has been chosen as an October selection of the Book-of-the-Month Club. About half the book appeared as a series of three articles in The New Yorker magazine last month.

A random sampling of opinion among trade associations and chemical companies last week found the Carson articles receiving prominent attention.

Many industry spokesmen preface their remarks with a tribute to Miss Carson's writing talents, and most say that they can find little error of fact.

What they do criticize, however, are the extensions and implications that she gives to isolated case histories of the detrimental effects of certain pesticides used or misused in certain instances.

The industry feels that she has presented a one-sided case and has chosen to ignore the enormous benefits in increased food production and decreased incidence of disease that have accrued from the development and use of modern pesticides.

The pesticides industry is annoyed also at the implications that the industry itself has not been alert and concerned in its recognition of the problems that accompany pesticide use.

Last week, Miss Carson was said to be on "an extended vacation" for the summer and not available for comment on the industry's rebuttal. Her agent, Marie Rodell, said she had heard nothing directly from chemical manufacturers concerning the book.

Houghton Mifflin referred all questions to Miss Rodell. The New Yorker said it had received many letters expressing great interest in the articles and "only one or two took strong objection."

American business has been subject to economic regulation at least since the 19th century. But environmental regulation was slow to arrive. In many ways, it owed its beginning to a book published in 1962—first as a series in The New Yorker—by Rachel Carson, a marine biologist formerly with the U.S. Fish and Wildlife Service. The book was harshly critical of the pesticide industry, saying that pesticides such as DDT were causing great damage to animals.

Within weeks, President Kennedy cited "Silent Spring" as he ordered a review of Goverment pesticide programs, but little was done by the Government until public concern crescendoed. In 1970, the Environmental Protection Agency was established, and two years later it banned DDT. Other "elixirs of death" that Miss Carson most deplored—such as chlordane, heptachlor, dieldrin and aldrin—also were banned. And while the use of pesticides rose, there was a shift away from long-lasting chemicals toward the types of pesticides that dissipate more quickly in the environment.

1960–1969

Rachel Carson, author of "Silent Spring."

In an interview, E. M. Adams, assistant director of the biochemistry research laboratory of the Dow Chemical Company, said he would be among the first to acknowledge that there were problems in the use or misuse of pesticides.

"I think Miss Carson has indulged in hindsight," he said. "In many cases we have to learn from experience and often it is difficult to exercise the proper foresight."

Emphasizing that he spoke as a private toxicologist, Mr. Adams said that in some procedures, such as large-scale spraying, the possible benefits had to be balanced against the possible ills.

He referred to the extensive testing programs and Federal regulations prevalent in the pesticides industry and said, "What we have done, we have not done carelessly or without consideration. The industry is not made up of money grubbers."

Tom K. Smith, vice president and general manager of agricultural chemicals for the Monsanto Chemical Company, said that "had the articles been written with necessary attention to the available scientific data on the subject, it could have served a valuable purpose—helping alert the public at large to the importance of proper use of pesticide chemicals."

However, he said, the articles suggested that Government officials and private and industrial scientists were either not as well informed on pesticide problems as Miss Carson, not professionally competent to evaluate possible hazards or else remiss in their obligations to society.

P. Rothberg, president of the Montrose Chemical Corporation of California, said in a statement that Miss Carson wrote not "as a scientist but rather as a fanatic defender of the cult of the balance of nature." He said the greatest upsetters of that balance, as far as man was concerned, were modern medicines and sanitation.

Montrose, an affiliate of the Stauffer Chemical Company, is the nation's largest producer of DDT, one of the pesticides that Miss Carson discusses at length. She also discusses the effect of malathion, parathion, dieldrin, aldrin and endrin.

"It is ironic to think," Miss Carson states at one point, "that man may determine his own future by something so seemingly trivial as his choice of insect spray." She acknowledges, however, that the effects may not show up in new generations for decades or centuries.

The Department of Agriculture reported that it had received many letters expressing "horror and amazement" at the department's support of the use of potentially deadly pesticides.

The industry had a favorite analogy to use in rebuttal. It conceded that pesticides could be dangerous. The ideal was to use them all safely and effectively.

The public debate over pesticides is just beginning and the industry is preparing for a long siege. The book reviews and publicity attendant upon the book's publication this fall will surely fan the controversy.

"Silent Spring" presages a noisy fall.

[July 22, 1962]

Steel: A 72-Hour Drama With an All-Star Cast

By WALLACE CARROLL

Special to The New York Times

WASHINGTON, April 22—It was peaceful at the White House on the afternoon of Tuesday, April 10—so peaceful that the President of the United States thought he might have time for a nap or a little relaxed reading.

Just to be sure, he called his personal secretary, Mrs. Evelyn Lincoln, and asked what the rest of the day would bring.

"You have Mr. Blough at a quarter to six," said Mrs. Lincoln.

"Mr. Blough?" exclaimed the President.

"Yes," said Mrs. Lincoln.

There must be a mistake, thought the President. The steel negotiations had been wound up the previous week.

"Get me Kenny O'Donnell," he said.

But there had been no mistake—at least not on the part of Kenneth P. O'Donnell, the President's appointment secretary.

Whether Mr. Blough—Roger M. Blough, chairman of the board of United States Steel Corporation—had made a mistake was a different question.

For when he walked into the President's office two hours later with the news that his company had raised the price of steel, he set off seventy-two hours of activity such as he and his colleagues could not have expected.

During those seventy-two hours, four antitrust investigations of the steel industry were conceived, a bill to roll back the price increases was seriously considered, legislation to impose price and wage controls on the steel industry was discussed, agents of the Federal Bureau of Investigation questioned newspaper men by the dawn's early light, and the Defense Department—biggest buyer in the nation—began to divert purchases away from United States Steel.

Also in those seventy-two hours—and this was far more significant—the Administration maintained its right to look over the shoulders of capital and labor when they came to the bargaining table and its insistence that any agreement they reached would have to respect the national interest.

And in those seventy-two hours, new content and meaning were poured into that magnificent abstraction, "the Presidency," for the historically minded to argue about as long as men remained interested in the affairs of this republic.

A full and entirely accurate account of those seventy-two hours may never be written. The characters were many. They moved so fast that no one will be able to retrace all of what they did.

Understandably, industry participants—facing official investigation now—would not talk much. Nor were Government participants willing to tell all.

Nevertheless, a team of New York Times reporters undertook to piece the tale together while memories were fresh.

Here is what they learned:

Early on that afternoon of April 10, Roger Blough had met with his colleagues of United States Steel's executive committee in the board room on the twentieth floor at 71 Broadway, New York. Three of the twelve members were absent, but Leslie B. Worthington, president of the company, and Robert C. Tyson, chairman of the finance committee, were there.

For several months these men had been giving out hints, largely overlooked in Washington, that the company would have to raise prices to meet increasing costs.

The Kennedy Administration had striven last fall to prevent a steel price increase, and there had been no increase. It had pressed again for a modest wage

---

In the early 1960's, inflation was viewed as a wage-price spiral. In the spring of 1962, President John F. Kennedy leaned heavily on the United Steelworkers union to accept a wage offer that he viewed as non-inflationary, but only days later U.S. Steel announced it was raising prices and some other companies joined the increase. Kennedy exploded with anger, beginning a confrontation that led to the steel companies backing down within three days.

The next month, the stock market fell sharply, and many blamed the anti-business tone of Kennedy's remarks. But the market recovered the next year, and no recession followed. The American economy, which had emerged from recession in 1961, was to avoid a new downturn until 1969, making the 1960's recovery the longest period of uninterrupted growth the country had yet seen. When inflation did begin to accelerate in the late 1960's, it was not because of greedy businessmen but because the Government had decided to fight a very expensive war in Vietnam without any cutbacks at home.

The Times covered the steel crisis as it happened, including a column by James Reston, published the day after U.S. Steel backed down, noting the challenges the industry would face in confronting international competition. But the most important contribution by The Times to the story was a long article that detailed all the tactics used by the Government to force a price rollback. That story was the first to report that Kennedy, shortly after learning of the price rise, had responded by recalling that his father had once told him that "all business men were sons-of-bitches, but I never believed it till now."

The report of the quote put Kennedy in a difficult position, and he told his next news conference that it was inaccurate; both he and his father had been referring only to steel executives, he said, not to all businessmen.

1960–1969

President John F. Kennedy, in 1962.

ASSOCIATED PRESS

contract this year, and a modest contract had been signed a few days earlier. The Administration expected no price increase now.

The company's executive committee reviewed the situation. The sales department had concurred in a recommendation to increase prices by 3½ per cent—about $6 on top of the going average of $170 a ton.

Mr. Blough had taken soundings within the company on the public relations aspects. Everyone realized that the move would not win any popularity prize, but the committee voted unanimously to go ahead.

With the decision made, Mr. Blough took a plane to Washington. Word was telephoned to the White House that he wanted to see the President and had something "important" to say about steel.

A few minutes after 5:45 the President received him in his oval office, motioned him to a seat on a sofa to his right and made himself comfortable in his rocking chair.

With little preliminary, Mr. Blough handed the President a four-page mimeographed press release that was about to be sent to newspaper offices in Pittsburgh and New York.

The President read:

"Pittsburgh, Pa., April 10—For the first time in nearly four years, United States Steel today announced an increase in the general level of its steel prices."

Mr. Kennedy raced through the announcement. Then he summoned Arthur J. Goldberg, the Secretary of Labor. Minutes later Mr. Goldberg reached the President's office from the Labor Department four blocks away.

Grimly, the President gave the paper to Mr. Goldberg and said it had been distributed to the press. Mr. Goldberg skimmed over it and asked Mr. Blough what was the point of the meeting, since the price decision had been made.

Mr. Blough replied that he thought he should personally inform the President as a matter of courtesy. Mr. Goldberg retorted it was hardly a courtesy to announce a decision and confront the President with an accomplished fact.

In the half-hour discussion that followed President Kennedy seems to have kept his temper. But Mr. Goldberg lectured Mr. Blough with some heat. The price increase, the Secretary said, would jeopardize the Government's entire economic policy. It would damage the interests of United States Steel itself. It would undercut responsible collective bargaining. Finally he said the decision could be viewed only as a double-cross of the President because the company had given no hint of its intentions while the Administration was urging the United Steelworkers of America to moderate its wage demands.

Mr. Blough, a high school teacher turned lawyer and company executive, defended himself and the company in a quiet voice.

When he had gone President Kennedy called for the three members of his Council of Economic Advisers. Dr. Walter W. Heller, the chairman, a lean and scholarly looking man, came running from his office across the street. Dr. Kermit Gordon followed in three minutes. James Tobin, the third member, hurried back to his office later in the evening.

Into the President's office came Theodore C. Sorensen, the White House special counsel, Mr. O'Donnell and Andrew T. Hatcher, acting press secretary in the absence of Pierre Salinger, who was on vacation.

Now the President, who usually keeps his temper under rein, let go. He felt he had been double-crossed—deliberately. The office of the President had been affronted. The national interest had been flouted.

Bitterly, he recalled that:

"My father always told me that all business men were sons-of-bitches but I never believed it till now!"

It was clear that the Administration would fight. No one knew exactly what could be done, but from that moment the awesome power of the Federal Government began to move.

To understand the massive reaction of the Kennedy Administration, a word of background is necessary.

Nothing in the range of domestic economic policy had brought forth a greater effort by the Administration than the restraint it sought to impose on steel prices and wages.

Starting last May the Administration worked on the industry, publicly and privately, not to raise its prices when wages went up in the fall. And when the price line held, the Administration turned its efforts to getting an early and "non-inflationary" wage contract this year.

Above all, the Administration constantly tried to impress on both sides that the national interest was riding on their decisions. A price increase or an inflationary wage settlement, it argued, would set off a new wage-price spiral that would stunt economic growth, keep unemployment high, cut into export sales, weaken the dollar and further aggravate the outflow of gold.

On Friday and Saturday, April 6 and 7, the major steel companies had signed the new contract. President Kennedy had hailed it as "noninflationary." Privately, some steel leaders agreed with him.

Thus, the President confidently expected that the companies would not increase prices. And the standard had been set, he hoped, for other industries and unions.

This was the background against which the group in the President's office went to work.

By about 8 P. M. some decisions had been reached.

President Kennedy would deliver the first counter-attack at his news conference scheduled for 3:30 the following afternoon.

Messrs. Goldberg, Heller and Sorensen would gather material for the President's statement. Other material of a statistical nature would be prepared in a longer-range effort to prove the price increase was unjustified.

While the discussion was going on, the President called his brother, Robert F. Kennedy, the Attorney General; Secretary of Defense Robert S. McNamara and the Secretary of the Treasury, Douglas Dillon, who had just arrived in Hobe Sound, Fla., for a short vacation.

At his home on Hillbrook Lane, Senator Estes Kefauver of Tennessee, chairman of the Senate Antitrust Subcommittee, was getting ready to go out for the evening. The phone rang. It was the President. Would Senator Kefauver publicly register "dismay" at the price increase and consider an investigation?

The Senator certainly would. He promised an investigation. So did the Justice Department.

In the President's office, meanwhile, there had been some talk of what could be done to keep other steel companies from raising prices. Most of the discussion centered on the economic rebuttal of the case made by United States Steel.

Mr. Goldberg and Dr. Heller decided to pool resources. Mr. Goldberg called Hyman L. Lewis, chief of the Office of Labor Economics of the Bureau of Labor Statistics, and asked him to assemble a crew.

Mr. Lewis reached three members of the bureau—Peter Henle, special assistant to the Commissioner of Labor Statistics; Arnold E. Chase, chief of the Division of Prices and Cost of Living, and Leon Greenberg, chief of the Productivity Division.

He told them what was wanted and asked them to go to Dr. Heller's office in the old State Department Building.

Dr. Heller, who had been working on the problem in his office, hurried off after a few minutes to the German Ambassador's residence on Foxhall Road.

Roger M. Blough, chairman of U.S. Steel.

1960-1969

The Ambassador was giving a dinner, a black tie affair, in honor of Prof. Walter Hallstein, president of the European Common Market. The guests were well into the meal when Dr. Heller arrived, looking, as one of the guests remarked, like Banquo's ghost in a tuxedo.

WEDNESDAY

Midnight had struck when Walter Heller, still in black tie, returned to his office from the German Embassy. With him, also in black tie, came another dinner guest, George W. Ball, Under Secretary of State.

Dr. Heller's two colleagues in the Council of Economic Advisers, Dr. Gordon and Dr. Tobin, were already there.

At about 2:45 A.M. the four men from the Bureau of Labor Statistics left the session. Their assignment from then on was to bring up to date a fact book on steel put out by the Eisenhower Administration two years ago.

The idea was to turn it into a kind of "white paper" that would show that the price increase was unjustified.

Toward 4 o'clock Dr. Heller and Dr. Tobin went home for two or three hours' sleep. Dr. Gordon lay down on the couch in his office for a couple of hours.

As the normal working day began, President Kennedy held a breakfast meeting at the White House with Vice President Johnson; Secretary of State Dean Rusk (who played no part in the steel crisis); Secretary Goldberg; Mr. Sorensen; Myer Feldman, Mr. Sorensen's deputy; Dr. Heller and Andrew Hatcher.

The meeting lasted an hour and forty-five minutes. Mr. Goldberg and Dr. Heller reported on the night's work. Mr. Sorensen was assigned to draft the President's statement on steel for the news conference. Mr. Goldberg gave him a two-page report from the Bureau of Labor Statistics headed:

"Change in Unit Employment Costs in the Steel Industry 1958 to 1961."

It said in part:

"While employment costs per hour of all wage and salaried employees in the basic iron and steel industry rose from 1958 to 1961, there was an equivalent increase in output per man-hour.

"As a result, employment costs per unit of steel output in 1961 was essentially the same as in 1958."

The latter sentence was quoted that afternoon in the President's statement.

During the morning the President had called Secretary Dillon in Florida and discussed with him the Treasury's work on tax write-offs that would encourage investment in more modern plant and machinery. The two decided that the course would not be altered.

The President also telephoned Secretary of Commerce Luther H. Hodges, who was about to testify before a House Maritime subcommittee. After giving his testimony Secretary Hodges spent most of the day on the phone to business men around the country.

In Wall Street that morning United States Steel

shares opened at 70¾, up 2¾ from the day before. But on Capitol Hill the company's stock was down.

Senator Mike Mansfield, the majority leader, called the price increase "unjustified." Speaker John W. McCormack said the company's action was "shocking," "arrogant," "irresponsible." Senator Hubert H. Humphrey, the Democratic whip, spoke of "an affront to the President."

Senator Albert Gore of Tennessee suggested a law that would empower the courts to prohibit price increases in basic industries such as steel until there had been a "cooling-off period."

Representative Emanuel Celler of Brooklyn, chairman of the House Antitrust subcommittee, scheduled a broad investigation of the steel industry. So did Senator Kefauver.

The pressures on United States Steel were beginning to mount. But now some of the other titans of the industry began to fall in line behind Big Steel.

As the President came out of the White House shortly before noon to go to the airport where he was to welcome the Shah of Iran, he was shown a news bulletin. Bethlehem Steel, second in size only to United States Steel, had announced a price increase.

Joseph L. Block, chairman of Inland Steel Co.

Others followed in short order—Republic, Jones and Laughlin, Youngstown and Wheeling. And Inland, Kaiser and Colorado Fuel & Iron said they were "studying" the situation.

When he faced the newsmen and television cameras at 3:30, President Kennedy spoke with cold fury. The price increase, he said, was a "wholly unjustifiable and irresponsible defiance of the public interest." The steel men had shown "utter contempt" for their fellow citizens.

He spoke approvingly of the proposed investigations. But what did he hope to accomplish that might still save the Administration's broad economic program?

In his conference statement the President had seemed to hold out no hope that the price increases could be rolled back. If the increases held what imminent comfort could there be in possible antitrust decrees that would take three years to come from the courts?

Actually, the possibility of making United States Steel retract the increase had been considered early in the consultation.

Drs. Heller and Gordon, and possibly some of the other economists, had argued that the principal thrust of the Administration's effort should be to convince one or two significant producers to hold out. In a market such as steel they said the high-priced sellers would have to come down if the others did not go up.

This suggested a line of strategy that probably proved decisive.

As one member of the Big Twelve after another raised prices, only Armco, Inland, Kaiser, C F & I and McLouth were holding the line. These five hold-outs represented 14 per cent or 17 per cent of the capacity of the Big Twelve.

Everything pointed to Inland as the key to the situation.

Inland Steel Corporation with headquarters in Chicago is a highly efficient producer. It could make a profit at lower prices than those of some of the bigger companies. And any company that sold in the Midwest, such as United States Steel, would feel Inland's price competition.

Joseph Leopold Block, Inland's present chairman, who was in Japan at the moment, had been a member of President Kennedy's Labor-Management Advisory Committee.

At 7:45 that Wednesday morning, Philip D. Block Jr., vice chairman of Inland, was called to the telephone in his apartment at 1540 North Lake Shore Drive in Chicago.

"Hello, P. D.," said Edward Gudeman, Under Secretary of Commerce, a former schoolmate and friend of Mr. Block's, calling from Washington.

THAT KENNEDY REMARK BERATED STEEL MEN, NOT ALL IN BUSINESS

By JAMES RESTON

Special to The New York Times

WASHINGTON, May 9—President Kennedy denied today that he had made a sharply critical remark about "all" business men. He told his news conference that he had had some unkind thoughts about some leaders of Big Steel during the recent price controversy but added: "That is all past. Now we are working together, I hope."

The quotation heard around the business world was printed in The New York Times on April 23. It said that, in his disappointment over U. S. Steel's decision to raise prices, the President had recalled and approved a violently offensive name once used by the President's father, Joseph P. Kennedy, about "all business men."

As it was printed, President Kennedy said, the story was "inaccurate." He implied that his father had used the derogatory epithet about some members of the steel industry in connection with a steel strike in 1937, and added that his father's opinion seemed appropriate during the recent steel crisis. But the President emphasized that the remark had been limited to a small group of steel officials.

The President spoke of the incident with regret but in good humor. Edward T. Folliard of The Washington Post raised the point:

MR. FOLLIARD—Mr. President, at the time of your controversy with the steel industry, you were quoted as making a rather harsh statement about business men. I am sure you know which statement I have in mind now.

THE PRESIDENT—Yes. You would not want to identify it, would you?

MR. FOLLIARD—Would you tell us about it, Mr. President? . . .

THE PRESIDENT—Oh, well, the statement which I have seen repeated, as it was repeated in one daily paper, is inaccurate. It quotes my father as having expressed himself strongly to me, and in this I quoted what he said, and indicated that he had not been . . . wholly wrong.

"What do you think of this price increase of United States Steel's?"

Mr. Block said he had been surprised.

"I didn't ask P. D. what Inland might do," said Mr. Gudeman several days later. "I didn't want them to feel that the Administration was putting them on the spot. I just wanted him to know how we felt and to ask his consideration."

Inland officials said they had not been coaxed or threatened by any of the officials who called them.

The approach, which seems to have developed rather spontaneously in many of the calls that were made to business men, was to ask their opinion, state the Government's viewpoint, and leave it at that.

But there also were calls with a more pointed aim—to steel users, asking them to call their steel friends and perhaps even issue public statements.

Another call to Inland was made by Henry H. Fowler, Under Secretary of the Treasury and Acting Secretary in Mr. Dillon's absence.

After Mr. Kennedy's afternoon news conference Mr. Fowler called John F. Smith Jr., Inland's president. Like other Treasury officials who telephoned other business men, Mr. Fowler talked about the effect of a steel price increase on imports and exports and the further pressure it would place on the balance of payments.

Though no concrete assurance was asked or volunteered in these conversations, the Administration gathered assurance that Inland would hold the line for at least another day or two.

Next came Armco, sixth largest in the nation. Walter Heller had a line into that company. So did others. Calls were made. And through these channels the Administration learned that Armco was holding off for the time being, but there would be no public announcement one way or the other.

Meanwhile, Mr. Gudeman had called a friend in the upper reaches of the Kaiser Company. Secretary McNamara had called a number of friends, one of them at Allegheny-Ludlum, a large manufacturer of stainless.

How many calls were made by President Kennedy himself cannot be told. But some time during all the activity he talked to Edgar Kaiser, chairman of Kaiser Steel, in California.

According to one official who was deeply involved in all this effort, the over-all objective was to line up companies representing 18 per cent of the nation's capacity. If this could be done, according to friendly sources in the steel industry, these companies with their lower prices soon would be doing 25 per cent of the business. Then Big Steel would have to yield.

Parallel with this "divide-and-conquer" maneuver, the effort moved forward on the antitrust line.

During the morning someone had spotted in the newspapers a statement attributed to Edmund F. Martin, president of Bethlehem Steel. Speaking to reporters on Tuesday after a stockholders' meeting in Wilmington, Del., Mr. Martin was quoted as having said:

"There shouldn't be any price rise. We shouldn't do anything to increase our costs if we are to survive. We have more competition, both domestically and from foreign firms."

If Mr. Martin had opposed a price rise on Tuesday, before United States Steel announced its increase, and if Bethlehem raised its prices on Wednesday after that announcement, his statement might prove useful in antitrust proceedings. It could be used to support a Government argument that United States Steel, because of its bigness, exercised an undue influence over other steel producers.

At about 6 o'clock Wednesday evening, according to officials of the Justice

Department, Attorney General Kennedy ordered the Federal Bureau of Investigation to find out exactly what Mr. Martin had said.

At about this same time, Paul Rand Dixon, chairman of the Federal Trade Commission, told reporters that his agency had begun an informal investigation to determine whether the steel companies had violated a consent decree of June 15, 1951.

That decree bound the industry to refrain from collusive price fixing or maintaining identical delivered prices. It provided penalties running up to $5,000 a day.

Meanwhile, more calls were going out from Washington.

The Democratic National Committee called many of the Democratic Governors and asked them to do two things:

First, to make statements supporting the President and, second, to ask steel producers in their states to hold the price line.

Among those called were David L. Lawrence of Pennsylvania, Richard J. Hughes of New Jersey and Edmund G. Brown of California. But the National Committee said nothing in its own name. The smell of "politics" was not to be allowed to contaminate the Administration's efforts.

Another call was made by Robert V. Roosa, an Under Secretary of the Treasury, to Henry Alexander, chairman of Morgan Guaranty Trust Company in New York. Morgan is represented on United States Steel's board of directors and is widely considered one of the most powerful influences within the company.

Thus by nightfall on Wednesday—twenty-four hours after Mr. Blough's call on the President—the Administration was pressing forward on four lines of action:

First, the rallying of public opinion behind the President and against the companies.

Second, divide-and-conquer operation within the steel industry.

Third, antitrust pressure from the Justice Department, the Federal Trade Commission, the Senate, and the House.

Fourth, the mobilization of friendly forces within the business world to put additional pressure on the companies.

THURSDAY

Archibald Cox, the Solicitor General, had left by plane on Wednesday afternoon for Tucson, where he was to make two speeches to the Arizona Bar.

On arriving at his hotel that night, he received a message to call the President. When he called he was asked what suggestions did he have for rolling back steel prices?

Mr. Cox had been chairman of the Wage Stabilization Board during the Korean War and had worked with young Senator Kennedy on statements about steel prices and strikes of the past.

After the call, Mr. Cox stayed up all night, thinking and making notes, mostly about legislation. From past experience Mr. Cox had concluded that the antitrust laws could not cope with the steel problem and that special legislation would be necessary.

Mr. Cox made his two speeches, flew back to Washington and stayed up most of that night working on the legislative draft.

At 3 A.M. Lee Linder, a reporter in the Philadelphia bureau of the Associated Press, was awakened by a phone call. It was the F. B. I. At first Mr. Linder thought he was being fooled. Then he determined that the call was genuine. The agents asked him a question or two and then told him:

"We are coming right out to see you."

Mr. Linder had been at the stockholders meeting of Bethlehem Steel in Wilmington on Tuesday and had quoted Mr. Martin about the undesirability of a price increase. Bethlehem Steel later called the quotation incorrect.

The agents were checking on that quotation. Mr. Linder said later that he had given them the same report he had written for The Associated Press.

Now, what was wrong with the statement was that, as it appeared in the daily paper, it indicated that he was critical of the business community and the phrase was "all business men." That is obviously in error, because he was a business man himself.

He was critical of the steel men, and he worked for a steel company himself, and he was involved when he was a member of the Roosevelt Administration in the 1937 strike, and he formed an opinion which he imparted to me, and which I found appropriate that evening. But he confined it, and I would confine it.

Obviously these generalizations are inaccurate and unfair, and he has been a business man, and the business system has been very generous to him. But I felt at that time that we had not been treated altogether with frankness, and therefore I thought that his view had merit. But that is past. Now we are working together, I hope.

The statement attributed by The Times to the President was:

"My father always told me that all business men were sons-of-bitches, but I never believed it till now!"

Since the publication of the quotation in The Times, several newspapers and magazines have reprinted it. It has also provoked editorial comment and a great deal of private comment to the effect that this was evidence of a bitter and hostile anti-business attitude on the part of the President.

This disturbed the President and his colleagues, especially since they have been consciously trying to reassure the business community ever since the steel controversy that the Administration's swift intervention then was a special case, not to be interpreted as a policy of hostility toward the business community.   [May 10, 1962]

1960–1969

GEORGE TAMES/THE NEW YORK TIMES

Clark Clifford took J.F.K.'s message to U.S. Steel.

At 6:30 A.M. James L. Parks Jr. of The Wilmington Evening Journal arrived at his office. Two F. B. I. Agents were waiting for him. He had talked to Mr. Martin after the meeting, together with Mr. Linder and John Lawrence of The Wall Street Journal. Later in the day the Federal agents interviewed Mr. Lawrence.

This descent of the F. B. I. on the newsmen was the most criticized incident in the seventy-two frenzied hours.

Republicans, who had kept an embarrassed silence up to this point, pounced on this F. B. I. episode. Representative William E. Miller of upstate New York, chairman of the Republican National Committee, compared it to the "knock on the door" techniques of Hitler's Gestapo.

In Chicago, as the day progressed, Philip Block and two other high officials of Inland reached a decision: prices would not be raised. They called Joseph Block in Kyoto. He concurred and they agreed to call a directors' meeting to ratify their decision the next morning.

No announcement was to be made until the morning and no one in Washington was told.

Back in Washington, the President was holding an early meeting in the Cabinet Room at the White House. Present were:

Attorney General Kennedy; Secretaries McNamara, Goldberg, Hodges; Under Secretary of the Treasury Fowler; Mr. Dixon, chairman of the Federal Trade Commission; Dr. Heller and Mr. Sorensen.

Roger Blough was scheduled to hold a televised news conference in New York at 3:30 that afternoon. The White House meeting decided that the Administration should put in a speedy rebuttal to his case for United States Steel.

Secretary Hodges had long-scheduled engagements that day in Philadelphia and New York. It was decided that he would hold a news conference in New York at 5 P.M. and try to rebut Mr. Blough point by point.

Meanwhile two of the most secret initiatives of the entire seventy-two hours had been set in motion.

The first involved a newspaperman—Charles L. Bartlett, the Washington correspondent of The Chattanooga Times. All Mr. Bartlett would say later was:

"I helped two friends get in touch with each other again."

One friend was President Kennedy—Mr. Bartlett and his wife are members of the Kennedy social set. The other friend was an officer of United States Steel. His identity has not been definitely established, but Mr. Bartlett knows Mr. Blough.

What came of this effort to reopen "diplomatic relations" is not known, although at least one Cabinet member thought it was useful. What came of the second secret initiative, however, can be reported.

At noon or earlier on Thursday President Kennedy phoned Clark Clifford, a Washington lawyer who had first come to national prominence as counsel for President Truman.

Secretary Goldberg, said the President, knew the officers of United States Steel very well and could, of course, talk to them on behalf of the Administration. But Mr. Goldberg, he went on, was known to the steel men mainly as an adversary.

For years he had been the counsel for the steel workers' union and one of their chief strategists in negotiations with the company. In view of this would Mr. Clifford, familiar as he was with the outlook of corporation executives through his law work, join Mr. Goldberg in speaking to United States Steel?

Mr. Clifford agreed, flew to New York and met Mr. Blough. He presented himself as a friend of the disputants, but he made clear that he was in 100 per cent agreement with the President. His purpose, he said, was to see if a tragic mistake could be rectified. The mistake, he left no doubt, was on the company's side.

For fourteen months, he continued, President Kennedy and Mr. Goldberg had worked for healthy conditions in the steel industry. They had tried to create an atmosphere of cooperation in the hope of protecting the national interest. Now all this was gone.

The President, he went on, believed there had been a dozen or more occasions when the company's leaders could easily have told him that despite all he had done they might have to raise prices. But they never had told him. The President, to put it bluntly, felt double-crossed.

What Mr. Blough said in reply could not be learned. But he indicated at the end that he would welcome further talks and he hoped Mr. Clifford would participate in them. Mr. Clifford returned to Washington the same day.

The Blough news conference was held in the ground floor auditorium at 71 Broadway.

"Let me say respectfully," Mr. Blough began, "that we have no wish to add acrimony or misunderstanding."

On several occasions, he said, he had made it clear that United States Steel was in a cost-price torque that could not be tolerated forever, that a company without profits is a company that cannot modernize, and that the price increase would add "almost negligibly" to the cost of other products—$10.64 for the steel in a standard automobile, 3 cents for a toaster.

One question and answer in the fifty-eight-minute session caught the ears of people in Washington: Could United States Steel hold its new price if Armco and Inland stood pat?

"It would definitely affect us," conceded Mr. Blough. "I don't know how long we could maintain our position."

A half-hour after Mr. Blough finished, Secretary Hodges held his news conference in the Empire State Building.

Meanwhile, Justice Department agents appeared at the headquarters of United States Steel, Bethlehem, Jones & Laughlin and other companies and served subpoenas for documents bearing on the price increase and other matters.

And at 7 P.M. Attorney General Kennedy announced that the Justice Department had ordered a grand jury investigation of the increase.

FRIDAY

The first big news of the day came from Kyoto, Japan. Joseph Block, Inland's chairman, had told a reporter for the Chicago Daily News:

"We do not feel that an advance in steel prices at this time would be in the national interest."

That news heartened the Administration but it did not stop planning or operations. Nor did Inland's official announcement from Chicago at 10:08 A.M., Washington time, that it would hold the price line.

At 10:15 Solicitor General Cox met in Mr. Sorensen's office with representatives of the Treasury, Commerce and Labor Departments, Budget Bureau and Council of Economic Advisers.

The discussion was on emergency wage-price legislation of three broad kinds:

First, ad hoc legislation limited to the current steel situation; second, permanent legislation imposing some mechanism on wages and prices in the steel industry alone, and third, permanent legislation for steel and other basic industries, setting up "fact-finding" procedures.

At 11:45 Secretary McNamara said at his news conference that the Defense Department had ordered defense contractors to shift steel purchases to companies that had not raised prices. Later in the day the department awarded to the Lukens

KENNEDY CAN BEAT 'EM BUT CAN HE CONVINCE 'EM?

By JAMES RESTON

CHICAGO, April 14—President Kennedy has defeated the leaders of Big Steel, but he has not convinced them. Even the sophisticated and progressive officials of Inland Steel here, who broke the deadlock, are asking not who won but what the President is going to do with his victory.

It is a good question. The President has proved what almost everybody but Roger Blough knew: that the United States is bigger than United States Steel. But this is just the beginning. Everything has been settled but the main problem, and the problem is not to modernize Mr. Blough—though that would help—but to modernize the steel industry: its machinery, its organization and, if possible, its mentality.

One of the remarkable things about the week's uproar out here is the contrast between the statements of Roger Blough and the comments of casual passers-by in the streets of Chicago or even in the streets of the Republican suburbs. Almost unanimously the casual comments in the street favor the President, and, what is more surprising, a great many people demand to know why Kennedy didn't "just take over and tell Blough what to do."

The cost of the week's skirmishing, therefore, is important. Big Steel has been hurt with the public, and after all those sharp words and all those nocturnal cops out of Washington, it has even been a little frightened. Even so, it is obvious that some cooperative way has to be found to deal not with the personalities of the past but with the causes of steel's economic problem and the future.

The industry is not building up enough capital to put in the necessary new equipment. The Government can help, as foreign governments have helped the overseas competitors of the United States companies. It can and does propose to provide tax relief for plant modernization. It can provide more cheap plant modernization capital than it now proposes to do. And it can help remove some of the sluggishness that now afflicts the industry in the

1960–1969

United States by subjecting it to tougher competition from overseas.

What steel company officials out here fear is that the Administration will, in its anger over the events of the last week, try to control prices the way the Interstate Commerce Commission controls transportation rates.

The view here is that this would not only be bad economics but bad politics because it would involve the President in every price change and every outcry following every price change. This, however, is probably an unjustified fear, for, while this approach to the problem has some support on Capitol Hill, there is very little evidence that it has the support of the President or the Secretaries of Labor and Defense, who have been so active in this week's fight.

What is perhaps a more serious danger is that the President, having won, will regard his victory as justification for carrying on the same policies he has followed in the past, and this will certainly not have the support of many of his advisers in the Administration.

Actually there are three groups now arguing what the President should do with his victory. There are the "planners," who do not believe that the steel industry can become competitive without state planning; there are the conservatives, who believe in the effectiveness of persuasion and "economics by admonition"; and there is a middle group that wants to use the latent powers of the Sherman Antitrust Act to reorganize the industry and at the same time help modernize it with more cheap capital, more liberal tax allowances for new modern equipment, and more competition.

How the President will react to all this remains to be seen. The Kennedys are more generous in victory than in defeat, and, judging from the President's remarks to the Inland officials after they broke the deadlock, he is in a mood to work things out by consultation rather than by legislation.

If this proves to be true, it may in due course be possible to turn the crisis of this week to advantage and this will be a gain. For the President and Mr. Blough, despite their difficulties, are in the same boat. A slight case of mutiny has been put down, but they are both heading into stormy international waters, and the boat is old, leaky and a little sluggish. [COLUMN, April 15, 1962]

Steel Company, which had not raised prices, a contract for more than $5,000,000 worth of a special armor plate for Polaris-missile submarines.

At 12:15 President Kennedy and most of the Thursday group met again in the Cabinet Room. It was estimated at that time that the price line was being held on 16 per cent of the nation's steel capacity.

Inland had announced. Armco had decided to hold but not announce. Kaiser's announcement came in while the meeting was on. This might be enough to force the bigger companies down again, but the sentiment of the meeting was that the retreat would not come soon.

Accordingly, preparations continued for a long struggle. Lists of directors of the companies that were holding the line were distributed, and each man present was asked to call men he knew.

Notably absent from this meeting was Secretary Goldberg. He was on his way to New York with Mr. Clifford in a Military Air Transport plane.

A secret rendezvous had been arranged with Mr. Blough and some of the other leaders of United States Steel at the Carlyle Hotel.

At this meeting, as in Mr. Clifford's talk with Mr. Blough on the previous day, no demands or threats or promises came from the Government side.

The discussion seems to have been a general one about what lay ahead. The outlook, said Mr. Clifford, was "abysmal."

United States Steel, he contended, had failed to weigh the consequences of its action. If it held this position, its interest and those of the industry would inevitably be damaged and the nation as a whole would suffer.

While the talk was going on Mr. Blough was called to the phone. Then Mr. Goldberg was called. Each received the same message. Bethlehem Steel had rescinded the price increase—the news had come through at 3:20 P.M.

President Kennedy heard the news while flying to Norfolk for a week-end with the fleet. It was unexpected.

The Administration had made no special effort with Bethlehem. To this day, officials here are uncertain what did it.

Among other things, Bethlehem's officials were struck by the Inland and Kaiser announcement that morning. Inland posed direct competition to Bethlehem's sales in the Midwest—the largest steel market—and Kaiser posed it on the West Coast.

Further, special questions were raised by the Pentagon's order to defense industries to shift their steel buying to mills that did not raise prices. What did this mean for Bethlehem's vast operations as a ship builder?

Whatever the compelling factors were, Bethlehem's decision brought the end of the battle clearly in sight. The competitive situation was such that United States Steel's executive committee was not called into session to reverse its action of the previous Tuesday. The company's officers acted on their own.

The big capitulation came at 5:28. Mrs. Barbara Gamarekian, a secretary in the White House press office, was checking the Associated Press news ticker. And there was the announcement—United States Steel had pulled back the price increase.

Mrs. Gamarekian tore it off and ran into the office of Mr. Sorensen, who was on the phone to the acting press secretary, Mr. Hatcher, in Norfolk.

"Well," Mr. Sorensen was saying, "I guess there isn't anything new."

Mrs. Gamarekian put the news bulletin under his eye.

"Wait a minute," shouted Mr. Sorensen.

Mr. Hatcher gave the news to the President as he came off the nuclear submarine, Thomas A. Edison, in Norfolk.

It was just seventy-two hours since Roger Blough had dropped in on Mr. Kennedy.   [April 23, 1962]

Pan Am Is Buying 25 New 490-Seat Jets

By ROBERT E. BEDINGFIELD

Pan American World Airlines, Inc., yesterday ordered $525-million worth of huge new jet airliners, each with a carrying capacity of 490 persons. This is about 2½ times the number than can be accommodated in today's standard jet airplane.

The company expects to get the first of the airliners—Boeing 747's—in September, 1969, and an entire fleet of 25 by May, 1970. The order is the biggest and most expensive for aircraft in commercial airline history.

The 747 will have a gross weight of 680,000 pounds, twice that of the biggest current long-range jets. It will be 228 feet 6 inches long, or half again as long as the big Boeing 707-321 jets Pan Am now uses. The wingspan will be 195 feet 7 inches, compared with 145 feet 9 inches for the 707.

The plane will have a range of 6,000 miles, which would enable it to fly from New York to Baghdad.

The world's largest plane now is the Soviet Ilyushin-62, which was shown last summer at the International Air and Space Show in Paris. It carries 186 passengers and has a length of 174 feet and a wingspread of 142 feet.

Though the 747 will not be a supersonic transport, such as is planned for service in the mid-nineteen-seventies, it will cruise about 10 per cent faster than today's jets—at an average of 633, rather than 580, miles an hour. It also will cruise at 45,000 feet, about a mile higher than most of today's jets.

Each of its four fan-jet engines, to be built by the Pratt & Whitney division of the United Aircraft Corporation, will deliver 41,000 pounds of thrust, about twice as much as any jet engine now in service.

Juan Trippe, chairman and president of Pan Am, said the decision to buy the jets had been his "most exciting" experience with the airline since 1927, when the company made its first flight in Alaska.

Mr. Trippe was guarded in predicting to what extent international air fares could be reduced with the 747, which will permit a 35 per cent reduction in operating costs per passenger mile.

"This will be a carrier for the great mass of people," he said when questioned on how it would differ from the supersonic airplane of the nineteen-seventies that is expected to fly at 1,500 to 2,000 miles an hour. The supersonic plane, he explained, probably will cost about as much to operate as today's standard jet airplane and will

The volume of air travel exploded in the 1960's with the introduction of commercial jetliners. Boeing, with first the 707 and then the 747, quickly came to dominate the business, and, in fact, commercial jets were for many years an industry that America completely dominated, with Douglas Aircraft (later to be merged into McDonnell Douglas) second to Boeing and Lockheed third.

The Soviet Union made some planes, but they never sold well outside the Soviet bloc. Lockheed eventually got out of the business, and McDonnell Douglas was acquired by Boeing in the 1990's. By then, however, European aircraft companies had formed a joint venture to create Airbus, which by the end of the century dominated the business with Boeing.

In 1966, The Times reported on the first order for the new Boeing 747, the first widebody jetliner with two aisles. The order from Pan American World Airways was then the largest ever in commercial aviation. Later that year, it reported on the boom being created in Seattle as Boeing geared up for 747 production.

Unfortunately, orders for the 747 were slower in arriving than expected, and development costs higher, and within a few years Boeing was forced to slash its work force. But orders recovered and the 747 became such a success that it was still being made as the century ended. Supersonic passenger jets, on the other hand, never succeeded. No such American plane was produced, and only a few European Concordes were placed in service.

1960–1969

Boeing's domination of the commercial jetliner business began with the 707 and continued with the 747, the first jumbo jet.

appeal to the traveler most interested in speed and first-class service.

The 747, he said, is designed to meet the demands of greatly increased travel. He said that conservative estimates were that international travel would increase 70 per cent over the next five years.

In addition to the 25 planes for which firm orders have been given, the airline has an option to acquire 10 more from Boeing. Of the 25 included in yesterday's order, 23 will be for passenger service and two for cargo.

Pan Am and Boeing both insist that because of advanced technology the 747 when compared to present jets will be quieter not only for the passenger but also for communities near airports. It will require no more runway strength and actually operate with shorter runways. Because it will fly higher than the average jet it also should relieve air traffic congestion at lower altitudes.

In Seattle yesterday, William M. Allen, Boeing president, said at a news conference that no decision had been made about where the 747 would be built. The company now produces all its commercial airliners in the Seattle area, but many of the components are made at its Wichita, Kans., plant.

Mr. Allen said a number of other airlines, both domestic and overseas, were interested in the 747. He said the company planned to be able to produce up to 200 of the planes by December, 1972, and a total of 400 by 1975.

Boeing's success in winning the Pan Am order was regarded in industry circles as a blow to the Douglas Aircraft Company, which had hoped to build a similar sized plane designated the DC-10, and to the Lockheed Aircraft Corporation, which has had plans for a commercial version of its giant C5A military transport.   [April 14, 1966]

BUSY BOEING CO. CROWDS SEATTLE

BY ROBERT A. WRIGHT
Special to The New York Times

SEATTLE, Sept. 24—Weekday attendance at the First Baptist Church of Renton near here has been heavy recently. The same is true at the First Methodist Church. The weekday visitors are not members of the congregation but trainees of the Boeing Company.

The big aircraft and aerospace company is expanding so fast it cannot build space quickly enough to accommodate all of its activities. So Boeing has rented space in churches, shopping centers, department stores and any other available locations it can find.

Boeing has been hiring in the Seattle area at the rate of 600 to 1,000 new employes a week. The company employs 85,000 persons in this area of a total Boeing payroll of 130,000, compared with 70,000 out of 100,000 a year ago. The need for people has become severe enough that William M. Allen, president, has appealed to Boeing stockholders to aid the company's recruitment of engineers, technicians and production workers.

Huge 707 jetliners are rolling out of the final assembly plant at Renton at the rate of 12 to 15 a month. Six to eight 727's a month emerge from the same plant. But at the Renton airstrip some 40 of the big planes, completely outfitted and painted with the various airline colors, line the runway awaiting engines. Boeing would build planes even faster if it could get all the components it wanted. Boeing has a backlog of unfilled orders on some $3.6-billion.

Next to the present Renton plant the company will soon complete a new assembly plant to supplement production of 707's and 727's. When this building, with 80-million cubic feet of space—slightly larger than the Pentagon—is completed, Boeing hopes to turn out the jetliners at the rate of two a day.

Twenty miles north of Seattle at Everett, Boeing is building what will be the largest building in the world to assemble the new 747 jetliner. The final-assembly plant at Everett will occupy part of a 700-acre site and enclose 160-million cubic feet of space.
[Sept. 25, 1966]

Chain Follows Road to Wall St.
McDONALD'S LOW-PRICED MENU LEADS TO LISTING

By JAMES J. NAGLE

A 10-item food menu, with no order costing more than 29 cents, has enabled a roadside hamburger chain to become so successful that it has met the requirements for a listing on the New York Stock Exchange.

The company is the McDonald's Corporation, Chicago, which operates 81 of its own units and has franchised 714 more roadside stands.

Among the items on all menus are hamburgers at 15 cents; milk shakes at 25 cents; soft drinks at 10 and 15 cents; and french-fried potatoes at 15 cents. The highest-priced order is a fish sandwich for 29 cents.

Including sales from the company-owned units, rentals, initial location fees, service and license fees and other income, the company had gross revenues last year of $35,427,779, contrasted to $6,274,758 in 1961. Net income came to $3,402,136 compared with $16,103 five years ago.

Two weeks ago in New York, when the stock was listed on the Big Board, Harry J. Sonneborn, president of McDonald's, emphasized that the company neither produced nor sold the food, equipment, fixtures or supplies used by the stands.

Its stock in trade, he said, is the "know-how" in operating such establishments. This is supplied constantly to the franchisees by a staff in five regional offices in addition to the Chicago headquarters.

It is the job of the company's personnel to advise operators of the stands in such matters as purchasing supplies and equipment, food preparation and serving methods, advertising and other details needed for the successful operation of a business, as well as in meeting the standards of quality fixed by McDonald's.

This kind of operation, Mr. Sonneborn said, has been so successful that there have been only eight or 10 failures of McDonald's roadside stands in the 11 years that the present management has been running the company.

The operators who have failed, he said, were either unwilling to follow the advice of the company's experts or had no aptitude for management.

All of the buildings are of similar design and construction, built according to company specifications. Each has an area of from 1,200 to 1,500 square feet. Most units are built on not less than 23,000 square feet of land and have parking space for about 50 cars.

All structures are built and owned either by the company or by the owner of the land and, for the most part, are leased or subleased to the operator by the company.

All equipment and fixtures are substantially the same but are purchased and owned by the unit operators.

Food preparation and service is prescribed by the company. Fresh food ingredients and some condiments are purchased from local purveyors, who must meet and maintain the standards set by the company.

There are a few stands in areas where pedestrian traffic is high but most are on highways and cater to motorists. There are no

The corner hamburger stand was a fixture in America long before Ray Kroc met the McDonald brothers in their Southern California restaurant and then persuaded them to sell him the rights to franchise their concepts. But, under Kroc, McDonald's became the first national fast-food chain— and eventually a symbol of American business around the world. In time, the price of a Big Mac was used by The Economist, a British publication, as a way of measuring whether currencies were overvalued, as The Times reported in 1997.

The Times first took note of the McDonald's story in 1966, when the company had become so successful—even with nothing on the menu costing more than 29 cents—that its stock qualified for trading on the New York Stock Exchange.

Ray Kroc opened his first McDonald's restaurant in 1955 in Des Plaines, Ill.

vending machines, no telephones, juke boxes or any of the other extra appurtenances found in many other roadside stands.

Only a handful have seats because the company has found it more profitable to concentrate on the drive-in and take-out trade.

To obtain a McDonald's franchise an operator must have $45,000 in cash. This covers various fees, a deposit against the lease, down payments on some equipment and inventory. Another $37,500 to complete the deal is usually financed by the operator on his own credit rating from some independent financial source. The company neither lends money not guarantees the obligations of its operators.

McDonald's system of drive-in self-service restaurants was originated in 1948 by M. J. and R. J. McDonald, brothers, with seven units, owned or licensed, in California. Six years later, the brothers' company, McDonald's Self-Service System, Inc., granted to Ray A. Kroc, now chairman of the company, an exclusive 10-year franchise to license operators of the restaurants.

That franchise was later transferred by Mr. Kroc to McDonald's System, Inc., which he organized in Illinois on March 2, 1955. On April 27, 1956, the Franchise Realty Corporation was organized by Mr. Kroc and a number of associates, including Mr. Sonneborn and Mrs. June Martino, to obtain, improve and lease unit locations licensed by McDonald's System, Inc. Mrs. Martino is now secretary-treasurer of McDonald's Corporation.

In 1960, the term of the franchise from the McDonald brothers was extended to 99 years from 1954. During the same year, the name of the Franchise Realty Corporation was changed to McDonald's Corporation and that company acquired all of the outstanding stock of McDonald's System, Inc. In 1961 the company bought out the McDonald brothers for $2.7-million.   [July 17, 1966]

IN CURRENCY TRADING, A McINDICATOR

By FLOYD NORRIS

The Chinese yuan is the world's most undervalued currency, selling for barely half its real value against the dollar. And the Swiss franc is the most overvalued, selling for 66 percent more than it is worth against the dollar.

At least that's what the Big Mac index says.

The somewhat whimsical index, developed by The Economist, the British weekly magazine, measures the average cost of a Big Mac at McDonald's restaurants around the world, and uses that figure to estimate just how much a currency's valuation deviates from real value.

The latest figures show that the average price of a Big Mac in the United States, including taxes, is $2.42. That compares to $4.02 in Switzerland and just $1.16 in China. The index assumes that if a Big Mac costs less than $2.42 under current exchange rates in another country, then the local currency is undervalued.

It sounds a little wacky, but as a forecasting device the Big Mac index hasn't done badly.

Two years ago, the index indicated that the Japanese yen was valued at almost twice its real worth. Now, since the dollar has soared against the yen, the conclusion is that the yen is just about fairly valued.

The Economist proudly notes that during the last year, when eight major currencies rose or fell by at least 10 percent in value, the Big Mac index got the direction right for seven of them. That record is, it reports, "better than some highly paid currency forecasters."   [April 13, 1997]

Door-to-Door Sales: The Lady Isn't Always Home

By ISADORE BARMASH

Door-to-door selling, as indigenous to America as apple pie and the corner drug store, is in a boom cycle. Across the country, cheery-voiced men and women are ringing doorbells, selling all manner of merchandise, and returning a few weeks later to sell more.

But the process is not as simple as it seems. The exceptional success of Avon Products, Inc., of New York, the nation's largest manufacturer of cosmetics and toiletries, all of which are sold directly to the consumer, has attracted a growing number of companies anxious to cash in on a $2.5-billion industry.

Few, however, have been prepared for the high cost of recruiting local sales representatives, or to take the pains of managing an intricate form of inventory-control, or to cope with the encroachment of increased selling costs.

Helene Curtis Industries, Inc., of Chicago, for example, expanded its door-to-door sales but lost millions because of inadequate planning and unexpectedly high expenses.

Direct selling, as the house-to-house selling process is called, has come into particular attention recently for at least two major reasons. One is proposed Federal legislation, namely the Magnuson Bill (S. 1599), also known as the "Door-to-Door Sales Act," which would purportedly protect consumers from abuses of door-to-door salesmen.

The other attention-getter has been the second consecutive year in which Avon emerged as the most profitable company in America in terms of its return on shareholder equity.

Other reasons why the direct-selling method has new appeal are the country's population boom, the rise in consumer affluence and the growth of leisure time. A new pool of potential selling representatives would seem to be available among young mothers and matrons freed by expanded "leisure time."

As far as Wayne Hicklin, chairman of Avon Products, is concerned, the proposed legislation will not hurt his giant company and may even help, if it serves to weed out the unscrupulous operator whose exploits have spurred the proposal of new regulations in the first place.

And, as far as the company's profitability is concerned, Mr. Hicklin, who declines to make any financial projections, indicated that plans were under way to increase sales and to expand the product array so that earnings should continue high.

In the year just ended, Avon's sales rose 16 per cent, to $474,814,000. Its net income increased 18 per cent to $65,383,000. Total expenses declined from the 1966 rate of 38.7 per cent of sales to 38.5 per cent, while total costs dipped from 35.1 per cent to 35 per cent.

These figures are the subject of much envy in the cosmetics industry, in which Avon is more than twice the size of the second-largest company. One reason why Avon's earnings are so high is its distribution costs, which are reduced by the fact that its advertising costs run less than 3 per cent of sales. In the rest of the cosmetics industry, the advertising percentage ranges between 15 and 30 per cent of sales.

Experience and refinement of its techniques appear to be two of the main reasons for Avon's success. Founded in 1886 by David H. McConnnell, a 28-year-old Oswego, N. Y., door-to-door salesman who sweetened his book sales with gifts of perfume, the company today employs 1,600 field supervisors who manage about 200,000 customers' representatives. All of these are women. Avon has 56 male divisional sales managers who are responsible for regional management.

The representative whose greeting is "Avon calling" is an independent contractor, who buys Avon Products at the wholesale price and sells them to the consumer at a retail price. This means that the representative buys the Avon merchandise at 60 per cent of the selling price and keeps 40 per cent.

In the late 1960's, Avon Products became one of Wall Street's favorites. It was cited in January 1968 by Forbes magazine as the most profitable company in the country over a five-year period, based on return on stockholder's equity. The company's success was rooted in its formula of using part-time salespeople, usually housewives, to call on other women at home and sell them cosmetics.

It sparked a host of imitators, as The Times noted in 1968, but its boom times were destined to end as more women entered the work force, depriving it both of potential workers and of customers for those workers to visit. Avon's stock, one of the best performers in the late 1960's, peaked in 1972 and has never returned to its old glory.

1960–1969

MIKE LIEBOWITZ/THE NEW YORK TIMES

Avon was calling and Wall Street was answering.

Avon had divided the year into 18 selling cycles, issuing new sales brochures every three weeks, which contain new or repackaged products. The agent pays for the merchandise when she personally delivers the shipment at the end of three weeks, shows the customer the new brochure and then obtains a new order. About 100 new or repackaged products are introduced a year.

Other cosmetics concerns issue about 30 new products a year, but Avon has cost advantages in this connection that are implicit in its mode of operation. One is that it is able to market new products at a much lower cost than the other cosmetics companies because its selling brochures are used to replace the retail selling counter, demonstrators, and other traditional retailing methods.

The overseas operation of Avon reached sales last year of $133.2-million, an increase of 36 per cent over the 1966 level. Net earnings of the international division rose 51 per cent.

Among the companies that saw mountains of gold in emulating Avon in the last few years was E. J. Korvette—now a division of Spartans Industries—with its Eve Nelson division selling cosmetics door to door. However, after several years of facing enormous costs of building a field organization, which sharply reduced its revenue, Korvette withdrew from the arena and now Eve Nelson beauty salons are the means by which the large retail chain hopes to cash in on the beauty-conscious American woman.

Helene Curtis, large producer of hair-care products, decided to enter the door-to-door field by acquiring Studio Girl, Inc., a direct-sales maker of cosmetics. It sought to quickly expand its sales and in a matter of about 5 years became the second largest direct seller of cosmetics.

In the process, however, it suffered substantial losses because of high recruiting costs, credit default by its representatives and excessive costs of mailings.

In Chicago, a spokesman for Helene Curtis said in a telephone interview that the company was now deliberately cutting back on its Studio Girl volume, tightening its credit procedures and mailing its recruiting literature "much more judiciously."

In Los Angeles, Vivian Woodard, Inc., a direct-selling company with sales of $5.7-million, is aiming at the more affluent customer with a referral, rather than a door-to-door selling approach.

Although most of the traditional-selling cosmetics companies are staying out of the direct selling field, their heavy consumer advertising has generated considerable interest among women for cosmetics, thus improving their response to the door-to-door saleswoman.

Other companies prominent in the direct-selling field are the Fuller Brush Company, Stanley Home Products and the Electrolux Corporation.

As the executive of a company that competes with Avon expressed it, "Looking at Avon's unique profit performance, you would think that this is a marvelous business and it ought to be easy to imitate them overnight.

"After all, what does it take! But what you tend to forget is that Avon has been at it for a long, long time and took its knocks before it began to hit its stride."

[Feb. 25, 1968]

'68 Sourdoughs Find Bonanza in Alaskan Oil

By WILLIAM D. SMITH

In oil—like boxing—it only takes one good shot to change a lot of things.

One of the biggest hits in the history of oil on the North American continent has apparently been scored on the bitterly freezing Arctic Slope of Northern Alaska, where the Atlantic Richfield Company and the Humble Oil and Refining Company have identified a field described as "one of the largest petroleum accumulations known to the world today."

This description was made by DeGolyer & MacNaughton, the internationally known oil-consulting concern. The concern places recoverable reserves of the field, which is located near Prudhoe Bay, about 390 miles north of Fairbanks and 150 miles southeast of point Barrow, at between 5 to 10 billion barrels of oil.

With the proven oil and natural gas liquid reserves of North America equal at present to about 49.6 billion barrels, this field could be equal to from one-tenth to one-fifth of the oil reserves of the entire continent, if preliminary estimates prove accurate.

It should be added that the consultants, DeGolyer & MacNaughton, have a reputation for being conservative.

"Although it is too early to completely assess, this is the most exciting development in the domestic oil industry in my memory or that of most other analysts on the street," Edward F. Carroll, the petroleum authority for E. F. Hutton, commented last week.

Atlantic, as would be expected, has been very close-mouthed about the field aside from the information released in original announcements. Students of the industry, however, have begun to form their own opinions beyond the material released by the company.

Norman R. Harvey, vice president of Auerbach, Pollak & Richardson, Inc., commented: "The characteristics of the oil discovered to date are indicative of a very desirable crude. It has low sulphur content, gravity ranges between 26 degrees and 31 degrees and its pour point is such that it may be possible to put the oil through an unheated pipeline."

In the oil business, it is often said that "it is a long way from the well-head to the gas pump," and this industry adage is particularly true in this case because of climatic and transportation problems.

Nonetheless, the Prudhoe Bay field and others that may develop hold the potential to affect the United States' balance of payments and foreign policy, not to mention "simple" oil affairs.

The field has not yet been completely proven, and as Robert O. Anderson, chairman of Atlantic, has explained, "Commercial development of the field will require a minimum of three to four years." Yet petroleum circles from Calgary to Beirut and many Government officials in between are reacting to the force of the area's potential.

Reaching the potential is a problem of large proportions, one that is probably as great as any that has ever faced the industry.

E. M. Benson Jr., vice president in charge of exploration and production for Atlantic Richfield's North American Petroleum Division, described the area:

"In the winter the temperature falls to 65 degrees below zero, but we have had to work then because during the summer, the perma-frost layer thaws and every piece of equipment sinks into the quagmire.

"There are no roads north of the Brooks Range 150 miles south and no lumber north of Fairbanks. When you put a rig up, you dig a hole in the ground, put in your pilings and pour water. When the water freezes, which is pretty soon, you have your foundations.

"The Arctic Ocean is only open two to eight weeks each year, and planes can

In 1968, a huge oil field was found in northern Alaska, near Prudhoe Bay, in some of the most inhospitable terrain on Earth. It would prove to be far more valuable than was estimated at the time, simply because oil prices were destined to rise sharply in the 1970's. The Times reported on the oil find in July 1968, noting that a pipeline was the most likely way to get the oil out of Alaska. Nine years later, that pipeline opened.

1960–1969

only land during the winter months, when the water is frozen."

The men who are now pursuing the riches of oil are facing conditions as severe as any met by the sourdoughs who went to Alaska in search of gold at the turn of the century.

Pulling pipe from a well is difficult even under the best of conditions, but in subzero weather, when the workers are bound in protective clothing, it is a near-miracle that the work is accomplished.

Mr. Benson said that guidelines connect the well with living quarters and all other buildings to prevent the men from being blown off course in the 100-foot walk from wellhead to bunkhouse.

Despite the hardships, Atlantic and Humble, which is Standard Oil Company's (New Jersey) principal domestic affiliate, will not want for company when winter comes sometime in October.

Now that the rush is on, drilling will likely be on a year-round basis with gravel or similar substances being used for insulation during the summer months.

Phillips Petroleum and the Mobil Oil Corporation, which hold joint acreage in the area, are moving a drilling rig down the Mackenzie River to the Beaufort Sea. The British Petroleum Corporation, which has 96,000 acres on wholly owned blocks in the area, is reported to be planning to fly in a rig from Southern Alaska.

Sinclair Oil; the Shell Oil Company; Texaco, Inc.; Standard Oil (Indiana); Union Oil of California and the Gulf Oil Company are among the companies with holdings in the area.

Although the task of finding and developing the oil reserves along the coast of the Arctic Ocean will be one of the most demanding in the history of the petroleum industry, the job of getting the oil out to markets may be even tougher.

There are three basic ways to move the oil to market. Each presents its own peculiar and formidable problems.

The first is by tanker shipments to West-Coast markets during the two-to-eight-week season when Arctic navigation is open. New ice-breaking devices, such as the Alexbow, may lengthen the season. Substantial developmental work on tankers would be necessary to make the operation feasible.

The second method is by pipeline to a year-round open water port on the Pacific Coast, 600 miles across Alaska's forbidding Brooks Mountain Range.

The third is by a pipeline, swinging 1,700 miles from Prudhoe Bay east along the Arctic coastal plain to the Mackenzie River, up the Mackenzie Valley across the Northwest Territories and Northern Alberta to Edmonton. At Edmonton, the line could connect with the Interprovincial system stretching another 1,560 miles across the United States Great Lakes to oil-hungry markets.

None of the transportation methods are likely to be considered in serious detail until several years of exploration have been completed to better define the potential of the whole Arctic coastal region, encompassing some 150,000 square miles.

[July 28, 1968]

The Time of the Conglomerates

THE URGE TO MERGE

By HARVEY H. SEGAL

An enchantment with innovation embraces all facets of contemporary society: the new writing, the new sound, the new politics. Micro-skirts and Nehru jackets, hirsute males and close-cropped females are conspicuous symbols of changing fashion. Computers and lasers, organ transplantation and space exploration foreshadow radical changes in the basis of physical life, while in business the revolution is heralded by the rise of the conglomerate, the corporation that grows rapidly by moving into unrelated markets through mergers.

To the geologist, a conglomerate is a rock composed of stone fragments held together by hardened clay or some other cement. Analogously, the conglomerate corporation is a group of companies which operate in separate markets and are held together by bonds of financial and administrative authority.

Last month, the world of finance was agog with the announcement of what could be one of the largest mergers on record, the offer by the Xerox Corporation to buy control of the CIT Financial Corporation. Xerox dominates the photocopying market and is moving into the fields of education, health and peripheral computer equipment. CIT, in addition to being the second largest commercial credit company, has moved into banking, X-ray equipment, insurance, office furniture and greeting cards. Clearly, a Xerox-CIT union would be of the conglomerate type. But despite the size of the merger—CIT has $3.4-billion in assets on its books, more than those of any company ever acquired by another—the merged corporation would not be nearly so diversified as some other conglomerates.

As an example of spectacular diversification consider the International Telephone and Telegraph Corporation. With $2.96-billion in assets at the end of 1967, I.T.T. ranked 17th among the nation's industrial companies. Originally an international

The 1960's saw stock prices rise to historic highs, with the Dow Jones industrial average almost reaching 1,000 in 1966 before slipping back. That bull market helped make possible a wave of mergers and takeovers as companies that were highly valued used their stock to buy other companies.

Many of the mergers took the form of conglomerates, in which companies acquired subsidiaries in widely disparate industries. That got around traditional antitrust concerns, although it raised fears of companies being able to use profits from one business to subsidize another and drive out competitors from that business. Investors were persuaded that, when it came to conglomerates, the whole was worth more than the sum of the parts.

In 1968, when The Times published a Magazine article analyzing the conglomerate phenomenon, it appeared that trend would continue for some time. But most conglomerates did not work out well for their shareholders—especially LTV, which had been put together by James J. Ling. A chart accompanying the Magazine article showed that LTV stock had risen from around 10 a share in 1964 to more than 160 in 1967. Its acquisition of the Jones & Laughlin steel company, however, proved disastrous and the company eventually succumbed to bankruptcy, with the stock becoming worthless.

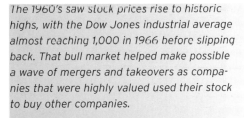

1960–1969

Drawing by James Flora

communications company that still operates telephone systems and other enterprises in 123 countries, I.T.T. branched out first into the manufacture of telephonic equipment, a natural enough development. But in recent years, under highly efficient and aggressive management, it has come to rent cars (Avis), operate hotels and motor inns (Sheraton), build homes (Levitt & Sons), bake bread (Continental), produce glass and sand, make consumer loans, manage mutual funds, and process data.

But if diversity were the only criterion for distinguishing a conglomerate, General Motors, Ford and General Electric would each outrank I.T.T. G.M. makes locomotives, refrigerators and washing machines. Ford produces a line of radios and household durables. G.E. produces jet engines, computers and synthetic diamonds in addition to its traditional lines of electrical equipment. But none of these is a true conglomerate.

What distinguishes I.T.T. is the source of its recent growth. Its assets grew by more than $2-billion in the period 1960–1967, and mergers accounted for more than a third of that total. In the same period, mergers made no contribution at all to the asset growth of G.M. or G.E. and accounted for a little more than 6 per cent of Ford's. Xerox's spectacular progress is the product of internal growth rather than expansion through merger.

In perusing the list of the 200 largest manufacturing corporations, conglomerates can almost invariably be distinguished by the high contribution of mergers to their asset growth. In 1966–1967, mergers accounted for nearly 46 per cent of Litton Industries' growth, and for others, the figures were as follows: FMC, 80 per cent; General Dynamics, 69 per cent; Gulf & Western, 47 per cent; Textron, 69 per cent; Martin Marietta, nearly 100 per cent, and Glen Alden, 94 per cent.

Only eight conglomerates ranked among the 200 last year, but they accounted for all the exciting merger action. Ling-Temco-Vought, which ranked 92d, bought control of the 63d-ranking Jones & Laughlin Steel Corporation with assets of

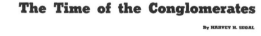
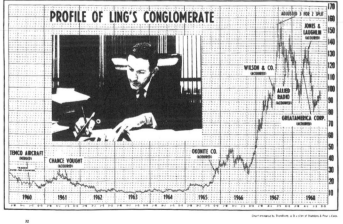

$1.1-billion. P. Lorillard, the tobacco company that ranked 184th was acquired by Loew's Theatres, a dazzling conglomerate that couldn't even qualify for the 200 club in 1967.

What accounts for this corporate acquisitiveness, this frenzied urge to merge? Is the driving force biogenetic in origin, a vestigial survival of prowess from man's primitive past? The evidence points to dollars, rather than chromosomes.

If a group of applied physicists is joined with an electronic equipment manufacturer, it's reasonable to suppose that the merged company will be able to take on new business—research and development contracts—which neither could have handled before the union. And with a greater capability for taking on larger contracts, it becomes easier for the company to borrow money that may be needed to finance work in progress.

But in the move from simple examples to corporate realities, synergism loses its force as an explanation of conglomerate mergers. In the case of Litton Industries and other conglomerates that reshape the managements of acquired companies and guide them through systems of centralized controls, some synergistic benefits might be realized. But the elements of the Ling-Temco-Vought complex function independently of one another and presumably the CIT's management would also remain intact after the proposed merger with Xerox. In such instances, therefore, especially when conglomerates are as widely diversified as I.T.T. or L.T.V., it's difficult to attach much weight to synergism.

The more decentralized the conglomerate becomes, the more it resembles a mutual fund or a pension trust account in a bank. Neither play active roles in the management of companies in which they hold stock.

Synergism implies greater efficiency in the production of goods and services, but it is doubtful whether such considerations weigh heavily in merger decisions. Yet there is no doubting the fact that managements which pursue aggressive merger policies can persuade investors to pay more for their stock. Thus, it is to the stock market rather than the production line that one must look for an explanation of the conglomerate corporation.

Conglomerates vary widely in size and maturity. Textron, which achieved success a decade ago in moving from textiles into optical instruments, electronic equipment, paper machinery, aircraft and a host of other fields, doesn't make news so often with announcements of acquisitions as Gulf & Western. Some conglomerate rockets have burned out (Merritt-Chapman & Scott) and others (Olin Mathieson, for one) have failed to reach their earnings targets. But the underlying strategy of conglomeration is essentially the same in every case: It consists in making investors willing, if not eager, to pay higher prices for shares in the company's stock, more in relation to each dollar that the conglomerate earns.

Conglomerate entrepreneurs—or conglomerators—must raise the price-earnings ratios of their stock if they are to expand, for unless it's loaded with cash, the rising conglomerate must depend on loans to acquire new companies. The higher the price of its common stock, the more it can borrow by pledging stock as collateral or the more it can raise by selling bonds that are convertible into common stock at a prearranged price. Where the merger is consummated through the exchange of stock, the higher the market price of the conglomerate's stock, the fewer shares it must give up in exchange and the smaller the dilution in the earnings per share.

The need for maintaining a rising P/E never ceases so long as the conglomerate continues to make acquisitions. And in order to avoid a decline or a slowdown in its earnings per share, it should seek to merge with companies whose P/E's are lower than its own.

It's not necessary for conglomerators actually to demonstrate that they can diminish risks and raise earnings per share through diversification. The mere intention to embark on the path of conglomeration may be sufficient to raise expectations. Franc

1960–1969

Ricciardi, an alumnus of Litton Industries who helped to turn Walter Kidde & Co. into a successful conglomerate, explains that the "stock market was very generous" with the new management from the start. As soon as they "threw their hats in the door," Kidde stock "went up 60 or 70 per cent, in the expectation that something might happen."

There are many stars in the conglomerate firmament, but none shines so brightly as that of James Joseph Ling, a 45-year-old high-school dropout who was born in Hugo, Okla., (population 6,287). In 22 years he has parlayed an investment of $3,000 in an electrical contracting shop into a diversified empire with more than $2-billion of assets and $3-billion in sales. A financial Archimedes, he has demonstrated what can be done with the leverage of rising P/E's.

After scoring a success as an electrical contractor—his skills were acquired in the Navy—Ling was able to go public when a Dallas investment banker agreed to underwrite stocks and bonds in Ling Electronics. That venture prospered, and in 1960, Temco Electronics and Missiles was acquired along with Altec, a major producer of sound equipment, and other companies. Two years later, in 1961, the Vought was added to Ling-Temco when Ling borrowed $10-million to gain control of Chance Vought, an aircraft, missile and electronics company with sales of $195-million. He was assisted by Troy Victor Post, a friend of Lyndon Johnson's. Post's own conglomerate, Greatamerica, which controlled insurance companies, a large bank and Braniff Airways, was merged into L.T.V. in 1967.

Texas tycoons are not noted for modesty in their personal tastes, and Ling is no exception to the rule. The cost of his home—a Palace of Versailles in the style of a Holiday Inn—is variously placed at figures in excess of $1.5-million, inclusive of a guest house, now under construction. "People don't live like that in the Northeast," a New York banker remarked, "even when they can afford it."

Ling once proclaimed that his goal was a combined sales total of $10-billion a year, and he took a giant step toward achieving it when he acquired control of Wilson & Co. in 1967. It was a performance that combined exquisite financial insight with perfect timing, one that made Ling the Lorenzo of the conglomerators.

Wilson was itself a conglomerate, producing sporting goods, meats and chemicals. Its sales were then nearly $1-billion, as against $468-million for L.T.V. Yet the python swallowed the pig.

In the spring of 1967, Ling was able to borrow $80-million from New York brokers, London merchant bankers, insurance companies and university trust funds in order to buy a controlling interest in Wilson stock. He paid a premium of 25 per cent over the market price to get it. The remaining Wilson stock was acquired by offering the owners a special L.T.V. convertible preferred stock.

Then he embarked on "Operation Redeployment," a tactic pursued in 1965 to reduce L.T.V.'s debts. He broke Wilson up into three independent companies, listed them on the exchange and sold blocks of stock to the public which in no case amounted to more than 25 per cent of L.T.V.'s holdings. Intrigued brokers referred to the new issues as "golf balls," "meat balls," and "goof balls."

The sale of Wilson stock brought in $44.4-million, enough to retire more than half of L.T.V.'s debt. But the real pay-off came a short time later when the market had an opportunity to appraise the prospects of the new Wilson companies and boost their P/E's. The happy result was that L.T.V.'s remaining holdings of Wilson stock were valued at a cool $250-million. With his highly appreciated bag of assets, Ling was in a position to offer collateral for bigger loans for bigger acquisitions. The opportunity came in May this year when he raised $425-million in cash to gain control of the Jones & Laughlin Steel Corporation. L.T.V. put in about $200-million from its own kitty and borrowed the rest, principally by tapping the Eurodollar market—U.S. dollars held on deposit in European banks.

Other conglomerators play variations on the same pecuniary theme. Meshulam Riklis, the scholarly chief of Glen Alden, accomplished less spectacular feats by selling convertible debentures, bond-like instruments that can be swapped for common stock. He once referred to them as "Castro (convertibles) pesos," and again, the ease with which they can be sold hinges on the crucial P/E of his common stock.

But none of the problems raised by the emergence of the conglomerate corporation are so complex—or politically explosive—as those relating to their impact on competition. Mergers once posed relatively simple antitrust problems. For the most part they were horizontal (one retail food store taking over another in the same market) or vertical (the acquisition of a slaughter-house by a retail food chain). Legality hinged on whether the mergers would lessen competition in the affected markets—not an easy judgment to make, but conceptually manageable. But conglomerates, which account for about 90 per cent of the assets acquired by merger—or for about $10-billion in 1968, according to preliminary estimates by the Federal Trade Commission—can't be fitted into a neat analytical scheme.

Conglomerates raise the issue of political power in a new and disquieting fashion. Litton, L.T.V., General Dynamics—to name only a few—owe their rise to defense contracts and a continuing relationship with the Federal Government. The "military-industrial complex," of which President Eisenhower warned before leaving the White House, is very much a reality.

Little light has yet been cast, however, on most of the antitrust issues. Veteran antitrust economists, whose survival in Washington's lobby jungle is a tribute to their courage, argue that conglomerates pose several clear threats to competition, and their contentions are mirrored in recent F.T.C. and Supreme Court decisions.

The first threat is from price subsidization—the use of profits, earned in a market where the position of the conglomerate is strong, to drive out the competition in another market by cutting prices below costs and subsequently raising them. If entry into the market is easy, the conglomerate's higher profits will soon attract competition. But if there are substantial barriers to entry, the gambit could pay off.

Second, if the conglomerate is very large and commands great financial resources, its move into a highly competitive market of small sellers could discourage potential entrants.

Third, there is reciprocity—the fear that the conglomerate will use its power to effect tie-in sales. Conglomerate X buys ball bearings from Company Y which in turn gets its steel from Company Z. If X acquires Z, it may then put pressure on Y to buy X-Z steel at an unfavorable price by threatening to patronize another manufacturer of ball bearings.

There are sharp disagreements among economists and lawyers as to whether these threats to competition are palpable. Nonetheless, the F.T.C., at the behest of Senator Philip Hart of Michigan, the chairman of the Antitrust and Monopoly Subcommittee, agreed to undertake a broad fact-finding investigation of conglomerates.

That decision elicited a loud blast from James J. Ling. He warned insurance company executives in Chicago of "the bureaucrats who would democratize and socialize all business and thus pave the way for the ultimate demise of the enterprise system. . . ."

The one certainty that emerges from the web of controversy is that the conglomerate issue isn't going to be resolved by Ling's rhetoric, the F.T.C.'s fact findings or the interpretations of the courts. A new, or at least novel, style of entrepreneurship is evolving, one based on raising expectations of rapid growth. It might disappear when the conglomerators, like Alexander, weep because there are no more worlds to conquer—but that isn't likely to happen for a very long time.

[THE NEW YORK TIMES MAGAZINE, Oct. 27, 1968]

James J. Ling, conglomerate entrepreneur.

1960–1969

Door to Executive Suite Opens Wider to Working Girls

The role of women in American business was basically set for most of the century. They occupied secretarial positions, of course, and other clerical jobs. Women who wanted to work in professions were generally expected to be nurses or teachers. There were exceptions, to be sure, but not until the 1960's did the idea of gender equality in the workplace begin to gain ground.

A 1969 Times article celebrated the progress being made. Read many years later, what seems most remarkable is just how little progress there had been, with one of the featured women saying it would take a lot of luck "and a unique group of men" before a woman was allowed into top management. While the road ahead was anything but smooth, it did become possible in the remaining years of the century for women to advance in corporate management and other fields long dominated by men.

By MARYLIN BENDER

Everyone knows it. Even male supremacists concede it. But no one can prove it by statistics.

It's just a realization—one could call it female intuition if so many men weren't asserting it—that women are going places at last in American business and industry.

Within the next decade, newspapers will no longer be recording female firsts. The first women to have been seated on the major stock exchanges, to have moved into the presidential suites of leading corporations on their own and not just because they inherited the stock, will be history rather than news.

Making a million, marrying the client (then losing his account), and finding new worlds to conquer will be the reasonable expectation of any dazzling blonde.

On the other hand, male executives need not fear being turned out to the kitchen. Given equality in business, women are unlikely to respond in droves. A majority will still prefer the reflected glory of their husbands.

Women have been playing an increasingly important role in the labor force since World War II. The number of working women has doubled in the last 25 years. The greater part of them are women over 35 who take jobs for money rather than identity. One out of three married women is working.

But these figures do not hint at the notable progress that women have begun to make in executive positions. The elevation of 64 women to key positions by the First National City Bank is more indicative.

They include four assistant vice presidents, such as Marian Schappel, a branch manager, and Diana Greer, a senior analyst in the investment research department. Miss Greer is one of the Harvard Business School's first three women graduates (class of 1960).

Christopher Rodgers, vice president for personnel administration for the bank, says: "We're doing some active recruiting in women's colleges, looking for women trained in the computer sciences, which evolves into systems analyst and programmer, but also on the professional banking and investment side."

Mr. Rodgers believes "it's a logical step" for the bank to have a woman vice president in the not-too-distant future.

Though the Harvard Business Review has stopped surveying executive opportunities for career women because "the barriers are so great that there is scarcely anything to study," the Harvard Business School has one of its 1965 graduates, Judith Chadwick, recruiting women. Miss Chadwick is executive assistant to the executive vice president and director of Moore-McCormack Lines, a middle management post she has just attained after two promotions in two years.

When she talks to college seniors, she points up the increasing number of opportunities for women holding the M.B.A. degree, "which opens many doors." As for a woman's chances of reaching top management, Miss Chadwick says:

"If she has the ability, if she is in a unique situation—this is going to sound like hedging, I know—and if she is working with a unique group of men and has a lot of luck, I think she can make it."

Miss Chadwick and James Foley, assistant dean for external affairs at the Harvard Business School, also hedge somewhat when they interpret discrimination against women in the light of starting salaries for the school's graduates.

The most recent of its 75 women graduates have, as a rule, been offered $11,500. The median salary for a graduate with one year's business experience (which most of the women don't have) has been $12,500. The median for graduates with engineering degrees (which most women don't have either) is $13,000.

This year's entering class of 780 enrolled 31 women. The women in the next class will be the first to live on campus.

There have not, however, been women in the Advanced Management Program or the newer, 16-week Program for Management Development (middle managers), both of which require co-sponsorship by the student's company. "How many companies are going to invest $3,000 tuition plus salary and fringes in a woman rather than a man?" Mr. Foley asked.

J. Fredric Way, director of placement for the Columbia Graduate School of Business, where the number of women in this year's entering class doubled to bring the female component of the school to 4 per cent, believes that companies have begun to realize that women may be able to manage as well as men.

"It may have taken the Fair Employment Practices Act to do it, but many more areas have opened up in the last few years," he said. Banks, accounting firms, even oil companies now see women in the same executive trainee category as men.

"Nobody says, 'We'll see men only,' and if they did, I'd raise merry hell," Mr. Way declared. "This is the start. A company officer finds himself talking to a woman, and discovers she's very qualified."

William Carothers, director of industrial relations for the chemical division of F.M.C., a diversified producer of chemicals, fibers, films and machinery, puts the situation this way:

"When we're looking for chemists, it's talent against talent. We recruit at 90 schools and the jobs are open to anybody in the disciplines we need."

But Mr. Carothers says few women "rush to us when we look for chemical engineers."

Mrs. Hilda Kahne, an economist and research associate of the Radcliffe Institute, finds that women "are not entering the fast-growing engineering and scientific categories at the same rate as men, with the exception of mechanical engineering, where the number is too small to be significant."

Only in medicine and law are their ranks multiplying faster than men. Women mathematicians, economists and psychologists are also proliferating, a fact that jibes with their presence in the marketing and analytical areas of industry and finance.

Discrimination against women in many of the clubs often considered vital to advancement is one roadblock in the path of business. Another is the refusal of women to take advantage of their new opportunities.

For the last three years, Barnard College has participated in recruitment interviews on the Columbia University campus. But last year, only 56 girls from a class of 440 crossed the street to be interviewed, according to Mrs. Jane Schwartz, Barnard's placement director.

"A woman is actually under less pressure to be a success," says Martha Peterson, Barnard's president. "Today's students want self-actualization for women as well as men, but whether it will lead to more top executive positions for women, I have my doubts. I think they will cut out their worthy pieces of work and do them. Maybe they will be leaders in innovation." [Jan. 6, 1969]

Big Board Defied by Member Firm
DONALDSON, LUFKIN PLANNING PUBLIC SHARE OFFERING

By TERRY ROBARDS

The New York Stock Exchange was confronted yesterday with a major uprising in its membership, when a leading member firm disclosed its intention to sell shares in itself to the public in defiance of an exchange rule.

Donaldson, Lufkin & Jenrette, Inc., perhaps Wall Street's most aggressive and best known institutional brokerage house, said it had filed a registration statement with the Securities and Exchange Commission covering the public offering of 800,000 of its shares for about $30 a share.

The action was expected to bring to a head the long-simmering controversy over public ownership of brokerage firms, as well as institutional membership on the stock exchange. The brokerage firm indicated that it had acted in a direct effort to confront the exchange's hierarchy with what many officials of the securities industry consider to be a highly significant issue.

"For nearly 200 years the New York Stock Exchange has been a cornerstone of the American free-enterprise system," said Richard H. Jenrette, chairman of the firm's executive committee. "Yet the lack of access by exchange members to permanent, public capital has begun to erode the exchange's historic role as the nation's central auction market."

The regulations of the stock exchange effectively prevent its member organizations from selling their shares to the public. The brokerage house said it was aware that it could be deprived of its status as a member if it went through with the public sale of its stock.

"In view of the substantial portion of the company's total revenues attributable to exchange commissions, it is hoped that means may be found whereby such membership may be retained," the concern said in its prospectus.

"However," it added, "D.L.J.'s ability to avail itself of opportunities for continued growth is a more important consideration. Capital additions can be effectively utilized immediately and are essential to the maintenance and improvement of its competitive position."

Robert W. Haack, president of the Big Board, responded with a statement noting that public participation through the issuance of debt securities is an issue that already has been submitted to the Securities and Exchange Commission.

"The issue is extremely complex by reason of its being closely woven into the matter of institutional memberships on stock exchanges, as well as the regulation and surveillance of its members," Mr. Haack said.

Dan W. Lufkin, chairman of D.L.J.'s board and a governor of the exchange, proposed amendments to the exchange's constitution at a board of governors meeting yesterday afternoon. Basically, these amendments would provide the mechanism and safeguards for public ownership.

Mr. Haack said the exchange's procedures on such constitutional matters were "clearly defined." He added that "they will of course be followed."

This means the proposed amendments will be tabled for two weeks before the board can take any formal action. If the board of governors decided to offer the amendments to the membership for ratification, S.E.C. approval would be sought.

The firm said the proceeds from its public offering, expected to be around $24-million, would be used to expand transaction services, including the handling of large blocks of stock for institutions. It said it had found it necessary to decline potential business in the past due to limitations of capital.

The volume of business for Wall Street exploded in the 1960's, and, without automation, the securities firms were ill-prepared to handle it. By 1968, there was chaos in the back offices as they tried to cope with the paperwork. Securities were misplaced and customer complaints proliferated. Finally, under prodding by the Securities and Exchange Commission, trading was halted on Wednesdays for much of 1968 to allow the back offices to catch up.

To solve the problem in the long run, however, Wall Street needed to automate. But it was not clear where the partnerships would find the money needed for the investments. The New York Stock Exchange had always barred brokerage firms from being publicly owned, on the theory that it needed to review every owner. But in 1969 an upstart firm, Donaldson, Lufkin & Jenrette, announced it planned to sell stock to the public. The stock exchange reacted with horror, but by the next year the rules had been changed, and D.L.J. was able to join the rest of corporate America in seeking money from public investors.

Unfortunately for D.L.J., by the time it could sell the stock in April 1970, a bear market was on and the most the firm could get for the shares was 15 each, about half the price it had expected when it originally filed. Nonetheless, a new era had dawned. One by one, all the major brokerage firms sold stock to the public, with Goldman, Sachs becoming the last of the group to do so, in 1999.

The company currently has a capitalization of about $24-million. This is derived mainly from the interests of its private stockholders. D.L.J. is a corporation whose shares are owned by employees and officers.

The public offering is being underwritten, ironically, by the First Boston Corporation, one of the world's largest underwriting houses, which has been prevented from becoming a member of the stock exchange because a number of its shares are in public hands.

The proposal of Donaldson, Lufkin & Jenrette comes at a time when the industry is being sorely pressed for new sources of capital in order to bring its securities-handling mechanisms up to date.

The failure of numerous brokerage houses to have automated procedures provoked an operational crisis in many back offices last year. Unlike virtually all other industries, the securities industry generally has not had the opportunity to use public capital, mainly because of the strictures of the stock exchange.

These strictures are based on the feeling that public ownership of brokerage firms would create a situation under which the exchange would be unable to police adequately the activities of its members.

The New York exchange's constitution and rules currently require approval by the board of governors before any individual can be admitted as a partner or stockholder of a member firm. Such approval obviously would be impossible to enforce if stock in member firms were made widely available to the public.

Donaldson, Lufkin & Jenrette is one of a small group of fast-growing brokerage concerns that have concentrated mainly on highly lucrative institutional business by providing extraordinary comprehensive investment research. Similar firms are Faulkner, Dawkins & Sullivan and Auerbach, Pollak & Richardson.

D.L.J. included a veiled threat in its announcement. It said that potential revenue losses, should it be deprived of its Big Board membership, ultimately could be made up through the greater use of regional exchanges and the over-the-counter market.

The Big Board is deeply fearful of a loss of business to the over-the-counter market and the out-of-town stock exchanges, lest the liquidity of the central auction market in New York be impaired. The desertion of the stock exchange by a firm as influential as D.L.J. could trigger similar moves by other houses.

[May 23, 1969]

Action on trading floors created expensive paperwork backlogs on Wall Street.

1960–1969

Bank Cards Thrive as Some Stores Say No

By ISADORE BARMASH

Credit cards have become a necessity of life for most Americans. Renting a car without one, for example, is virtually impossible. Many stores will not take checks from people they do not know, or will take them only with credit cards for identification.

But the modern credit card accepted by more than one merchant is an invention of the last half of the 20th century. Diners Club was the first to offer such a card, in 1949. It concentrated on an upper-income clientele, with a card that was accepted at restaurants but that soon expanded into other establishments. It was eight years before competition arrived from American Express and Carte Blanche. All were aimed at richer Americans.

In 1958, the Bank of America began the revolution that brought general credit cards to most people by issuing a card called BankAmericard in Fresno, Calif. The initial effort was a fiasco, marked by big losses from abuse of cards by some of the people who received them. But the bank persevered and was soon imitated by banks across the country.

In 1969, The Times reported that the bank cards were thriving, although major department stores that made money from their own credit cards refused to accept the upstarts. Not long afterward, however, the Franklin Simon fashion apparel chain broke ranks and decided to begin taking bank cards.

In the end, the bank cards consolidated into two groups, Bankamericard, which eventually changed its name to Visa, and Master Charge, which became Master Card. There were few stores that did not accept both of them.

In your mail box or even under your door, often unwanted and unwelcomed, they keep coming—a maze of bright new, plastic credit cards to be heaped on top of all the others you already have.

Your favorite bank and banks you may never have heard of are on the prowl, both for your money and for the charge and installment business heretofore claimed as their own by the big, local stores.

In New York Interbank, the clearing house for the Master Charge bank card, said yesterday that some 3 million cardholders are now listed in the metropolitan New York area. And BankAmericard, the credit card franchised by the Bank of America of San Francisco to the Bankers Trust Company here, is said to have 600,000 card holders in the metropolitan area.

But the big New York stores, such as Macy's, Gimbels, Abraham & Straus, Bloomingdale's, B. Altman and others, say they have no intention of honoring these cards. "They're not for us," said one credit man yesterday.

However, thousands of smaller stores, as well as the discount or promotional stores that have either not been in the credit field very long or haven't reached anything like the credit customer saturation they want have signed on with either Master Charge or BankAmericard or both.

And the situation is true in almost every major city in America.

The traditional department stores do not like bank cards because they say it is new competition, rather than an aid to them.

Robert Thiel, vice president of the National Retail Merchants Association and manager of its credit management division, said yesterday, "I don't think the bank cards have hurt the department stores, although it is probably too early to tell. At the same time, it is providing new competition because many small stores and specialty shops now subscribe

Workers validate transactions at a credit-card center in Jericho, N.Y.

CARL T. GOSSETT JR./THE NEW YORK TIMES

to the bank cards and are offering credit for the first time."

Other merchants fear that honoring the bank cards would mean giving up control of the credit policy that they maintain as a competitive measure.

"Setting the terms, deciding on maturity dates, how and when to get tough on slow payers—these have been considerations that we have made for years," a retail credit manager said. "Now, we are asked to give up what we consider to be a competitive edge over the other stores. Why?"

The bank-credit-card community, however, sees this as only a short-term view. On a long-term basis, several prominent bank-card officials feel, they will triumph—and it will be to the great advantage of the retailer.

The end of 1969 will probably see 50 million card holders signed up between the two big bank credit cards, said Garrison A. Southard, president of the Interbank Card Association, the clearing house for Master Charge and other cards in other cities.

"The great market we can provide for stores, plus the strong possibility that we can develop an important direct-mail program for selling merchandise, are elements that stores can only use to their great benefit," he said. Because of the "great volume" of bank cards, he added, "we can handle the big stores' credit system and mail-order selling more efficiently and economically."

Asked how the bank cards were affecting the standard credit cards Richard Howland, General Manager of American Express' credit-card division, replied, "Our business remains 33 per cent higher this year on a base of $1.3-billion, which makes us about the biggest credit card in the country."   [July 8, 1969]

1960–1969

WHY FRANKLIN SIMON ADOPTED BANK CARD

By ISADORE BARMASH

The Franklin Simon Company, one of the country's leading fashion apparel chains, recently decided to adopt the Master Charge bank credit card because its own credit-card operations had been unprofitable and early tests with the bank card in three cities had proved encouraging.

In a move officially effective next week, the apparel-store division of the City Stores Company will attempt to add to its own 500,000 credit customers several million holders of the credit card offered by the Chemical Bank and others across the country. The chain is the first to break the heretofore solid ranks who have steadfastly refused to honor the proliferating bank cards.

Edwin G. Roberts, president of Franklin Simon, said yesterday that adding the Master Charge card as a supplement to his concern's own 30-day charge accounts and budget account plans was "simply bowing to the inevitable."

Acknowledging that he had encountered some negative reaction to his plan from other merchants, Mr. Roberts said he believed that other retail chains would eventually take on bank cards. Such companies would probably be those that have "decentralized operations such as ours, in which we have to service from New York our credit customers in 56 relatively small stores located in 17 states," Mr. Roberts said.

But, he added, he expected the department stores to be the last retailers to join the bank-credit-card parade, because of their own strong credit-card systems and ability to operate them profitably.

Within the last three months, Franklin Simon has tested the bank card in Washington, Atlanta and Detroit, found only a small overlap with its own credit-card holders but derived there the largest city sales increases in its chain.

"We think that our business gains in those cities during those months is more than a mere coincidence," he added.

As additional advantages of accepting the bank card, the Franklin Simon chief cited the opportunity to attract business from many tourists who come to New York and other major cities with their bank cards and the greater opportunity for sales offered by the bank's 24-month maturity time for payment, as opposed to Simon's six months.   [Sept. 26, 1969]

1970–1979

Last gasp of the gas guzzlers. As on Route 17 in Lodi, N.J., rising oil prices and gasoline shortages plagued motorists in the 70's.

The New York Times

NEW YORK, MONDAY, AUGUST 16, 1971

Doubts and Deregulation

THE 1970'S WERE THE YEARS that America came to doubt itself. Inflation rose relentlessly and the country seemed to be at the mercy of oil sheiks and oil company executives. The dollar, for long a symbol of American supremacy in the world, was devalued as the Bretton Woods system of fixed currency rates was ended by President Richard M. Nixon. By the end of the decade, a dollar was worth far less than it had been by any measure—whether in purchasing power or in the number of marks or yen that it could buy. "Sound as a dollar" was viewed as an insult.

The stock market, which had risen reliably for most of the time since World War II, went into reverse. The worst bear market since the Great Depression sent the Dow Jones industrial average down 45 percent, and when the decade ended the average was below where it had been 14 years earlier. By then, investors had concluded that stocks and bonds were dubious investments but that commodities, particularly precious metals, could only rise in price.

The discontent brought on by troubled economic performance was reflected in politics. President Nixon might have survived the Watergate scandal had the economy not looked so bad in 1974. He was forced to resign, and his successor, Gerald Ford—who had been appointed to the Vice Presidency—was turned out of office at the next election. The winner of that election, Jimmy Carter, in 1980 would become the first elected President to be defeated in a run for re-election since Herbert Hoover in 1932.

The oil price increases that plagued the decade brought about changes in the way America lived. Cars got smaller and more fuel-efficient, and speed limits were lowered to cut fuel consumption. It became patriotic to turn down thermostats in winter. American industry began to invest heavily in ways to cut energy costs. Those investments would pay off in future years, but at first they seemed to have little impact. The enduring image of 1979 was of long lines to buy gasoline.

For most of the decade, the response from Washington was to try to place controls on the economy to make it behave better. President Nixon imposed wage and price controls. President Ford had a "Whip Inflation Now," or WIN, campaign. President Carter tried to step up enforcement of controls meant to hold down the costs of domestically produced oil.

But even as controls were being tried, the advocates of deregulation and free competition were winning converts. The tradition of allowing Wall Street to set fixed minimum commissions on stock trades was outlawed in 1975, and baseball teams were forced to compete using salaries to lure players. President Carter ended Government controls on airline fares and eventually decided to phase out the controls on domestic oil prices.

Paul Volcker, who became chairman of the Federal Reserve Board when the decade was ending, was given free rein to use monetary policy to fight inflation. He eventually won, but not before high interest rates helped to bring about two recessions.

1970 Students protest as the U.S. invades Cambodia.

The Penn Central railroad declares bankruptcy.

1971 The Supreme Court approves busing to integrate schools.

President Nixon orders a freeze on wages and prices.

1972 President Nixon is re-elected in a landslide.

The Dow Jones industrial average closes above 1,000 for the first time.

1973 Vice President Spiro T. Agnew resigns, admitting tax evasion.

The Arab oil embargo sends gasoline prices soaring.

1974 President Nixon resigns amid the Watergate scandal; Gerald R. Ford becomes President and pardons Nixon.

1975 The last Americans evacuate Saigon as South Vietnam falls to North Vietnam.

1976 The Viking I and II robots land on Mars.

Jimmy Carter is elected President.

1977 The TV mini-series "Roots" draws 130 million viewers.

The U.S. confirms testing of the neutron bomb.

1978 The first test-tube baby is born, in Britain.

Egypt and Israel reach Camp David accord.

1979 President Carter deregulates oil prices.

Margaret Thatcher becomes prime minister of Britain.

Blacks Snubbed in Business

By MARYLIN BENDER

The civil rights movement of the 1960's had focused on political rights as the Voting Rights Act gave blacks political power in parts of the South. But by the 1970's there was additional emphasis on economic progress. Black executives began to speak out about how they were treated, discussing the lack of respect they received at work and in social situations related to the job. The Times reported in 1970 on the complaints of black managers and on the need for companies to embrace diversity.

One black manager who concluded that it was far better to run his own company—and did so with great success—was John H. Johnson, the owner of Ebony and Jet magazines. In 1990, on the 45th anniversary of the start of Ebony, The Times reported on his business.

His secretary doesn't pass on the office scuttlebutt because their relationship is more reserved than most. As a middle manager in a billion-dollar corporation, he has access to the executive dining room but he can't envision himself at the "big table" with the chairman and the senior officers. He certainly never meets them at their clubs.

At company parties, he doesn't dare ask his immediate boss' wife to dance and he worries about his own wife's uneasiness with a patronizing vice president.

On the few occasions when he stops for a drink with his peers after a late conference, he knows he will be required to answer for the Black Panthers.

When they leave the bar, his colleagues head for the same suburban trains on which they will continue their office politicking. He goes north by subway (unless he's in a mood for cabdriver confrontation) to his integrated apartment house where few if any of his neighbors are trying to climb the executive ladder of American industry.

Given his social handicaps can a black manager or executive (here described in a composite) reasonably hope to attain the higher official levels?

Or is the corporation "the last bastion of resistance to social integration"? Richard Clarke, a minority executive recruiter who has placed 11,500 men and women in positions paying $12,000 to $45,000, charges that it is. "It is shortsighted of industry to hire people, turn them on at 9 and turn them off at 5," he asserts. "Lack of social mobility on and off the job is a definite denial of some of the extra tools needed to put a good finish on the job he's hired for."

But what are blacks hired for other than window dressing and do they move anywhere except laterally? Part of young black disenchantment with business is the conspicuous lack of black faces at the top. In a study conducted by the American Jewish Committee as part of its inquiry into executive suite social prejudice, 90 per cent of the business leaders queried said they considered being black a handicap to chances for executive promotions.

There is a paucity of experienced black executive manpower partly because, says George Carter, a former Peace Corps director and now assistant to the president of the systems manufacturing division of the International Business Machines Corporation, his college generation now 35 to 45 years old found the professions more hospitable than business to blacks.

Moreover, many black department heads or vice presidents are sidelined, however grandly, in public relations, community or urban affairs, special markets or equal employment opportunities.

Rare are such mainstream executives as Dr. Albert Stewart, marketing manager for rubber chemicals at Union Carbide; Frederick Wilkinson Jr., vice president and director of Macy's Jamaica, and E. Frederic Morrow, vice president of the Bank of America-New York working in international business development.

Mr. Wilkinson, Harvard Business School '48, insists, "I've never encountered any obvious occasions of prejudice." He lives in an integrated section of Mount Vernon, N.Y.; and still teaches Sunday school in his former East Bronx neighborhood.

Mr. Morrow, administrative assistant to President Eisenhower for six years, deplored "the jungle of racial barriers" that kept him from an executive position in

A black office worker among whites in 1973 in White Plains, N.Y.

EDWARD HAUSNER/THE NEW YORK TIMES

industry when he left the White House. After two and a half "stop-gap" years with the African-American Institute, he was recommended to the Bank of America by Robert Anderson, former Secretary of the Treasury.

Mr. Morrow and his wife live in an integrated cooperative on upper Fifth Avenue ("not necessarily where I'd like to live but it's still almost impossible for a black person to penetrate those apartment houses on Fifth and Park"). Because of his White House, international and U.N. contacts, "we have a well-rounded, happy social life," he says. "We've not had to depend on business acquaintances."

The chief social sticking points pertinent to black advancement in the executive suite are:

HOUSING: "Give us the option. Don't tell me I have to live in Harlem or that I can't move to Scarsdale," says Adolph Holmes, the National Urban League's economic development director.

Some companies like General Electric and I.B.M. that have had to attract professionals to suburban or remote areas, have gone to bat for black employes whose problems in finding and financing houses are more complicated than those of their white counterparts.

CLUBS: "It may be all right at the lower level to conduct business at 21 or Four Seasons but in the top league it's essential to have access to the big boys in their havens of relaxation," says Ulric Haynes Jr., a minority executive recruiter, alumnus of Amherst, Yale Law and the State Department and now a Lincoln Center board member. "One thing keeps the issue from being joined. We don't want to go where we're not wanted," he adds. Like other self-assured, achieving black executives, he wryly acknowledges "the collective heart attack at the University Club" when he has lunched there as someone's guest.

One alternative to Establishment club barriers is the New Yorker Club, recently organized as a business and professional meeting ground with a membership that is non-exclusive as to race, creed and sex.

SEXUAL MYTHS: In the April issue of The MBA magazine (entitled "Black Management 1970"), James Spain, urban affairs director of Allied Chemical, writes of the "sick fear" of corporate leaders that blacks in the executive suite will "somehow insinuate themselves into the world of private clubs and then living rooms, and ultimately . . . into the sacred confines of the white bedrooms . . ."

On the business cocktail circuit, the white man's view of the black "stud" crops up explicitly. It is snidely expressed at company parties where wives are present and in the office when black managers are pointedly assigned black secretaries or denied clerical support.

Black responses toward social handicaps in the corporation range from an insistence on black identity to accommodation with the white businessman's view of the black man as hard-core unemployed.

"When young blacks call guys like me Oreo—black on the outside, white on the inside—they're absolutely right," says George Carter of I.B.M. "The problem is for

1970–1979

white institutions—and institutions are white—to somehow develop a style which can accommodate real cultural differences."

Meanwhile, efforts at recruiting more black students for business schools increase. The Alfred P. Sloan Foundation has allotted $1-million for fellowships and counseling and has funded the Council for Opportunities in Graduate Management Education representing 10 top business schools. The five-university Consortium for Graduate Study in business for Negroes, originally founded by the Ford Foundation, awarded 65 fellowships last year.

"In the next 10 years, we'll be hearing a lot from these people," predicts Dr. Herbert R. Northrup, professor of industry at the Wharton School who has been studying racial politics in American industry. "You can't make an instant executive but the black executive is a precious commodity today."   [April 19, 1970]

BLACK MEDIA GIANT'S FIRE STILL BURNS

By ROGER COHEN
Special to The New York Times

CHICAGO—John H. Johnson, the owner of Ebony and Jet magazines and one of the richest black men in America, is not altogether happy that 12 percent of his readers are white. "That is more than I would like to have," he said. "I want to be king of the black hill, not the mixed hill."

Having worked his way from being a penniless kid on the banks of the Mississippi to having great wealth and influence on Chicago's glittering North Shore, Mr. Johnson, who estimates his net worth in excess of $200 million, is still a man whose rancor can easily flare.

He says he would never invite a white person to dinner unless that person had first invited him. His advice to young blacks considering joining a white-run corporation is: "If you're satisfied with vice president, fine. But if, like me, you are temperamentally unsuited to that and want to reach the top, do something else."

Mr. Johnson's advice carries much weight within the black business community. As a pioneer in black entrepreneurship—Mr. Johnson founded the Johnson Publishing Company in 1942 with a $500 loan secured by his mother's furniture—his stature is considerable.

Previously, he was more optimistic about race relations, but the Reagan years appear to him to have left more blacks poorer and less educated, reversing earlier progress.

Mr. Johnson, who is 72 years old, has fought barriers all his life. He grew up in Arkansas, where his mother was a domestic, came to Chicago when he was 15 and, when he first tried to borrow money at the age of 24, was waved away by bankers who contemptuously called him "boy."

Today, Mr. Johnson occupies offices taking up the entire 11th floor of the building he owns overlooking Grant Park. The office walls are adorned with photographs of himself with Presidents from Kennedy to Reagan.

Mr. Johnson owns all of Johnson Publishing, whose top officers are his daughter, Linda Johnson Rice, and his wife, Eunice. He favors what he calls a "hands-on, hands-in, hands-wrapped-around management" and still signs every check himself.

The company's sales have soared to $241 million last year, from $72 million in 1980, and it is the second-largest black-owned business in the country, behind TLC Beatrice International Holdings Inc., a multinational food products company operated by the financier Reginald F. Lewis. Johnson publishes three magazines—the flagship Ebony, a general-interest monthly that emphasizes black achievements; Jet, a weekly news magazine, and EM, a men's monthly. A superstitious man, Mr. Johnson started all the magazines in November—of 1945, 1951 and 1985 respectively.

The company also owns the Fashion Fair line of cosmetics for blacks, which was introduced in 1973 and now accounts for about 35 percent of its revenues; the nationally syndicated television series "Ebony/Jet Showcase," and three radio stations.

Ebony and Jet have suffered from the general advertising downturn, with their ad pages falling about 10 percent from 1989 levels in the first eight months of this year. Because they had attracted much advertising from two shrinking industries—liquor and tobacco—the magazines have been particularly hard hit.

Still, their dominance over black publishing remains overwhelming. Ebony, whose circulation has grown to almost 1.9 million, from 1.2 million, during the last 10 years, outsells other black magazines like Essence and Emerge by well over a million copies. And Jet sells nearly a million copies a week.

Mr. Johnson will not disclose his profits but says they are consistently high.

He continues to be angry with what he sees as continuing oppression of blacks, despite the radical change in black-white relations since Ebony was introduced in 1945.

When Mr. Johnson founded Ebony, there were no black players in major-league baseball and no black mayors in big cities. The income of blacks being what it was in the 1940's, the very idea of a black publishing company was widely dismissed. "I've lived through all the changes—from nigger to Negro to black to Afro-American to African-American," he said. "We've come a long way."

These changes used to make him optimistic, but his optimism has faded. "There is still a pattern of discrimination and denial," he argued. "It's tough being black in America. I'm at the top, but not a day goes by without someone reminding me in some way that I am black."

Mr. Johnson has named his daughter as his successor but has no plans to retire. He also has no plans to take his company public. "I'm much too old to get a boss," he said.   [Nov. 19, 1990]

Penn Central Is Granted Authority to Reorganize Under Bankruptcy Laws

By LINDA CHARLTON

The Penn Central Transportation Company, which operates the country's largest railroad system, told a Federal judge yesterday that it could not pay its bills and was granted its petition for reorganization under the bankruptcy laws.

The action will prevent the company's creditors from moving for immediate collection of debts pending the appointment by the judge of trustees to oversee the company's affairs. The company has reported a net loss of $62.7-million in the three months that ended March 31.

Despite the emergency nature of the company's seeking court protection on a Sunday, the Penn Central Board of Directors said that none of its passenger or freight operations would be immediately affected.

All 94,000 of the company's employes were instructed to continue work on the Penn Central lines, which carry thousands of passengers and millions of tons of freight on routes stretching from new York through Chicago and St. Louis, north to the Canadian border and south to Cape Charles, Va.

Governor Rockefeller, in a statement, declared: "The bankruptcy of the Pennsylvania Railroad is a most regrettable development, but I can assure commuters in the New York metropolitan area that the state's emergency program to improve the Penn Central equipment and service will continue without interruption."

The Governor said also that the Metropolitan Transportation Authority, which oversees the operations of railroads in the commuter area, "is prepared for immediate negotiations with the court-appointed new management" on the commuter service.

There was uncertainty last night about the impact the court action would have on the financial markets, which reopen for business this morning.

The timing of the action, while undoubtedly due in part to the failure of all efforts to reach an alternative solution, may also have been related to today's resumption of business. Penn Central had $75-million in short-term notes, or loans, that would have had to be repaid by June 30. It was not known how much, if any, of this indebtedness had been already met or could be met by the railroad.

A spokesman for the New York Stock Exchange said that the Big Board's floor governors would meet this morning to decide whether trading in Penn Central stocks and bonds listed on the exchange should be delayed beyond the normal 10 A.M. opening. In view of the situation, the spokesman said, such a delay appeared likely.

The railroad filed its petition yesterday in Philadelphia, the company's headquarters. It was signed by United States District Court Judge C. William Kraft Jr. in his home at 5:45 P.M. after a long day of meetings by company officers.

The petition was sought under Section 77 of the Federal Bankruptcy Act. It came two days after the announcement that the Nixon Administration had decided not to guarantee loans of up to $200-million to the Penn Central Company and Penn Central Transportation, its railroad subsidiary.

The directors' statement said the action had been taken "because of a severe cash squeeze" and the company's inability "to acquire from any source additional working capital."

Until the petition was granted, the company refused to comment on the crisis through the day, although the 18-story Penn Central headquarters building, normally quiet on Sundays, was filled with activity. The directors themselves held a meeting beginning at 11 A.M. and stretching into the middle of the afternoon.

Other efforts were reportedly under way in Washington to obtain emergency

---

In 1970, the Penn Central railroad was desperately searching for money to stay afloat, but it came as a shock to the public nonetheless when the line was unable to get the Federal Government to guarantee bank loans and was forced to file for bankruptcy.

The railroads had been important parts of the American economy for a century. But the Penn Central had failed to solve any of the problems that had led to its creation in 1968, as a merger of the Pennsylvania Railroad and the New York Central. The two managements had not been able to work well together, nor had the combination achieved the hoped-for savings.

For decades, the nation's railroads had ignored the competing technologies that were taking away their business and had made no effort to expand into trucking or airlines, something they could have easily done with their financial might.

In the aftermath of the Penn Central failure, the Government had to step in to preserve needed rail service. Conrail, a Government-owned company, took over freight service in the Northeast. Recognizing that all railroads were losing money moving passengers, Congress established Amtrak to take over that service.

By the end of the century, most railroads were healthy again, thanks in part to progress in working with trucking companies to haul freight trailers for long distances, with the trucks then being driven to their final destinations. Conrail had been sold to investors, and then taken over and carved up by two other railroad lines.

1970–1979

financial relief for the 28-month-old-line that was formed by the merger of the New York Central and Pennsylvania Railroads.

The appeal for a Government loan guarantee followed the line's failure last month to float a $100-million debenture, or unsecured bond issue, even at interest rates of 11.5 per cent. With Wall Street confidence in the huge system's stability impaired, the company was unable to refinance its short-term indebtedness as loans came due for payment.

As a result of high-level conferences between Penn Central executives and Administration officials, the Defense Department under Section 301 of the Defense Production Act of 1950, agreed to guarantee up to $200-million of bank loans until Congress acted on pending legislation that would allow the Department of Transportation to guarantee such loans to railroads.

After the announcement Friday that the Defense Department, apparently as a result of Congressional pressure, had reversed itself and decided not to guarantee the loan, Penn Central executives met Saturday with Representative Wright Patman, the Texas Democrat who is chairman of the House Banking Committee. The lengthy meeting was an unsuccessful attempt to persuade Mr. Patman to withdraw his opposition to an immediate Government loan guarantee.

The negotiating efforts reportedly continued yesterday at the White House level. William A. Lashley, vice president in charge of public relations for Penn Central, when asked if the continued silence regarding the crisis earlier in the day had been maintained in the hope that some solution would be worked out in Washington, said this interpretation was correct.

The White House refused to comment on the reports. President Nixon was at his weekend retreat of Camp David, in Maryland.

A Senate aide conversant with the situation said the banks that were Penn Central's creditors would accept no assurances except from the White House. When these were not given, he said, the line was left with no alternative except the Section 77 proceeding.

Section 77 of the Bankruptcy Law was signed into law by President Herbert Hoover as his last official act on March 3, 1933, and amended somewhat in 1934.

This section provides for railroads the opposite of what is provided for industrial concerns by bankruptcy laws.

In an ordinary bankruptcy proceeding, the concern's properties and assets—whatever are left—are turned into cash, which is then distributed among its creditors. Under the section concerning railroads, however, a trusteeship is set up with the aim of adjusting the line's debts, preserving its properties and keeping the railroad going.

"The court order," the directors' statement said, "permits Penn Central Transportation Company to retain possession of and continue operation of the railroad system and to conduct other normal business, pending the appointment of trustees by the court."

Since the Depression days of the nineteen-thirties, more than one-third of the railroad mileage of the country has been reorganized under Section 77. Between the early thirties and the mid-forties, about three dozen railroads have operated under the provisions of Section 77 at one time or another.

The Penn Central Transportation Company has substantial real-estate holdings in New York City, including Grand Central Terminal and much of the land along Park Avenue as far north as the Waldorf-Astoria on 50th Street, as well as a number of hotels, office and apartment buildings.

The railroad, which operates 20,530 miles of line in 16 states and two provinces of Canada, provides 35 per cent of all railroad passenger service in the United States. East of the Mississippi, Penn Central accounts for 65 per cent of all passenger service.

The bankruptcy-law action might result in improved service for the Penn Central's 100,000 commuters since, by relieving the line at least temporarily of its immediate financial obligations, more money might be available for improvements. Governor Rockefeller, in his statement, cited at length the improvements under way and planned in the line's commuter service under the state's emergency program.

Penn Central Company, the parent organization, has a variety of nonrailroad subsidiaries including real estate and pipelines, with total assets of more than $6.5-billion. Its annual revenues make it one of the largest private corporations in the United States. The transportation company, however, reported a net loss of $56.3-million last year.

Penn Central stock, which reached a high of $86 a share in 1968, closed Friday at 11⅛. This apparently reflected a continuing investor concern about the company's future despite a recent high-level reshuffling of executives. This step, taken June 8, involved the resignation of two top officers, a third being "relieved" of his duties, and the assumption by Paul A. Gorman, president of the railroad since last December, of the positions of chairman and chief executive officer.

The railroad's long-standing financial problems have been attributed by both its management and the Interstate Commerce Commission largely to the drag of maintaining unprofitable passenger services. The Penn Central's freight profits are not sufficient to offset its steadily growing loss on passenger operations.

Penn Central has been a substantial borrower in the commercial paper market—the Wall Street term for the process by which major corporations obtain short-term loans in the open market rather than through banks or finance companies—and it was uncertain what effect its action would have on investor confidence today.

Secretary of Transportation John A. Volpe said last night that his department "tried desperately to salvage the situation, so that the railroad wouldn't have to file reorganization."

At a news conference Friday, Mr. Volpe said the Government had agreed to guarantee the Penn Central's borrowing because: "If the Penn Central goes down, others will suffer and possibly bring about a complete collapse of our railroad picture."

The department, a spokesman said, would continue to push for Congressional approval of proposed legislation that would put the Government's guarantee behind as much as $750-million in loans to the nation's railroads.

In his Wednesday speech on the economy, President Nixon said that to "strengthen our railroad industry," he was asking Congress "for legislation that will enable the Department of Transportation to provide emergency assistance to railroads in financial difficulty." [June 22, 1970]

1970–1979

The Penn Central experimental Turbo train required millions for track improvement.

Rate War Rages Among Brokers

DEATH OF WALL STREET FIRMS IS FEARED AS A RESULT OF INSTITUTIONAL DISCOUNTS

The New York Stock Exchange traces its roots to a meeting of brokers under a Buttonwood Tree on Wall Street in 1792. The agreement signed then set fixed commissions that the brokers agreed to charge.

For more than 180 years afterward, price competition was forbidden among brokerage houses, and the fixed rates offered only small discounts for the size of an order. The result was that, as trading of big blocks of stock grew, the commissions generated were far in excess of reasonable levels. Then, on May 1, 1975–May Day–a new law took effect requiring negotiated commissions.

At first, commissions charged to institutions fell only a little, but within a month the rates had fallen by more than half, as The Times reported on May 30. Much larger cuts were to come, and institutions grew accustomed to paying only pennies a share for trades. Rates held up for individuals at full-service firms, but discount brokers soon appeared. Even so, it was costly to process small trades, and within a decade even discount brokerage commissions on such transactions were higher than the old fixed rates.

The law led to a shakeout on Wall Street. Firms that primarily served institutional investors found the profits were available not in executing trades–or in the research that traditionally was paid for by commissions– but in trading for the firm's account and in investment banking services such as arranging mergers and underwriting stock offerings.

By ROBERT J. COLE

A month after the end of fixed commissions, a rate war is raging among stockbrokers, and some of the nation's leading financial institutions warned yesterday that it could lead to the death of one or more Wall Street houses.

A spot check of a number of leading banks, insurers, other major institutions and stockbrokers showed that brokers are cutting their fees for the most part by 25 to 35 per cent, and in some cases by 50 and 60 per cent.

The reductions are going almost entirely to major financial institutions, rather than to small investors. In fact, rates charged many small investors have actually increased slightly.

Some financial institutions, moreover, warned that the reduction in rates had become so deep as to endanger the future of the industry and to threaten its ability to handle highly complex financial transactions.

The extent of the cuts, however, is creating genuine concern.

Edward I. O'Brien, president of the Securities Industry Association, the industry group, in a speech yesterday to the Association of Investment Brokers, called the cuts "a form of Russian roulette." Brokers have "scrambled for positions of leadership in a march to the precipice," he said.

He called on the Securities and Exchange Commission, the institutions and brokers to take "a reasoned approach to commissions" to "purge the panic psychology" that he said now gripped institutional securities trading.

"Perpetuation can only lead eventually to drastic deterioration of the broker/dealer network and emaciation of its research capability," he asserted.

Robert D. McEvers, senior vice president in charge of the trust department at the First National Bank of Chicago, Dexter D. Earle, first vice president in charge of securities for the Bankers Trust Company of New York, and others in similar posts who declined to be identified warned of the dangers of the deep reductions.

"Fifty per cent is suicide," Mr. Earle contended, "The laws of economics will prevent it from lasting indefinitely."

"I don't believe the rates will stay where they are," Mr. McEvers said. "They're below what the brokers can afford and stay solvent." He forecast "solvency problems" for some brokers "over the next six months."

Most institutions, however, felt they had little to do with the present situation. "We don't set prices. We just react to them," Mr. McEvers said.

"If the man insists his rate is 50 per cent," Mr. Earle said, "we're not going to argue with him."

"We don't necessarily agree that this wholesale cutting of rates is good," the Bankers Trust officer said. "It doesn't appear to be well thought out on the part of the broker. If they discount too long at too steep a rate, it's going to have a very negative impact. . . . It's no sense charging a level that's unprofitable. They'll go out of business. The market will become less liquid. There will be fewer firms in the business."

One of the nation's leading brokerage houses, Bache & Co. Inc., also warned of the dangers. Speaking in Hawaii yesterday, Harry A. Jacobs Jr., president, decried industry complacency to what he called the "unprofitable deep discounts" being offered by some firms and warned that it was "a practice that can easily lead to the dissolution of some houses" in a poor market.

The Securities and Exchange Commission, which ordered full competition, has the power to reinstitute fixed rates. But Ray D. Garrett Jr., chairman, clearly has no such intention. Mr. Garrett told executives here earlier this week that he was well aware of the price-cutting, but he said that "we don't want to contribute to fear by displaying dramatic consternation ourselves.

"We simply must let things work themselves out until everyone can see a clearer picture."

Last January the S.E.C. ordered the industry to unfix its rates effective May 1 after it concluded that "the free play of competition can provide a level and structure of commission which will better serve the interests of the investing public, the securities markets, the securities industry, the national economy and the public interest than any system of price fixing which can reasonably be devised." It ended a system that had existed on Wall Street since 1792.

Under the former fixed-rate system, brokerage fees quoted for big customers in cents per share—typically ranged from about 15 cents to 50 cents a share, depending on the size and nature of the transaction.

An executive for one of the nation's major life insurance companies commented, "Brokers suddenly realized that the pie had grown smaller, and they wanted to keep their share. So they're competing aggressively on price. It's bad for them, but that's what they're doing."

This executive said that the brokerage houses that are now suffering the most were those that "didn't want to be the leaders in cutting prices and, as a result, lost a lot of business." He declined to identify them other than as "research-oriented" brokers—firms that are widely known for maintaining close watch on industry groups, often paying well for talented research associates.

Edwin R. Olsen, trading director of H. C. Wainwright & Co., a research-oriented brokerage firm, conceded that Wainwright had been outpriced last week, but by deepening its discounts, he said, the firm had won back its clients.

Mr. Olsen said that Wainwright attempted to hold its discounts in early May to no more than 10 per cent, a level maintained by many top-level firms. By mid-month, he said, Wainwright became "more competitive." A few days later, he added, the market "changed substantially."

What happened was that Oppenheimer & Co., heretofore a leader in holding the line, decided to join in cutting rates in order to recover lost business.

"We watched the market until late in May," the Wainwright executive said, "and then we became competitive with most other brokers on the street." He refused to say how deep he would discount but stressed that even today he was conducting some business with little or no discount.

Meanwhile, at Oppenheimer, a spokesman said Oppenheimer's market share had improved since it cut rates. He noted that the firm originally had sought to hold its rate reductions to 8 per cent but then decided to cut fees by 15 to 20 per cent because "our market share was down somewhat."

But can Oppenehimer make money cutting its rates 15 to 20 per cent? "The chances are we can," the spokesman said, "but it's harder to do than at 8 per cent off."

[May 30, 1975]

1970–1979

Nixon Orders 90-Day Wage-Price Freeze, Asks Tax Cuts, New Jobs in Broad Plan; Severs Link Between Dollar and Gold

Richard M. Nixon was elected as a conservative, and he is still remembered that way despite the fact that the most important decisions of his Administration directly challenged conservative orthodoxy. His opening to China is still celebrated as a bold and necessary step, but his economic policy, while equally bold and stunning, was far less wise.

In 1971, he froze wages and prices and then instituted an elaborate system of price controls that lasted for several years but did nothing to really defeat inflation. Interest rates continued to rise, and by the end of the decade the 5 percent inflation rate that had so alarmed Nixon would seem to be amazingly low. Nixon also announced plans to cut taxes. The result was a strong economy with apparently low inflation as he easily won re-election in 1972. But his program left the economy vulnerable to the shocks that were to come, most notably in oil.

The more enduring aspect of the Nixon program was the decision to decouple the dollar from gold. The world was so accustomed to fixed currency exchange rates that there was initial confusion regarding what the action meant, with some banks continuing to change dollars at the old rates while others offered a lower rate and imposed limits on the number of dollars they would accept. Nixon's aides said privately that they expected the result would be a devaluation of the dollar by 12 percent to 15 percent, but it eventually proved to be much greater. By the end of the decade, the dollar had lost half its value against the German mark and a third against the Japanese yen. The age of floating exchange rates had begun, giving international markets a tool to register immediate opinions of a country's economic policies and prospects.

By JAMES M. NAUGHTON

Special to The New York Times

WASHINGTON, Aug. 15—President Nixon charted a new economic course tonight by ordering a 90-day freeze on wages and prices, requesting Federal tax cuts and making a broad range of domestic and international moves designed to strengthen the dollar.

In a 20-minute address, telecast and broadcast nationally, the President appealed to Americans to join him in creating new jobs, curtailing inflation and restoring confidence in the economy through "the most comprehensive new economic policy to be undertaken in this nation in four decades."

Some of the measures Mr. Nixon can impose temporarily himself and he asked for tolerance as he does. Others require Congressional approval and—although he proposed some policies that his critics on Capitol Hill have been urging upon him—will doubtless face long scrutiny before they take effect.

Mr. Nixon imposed a ceiling on all prices, rents, wages and salaries—and asked corporations to do the same voluntarily on stockholder dividends—under authority granted to him last year by Congress but ignored by the White House until tonight.

The President asked Congress to speed up by one year the additional $50 personal income tax exemption scheduled to go into effect on Jan. 1, 1973, and to repeal, retroactive to today, the 7 per cent excise tax on automobile purchases.

He also asked for legislative authority to grant corporations a 10 per cent tax credit for investing in new American-made machinery and equipment and pledged to introduce in Congress next January other tax proposals that would stimulate the economy.

Combined with new cuts in Federal spending, the measures announced by Mr. Nixon tonight represented a major shift in his Administration's policy on the economy.

Only seven weeks ago, after an intensive Cabinet-level study of economic policy, the President announced that he would not seek any tax cuts this year and would hew to his existing economic "game plan," confident of success.

Eleven days ago, Mr. Nixon reasserted his opposition to a wage and price review board—a less stringent method of holding down prices and wages than the freeze he ordered—and said only that he was more receptive to considering some new approach to curtailing inflation.

The program issued tonight at the White House thus came with an unaccustomed suddenness, reflecting both domestic political pressures on the President to improve the economy before the 1972 elections and growing international concern over the stability of the dollar.

The changes represented an internal policy victory for Paul W. McCracken, chairman of the Council of Economic Advisers, and Arthur F. Burns, chairman of the Federal Reserve Board, both of whom had pushed over a number of months for a wage-price curtailment. It marked the first major defeat for George P. Shultz, Mr. Nixon's director of management and budget, who has vigorously opposed such an incomes policy.

The President adopted the new tactics following a weekend of meetings at the Presidential retreat at Camp David, Md. With him there were Dr. Burns, Mr. McCracken, Mr. Shultz and John B. Connally, the Secretary of the Treasury.

"Prosperity without war requires action on three fronts," Mr. Nixon declared in explaining his new policies. "We must create more and better jobs; we must stop the rise in the cost of living; we must protect the dollar from the attacks of international money speculators."

"We are going to take that action—not timidly, not halfheartedly and not in piecemeal fashion," he said.

As a corollary to his tax cut proposals, the President announced that he would slash $4.7-billion from the current federal budget to produce stability as well as stimulation. The budget cutback would come from a 5 per cent reduction in the number of Federal employes, a 10 per cent cut in the level of foreign aid and through postponement of the effective dates of two costly domestic programs—Federal revenue sharing with states and localities and reform of the Federal welfare system.

Mr. Nixon's sudden adoption of a wage and price freeze represented his most drastic reversal of form. He established an eight-member Cost of Living Council to monitor a program under which management and labor must keep wages and prices at the same levels that existed in the 30 days prior to tonight.

Wage or price increases that had been scheduled to go into effect during the next 90 days, such as a 5 per cent raise for the nation's rail workers due to take effect on Oct. 1, must be postponed at least until the 90 days expire. But wage improvements that took effect tonight, including the 50-cent-an-hour increase won by the steelworkers on Aug. 2, will not be affected.

The White House did not include interest rates in the freeze on the theory that they cannot properly be kept under a fixed ceiling. Although describing the freeze as "voluntary," officials noted there was a provision for court injunctions and fines as high as $5,000 for failure to adhere to the ceiling.

Political pressures for some form of an incomes policy have been building for weeks. Public opinion polls have certified concern over unemployment and prices as the No. 1 domestic issue. Democratic Presidential hopefuls have singled out the economy as the primary area for criticizing Mr. Nixon.

At a White House briefing just before the President's address, Secretary Connally said that the changes had been "long in the making." But he conceded in response to questions that he had left last week on vacation without any expectation that Mr. Nixon would put the program into effect tonight.

In explaining why the White House had shifted its economic strategy since he expressed confidence on June 20 that "we're on the right path," Mr. Connally cited tonight an "unacceptable" level of unemployment—currently running at an annual rate of 5.8 per cent—as well as continued inflation, a deteriorating balance of trade and an "unsatisfactory" balance of payments in dealings abroad.

Congress, which is in recess until after the Labor Day weekend, must approve the President's request for new consumer tax breaks and investment credits.

"Every action I have taken tonight is designed to nurture and stimulate [the] competitive spirit, to help snap us out of the self-doubt, the self-disparagement that saps our energy and erodes our confidence in ourselves," the President said.

In calling for repeal of the tax on automobiles, the President said it would represent an average drop of about $200 in the price of a new car. "I shall insist that the American auto industry pass this tax reduction on to the nearly eight million cus-

1970–1979

President Richard M. Nixon, in 1971.

MIKE LIEN/NEW YORK TIMES

tomers who are buying automobiles this year," he emphasized, but did not say how he would keep that pledge.

Mr. Nixon's political advisers have been hoping to cast him as the President of peace and prosperity in a bid for re-election next year.

With every speech in recent weeks emphasizing his initiatives toward global peace—his forthcoming journey to Peking, disengagement from Vietnam and negotiations on arms, the Middle East and Berlin with the Soviet Union—Mr. Nixon has faced a proliferation in Democratic statements criticizing him for permitting continued unemployment and inflation.

Mr. Nixon's address tonight contained the kernels of what could become, if his policies have the desired impact, the prosperity rhetoric of 1972.

"Today we hear the echoes of those voices preaching a gospel of gloom and defeat," he said.

"As we move into a generation of peace, as we blaze the trail toward the new prosperity," he added, "I say to every American—let us raise our spirits, let us raise our sights, let all of us contribute all we can to this great and good country that has contributed so much to the progress of mankind." [Aug. 16, 1971]

UNILATERAL U.S. MOVE MEANS OTHERS FACE PARITY DECISIONS

By EDWIN L. DALE JR.
Special to The New York Times

WASHINGTON, Aug. 15—President Nixon announced tonight that henceforth the United States would cease to convert foreign-held dollars into gold—unilaterally changing the 25-year-old international monetary system.

How many pounds, marks, yen and francs the dollar will buy tomorrow will depend on decisions of other countries. In some countries, the value of the dollar may "float," moving up and down in day-to-day exchanges. A period of turmoil in the foreign-exchange markets is all but certain, which means uncertainty for American tourists, exporters and importers.

The President said he was taking the action to stop "the attacks of international money speculators" against the dollar. He did not raise the official price of gold, which has been $35 an ounce since 1934.

Mr. Nixon said he was not devaluing the dollar. But, he said, "if you want to buy a foreign car, or take a trip abroad, market conditions may cause your dollar to buy slightly less."

In addition to severing the link between the dollar and gold, the President announced a 10 per cent extra tax on all dutiable imports, except those that are subject to quotas, or quantitative limits.

The tax will thus apply to cars but not to coffee, to radios but not to sugar, to shoes but not to oil. Coffee and other items, such as bananas, grown in tropical countries are exempt because no duty is charged on them. Oil and sugar are exempt because they are under quota. The President said he had legal authority for the new surcharge.

The change in the world monetary system brought about by the President's decision to cease converting foreign-held dollars into gold is entirely uncertain. That was the word used by

Secretary of the Treasury John B. Connally. What matters most is exchange rates among currencies and Mr. Connally said he did not know what would happen.

The purpose of Mr. Nixon's move was clear. The President said, "The time has come for exchange rates to be set straight and for the major nations to compete as equals." This means a desire for other countries to raise their currencies' value in terms of the dollar. In effect, therefore, the dollar would be devalued.

Mr. Connally said, "We anticipate and we hope there would be some changes in exchange rates of other currencies."

But this will depend on other countries. For 25 years non-Communist nations have maintained the international exchange value of their currencies by "pegging" them to the dollar. Their central banks would buy or sell their own currencies in daily trading in the foreign-exchange market to keep the value within one per cent either side of "par," expressed in a precise dollar amount for each unit of the other currency.

After Mr. Nixon's action tonight, they can still do so, if they so wish. But they are no longer obligated to do so under the rules of the International Monetary Fund. Their obligation to peg their currencies to the dollar was a counterpart of the United States's obligation to exchange dollars for gold. The United States has now renounced that obligation.

Referring to the 1944 conference in New Hampshire that established the I.M.F. and the present rules for monetary exchange, Arthur M. Okun, Chairman of the Council of Economic Advisers under President Johnson, said tonight, "We just ended the Bretton Woods system forever."

Mr. Okun said he could not say by what degree other currencies would rise in value relative to the dollar, but he was certain that they would rise. [Aug. 16, 1971]

Young Workers Disrupt Key G.M. Plant

By AGIS SALPUKAS

Special to The New York Times

LORDSTOWN, Ohio, Jan. 22—Production on the world's fastest assembly line, on which the General Motors Corporation has pinned its hopes of being able to meet foreign competition, has been seriously disrupted by mostly young workers who say they are being asked to work too hard and too fast to be able to turn out quality automobiles.

The outcome of the labor dispute, in which the youngest local of the United Automobile Workers is confronting one of General Motors' toughest management teams, could have wide repercussions for United States industry.

The struggle has raised a wider issue of how management can deal with a young worker who is determined to have a say as to how a job should be performed and is not so easily moved by management threats that there are plenty of others waiting in line if he does not want to do the job.

It also comes at a time when the Nixon Administration is stressing rising productivity as the way to stop inflation and the influx of foreign goods.

The costly dispute centers on whether management has eliminated jobs and distributed extra work to the remaining men to the extent that they are unable to keep up with the assembly line in the Lordstown plant.

General Motors estimates that it has lost the production of 12,000 Vega automobiles and about 4,000 Chevrolet trucks worth about $45-million. Management has had to close down the assembly line repeatedly since last month after workers slowed their work and allowed cars to move down the line without performing all operations.

A. B. Anderson, the plant manager, said in an interview, "We've had engine blocks pass 40 men without them doing their work."

Management has also accused workers of sabotage, such as breaking windshields, breaking off rear-view mirrors, slashing upholstery, bending signal levers, putting washers in carburetors and breaking off ignition keys.

The union, which concedes that there may have been some sabotage by a few angry workers, maintains that the bulk of the problems with the cars were a result of cutbacks in numbers of workers in a drive by management to increase efficiency and cut costs. According to the union, the remaining workers have had to absorb the extra work and cannot keep up with the assembly line. The result, the union men say, is improperly assembled cars.

The dispute is taking place in one of the most modern and sophisticated assembly plants in the world, built in 1966 on a farm field near Lordstown.

Through better design, a variety of new types of power tools and other automated devices, much of the heavy lifting and hard physical labor has been eliminated in the plant. Workers on the assembly line have easier access to the car body and do not have to do as much bending and crawling in and out as in the older plants in Detroit. The Vega also has 43 per cent fewer parts than a full-size car, making the assembly easier.

But, as the jobs become easier and simpler, the rate at which they can be done can be increased. On a regular assembly line, which runs at about 55 cars an hour, a worker takes about a minute to perform a task, while workers at the Lordstown plant need only about 40 seconds.

The wages are good. Workers start out on the line at $4.37 an hour, get a 10-cent-an-hour increase within 30 days and another 10 cents after 90 days. Benefits come to $2.50 more an hour.

The late 1960's had seen student rebellions and the growth of a widespread drug culture on college campuses. But it came as a great surprise to America—and to the executives who ran manufacturing firms—that working-class youths had many of the same rebellious attitudes. The problems that General Motors encountered in dealing with the young workers at a new plant in Ohio were detailed by The Times in 1972.

A few weeks after the article appeared, the workers at the plant went on strike, angry about the company's efforts to speed up work in its attempt to compete with low-cost imports. The strike was settled after a few weeks, but the incident at the Lordstown plant became a symbol of worker unrest.

1970–1979

The plant sits almost in the center of the heavy industrial triangle made up of Youngstown, with its steel plants; Akron, with its rubber industry, and Cleveland, a major center for heavy manufacturing.

The plant, which produces all the Vegas made by General Motors, draws its 7,700 workers, whose average age is 24 years, from areas that have felt the sting of foreign competition and where unemployment and layoffs have been heavy. Many of the fathers of the young auto workers are employed in steel and rubber and have watched their jobs dwindle because foreign products have undercut their industries.

But the threat of unemployment and pressure from mothers and fathers, from the local press and public officials, have so far had little effect on the militant young workers who began their struggle with General Motors last October.

It was then that the General Motors Assembly Division, a management team that has developed the reputation for toughness in cutting costs and bettering productivity, took over the operation of the Fisher Body Plant and Chevrolet assembly plant here and began to consolidate the operations.

From the point of view of management, the two plants had not been operating at their peak efficiency. A major reorganization of work began. According to management it consisted mostly of changing jobs to make them more efficient, although management conceded that about 300 jobs had been eliminated and some workers had been given additional work.

Mr. Anderson explained that changes had to be made to bring the assembly line, which can turn out 100 Vegas in an hour, up to the potential it was designed for.

"If we are to remain competitive, we will have to take advantage of those sections of the contract on making the work more efficient," he said.

But across the Ohio Turnpike, Gary Bryner, the 29-year-old president of Local 1112, in an interview in his office in a modern brick union hall, said that about 700 jobs had been eliminated and that much of the extra work had been shifted to men who had no time to do it.

Striking auto workers picket outside the General Motors plant in Lordstown, Ohio.

CORBIS/UPI

"That's the fastest line in the world," Mr. Bryner said. "A guy has about 40 seconds to do his job. The company does some figuring and they say, 'Look, we only added one thing to his job.' On paper it looks like he's got time.

"But you've got 40 seconds to work with," he continued. "You add one more thing and it can kill you. The guy can't get the stuff done on time and a car goes by. The company then blames us for sabotage and shoddy work."

He said that before the new management team took over, there were about 100 grievances in the plant. Since then, he said, grievances have increased to 5,000—about 1,000 of which consist of protests of too much work added to a job.

Mr. Bryner, on whose desk sit a peace symbol and a little book of "Revolutionary Quotations by Great Americans," said that a decision by the workers to work at their old pace to protest the changes had come from the rank and file and not from the union leadership.

"These guys have become tigers," he said. "They've got guts. You used to not see them at union meetings. Now we've got them in the cafeteria singing 'Solidarity'"

Management has attempted conciliation and has instituted sensitivity sessions with groups of workers to find out what the complaints are.

But the over-all management strategy so far has been one of toughness, of hoping for results from the smaller pay checks that are issued when workers are sent home early when there is a slowdown and from foremen's disciplining workers by sending them home without pay.

When the workers went into the plant yesterday they found on the bulletin boards a notice saying that not only would work slowdowns be dealt with through disciplinary measures but also that workers could be dismissed.

Many young workers said in interviews that the tougher the company became, the more they would stiffen their resistance, even though other jobs were scarce and many of them had recently been married and had families.

Nick Schecodonic Jr., 27, a repair spot welder, said, "In some of the other plants where they did the same thing, the workers were older. They took some of this. But I've got 25 years ahead of me in that plant."

Mr. Schecodonic, who is married and has children, added, "I actually saw a woman in the plant running along the line to keep up with the work. I'm not going to run for anybody."

Another worker who is worried about keeping his job said that he decided to support the union rank-and-file when he saw a gap between the body of a car and the instrument panel and brought it to the attention of the foreman.

The worker, who has a job as an inspector, said the foreman told him, "To hell with it. Ship it to the dealer." He said that after he refused to approve the car, the foreman signed the paper himself.

Andrew O'Keefe, public relations director at the plant, denied that any defective cars had been shipped and said that any foreman passing on a defective car would "be fired on the spot."

Mr. Anderson attributed part of the dispute to the attitude of the young worker. But he also laid much of the resistance to the fear that a worker's job would be changed.

But many industrial engineers have recently been questioning whether the direction of management toward assembly line work can continue.

Most of the efforts, brought to a highly advanced state in the Lordstown plant, have been to make the job simpler and easier, but they have often resulted in removing the last traces of skill.

Some of the industrial engineers are saying that perhaps it is not so much the physical nature of the work as its constant, repetitive unskilled nature that is being resisted by assembly line workers, particularly young workers who are more educated and have higher expectations.

[Jan. 23, 1972]

1970–1979

Baseball's Exempt Status Upheld by Supreme Court

As professional sports became one of America's most popular entertainment industries, baseball clung to a system that prevented athletes from moving from one team to another in search of higher pay, although the clubs were perfectly free to trade them to other teams.

That system was challenged in 1970 by Curt Flood, a St. Louis Cardinals all-star outfielder who was angered at being traded to the Philadelphia Phillies. He asked the courts to rule that professional baseball's exemption from the antitrust laws, first established by a Supreme Court decision in 1922, made no sense in light of the big business it had become.

Flood lost his suit in 1970 and appealed to the Supreme Court, which ruled that it was up to Congress to change the system if it wanted to do so, as The Times reported in 1972. Flood never played baseball again after he lost the appeal.

But baseball's system was nonetheless in jeopardy. Players were tied to teams by the reserve clause in each contract, which held that the team had the right to renew the contract for the next season. As far as the teams were concerned, that meant they could keep a player forever—or at least until he was no longer able to play well enough. But in 1975 two pitchers—Andy Messersmith, of the Los Angeles Dodgers, and Dave McNally, a long-time Baltimore Orioles star who had been traded to the Montreal Expos—filed for arbitration, arguing that the fact the contract said it was renewable for one year meant it could be renewed for only one year. The arbitrator agreed, and free agency came to baseball after the courts refused to overturn that decision.

Other sports, which lacked baseball's historic antitrust exemption, had made deals with player unions for limited free agency that slowed the escalation of salaries. Baseball no doubt could have gotten a similar deal. But the team owners insisted on appealing every ruling, and when they lost they had little bargaining power left. Baseball players became among the best-paid workers in America.

By LEONARD KOPPETT

Special to The New York Times

WASHINGTON, June 19—Baseball, and only baseball, remains exempt from the antitrust laws, the Supreme Court ruled today by a 5–3 margin. But the Court again urged Congress to resolve the problem.

The decision ended the Curt Flood case in defeat for the player who challenged baseball's reserve system, a set of arrangements that ties a player to one club indefinitely.

Flood, then a 32-year-old outfielder earning $90,000 a year, objected to being traded from St. Louis to Philadelphia after the 1969 season. He sued for $3-million in damages, claiming that reserve rules had prevented him from playing for any other club. The Major League Players Association supported his suit financially and former Justice Arthur Goldberg represented him.

A trial in May, 1970, resulted in a lower court decision that the merits of the case need not be considered because baseball was made exempt from antitrust laws by Supreme Court decisions in 1922 and 1953.

Today's decision, delivered by Justice Harry A. Blackmun, also bypassed the merits of the reserve system and stressed the Court's refusal to overturn previous rulings. It acknowledged that baseball's special status was an "aberration" and an "anomaly," but re-affirmed the position taken in several prior cases that it was up to Congress to remedy the situation with legislation.

Voting with the majority were Chief Justice Warren E. Burger, who expressed "reservations," and Justices Byron R. White, Potter Stewart and William E. Rehnquist.

Justices William O. Douglas and Thurgood Marshall filed dissenting opinions, in which Justice William J. Brennan Jr. joined. Justice Lewis F. Powell Jr. did not participate.

The 1922 ruling, referred to as Federal Baseball, stated that baseball was not the sort of business that the antitrust laws were intended to cover.

In 1953, in a case called Toolson vs. New York, the Court ruled, 7–2, that the exemption should be continued, even though legal philosophy had changed, because the industry had been allowed to develop for 30 years on the assumption of its immunity.

Justice Blackmun stressed this point.

"We continued to loathe, 50 years after Federal Baseball and almost two decades after Toolson, to overturn those cases judicially when Congress, by its positive inaction, has allowed those decisions to stand for so long," he wrote.

During the last 20 years,

Curt Flood challenged baseball's reserve system.

many bills have been introduced to grant uniform antitrust exemptions to all major professional sports, but none has passed both houses of Congress in the same session.

Even as the Supreme Court was issuing today's ruling, a Senate hearing was in progress on a proposed Federal sports commission that would have jurisdiction over professional team sports, and the House Judiciary Committee was scheduling hearings starting July 24 on the general topic of sports and antitrust regulations.

Justice Douglas, in a footnote to his dissent, declared: "While I joined the Court's opinion in Toolson, I have lived to regret it, and I would now correct what I believe to be its fundamental error."

He argued that the inaction of Congress could be seen two ways:

"If Congressional inaction is our guide, we should rely upon the fact that Congress has refused to enact bills broadly exempting professional sports from antitrust regulation. . . . There can be no doubt that were we considering the question of baseball for the first time upon a clean slate, we would hold it to be subject to Federal antitrust regulation. The unbroken silence of Congress should not prevent us from correcting our own mistakes."

But Chief Justice Burger, in his brief concurring opinion, said:

"Like Mr. Justice Douglas, I have grave reservations as to the correctness of Toolson; as he notes in his dissent, he joined in that holding but has 'lived to regret it.'" The error, if such it be, is one on which the affairs of a great many people have rested for a long time. Courts are not the forum in which this tangled web ought to be unsnarled.

"I agree with Mr. Justice Douglas that Congressional inaction is not a solid base, but the least undesirable course now is to let the matter rest with Congress; it is time the Congress acted to solve this problem."

Justice Marshall, in his dissent, stressed the importance of upholding antitrust laws in the general interest. "They are as important to baseball players as they are to football players, lawyers, doctors, or members of any other class of workers."

He pointed out, however, that overruling Federal Baseball and Toolson would not necessarily mean that Flood won. "I would remand this case to the District Court for consideration whether . . . there has been an antitrust violation."

The prevailing view, however, was Justice Blackmun's: He found that Federal laws took precedence over state antitrust suits, and that there was no need to consider the argument that the reserve system was a matter for labor negotiation and therefore exempt from antitrust.

"If there is any inconsistency or illogic in all this, it is an inconsistency and illogic of long standing that is to be remedied by the Congress and not by this Court," he wrote.

"Under these circumstances, there is merit in consistency even though some might claim that beneath that consistency is a layer of inconsistency." [June 20, 1972]

1970–1979

ARBITRATOR FREES 2 BASEBALL STARS

By JOSEPH DURSO

A labor arbitrator ruled yesterday that two pitchers, Andy Messersmith and Dave McNally, were free agents who were no longer bound by their baseball contracts and could sell their services to the highest bidder.

If upheld, the ruling could topple the major-league teams' legal right to "own" players indefinitely under their contracts. But it was expected to be challenged, and perhaps modified, either in court or in collective bargaining between the players and their clubs.

The decision by the arbitrator, Peter M. Seitz, was immediately cheered by the Players' Association as a major erosion of the controversial "reserve system" which binds an athlete to his team until he is traded or retires.

But it was denounced by the commissioner of baseball, Bowie Kuhn, who said: "If this interpretation prevails, baseball's reserve system will be eliminated by the stroke of the pen."

Both sides, though, agreed that the arbitrator had fired the first shot—but by no means the last—in a struggle that now would be waged in two places: in face-to-face bargaining between the 960 players in the big leagues and the 24 club owners, and ultimately in the courts.

The stakes and the emotions in the dispute were so high that the arbitrator barely survived his own blockbuster. As the ruling was announced, the owners handed Seitz a written notice to terminate his role as chairman of the three-man panel that had heard the two cases. The reason was that "professional baseball no longer has confidence in the arbitrator's ability to understand the basic structure of organized baseball."

At the heart of the controversy was the fact that baseball had long enjoyed stricter control over its players than the other professional sports. Twice in the last half-century, the Supreme Court has reviewed the game's "reserve system" and allowed it to stand.

But in recent years, the contract system has been increasingly challenged in Congress and in collective bargaining; and one year ago Seitz declared Catfish Hunter free of his contract with the Oakland A's, after which Hunter auctioned himself to the New York Yankees for $3.75 million.

But that dispute involved a breach of contract by the Oakland team, which owed $50,000 to the pitcher. In the two cases yesterday, the issue was more basic: both Messersmith and McNally refused to sign contracts for 1975, pitched without contracts and then demanded their freedom in the open market.

Their appeal was heard by three officials: John Gaherin, who represents the teams' owners in labor matters; Marvin Miller, the economist who is executive director of the Baseball Players' Association, and Seitz, a professional arbitrator from New York who served as an "impartial chairman." In a 70-page opinion, Seitz cast the deciding vote that ruled Messersmith free of the Los Angeles Dodgers and McNally free of the Montreal Expos.

"It was represented to me that any decision sustaining Messersmith and McNally would have dire results, wreak great harm to the reserve system and do serious damage to the sport of baseball [and] would encourage many other players to elect to become free agents.

"The panel's sole duty is to interpret and apply the agreements and understandings of the parties. If any of the expressed apprehensions and fears are soundly based, I am confident that

Andy Messersmith.

the dislocations and damage to the reserve system can be avoided or minimized through the good-faith collective bargaining between the parties."

The bargaining, in fact, has already been under way because the current "basic agreement" between the teams and players expires next Wednesday. It covers minimum pay, working conditions, the length of the season and the teams' legal hold on the players—that is, their right to "reserve" their services year after year.

In professional football, basketball and hockey, a team's control over its players is considerably less sweeping. A team generally may "own" an athlete for the length of his contract plus one year—the "option year."

Dave McNally.

During the extra year, the player may take the option of working without a contract; after it, he is free to sign with another club. But the team that lost him usually receives some compensation in return, a procedure (now under legal attack) known as the "Rozelle rule" because it was instituted by Pete Rozelle, now commissioner of the National Football League.

In baseball, though, a team's control has been maintained through a paragraph in each player's contract. It permits the club to renew the contract the following year, even if the player refuses to sign again. The players recently have argued that the renewal was good for only one year; the owners insisted it could be invoked indefinitely. Seitz sided with the players.

"I am not an Abraham Lincoln signing the Emancipation Proclamation," the arbitrator said at a news conference in his home after the ruling had been announced. "Involuntary servitude has nothing to do with this case. I decided it as a lawyer and an arbitrator. This decision does not destroy baseball. But if the club owners think it will ruin baseball, they have it in their power to prevent the damage."

But Commissioner Kuhn, a lawyer, said:

"I am enormously disturbed by this arbitration decision. It is just inconceivable that after nearly 100 years of developing this system for the over-all good of the game, it should be obliterated in this way. It is certainly desirable that the decision should be given a thorough judicial review."   [Dec. 24, 1975]

Life to Cease Publishing Dec. 29

By ERIC PACE

Life magazine, whose birth 36 years ago helped make photo journalism an art form as well as a news medium, will publish its last issue Dec. 29, Time Inc. announced yesterday.

Tears welling in his eyes, Andrew Heiskell, the chairman of the board of Time Inc., said there had been "emotional agony in the decision" to end publication of the magazine, which has lost more than $30-million in the last four years.

The demise of Life, following the folding of Look, The Saturday Evening Post and Collier's in the last 15 years, leaves the country without a major, general interest, text-and-picture magazine for the first time since well before World War II.

Hedley Donovan, the editor in chief of Time Inc., said that competition from television, rising postal rates and predictions of further heavy losses had been prime considerations in the decision to close Life. It was taken Thursday at a directors' meeting in Mr. Heiskell's 34th-floor office in the Time-Life Building.

Mr. Heiskell said that closing down Life "is obviously going to improve the financial outlook of the corporation—otherwise why did we do it?" All told, Life's demise will cost the corporation about $7-million in severance pay, unexpired printing contracts and other closing expenditures.

Asked what Henry R. Luce, the firm's late head, would think of Life's end, Mr. Heiskell said, "Surely he would have shed a very big tear on this occasion."

In Honolulu, meanwhile, Mr. Luce's widow, Clare Boothe Luce, said the cessation of publication was "very sad," but she added: "There's no place for something that can't survive." Mr. Luce had been "quite aware that Life was ailing before he died," she said.

Mr. Heiskell and Mr. Donovan, both grim-faced six-footers wearing somber gray suits, appeared at a news conference in the sumptuous eighth-floor auditorium of the building, which is to keep its name unchanged. Upstairs, in the Life offices, raucous, desperate laughter rang out, and fists flew briefly when a Life staff member objected to being filmed by a television cameraman.

Time Inc. executives said they did not know how many of the more than 300 Life staff members would be given other jobs within the corporation.

Asked at the news conference what would happen now to the collection of millions of pictures taken by Life photographers, Mr. Heiskell paused an instant, and then said, "I haven't thought about that."

But an aide said later that the collection would continue to be used by Time Inc. magazines. These are Time, Fortune, Sports Illustrated and the newly founded specialty magazine Money. Mr. Donovan said all four publications were doing well.

Mr. Donovan and Mr. Heiskell issued a joint statement that gave this explanation of the decision to cease publication:

Life magazine was an American institution in 1972, legendary for its photo essays that had brought the world to every town in America. But now television was doing that, and Life was losing money. Like Look and the Saturday Evening Post, both of which had died within the previous three years, Life had tried to cut circulation while charging premium rates to advertisers. Once again, the strategy failed. There was, it seemed, no place for a general interest magazine in the television era. The Times reported on and analyzed its demise that December.

1970–1979

A layout artist works on the last issue of Life magazine.

MICHAEL EVANS/THE NEW YORK TIMES

"We have published Life at very substantial deficits in 1969 and 1970, and smaller deficits in 1971 and 1972. As our projections for 1973 took shape, however, they showed a resumption of heavy losses, and the indications for 1974 were even more unfavorable.

"We have persevered as long as we could see any prospect, within a reasonable time span, of a turnaround in Life's economy. We can no longer see such a prospect, and we believe that publication of Life beyond 1972 could be a burden on the other magazines and activities of Time Inc. and the long-term growth of the company.

"From the late nineteen-fifties on, Life's form of photo journalism, and the magazine's appeal as an advertising medium, have encountered increasingly severe competition from television . . . the cost pressures and the competitive pressures kept building up, and we have been running out of economies.

"In late 1970 we decided on a change in circulation policy, and in two moves lowered total circulation from 8.5 million to 5.5 million, at the same time increasing the effective price per copy to the subscriber. The benefits of these moves are offset, however, by the postal rate increases of about 170 per cent which were facing Life over five years."

And, the statement continued, "it should be remembered that the Administration exempted the Postal Service, but not the press, from price controls."

Ralph Graves, Life's managing editor who has spent 24 of his 48 years at Life, attended the news conference, but said nothing. Earlier, he had told a meeting of Life staff members, "We worked on a great and famous magazine, we published many wonderful stories and we had a remarkable experience together." [Dec. 9, 1972]

DATED PUBLISHING STRATEGY LINKED TO DOWNFALL OF LIFE

By PHILIP H. DOUGHERTY

Life magazine, once the nation's leading national advertising medium, is sharing the fate of other once-great, mass-circulation, general-interest magazines—Look, the weekly Saturday Evening Post, Collier's and Liberty.

It is the victim of television, the special-interest magazine and the proposed drastic postal-rate increases.

It is the victim also of an outmoded publishing philosophy it was trying to change even as it sank.

The philosophy, born during the circulation war that waged from the late nineteen-forties through the mid-nineteen-sixties, had Curtis Publishing's Post, Cowles Communications' Look and Time Inc.'s Life practically giving away subscriptions through special offers to increase circulations and charge advertisers more.

Today most magazines are insisting that their readers carry their share of the costs, and that was the announced intention of J. Garry Valk when he became publisher of Life three years ago.

By that time the Post had been dead a year, having cut its circulation in half in an effort to survive, and Life—still following the circulation-war philosophy—picked up 1.5 million of the Post circulation, bringing its own to 8.5 million. Life then increased the advertising rate for a four-color page to an unheard-of $64,200—far higher than for the average commercial minute on TV.

In the spring of 1970, Look cut its circulation from 7.75 million to 6.5 million, concentrating on metropolitan areas. It ceased publication last year.

And when Life in late 1970 cut its circulation twice, bringing it to its present 5.5 million, there were those in advertising and publishing circles who said it was the beginning of the end.

But while the circulation was cut 21.4 per cent, the advertising rates were lowered only about 15 per cent. This year, Life, which in its 36 years has carried $3.5-billion in advertising, dropped below $100-million in annual advertising revenue for the first time since 1952. From a high of $169.6-million in 1966, revenues have fallen this year to an estimated total of $91-million.

Meanwhile, according to the Magazine Publishers Association, production costs are increasing year by year. The physical production cost of an issue of Life, not including editorial costs and subscription promotion, is about 20 cents, Mr. Valk said. In the past, the magazine sold by subscription for as little as 10 cents a copy.

Only 175,000 copies of each issue were being sold on newsstands at the cover price of 50 cents. Mr. Valk said that subscription rates had been raised to about 16.8 cents a copy, and that plans had called for an increase to 19 cents next year.

The magazine industry generally is doing well this year with special-interest publications, such as women's magazines and Time Inc.'s Sports Illustrated, the healthiest. These allow advertisers to be selective in addressing their costly messages. [Dec. 9, 1972]

Anatomy of an Insurance Scandal

By ROBERT J. COLE

The Equity Funding Corporation of America, once among the most promising companies in mutual funds and life insurance, today lies smoldering in the ruins of what may yet become one of the biggest financial disasters in modern history.

Raymond L. Dirks, a recognized stock-market analyst, following a phone call from a disgruntled former employe uncovered the incredible story that Equity Funding officers were masterminding a scheme to create insurance policies by the thousands and then sell these policies for cash to other major life insurers.

The almost unbelievable part of the story is that the widespread fraud was known at many levels of the company, by perhaps as many as a thousand people. Those closest to it were believed to have cleverly concealed their tracks through intimidation, subterfuge, threats of violence and the use of doctored computer tapes.

The apparent purpose was to create sufficient profits, at least on paper, to keep the price of Equity Funding stock up.

If the price was high enough, so the reasoning went, Equity Funding might one day be able to buy a major insurance company with legitimate life insurance and then "go straight."

Even more unbelievable, however, is the fact that until Mr. Dirks took his wild tale to a blue-chip list of clients who held stock in the company, some of whom refused to take the story seriously, Equity Funding managed to deceive the auditors who checked their books, the companies that bought their insurance, the experts who influence Wall Street and even the insurance watchdogs in several key states.

The mind-boggling scandal may take years to resolve, but the issues it raises are commanding attention now.

THE AUDITORS

It does not take much imagination to conclude that the auditing techniques of even the establishment certified public accounting firms—as good as they might be— need improvement.

The firm of Wolfson, Weiner, Ratoff & Lapin, now part of Seidman & Seidman, for example, examined the financial statements of Equity Funding for the four years ended in 1970 and concluded that they "present fairly the consolidated results of operations."

Seidman & Seidman, in a subsequent examination of the company as of Dec. 31, 1971, said the statements "present fairly the consolidated financial position of Equity Funding Corporation of America and subsidiaries."

If even only part of the charges prove to be true, namely, that an ingenious system of computer codes was programmed to handle bogus insurance policies, phantom death benefits and nonexistent policy lapses, it would mean that the operation was so cleverly devised that some of the top accounting firms in the country were unable to detect it.

When Equity Funding said it had $25-million in negotiable bonds in the American National Bank and Trust Company in Chicago, why did no one discover that the bonds were not there, if they ever existed, until the Illinois Insurance Department looked last month? By then, however, it was too late.

When Equity Funding said it had a number of certificates of deposit, why was it that some auditor, not yet identified, allegedly accepted a written list of the documents as proof instead of asking to see the real thing?

Auditors already concede that changes are coming as a direct result of the Equity Funding scandal and some auditors are already at work to try to make certain it cannot happen again.

For a time in the late 1960's and early 1970's, the Equity Funding Corporation of America was thought to be one of the most innovative financial companies in the country. It sold life insurance tied to mutual funds, supposedly providing the best of both worlds for its customers and rapidly rising profits for itself.

In fact, for several years it was a huge fraud, reporting sales vastly in excess of reality. It fooled auditors with computer printouts and with paper files that were created during late-night parties after the auditors asked to see random files.

The scandal broke after a former employee tipped off a Wall Street analyst, Raymond L. Dirks, who then told favored institutional clients and alerted the Securities and Exchange Commission. There was a mad dash by clients to get out of the stock, with the shareholders who did not hear the story, or who failed to act on it quickly enough, left with worthless shares.

The case revealed shortcomings in the ways audits were conducted and in the quality of state regulation of insurance companies, as was explained in a Times article published two weeks after the scandal erupted in 1973.

Stanley Goldblum, the founder of Equity Funding, was convicted of fraud and sentenced to eight years in prison, but the most enduring legal precedent was set in a case involving Dirks, the analyst who first learned of the fraud.

Dirks considered himself a hero, but to the S.E.C. he had profited from passing on inside information. The agency censured him, and Dirks took the case to the Supreme Court, which cleared him. For a recipient of a tip to be guilty of insider trading, the court said, the insider who provided the tip must have been seeking to profit from the tip.

1970–1979

THE REINSURERS

The insurance industry today is probably one of the most closely knit institutions of its kind in the world.

Millions of dollars of business is done over the telephone on faith alone. To violate that trust would be to invite immediate ostracism.

Consequently it was no surprise that among the big-name insurers who had bought insurance from Equity Funding were Anderson, Clayton & Co., Ranger National Life Insurance Company, the Connecticut General Life Insurance Company, the Pennsylvania Life Insurance Company and the Kentucky Central Life Insurance Company. In all, a trusting insurance industry, according to a preliminary search by the California Insurance Commission, bought and paid for 56,000 fake life insurance policies.

What is even more surprising is that Peat, Marwick, Mitchell & Co., the auditing firm, was asked by Anderson, Clayton, its client, to look over the Equity Funding business. It looked so closely by the third time it was on company premises that Equity Funding ordered Peat, Marwick away before it really got started. Anderson got the report but continued to do business with Equity.

Now, in the light of the Equity Funding lesson in apparently misplaced trust, will insurance men tighten their warning systems? Initial indications suggest that they will. For one thing, even the most innocent-looking business will be subject to careful scrutiny. Outside auditors will be called on to do more work and, consequently, will have to hire more people to do it.

The computer, regarded as a useful tool, but never entirely understood, will become even more suspect, but a major effort to head off its use in a future deception needs to be undertaken. Policyholders, moreover, who rarely hear from the company after the sale is made, might also discover that someone will be knocking on their door one day to ask if they really bought the policy.

THE WATCHDOGS

New York State is generally regarded as having the best insurance regulation in the nation. Ever since the Armstrong Investigation of 1905 uncovered widespread insurance scandals here, New York's insurance department has been so strict that many insurance companies cannot or will not operate here.

The Equity Funding Life Insurance Company, with headquarters in Illinois, was one such company. Its watchdog was the Illinois Insurance Department. The California Insurance Commission also has a tenuous hold on the company because its parent maintained its headquarters in Century City, Calif.

New Jersey watched over another subsidiary, the Bankers National Life Insurance Company, while Washington watched over the Northern Life Insurance Company and New York watched over a separate concern operating only here, the Equity Funding Life Insurance Company of New York.

New York, New Jersey and Washington all moved in swiftly to protect the assets of their respective companies and, as a result, these companies are believed to be sound.

But by the time Illinois and California got wind of the situation, it was too late.

The surprising thing is that both of these states have a strong regulation, particularly California. Nevertheless, neither of these states, despite protests by California, comes close to New York in putting insurers under a microscope.

State regulators have asked for more funds repeatedly, but, with the low profile most of them maintain and the widespread mystery about what they actually do to protect the public, the chances that more money will be allocated to them seem remote.

But if the regulators cannot do the job on a state level, the chances of the Federal Government's doing it for them are considered very strong.

THE ANALYSTS

The stock-market analyst, unlike the analysts who treat the Hollywood stars, has no couch. The tools of his trade are an inquisitive mind and very good contacts.

When Mr. Dirks, senior vice president of Delafield, Childs, Inc., started out to uncover the scandal at Equity Funding, all he had to go on—at first—was a phone call from a former employe who piqued his curiosity with a tale of phantom insurance. By the time he decided the story was real, Mr. Dirks had personally talked to 20 or 30 others who corroborated it in great detail.

Even then Wall Street analysts were widely convinced the story had little merit.

As late as February, Cowen & Co., in a report signed by its analyst, recommended purchase of Equity Funding "for aggressive accounts."

Burnham & Co., Inc., in a Jan. 30 report from its analyst, said: "We regard the stock, selling at 9.9 times estimated 1973 earnings, an excellent value and rate it a Buy."

And on March 26, a day before the New York Stock Exchange halted trading as the price of Equity Funding stock plunged, Hayden, Stone, Inc., in a lengthy memo by its analyst, said flatly that "several rumors have been circulating which have affected Equity Funding's stock; we have checked these rumors, and there appears to be no substance to any of them."

The Hayden, Stone memorandum went on to say that the rumor had been checked with the insurance departments of Illinois, New Jersey and Washington and that "each man told us that he is not conducting an investigation of Equity Funding or any of its subsidiaries, has no present intention of conducting such an investigation, and knows of no other insurance department that is conducting such an investigation."

Although analysts were unable to find proof of deception, a poll conducted among them during the height of the rumors disclosed that a surprisingly large number on intuition alone felt uneasy about Equity Funding.

After listening to Mr. Dirks for less than 15 minutes, an analyst for the Bankers Trust Company said he had "heard enough." Mr. Dirks said he told the Securities and Exchange Commission that this analyst said that he "never liked" Equity Funding and was going to recommend its immediate sale even if the Dirks story turned out to be untrue.

Will it happen again? No on can say with certainty. But analysts may be in for difficulty from almost everyone.

The next time a situation like Equity Funding develops, many analysts will remember what happened to Mr. Dirks. The New York Stock Exchange late last week brought disciplinary charges against him and his firm. It charged him with circulating rumors of a sensational nature, furnishing his clients and others with material adverse information not publicly available and failing to inform the exchange before he went to the regulatory authorities.

THE INSIDERS

Some lawyers argue that there are no statutes or rules that define insiders. The American Stock Exchange defines them, in part, as "all persons who

Raymond L. Dirks, stock analyst.

come into possession of material inside information before its public disclosure."

It further states that such persons include "control stockholders, directors, officers and employes, and frequently also include outside attorneys, accountants, investment bankers, public relations advisers, advertising agencies, consultants and other independent contractors." Husbands, wives, immediate families and those "under the control of insiders," the exchange said, may also be regarded as insiders.

A landmark case against Merrill Lynch involved an underwriter as an insider. The Texas Gulf Sulphur case, also well-known, involved employes as insiders. But, some lawyers maintain, there appears to be no case that decides whether a former employe, the source of Mr. Dirks's information, is considered an insider, too.

But Salomon Brothers, the nationally known investment banking firm, is suing John W. Bristol & Co., Inc., the Boston Company, Inc., Boston Company Institutional Investors, Inc., and 69 of their clients—all former owners of Equity Funding stock—on charges that they sold Salomon $8-million of the stock on the basis of information obtained from insiders without telling Salomon that they had such information.

William W. Wolback, president of the Boston Company, maintained that the firm "did not have inside information" and that, therefore, its sale to Salomon was "bona fide."

[April 15, 1973]

HIGH COURT BACKS STOCK ANALYST WHO TOLD CLIENTS ABOUT A FRAUD

By LINDA GREENHOUSE
Special to The New York Times

WASHINGTON, July 1—The Supreme Court vindicated Raymond L. Dirks today, ruling that the securities analyst did not misuse inside information in warning several clients that the Equity Funding Corporation was about to collapse.

The Court's 6-to-3 ruling went well beyond the Dirks case. It set significant new limits on the legal liability of those who make use of nonpublic information they receive from a corporate insider, usually an officer, director or major stockholder.

In a strongly worded opinion today, Associate Justice Lewis F. Powell Jr. said not only that the Securities and Exchange Commission was wrong to censure Mr. Dirks but also that the commission had taken an unduly rigid view of the law on insider trading.

The Court agreed with the Justice Department, which backed Mr. Dirks in his Supreme Court appeal and told the Justices that the S.E.C.'s view of what constituted insider trading "threatens to impair private initiative in uncovering violations of the law."

Mr. Dirks is widely credited with bringing the Equity Funding scandal to light in 1973, after first learning about it from a former Equity vice president. His role in exposing the large insurance fraud made him a folk hero in some circles. But his admirers did not include the S.E.C., which censured him for allegedly violating the antifraud provisions of the securities laws by taking advantage of inside information he had received.

Equity Funding, based in Los Angeles, grew rapidly in the early 1970's, attracting many investors to its shares, in large part as a result of the sale of bogus insurance policies to reinsurers, transactions that inflated the company's apparent assets and earnings.

Mr. Dirks's censure was a mild form of penalty that did not bar him from the securities business. But as a matter of principle, he challenged the commission in the United States Court of Appeals for the District of Columbia and thus began a battle for vindication that lasted a decade, until today. Mr. Dirks, now 49

years old, said that he spent $500,000 in legal fees on the case. He is now a consultant to companies seeking to raise capital through new stock issues.

The Court said the commission was mistaken as a matter of law in its view that anyone who received nonpublic information from a corporate insider "inherits" the insider's legal obligation to either make the information public or to refrain from trading.

Rather, the Court said, the duty of a person who receives an inside tip—known in securities jargon as a "tippee"—depends entirely on whether the source of the tip has himself breached a legal duty to the corporation's shareholders in passing the information along.

Whether the insider has breached a duty, the Court said, depends in turn on his motive and on whether he stands to gain from passing the information further along the chain.

"The test is whether the insider personally will benefit, directly or indirectly, from his disclosure," Justice Powell said. "Absent some personal gain, there has been no breach of duty to stockholders. And absent a breach by the insider, there is no derivative breach."

Justice Powell was the author of the Supreme Court's last opinion on insider trading, a 1980 decision known as Chiarella. That case involved a financial printer who broke the code used by his employer's clients and used the information he gleaned about impending mergers to make money in the market.

The Court held in Chiarella that the mere fact that the printer had access to nonpublic information did not give him a duty to disclose it or to refrain from trading on it. As an employee of a printing company, he had no particular relationship of trust to the companies' stockholders and consequently did not breach any duty to them when he acted on the basis of the inside information.

"We reaffirm today," Justice Powell said, "that a duty to disclose arises from the relationship between parties and not merely from one's ability to acquire information because of his position in the market."

[July 2, 1983]

A Saudi Threat on Oil Reported

MINISTER IS SAID TO PREDICT PRODUCTION SLASH IF U.S. RESUPPLIES ISRAELIS

By EDWARD COWAN

Special to The New York Times

WASHINGTON, Oct. 15—The Saudi Arabian Oil Minister was reported today to have told Western oil executives that if the United States overtly undertook to resupply Israel's fighting forces, Saudi Arabia would cut crude-oil production by 10 per cent at once and by 5 per cent a month thereafter.

Sources close to the oil price negotiations held in Vienna last week gave this account shortly before the United States announced that it was dispatching military equipment to Israel.

"The Arabs have it now," an industry executive commented after the announcement. "It's a question of what they do."

Although Washington has repeatedly urged the Arab oil states not to use oil as a political weapon, officials here have said privately that King Faisal of Saudi Arabia was under intense pressure to make a show of solidarity with the other Arab states. Accordingly, Saudi action to deny oil to the United States would come as no surprise.

The crucial question, officials here said, is how far-reaching such action might be. Saudi Arabia produces 8.5-million barrels of crude a day, with 600,000 going to refineries in the United States.

The United States consumes about 17 million barrels of crude oil and refinery products a day, of which about 6.4 million are imported. Imports of crude from Arab states have been estimated by Government officials at 1.1 million barrels a day and by industry sources at 1.4 million.

In addition, imported refinery products, principally heating oil and heavy fuel oil for utility boilers, account for 400,000 to 500,000 barrels a day of Arab oil, according to Government sources.

Instead of cutting production, Saudi Arabia could attempt to embargo deliveries of her crude to the United States. With production unchanged, the volume of crude flowing to European and Japanese refineries would presumably increase. Some additional scarcity in this country would occur, but over time the industry would probably find ways to reroute other crude and refinery products to minimize the impact.

If an embargo and a production cutback were undertaken, the consequences could be more acute. Production cutbacks of the magnitude mentioned by the Saudi Oil minister, Sheik Ahmed Zaki al-Yamani, could cause pronounced dislocations in Western Europe and the United States.

Sheik Yamani was described by informed sources as taking a more temperate tone in public statements than in the private negotiating sessions with the Western oil executives.

Robert J. McCloskey, the acting State Department spokesman, again denied reports that the United States had received official threats of a Saudi oil cutback.

Meanwhile, authoritative sources reported that the Foreign Ministers of Saudi Arabia, Kuwait, Libya and Algeria, who have been attending the United Nations General Assembly, had asked to see President Nixon. There was no immediate comment from the State Department.

Arab diplomats reported that Kuwait would seek to stop shipments of her crude, estimated at 65,000 barrels a day, to the United States.

A meeting of Arab oil countries scheduled for tomorrow in Kuwait was put off

In 1973, oil supplies were tight and the United States experienced some shortages of home heating oil because of a lack of refining capacity. The oil-exporting countries were pressing the international oil companies for a price increase, but the companies were resisting.

Then came a new Arab-Israeli war. The Arab oil producers quietly threatened to stop selling oil to the United States if it resupplied arms to Israel, and, when it did, they carried out the threat. Oil prices headed up. Soon gasoline lines appeared, and the Nixon Administration was forced to bar gasoline sales on Sunday and take other steps to conserve oil. For the rest of the decade, energy became a national obsession. Oil prices shot up again in 1979 after the fall of the Shah of Iran, sparking new shortages and gas station closings. Blamed by many for the high prices, energy companies became the darlings of the stock market for their increasing profits, and meetings of the Organization of Petroleum Exporting Countries were viewed with dread because the cartel was widely seen as having the power to move prices as high as it wished.

Throughout the decade, the Government tried to hold down inflation through controls on the prices of oil produced from domestic wells. That led to an extensive bureaucracy and lots of cheating. In 1979, President Carter gave up. He said he would end the price controls, but he asked Congress for a "windfall profits" tax on oil companies, which was enacted the following year but had little effect.

Oil companies made high profits during the decade but became objects of suspicion by many. The White House called Exxon's profits "enormous" and oil companies took to running ads explaining that their profits were not as large as they appeared to be. When a Mobil gas station just happened to stay open while a Mobil executive's daughter was getting married nearby, it became a cause célèbre.

The forecasts of gloom and doom proved wrong, eventually. Higher oil prices led to conservation as small cars became popular and companies revised their methods of operating to save energy. In the 1980's oil prices were to plunge, creating a new set of problems.

1970–1979

until Wednesday for unannounced reasons. Experts here regarded it as a crucial event, at which the major combatants against Israel—Egypt, Syria, and Iraq—would seek to put pressure on other Arab countries to use oil to support them.

With anxiety about Middle Eastern oil supplies mounting each day that the war goes on, officials here have been reviewing emergency plans. One calls for the establishment of a foreign petroleum-supply committee consisting of Government officials and representatives of 21 American oil companies with foreign operations.

Officials said that consumer rationing was an ultimate measure that might have to be taken but that there was no workable rationing plan at present. Before limiting the volume that households, stores and factories could burn, the Government would seek to reduce consumption by adopting a system of priorities and by appealing for restraint.

With one eye on the Middle East, William F. Simon, Deputy Secretary of the Treasury and chairman of the Inter-Agency Oil Policy Committee, said in a statement that energy-conservation measures alone could cut consumption of oil by three million barrels a day. Some Treasury officials encouraged the interpretation that the United States could get along without Arab oil if conservation was invoked.

Other analysts found the conclusion far too optimistic because of the assumptions that underlay the figure of three million barrels. For example, the Treasury assumed that all autos would be tuned up twice a year, that all household laundering would be done in cold water, that all cars would be driven no faster than 50 miles an hour and that intensified pooling would raise the average number of persons in commuter cars to 2.3 from 1.3.

Officials acknowledged that there had been "maximum assumptions" and said the statement was "meant to have a calming effect."

Another sign of the apparently growing willingness of the Arab states to use oil as a lever on Washington came from Bahrain, the island-state in the Persian Gulf. Its Foreign Minister, Mohammed Bin Mubarak al-Khaifa, was reported to have summoned the United States chargé d'affaires to protect what was termed United States support of Zionism. The Minister was reported to have said that such support would have a serious effect on his country's relations with Washington.

Analysts of Middle Eastern affairs here said that, although Libya had been regarded as more radical and anti-American than other Arab states, it appeared that Col. Muammar el-Qaddafi, the Libyan leader, was reserved in his support of Egypt and Syria. Diplomats and industry sources believe he is irritated because he had little or no advance notice of the attack.

Libya, Kuwait and Saudi Arabia, all of which have large financial reserves in relation to their populations, are regarded as the countries best able to reduce output for political reasons.

Cutbacks would create more of a burden for Iraq and Algeria, according to the analysts here.

[Oct. 16, 1973]

Carter to End Price Control on U.S. Oil and Urge Congress to Tax Any 'Windfall Profits'

By MARTIN TOLCHIN

Special to The New York Times

WASHINGTON, April 5—President Carter told the nation tonight that he would gradually lift price controls on domestic crude oil, and ask Congress for a tax on any "windfall profits" that resulted for oil producers, as part of a complex and potentially controversial plan to end America's dependency on foreign oil.

"Our national strength is dangerously dependent on a thin line of oil tankers stretching halfway around the earth, originating in the Middle East and around the Persian Gulf—one of the most unstable regions in the world," Mr. Carter said in a 23-minute nationally televised speech from the Oval Office.

In stern, blunt words, the President declared that Americans would have to change their living and working habits and must be prepared to be colder in winter and warmer in summer, to drive less and in smaller cars.

"This is a painful step, and I'll give it to you straight: Each one of us will have to use less oil and pay more for it," he said.

Presidential advisers estimate that the plan would increase the price of gasoline and other oil products by 4 or 5 cents a gallon by 1982.

Mr. Carter minimized the obviously difficult choice he had made between allowing oil price increases, on the one hand, and seeking to control inflation on the other. He said that although decontrol of oil prices would lead to short-term increases in the rate of inflation, in the long run it would be anti-inflationary.

Presidential advisers said at a background briefing that decontrol would increase the rate of inflation by only one-tenth to three-tenths of 1 percent a year.

The Speaker of the House, Thomas P. O'Neill, Jr., gave his crucial support to the President's proposals, saying he would work "to encourage prompt passage of a tax to recoup the lion's share of the windfall." Senator Russell B. Long of Louisiana, chairman of the Finance Committee, praised the President's "initiative" on energy but did not say he would support the proposed tax.

Unlike his energy plan of almost two years ago, when Mr. Carter called the effort to achieve energy independence "the moral equivalent of war," today's proposals resulted from extensive consultation between Mr. Carter and Congressional leaders, and the plan reflected some of the Congressional proposals.

"We learned something in two years," said a member of the White House senior staff. "An energy plan didn't have to come down as tablets from Mount Sinai."

The President sought to offset the expected complaints that oil companies would reap extraordinary profits from higher oil prices by proposing the "windfall profits" tax. The President declined, however, to make decontrol contingent upon enactment of the proposed

1970–1979

DAUGHTER OF MOBIL OFFICIAL WED; STATION STAYS OPEN

By ROBERT E. TOMASSON

Special to The New York Times

NEW CANAAN, Conn., June 7—Last Saturday, the Mobil gasoline station at the corner of Cherry Street and South Avenue in this suburb was open from 6:30 P.M. to 10:30 P.M. It was unusual because, for the last several weeks, the station had closed its pumps at 11 A.M.

The station's new hours coincided with the reception on nearby Lee Lane for 200 guests who were celebrating the wedding of Lee Ann Wolfe, daughter of Paul J. Wolfe, executive vice president and director of the Mobil Oil Corporation.

"There is absolutely no connection between the two incidents," said Anthony DeNigro, manager of media projects for Mobil in New York. "It is inconceivable to believe that a special allocation was given the station to provide for the guests."

But the company acknowledged that the reopening of the pumps around the time of the wedding and reception was a "very unfortunate coincidence."

The Mobil spokesman said the reopening of the company-owned station was part of an experiment designed to vary hours of sale so that gasoline would be available to more people, specifically in the suburbs.

Mr. DeNigro said the staggered system had been tried at 35 Mobil stations in seven Southwestern cities: Dallas, Houston, San Antonio, and Little Rock, Ark., and Shreveport, Alexandria and Lafayette, all in Louisiana.

Forty-five other Mobil-owned stations in the South and Southwest that use brand names other than Mobil were also part of the experiment, he said.

There was no advance notice of the New Canaan station's late hours and unlimited gasoline sales, Mr. DeNigro said, adding that it was felt that an announcement of the additional hours would only create new traffic jams.

"I knew absolutely nothing about that station being open," Mr. Wolfe said. "As far as I later learned, it was part of an experiment."

Among the wedding guests was Raleigh Warner, board chairman of Mobil, who lives in New Canaan.   [June 8, 1979]

tax. Instead, the White House aides indicated that they expected constituent pressure to persuade members of Congress to enact the tax, and create the linkage.

The President alluded to the Iranian revolution of barely two months ago, and the 9 percent rise in oil prices put into effect last Sunday by the Organization of Petroleum Exporting Countries, as well as the nuclear accident at the Three Mile Island reactors near Middletown, Pa.

The President said that he would insist that the oil companies plow their new profits back into research and development.

"I will demand that they use their new income to develop energy for America, and not to buy department stores and hotels, as some have done in the past," he said.

Mr. Carter, seeking to build a national constituency for the energy plan, proposed benefits for the poor, urban dwellers and the Northeast.

Since August 1971, the price of domestic crude oil has been controlled by the Government while the price of imported oil has been set at much higher levels by foreign producers. As a result, the President said tonight in adopting the decontrol philosophy long urged by the oil industry, domestic oil production had been discouraged and an increasing national reliance upon foreign oil had been encouraged.

Mr. Carter also disclosed that, if Congress gave him the authority to do so, he would immediately require that thermostats in nonresidential buildings be set no higher than 65 degrees in winter and no lower than 80 degrees in summer. The bill is already pending in Congress.

Exceptions to the thermostat settings would be allowed for hotels, motels and other lodgings and for hospitals and other health-care facilities, but office buildings and entertainment facilities would apparently have to abide by the regulation.

The President said that he would set gasoline consumption targets for each state and would order mandatory steps, assuming Congress allows him to do so, if the states fail to save as much gasoline as they are supposed to do. One such step, he added, might be the weekend closing of service stations.

The President said that the gradual price lifting would begin in June when newly discovered oil may be sold for the world market price. The average domestic price is $9.65 a barrel, while the world price is more than $16.

The purpose of starting by raising the price of new oil, according to a White House fact sheet distributed today, is to begin "by providing special new incentives to those categories of oil where the maximum amount of new exploration and production will result."

[April 6, 1979]

Oil prices leaped after a revolution brought the Ayatollah Khomeini to power in Iran in 1979.

Why This Bear Market Is Different

By VARTANIG G. VARTAN

After the close on the New York Stock Exchange last Tuesday, a vice president of a Wall Street brokerage firm stopped by to check the Dow Jones ticker that was humming with gentle, cricket-like chirps. "Good Lord!" he exclaimed. "The Dow is down another 16½ points!"

The blue chip average limped in that day with a finish at 671.54, rounding out a decline of 126 points within 14 trading sessions, a period that encompassed President Ford's ascendancy to the White House.

The broker took a sip of cold coffee and grunted. "You know the trouble with this market?" he said. "The persistent grinding away of prices. Every time you think it's going to improve, you raise your head—and then get it handed back to you on a platter."

Bad as it appeared, the true significance of that Tuesday closing eluded the disconsolate Wall Street broker and virtually all of his counterparts across the United States. It meant that the current bear market had exceeded the 1969–70 rout in the modern record books and, in the process, invited fresh comparisons with the granddaddy of all stock smashes, the 1929–32 Crash when the drop was 89 per cent.

From its high-water mark of 1,051.70 on Jan. 11, 1973, through last Tuesday, the Dow plummeted 36.15 per cent and, in the process, rubbed out more than $200-billion in the market value of Big Board stocks alone. This compares with a decline of slightly under 36 per cent—and a less cataclysmic erosion of dollar values—during the 1969–70 break.

But, after all, the securities business went through a bear market in 1957, in 1962 and again in 1966, only to see stock prices and the public's speculative urge run higher than ever before. The tide comes in and the tide goes out; the market goes up and the market goes down, in cycles. Isn't that the way it always works?

Well, the chilling figures of the current decline tell only part of the story. There is plenty of evidence to suggest that when the tide finally quits going out for this market, it will leave behind a vastly different topography for the securities industry. The results seem bound to affect the nation's 31 million shareholders, the big institutions, and publicly owned corporations.

So far, the prolonged decline—since the end of 1968, the typical stock has dropped 70 per cent in value, according to a broadly based Value Line index—has meant lost confidence along with lost dollars for investors.

"Customers don't want to talk to me when I call them up," reports one stockbroker. For people who hold stock on margin, those calls may be a request to put up more money—or be sold out. For strapped-for-cash individuals who use securities as collateral for bank loans, a long market slump similarly becomes a real worry.

Brokers also worry, and more than 7,000 of them have departed the sales ranks for other jobs in the last few years. Lawrence G. Myers left Dean Witter & Co. in Chicago for a bank job last year. "My peak year was 1971 when I made $30,000," he said. "By the middle of 1973, my income had dropped to where I was earning [at] the annual rate of $10,000. That's when I got out."

Many investors who abandoned the ailing stock market, or changed investment strategy, have not done too badly, thanks to new, or newly discovered, opportunities. They have benefited chiefly from the dramatic rise in yields on short-term instruments.

Last week, the Treasury Department paid a record 9.93 per cent to borrowers at its auction of 180-day Treasury bills. The average rate on the companion 91-day issue was 9.9 per cent, also a record. Treasury bills of somewhat longer maturities—but all less than one year—recently have yielded better than 10 per cent.

The service charge on a $10,000 bill, the minimum purchase, is just $15 and these securities are backed by the full faith and credit of the Federal Government. Further-

The great bull market of the 1950's and 1960's reached its culmination in 1972 with the final run of the stocks that became known as the "Nifty Fifty," including such companies as Polaroid and Avon. They had grown rapidly for years, and money managers had concluded that there was no price too high to pay for such growth.

With those stocks as the leaders, the Dow Jones industrial average first closed above 1,000 on Nov. 14, 1972, and reached a peak of 1051.70 on Jan. 11, 1973. It was a record that was not to be broken until 1982. At first, the market's setback seemed mild, and by October the Dow was back almost to 1,000. Then came the Arab oil embargo, rising inflation and interest rates and a severe recession, as well as Watergate revelations that led to President Nixon's resignation in August 1974. By the time the Dow hit bottom on Dec. 6, 1975, at 577.60, it had lost 45 percent of its value and a new generation had come to fear the stock market.

Near the end of that decline, The Times looked at its causes and the depressing effect the bear market was having on Wall Street spirits and property values.

1970–1979

more, Treasury bills are not subject to state or local income taxes. Various Government agency issues also offer high yields to investors. In early August, when the Treasury sold a $4-billion package of 9 per cent notes, the public's response was tremendous.

And sales of the new money-market mutual funds rose to $176.5-million in July from $81.5-million in June.

Meanwhile, on a 40-year debenture issue, Northwestern Bell Telephone offered last week a 10 per cent return, or the highest ever for a Bell System member.

These competitive yields are as much a part of the stock market's problem as the 12 per cent inflation rate, general investor disenchantment and economic uncertainty. With higher returns now available elsewhere, many investors are showing far greater sophistication as to where they put their cash.

After all, when an old stock favorite like Polaroid plunges from 143½ to 18⅛ within a year, that isn't exactly conducive to forming bull-market psychology.

One service the current bear market may have rendered, in fact, is to put to rest the overworked, and misapplied, thesis that the stock market offers a consistent hedge against inflation.

Harold B. Ehrlich, president of the investment counseling firm of Bernstein-Macaulay, Inc., and a man who some time ago advised investing cash reserves in short-term debt instruments rather than in stocks, made this observation:

"Common stocks have been good 'inflation hedges' historically only when the rate of inflation has been moderate and relatively predictable. Stocks have done poorly during periods of rapidly accelerating inflation."

Meanwhile, down on Wall Street, the American flags still flutter, there are pretty girls around and the men sport vacation tans and tryout beards.

And high above the pediment of the New York Stock Exchange, serene in white Georgia marble, stands the massive statue of Integrity, sculpted to represent the just government of financial transactions.

Are things really changing behind this placid façade? As if in reply to that question, the Cities Service Company announced plans a few days ago to tear down six buildings it owns in the heart of the Wall Street area. This would leave a vacant tract of more than an acre, a sign of the downtown building vacancy rate of 20 per cent.

It was all so different back in the golden days of 1968 when one broker installed a sauna with a cork backgammon table in his private office and when, on a sunny September day, a cheering crowd of more than 10,000 jammed the corner of Broad and Wall Streets to watch Francine Gottfried of Brooklyn, a tight-sweatered bank employe with measurements of 43-25-37, exit from the subway.

The cheers have died away, to be replaced by the threat of commercial bank competition and dwindling share volume and the search for new capital and the wasteland of the over-the-counter market and even a few privately voiced worries about how long the American Stock Exchange can exist in its present form if business does not pick up.

As for the market, nobody knows really what's going

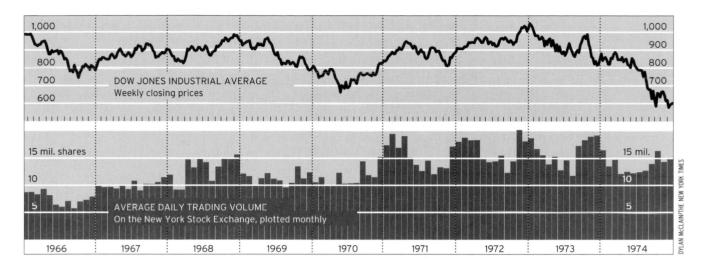

DOW JONES INDUSTRIAL AVERAGE
Weekly closing prices

15 mil. shares

AVERAGE DAILY TRADING VOLUME
On the New York Stock Exchange, plotted monthly

1966 1967 1968 1969 1970 1971 1972 1973 1974

DYLAN McCLAIN/THE NEW YORK TIMES

to happen, but just about everybody agrees that a Sixties-type boom is nowhere on the horizon. Right now, most brokers would settle happily for a 100-point rally in the Dow.

Warning flags were hoisted a month ago by Robert H. B. Baldwin, president of Morgan Stanley & Co., Inc., a prestigious firm that has left the Wall Street area for a new home in a mid-Manhattan skyscraper. He said that 100 to 200 brokerage houses were in danger of disappearing within the next year if the stock market does not improve and if short-term rates don't fall substantially.

The Big Board only numbers a shade more than 500 firms and three of them recently have merged or are in the process of being acquired by other houses. The three, all medium-sized retail operations with no distinctive franchise to keep them going alone, are W. E. Hutton; Shearson, Hammill, and Clark, Dodge.

But it was Mr. Baldwin's third big "if" that could crumble the façade of Wall Street more swiftly than anything else. He, along with a number of other industry leaders, is opposed to the scheduled advent of competitive brokerage rates on all trades next May 1. At present, rates are negotiated between brokers and large clients only on trades involving more than $300,000.

But last Tuesday—it was a red-letter day, indeed, on the Street—the Securities and Exchange Commission reaffirmed its long-standing decision to abolish all fixed rates by the May, 1975, deadline. In a move that surprised any number of industry leaders, the S.E.C. said, in effect, that if stock exchanges failed to change their rules it would take steps to accomplish the same end.

Most brokers are against a fully competitive rate structure on the rationale that it will reduce income and, in some cases, cause houses to go under. But the alternative argument, which even some Wall Streeters admit in private, is that fixed rates provided a protective umbrella for many poorly-managed firms.

"Let's face it," declared one broker. "This business has been an ego trip for many of the principals in firms. You have some fun and you make money with fixed rates."

If competitive rates become a way of life, it will mean lower commission costs for institutions, which account for triple the total volume of individuals, and higher commissions for small customers.

In the short term, the little fellow is going to pay higher commissions anyway, in all probability. The Big Board recently asked S.E.C. approval for a 6 per cent to 8 per cent increase in rates on orders between $2,000 and $300,000.

A few days ago, amid the gathering gloom on Wall Street, one institutional sales-man demonstrated that *joi de vivre* is not dead downtown. He mailed out brochures on "Five Solutions For A Summertime Bear Market." One solution was a Ward 8 cocktail, another a Planter's Punch.   [Sept. 1, 1974]

1970–1979

U.S. Company Payoffs Way of Life Overseas

A series of scandals erupted in the 1970's in which American businesses were suspected— or clearly guilty—of bribing foreign officials for business. Companies said they had to do it or the contract they sought would go to a foreign competitor. But Congress eventually decided that the practice was damaging America's reputation, and it passed the Foreign Corrupt Practices Act in 1977. The law certainly reduced the instances of such payoffs, although it did not eliminate them. And, contrary to warnings, American companies continued to be able to do business overseas.

In 1975, The Times reviewed the many cases of bribery that had arisen.

By MICHAEL C. JENSEN

American companies doing business abroad are spending hundreds of millions of dollars each year for agents' fees, commissions and outright payoffs to foreign officials.

The payments range from $5 bribes for customs agents and other minor officials to multimillion-dollar rake-offs on defense contracts. Sometimes even heads of state are involved.

The practice of funneling cash into the hands of government officials or their representatives is long-standing and is defended by many businessmen as the only way they can compete effectively abroad. Indeed, some such payments are officially sanctioned by the United States Government.

Nevertheless, the practice is coming under increased scrutiny in the United States, spurred by disclosures that the United Brands Company, based in New York, paid more than $2-million in bribes to officials in Honduras and Europe.

The Senate Foreign Relations subcommittee on multinational corporations has begun a full inquiry into the United Brands case.

It is also looking into expenditures by the Northrop Corporation, which paid out more than $30-million in agents' fees and commissions, much of it for overseas sales, from 1971 to 1973.

The Gulf Oil Company's disbursements of more than $4-million overseas, most of it reportedly to a single unidentified country, is also being investigated.

Until now, most of the Government attention to corporate bribery has come from the Securities and Exchange Commission, which is responsible for insuring adequate disclosure of corporate activities to shareholders. The current investigations are an outgrowth of the Watergate prosecutions of illegal campaign contributions.

The Internal Revenue Service, which is concerned with the proper handling of foreign transactions for tax purposes, also is looking into some of the foreign situations.

It is apparently not a violation of United States law for an American corporation to bribe foreign officials. Such action may be illegal in the host country, but bribery laws are seldom enforced in many parts of the world.

Few American businessmen will discuss their companies' payoff practices openly, although some agreed to interviews with news reporters with the understanding that they not be identified.

Some of the most blatant cases of bribery have become public, however, and a few have spawned major scandals overseas.

In the United Brands case, for example, Eli M. Black, the chief executive of the company, committed suicide shortly before the company's overseas bribes become known publicly. The ensuing scandal also resulted in the overthrow of the chief of state of Honduras, Gen. Oswaldo Lopez Arellano.

In other cases, there is almost certain to be a growing furor as further details become known. For example, the reported testimony of Bob R. Dorsey, chairman of the Gulf Oil Corporation, about cash "contributions" abroad is being studied by the S.E.C.

Mr. Dorsey and other Gulf officials reportedly told the S.E.C. that foreign politicians had forced them to pay large amounts of cash in order to stay in business.

While some commissions and agents' fees are nothing more than thinly diguised bribes, others are said to be legitimate payments to local representatives overseas, designed to cut through red tape.

The Defense Department authorizes defense contractors to pay "reasonable" agents' fees as part of their "cost of sales" and to pass these costs along to the Pentagon when it acts as the middleman in arms contracts.

In an advisory memorandum issued to several defense contractor associations last summer, the Defense Security Assistance Agency said United States arms manufacturers selling major systems usually limited their standard agents' fees to 4 to 6 per cent of the selling price. It added, however, that on less expensive equipment the percentage sometimes exceeded 25 per cent.

Some Middle Easterners have gotten rich on such fees. Persian Gulf sources say that Adnan M. Khashoggi, a Saudi Arabian businessman who has an international string of industrial and financial ventures, including a bank in California, made his initial capital as the Saudi agent for Raytheon Hawk missiles and Lockheed aircraft bought by Saudi Arabia. Mr. Khashoggi's connection is said to be his friendship with Prince Sultan, the Saudi Defense Minister, and his commissions were said to run to $10-million to $20-million.

American executives say the Middle East is one of the world's most vexing regions as far as doing business is concerned. An illustration of the problems they face there was contained in a limited-circulation Defense Department memorandum entitled "Agents' Fees in the Middle East."

"There is the classic example," the memo said, "of a new vice president of a United States firm who, after reviewing agents' fees, decided that a local Middle East agent's contract could be canceled. All that the company had in the country at that time was a continuous but lucrative servicing contract that had been negotiated many years ago.

"Within 48 hours after the agent had been canceled all local work permits of the company's employes were withdrawn. Needless to say, the agent was reinstated immediately."

Although the most dramatic instances of corruption are those involving millions of dollars, a far more widespread type of bribery takes place at a much lower level. It is variously called baksheesh, la mordita or dash, depending on whether it is offered in the Middle East, Latin America or Africa.

One businessman in Africa said in an interview: "In countries like Nigeria and Zaire, you have to pay small bribes, called 'dash,' to get anything done. It's part of the price of visas, getting customs clearance on materials— even getting your suitcase in the instance of Nigeria."

In other parts of the world, the pressures take a different form. For example, one type of harassment for American companies in the Philippines is the stream of requests for donations for charities from government and military officials or members of their families. Such requests, invariably granted, sometimes run to more than $100,000.

In Italy, on the other hand, requests are more likely to be for contributions to political parties.

An executive of a United States-controlled multinational electronics group, who insisted on anonymity, said: "To do business in Italy, as in other European countries, you have to render all sorts of favors, including outright bribery.

"It's up to your ingenuity to disguise such practices in reports to your board and in financial statements. You send lavish gifts to key people and their wives. You have your own workers install costly appliances in their

Eli M. Black, chief executive of United Brands.

seaside villas free of charge. You hire their relatives and protégés if you have staff vacancies. Sometimes cool cash changes hands.

"Don't expect company headquarters to give you any instructions on how to handle such situations," he continued. "You are completely on your own—just keep the sales performance going up."

Although many Americans profess astonishment and sometimes disgust at reports of bribery and under-the-table gratuities offered abroad, such practices are also widespread in this country.

Gifts, some of them lavish, often are pressed on officials with purchasing responsibilities in the United States, and a number of corporate contributions to political campaigns were uncovered during the Watergate investigations.

Furthermore, American companies are quick to point out that overseas competitors also employ such methods, making it more difficult to resist the pressures.

For example, the president of a French-based company in international transport won contracts from a foreign ministry official by seeing that he found his way to one of the exclusive and illegal brothels of Paris. He said he clinched the contract by giving the official's wife a high-speed, electric sewing machine from Switzerland.

The importance that American companies attach to employing local representatives was vividly demonstrated by the International Telephone and Telegraph Corporation in mid-1971 after Salvadore Allende Gossens, a Marxist who was opposed by I.T.T., was elected President of Chile.

Confronted with a hostile regime and anxious to protect its telephone properties, I.T.T. moved quickly to foster better relations. In a memo to P. J. Dunleavy, who is now president of I.T.T., J. W. Guilfoyle, another I.T.T. executive, related what had been done to try to improve matters for the company.

He said that two I.T.T. officials were meeting with a Dr. Schaulson, "the consultant I obtained on our last trip," to determine the outcome of Dr. Schaulson's discussions with President Allende. "Schaulson is a lawyer and a former politician," Mr. Guilfoyle wrote, "and is considered friendly with Allende and, as a Christian Democrat, is not committed to the U.P. [Allende's party]."

Later, despite the hiring of Dr. Schaulson, Chile expropriated the telephone company, and I.T.T. was subsequently compensated by a United States Government agency which insures overseas investments.

I.T.T., in response to a query, confirmed that it had hired a Chilean legal consultant but declined to confirm that it was a Dr. Schaulson. The company said it had hired the consultant on the advice of its Chilean outside counsel.

In the Northrop case, a private report written by the accounting firm of Ernst & Ernst disclosed that Northrop made more than $9-million worth of consultants' payments in 1971, then $7.8-million in 1972 and $12.9-million more in 1973. The report pointed out that the big aircraft manufacturer employed 400 to 500 consultants and agents in the 1971–73 period.

The S.E.C. is looking into these overseas disbursements, which it says were made "without adequate records of controls." The commission also says there was no indication whether services provided in exchange for the $30-million were "commensurate with the amounts paid."

"People have said what can we do," said Irving Pollack, an S.E.C. commissioner. "If we don't do it, the customer will go to the Japanese, or the Germans or someone else, and they will pay off."

"The only answer I can see is if the contract goes to the Japanese or the Germans, the Americans should speak up and say, 'You know, we were offered it, but we didn't take it because they wanted us to put $5-million into a Swiss bank account.'"

[May 5, 1975]

Anti-Inflation Plan by Federal Reserve Increases Key Rate

By STEVEN RATTNER

Special to The New York Times

WASHINGTON, Oct. 6—Paul A. Volcker, the chairman of the Federal Reserve Board, tonight announced a new package of measures, including higher interest rates, aimed at bringing inflation under control, calming financial markets and indirectly bolstering the dollar.

In a rare Saturday night news conference, Mr. Volcker said that the board of governors of the nation's central bank had voted unanimously to increase what is called the discount rate—the rate at which banks borrow from the Federal Reserve—by a full percentage point to a record 12 percent. The only other one-point increase in the Fed's history occurred as part of a dollar-rescue package last Nov. 1.

In addition, Mr. Volcker unveiled a new reserve requirement on certain bank borrowings that had helped promote an unhealthy expansion of bank credit, in the view of the Federal Reserve. Finally, the Fed plans to change the way it manages the money supply, with the prospect of more volatile but generally higher interest rates.

In addition to higher interest rates, the new actions are likely to put further brakes on an American economy that most economists believe is already moving into recession. The actions are expected to slow the economy as they discourage all kinds of business loans by making them more expensive.

The actions came after a week of rumors and unrest on the international financial markets, particularly those in Europe, which have been increasingly uncomfortable about the United States' mounting and persistent inflation problem.

A dollar-rescue plan had been rumored, but no measure to help the dollar on foreign-exchange markets would be credible without serious action to control domestic inflation. A higher rate of interest would also, monetary authorities say, help the dollar by attracting foreign funds, but with the rate of inflation still running at above 13 percent on an annual basis, the markets may deem this inadequate.

With President Carter in political difficulties, foreign financial officials have become more concerned that the United States lacked the ability to bring inflation under control.

"We consider that these actions will effectively reinforce actions taken earlier to deal with the inflationary environment," Mr. Volcker said tonight. He also predicted a "healthy effect on expectations."

Unlike the decision to institute a dollar-rescue package a year ago, the White House was not directly involved in tonight's announcement. However, within moments, the President's press secretary, Jody Powell, said in a statement that the action would "help reduce inflationary expectations, contribute to a stronger United States dollar abroad and curb unhealthy speculations in commodity markets."

On the surface, the plan announced tonight resembles last year's package. Mr. Volcker main-

By 1979, the Government had tried a variety of controls and guidelines as a way to hold down inflation during the decade, but none had really worked. Americans had largely concluded that inflation was here to stay and that the wisest course was to buy before prices went up further.

Then an extraordinary bureaucratic fight broke out. The Treasury Secretary, W. Michael Blumenthal, decided that only much tighter monetary policy—that is, higher interest rates—could bring inflation under control. But the chairman of the Federal Reserve Board, G. William Miller, thought monetary policy was fine as it was and resisted raising interest rates further. The fight became public in April.

In July, Blumenthal lost the battle; he was fired by President Carter and replaced by Miller. But Blumenthal's views nonetheless prevailed. Paul Volcker was chosen as Fed chairman to replace Miller, and in October Volcker announced on a Saturday night that the Fed was changing the way it did business. Henceforth, the Fed would target the money supply numbers and raise or lower interest rates to meet those targets. In practice, that meant that interest rates, already high by historic standards, were headed much higher. Two recessions resulted—a brief one in 1980 and a longer one in 1982-83. But the medicine imposed by Volcker's "Saturday Night Massacre" eventually worked.

1970–1979

Paul A. Volcker, Federal Reserve chairman.

CHESTER HIGGINS JR./THE NEW YORK TIMES

RIFT OVER RATES: MILLER VS. BLUMENTHAL

By JUDITH MILLER
Special to The New York Times

WASHINGTON, April 19—A sharp rift seems to have developed between G. William Miller, chairman of the Federal Reserve Board, and the senior economic policy makers of the Carter Administration over the conduct of economic policy.

The rift follows a year in which they worked together unusually closely. It has placed Treasury Secretary W. Michael Blumenthal, who has led the campaign for further tightening of credit to stem inflation, squarely at odds with Mr. Miller, who repeated today his belief that higher interest rates are not needed now.

Mr. Blumenthal's unsuccessful effort to persuade Mr. Miller to support credit tightening has led to deep pessimism among several senior economic advisers in the Carter Administration. In interviews, they said they were concerned that, in the absence of action by the Fed, the Administration had run out of ammunition to fight inflation. Despite the surprising economic slowdown during the first quarter, these advisers say further steps are necessary to bring inflation under control.

The events of the last two weeks have graphically illustrated the disarray over monetary policy that has plagued the Administration for some time. The events have led some officials to feel that they were misled by Mr. Miller at a meeting early last week. According to officials familiar with the meeting, Mr. Miller agreed that tighter credit was in order. He has refused to answer questions about the meeting.

The rift is based in actions that began several weeks ago when, according to senior economic advisers, the Administration's economic policy group—made up of top officials of the Treasury Department, the domestic policy staff, the Council of Economic Advisers, the Office of Management and Budget and other senior advisers—concluded after weeks of study that nothing further could be accomplished to curb inflation through either budgetary policy or wage-price restraints.

Two weeks ago, according to a White House official, Mr. Blumenthal finally succeeded in persuading other members of the economic policy group that tighter credit was necessary, and the group recommended to the President that he encourage further credit restraint.

Early last week Mr. Miller and Mr. Blumenthal met and agreed that some credit tightening was in order. They also agreed, according to senior officials, that selective credit controls were not warranted.

On April 10 Mr. Blumenthal turned his initially private campaign into a public one. In a speech in Dallas, he advocated further tightening of economic policies to combat the rate of inflation, now running at 14 percent annually.

The Dallas speech was followed by a series of newspaper articles hinting that further credit tightening was in the offing.

On April 12, according to Administration officials, President Carter, apparently dismayed by the spate of news articles focusing on the policy debate, wrote notes on the margin of a memo to Charles L. Schultze, chairman of the Council of Economic Advisers, and Mr. Blumenthal, ordering them to stop putting pressure on the Fed in public.

Last Monday Mr. Miller, in an extraordinary move, responded to the Blumenthal campaign by giving interviews to several major publications expressing satisfaction with the current level of monetary restraint. Mr. Miller gave his interviews on the eve of the monthly meeting of the Federal Reserve Open Market Committee.

By tradition, Federal Reserve chairmen almost never speculate publicly on future monetary policy. Market analysts expressed amazement and dismay about both the timing—the day before a meeting of the Open Market Committee—and the substance of Mr. Miller's remarks.

"I truly cannot understand why some central bankers prefer to act as private economists, making predictions and going out on limbs," said Lawrence A. Kudow, vice president and money market economist at Paine, Webber, Jackson & Curtis.

Mr. Blumenthal, who is on vacation in Florida, could not be reached today.

Mr. Miller called reports of a rift "utter rubbish," but he declined today to entertain specific questions about his relationship with the Carter Administration.

In the past Mr. Blumenthal and Mr. Miller have had a close working relationship, and Mr. Miller has taken part in some of the Administration's key economic decisions. For example, he was one of the architects of the policy set forth Nov. 3 to bolster the international value of the dollar.   [April 20, 1979]

---

tained, however, that the new effort was based on the belief that over the longer term, the only way to deal with the dollar's problems is by curing inflation.

"I would emphasize that the fundamental solution to instability in foreign-exchange markets does not lie in intervention," said the new Federal Reserve chairman, who assumed his post Aug. 6.

Accordingly, tonight's announcement appears principally directed toward the domestic economy. Although economists believe that a recession is either under way or imminent, the Federal Reserve appeared to be relying more heavily on the last week's statistics.

Those figures show that jobs are continuing to expand, as evidenced by the fall in the unemployment rate. Meanwhile, the expansion of credit has continued and on Thursday, the Labor Department reported that producer prices in September took their largest monthly jump in five years.

"Business data has been good and better than expected," Mr. Volcker said at the news conference held to announce the moves. "Inflation data has been bad and perhaps worse than expected." Nonetheless, Mr. Volcker's comments suggested that he still expected the economy to endure a recession.

Besides following the release of more promising economic data, the actions came after top economic officials, including Mr. Volcker, spent several days at the International Monetary Fund meeting in Belgrade, hearing the Europeans' warnings.

Those events apparently persuaded the Federal Reserve to shift its posture dramatically. When Mr. Volcker first arrived on the scene at the central bank, the result was the fastest run-up in interest rates in its history. But since mid-September, when the Board of Governors split 4–3 on a rise in the discount rate, interest rates directly controlled by the Federal Reserve have remained mostly stable.

One question left unanswered in tonight's announcement was how high other interest rates—such as the prime rate (the rate banks charge their most creditworthy customers for short-term loans) and mortgage rates—will go. As part of the new package, the Fed will now focus almost exclusively on controlling the money supply and will let interest rates fall where they may. Because all of the monetary statistics watched by the Fed have been growing faster than the central bank would like, this change points to additional restraint and higher interest rates in the days ahead.

"The broad thrust is to bring monetary expansion and credit expansion within ranges established by the Federal Reserve a year ago," Mr. Volcker said.

In part, the Fed's actions today appeared to be an acknowledgement that despite record-high interest rates, business has continued to borrow at high levels. Mr. Volcker said firmly that the program was not aimed at consumer borrowings.

Toward that end, the Fed will now impose a special 8 percent reserve requirement on additional borrowings by banks by means of certificates of deposit, Eurodollars, which are dollars held overseas, and certain other similar sources of funds. In its formal statement, the Fed said that a surge in these sources of funds in the last three months had been responsible for half of the increase in bank credit.

At present, the reserve requirement on these special sources of funds are quite low and on Eurodollars, it is zero. The new requirement applies only to borrowings above current levels. All of the changes announced today take effect Monday.

An 8 percent reserve requirement forces banks to set aside 8 percent of those special funds, including the Eurodollars, which will increase the cost of borrowing the money because the bank will have to pay interest on the 8 percent that it cannot lend. Because banks cannot charge higher interest than they have established for loans made with other funds, they will have to offset their added cost by lowering the interest rates paid to depositors of the special funds. The result, the Fed hopes, would be a reduction in the growth rate of those deposits. [Oct. 7, 1979]

1970–1979

CHAPTER NINE

1980–1989

MARTY KATZ/THE NEW YORK TIMES

Workers in Silicon Valley assemble video display terminals during the 1982 computer boom.

The Great Turnaround

THE 1980'S BEGAN on an uncertain note, as the United States worried about its ability to compete in the world and feared that inflation would never be contained. The decade ended with confidence rising as the economy weathered a stock market crash without a recession.

At the start of the decade, Washington was working on a controversial plan to bail out Chrysler, an industrial giant that had fallen on hard times in large part because the American automobile industry had found it increasingly difficult to compete with Japanese auto makers.

"Lemon" socialism was the phrase applied to risking the taxpayers' money on unsuccessful enterprises, and there were widespread forecasts that any aid to Chrysler would be wasted. But it wasn't. Chrysler recovered with the help of a drastic reduction in its work force, which set a precedent that others would follow in later years.

There was also a turnaround in the world of money. Gold and silver—whose value had been rising throughout much of the previous decade—peaked early in 1980 and then came down rapidly. It was a sign that inflation was headed lower.

But first came the recessions. A short one in 1980 was followed by a longer one in 1982–83, as the Federal Reserve, under the chairmanship of Paul A. Volcker, showed it was determined to halt rising prices through a tight money policy—even if there were a lot of complaints as the prime rate climbed, reaching 21½ percent in late 1980.

In the summer of 1982, with the country mired in recession, interest rates were falling and the stock market began to rise even as Mexico was defaulting on its debts. The Latin American debt crisis would last for years, damaging banks, and the financial system would come under additional strain from the savings and loan crisis. But none of that derailed the stock market. The Dow Jones industrial average not only sailed past 1,000, but in 1987 it cleared 2,000 as well.

Then the market crashed. The 22.6 percent plunge in the Dow Jones industrial average, a 508-point drop, on Oct. 19, 1987, was unprecedented. But it proved to have remarkably little impact on the national economy. No recession arrived, and stock prices resumed their upward march, with the Dow ending the decade up 228 percent over the 10-year period.

That rise in stock prices seemed puny, however, compared with the bull market under way in Tokyo, where the dollar value of the Nikkei 225 rose 890 percent over the decade. The Japanese economic machine was widely viewed as unstoppable, and every sign of its advance in such areas as semiconductors was viewed as evidence of another American defeat at the hands of the mighty Japanese.

And yet there were already signs that it was American ingenuity that was making the great technological advances, whether in personal computers—where I.B.M. entered the market in 1981 with a computer that relied on an operating system made by an unknown young company called Microsoft—or in biotechnology, an industry that was effectively legalized by the Supreme Court in 1980. As the decade ended, the Japanese bubble was ready to burst.

1980	Gold peaks at $875 an ounce; silver tops $50.
	Ronald W. Reagan is elected President.
1981	Iran releases American hostages after 444 days in captivity.
	President Reagan is wounded in an assassination attempt.
1982	The Equal Rights Amendment dies as states fail to ratify it.
	Mexico defaults on its debt payments.
1983	Terrorists in Lebanon blow up the U.S. Embassy and a Marines barracks.
1984	A.T.&T. spins off the "Baby Bells."
	President Reagan is re-elected in a landslide.
1985	Mikhail Gorbachev becomes head of the Soviet Union.
1986	The space shuttle Challenger explodes, killing all seven aboard, including the first teacher in space.
1987	The Dow Jones industrial average plummets 508 points, or 22.6 percent, for the market's worst day ever.
1988	Vice President George Bush is elected President.
	Kohlberg, Kravis, Roberts agrees to pay $24.88 billion for RJR Nabisco.
1989	Chinese authorities crush student protest in Tiananmen Square.
	The *Exxon Valdez* spills 11 million gallons of oil off the Alaska coast.

Congress Approves a Compromise Plan on Aid to Chrysler

$1.5 BILLION LOAN GUARANTEE; UNION IS CRITICAL OF $462.5 MILLION IN REQUIRED CONCESSIONS—IACOCCA CALLS BILL STRONG

Chrysler, the third-largest car company in the United States, was in desperate condition as the 1970's ended. It owed too much money, and banks were not interested in lending it more. After some hesitation, President Carter proposed bailing out the company, and Congress passed a rescue bill in the waning days of 1979, although the aid did not begin arriving until negotiations were completed with lenders and workers in 1980. If Chrysler survived, the Government's agreement to guarantee up to 1.5 billion in loans would cost the Government nothing. In fact, it might even make a profit since the Government was given the right to buy 14.4 million shares of Chrysler stock at 13 each at any time before 1990. The shares were then trading at 5.

To the surprise of many, the bailout worked. Using 1.2 billion of the guarantees, Chrysler developed new cars that people wanted to buy. The company was forced to cut costs, and it laid off thousands of workers, as The Times reported in 1983 when Chrysler paid back the money it had borrowed with the Government guarantee. Its harsh restructuring was a precursor of steps that would be taken by many large companies in the early 1990's.

The Government ended up making 311 million when it sold back to Chrysler its right to buy shares in the company. It could have done better if it had held on. Its stake would have been worth 2.9 billion in 1998, when Chrysler merged with Daimler-Benz to form Daimler Chrysler.

By JUDITH MILLER

Special to The New York Times

WASHINGTON, Friday, Dec. 21—Congress gave final approval early today to compromise legislation to provide $1.5 billion in Federal loan guarantees to the struggling Chrysler Corporation, the largest Federal rescue plan ever for an American company. The bill now goes to President Carter, who is expected to sign it by Christmas.

The $3.5 billion package of public and private aid, calling for higher wage concessions by the United Automobile Workers than the union had wanted, was approved by both houses after a conference committee hastily crafted a compromise yesterday afternoon between the measures approved by each house earlier this week.

Last night's vote in the House, 241 to 124, came after less than an hour of debate. But the Senate vote, 43 to 34, was stalled until early this morning by Senator William Armstrong, Republican of Colorado, who held the floor for more than an hour to object to what he called too hasty an action.

"It is almost traditional that the most important legislation considered in this chamber comes before us in the dark of the night," Senator Armstrong said.

The conference bill provides the loan guarantees on the condition that those with a stake in the future of the third-largest auto maker—banks, unions, suppliers, dealers and state and local governments—must first provide "adequate assurances" that they will contribute $2 billion in loans, wage and other concessions to help Chrysler survive.

The company contends that without the aid, it would be forced into bankruptcy by mid-January.

It must still line up fast, short-term loans from private creditors on its own to survive, as the Federal plan will take several months to assemble, but Chrysler officials have expressed confidence that they will be able to do that.

Approval of the package came swiftly despite warnings from some Congressmen that it set a dangerous precedent that would force the Government to "bail out" other failing enterprises. But supporters of the measure had argued that a Chrysler failure would mean the loss of hundreds of thousands of jobs that could help set off a deep recession.

Passage was a victory for the Carter Administration, which supported the bill, the auto workers' union, which lobbied intensively, and for Chrysler.

These are the major provisions of the compromise bill:

¶ It provides Chrysler with the $1.5 billion in guarantees on the condition that the company's unionized workers contribute $462.5 million in wage and benefit concessions and that management and nonunionized employees contribute $125 million in salary cuts or holds on salaries. This provision will probably require the United Automobile Workers to renegotiate its recently ratified three-year contract with the company.

¶ It requires banks involved in Chrysler financing to provide $400 million in new credit before the company can qualify for the Federal loan guarantees.

¶ It requires Chrysler to distribute $162.3 million to its employees in a stock ownership plan to compensate them for deferred and lost benefits.

¶ It establishes a three-member Government board, made up of the Secretary of the Treasury, the Federal Reserve Board's chairman and the Comptroller of the Currency, to monitor the loan guarantee program; the Secretary of Labor and the Secretary of Transportation would be nonvoting members.

¶ It requires the board to set a guarantee fee of between one-half and 1 percent of the value of the loans.

¶ It gives both the banks and the Government an equal credit footing so that they would share in the payback of loans in the event the company goes into bankruptcy. Under present law, the Government has what is called senior credit status, meaning it would have the first claim on Chrysler's assets in a bankruptcy.

As expected, the conferees decided on contributions from workers and management—pivotal issues in the debate—that were halfway between the contributions required in the versions of the bill approved by the Senate and House of Representatives.

Howard Paster, legislative director of the union, called the compromise "unfair, rough medicine that forces workers to accept a disproportionate share of the contributions required to save the company." He said that Douglas A. Fraser, the U.A.W.'s president, would meet with union leaders soon and ask them to renegotiate the contract, but he would not predict the outcome.

Lee A. Iacocca, Chrysler's chairman and chief executive, called the compromise "tough, but a strong bill that will provide the financing needed to return Chrysler to profitability."

Another major issue resolved late this afternoon by the conferees concerned the Government's credit seniority in terms of the guarantees. They permitted the Government board that would monitor the guarantee program to waive the Government's right to have its loans paid first, if the company went bankrupt, on up to $400 million of new credit.

Deputy Treasury Secretary Robert Carswell told the conferees that banks and other potential lenders would probably not extend credit to Chrysler without such a provision.

The bill originally approved by the Senate would have required unionized workers to provide $525 million in wage and benefit concessions to Chrysler as a condition of the guarantees and would have asked nonunionized white-collar workers to contribute $150 million in wage concessions. In addition, the company would have been required to distribute $150 million in common stock to employees as part of an employee stock ownership plan.

The House bill, on the other hand, would have required $400 million in wage concessions by unionized workers, $125 million less than the Senate bill; wage concessions by nonunionized, salaried employees of $100 million, $50 million less than the Senate version, and an employee stock ownership plan of $175 million, $25 million more than the Senate bill.

[Dec. 21, 1979]

CHRYSLER'S SHARP TURNAROUND

By JOHN HOLUSHA

Special to The New York Times

HIGHLAND PARK, Mich., July 14—The Chrysler Corporation's announcement that it will repay within weeks the remaining $800 million of Government-guaranteed loans that saved it from bankruptcy just a few years ago is a dramatic indication, as it was intended to be, of the sharp reversal of the company's fortunes.

It is hard to overstate the magnitude of the turnaround. As recently as 1980, Chrysler lost $1.7 billion and, at times, was just hours from failure. Now it has $1.5 billion in cash on hand and is expected to earn a profit of about $900 million this year.

How was it possible to turn such a desperately sick company around so quickly? There was no single answer. Rather, the change came about through a combination of factors—management's determined decision to slash the company to its essentials, concessions granted by workers, lenders and suppliers under pressure from the Federal Government, more attractive, better engineered products and some inspired salesmanship on the part of Lee A. Iacocca, Chrysler's chairman.

The company's ability to continue to draw funds from the market-

The pressure of fending off imminent collapse made the company quick on its feet. The early K-cars were offered loaded with optional extras in the hope of increasing profit margins. But when sales fell below expectation, Chrysler quickly began featuring lower-priced, plainer versions of the cars. The General Motors Corporation, in contrast, waited almost a year before conceding that its J-cars were overloaded and overpriced.

"When the alternative is oblivion, you move fast," observed Maryann N. Keller, an analyst and investment manager at Vilas-Fischer Associates.

Although the $1.2 billion that Chrysler borrowed with Government backing kept it in business, that amount was less than half the amount raised as a result of the terms of the guarantee program. Before the Government would agree to back the loans, it insisted that everyone else with a stake in the company's fortunes—blue- and white-collar employees, banks, suppliers and dealers— make financial contributions. Mr. Iacocca said these concessions ultimately totaled $2.2 billion.

Almost as important as the amounts of money involved was the sense of common purpose the concessions

Lee A. Iacocca celebrates repayment of the Government-guaranteed loan by Chrysler in 1983.

ASSOCIATED PRESS

place—made possible only by the Government's $1.2 billion loan guarantee—was clearly also a factor, buying the company time to develop new products. The company's success, however, has in no way ended the debate over the appropriate role for Government in helping ailing companies.

Another important ingredient, according to some Chrysler executives, was the very desperation of the company's situation. "You get to a low break-even point by not listening to your own or anybody else's myths," Gerald Greenwald, the vice chairman of Chrysler, said today. "You don't make studies, you make decisions."

Those decisions included a sharp reduction in the number of Chrysler employees from more than 130,000 in 1979 to an average of about 74,000 last year, which helped to cut the company's break-even point in half, to 1.2 million cars and trucks. Whole divisions and layers of management were eliminated; the only area that was sacrosanct was the one developing new products, such as the compact K-cars that were introduced in late 1980. Those and other new products helped Chrysler to raise its share of the market from a low of about 7 percent to the current level of more than 10 percent.

produced, said Martin L. Anderson, a researcher with the Massachusetts Institute of Technology.

The result was that factory workers could see a clear connection between product quality, the company's earnings and their paychecks; bankers were not simply bailed out by the Government, and dealers realized they had to sell and service more effectively.

The company is also given high marks for cleverly developing variations of its limited number of products, so that it appears to offer the same range of choice as its larger competitors.

"The marketing was masterfully done," Mr. Anderson said. "They took two basic platforms and made them look like five full lines of cars."

Mr. Iacocca is acknowledged as the key figure in Chrysler's survival. In addition to his television commercials, which helped persuade customers to buy cars when it did not seem as if the company would last another year, his blunt, usually profane, sales pitches helped convince union leaders to sell unpopular concessions to rank and-file workers, bankers to swallow loan losses and lawmakers to vote for the none-too-popular loan guarantees.   [NEWS ANALYSIS, July 15, 1983]

Silver's Plunge Jolts Hunts' Empire and Brings Turmoil to Wall Street

By STEVE LOHR

The plummeting price of silver yesterday shook the enormous $2 billion silver empire of Nelson Bunker Hunt and W. Herbert Hunt of Dallas, pressing them to raise millions of dollars in cash and throwing Wall Street into a furor.

Fears of a headlong sell-off in silver and the possible collapse of the Hunt empire sent the Dow Jones industrial average down more than 25 points at one point in hectic trading of more than 60 million shares.

The upheaval threatened at least one major brokerage house, prompting Government intervention to prevent stampede selling in its shares and driving the price of silver still lower. Silver closed the day at $10.80 an ounce, down $10.82 from Wednesday's price and far below its January high of $50.05.

The tumult was touched off by a sharp fall in silver futures prices Wednesday, which generated a flurry of margin calls by brokerage houses. That meant that investors who bought silver on credit had to put up more cash to maintain their equity in their holdings. Investors routinely buy silver and other commodities largely on credit, or margin, a down payment of a small percentage of the total purchase price. Margin calls often lead to forced selling if investors decide not to provide additional collateral. That can send prices even lower.

A futures contract is an agreement to buy or sell a certain amount of goods at a fixed price during a specified period of time. The value of the contract increases or decreases depending on how the price of the commodity rises or falls during the period of the contract. The contract can be sold at any time at the prevailing market price, resulting in either a loss or a gain.

Hardest hit by the margin calls were the Hunt brothers, who since last summer have built up silver holdings of more than 200 million ounces. Their widely publicized purchases of silver helped push its price up from $6 in early 1979. According to bankers and silver traders at least some of those purchases were made on credit.

With falling silver prices and soaring interest rates, their hoard has become all the more costly to carry. Apparently strapped for cash, the Hunts reportedly were forced to sell some of their securities holdings to raise money on their silver futures positions.

Late last night officials of the Commodity Exchange Inc. disclosed that they were holding discussions "with major financial institutions concerning market conditions and methods to resolve the situation." The

The Hunt brothers of Texas: W. Herbert, left, and Nelson Bunker at House hearings in 1980.

GEORGE TAMES/THE NEW YORK TIMES

Throughout the late 1970's, the prices of precious metals rose as investors lost faith in paper money. No one was more certain that the rise would continue than the brothers Nelson Bunker Hunt and W. Herbert Hunt, Texas oilmen who set out to accumulate as much silver as they could.

In early 1980, gold peaked at 875 an ounce, and silver briefly topped 50 an ounce. The high prices produced two reactions the Hunts had not counted on. New silver supplies appeared as people decided that grandma's old silver tea service was worth too much to keep and sold it to be melted down. And the Commodity Exchange of New York, where silver contracts were traded, changed its rules to make it harder for speculators to accumulate positions.

As silver prices came down in February and March, the Hunts were increasingly squeezed because they had been buying more and more silver on credit as the price had risen. On Wednesday, March 26, Nelson Bunker Hunt said he and associates were considering selling bonds backed by silver. That was a sign that the Hunts needed cash, and the next day–known as "Silver Thursday" on Wall Street–the value of silver fell by half, to 10.80 an ounce. Amid rumors that the Hunts' main brokerage firm, Bache Halsey Stuart Shields, would go under, the stock market also plunged, and the Dow Jones industrial average was down 3.3 percent at 3:30 P.M., half an hour before the market closed. But stocks then turned around, and the Dow recovered almost all its losses by the end of the day.

The Hunt brothers were virtually wiped out and would eventually have to give up much of their oil wealth to satisfy creditors. Bache survived, but was weakened. Silver never did come back. In 1999, nearly two decades later, it traded at less than 5 an ounce, a tenth of the 1980 peak.

1980–1989

officials declined to disclose the types of financial rescue operations under consideration to aid the Hunts.

Brokerage house officials said that W. Herbert Hunt and others representing Hunt family interests met yesterday afternoon with executives of Merrill Lynch, Pierce, Fenner & Smith on the 46th floor of Merrill's headquarters at Liberty Plaza near Wall Street. Mr. Hunt reportedly requested that Merrill not impose margin calls of $44 million against his positions so that the Hunts could meet the margin requirements of smaller, less highly capitalized brokerage houses with which the Hunts have accounts.

Merrill executives could not be reached for comment last night, but exchange officials and others confirmed that the meeting took place and that such a request was made.

According to traders, the Hunts were caught in the classic pinch. If they sold silver to raise the needed cash, they faced the near-certainty of driving down the price still further and touching off a snowballing process. By market accounts, the Hunts have lost more than $1 billion in recent weeks.

Equally hard pressed was Bache Halsey Stuart Shields, a brokerage firm that has been the Hunts' silver brokers for years and that is 5.6 percent owned by the Hunts.

A Bache spokesman said the Hunts had failed to meet the margin requirements first imposed late Tuesday, and that the firm had proceeded to liquidate some of the Hunt silver holdings to meet the margin calls on Wednesday morning.

"We've been dealing with the Hunts for about eight years, and Tuesday of this week was the first time they didn't meet one," said Elliot J. Smith, executive vice president of Bache.

Mr. Smith said that, in accord with the policy of his firm, the Hunts were informed by telephone Wednesday morning that, unless the position were covered, Bache would begin liquidating some of their silver holdings. "They said they were not sending money or collateral," Mr. Smith said.

Apparently as a result of the liquidation, the margin debt by the Hunts to Bache Halsey Stuart Shields currently stands at about $100 million, down from more than $300 million a few days ago, according to Wall Street sources. "That's about right," said one Bache executive, who declined to provide any other details.

Mr. Hunt could not be reached for comment yesterday.

In an unusual afternoon action, the Securities and Exchange Commission yesterday suspended trading in the Bache Group Inc., the parent company of the brokerage house, because of "undisclosed material corporate events relating to commodities futures trading accounts maintained by customers with the firm."

Although commission officials would provide no further details on that action, the statement clearly referred to the Hunts' failure to meet their margin call.

Underscoring the urgency of the Hunt situation and the possible effect on the financial markets, the Government decision to suspend trading in Bache took place at an unusual emergency meeting of top S.E.C. and Treasury Department officials yesterday afternoon. [March 28, 1980]

Industry of Life: The Birth of the Gene Machine

By ANTHONY J. PARISI

ROCKVILLE, Md.—Leslie Glick makes a living making living things. By carefully mixing solutions in test tubes, he modifies the genes of garden-variety bacteria to create more talented ones tailored for specific tasks, like making insulin or converting garbage into fuel.

Dr. Glick is a genetic engineer; he creates forms of life that create goods. And, although he tends to take this feat for granted, he seems acutely aware that he and his colleagues in his remarkable profession are shaping a new industry: the industry of life. "It's the same as with any technology," he said off-handedly. "The only difference is that, for the first time, it's the biologist who has come up with something that has commercial potential."

That something is the almost mystical technique known as recombinant DNA. With it, molecules of deoxyribonucleic acid—the long, twisting strands of atoms that are found in the cells of all living things and that contain the genes that are the "blueprints" of life—are snipped apart and reassembled in novel forms. The new bacteria might be used to make pharmaceuticals cheaper, produce whole new classes of drugs, turn out chemicals more efficiently, clean up toxic wastes or accelerate food production.

It was only eight years ago that scientists in California, building on the groundbreaking work of James Watson and Francis Crick, the Cambridge University researchers who had deciphered the double-helix configuration of the DNA molecule two decades earlier, learned how to insert genes from the DNA of one bacterium into the DNA of another in such a precise way that they could fashion an organism that possessed the desired features of both. Although there were and are other ways to create micro-organisms, recombinant DNA made all of them seem clumsy by comparison, and scientists promptly declared that recombinant DNA would do for bioengineering what the transistor did for electronics.

They were right. Already, a dozen small companies seem on the verge of introducing commercial products made with the recombinant DNA process, and advances may come even faster now that the Supreme Court has ruled that new life forms created in the laboratory can be patented.

One of the promising DNA companies is the Genex Corporation, formed in 1977 by Dr. Glick, a molecular and cell biologist by training, with seed money from a venture capital company called InoVen. Last year, the Koppers Company bought 30 percent of Genex for approximately $3 million, and today Dr. Glick says his company is worth about $75 million. InoVen, whose backers include the Monsanto Company and the Emerson Electric Company, now holds 25 percent.

Other companies are concentrating on the older techniques of making new micro-organisms, aware that there is still plenty of room for innovation in the burgeoning business of bioengineering. Still others are specializing in the materials and equipment needed by the companies conducting all this research.

"There are now a thousand research labs in the U.S. doing some kind of cloning; that's a market," observed Stephen Turner, the 35-year-old president and principal owner of Bethesda Research Laboratories Inc., also based in Rockville. His four-year-old company sells research enzymes, the raw materials of the genetic engineer, to those labs. Some of the enzymes are made with recombinant DNA. "It's not as sexy as interferon cloning," said Mr. Turner, an economist, "but it's a real-world business."

The big companies are rushing into the business, too. Although an assortment of major corporations had been entwined with the small cloning companies for some time through a web of equity interests, joint ventures and research contracts, most refrained from establishing their own programs, until recently. Their reluctance

It is one thing to patent a new machine. But can you patent a new form of life?

Advances in biochemistry raised that question, and in 1980 the Supreme Court ruled, 5 to 4, that the answer was yes. A General Electric scientist, Ananda M. Chakrabarty, had invented a micro-organism that degraded crude oil, and Chief Justice Warren E. Burger wrote for the majority that Dr. Chakrabarty's discovery was patentable because it was "not nature's handiwork, but his own."

That decision cleared the way for a then fledgling industry: biotechnology. Biotech companies produced drugs and then produced modified foods—corn, for instance, with a pesticide built in. The possibilities scared many people, and at the end of the century, even while such foods became plentiful in the United States, where regulators decreed that they need not be labeled as genetically modified, they became very controversial in some European countries.

In 1980, The Times followed up the Supreme Court ruling with an assessment of where the biotechnology industry then stood.

1980–1989

stemmed in part from the early furor over the possible hazards of recombinant DNA research. They feared the controversy would lead to bad publicity and a permanent tangle of Government regulations. Indeed, in 1978, following a two-year moratorium on recombinant DNA research, during which the dangers were studied, the National Institutes of Health did issue tight guidelines for DNA research.

Gradually, though, as hours upon hours of laboratory work piled up without some killer strain of bacterium accidentally escaping from a lab, the agency greatly relaxed its rules. The researchers found that their experiments yielded few surprises. But to be sure, they created a particularly weak bacterium to work with; if a troublesome mutation did get loose, it would have a hard time surviving. Even the bacterium developed to eat oil from off-shore spills that was involved in the Supreme Court decision, a bacterium that was not created with recombinant DNA, has happy limitations: It cannot survive without water, and once it gobbles up the oil, it simply dies and becomes part of the food chain.

As the concern over safety eased, most of the major pharmaceutical concerns started setting up in-house research programs, and the chemical companies and others are now following suit. Earlier this month, the Shell Oil Company donated $2 million to clinical research on interferon, and the company says it is now negotiating to set up a joint venture with a genetic engineering company. E.I. du Pont de Nemours & Company started a broad program in genetics more than a year ago.

So far, researchers concentrating on pharmaceuticals have made the greatest strides, probably because the science is most closely related to that industry. They have duplicated several hormones, including one that stimulates growth and might be used to treat dwarfism and accelerate healing. They have made human insulin for the treatment of diabetes, which is expected to replace the increasingly costly kind that comes from pigs and cows and causes unacceptable side effects in nearly 20 percent of the diabetics who must take the drug. They have learned how to produce two types of

Dr. Ananda Chakrabarty opened the door for biotechnology.

interferon, a substance made sparingly by the body that, in quantity, may prove invaluable in combating viruses and cancer.

Genetic engineers say there is no inherent reason why recombinant DNA should lend itself more to the drug business than others, and many believe that it may have even greater impact in the chemical industry.

"It's a technology that's just waiting for industrial application," said William F. Amon Jr., vice president of the Cetus Corporation, of Berkeley, Calif., one of the oldest and largest DNA companies.

Cetus, which is 61 percent owned by the Standard Oil Company of California, the Standard Oil Company (Indiana) and the National Distillers and Chemical Corporation, operates out of 12 different buildings, has 250 employees and is worth about $300 million, according to Mr. Amon, although its capitalization currently amounts to only about a tenth of that figure.

In its production facilities, the company uses conventional genetic engineering to make organisms for manufacturing antibiotics. But in the lab, it has turned to recombinant DNA to make ethylene oxide, a petroleum derivative that is a starting material for making other chemicals and plastics; ethylene glycol, the basic ingredient in antifreeze, and fructose, the simple form of sugar found in fruit. It is also trying to perfect a yeast bacteria that could withstand high temperatures and greater concentrations of alcohol, which would aid in the production of gasohol. And Mr. Amon said Cetus would soon announce a new joint venture to produce interferon, the antiviral drug.

The first company to make interferon was Biogen S.A., of Geneva, Switzerland, which is 16 percent owned by the Schering-Plough Corporation and 24 percent owned by Inco Ltd., formerly International Nickel. Schering-Plough recently applied to the National Institutes of Health to begin pilot production of the drug using Biogen's bacteria. That seemed to put Biogen in a race with the Genentech Corporation, of South San Francisco, which many industry analysts consider the leading company in recombinant DNA.

Genentech, which concentrates mainly on pharmaceuticals, has announced a half-dozen drugs and hormones, including interferon, that were made with recombinant DNA, more than any other company. It has formed a joint venture with Eli Lilly & Company, which plans to market human insulin made with Genentech's micro-organisms. Small quantities of insulin are now extracted from the pancreases of cadavers for diabetics who cannot take animal insulin, but the supply is limited. Lilly will begin testing its synthesized variety later this year, and human insulin could become the first product made with recombinant DNA that is distributed to consumers.

"At this point, it's a matter of getting the necessary Government approval," said Robert Swanson, Genentech's 31-year-old president.

Mr. Swanson, who studied both organic chemistry and business administration, started Genentech in 1976 with money from a half dozen venture capital firms, including a subsidiary of the Lubrizol Corporation, which makes lubricating oil, and InoVen, the firm that Monsanto and Emerson Electric are involved in. Today, the officers, directors and staff of Genentech own half the company, Lubrizol holds 20 percent and the rest is split among InoVen and the other investors. The company says its market value exceeds $100 million.

Relatively little is known about the finances of the DNA companies because all but one, Enzo Biochem, are still privately held. Founded in 1976, the company went public just two weeks ago. The owners offered 770,000 shares, or 60 percent of the business, at 6¼ a share. Even though the prospectus said Enzo Biochem lost money during its last fiscal year on a gross income of just $133,000, mainly from the sales of enzymes, the company had no trouble selling its stock. Investors have since bid the price of the shares up by a third, to 8⅜ bid, by late last week.

Based on recent transactions, the paper value of the four pacesetters has doubled since the start of the year, to more than $500 million, or about a fourth of what the common stock of Monsanto is currently worth. Yet their sales are insignificant, and all they have to show is a lot of potential. Only one, Genentech, says it operates in the black. Research companies often run up big deficits, of course, but many of the DNA products that now seem so promising, such as interferon, may prove to be duds, and fierce competition could cut deeply into the profitability of even the successful genetic inventions.

"I agree with most of the optimistic assessments of what this technology will lead to," said Scott R. King, an analyst with F. Eberstadt & Company. "I just question the time frame that many people have in mind. Sure, recombinant DNA is like the discovery of semiconductors. But keep in mind that we didn't see cheap pocket calculators until 25 years after the transistor was developed." [June 29, 1980]

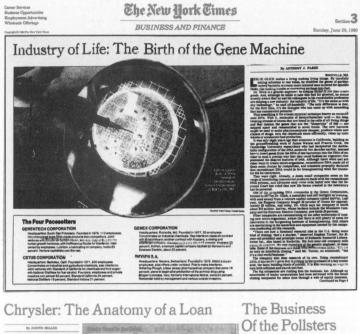

1980–1989

The Great Repression

The economy looked horrible in the early 1980's, as interest rates climbed to unprecedented heights while inflation and unemployment also rose. It appeared to be the worst of all possible worlds.

In the spring of 1982, Leonard Silk, The Times's economic columnist, traced all that had gone wrong and argued that the Federal Reserve's monetary policy was too tight. In fact, the recession then going on had nearly another year to run, but when it was finally over, inflation would be headed lower and the United States would begin a long period of growth.

By LEONARD SILK

How to describe the underlying condition of the American economy? Short-term, it is obviously in a recession that started last fall; but this is the second recession since 1980, the third since 1975, and many economists believe that, even if recovery begins in the second half of this year, a fourth recession is just around the corner. It's been a long sequence of recessions and weak, aborted expansions.

Is this, then, a depression we are in? Looking backward, the term seems too strong. The economy has been stagnating, not collapsing. If the roof were to fall in later this year, or next, it could become a depression, but the odds are still against it.

Call it repression—a chronic state of underemployment and industrial slack that has dogged the economy for the greater part of the past decade, a condition brought on by repressive actions of governments in the industrial world to cope with inflation, energy shortages and currency disorders.

In American terms, the accompanying charts tell the story. The utilization of manufacturing capacity, which ran as high as 90 percent in the mid-1960's, averaged in the low 80 percent range during the 1970's and in the final quarter of 1981 was down to 74.8 percent.

The jobless rate, only 3.5 percent of the labor force in 1969, President Richard M. Nixon's first year in office, has been on a rising trend since then, and was last clocked at 8.8 percent in February. Since unemployment lags behind the production data, it almost certainly will go higher.

New housing construction, which peaked at 2,378,000 units started in 1972, is currently running below 1 million starts. Business failures are climbing sharply. They soared from 24 per 10,000 in 1978 to a rate of 83 per 10,000 now. And the stock market, which has on the surface wobbled up and down without getting anywhere, actually has been in a long quiet crash if results are adjusted for inflation. Measured in constant 1981 dollars, the Dow Jones industrial average has fallen from an adjusted level of 2,624 in 1965 to less than 800 now, a decline of nearly 70 percent.

When did this Great Repression begin? Since history is a seamless web, it is hard to date it precisely. But the escalation of the Vietnam War in 1965 and 1966 seems the logical point, since that is when a price-stable phase of economic growth gave way to an inflationary phase. The Johnson Administration tried to mount a medium-sized war on top of an almost fully employed economy without raising taxes lest Congress slash the President's eagerly sought Great Society program. The first act of repression came in 1967 when L.B.J. belatedly called for and got a tax increase, which helped to jerk the economy into a mini-recession.

But the new era of inflation was not so easily ended. President Nixon sought to repress the rising trend of inflation first in 1969–70 by a policy of "gradualism" in fiscal and monetary policy, which caused a recession; then, fearing the possible damage to his electoral prospects, he resorted to price and wage controls in 1971–72, while

speeding up the growth of the economy with the help of a cooperative Arthur F. Burns as chairman of the Federal Reserve Board.

The inflationary trend was implanted even more deeply, both at home and abroad, in 1973, when the economies of the Western world boomed together, driving up commodity prices.

The most dramatic episode in that inflationary trend came with the outbreak of the Arab-Israeli war in October 1973, and the Arab oil embargo against the United States and a few other countries, setting the world up for the enormous increases in oil prices by the Organization of Petroleum Exporting Countries, including not only the Arabs but our then close ally, Iran.

During the 1970's, the main method of checking inflation in the United States was a repressive monetary policy. The money supply, defined as currency in circulation and demand deposits plus other checkable accounts, was reduced from 21 percent of gross national product in 1971 to 15 percent at present.

But this means of braking inflation has come at a high cost. John Winthrop Wright, head of an investment advisory service, states: "The United States has suffered through 10 years of record-breaking inflation, a surge in business bankruptcies, mostly among small companies during the past 18 months, and an unprecedented shrinkage in the auto, housing, savings and loan and farm equipment industries.

"This excessive inflation and related business casualties occurred despite the Federal Reserve Board's unprecedentedly vigorous employment of tight money policies. It can, therefore, scarcely be doubted that the unselective nature of the established methodology is an unmitigated failure and that it is time for a thorough, constructive reformation of the nation's economic and monetary management."

Mr. Wright is far from alone these days in his rejection of the current methods of monetary repression, based on the formula of trying to restrict the rate of growth of the money supply within narrow bands.

David M. Jones, vice president and economist of Aubrey G. Lanston & Company, a leading government securities dealer, recently declared: "The United States economy is currently in the throes of a deepening and widening recession.

1980–1989

A GLOSSARY OF UPS AND DOWNS

By LEONARD SILK

Economies never stand still. They're always rising and sinking and, on rare occasions, collapsing. Here are some of the words economists and politicians use to characterize an economy's ebbs and flows:

BUSINESS CYCLE: The sequence of expansion and contraction of capitalist economies. The cycles are highly irregular. Sometimes an economy can run through an entire cycle in a year; sometimes it can take a decade or more. Some economists believe in a Kondratieff cycle, lasting about 50 years, with minor cycles within it, and ending in a mighty crash.

TROUGH: The bottom of an ordinary, short-term cycle, when such important, so-called coincident indicators as the gross national product and industrial production stop falling.

RECOVERY: The phase when G.N.P., industrial production, employment, housing, retail sales and other indicators are rising, some sooner, some later. Business investment and the drop in unemployment tend to lag behind in recoveries.

PEAK: The end of the expansion.

RECESSION: The slide downhill. The current recession is the 20th of this century.

DEPRESSION: An ill-defined term meaning a spell of hard times and high unemployment. Originally the term was used as a euphemism for such harsh words as panic or slump. But depression exhausted its euphemistic appeal by 1937 when the recovering economy seemed to be relapsing into depression, and President Franklin D. Roosevelt said it was only in a "recession."

STAGNATION: When the economy seems to stall, with frequent recessions followed by weak recoveries. Over the years of stagnation, real economic growth is sluggish.

INFLATION: When price levels are rising and the dollar shrinks in value.

DEFLATION: When price levels are falling and the dollar gains in value. Hasn't happened since the early years of the Great Depression of the 1930's.

DISINFLATION: A slowing of the rate of inflation.

STAGFLATION: The combined phenomenon of stagnation and inflation.

SLUMPFLATION: An inflationary slump. [March 14, 1982]

It may turn out to be the worst slump since the Great Depression of the 1930's.

"The main cause of this cumulating downturn has been the Federal Reserve's excruciatingly tight money and credit policy over the past year or so. This Fed restrictive overkill took the form of an abrupt and irregular series of Fed restrictive responses to unexpected spurts in money demand."

While Mr. Jones generally commends the Fed's anti-inflation stance, "particularly in the face of an irresponsibly stimulative fiscal policy," he holds that the "prolonged and excessive Fed restraint in 1981 will almost certainly produce higher unemployment and more economic pain than would have been required to crush inflation and inflation psychology."

Perhaps the best indicator of what Mr. Jones calls the Fed's "strangle-hold on the economy" is the real interest rate—the market rate less inflationary expectations. Since one cannot precisely quantify inflationary expectations, it is conventional to measure real interest rates by taking selective market rates of interest against the annual rate of increase in consumer prices.

Irwin Kellner, senior vice president and chief economist of Manufacturers Hanover Trust, calculates that, using the spread between the prime rate and inflation, the real rate of interest is now 8.08 percent, compared to an average of 2 percent or less in most earlier years. The spread between market rates on utility bonds and inflation is now 7.53 percent, the highest of the postwar years; one must go back to the early years of the Great Depression of the 1930's to find higher long-term real interest rates.

The world slump has resulted from comparable efforts of most other nations and their central banks to fight inflation, partly in response to the pressure of high oil import prices, and partly, they say, to protect their own currencies against the pull of high interest rates in the United States.

Kurt Richebaecher, an economic consultant who formerly was chief economist of the Dresdner Bank in West Germany, contends that the current economic crisis, which he considers the worst since World War II, dates back to the second big increase in oil prices by OPEC in 1978. "But," he adds, "although that triggered the crisis, we should beware of making it solely or even mainly responsible for our present worldwide economic predicament."

Rather, he contends, the emphasis on oil distracts attention from "the real causes and the real culprits—namely our governments, and in most cases central banks." Anyone who finds that hard to believe, he says, should look at Japan, "which has coped with the oil price jump in masterly fashion despite its unmatched dependence on energy imports."

The world appears to be suffering from the effort to cope with inflationary strains by periodic bouts of tight money, which, when they induce recession and climbing unemployment, give way to bigger inflationary injections, which, in turn, seem to have undermined productive power.

Huge budget deficits, created by the Reagan Administration's tax cuts adopted for their alleged "supply-side" stimulative effects, together with sharp increases in military spending, further undermine national productivity by taking private saving away from investment in plant and equipment.

By some calculations of projected budget deficits and savings rates, the United States Government in the next three years could absorb more than three-fourths of all private saving, thereby choking off capital formation and productivity growth, worsening the nation's competitiveness in world markets.

Thus, as the Orwellian year of 1984 approaches, stimulus has become repression. And, until the nation's fiscal and monetary policies are changed, along with the building of new industrial policies, repression is likely to continue.   [March 14, 1982]

Mexico Seeking Postponement of Part of Debt

By ROBERT A. BENNETT

Mexico's acute financial problems sent international bankers scrambling yesterday to arrange a sweeping financial program intended to prevent the Government from running out of cash and to stop a run on the peso.

Leading Mexican officials met with several New York banks yesterday in an effort to postpone at least some payments on about $40 billion of debt interest and principal that is due within a year.

The officials will meet today at the Federal Reserve Bank of New York with representatives of about 55 leading international banks from around the world. "It's a who's who in the international bank list," said one banker who is to attend the meeting.

Several banking sources said that they expected that Mexico would ask today for between $1 billion and $2 billion in new credits from the commercial banks.

A default by Mexico could have serious effects on the American banking system and on banks throughout the world. According to one American banker, some United States banks have as much as 90 percent of their capital on loan to Mexico. Even at banks with relatively small exposure, the Mexican loans represent 30 percent of their capital.

Meanwhile, Mexico has arranged for about $3.5 billion in immediate aid from the United States Government and from the Bank for International Settlements, which is made up of central banks from around the world. Mexico also is said to be negotiating for a large credit, perhaps as much as $4.5 billion, from the International Monetary Fund.

The aid from the United States Government consists of $1 billion in advance payments by the Treasury for oil destined for this nation's strategic reserve, and $1 billion in loans from the Commodity Credit Corporation.

In Mexico, the foreign exchange markets reopened yesterday for the first time since last Thursday. The free-market rate first rose to 130 pesos per dollar, from only about 70 pesos last week, but the rate settled later in the day at about 115 pesos.

In the late 1970's, international banks lent more and more money to foreign Governments–to nations that needed the money to buy ever-more-expensive oil as well as to those countries, like Mexico, that were deemed rich because they had oil but that wanted to borrow to speed their development. In 1982, Mexico ran out of money as the peso fell sharply. Developing countries that did not have oil were already suffering as a weak world economy shrank the markets for their goods. Soon, much of Latin America was in dire straits as well.

For the big banks, most of them American, a time of trial had begun. Efforts to sweep the problem under the rug continued for years, but eventually the banks had to take significant losses as loans were restructured. By 1990, there was fear that many large banks would go broke.

In the end, few did. The Federal Reserve began driving down short-term interest rates in 1982 while longer-term rates remained relatively high. That meant banks could make good profits by taking in deposits and buying Treasury securities–and in an era of huge budget deficits there were plenty of those to be had. Those profits helped banks to offset their losses on Third World debt.

At the end of the decade, the Bush Administration came up with a plan to help reduce Third World debt through the issuance of "Brady bonds," named for Nicholas Brady, Bush's Treasury Secretary. Investors got these new bonds, whose principal was secured by United States Treasury issues, in return for accepting losses. The economies of Latin America, meanwhile, basically stood still throughout the 80's.

1980–1989

President Ronald Reagan and Miguel de la Madrid, president of Mexico, in 1986.

PAUL HOSEFROS/THE NEW YORK TIMES

But the Mexican Government offered far more favorable rates to companies that needed the dollars to meet interest payments to foreign creditors. This was intended to avoid defaults. In contrast to the free-market rate of about 115 pesos to the dollar, Mexicans had to pay only 49 pesos if the dollars were to be used to meet interest payments on foreign loans that had been registered with the Government.

"It's a problem we've seen coming for a long time and it's the result of a lot of factors," one New York banker said. In addition to an annual inflation rate approaching 100 percent, the factors included a decline in oil prices and in oil exports, reducing Mexico's oil export earnings by $6 billion; the recession in the United States, which reduced demand for Mexican products, and about $7 billion in cash outflows from Mexico resulting in part from expectations that the peso would be devalued.

In addition, the war earlier this year between Britain and Argentina over the Falkland Islands caused a number of European and Japanese banks to reduce their lending to all of Latin America, including Mexico.

West German banks, in particular, were reported by bankers to have pulled back on their loans to Mexico in response to demands by Bonn that they reduce their overall lending, especially in light of the German banks' heavy exposure in Poland. Canadian banks, too, have reduced their foreign lending because of potentially large losses at home.

According to American bankers, Mexico's financial situation deteriorated last week after a number of European banks refused to refinance credits that were falling due. It was then that the Government decided to take the drastic step of closing the foreign exchange markets and imposing foreign exchange controls.

Estimates of the amount that American banks have on loan to Mexico vary widely. One banker put it at between $18 billion and $24 billion, but another said the figure might be as high as $34 billion.

A major problem is that much of these debts fall due within a short period. About $21 billion of Mexico's foreign debt will mature in less than 12 months. In ordinary times, much of this would be automatically refinanced by the lenders. But because of Mexico's difficult situation, some lenders, like the European banks, might be unwilling to roll over their credits. Mexico owes money to about 1,000 banks around the world.

Mexico also is scheduled to repay about $8 billion in principal and about $11.5 billion in interest this year on its medium-term debt. It is expected that the banks will agree to postpone the payments of principal, but a tougher stand is expected on interest payments.

Mexico's foreign debts total about $81 billion, making it one of the biggest debtors among the world's less developed countries. Poland, for example, another country that is having severe difficulty in meeting its commitments, has total debt of only about $26 billion, of which only $1.3 billion is to American banks.

Rumors charged through the financial markets yesterday that a major American bank had an exposure of hundreds of millions of dollars in the Mexico peso, but bankers denied there were any major losses. [Aug. 20, 1982]

Television's 'Bad Boy' Makes Good

By SANDRA SALMANS

ATLANTA—He is best known as "Captain Courageous"—the skipper of the yachts that won the 1977 America's Cup and the stormy 1979 Fastnet race, off the south of England, in which 15 other sailors drowned. At Fastnet last week, Ted Turner tried for another victory at sea. But the waters were calmer this year, and another boat came in first.

If Ted Turner thrives in stormy weather, it is not only at sea. While the rest of the cable industry is going through a shakeout, R. E. (Ted) Turner, television's bad boy, and his company, Turner Broadcasting System Inc., appear to be on the verge of turning a profit for the first time since 1978.

After losing $3.4 million last year on revenues of $165.6 million, TBS has reported a profit of $6.3 million for the first half of this year—roughly equivalent to its loss in the period a year ago—and is estimating a $20 million profit for 1983.

Compared with the three major networks, that is a modest sum, but it contrasts quite favorably with the three networks' experience in cable. In the past year, CBS Cable and RCTV—which was half-owned by NBC's parent, RCA—have gone under, and ABC's services are foundering.

"Everybody decided the ship was sailing and they'd better get on," the 44-year-old Mr. Turner said in an interview at TBS headquarters here. "It's a highly competitive environment right now." He and TBS are responsible for much of that competition.

If cable has a single pioneer, it is arguably brash, outspoken Ted Turner. The so-called "Mouth of the South," Mr. Turner has shaken up the television industry repeatedly since he entered it in 1970 with the purchase of a failing Atlanta UHF channel, which in 1976 he turned into a superstation—beaming its signal via satellite to cable television systems across the nation.

While he is still a controversial and perhaps unpopular figure in broadcasting, there are few who would quibble with his claim—widely publicized in his trade promotions—that "I was cable before cable was cool." Cable is "cool" now, and so is Mr. Turner. After creating his superstation, WTBS, Mr. Turner broke new ground with Cable News Network, a 24-hour-a-day all-news cable channel that has forced the broadcasters to increase their late-night news programming. Most recently, he has been talking up an ad hoc fourth network of broadcast stations to which TBS would transmit shows—from sports to the 1983 Miss World contest—that were once the automatic property of the big three.

For the past two years, TBS has taken in about half of the entire cable industry's advertising revenues, which were $241.8 million last year, according to Paul Kagan, the cable industry analyst. Most of the sales have been generated by the superstation, WTBS, which today offers a diet mainly of old movies, reruns and sports, and goes into 26 million homes. CNN, which was begun in 1980, is now received in 20 million households via satellite relay. Its spinoff, CNN Headline News, television news in 30-minute formats akin to all-news radio, is offered in 4.5 million cable households and, in addition, is carried by 131 broadcast stations.

"This place has the opportunity to be very profitable by 1986 or 1987," said Robert Wussler, the former president of the CBS television network who is executive vice president of TBS and president of WTBS. Conceivably, some TBS executives say, its revenues could match any one of the big three networks by 1990.

It is a considerable boast. Last year, both CBS's and ABC's broadcast divisions had revenues of more than $2 billion. Other Turner executives remain more skeptical. In terms of advertising, "the networks are still the only game in town," said one. "We're not replacing the networks, we're supplementing them."

The spread of cable television opened up opportunities to those who could provide programming, and no one took better advantage of those opportunities than Ted Turner, who bought a down-and-out Atlanta independent television station, named it WTBS, and turned it into cable's first "superstation." Eventually he added other channels, and then, in June 1980, he started CNN—the Cable News Network—which became a principal provider of news to viewers around the world.

In 1983, when it appeared that the Turner Broadcasting System was about to report a profit, something that had been rare for it as it invested in the future, The Times profiled Turner. His days of taking risks were not over at that point, by any means. He bid to buy CBS, but was rejected. His efforts to expand left the company financially extended, and cable operators had to help save it. But it recovered its health and eventually was acquired by Time Warner. Turner became vice chairman of that company and remained a power in the broadcasting industry.

1980–1989

And in the short term, Mr. Wussler and others at TBS recognize, the company's flamboyant chairman and president could well have an idea that would jeopardize the company's newfound profitability. Each time that TBS has appeared to be entering a period of financial stability, it seems, Mr. Turner has headed into uncharted and risky waters—first with CNN, then with CNN Headline News.

Now, Mr. Turner talks of making movies for families, and even building a studio in Atlanta. According to Mr. Kagan, TBS is contemplating a joint venture with Home Box Office to set up a satellite programming delivery service. While TBS management declined to comment on the report, it acknowledged that anything was possible. "Ted's always going to be that way," Mr. Wussler said. "I wait every day for Ted to call me in and say, 'Here's what we're going to do.'"

All those ventures are tangential to TBS's real business, in Mr. Wussler's view. "We're in the circulation business," he said. "The future is getting WTBS and CNN into as many homes as possible."

Mr. Turner, for his part, said that he has no new ventures planned that would upend the company. "I hope not to be in the red again," he said. Due to the company's hard-won financial stability, he said at a party in June to celebrate CNN's third birthday, TBS was no longer looking for a merger with another television network.

In fact, his widely reported talks earlier this year with the three major networks have been interpreted as an effort by Mr. Turner to put a value on his holdings; he owns 87 percent of TBS, which is traded over-the-counter. A merger would thus have made him a substantial shareholder in one of the three major networks, but none of the major networks apparently took him seriously. "I said that I wanted a merger, I didn't want to sell," Mr. Turner recalled. "It was all or nothing."

Even if Ted Turner does not go off on another speculative venture, WTBS's and CNN's circulation—and thus their future—is under challenge. For one thing, the news services are facing competition from the Satellite News Channel, a joint venture of the Westinghouse Corporation—which owns Group W Cable—and ABC Video Enterprises. Introduced a year ago with bonuses of up to $1 per subscriber to system operators, SNC has signed up 7.3 million households and is projecting that it will be in more than 10 million by year-end.

"SNC is absolutely eating into our market, they're costing us a large fortune," Mr. Turner complained.

Another threat to WTBS are the significantly higher copyright royalty fees that cable system operators must pay now for each distant signal. So far, WTBS has lost only 300,000 subscribers, but the fee increase could make it more difficult to add subscribers in new systems.

The royalty fees are worrisome mainly because the superstation is TBS's only guaranteed moneymaker. Last year, WTBS contributed $96.6 million to revenues and $31.2 million to operating profits. That was an impressive profit margin, but the sum was not enough to make up for the losses of the news channels and the Turner baseball and basketball teams, the Atlanta Braves and Hawks.

"WTBS continues to be the locomotive of the corporation," said Mr. Wussler. WTBS "is all we've got," said William Bevins, TBS's chief financial officer.

CNN was actually profitable between last October and May, Mr. Bevins said, but the ink reddened again this summer with the renegotiation of contracts with systems operators. With SNC offering an alternative, systems operators reduced their per-subscriber payment to TBS to 10 cents from 15 cents, "and it's going to go on down," said Mr. Bevins. (Such fees are important, as CNN sells only 40 percent of its commercial time. WTBS sells the same percentage over all, but it sells between 65 and 70 percent of its commercial prime time, for which advertisers pay a higher rate than for daytime.) This year, as in 1982, he said, CNN will probably lose $6 million and CNN Headline News will lose another $10 million.

While CNN Headline News may be profitable next year, he said, "it's too early to say if CNN will be profitable. We could make it profitable if we cut back service, but that's not in the cards." Instead, money is being plowed into the news-gathering operations, with two more overseas bureaus—Paris and Mexico City—opening next year.

The sports teams, even the high-flying Braves, are also a drag on profits, said Mr. Bevins, "but for us, the ball clubs are a program. If the club performs well, we have a free program, one of our best-rated. We will make a lot more from televising them than the clubs will lose." The Braves games, along with 4,200 movies under license, give WTBS a reliable source of supply.

Still, TBS has spent more than $20 million in the past year or so to make or acquire programming. It has given $6 million to Jacques Cousteau for a series on the Amazon, which will run on WTBS next spring and be syndicated worldwide, and which nobody expects to pay its way. "Someone had to keep Cousteau going, and it's a prestige thing to do, like a loss leader in the supermarket," said Mr. Turner.

The plan is to build up a substantial syndication business with the Cousteau show, other original programming and acquisitions that include some British family series, the Miss World contest and "Centennial," the miniseries based on the James Michener novel. Some of the shows will be fodder for a fourth network; others will be sold outright for cash. But whether WTBS has the expertise for syndication is debatable. "I'm not sure you can run something like that out of Atlanta," said one television executive. "You need to be on the streets of Los Angeles or New York."

If Turner Broadcasting System is going to create more original programming, the likelihood is that it will be relatively high-toned, family-oriented and in keeping with Ted Turner's personal brand of morality and politics—"archconservative with some big liberal holes," in the view of Robert Wussler, executive vice president of TBS and head of WTBS.

Accordingly, the shows that WTBS has originated to date tend to be patriotic and upbeat. There is "Portrait of America," a five-year project that has vowed to take an in-depth look at each of the 50 states. Another is "Nice People" which, as the publicity notes, focuses on "unsung heroes who, as ordinary people, do extraordinary things for the well-being of others." Next week will bring the debut of "Good News," a nightly news-format show that will recap the happier events of the day.

Is that a Ted Turner inspiration? "They're all his inspirations," said Mr. Wussler.

[Aug. 14, 1983]

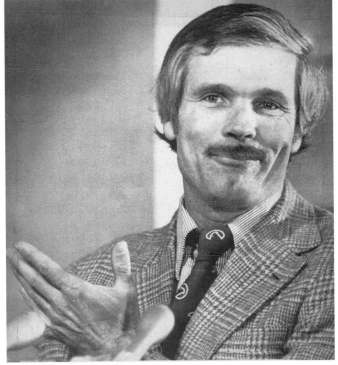

ASSOCIATED PRESS

Ted Turner's Atlanta superstation paved the way to CNN.

1980–1989

Bell System Breakup Opens Era of Great Expectations and Great Concern

The American Telephone & Telegraph Company was the unchallenged giant of the American communications business until the 1970's, when rivals began trying to pick off pieces of the lucrative long-distance business. In 1974, the Justice Department sued A.T.&T., claiming that it had abused its monopoly to keep competitors out of the markets for equipment and long-distance service. The case went to trial in March 1981, and A.T.&T. was presenting its defense when the trial broke for a holiday recess at the end of that year. On Jan. 8, a settlement was reached, with A.T.&T. agreeing to spin off its local telephone companies—soon to be known as "Baby Bells"—on Jan. 1, 1984.

The breakup did bring on increased competition. It also left A.T.&T. a giant in search of a strategy, given that its long-distance business was losing market share. It tried computers, with disastrous results, and at the end of the century was trying to get back into the local telephone business through cable television wires.

On the day of the breakup, The Times analyzed the emerging shape of the telecommunications business, including the forecast that telephones "will become increasingly used not only to convey voice communications but also to convey computer data, electronic mail and video images, and all at the same time." Sounds remarkably like the Internet, which was to become the most exciting business of the 1990's.

By ANDREW POLLACK

A new era for American telecommunications and for American business begins today as the once-unified Bell System begins life as eight separate companies. It is a time of great expectations and great concern for both the telephone industry and the nation as a whole.

No company so large and technologically integrated as the Bell System has ever split itself into pieces before, not even in the great trust-busting days early in the century.

No nation has ever made a determination to let the forces of competition, rather than government-backed monopoly, determine the future of something so vital as its telephone network.

It is an especially daring course for the nation that, by almost all accounts, already has the best phone system in the world. If the gamble is lost, quality of telephone service could deteriorate.

"To break up a very tight network is something quite unprecedented," said Alfred D. Chandler Jr., professor of business history at the Harvard Business School. "It was one of the best managed companies in the world for a long time. You go overseas and people there can't understand why we're breaking up A.T.&T."

For the consumer, the breakup might appear to mean only new and bewildering choices about which long-distance company to choose or which telephone to buy.

But more is at stake. The telephone network has served to bind the nation together. It is vital for the nation's defense. And it is increasingly becoming vital for industry of all types as the nation enters an age when the movement of information, from person to person or computer to computer, is as crucial as the movement of goods. The telephone system is, in effect, the highway system of the Information Age, and its health affects the competitiveness of all American industry. If the telephone breakup spurs innovation, it could help all industries.

"We'll get new technologies rushing forward," said Ithiel de Sola Pool, director of the research program on communications policy at the Massachusetts Institute of Technology.

In the divestiture, which took effect at midnight, A.T.&T. has kept the long-distance business, equipment manufacturing operations and Bell Laboratories and is free to enter new businesses, such as computers. The local operating companies are now seven independently owned regional holding companies mainly engaged in providing local telephone service.

What might the phone system look like five years from now? Ten years? At the turn of the century?

Despite great promises on the one hand and forecasts of doom on the other, the truth is that no one really knows how the divestiture will turn out in the long run. Alexander Graham Bell, the inventor of the telephone, was trying to help the deaf. Instead, he invented a device that shifted the world from written communications to spoken communications, shutting the deaf out even more from the events around them. The effects of the breakup of A.T.&T. might be just as unpredictable, and just as dramatic.

Nevertheless, experts are already predicting that the new evolution in communications will have these results:

¶ Several networks will be competing with the new A.T.&T. to carry long-distance calls. They will include those of the MCI Communications Corporation and GTE Sprint, and perhaps one or two other major ones. There will be specialty networks for computer communications and some networks that are only regional, as opposed to national. Large companies will increasingly build their own networks that will interconnect with the public networks in a complex web.

¶ Communications capacity will become a commodity, such as wheat and corn, to be bought in bulk and resold for a profit. Hotels will resell communications capacity to their guests, landlords to their tenants and companies to their employees. Much of the profit will come from providing the information that flows over the network, rather than mere transmission.

¶ The telephone system will become increasingly used not only to convey voice communications but also to convey computer data, electronic mail and video images, and all at the same time. The telephone system itself will become much more computerized and "intelligent." It will be able to tell you who is calling before you pick up the phone. You might be able to program the phone system with your daily schedule, so that calls could be automatically routed to you any time of day.

¶ The already healthy industry that makes telephone equipment should continue to grow but will also experience a period of intense competition. One of the more popular products will be a combination computer-telephone.

Many of these trends are already under way, but the increasing competition spurred by the Bell breakup is expected to speed them up.

However, the breakup could also impede innovation in some cases, according to some experts. Bell Laboratories, no longer supported by telephone ratepayers, might see its research funds shrink and its focus become more oriented toward short-term product development rather than the long-term research that has made it a national electronics resource. Also, if the phone system is Balkanized, it might take longer to introduce new services because many companies would have to agree to them. In the past, A.T.&T. alone decided what to do.

Opponents of the divestiture say that it will probably lead to a rise in local rates because they will no longer be subsidized by long-distance rates, although the Government has yet to sort this out.

In addition, the opponents argue, with no company having responsibility for end-to-end communications and with each company cutting corners to lower costs, the quality of telephone service will deteriorate.

"It is the dumbest thing that has ever been done," said Charles Wohlstetter, chairman of Continental Telecom Inc., an independent telephone company. "You don't have to break up the only functioning organization in the country to spur innovation."

But such potential drawbacks could be balanced out by reduced long-distance rates and by the money people can save by buying their phones rather than renting them. In addition, many people might prefer lower-quality phone service if they can pay less.

The restructuring of the phone industry was done without much public debate and planning. The phone system monopoly unraveled gradually, and no one, particularly Congress, ever really sat down and decided how the telephone system should be redesigned.

"Most of those decisions were made one at a time on an ad hoc basis," said William M. Ellinghaus, the president of A.T.&T.

Charles L. Brown, chairman of A.T.&T., at a shareholders meeting in 1980.

IRA WYMAN/THE NEW YORK TIMES

1980–1989

"Nobody had any grand design on what telecommunications ought to be."

Nor was there much concern from the general public about the size of A.T.&T. Indeed, the breakup is occurring at the time of an Administration that believes bigness in itself is not badness.

But some sort of Bell restructuring, many experts contend, was virtually inevitable. They argue that a traditional regulatory approach was not suited to an era of rapidly changing economics and technology. While the public may feel that the Bell System was not broken, and thus did not need fixing, the huge communications monopoly actually started unraveling sometime after World War II, and the pace of that unraveling has been picking up ever since.

As air transportation became more commonplace, large companies began dispersing their operations. This made communications more important to a company both strategically and as a percentage of its budget. Pressure increased to find new services and cut costs.

At the same time, there was a veritable explosion in the technologies of electronics, in general, and computers, in particular. With microwave radio, it no longer was prohibitively expensive to duplicate the telephone system, as it was in the days of wire. And computers allowed for new services and a burst of innovation. So much was made possible, and so much was demanded by users, that the Bell System could not keep up.

Ironically, Bell pioneered in many of these innovations, such as the transistor, that powered the computer revolution. But Bell had a vast investment in equipment that was already installed and did not want to make its investment obsolete. It was slow in installing high-speed communications needed by computer users and in allowing the computer equipment of other manufacturers to be attached to its lines.

By 1959 the Federal Communications Commission had ruled that big companies could build their own microwave systems. In 1968 the F.C.C. said non-Bell equipment could use the telephone lines. A year later, MCI was authorized to begin limited long-distance service. Bell tried to fight back, but its position as a regulated monopoly prevented it from focusing on the biggest customers at the expense of the rest. And prior legal agreements kept it restricted to the telephone business, leaving the F.C.C. with the virtually impossible task of trying to define where telephones ended and computers began.

Most experts expected some sort of resolution that would have allowed others into Bell's business and allowed Bell into new businesses. They assumed there would have to be an elaborate regulatory system to prevent Bell from subsidizing its competitive businesses with its regulated businesses.

So the breakup of the Bell System was a dramatic and unexpected development. But, in many ways, it does the same thing the F.C.C., perhaps in a more elegant manner, might have done, and allows for less regulation rather than more. The breakup, therefore, is in keeping with the current deregulatory trend. It will finally allow the communications industry's competition to shift from courtrooms and regulatory agencies to the marketplace.

[Jan. 1, 1984]

For Apple, a Risky Assault on I.B.M.

By DAVID E. SANGER

When Apple Computer Inc. introduces its long-awaited Macintosh computer tomorrow, it may represent the last serious assault on the dominance of the International Business Machines Corporation in the personal computer industry.

The Macintosh, unlike many personal computers introduced over the past year, is completely incompatible with the I.B.M. Personal Computer. Thus, it is a gamble for Apple because many of the most widely used computer programs on the market are designed for the I.B.M. machine.

"They are taking an awesome risk," said David Lawrence, an analyst for Montgomery Securities in San Francisco. "The bottom line is 'Can you establish an alternative to I.B.M.?'"

Whether Apple is successful will depend largely on whether consumers believe that the Macintosh represents such a large technological advance, in computing power and ease of use, that they will choose it over the more secure I.B.M. alternative.

Steven P. Jobs, Apple's chairman and co-founder, and John Sculley, the president and chief executive, said in an interview last week that more than Apple's future rides on the Macintosh. "This industry survives on constant innovation," said Mr. Sculley. "Unless Apple does it, no one will be able to innovate except I.B.M. But if we are successful, it means there still is a place for new ideas."

Most of those who have seen the Macintosh, which Apple has previewed for the press and industry analysts, agree that it is refreshing. "Everything else in the past year has been an echo of I.B.M.; this is a choice," said Esther Dyson, editor of Release 1.0, an industry newsletter. "It won't dislodge the I.B.M. standard, but it is a good No. 2."

Much about the Macintosh departs from the I.B.M. standard. Instead of 5¼-inch disks, which store information permanently, it uses a 3½-inch format. Moreover, the computer is driven by the 32-bit Motorola 68000—a microprocessor that handles 32 pieces of information at a time. That is about twice as powerful as the Intel chip at the heart of the I.B.M. And like Apple's Lisa machine, which floundered last year, the Macintosh relies on a handheld device called a mouse.

Instead of typing instructions, the user rolls the mouse on a desktop. As it moves, the cursor—an arrow that points to specific points on the screen—moves accordingly. The user can give instructions by pointing the mouse to pictures on the screen, such as a file cabinet or wastepaper basket. Or, by using a graphics package called MacPaint, he can draw his own creations.

The mouse is the Macintosh's biggest selling point because it takes almost no

MARILYNN K. YEE/THE NEW YORK TIMES

Steven P. Jobs and a new Mac in 1984.

I.B.M. was the leading computer company in the world in 1981 when it entered the growing but fragmented personal computer market. That decision instantly lent cachet to the product category and offered the possibility of establishing the industry standard.

That is just what happened, but I.B.M. did not wind up as the prime beneficiary. That honor went to Microsoft, a little-known company that I.B.M. chose to design the operating system for the new computer. I.B.M. failed to use its power to get an ownership stake—either in the operating system itself or in Microsoft.

That error was not apparent for years. In 1984, when Apple Computer introduced its Macintosh computer—with a strange device known as a mouse—it was still viewed as being the last competitor left standing against I.B.M., even though other companies were making I.B.M.-compatible machines.

In 1991, after Microsoft and I.B.M. had become rivals, if not enemies, The Times analyzed the success of Microsoft and noted that some experts thought it would have a difficult time competing with I.B.M. They were wrong. I.B.M.'s own operating system failed to win market acceptance and was dropped.

Why did I.B.M. make the mistake of letting Microsoft own the crucial element? There is no clear answer. Probably its executives did not anticipate how the industry would develop. Perhaps they felt constrained by antitrust considerations, since a major antitrust case against I.B.M. was still pending, although it would be dropped in 1982. By 1999, it was Microsoft that was on trial as a monopolist, with an I.B.M. executive among the prosecution witnesses.

The stock numbers show who won. An investment of 1,000 in I.B.M. on March 13, 1986, the day Microsoft went public, would have grown to 3,000 by June 7, 1999, the day an I.B.M. executive testified against Microsoft. Apple did better, with 1,000 growing to 4,000. But 1,000 invested in Microsoft at the close of its first day of trading would have been worth more than 400,000 in 1999. It was the most valuable company in the world, and Bill Gates, its chairman and chief executive, was the richest person.

1980–1989

prior knowledge of computers to run the machine. As a result, Apple hopes the computer will appeal to a new market: executives, students and home users who want to use a computer without having to understand its inner workings. Analysts say that the image of simplicity should give the Macintosh a strong position in the marketplace. "People will like it, because it is a cuddly machine," said Mr. Lawrence, the industry analyst. "The question is whether the simplicity will prove compelling to someone deciding whether to buy a computer."

But the success of the Macintosh may depend less on the design of the hardware than on the availability of software, the programs that give the machine its operating instructions. I.B.M.'s success has snowballed because it made the technical specifications of its Personal Computer available to third parties, and as a result, thousands of specialized programs are on the market.

Similarly, Apple put prototypes of the Macintosh in the hands of some software manufacturers as long ago as early last year. And it will announce tomorrow that more than 80 software manufacturers have agreed to write programs for the machine.

Among them are Microsoft Corporation, which developed the operating system for the I.B.M. Personal Computer, and Lotus Development Corporation, which soon will have a version of its Lotus 1-2-3 spreadsheet program for the Macintosh.

One of the biggest attractions of the Macintosh may be its price. For $2,500, purchasers will receive a keyboard, a mouse, a high-resolution video screen, 128,000 characters of internal memory and one disk drive. A similar configuration from I.B.M. would cost about $1,000 more.

[Jan. 23, 1984]

One Day, Junior Got Too Big

By ANDREW POLLACK

REDMOND, Wash.—Ten years ago this month, the International Business Machines Corporation introduced its first personal computer, changing the computer industry forever. Almost overlooked at the time was the company chosen to provide key software for the machine, headed by a nerdy programmer young enough to be the son of many of the I.B.M. executives.

No one is overlooking the results of that decision today. Seizing on that initial opportunity to provide the MS-DOS operating system for I.B.M. personal computers and the clones that followed, the Microsoft Corporation has grown into the world's largest software company, with revenues of $1.8 billion for the fiscal year ending in June. Its reach expands into nearly every nook and cranny of the software business.

With a market capitalization of $12.8 billion, Microsoft is also one of the 50 most valuable companies in the nation, according to a Business Week ranking, ahead of all computer companies except I.B.M. and Hewlett-Packard and in the company of Ford Motor, Dow Chemical and other industrial giants with many times its revenues. The nerdy programmer, William H. Gates, now 35, owns enough of Microsoft to make him worth $4 billion, more than the gross national product of Nicaragua.

But it is getting lonely at the top. On the way to its current dominance, Microsoft and the intensely competitive Mr. Gates have angered many rivals and even some former partners, including I.B.M. Now, almost everyone in the industry is hatching plans to try to compete with Microsoft for control over the industry's direction. And the resulting massive realignment of forces that is reshaping the industry could pose a severe challenge to Microsoft's hegemony.

"Our belief is that Microsoft has peaked," said George Colony, president of Forrester Research, a market research firm in Cambridge, Mass. "They have enough hubris now to believe they don't need I.B.M., that they don't need anybody. I think Microsoft will be a big, struggling company in two years."

Microsoft's relationship with its former mentor, I.B.M., indeed is in a shambles. After a falling out over the joint development of a successor to MS-DOS, I.B.M. is now competing head to head with the software company in what promises to be one of the nastiest personal-computer industry battles of the 1990's. Each company is already trashing the other's product in public. Under the old rubric that "My enemy's enemy is my friend," I.B.M. has even joined forces with its former rival, Apple Computer Inc., to develop software that will compete with Microsoft's offerings.

Novell Inc., which so far has bested Microsoft in software for controlling networks of personal computers, recently strengthened its hand by buying Digital Research Inc., which makes a program that competes with MS-DOS.

And the Federal Trade Commission is investigating Microsoft's practices, spurred in part by complaints from competitors that Microsoft's dominance in operating systems gives it unfair advantages in other categories.

The key threat to Microsoft, however, is not other companies but a big technology change. With MS-DOS and its newer product called Windows, Microsoft dominates the market for software that controls personal computers. But personal computers are increasingly being linked in networks and with larger machines called servers to handle computing tasks now handled by centralized mainframe computers.

Not only has Microsoft had little experience with networked systems, but such an interconnected computing world is likely to require cooperation among companies. Some say Microsoft will have a tough time going it alone, especially against I.B.M., which wields considerable influence with corporate data processing departments.

"No one really likes to do business with Microsoft," said Philippe Kahn, the founder and president of Borland, who predicts the falling out with I.B.M. will hurt the software company. "He didn't need to declare war on I.B.M.," Mr. Kahn said, referring to Mr. Gates. "That will turn out five years from now to look like his biggest mistake. That's ego."

To be sure, there is an element of wishful thinking and jealousy in predictions of Microsoft's downfall. For all their moaning that Microsoft was lucky to be anointed by I.B.M., or that it abuses its control over the key operating software, rivals also acknowledge that Microsoft is a superb competitor and has executed its strategy with precision.

Moreover, most of the threats to

Bill Gates of Microsoft in the mid-1970's.

Microsoft from new alliances might take two or more years to materialize. In the meantime, Microsoft will likely continue its rapid growth merely by selling Windows to as many as possible of the 70 million users of MS-DOS PC's. "Until anyone sees evidence of a broadside hit, it's just a war of words in my opinion," said David Readerman, a software analyst at Shearson Lehman Brothers. "The product momentum is very much on Microsoft's side."

And what momentum it is. Net income has been growing at an average of 64 percent a year over the last five years and revenues at 56 percent. With 8,200 employees, Microsoft has been hiring 10 new people a day.

Mr. Gates is not unaware of the challenges. "I think I need to work extremely hard if we are to do anywhere near as well as we've done," he said.

Mr. Gates also dismissed talk that his behavior has angered his partners and that he, or his competitors, were driven by emotion and ego instead of business sense. "This is business. This is not Divorce Court or Psychology Today," he said. In forming their alliance, he said, I.B.M. and Apple are acting out of perceived needs.

"I won't take any credit for that wildness," he said, explaining that he thinks the partnership makes little sense, particularly for Apple, which will sacrifice its uniqueness by sharing software development with I.B.M.

I.B.M.'s need for Apple and other partners stems in large part from the void left by Microsoft. I.B.M. and Microsoft initially worked together on OS/2, which was supposed to be a successor to MS-DOS, with more sophisticated features. But now Microsoft is backing its own program, Windows, which it began developing long before it started work on OS/2.

For I.B.M., OS/2 is crucial to tying personal computers to its larger machines. It also needs its own operating system to help differentiate its personal computers from the legions of cheaper clones that have severely cut its market share.

With relations with I.B.M. broken off, however, Microsoft is fully committed to Windows. It has sold more than 4 million copies since a revamped version appeared a little more than a year ago, dwarfing the 600,000 copies of OS/2 sold since 1987. Windows works on top of MS-DOS, making it an easier transition than OS/2, a replacement for DOS.

But being tied to the older technology of MS-DOS could also be a drawback for Windows. So Microsoft is developing a new operating system, known as Windows NT, which it says will be ready next year. NT—which stands for new technology—will run on powerful personal computers using different kinds of microprocessors and will be better geared for use in networks.

Windows, however, is more than just an operating system. Microsoft is using it to increase sales of applications products like Microsoft Word, its word-processing program, and its Excel spreadsheet by tailoring these programs to run with Windows.

Competitors are following suit, after having initially ignored Windows in favor of OS/2. Some, in fact, say Microsoft misled them into supporting OS/2, a charge Microsoft denies.

In any case, Microsoft has had the market for applications that work with Windows nearly to itself. "It's almost like taking candy from a baby," said Scott Oki, senior vice president of sales, marketing and services for Microsoft.

Microsoft said that in the last year its share of the United States markets for spreadsheets and word processing for I.B.M. and compatible personal computers have both doubled to about 30 percent, as measured by revenues.

Mr. Gates seems determined to enter every major area in the personal computer software business. To develop new software concepts, the company has started a lab, headed by Nathan P. Myhrvold, a physicist who worked with the noted British astrophysicist Stephen Hawking before being bitten by the software bug.

Rivals have long complained that the rest of the industry has served as Microsoft's R.& D. lab. Windows was clearly inspired by Apple's work with the Macintosh, so much so that Apple is suing Microsoft for copyright infringement. While the Go Corporation has pioneered development of new software to control pen-based computers, Microsoft is adding extensions to Windows to handle pen input. Even MS-DOS, the program that put Microsoft on the map, was acquired from another company.

"You will have a hard time finding anything that Microsoft pioneered," said Mr. Kahn of Borland. "Guys like Steve Jobs have contributed tons more to the industry than Bill," he added, referring to the founder of Apple and of Next Computer Inc.

That might be somewhat unfair. Microsoft has been early in some technologies like combining video with computing, and has kept up its investment for years even though a big market has yet to materialize. As the Japanese have proved, what matters most is not the basic invention but the ability to commercialize it. Mr. Gates has proved to be a master at quickly positioning Microsoft to take advantage of new developments.

Mr. Gates is, by all accounts, a demanding boss. Employees who enter meetings not fully prepared can leave carrying their head in their hands. "At least three times in a meeting he'll say 'That's the stupidest thing I've ever heard,'" said Paul Maritz, vice president for advanced operating systems.

But Mr. Gates also inspires loyalty. Microsoft has had very little turnover in its top management.

Mr. Gates works at the same relentless pace as in 1975, when he dropped out of Harvard at age 19 to start Microsoft, staying up late to reply to some of the more than 100 electronic mail messages he gets each day. "You see mail from Bill at 2 in the morning," said Mr. Oki, the senior vice president. It is somewhat disconcerting to Mr. Gates, then, that some of his thirtysomething lieutenants are starting to marry and have kids, and sometimes can't reply to his messages until the morning. A couple of executives have retired to enjoy the wealth they've earned from Microsoft.

Mr. Gates has not had much time to enjoy his fortune, with the exception of a penchant for fancy cars and of a new house he is building, most of it underground, with a garage the size of an airplane hangar and space to seat 250 people for dinner. The house will also have four children's bedrooms, perhaps a sign that Mr. Gates will someday settle down and marry.

But most of Mr. Gates's efforts will be occupied with making Windows a broad-based success and extending Microsoft's reach throughout the software business, which could be among the most important industries of the coming decade.

Said Paul Grayson, chairman of Micrografx, a Dallas software company that was an early supporter of Windows but is now working with I.B.M. on OS/2: "If Bill succeeds in his strategy, in my opinion he'll become the wealthiest, most powerful person in the history of mankind."

[Aug. 4, 1991]

1980–1989

'Old' Coke Coming Back After Outcry by Faithful

By 1985, Coca-Cola was perhaps the most famous brand name in the world. But Coca-Cola officials were worried about their perennial shadow in the soft-drink wars, Pepsi-Cola. Its ads featured blind taste tests in which Coke drinkers concluded that Pepsi tasted better. To make things worse, Coke's own taste tests produced the same result.

So Coca-Cola took the radical step of producing a "new" Coke that tasted more like Pepsi, and letting it replace the old one. The decision, said Roberto C. Goizueta, chairman of Coca-Cola, was "one of the easiest we have ever made."

It was also one of the dumbest. A few months later, Coca-Cola found out that millions of people had liked the old formula, no matter what the tests said. It brought back the old Coke. The new Coke remained available for a few years, but eventually vanished.

By KENNETH N. GILPIN

In one of the most stunning about-faces in the history of marketing, the Coca-Cola Company yielded to thousands of irate consumers yesterday and said it would bring back the original Coke formula that it scrapped three months ago.

The product will be sold under the brand name Coca-Cola Classic, the company said, emphasizing that it would continue to market the new, sweeter soft drink that it introduced with great fanfare last April.

"It's a multimillion-dollar reversal," said James G. Shennan, president of S&O Consultants Inc., a San Francisco marketing and design firm. "I am very surprised."

Explaining the move, Thomas Gray, a spokesman for Coca-Cola, said: "Over 40 million consumers every day in the United States enjoy Coca-Cola but thousands of dedicated Coca-Cola consumers have told us they still want the original taste as an option. We have listened and we are taking action to satisfy their request."

Indeed, the abandonment of the original formula had unleashed a groundswell of protest from Americans who contended, among other things, that the soft-drink company was depriving them of a national institution.

Marketing experts suggested that Coca-Cola's original studies, which were based on taste tests, had failed to take into account the nation's loyalty to the 99-year-old drink. But they also said that while Coca-Cola might have briefly earned itself a reputation as insensitive to consumer sentiments, it had done much to redeem itself with its quick and dramatic response.

Some analysts suggested that the company may have been contemplating a reintroduction all along, despite the pledge of Coca-Cola's chairman, Roberto C. Goizueta, last April that the old formula would be placed in a vault at the Trust Company of Georgia, never to be used again.

"They may be bringing it back somewhat earlier than originally planned," said Hugh Zurkuhlen, an analyst at Salomon Brothers, "but I wouldn't be surprised if they hadn't considered bringing the old formula back once the new product was launched."

However long in planning the reintroduction may have been, the product will be reaching store shelves at the peak point during the sales year. Coca-Cola Classic, which is to be formally introduced at a news conference at 1 P.M. today at company headquarters in Atlanta, will be available in some markets within weeks, according to Mr. Gray.

The company lost no time in getting television commercials for the product on the air either: Spots were broadcast last night, featuring Donald R. Keough, president of Coca-Cola, thanking consumers who tried new Coke and promising the loyalists the return of the original formula.

The company also picked up an extraordinary amount of free air time. Reports on the original formula's return were prominently featured in news reports by all three television networks.

With the reintroduction, there will be six soft drinks carrying the Coke name: Coca-Cola, Diet Coke, Caffeine-Free Coca-Cola, Caffeine-Free Diet Coke, Cherry Coke and Cola-Cola Classic.

Until four years ago, the company had reserved the brand name for only one product, selling its other soft drinks under a variety of other names, including Tab and Sprite.

But Mr. Gray said that "new" Coke would remain the company's flagship brand.

Bottlers and retailers welcomed Coca-Cola Classic, but said it would create production and space problems.

A spokesman for Pepsico Inc., the nation's No. 2 soft-drink manufacturer, was triumphant.

Coke's big mistake.

"We now have the opportunity to compete with one product that lost to Pepsi in millions of taste tests and against one product that the public hates," said Ken Ross, the Pepsico spokesman.

The new Coke was introduced with the support of a $4 million research project and an advertising campaign that analysts estimate cost Coca-Cola at least $10 million. While sales figures are not yet available, analysts say they appear to have been spotty so far.

"New Coke has not been selling particularly well, particularly in the South, where there was a visceral reaction to what Coke did when it scrapped the old formula," said Emanuel Goldman, an analyst at Montgomery Securities Inc. in San Francisco.

Indeed, today's announcement seemed to represent a clear admission that a long-studied and carefully orchestrated marketing move had gone awry.

Coca-Cola, generally viewed as one of the nation's most conservatively run companies, spent two years conducting consumer tests before it introduced the new formula. Mr. Goizueta told reporters at the time that Robert W. Woodruff, the driving force behind the growth of the company, had personally approved the switch shortly before his death earlier this year.

With its sweeter, less fizzy taste, the new Coke was intended primarily to regain market share lost in recent years to Pepsi-Cola. According to Beverage Digest, a widely followed industry newsletter, Coke held a 21.7 percent market share compared with 18.8 percent for Pepsi at the end of 1984.

But while Coca-Cola's taste tests, involving more than 190,000 consumers, showed that a majority preferred the taste of the new Coke to the old formula, analysts said the company apparently did not research, or count on, consumers' reaction to withdrawing the old product.

"There was some research they should have done that they didn't do," Mr. Goldman said. "This will provide material for quite a few case studies at major business schools in years to come."

In Seattle, one man filed suit to make Coca-Cola provide the old Coke to consumers. Nationwide, people stockpiled the old-formula soft-drink before it ran out. Atlantans, who had been drinking the old Coke longer than anyone else, particularly mourned its passing.

Coca-Cola issued a three-paragraph statement acknowledging the return of the old formula after analysts, including Jesse Meyers, publisher of Beverage Digest, said the company intended to do so.

Mr. Meyers, who in April reported the arrival of the new Coke several days in advance of its introduction, said yesterday that the decision to reintroduce the old formula represented two things: "One, the market is getting incredibly diversified, and Coke sees the opportunity to add another segment." He continued, "Secondly, the diehard, very vocal Coca-Cola drinker wants his old friend back. This became a cultural offense to some people and Coke is now saying, 'Hey, we're listening to you.'"

[July 11, 1985]

Stocks Plunge 508 Points, a Drop of 22.6%; 604 Million Volume Nearly Doubles Record

The 1980's bull market began on Aug. 13, 1982, after the Dow Jones industrial average hit bottom the preceding day at 776.92. By the summer of 1987, the Dow had climbed above 2,700 and bullishness was widespread.

Then it slipped a bit in September, and fell sharply during the second week of October, ending that week with its first ever daily loss of more than 100 points. The average fell 9.5 percent that week, the biggest decline for any week since 1940, when German troops were sweeping across France and it was easy to understand why stocks were being dumped. In 1987, the decline was not as easy to explain. Germany and the United States were having arguments about currency exchange rates, interest rates had been rising and stock prices were very high by traditional valuation measurements. But it was not obvious why the market should react so violently to any or all of those things.

In fact, it now appears to have been a classic market failure. Many institutional investors had signed up for "portfolio insurance," hiring money managers to sell stock index futures for them if prices fell. The sales would have the effect of protecting the value of the investors' portfolios if prices fell further.

In fact, those sales unnerved investors in October. The buyers of the futures contracts tried to hedge their exposure by selling stocks, which drove prices lower and led the portfolio insurers to sell more futures.

On Monday, Oct. 19, the Dow plummeted 508 points, or 22.6 percent. It was by far the worst day in the stock market's history, and it was widely—but wrongly—interpreted as indicating a recession was coming. The Federal Reserve quickly lowered interest rates. Many companies bought back their own shares. The market stabilized, and then began to slowly recover. In the summer of 1989, the Dow exceeded its 1987 high. And while the market fell during the brief 1990-91 recession, prices continued to rise for the next decade. Americans came to view the 1987 crash as a gigantic buying opportunity and reacted to future bad days as being new opportunities for profit. By the spring of 1999, the Dow had passed 10,000.

By LAWRENCE J. DE MARIA

Stock market prices plunged in a tumultuous wave of selling yesterday, giving Wall Street its worst day in history and raising fears of a recession.

The Dow Jones industrial average, considered a benchmark of the market's health, plummeted a record 508 points, to 1,738.74, based on preliminary calculations. That 22.6 percent decline was the worst since World War I and far greater than the 12.82 percent drop on Oct. 28, 1929, that along with the next day's 11.7 percent decline preceded the Great Depression.

Since hitting a record 2,722.42 on Aug. 25, the Dow has fallen almost 1,000 points, or 36 percent, putting the blue-chip indicator 157.5 points below the level at which it started the year. With Friday's plunge of 108.35 points, the Dow has fallen more than 26 percent in the last two sessions.

Yesterday's frenzied trading on the nation's stock exchanges lifted volume to unheard-of levels. On the New York Stock Exchange, an estimated 604.3 million shares changed hands, almost double the previous record of 338.5 million shares set just last Friday.

With the tremendous volume, reports of brokers' trades on the New York Stock Exchange were delayed by more than two hours at one point. The New York Stock Exchange said that, as a result, it would not have definitive figures for the Dow's point decline and the exchange's volume until today.

Yesterday's big losers included International Business Machines, the bluest of the blue chips, which dropped $31, to $104. In August the stock was at $176. The other big losers among the blue chips were General Motors, which lost $13.875, to $52.125, and Exxon, which dropped $10.25, to $33.50.

According to Wilshire Associates, which tracks more than 5,000 stocks, the rout obliterated more than $500 billion in equity value from the nation's stock portfolios. That equity value now stands at $2.311 trillion. Since late summer, more than $1 trillion in stock values has been lost.

The losses were so great they sent shock waves to markets around the world, and many foreign exchanges posted record losses. In a sign of the continuing effect, the Tokyo Stock Exchange fell sharply today. The Nikkei Dow Jones average plummeted a record 3,395.95 yen, to 22,350.61, a drop of 13.2 percent, by late afternoon. Also, the Hong Kong exchange decided to close for the week.

In Washington yesterday, the White House spokesman, Marlin Fitzwater, issued a statement saying that President Reagan had "watched with concern" the stock market's collapse. But Mr. Reagan remained convinced that the economy was sound.

Mr. Fitzwater said the President had directed Administration officials to contact leading financial experts. "Those consultations confirm our view that the underlying economy remains sound," he added.

Stock market analysts scrambled for explanations, which ranged from rising interest rates to the falling dollar to the possibility of war between the United States and Iran.

Indeed, the panic selling may have been bolstered by the news that the United States Navy destroyed an Iranian offshore oil platform in the central Persian Gulf yesterday, and Iran vowed retaliation.

But many experts seemed to think that a major catalyst was fears of a breakdown in accords to maintain trading and currency stability between the United States and its major trading partners.

Some others, meanwhile, blamed program traders for the debacle, and predicted that regulators would curb, and perhaps outlaw, the practice. In program trading, huge blocks of stock are traded by arbitragers seeking to profit from the difference in value between the actual cash value of the stocks and futures contracts based on those stocks.

Discussing yesterday's collapse, John J. Phelan Jr., chairman of the Big Board, said: "It's the nearest thing to a meltdown that I ever want to see. We were fortunate this occurred when the American economy is very strong. We are not operating in an environment of weakness."

Meanwhile, Treasury Secretary James A. Baker 3d met in Frankfurt, West Germany, with top economic officials, who agreed to keep currencies "around current levels." For several days, Mr. Baker had been criticizing West Germany's recent increase in interest rates.

Some analysts said that Mr. Baker's public criticism of Bonn was taken by stock investors as a sign that recent currency accords were crumbling and the dollar was likely to weaken further. A volatile dollar discourages huge foreign investors, such as the Germans and the Japanese, because it does not allow them to make reasonable assumptions about the return on their investments in American securities.

To defend the dollar, the Federal Reserve could allow American interest rates to move higher, which would have the effect of drawing funds into Treasury securities. Foreign buying of those instruments is important, in that it helps to pay for the nation's huge budget deficit.

Robert C. Holland, a former member of the board of governors of the Fed, and now president of the Committee for Economic Development, said that the United States, the world's largest debtor nation, had made itself too vulnerable to foreign financial influence because its budget and trade deficits are "sucking in foreign capital."

In a news conference, Mr. Phelan, at the Big Board, said that the exchange had

1980–1989

DOES 1987 EQUAL 1929?

By ERIC GELMAN

As stock prices soared this year, a chorus of pessimists warned that 1987 was looking more like 1929, when a stock market crash helped to usher in the Great Depression. Yesterday, after a plunge reminiscent of the worst days of 1929, one pressing question was whether the aftershocks would be as devastating to individuals and the nation.

The quick answer, many economists say, is no. The huge losses on Wall Street constitute a substantial blow to the economy at large. But there are many safeguards in place today—some instituted directly in response to the Depression—that would tend to prevent the cascading financial collapse that characterized the crash, impoverishing millions of Americans.

"A stock market crash doesn't ripple out into the economy with the same force" as it did in 1929, said Geoffrey H. Moore, director of the Center for International Business Cycle Research at Columbia University.

To be sure, there are some unsettling similarities between the current era and the pre-Depression years. Like the Roaring Twenties, the 1980's have seen an astonishing boom on Wall Street. Now as then, individual and corporate debt are high, and some sectors of the economy are extremely weak. Trade relations are strained, with protectionist sentiment growing.

But today's economy is better equipped to handle financial shocks. "I don't see this decline in the stock market leading to a great breakdown in the economy," said Robert A. Kavesh, a professor of finance and economics at the New York University

School of Business. "There are still many elements of strength in the economy—profits are strong, for example."

Among the important differences between today and 1929 are Federal deposit insurance, unemployment insurance and Social Security insurance and other elements of what has come to be known as the safety net. These not only guarantee against widespread destitution; their very existence should also help to prevent the kind of financial panic that fed on itself in the Depression.

"In 1929, you didn't have insurance of bank deposits, you didn't have the Securities and Exchange Commission, you had much less knowledge of how the economy worked," Professor Kavesh said.

Today the Government is much more willing to intervene to keep the economy growing. "All governments, liberal and conservative, have assumed that responsibility, which wasn't the case in 1929," said John Kenneth Galbraith, a retired professor of economics at Harvard University and author of "The Great Crash." Huge Federal budget deficits make it difficult for Washington to increase Government spending, however, which has been one response to economic slowdowns.

The Federal Reserve would be the first line of defense if the financial system began to falter. "If necessary—and I don't think it will be—the Federal Reserve could provide additional bank reserves and other support to make sure any loans that turned sour because of what's happened in the market wouldn't result in a banking crisis," said Charles L. Schultze of the Brookings Institution. [NEWS ANALYSIS, Oct. 20, 1987]

been in "constant" contact with the Securities and Exchange Commission throughout the day, but had never seriously considered closing. "If the S.E.C. had asked us to do so, we would have," he added.

Rumors that the commission would seek a stock trading halt swept Wall Street all afternoon. Many economists and analysts said such an unprecedented move would almost surely destroy any lingering confidence in the securities markets. The fact that it was even suggested was an indication of the completeness of Wall Street's dismay.

The Securities and Exchange Commission's chairman, David S. Ruder, said at one point: "I'm not afraid to say that there is some point, and I don't know what that point is, that I would be quite anxious to talk to the New York Stock Exchange about a temporary, and very temporary, halt of trading."

Late in the day, it was announced that the Pacific Stock Exchange would close a half-hour early, at 4 P.M. Eastern time. Ordinarily, the Pacific exchange's normal 4:30 P.M. close allows East Coast investors to transact business after the close of their own markets. Had they been able to do so, yesterday's selloff might have been even greater.

Hugh A. Johnson Jr., an economist at the First Albany Corporation, said the market collapsed because "so much damage has been done to confidence in the financial markets" by the apparent falling out of the United States, West Germany and Japan.

The current crisis "has to be dealt with quickly," Mr. Johnson said, adding that "they should call Paul Volcker back" to head up an international meeting of finance ministers and central bankers to restore confidence. Mr. Volcker is the former head of the Federal Reserve Board.

People in New York City watching stock prices plunge on Oct. 19, 1987.

"This is the stuff of history," he said. "We can't forget this one. Historians generally refer to these things as genuine financial panics."

The rout was of such magnitude that Wall Street's professionals were at a loss for words. Many had, in fact, not even recovered from Friday's 108.35-point decline in the Dow, which was the first time the blue-chip indicator had ever lost more than 100 points.

While many brokers and analysts were concerned that trouble was brewing over the weekend, as investors at home and abroad digested the news from the financial markets, no one conceived that the Dow, which had tripled since August 1982, could lose 500 points in one day.

Traders suspected that there might be a big increase in mutual fund redemptions and, because many people have bought stock on credit, in margin account selling as brokerages demanded more collateral for customers' accounts. And there was concern that mutual fund redemptions and margin calls would snowball even further today.

In addition, rumors began to spread yesterday that some financial institutions might have lost heavily in the frantic trading, and might be in trouble. Small firms may have liquidity problems, and be forced to close. Individual traders and investors have undoubtedly been wiped out. Large firms may have to cut back, and it is not inconceivable that the ripples may spread to the banking community, which has been edging into the securities business.

"One word is operative out there now," said one very shaken trader. "Fright."

[Oct. 20, 1987]

DOW FINISHES DAY OVER 10,000 MARK FOR THE FIRST TIME

1980–1989

By GRETCHEN MORGENSON

The Dow achieved a perfect 10 yesterday. Thousand, that is.

After nearly two weeks of thrust and parry, traders pushed the Dow Jones industrial average above 10,000 and kept it there until trading ended. The Dow closed at 10,006.78, up 184.54 points, or 1.9 percent.

Although 10,000 is little more than a psychological hurdle for investors, the market's move is significant in what it reflects: the unparalleled strength of the economy and the dominance of the world economic stage by American corporations.

More and more of the world's profits are being claimed by the nation's corporations. "Back in 1990 the U.S. share was 36 percent; last year, it was 44 percent," said Jeffrey M. Applegate, chief investment strategist at Lehman Brothers in New York. "That goes a long way toward explaining why U.S. equities have had such exemplary performance."

The Dow has doubled in less than four years; it reached 5,000 in November 1995. It is up nearly tenfold since 1982.

"The market's ability to sustain itself through all sorts of climates and economic conditions—inflation/deflation, growth/lack of growth—has been impressive," said Laszlo Birinyi, president of Birinyi & Associates in Greenwich, Conn., and a global trading consultant for Deutsche Bank.

A lurking concern, however, is just how narrow the market's advance has been. A growing portion of Americans' investment money is devoted to the 30 well-known companies in the Dow and the components of the Standard & Poor's 500-stock index, which rose near its record yesterday. But many portfolios have not matched the performance of the Dow and the S.& P. That is because a relatively small number of stocks have pulled the indexes higher. The winners have been the best-known stocks with household names, stocks like General Electric, American Express and Wal-Mart Stores.

Neither has the road to Dow 10,000 been pothole free. The financial crisis that began in Asia with the devaluation of the Thai baht in July 1997 and migrated to Russia last summer and then to Brazil gave stock market investors their first taste of significant losses in eight years. But three cuts in interest rates by the Federal Reserve Board turned stocks around last fall.

Economic problems still simmer overseas: fourth-quarter data from Japan, Germany and much of Latin America show declines in gross domestic products there. But difficulties abroad have only served to make the United States stock market more of a haven to investors worldwide. Because the United States is almost alone in experiencing solid growth now, stocks of big American companies are viewed as enticing.

Behind the long bull market are several factors—declining interest rates, low inflation, increasing productivity as a result of advancements in technology—that have helped propel corporations to new levels of efficiency.

"The lower rate structure has clearly been the majority of strength in the market," said Ned Riley Jr., chief investment officer at BankBoston. He contends that lower rates account for 80 percent of the return in the stock market this decade. "Only 20 percent was the result of expanding earnings," he said.

But interest rates would never have fallen had inflation not dwindled. On an annualized basis, consumer prices are rising 1.6 percent, well below the average annual rate of 3.2 percent since 1926.

One reason inflation is virtually nonexistent even after years of economic strength is that labor costs remain in the cellar. So even as the economy expands, usually a precursor to higher inflation, there is little threat of overall price increases.   [March 30, 1999]

Who to Thank for the Thrift Crisis

By NATHANIEL C. NASH

Not since the 1930's, before deposit insurance, had financial institutions failed at the rate they did in the 1980's. The problem began when interest rates rose to the sky, squeezing savings and loan associations that had lent money in fixed-rate mortgages. It got worse after the Government cleared the way for savings and loans to make riskier investments and when Congress refused to provide enough money to close down insolvent institutions. That was an invitation to such associations to gamble, realizing that, if they lost, the loser would be the taxpayer but, if they won, they might get to keep the money as the association became solvent again. Few such gambles worked; some were simply crooked.

Eventually, Congress created the Resolution Trust Corporation, which took over bad assets as insolvent institutions were shuttered. But the losses were far greater than they need have been.

In 1988, The Times reported on how the country had gotten into the mess.

Charles H. Keating Jr., who ran Lincoln Savings and Loan in California, came to symbolize the crisis. His contributions to politicians were large, and five senators helped him delay the closing of his thrift institution. He won appeals of fraud convictions in both Federal and California state court after serving more than four years in prison. He eventually pleaded guilty to four counts of fraud, admitting taking 1 million from a company that he knew to be insolvent.

WASHINGTON—However you look at them, the numbers are staggering. Last week, the Federal Home Loan Bank Board said it would pay $1.35 billion to liquidate two California savings and loan associations that had gone bankrupt, producing the most expensive liquidations on record. It will devour more than 40 percent of the cash on hand at the Government's deposit insurance fund, whose paper losses already total almost $14 billion, according to the General Accounting Office.

The bleeding does not stop there.

Almost one-third of the nation's 3,120 savings and loan institutions lost money last year—a staggering total of $13.4 billion—and analysts expect losses to be just as big this year. More than 500 savings and loans are bankrupt and another 300 to 500 are nearly insolvent. In all, experts estimate that it will cost anywhere from $20 billion to $70 billion—and maybe more—to shut institutions that have already been found insolvent and to cover their losses.

This is shaping up to be the biggest financial disaster of the postwar era. It is a crisis that could produce the largest Government bailout in history and the possibility that the thrift industry, born in the Depression to bolster home ownership, will not survive the turbulent, deregulated 1980's as an independent industry.

As the scope of the disaster becomes increasingly clear, so does a picture of how the situation managed to get so out of control.

Fingers point in different directions, and many take aim straight at the depressed Texas economy, whose plummeting oil prices brought down the real estate industry to which savings and loans had lent heavily. But there was not just one culprit, nor a single big mistake. Rather, from the late 1970's on, there was a confluence of error and ineptitude, at times compounded by fraud. Congress, regulators and the industry, all failed. Together, they produced a maelstrom of legislation, regulatory measures and lending practices that were too lenient, shortsighted, poorly conceived, politically compromised or inadequate.

"There's an awful lot of blame to go around," said M. Danny Wall, chairman of the Federal Home Loan Bank Board.

Federal legislators, who frequently bowed to political pressure from an industry known for its powerful grass-roots lobbying, have come under fire for deregulating the thrift industry piecemeal and granting too much leeway in accounting practices. The Bank Board, the industry's primary regulator, is criticized for being too close to the thrift units it regulated, and for responding with inadequate resources and ill-trained examiners when the situation began to unravel.

And the industry, for its part, was unable to cope with the high interest rates that sprang from the late 1970's and spurred deregulation. Many executives lacked expertise to compete in the new world of finance. More troubling were the aggressive entrepreneurs, wheeler-dealers and gamblers who saw an opportunity to make a bundle at the expense of the Federal Government.

Now, in sorting through the rubble, several questions emerge. One is the scope of the problem; how many billions of dollars will be needed to resolve it depends partly on how much the government can salvage from real estate loans gone bad. Another is whether the policies pursued by the Federal Home Loan Bank Board will be enough to halt the industry's deterioration.

Senator William Proxmire minces no words when he speaks of how Congress handled industry problems in the last 10 years.

"Repeatedly, Congress moved too late or failed to produce legislation" to halt the industry's demise, said the Wisconsin Democrat who is chairman of the Senate

Banking Committee. "We created a whole new ball game in 1980," he said, referring to Congressional deregulation of interest rates. But, he added, the Federal Government was unwilling "to appropriate funds to adequately police the new systems."

Although some candid lawmakers blame themselves for insufficient action in the late 1970's and 80's, some analysts believe the roots of the crisis lie deep in the structure of the industry, established by Congress in 1932. The savings and loans—or building and loans, as others were called—were intended to take short-term deposits and use them to make 15-, 20- and 30-year mortgages.

"The whole thrift financial structure was fundamentally flawed from the beginning," said Bert Ely, a banking and thrift consultant based in Alexandria, Va. "It is borrowing short to lend long. Sooner or later you are going to have a disaster."

While interest rates held steady over the next few decades, the system worked. Congress had established an interest-rate ceiling for deposits and the business developed essentially risk-free. But when the Federal Reserve Board, to tame inflation, dramatically pushed up interest rates in the late 1970's and early 1980's, the system's fatal flaw was revealed: savings and loans were forced to pay more for deposits than their mortgage portfolios were yielding.

The interest-rate ceiling that had long provided the industry with handsome profits began to suffocate it. Depositors, knowing that they could earn higher rates from money-market mutual funds, began massive withdrawals of their money. To finance that, the industry began selling assets at a loss. The result: Almost 500 institutions failed between 1980 and 1983, and the underlying net worth—the capital cushion used in times of stress to absorb losses—plummeted from $32.4 billion in 1980 to $20.3 billion by 1982.

As losses mounted, Congress was urged to rescue the system it had created. But the steps it took had the unanticipated effect of making matters worse.

"I don't think that most of us really understood just how serious the problem was," said Senator Jake Garn, Republican of Utah. "When we began to realize how big it was, we did not have the resources to handle it."

First, in 1980, Congress deregulated interest rates that depository institutions could pay on deposits. It also allowed the industry to offer adjustable-rate mortgages to help protect itself from interest-rate fluctuations. Then, in 1982, Congress passed the Depository Institutions Act, permitting the industry to enter new businesses, such as commercial loans like those from banks. The idea was to let the industry diversify its asset portfolio and to shore up its finances.

The new powers allowed institutions with skilled managers to benefit. But Congress and the state legislatures failed to take into account the existence of more than 1,000 severely weakened institutions. With diminishing resources, they began committing funds to new, risky ventures: horse and fish farms, racetracks and building projects that made no economic sense. Many of these projects carried no proper documentation and had no valid appraisals. And state regulators proved particularly lax in supervising such transactions.

1980–1989

A MAN OF INFLUENCE: POLITICAL CASH AND REGULATION

By NATHANIEL C. NASH
with PHILIP SHENON
Special to The New York Times
WASHINGTON, Nov. 8—To his critics, Charles H. Keating Jr., the Phoenix financier who built and lost the Lincoln Savings and Loan Association, represents all that is wrong with a political system in which wealth grants access and influence. To his defenders, Mr. Keating is simply a hard-driving entrepreneur who is being made the fall guy for the savings industry's plight.

But there is no dispute that Mr. Keating has become the central figure in the savings and loan crisis, a breakdown stemming from lax regulation and speculative excess. The Federal bailout of the industry will cost taxpayers more than $100 billion over the next decade, and Lincoln's collapse alone will cost at least $2 billion.

Mr. Keating has never minced words about buying political influence in defense of his financial interests.

"One question, among many raised in recent weeks, had to do with whether my financial support in any way influenced several political figures to take up my cause," he told reporters in April after Federal regulators had taken over Lincoln, with its $6 billion in insured deposits, almost $4 billion of which went to speculative investments in real estate and high-risk "junk bonds."

"I want to say in the most forceful way I can: I certainly hope so."

Mr. Keating, who is scheduled to appear before the House Banking Committee soon to discuss the Lincoln failure, stands accused of fraud and making illegal loans.

For his part, Mr. Keating protests his innocence, denying any wrongdoing, saying that if you do not have money your chances of being heard are greatly reduced. Influence is the way the political system works, he says, and he intends to use it. If regulators had permitted him to keep running Lincoln, he argues, he could have earned his way out of the hole.

[Nov. 9, 1989]

A disaster was in the works because the industry's deposits were insured by the full faith and credit of the United States Government. In 1980, when Congress deregulated interest rates, it increased deposit insurance for thrift institutions, banks and credit unions to $100,000 per account, from $40,000. But the mechanism, intended to protect depositors, enabled thrift executives to attract funds, even while they took big risks with large amounts of money. If they lost, the Government would pay the tab.

As the Bank Board tried, in the 1980's, to give sick institutions enough time to recover, it approved new regulations that most experts, in hindsight, call accounting gimmickry. Those measures hid real losses, delayed big write-downs on bad loans and permitted thrift institutions to lend at levels that far exceeded prudent lending practices.

"In retrospect, the relaxation of controls caused, or at least facilitated, the current crisis," stated R. Dan Brumbaugh Jr., a former economist at the Bank Board, and Andrew S. Carron, an analyst for the First Boston Corporation, in a report for the Brookings Institution last year.

Facing explosive growth in lending, thrift examiners—from the Bank Board and the state agencies—were underpaid and undertrained; there were also not enough of them. The annual starting pay of Bank Board examiners in the early 1980's averaged about $14,000. And Reagan Administration budget cuts trimmed the staff just when the Bank Board needed skilled personnel the most.

By 1984, the Bank Board began to realize how large the problem was. But by then, the assets of the Federal Savings and Loan Insurance Corporation, used to shut thrifts and pay depositors, had begun to dwindle to finance the closures of almost 500 institutions in the previous five years.

Beginning in 1985, the Bank Board—finally recognizing that leniency would only deepen the problem—began trying to institute regulatory changes to reverse the loose accounting measures and to restore credibility to the industry's balance sheets. It approved regulations that limited the amount of direct investment that savings and loans could make in building projects; limited the amount that they could grow each year; phased in increases in minimum capital requirements to 6 percent, and phased out regulatory accounting principles and ushered in a return to generally accepted accounting practices.

But many argue that the measures were too few—and too late. Failure to recognize the problems sooner meant the insolvent institutions were piling losses higher.

"The losses in Texas are averaging $500 million a month, and they get bigger with time until you finally do something about it," said William K. Black, senior associate general counsel at the Federal Home Loan Bank of San Francisco. "That is the magic of compound interest, and the blood letting will continue. You get very scary numbers."

In Jimmy Stewart's movie, "It's a Wonderful Life," the local building and loan society brought joy and prosperity to the middle-class town of Bedford Falls. Residents were prudent savers, homes were built—and the ending couldn't have been happier.

Hollywood would be hard-pressed to make such a movie today. Instead it would have to show a crippled industry whose members include thrift owners wooing members of Congress, building huge, high-risk projects and, not infrequently, engaging in kickbacks, land-flips and other fraudulent acts.

Bank Board officials say that 75 percent of the thrift insolvencies include fraud or criminal conduct. "That does not mean 75 percent of the failures are caused by fraud, but in 75 percent, fraud is a contributing factor," said Mr. Black. Fraud has cropped up all over the country, but Bank Board officials say it has been most apparent in Texas, California and Florida, which have the most liberal investment regulations for their state-chartered thrifts, and the weakest state regulators.   [June 12, 1988]

RJR Nabisco Suitor Claims $24.88 Billion Victory

By JAMES STERNGOLD

In one of the roughest, most confusing and dramatic finales to a takeover battle, the small but powerful buyout firm of Kohlberg, Kravis, Roberts & Company claimed victory late last night in the contest for RJR Nabisco Inc. with a staggering offer of $24.88 billion, the largest sum ever paid for a corporation.

But its rival, an investment group led by RJR Nabisco's top executives, said in a bitter response that it had bid more—$25.42 billion—but had been cheated out of the prize because of an unfair bidding process. The group hinted that it was not yet ready to concede defeat but gave no indication of what further action it might take.

It was the second time that RJR Nabisco's board had set a supposedly firm bidding deadline, only to alter the rules and allow more haggling. Any pretense of rules, procedures or order was dropped yesterday as the auction turned into a free-for-all.

The auction pushed the bidding to levels where the risk of suffering losses just to complete the deal grew substantially. The result will be enormous short-term profits for RJR Nabisco's shareholders, but it is likely to weigh the company down with an unprecedented debt burden and will force the sale of billions of dollars of its assets.

At the winning purchase price, the company will be saddled with more than $20 billion in debt, more than the combined national debts of Bolivia, Jamaica, Uruguay, Costa Rica and Honduras.

The winning offer was almost double the previous record takeover, the $13.4 billion paid in 1984 for the Gulf Oil Corporation by another oil company, the Chevron Corporation. After two previous deadlines set by RJR Nabisco's board, the management group believed it had won, only to be frustrated in the end.

The conclusion to the six-week spectacle was the product of a deft series of maneuvers by Kohlberg, Kravis, which finished last in previous bidding, and some hardball tactics that showed Wall Street at its best and at its worst.

It seems certain that the remarkable sight of the nation's 19th-largest industrial company being hoisted on the auction block by its management and its board, and then fought over so bitterly by some of the sharpest financial minds in the country, will help make the takeover a watershed.

Already, Congressional leaders have expressed some misgivings about the ferocious battle and the amount of debt that will be piled on top of RJR Nabisco to complete the transaction. They have promised hearings into the issue next year.

Kohlberg, Kravis offered cash and securities worth $109 for each of RJR Nabisco's 227 million shares. In addition, it will pay $108 for each of the company's 1.3 million outstanding shares of preferred stock.

The management group said its offer was worth $112 a share, but the company's advisers judged the offers to be "substantially equivalent," according to a company statement.

The company's statement, issued at midnight, said that a special committee of RJR Nabisco outside directors who had been considering the offers decided to recommend that

Henry R. Kravis, takeover strategist.

In the 1980's, a new form of takeover took shape: the leveraged buyout. In such a deal, the buyers put up little of their own money to buy stock. Instead, they borrow nearly all the money.

They were highly profitable in the early 1980's, a fact that attracted more money to them as years went by. But the profits derived from two advantages that disappeared as the years wore on—low prices and falling interest rates. By paying relatively little for companies, the buyers had a margin of safety. With interest rates declining, the loans could be refinanced at lower rates, freeing up more cash to pay down loans.

The peak of the L.B.O. boom came in 1988 with the takeover of RJR Nabisco, the giant tobacco and food company. F. Ross Johnson, the company's chief executive who had been head of Nabisco before its merger with RJR in 1985, bid 17 billion for the company on Oct. 20. But Kohlberg, Kravis, Roberts & Company, the largest of the L.B.O. firms, leaped in with an offer, and the battle was joined. Kohlberg, Kravis won at the end of November by agreeing to pay almost 25 billion. By then, Johnson had been widely painted as being greedy and the RJR Nabisco board had turned against him. It allowed Kohlberg, Kravis to win even though the firm was bidding a bit less.

The deal was not a failure—at least in the sense that the company never went broke. But investors in the Kohlberg, Kravis fund that financed its deals did poorly, as did those investors who bought when the company went public again in 1991. In 1999, years after Kohlberg, Kravis had gotten out by trading its remaining interest for control of Borden, a troubled food company, RJR and Nabisco were split up, separate companies once again.

1980–1989

the Kohlberg, Kravis proposal be accepted. The company's full board then voted to accept the proposal, the statement said.

While Kohlberg, Kravis expressed its satisfaction, F. Ross Johnson, RJR Nabisco's chief executive and the leader of the losing group, issued a one-sentence statement that captured his group's disappointment. "I am proud of the fact that we put the best bid on the table the first time and this time," he said.

Shearson Lehman Hutton, the Wall Street firm that was one of Mr. Johnson's key financial partners, said in a statement: "From what we know our bid was the best. We are mystified about the process and the standards that the board used to reach its decision. We are going to continue to keep our options open. We believe the RJR shareholders will have a lot of questions as well."

One person close to the management group, which included Salomon Brothers, another Wall Street firm, said the group was unlikely to initiate legal action itself, but was hoping some shareholders might sue to force the board to reconsider.

Both bids involved borrowing about 90 percent of the acquisition price, using the company's assets as collateral, a transaction known as a leveraged buyout.

The final skirmishes began with a bidding deadline of 5 P.M. on Tuesday. At that time Kohlberg, Kravis was ahead with a bid of $106 a share, a total of $24 billion.

The management group had offered $101 a share. A third bidder, a group led by the First Boston Corporation, dropped out because the bank financing of its bid was uncertain.

Kohlberg, Kravis worked through the night with the advisers to RJR Nabisco's board of directors to fashion a final agreement, assuming it had won as of the deadline. To reverse the pressure, Kohlberg, Kravis then told the special committee that its bid was only good until 1 P.M. yesterday, and then it would be dropped.

Around midnight Tuesday night, the management group learned that Kohlberg, Kravis was with the special committee's legal advisers working out a deal. Outraged that they were being left out, the lawyers for the management group fired off two letters to the special committee demanding to know what Kohlberg, Kravis had offered and insisting that they be given a chance to better their bid.

Yesterday morning the management group stepped up with a new bid of $108 a share, or $24.5 billion, and demanded that it be considered, no matter what the original rules of the competition had been. To Kohlberg, Kravis' chagrin, a special committee of directors running the auction allowed the group to submit the new offer, setting up the real showdown.

At around midday, both bidding groups and their key advisers were put into conference rooms and told they had just a few minutes to formulate a final proposal.

The management group went to $112 a share, or $25.42 billion. Kohlberg, Kravis went to $108.

The two sides were left to sit while the special committee and its advisers mulled the new offers. They went back to Kohlberg, Kravis at about 7:30 in the evening and asked if they wanted to raise their offer. Kohlberg

Kohlberg, Kravis demanded several conditions, including one that Mr. Johnson, a member of the board, not be allowed to learn of any new bid by joining a board meeting. The special committee agreed after a half hour, and Kohlberg, Kravis responded by increasing the offer to $109.

Kohlberg, Kravis then turned up the pressure. It handed the committee's advisers a signed merger agreement and said they had a half-hour to add their signatures or the deal was off, people with knowledge of the situation said.

The advisers came back in 40 minutes with the documents signed by Charles Hugel, RJR Nabisco's chairman and head of the special committee. The battle was over.

[Dec. 1, 1988]

END OF A DISASTER: DISMEMBERING RJR NABISCO

By FLOYD NORRIS

It's over. A decade after RJR Nabisco was bought in the largest leveraged buyout in history, the company is being sliced into three pieces. It is a sad saga for almost all involved.

"The story is what happens when you really overpay for a company, and the debt levels are just too high," said Stephen F. Goldstone, who will be the last person to hold the job of chairman and chief executive of RJR Nabisco.

When all is finished, the only real winners will be those who cashed out in 1989—primarily the shareholders who sold and the investment bankers who arranged the buyout.

The losers include R.J. Reynolds and Nabisco, which almost certainly would have been more vigorous competitors had they not been saddled with more than $25 billion in debt from the buyout. Kohlberg, Kravis, Roberts, the leveraged-buyout firm that engineered the deal, lost more in reputation than it made in money.

Among the sufferers are investors who bought RJR Nabisco stock in 1991, when the company went public again, two years after Kohlberg, Kravis took it private. A $100 investment then is

now worth $51. Over the same period, the Dow Jones industrial average more than tripled.

Kohlberg, Kravis gave up in 1994, trading its RJR Nabisco stock for ownership of Borden Inc., the troubled food company. So far that looks like a doubtful investment at best.

What went wrong at RJR Nabisco? The tobacco business proved not to be as good a cash cow as the buyers thought it would be. The great advantage of selling to addicted customers was reduced when price wars broke out among cigarette companies. Tobacco litigation proved to be a significant threat.

Those problems hurt RJR Nabisco more than its competitors. Philip Morris, the largest tobacco company and the owner of Kraft Foods, has seen its share price about double since 1991, while RJR Nabisco's price has been cut in half. One difference was that Philip Morris had enough financial flexibility to invest in promoting its products, including Marlboro cigarettes and Maxwell House Coffee, while debt-ridden RJR Nabisco was forced to cut back on promotional spending for Winstons and Oreos. Over time, it hurt.

Now RJR Nabisco will sell its international tobacco business for $8 billion to Japan Tobacco. That money, after taxes, will go to pay debt. Then the domestic tobacco business will be spun off into a separate company, with just $1 billion of debt. Shareholders of the current RJR Nabisco will get the shares in that operation.

The remainder will be Nabisco, which will have two kinds of common stock. One type, the Nabisco Holdings shares that already trade, will have a stake in the profits from such products as Chips Ahoy and Ritz Crackers. The other will have a stake in the same profits. But as the former parent of the tobacco company, it will also be burdened with the possibility of residual liability if lawsuits manage to bankrupt the tobacco company. The discount between those two prices will show just how scared investors are of tobacco litigation.

When all that is done, things will be almost back to where they were in 1985, before R.J. Reynolds acquired Nabisco. Nabisco will again be an independent company, albeit a weaker one than its predecessor. R.J. Reynolds will also be independent, with a smaller market share in this country and an international business that had to be sold to pay debt taken on in one of the most misguided deals in Wall Street history.

In a more just world, the investment banks that made hundreds of millions from the RJR Nabisco buyout might now join in the suffering. Instead, they will collect more fees for their services in dismembering the hobbled company.

[EDITORIAL OBSERVER, March 10, 1999]

Nabisco: from snacks to merger feast.

1980–1989

Sony Aims to Marry Best of Two Nations

By DAVID E. SANGER

Special to The New York Times

By the end of the 1980's, Japan appeared to be the most successful economy in the world. It ran huge trade surpluses, bringing in billions of dollars that were being used, it seemed, to buy up most of America. The Pebble Beach golf course, Rockefeller Center and Columbia Pictures all were bought by Japanese companies. It was almost universally agreed that Japan's corporate might could only grow.

Sony bought Columbia at the end of 1989, which–although no one knew it at the time–marked the peak of Japanese economic success. The Japanese stock market bubble burst early in 1990, and the economy soon followed. It turned out that the Japanese had overpaid for many of their American treasures, Columbia included. The investment proved a poor one for Sony, but at least Sony still owns it. Crushed by debt, the buyers of both Pebble Beach and Rockefeller Center ended up surrendering their assets.

TOKYO, Sept. 27—By the time Norio Ohga left Sony headquarters here tonight, certain that his quest for one of Hollywood's hottest properties was finally successful, he was well on his way to transforming the company that more than any other has symbolized the breakthroughs of Japanese business in the decades since World War II.

As expected, the board of Columbia Pictures Entertainment Inc. today accepted the Sony Corporation's $27-a-share, $3.4 billion cash offer. Sony also said it had signed an agreement to buy the Coca-Cola Company's 49 percent stake in Columbia, subject to approval by Coke's board.

Mr. Ohga's mentor, Akio Morita, built Sony from a transistor-radio maker into a symbol of Japanese innovation, a rebel that always seemed to appeal to American buyers far more than giant Matsushita or Hitachi; Sony repeatedly sold Americans gadgetry they had not known they needed. But Mr. Ohga, now president and chief executive, is leading a post-Morita generation at Sony that concluded four years ago that the company's well-honed act needed more than new gadgetry.

The future course, they became convinced, was to marry Japan's seemingly unassailable lead in consumer electronics with America's in "entertainment software," the industry term for movies and programming, using "Rambo" and "Ghostbusters" to propel demand for innovations like pocket-sized videocassette players and high-definition television.

Now, with the purchase of Columbia Pictures at hand—bringing Sony movie and television studios, theaters and, most important, a giant film library—Mr. Ohga spent this evening talking about "the synergy of audio and video hardware and software."

He spoke of Japan's insatiable appetite for American programming, and of bringing together two American institutions, Columbia Pictures and CBS Records, which Sony bought last year for $2 billion. But the key to success, said Mr. Ohga, who is 59 years old, will be to make Japan's presence virtually invisible to Americans, who fear they are losing control of a vital cultural asset.

"If we act" like the American occupying army that controlled postwar Japan, "we will be bashed," he said, "but if we manage to keep it totally as an American company, everything will work out fine."

Mr. Ohga entered Sony as a baritone, not a businessman. He was trained at a Tokyo university specializing in music and fine arts and moved to Germany to study opera singing, his true love. When he returned to Japan, he met Mr. Morita and was drawn into Sony as a consultant on the quality of its tape recorders, which had left him unimpressed. He soon joined the company full time, focusing on the output of Sony's equipment rather than on engineering.

Not everyone is convinced Mr. Ohga can make the acquisition work. Some question whether Sony is inviting political repercussions. "This is part of the culture of the United States," said Koji Iwata, the general manager of planning and strategy for the software group at the Victor Company of Japan, or JVC. "If a Japanese company buys it, the perception will be that foreign capital is taking over American culture." JVC decided last month to create a new movie production company with Lawrence Gordon, a former president of 20th Century-Fox, rather than to buy an existing company.

ROBERT C. WALKER/THE NEW YORK TIMES

Akio Morita, chairman of Sony, demonstrating a videocassette recorder.

Others note that Japanese companies made their mark by exercising a strict discipline in manufacturing and miniaturization, design and efficiency—the antithesis of Hollywood's style. But the record industry, too, is part of American show business, and Sony boasts that CBS Records is already proving highly profitable, sooner than anyone expected.

The outlines of the new Sony began to come together five years ago when a team of Sony's senior managers began reassessing some of the fundamental principles that Mr. Morita used to build the company.

The first was that Sony should no longer hold its hardware innovations close to the chest. Mr. Ohga decided the company could make money by selling its technology—from chips to miniature video recording heads—even to its competitors. Now Sony has grown so vertically integrated that it recently purchased a small American maker of semiconductor production equipment, to bolster its components business.

The second was the discovery that the key innovations in consumer electronics are increasingly driven by the computer industry. Sony entered that field too, and it has enjoyed modest success with its News work station, a competitor with American companies like Sun Microsystems and I.B.M. And it started a major effort in industrial electronics, making not only small videocameras for home use, but also some of the early production equipment for high-definition television, which creates images as sharp as movies and makes enhanced special effects possible.

Innovations in consumer electronics continue, from Sony's filmless Mavica camera—which stores images electronically on a small floppy disk—to a new, lightweight videocamera that the company advertises as smaller than a Japanese passport. The white-haired Mr. Morita, 68, still revels in such breakthroughs, but he has turned everything but his chairman's title over to Mr. Ohga, and spends most of his days talking about trade and competitiveness.

But profits are increasingly scarce in consumer electronics, and Sony has learned that the field is full of pitfalls.

South Korea's enormous success at the lower end of the market—especially in basic VCR's—convinced Sony's leadership that the company must find niches where its innovative touches could not easily be imitated. For example, the Video Walkman, the year-old portable VCR with a miniature television screen, which has become a favorite of train commuters here, is crammed with specialty components that Korea would be hard pressed to replicate, at least for a while.

"The Walkman was a brilliant product," one Sony executive said recently of the original audio player. "It changed the way people listen to music. But these days, the lead time on a technology like that is far too short. We can't depend on that kind of advance any longer."

For tonight at least, Mr. Ohga said he was thinking less about how to make the most of the Columbia Pictures purchase than about how to become a movie mogul. "The most important thing is to raise the image of Columbia," he said. "For a start, it would be nice to get a few big hits."   [Sept. 28, 1989]

1980–1989

CHAPTER TEN

1990–1999

The Internet became the most important technological tool of the Information Age, for business, the economy and much more.

The American Decade

THE 1990'S BROUGHT a great resurgence of American economic power and pride. As the decade neared an end, the United States economy seemed to be functioning better than at any time in history and to be the clear leader in the world. The self-doubt of two decades before had been replaced by a growing self-confidence, and warnings of a stock market "bubble" were dismissed as the profits rolled in.

The crumbling of the Soviet Union had left the United States with clear military superiority, which it used in 1991 to force Iraq out of Kuwait. Iraq's 1990 invasion of Kuwait, however, had sent oil prices soaring and helped bring on a brief recession in this country.

The recovery was a gradual one, with unemployment falling only slowly. That produced great concern—and helped Bill Clinton win the Presidency over incumbent George Bush in 1992. The slow gains in employment reflected corporate restructurings, which produced substantial layoffs of executives and other office workers. In the past, layoffs had been cyclical, not structural, and were largely confined to blue-collar workers.

But while downsizing was painful for many, it also made the economy more efficient by moving workers into jobs where they were needed. And it reflected the fact that advances in computer technology were finally bringing long-anticipated improvements in productivity.

Those advances brought computers into millions of homes and produced an Internet that was revolutionizing the economy by making it far easier to distribute information.

Internationally, it was a lost decade for Japan, which was unable to deal with the bursting of its 1980's bubble economy in real estate and stock prices. American companies that had feared losing market after market to the Japanese, particularly in technology, instead recovered markets. Other Asian countries that had grown very rapidly suddenly saw their currencies collapse, exposing significant economic problems. But the world avoided a recession, thanks largely to continued strong purchases by American consumers.

By the end of the decade, there were pressures in both Japan and Europe to imitate the flexible labor markets of the United States, where unemployment was falling. It appeared that employers who knew they could fire workers if they had to—either because of a business setback or because an employee was not doing a good job—were more willing to take the chance of hiring workers in the first place.

In America, the Federal Reserve Board chairman, Alan Greenspan, became something of a national hero as interest rates and inflation declined while the economy kept growing. Gold prices dropped as confidence in paper money increased.

The United States stock market reflected and encouraged American self-assurance. Stock prices zoomed, and so did the public's investment and faith in the market. Economic turbulence abroad encouraged foreign investment in the United States, and that helped offset the massive trade deficit the United States was running as the century ended. Stock valuations reached levels never seen before in America, but they were justified, investors believed, by the economic growth the nation was enjoying—growth that was being produced by technology as the Internet age began.

1990	"Junk bond" pioneer Michael Milken is fined $600 million and sentenced to prison.
1991	U.S. Operation Desert Storm drives Iraq's armed forces out of Kuwait.
	The Soviet Union disbands.
1992	Bill Clinton is elected President.
	Johnny Carson retires after 29 years as host of "The Tonight Show" on NBC.
1993	A car bomb kills 7 at the World Trade Center in New York.
1994	Nelson Mandela becomes the first black President of South Africa.
	The Chunnel connects England and France.
1995	A car bomb kills 169 at a Federal building in Oklahoma City.
	Israeli Prime Minister Yitzhak Rabin is assassinated.
1996	TWA Flight 800 explodes and crashes into the Atlantic; all 230 aboard die.
	President Clinton wins re-election.
1997	A scientist from Edinburgh announces the cloning of a sheep.
	China resumes control of Hong Kong.
1998	Citicorp and Travelers Group agree to combine in the biggest merger ever.
	Pope John Paul II visits Cuba.
1999	The euro is introduced as the currency of 11 European nations.
	The Senate acquits President Clinton of impeachment charges.

Milken Defends 'Junk Bonds' As He Enters His Guilty Plea

For a time in the 1980's, Michael Milken was the most powerful—and, in some circles, the most feared—man on Wall Street. He was head of the high-yield—or "junk"—bond desk at Drexel Burnham Lambert, and as such he could raise billions for clients he chose to underwrite.

That ready access to capital meant that virtually any Drexel client could mount a credible raid on a company. Target companies began buying back stock from such raiders—a practice known as "greenmail." Some companies not only got promises from a raider that he would stay away, but demanded and got promises that Drexel would finance no more raids.

Milken's downfall began when Dennis Levine, a Drexel investment banker who had previously worked for Smith Barney and Lehman Brothers, was caught violating the insider trading laws. He had provided inside information to Ivan Boesky, the best-known speculator in takeover stocks, and was willing to incriminate him. Boesky, meanwhile, knew of crimes committed by Milken and talked after he was caught.

Milken and his supporters believed that major corporations were out to get him—and they were right. But Milken also had committed crimes, and in due course first Drexel pleaded guilty to felonies and then, early in 1990, Milken did the same. He served 22 months in prison and paid 600 million in fines. After he was released on parole, he paid another 47 million in penalties to settle charges that he had violated the terms of his parole. Still, he remained a very rich man with "a certain air of unrepentance," as The Times reported in 1993. Drexel, without Milken, went broke.

By KURT EICHENWALD

Apologizing for his crimes but defending the "junk bond" market he created, Michael R. Milken pleaded guilty yesterday to six felony charges of securities fraud and conspiracy. The 43-year-old financier agreed to pay $600 million in fines and penalties.

Mr. Milken had long maintained his innocence and had not let the pressure of the Government investigation show in public. But yesterday, during his 35-minute appearance in a packed Manhattan courtroom, Mr. Milken broke down and cried, saying he had "hurt those who are closest to me."

In his statement to the Federal District Court, Mr. Milken admitted that he had committed several illegal acts in cooperation with others intended to enrich his firm, Drexel Burnham Lambert Inc., and to help the firm complete trades for itself and its clients.

"I transgressed certain of the laws and regulations that govern our industry," Mr. Milken said. "I was wrong in doing so and knew that at the time and I am pleading guilty to these offenses."

In essence, Mr. Milken admitted to cheating some Drexel customers, aiding others in the violation of securities and tax laws, and manipulating the securities market to benefit a client.

The plea by Mr. Milken brings to a close the largest criminal prosecution in Wall Street history. He agreed to the plea and the largest monetary penalty ever last week.

Mr. Milken, the former head of the junk bond division at the now-defunct Drexel, had been at the center of the giant Wall Street inquiry that bloomed in 1986. In November that year, Ivan F. Boesky, the former stock speculator, agreed to settle insider trading charges, pay a fine of $100 million and provide evidence about other wrongdoing on Wall Street. The junk bond market Mr. Milken pioneered financed many of the corporate takeovers of the 1980's.

Mr. Milken will be sentenced on Oct. 1 and faces a maximum prison term of 28 years. Securities lawyers say they expect his prison term will not exceed five years.

Mr. Milken appeared in a courtroom that was overflowing. The walls were lined with officials from the Securities and Exchange Commission, the United States Attorney's office, lawyers and reporters. Mr. Milken's wife, Lori, sat in the front row of the courtroom next to his brother, Lowell Milken, who had been indicted in the case, but the charges against him were dropped as part of the settlement.

Throughout most of the proceeding, Mr. Milken remained stoic, staring intently at the judge with his hands folded at his waist, while answering a litany of questions to assure the judge that his plea was being voluntarily given and that he was aware of the maximum possible sentence.

Only once did he divert from quickly answering the questions with a curt "Yes, Judge," or "No, Judge." When asked if he was making his plea under any force or threats, he hesitated for a few seconds and then replied, "No."

Reading from his statement, Mr. Milken said, "This long period has been extremely painful and difficult for my family and friends as well as myself. I realize that by my acts I have hurt those who are closest to me." Mr. Milken hesitated as tears began to well in his eyes, and he placed his right index finger under his nose.

"I am truly sorry," he continued, his face reddening. He then uttered while sobbing, "I thank the Court for permitting me to add this apology and for its fairness in handling this complex case."

Mr. Milken's lawyer, Arthur Liman, then put his arm around his client and raised his hand slowly to the judge, indicating that his client needed a moment to recover. Judge Kimba M. Wood then thanked Mr. Milken for his statement, and he sat down.

Seconds passed until Mr. Milken regained his composure, drinking from a plastic cup of water. He then stood again, and Judge Wood said, "Mr. Milken, how do you plead?"

With his voice cracking with emotion, the financier replied, "Guilty, Your Honor."

The charges to which Mr. Milken pleaded guilty involved a series of illegal transactions with Mr. Boesky, as well as other illicit deals with David Solomon, a former junk bond trader and founder of Solomon Asset Management. The charges portray a man who ignored some legal restrictions in an effort to benefit his firm and clients of his division.

Mr. Milken engaged in a conspiracy that allowed Mr. Boesky to violate the rules on capital that governed his stock trading firm, as well as to file inaccurate financial statements to Government regulators. He also conspired with Mr. Boesky to inflate the price of a stock to benefit one of Drexel's clients.

In addition, Mr. Milken entered into an illegal agreement with Mr. Solomon under which the cost of some trades was misstated to repay Drexel for the cost of paying commissions on those trades. Also, he conducted a complex series of trades that allowed Mr. Solomon to illegally claim losses to reduce his 1985 Federal income tax return.

None of the crimes to which Mr. Milken pleaded guilty involved illegal activities in the junk bond market, but rather in other securities markets. In his court statement, which was approved by the Government, Mr. Milken said the crimes were "not a reflection on the underlying soundness and integrity of the capital markets in which we specialized." He added: "Our business was in no way dependent on these practices."

After the hearing, Mr. Liman read a statement on the steps of the courthouse, saying the charges described were "instances in which Michael went too far in helping clients" and an arrangement "to recoup expenses incurred by Drexel."

He said, "It is Michael's hope that in the long run, history will see his violations in context and judge him not just on the basis of his lapses, but on the basis of the contributions that he made to the economy."

One trader who was caught up in the scandal that enveloped Wall Street after Mr. Boesky began to turn over information to the Government said he was not surprised by Mr. Milken's fate.

"It's anti-climactic," said Boyd L. Jefferies, a former stock trader who is on probation for engaging in illegal activities with Mr. Boesky. "I don't think anybody in this whole thing has gotten anything but what they deserved."

Mr. Jefferies added: "When I was doing these favors for clients, I knew I was breaking the law. We all knew we were breaking the law."

While the charges Mr. Milken pleaded guilty to were serious, some securities lawyers expressed surprise yesterday at how mild they turned out to be. Mr. Milken did not plead guilty to insider trading or racketeering, the two most serious crimes in the original indictment in March.

Mr. Milken agreed yesterday to pay $600 million in

1990–1999

Michael Milken, before a House committee in 1988.

ASSOCIATED PRESS

fines and penalties to settle both the criminal case against him and the civil case brought in 1988 by the Securities and Exchange Commission. He will pay $200 million in fines and, as part of the S.E.C. settlement, will set aside $400 million to satisfy civil claims that have been filed against him.

Despite the fines and penalties, Mr. Milken will remain a rich man. He was paid more than $1.1 billion by Drexel from 1983 to 1987, and earned income from his large number of investments as well.

In his statement, Mr. Milken also described his personal relationship with Mr. Boesky. Mr. Milken said his dealings with Mr. Boesky constituted less than 1 percent of the business of Drexel's junk bond unit.

"He traded in stocks, and I traded in bonds or their equivalent," Mr. Milken said. "But because he was a major factor in the securities markets, he had the potential to become a more significant account."

Mr. Milken said he and Mr. Boesky "were not social friends, and had little in common." He added: "His philosophy of business was different from mine. The relationship started as an arm's length and correct one."

But over time, Mr. Milken said, the two men began to enter into transactions that violated the law.

After the hearing was over, Mr. Milken left the courtroom through the judge's chambers. Unlike last year when he pleaded not guilty to the original indictment, there was no crowd of supporters waiting for him outside the courthouse. A handful of people did cheer for him, but others also booed as he left.   [April 25, 1990]

AN UNFETTERED MILKEN HAS LESSONS TO TEACH

By FRANCIS X. CLINES
Special to The New York Times

LOS ANGELES, Oct. 14—Michael Milken is back from prison and forever barred from the Wall Street world of high-risk financing where he fell from reigning master to disgraced convict. But the tattered mogul hardly seems east of Eden these days as he buoyantly teaches his weekly class of young M.B.A. candidates much, if not all, that he has learned.

"Can you suggest when you'd use the zero-coupon bond?" he asks, endlessly animated as he moves about the classroom of 57 students who seek to enter that chastened world now forbidden to him. They sit raptly, knowing they are being taught by a man of fabulous wealth and considerable resiliency, a man who chuckles at academic business notions and stands as the epitome of real-world experience, 22 months of prison time for securities fraud included.

Across the corridor from his class here at the University of California at Los Angeles, an overflow crowd of worshipful undergraduates, a few commuting for the night from distant campuses, audit the master's lessons. They watch the television screen as if it were a futuristic stock ticker.

"We're going to look at securitized business loans," Mr. Milken announces with a boyish smile that acknowledges his own notoriety. "I think that sounds better than 'junk bonds,'" he says of the risky but lucrative financial tool that he made his virtuoso instrument and that finally broke him as the most celebrated miscreant of what became known as the greed decade, the 1980's.

All of this is not quite behind him as the 47-year-old Mr. Milken, a bald, lean, avid-eyed figure who resembles the actor John Malkovich, scrambles back into public life with a certain air of unrepentance.

Ask him about the financing techniques that eventually scandalized Wall Street and saw him confess to six counts of securities fraud, and Mr. Milken discusses Galileo and other penalized visionaries proved right by history. Ask him about the decade of greed, and he talks of misperception becoming reality, citing data to argue that donations adjusted for inflation show Americans in general as charitable, not greedy, in the 1980's.

"If there's no risk, there's no future," he says repeatedly, having to marshal his comeback on the cusp of the financial world since he left prison in January.

"He is a great man—a martyr, not a crook," insists one student, Scott Ragsdale, ardently absorbing all the Milken he can. "It's not fair, punishing him simply because society cannot understand how one man could make $500 million in a single year."

Free and full of ideas, Michael Milken would have us believe his prison time was only another pragmatic deal in a life of dealing. He can be amused in recalling parts of it. Among the jailhouse sustenance offered by outside fans were 22 copies of "Atlas Shrugged," the cult novel by Ayn Rand about willful, Promethean characters.

"I had not read it since the 60's," says Mr. Milken, chatting after teaching his fledgling successors all about Wall Street. "In retrospect, I'd have been better off had I re-read it in the early 80's," he adds, smiling and admitting he could have used a caution against hubris in that especially rich time right before his downfall.   [Oct. 16, 1993]

Tobacco Chiefs Say Cigarettes Aren't Addictive

By PHILIP J. HILTS

Special to The New York Times

WASHINGTON, April 14 - The top executives of the seven largest American tobacco companies testified in Congress today that they did not believe that cigarettes were addictive, but that they would rather their own children did not smoke.

The executives, sitting side by side at a conference table in what seemed to many a counterpoint to the growing antismoking sentiment in Congress, faced more than six hours of sharp questioning by members of the House Energy and Commerce Subcommittee on Health and the Environment.

Under persistent questioning, each of the executives agreed to give Congress extensive, previously unpublicized research on humans and animals that their companies had done concerning nicotine and addiction.

Democratic Congressmen on the panel, inspired by recent news reports, pressed the executives on whether their companies manipulated the content of nicotine to keep smokers addicted to cigarettes. The executives acknowledged that nicotine levels could be and were controlled by altering the blends of tobacco, but they said this was done to enhance flavor, not to insure addiction.

The executives also made a number of other notable admissions, including these:

¶ Cigarettes may cause lung cancer, heart disease and other health problems, but the evidence is not conclusive.

¶ Despite earlier denials, a Philip Morris study that suggested that animals could become addicted to nicotine was suppressed in 1983 and 1985.

The hearing was televised live by the Cable News Network and C-Span cable channels, as an overflow crowd stood or sat in the hallways of the Rayburn House Office Building for what several members of Congress said marked a high tide of antismoking sentiment.

The executives seemed to agree, saying that they felt besieged and that the sweep of antitobacco fervor in recent months had led them to fear that the Government would try to ban cigarettes.

What the "antitobacco industry wants is prohibition," said James W. Johnston, chairman and chief executive of R. J. Reynolds. "We hear about the addiction and the threat. If cigarettes are too dangerous to be sold, then ban them. Some smokers will obey the law, but many will not. People will be selling cigarettes out of the trunks of cars, cigarettes made by who knows who, made of who knows what."

Among the most significant statements by the executives were those that confirmed that tobacco companies could control the amount of nicotine in cigarettes by varying the types of tobacco and the parts of the tobacco plant that were used in a particular blend. They said a number of their cigarettes, primarily low-tar brands, did use high-nicotine blends, which gave more nicotine to the smoker than the cigarettes might have otherwise given. They use these blends for flavor, they explained.

On the Reynolds company's widely criticized use of the cartoon figure Joe Camel to promote its Camel brand, Mr. Johnston of Reynolds apologized for an ad that recommended that young men seeking dates at the beach drag women from the water, pretending to save them from drowning.

"That ad ran once," he said. "It never should have run. I apologize. It was offensive. It was stupid. We do make mistakes."

While most of the exchanges focused on the health risks of cigarettes, the executives were also asked about other risks posed by their products, like fire. The president and chief executive of Philip Morris, William I. Campbell, was asked about the feasibility of making cigarettes whose paper tubes would pose less danger of starting

The tobacco industry has long been one of the nation's most profitable, largely because addicted customers are not price-sensitive ones. But in the last half of the century its products became increasingly unpopular with a growing part of the population—and many of those people were determined to punish the industry.

In the 1950's, it was considered polite to offer a cigarette to a guest after dinner, even if the host did not smoke. By the 1990's, it was illegal to smoke cigarettes in restaurants in many communities, and it was a common sight in even the worst weather to see office workers huddled outside buildings, smoking cigarettes.

The industry's procession from popular to pariah began with the 1964 Surgeon General's report concluding there was clear evidence that smoking caused lung cancer. Within a few years, warning labels were required on cigarette packs and then, in 1971, television advertising was banned.

Until the 1990's, however, efforts to hold cigarette companies legally responsible for health problems caused by smoking were largely ineffective. But eventually the industry agreed to pay billions to states that were suing to recover money that Medicaid spent on treating smoking-related diseases. That settlement led to a large increase in cigarette prices and to an end to billboard advertising in 1999.

By 1994, the public had long since accepted that cigarettes were harmful, but many agreed with the companies that smokers had made the decision to ignore the warning labels on cigarette packages and should bear responsibility for their actions. But anger mounted after the chief executives of the major tobacco companies told a Congressional hearing that cigarettes were not addictive. That played into the hands of industry opponents who said the companies had misled smokers regarding the danger. The pressure on the industry intensified and made the companies more willing to seek a settlement.

One indication of the industry's reduced willingness to fight came in 1997 when R. J. Reynolds, barraged with charges that its Joe Camel character was enticing children to smoke, surrendered and retired the cartoon character.

1990–1999

fires. Cigarette companies have said this type of cigarette would be difficult to draw smoke through and would taste bad. Representative Albert R. Wyden, Democrat of Oregon, noted that the Virginia Slims brand was considered less of a fire hazard than others, and he asked Mr. Campbell, whose company makes the brand, if a Virginia Slim was difficult to smoke.

"As a matter of fact, it is too hard to smoke, and doesn't taste very good," snapped Mr. Campbell. He said the company had been unable to make a commercially acceptable and fire-safe cigarette.

Pressed by the subcommittee's chairman, Henry A. Waxman, Democrat of California, and by Representatives Wyden and Mike Synar, Democrat of Oklahoma, the companies agreed to supply many private company papers, including all the research on humans and animals concerning nicotine and addiction, all the market research and internal memoranda on Reynolds' Joe Camel advertising campaign and all the research done by the Philip Morris researcher whose scientific paper on addiction was blocked from publication by company executives.

At one point during the hearing, Mr. Wyden presented a stack of data from medical groups and a 1989 Surgeon General's report on the perils of smoking, asking each executive in turn if he believed that cigarettes were addictive. Each answered no.

When Mr. Johnston said that all products, from cola to Twinkies, had risks associated with them, Mr. Waxman replied, "Yes, but the difference between cigarettes and Twinkies is death."

"How many smokers die each year from cancer?" Mr. Waxman asked Mr. Johnston.

"I do not know how many," he replied, adding that estimates of death are "generated by computers and are only statistical."

Mr. Waxman asked, "Does smoking cause heart disease?"

"It may," Mr. Johnston said.

"Does it cause lung cancer?"

"It may."

"Emphysema?

"It may."

The list continued through several other ailments. Mr. Waxman asked Andrew H. Tisch, the chairman and chief executive of the Lorillard Tobacco Company, whether he knew that cigarettes caused cancer. "I do not believe that," Mr. Tisch answered.

"Do you understand how isolated you are from the scientific community in your belief?" Mr. Waxman asked.

"I do, sir," Mr. Tisch said.

Although each of the six executives who have children said he would prefer that his own children not smoke, several added that they would give no advice to their children but let them decide on their own.

In his testimony, Mr. Campbell of Philip Morris admitted twice stopping publication of a study, in 1983 and 1985, that showed that laboratory animals could be conditioned to press levers repeatedly to get nicotine, the sort of study that is key to proving that a drug is addictive.

[April 15, 1994]

JOE CAMEL, A GIANT IN TOBACCO MARKETING, IS DEAD AT 23

By STUART ELLIOTT

Joe Camel, the cartoon character that became the focus of perhaps the most intense attacks ever leveled against an American advertising campaign, is being sent packing by the R. J. Reynolds Tobacco Company, which will replace it with stylized versions of Camel cigarettes' original camel trademark.

The unexpected decision, announced yesterday, ends a nine-year run in this country for Joe Camel. The embattled ad figure and his brethren, bearing names like Buster, Max and Floyd, will disappear from billboards, print advertisements, display signs and even store-door stickers. Joe Camel's goofy grin, oversized nose and exaggerated depictions of masculine behavior had helped Reynolds stem a decades-long sales slide for Camel by imbuing the brand with a hipper image.

But the gains in sales and market share for Camel, the nation's No. 7 cigarette brand, came only at a high cost as anti-smoking activists convinced President Clinton, the American Medical Association, several Surgeons General, the Federal Trade Commission and other authorities that Joe Camel was emblematic of what they maintained were the insidious, underhanded marketing gimmicks by which cigarettes are sold in America. Particularly, the activists hit home with contentions that slick, colorful presentations of a grinning cartoon animal were intended to appeal specifically to children to take up smoking.

"Joe Camel represented an icon that refueled the moral outrage of the antismoking movement," said Eric Solberg, executive director of Doctors Ought to Care, an antitobacco group in Houston. Reynolds has always denied that Joe Camel—introduced to Americans in 1988 after more than a decade of selling cigarettes to Europeans— was anything but a standard marketing tactic meant to persuade adult smokers to switch to Camel from bigger brands like Marlboro.

The White House cheered the demise of Joe Camel, which now appears only in the United States. "We must put tobacco ads like Joe Camel out of our children's reach forever," President Clinton said in a statement.

Bruce Reed, the President's chief domestic policy adviser, was more succinct. "Joe Camel is dead," he said. "He had it coming."

A brief statement from Reynolds that disclosed Joe Camel would be extinguished did not mention a ban on cartoons as part of a landmark $368.5 billion settlement reached on June 20 by Reynolds and other tobacco marketers.

Rather, the abrupt change is being made, said Fran Creighton, vice president of marketing for Camel at Reynolds, a unit of the RJR Nabisco Holdings Corporation in Winston-Salem, N.C., because "like other consumer product marketers,

Joe Camel was banished in 1997.

we embrace the theory that variety is the spice of life."

While the Reynolds release did not address the castigation of Joe Camel, Richard L. Williams, a company spokesman, said: "The controversy that swirled around Joe Camel was a reason we began looking for alternatives. The issue our critics have raised over and over again was Joe Camel. With this new campaign, that's off the table."

Also unmentioned by Reynolds was the most recent effort to eliminate Joe Camel by the Federal Trade Commission, which voted 3 to 2 on May 28 to declare that the character attracted underage smokers. Attempts by the commission to have Joe Camel deemed an unfair advertising practice were rejected in 1994.

The commission will continue pursuing its case against Reynolds, even though the company has "finally terminated an advertising campaign that we believe has caused substantial injury to children and adolescents," said Jodie Bernstein, director of the F.T.C.'s bureau of consumer protection in Washington.

The new Camel campaign, carrying the theme "What you're looking for," supplants Joe Camel with representations of Old Joe, the camel drawing that inspired Joe Camel, which has appeared on packs of Camel cigarettes since the brand's introduction as the first nationally advertised cigarette in 1913. As smokers light up, puff away or enjoy a cigarette with a drink in the new ads, versions of Old Joe are seen inside a flame, in smoke plumes and as a water mark left by a glass.

The replacement campaign will begin on billboards this week and in August issues of national magazines. They had been tested since March in some smaller publications.

"Joe Camel accomplished what Reynolds wanted, which was to give the Camel brand an identity that went from being 'your father's Oldsmobile' to something much more contemporary," said Emanuel Goldman, an analyst who follows the tobacco industry for Paine Webber in San Francisco.

The furor against Joe Camel began building after the Journal of the American Medical Association published in December 1991 studies indicating that the character was widely recognized by and popular among children. This broadside in March 1992 from Antonia Novello, then the United States Surgeon General, was typical: "In years past, R. J. Reynolds would have us 'walk a mile for a Camel.' Today, it's time we invite old Joe Camel himself to take a hike."

Joe Camel was a new twist on the tobacco industry's decades-old crusade to portray smoking as an intrinsic part of a fashionable, pleasure-filled life style. The character, based loosely on Old Joe, was created in 1974 by a British artist, Nicholas Price.   [July 11, 1997]

On the Battlefields of Business, Millions of Casualties

When the American economy was largely a manufacturing one, layoffs were a mostly cyclical phenomenon, confined to industries that saw demand fall off with the economy.

But in the 1990's layoffs ranged much farther up the corporate ladder. As companies restructured, whole layers of middle management were sometimes eliminated. That led to great uncertainty for a class that had never felt vulnerable before, and it slowed the recovery from the 1990-91 recession.

But the long-term effects of downsizing seem to have been largely positive. Notwithstanding the pessimism at the time, the economy created more than enough jobs to offset those lost through downsizing. While some of those laid off no doubt suffered a permanent reduction in income, the overall effect was to make the economy more productive.

In a major series in 1996, The Times explored the downsizing phenomenon, which it summarized at the start of the opening article.

By LOUIS UCHITELLE and N. R. KLEINFIELD

Drive along the asphalt river of Interstate 95 across the Rhode Island border and into the pristine confines of Connecticut. Stop at that first tourist information center with its sheaves of brochures promising lazy delights. What could anyone possibly guess of Steven A. Holthausen, the portly man behind the counter who dispenses the answers?

Certainly not that for two decades he was a $1,000-a-week loan officer. Not that he survived three bank mergers only to be told, upon returning from a family vacation, that he no longer had a job. Not that his wife kicked him out and his children shunned him. Not that he slid to the bottom step of the economic ladder, pumping gas at a station owned by a former bank customer, being a guinea pig in a drug test and driving a car for a salesman who had lost his license for drunkenness. Not that, at 51, he makes do on $1,000 a month as a tourist guide, a quarter of his earlier salary. And not that he is worried that his modest job is itself fragile, and that he may have to work next as a clerk in a brother's liquor store.

That, however, is his condensed story, and its true grimness lies in the simple fact that it is no longer at all extraordinary in America. "I did not realize on that day I was fired how big a price I would have to pay," Mr. Holthausen said, in a near whisper.

More than 43 million jobs have been erased in the United States since 1979, according to a New York Times analysis of Labor Department numbers. Many of the losses come from the normal churning as stores fail and factories move. And far more jobs have been created than lost over that period. But increasingly the jobs that are disappearing are those of higher-paid, white-collar workers, many at large corporations, women as well as men, many at the peak of their careers. Like a clicking odometer on a speeding car, the number twirls higher nearly each day.

Peek into the living rooms of America and see how many are touched:

¶ Nearly three-quarters of all households have had a close encounter with layoffs since 1980, according to a new poll by The New York Times. In one-third of all households, a family member has lost a job, and nearly 40 percent more know a relative, friend or neighbor who was laid off.

¶ One in 10 adults—or about 19 million people, a number matching the adult population of New York and New Jersey combined—acknowledged that a lost job in their household had precipitated a major crisis in their lives, according to the Times poll.

¶ While permanent layoffs have been symptomatic of most recessions, now they are occurring in the same large numbers even during an economic recovery that has lasted five years and even at companies that are doing well.

¶ In a reversal from the early 80's, workers with at least some college education make up the majority of people whose jobs were eliminated, outnumbering those with no more than high school educations. And better-paid workers—those earning at least $50,000—account for twice the share of the lost jobs than they did in the 1980's.

¶ Roughly 50 percent more people, about 3 million, are affected by layoffs each year than the 2 million victims of violent crimes. But while crime bromides get easily served up—more police, stiffer jail sentences—no one has come up with any broadly agreed upon antidotes to this problem. And until Patrick J. Buchanan made the issue part of the Presidential campaign, it seldom surfaced in political debate.

Yet this is not a saga about rampant unemployment, like the Great Depression, but one about an emerging redefinition of employment. There has been a net increase of 27 million jobs in America since 1979, enough to easily absorb all the laid-off workers plus the new people beginning careers, and the national unemployment rate is low.

The sting is in the nature of the replacement work. Whereas 25 years ago the vast majority of the people who were laid off found jobs that paid as well as their old ones, Labor Department numbers show that now only about 35 percent of laid-off full-time workers end up in equally remunerative or better-paid jobs. Compounding this frustration are stagnant wages and an increasingly unequal distribution of wealth. Adjusted for inflation, the median wage is nearly 3 percent below what it was in 1979. Average household income climbed 10 percent between 1979 and 1994, but 97 percent of the gain went to the richest 20 percent.

The result is the most acute job insecurity since the Depression. And this in turn has produced an unrelenting angst that is shattering people's notions of work and self and the very promise of tomorrow, even as the President proclaims in his State of the Union Message that the economy is "the healthiest it has been in three decades" and even as the stock market has rocketed to 81 new highs in the last year.

Driving much of the job loss are several familiar and intensifying stresses bearing down upon companies: stunning technological progress that lets machines replace hands and minds; efficient and wily competitors here and abroad; the ease of contracting out work, and the stern insistence of Wall Street on elevating profits even if it means casting off people. Cutting the payroll has appeal for gasping companies that resort to it as triage and to soundly profitable companies that try it as preventative medicine against a complicated future.

The conundrum is that what companies do to make themselves secure is precisely what makes their workers feel insecure. And because workers are heavily represented among the 38 million Americans who own mutual funds, they unwittingly contribute to the very pressure from Wall Street that could take away their salaries even as it improves their investment income.

The job apprehension has intruded everywhere, diluting self-worth, splintering

1990–1999

ANDREA MOHIN/THE NEW YORK TIMES

Steven A. Holthausen, once a loan officer, dispensed tourist tips at a highway stop in Connecticut in 1996.

families, fragmenting communities, altering the chemistry of workplaces, roiling political agendas and rubbing salt on the very soul of the country. Dispossessed workers like Steven Holthausen are finding themselves on anguished journeys they never imagined, as if being forced to live the American dream of higher possibilities in reverse.

Many Americans have reacted by downsizing their expectations of material comforts and the sweetness of the future. In a nation where it used to be a given that children would do better than their parents, half of those polled by The Times thought it unlikely that today's youth would attain a higher standard of living than they have. What is striking is that this gloom may be even more emphatic among prosperous and well-educated Americans. A Times survey of the 1970 graduating class at Bucknell University, a college known as an educator of successful engineers and middle managers, found that nearly two-thirds doubted that today's children would live better. White-collar, middle-class Americans in mass numbers are coming to understand first hand the chronic insecurity on which the working class and the poor are experts.

All of this is causing a pronounced withdrawal from community and civic life. Visit Dayton, Ohio, a city fabled for its civic cohesion, and see the detritus. When Vinnie Russo left his job at National Cash Register and went to another city, the 85 boys of Pack 530 lost their Cubmaster, and they still don't have a new one. Many people are too tired, frustrated or busy for activities they used to enjoy, like church choir.

The effects billow beyond community participation. People find themselves sifting for convenient scapegoats on which to turn their anger, and are adopting harsher views toward those more needy than themselves.

Those who have not lost their jobs and their identities, and do not expect to, are also being traumatized. The witnesses, the people who stay employed but sit next to empty desks and wilting ferns, are grappling with the guilt that psychologists label survivor's syndrome. At Chemical Bank, a department of 15 was downsized to just one woman. She sobbed for two days over her vanished colleagues. Why them? Why not me?

The intact workers are scrambling to adjust. They are calculating the best angles to job security, including working harder and shrewder, and discounting the notion that a paycheck is an entitlement. The majority of people polled by The Times said they would work more hours, take fewer vacation days or accept lesser benefits to keep their jobs.

Even the most apparent winners are being singed. A generation of corporate managers have terminated huge numbers of people, and these firing-squad veterans are fumbling for ways to shush their consciences. Richard A. Baumbusch was a manager at CBS in 1985 when a colleague came to him for advice: Should he buy a house? Mr. Baumbusch knew the man's job was doomed, yet felt bound by his corporate duty to remain silent. The man bought the house, then lost his job. Ten years have passed, but Mr. Baumbusch cannot forget.

[March 3, 1996]

Japan's Economic Report Card: Where Did the A's and B's Go?

By SHERYL WuDUNN

TOKYO, Jan. 23—Many Japanese used to think that the next century would be the Japanese century. But after years of unremitting economic struggles and a convulsing stock market, that now sounds like a bitter joke to people like Yukiko Shinya.

"As a shareholder, I'm just terrified," said Mrs. Shinya, a 70-year-old retiree, as she watched stock prices fall recently on an electronic securities board. "There is just no future."

Mrs. Shinya's bleak mood may sound unduly alarmist here in Japan—one of the richest countries in the world and one where only about 7 percent of all Japanese own stock. But her pessimism is widely shared by business leaders, some best-selling authors, top Government officials and economists, many of whom feel that drastic changes are needed to recover lost dynamism.

Despite Japan's overall economic strength, the 11 percent drop in the stock market so far this year and the continued slide of the yen against the dollar amounts to, in the psyche of many Japanese, a "D" report card for the nation's stagnant economy. The Japanese, of course, are celebrated for their pessimism and modesty, but now the discontent seems to be stirring a movement that something must be done.

Japanese books, business magazines and dailies are arguing that like Britain a century ago Japan may be in an inexorable decline in international prestige and economic might. Headlines and articles blare: "Japan Is Disappearing," "Japan Is in Danger, Starting to Decline," "Japan Is Heading Toward Collapse." Commentators argue that Japan will be carried into the sea of sclerotic countries burdened by complacency and overregulation.

"Japan stands at a crossroads," Shoichiro Toyoda, chairman of Keidanren, the nation's most influential business organization, said in a recent speech. "If we take no action and let these problems linger on, the Japanese economy will be headed for catastrophe and will be left out of the world's prosperity in the 21st century."

Mr. Toyoda is no Cassandra. He is also chairman of the Toyota Motor Corporation, and he stressed that unless the economy was freed of regulatory barriers, the bureaucracy reorganized and the approach to policy-making changed, Japan's aging society and the flight of manufacturing industries to lower-wage countries would present even greater challenges than the ones that burden Japan today.

Prime Minister Ryutaro Hashimoto has called for broad changes, from reorganization of the bureaucracy to reform in fiscal budgeting, social security, education and drastic restructuring in the financial industry and the overall economy. Ten years ago, the Maekawa Reports also laid out a wide-ranging plan for change, but those changes were never fully put into effect. Thus, many voters and investors are now skeptical that Mr. Hashimoto can bring about real change.

Since the first trading week of the year, stocks have spiraled way up and way down, and the yen has further weakened against the dollar, offering opportunity for some but serious concern for many. The benchmark Nikkei index of 225 issues closed today at 17,909.46, down 104.42 points from Wednesday's close. In late New York trading, the yen flirted with 120 yen to the dollar, its weakest point in nearly 4 years.

Some people, including financial officials, are quietly grateful for the recent stock market crash because it may jolt the nation into taking the extreme steps they say are necessary to bring about far-reaching change. The market's incremental declines, they argue, have brought about only incremental change.

"I would like to see it go to 13,000 or so, for that would cause a shock wave," Masao Miyamoto, a social commentator and author of a best-selling book critical of

---

For Japan, the 1990's was an anxious time, one in which the economy fell into repeated recessions and showed little growth in between. The economic system that had seemed to serve the country so well in the 1980's was no longer working. Stock prices tumbled from the inflated levels of the 1980's, and so did real estate prices. At the low point in 1998, the Nikkei 225 stock index was down 67 percent from its peak and lower than at any time since 1985.

The fall in asset values meant that many banks were in trouble, but there was great hesitancy to accept that fact, and both banks and the Government spent the better part of the decade trying to cover up the problems in the hope they would go away if given enough time.

Japan continued to run huge trade surpluses, however, which meant it could afford to take that attitude, at least for a while. Companies kept workers on the payroll, getting annual raises based on seniority, long after there was no work for them to do. The Government provided subsidies to avoid layoffs.

But by 1997, as The Times reported, there was growing pressure for American-style reforms in Japan as the kind of pessimism that had been pervasive in the United States 20 years before began to take root in Japan. By 1999, layoffs were becoming less of a rarity, but it was not clear how far the changes would go.

1990–1999

A broker rested after watching prices plummet at the Tokyo Stock Exchange.

REUTERS

Japan's bureaucracy and society, said of the Nikkei. "Japan has to go through some devastating experience before people will say we have to start doing something."

For now, the recent wild fluctuations in the currency and stock markets reflect more immediate concerns, such as an anemic economic outlook, tightened Government spending and an overregulated financial system plagued by bad bank debt and a real estate crash. But longer term, the market jitters expose a deeper uneasiness about Japan's future and its global economic role as it moves into the next century.

What a difference a half-dozen years can make. When the Japanese stock market was at its peak, in 1989, many experts around the world foresaw Japan capturing global economic and industrial leadership from America. Japanese companies bought up chunks of Hollywood and New York real estate, they spoke of their nation's gross national product surpassing America's in the next century, and some people here felt so rich that they sprinkled gold on their food. Americans and Japanese alike came to believe that Japanese corporations were simply more efficient than American ones, that Japanese products were more durable, and that the next century belonged to the industrialists who created the Walkman and the virtually flawless car.

Now it is Americans who are seeing their stock market soar and believing that their economy is blessed. And while some Japanese and Americans wonder if Americans are not imitating the Japanese hubris of the 1980's, the New York stock market does not think so—at least not yet.

"Asian countries are now seeking their models in the United States, not Japan," said Heizo Takenaka, an economist at Keio University. "Japan was an important model for economic development, but from now on, Japan is no longer a model."

Japan's economy is the second largest in the world, partly powered by top competitors like Toyota, Canon Inc., and the Matsushita Electric Industrial Company. But about four-fifths of the economy, including the financial industry, lumbers through commerce under heavy regulation, cartel-like behavior or a herd mentality.

Trucking companies, for instance, mutually agree to charge almost identical rates; wholesale prices for rice, wheat and barley are controlled by the Government; the three largest daily newspapers charge the same price, and a fourth just joined the price club this year.

This used to be thought of as a strength of mighty Japan Inc. But now, to many Japanese, it is pitied as a failing of a economy in decline.

For the regulated swath of the economy, the transition toward the market mechanism is fraught with growing pains. Some economists worry that the best of Japan is moving out of the country as manufacturers build their cars and television sets abroad, leaving some smaller, inefficient operations at home.

What changes have taken place have been slow in coming.

In a country dominated by small shops and high prices, large retailers and discounters are growing, and more companies bucked the trend and opened for service during the traditional New Year holidays.

Still, critics say the pace of change is neither fast nor substantial. Prime Minister Hashimoto has talked about transforming Japan's economy and financial system, but the Government's latest budget proposals offered little encouragement to financial markets.

While bureaucrats reined in spending, Japan's transportation lobbyists somehow ended up with a $10 billion bullet-train extension. Farmers won $85 million in subsidies to plant less rice, and $2.6 billion once scheduled for economic restructuring is going to support farmers, construction workers and the oil industry.

Meanwhile, a national sales tax will rise to 5 percent from 3, and other income tax breaks will end. The comparison with America makes Japan's difficulties look even more acute.

"Twelve years ago, American corporate managers were almost losing confidence against the Japanese," who were buying up properties like Rockefeller Center, said Tetsundo Iwakuni, a member of Parliament and former head of Merrill Lynch in Japan. "Now the Japanese are selling back and Americans are buying back, regaining confidence against Japanese competition."

Yet, for all the talk of gloom, many business leaders say that beyond financial and property circles, there still may not be enough of a crisis among voters to bring about significant change. Only a minority of Japanese individuals invest in the stock market and fewer trade yen for dollars, so the recent volatility touches only a relative few.

Moreover, at 3.3 percent, unemployment is extremely low; company salaries still rise essentially in lock step with seniority; small store owners still benefit from regulatory support; inflation is virtually zero though it threatens to rise; and there is a buying boom now as people try to make large purchases before the national sales tax increases in April.

Indeed, there is tacit resistance to change, and not only from bureaucrats who stand to lose regulatory influence. The Prime Minister's grand plans to impose greater competition will produce winners and losers, even bankruptcies and probably greater unemployment. So Japan's efforts to change are like Americans and taxes: let the next person pay more.

"As a general argument, the businessman says, yes, this is the trend and deregulation is necessary," said Masao Ogura, the former chairman of Yamato Transport who has fought bitterly against regulatory barriers. "But once you go into specific industries, if the question comes down to my company, they say, we don't want it."

Even so, the recent pessimism and the currency and stock market declines may have worried some leaders to spin sentiment in the opposite direction. The Finance Ministry released a mildly optimistic report this week, and Jiro Ushio, chairman of Keizai Doyukai, the Japan Association of Corporate Executives, suggested that business leaders be "prudent so that negative factors not be written about too much." [Jan. 24, 1997]

IN JAPAN, FROM A LIFETIME JOB TO NO JOB AT ALL

By STEPHANIE STROM

TOKYO, Feb. 2—Last June, Takaharu Akimoto's boss politely and apologetically asked him to quit his job as a production manager at the Shoshiba Manufacturing Company, a midsized engine parts maker affiliated with the beleaguered Nissan Motor Company.

"I said to myself, 'Impossible!'" Mr. Akimoto recalled. "I told him I didn't want to quit, please let me stay longer."

But in today's Japan, the impossible has become possible, and in December, seven years shy of his retirement, Mr. Akimoto "quit" and joined the 2.91 million other Japanese who are officially looking for a job.

"This is the worst period of my life," he said. "I've had some serious setbacks before, but this is totally different."

Japan is suffering its highest rate of unemployment, 4.1 percent, since the Government started keeping statistics in 1949. Almost twice as many people are looking for jobs as there are job openings, and many of the available positions are in low-paying, unskilled areas.

That strikes a blow to the heart of Japan's self-image, and the whole country is reeling. Although Japan's unemployment is low compared with the rate in many other countries, full employment, or close to it, is a key clause in the social contract that has kept the public complacent and one political party in power almost consistently since World War II. Now, for the first time since the lean years after Japan's defeat in the war, most people here know someone who is out of a job—and fear that they could be next.

In addition to the challenge of finding work, the jobless battle shame and despair. Mr. Akimoto, for instance, kept his job loss a secret from his wife for a week. "I was at a loss as to how we would survive," he said.

The Japanese employment system, heavy on lifetime loyalty guaranteed by seniority-based pay, has been crumbling since 1993, when a slew of corporate titans started campaigns to trim their work forces.

But that erosion moved at the pace of molasses compared with what happened last year, when the unemployment rate jumped an alarming seven-tenths of a percent, to 4.1 percent. Compounding the problem, companies struggling to avoid layoffs cut wages, which fell 6.8 percent in December, the worst decline on record.

These statistics have rocked the psyche of a nation that has previously regarded itself as blessedly immune from the economic woes suffered by other developed countries.

A lifetime employee of Shoshiba whose salary had increased in lock step with his seniority, Mr. Akimoto had expected to work at the company until he retired at age 60 and received a fat, lump-sum payment to finance his retirement. But with Nissan fighting for its life, Mr. Akimoto's company could no longer afford to keep him on, or even to find him a job at a smaller Nissan affiliate, as it would have done in the past.

"I am angry," he said. "But I don't know where to direct my anger. The company did try to help me find another job at least."

The only jobs he has found so far are as a driver or as the man who waves a light baton at construction sites to direct traffic. He would earn less than the unemployment benefits he receives, but those will run out in late March unless he enrolls in a job training course.

"Right now, rather than immediately taking a job as a driver, I would like to continue to look for a while," Mr. Akimoto said. "But there is no question that my income will be less than half what I was earning."

Fearful of the social costs that may accompany frustration of the sort Mr. Akimoto is experiencing, the Government goes to great lengths to try to keep unemployment figures from rising, providing generous public subsidies to companies to keep workers on their payrolls.

"There is so-called invisible unemployment in corporations today that may become visible in the future, in which case the rate will become much higher than it is now," warned Akira Amari, the Labor Minister, at a recent press gathering.

Mr. Amari refused to make any estimates about what the real level would be. "These kinds of figures can drive up the insecurity of the Japanese consumer, so, excuse me, I cannot say what the figures are," he said. "It's my corporate secret."

It is no secret, though, that the need to create jobs provides much of the impetus behind the vast sums of money the Government has spent on public works during the last several years.

Despite the record unemployment rate, what is remarkable is that so many workers have retained their jobs. Automobile production dropped more than 8 percent last year, for instance, and yet it is rare to hear of an unemployed auto worker.

Reducing the head count is often the last resort for struggling companies. The obligation binding employer to employee is still strong here—so strong that in some cases, business owners have committed suicide so that their life insurance premiums can be used to pay workers and creditors.

The Honda Motor Company halted production at its plant in Thailand last year but has kept workers on the payroll, even flying some managers to Japan for three-month training courses.

And the Mitsubishi Corporation encourages marginal workers to take a year off for retraining at its expense, after which they can either find work elsewhere or come back to the company. "We cannot restructure in the U.S. way," said Minoru Makihara, the chairman of Mitsubishi and an outspoken proponent of greater labor mobility in Japan. "The Japanese way of insuring the way of life and living is a very respectable thing."

He noted that there are shortages of labor in important areas of the economy, like computer technology. "We're very good at making computers but not so good at using them," he said. "This is a highly educated population. In six months, we could produce a whole new corps of people who would be in great demand."

Masue Otani is someone who lost out to a computer. After working seven years in the mail room at the Ministry of Posts and Telecommunications, she left her job in part because some of her work was being computerized and because she felt unable to operate a computer. "Because I cannot use a computer, I'm afraid I cannot find a job," she said as she scanned the job offerings at the Hello! Work office. "Every available job asks for someone who can use a computer."

Mrs. Otani, whose husband cannot work because of a chronic stomach problem that periodically puts him in the hospital, is making ends meet with her unemployment insurance, and her sons, who live at home, give her a portion of their incomes. "It's very difficult and frightening," she said. "I don't know what will happen to us."

[Feb. 3, 1999]

As Currency Crisis Roils Asia, Thais Ask I.M.F.'s Help

By EDWARD A. GARGAN

HONG KONG, July 28—The fast-growing countries of South and Southeast Asia, regarded for years as the most economically promising of the world's developing nations, have been shaken by a plunge in their currencies.

While the crisis has reached outward to Malaysia, Indonesia and the Philippines, its center has been Thailand, where hard-willed global currency traders first sensed profit in a looming financial crisis stemming from a buildup of debt and a slowdown in growth.

Today, the Thai Government formally decided to seek International Monetary Fund assistance, underscoring the severity of its troubles and its inability to contain them.

In return for a special credit line that could total billions of dollars, however, the I.M.F. might ask for politically unpopular measures to patch up an economy that the Thai Finance Minister, Thanong Bidaya, compared tonight to "a water tank with a leak."

Thailand's action brings full circle a series of events that began on July 2, when the nation's central bank took steps to ease the pressure on its currency, the baht—in effect, a devaluation. In the three weeks or so since, the Philippines has sought assistance from the I.M.F., and the currencies of Malaysia and Indonesia have fallen, making life more expensive and creating a welter of economic and political problems for governments.

From small towns to meetings of top Asian leaders, the talk is of devaluation, of economic stability (or instability) and of the perfidy of the West. But underlying the pain and the polemics, there is spreading concern over whether the supercharged growth of the past is ending.

"Asia has to be prepared for much slower growth in the coming 10 years," said Nikhil Srinivasan, a vice president at Morgan Stanley in Bangkok. "These tigers are going to be roaring much less loudly."

Indeed, Thailand, long considered one of the region's most robust economies, faces a five-year supply of residential and commercial real estate, the result of a wild lending and construction boom at a time when growth indicators seemed to point only upward. The country's exports are sharply down compared with last year, and the Thais are facing their first budget deficit in a decade.

Economic growth this year, by some estimates, is expected to cool to 3.2 percent. While that might invite envy in Europe or the United States, it is sharply off from a pace of nearly 9 percent two years ago.

In Bangkok today, the suggestion of an I.M.F. rescue sent the Stock Exchange of Thailand index up more than 5 percent. Since the Thai baht was cut loose to float at market rates, stocks have risen 29 percent.

After the request for I.M.F. aid was announced, the governor of the Bank of Thailand, Rerngchai Marakanond, who had been orchestrating the defense of the baht, resigned.

Michel Camdessus, I.M.F. managing director.

MR. CAMDESSUS

AGENCE FRANCE-PRESSE

For much of the 1980's and 1990's, Asian countries such as Thailand, South Korea and Indonesia were among the fastest-growing economies in the world, with export-oriented policies that were widely praised.

Then, in 1997, that ended. Thailand was the first economy to quiver as its currency, the baht, came under pressure from speculators. The country raised interest rates and seemed to win. But the reality was that its currency was overvalued, and, in the wake of the speculative attack, many Thai companies and individuals began buying dollars, just to be on the safe side. Soon, the currency collapsed.

The story was repeated in South Korea and Indonesia, with local variations. All underwent changes in Government and had to turn to the International Monetary Fund for help. All had corporate sectors that were overly indebted and banks that were in financial trouble.

For a time, it appeared that the Asian crisis would bring on a world recession. But that was averted, in part because central banks in the United States and Europe cut interest rates repeatedly to stimulate those economies. By 1999, the economies in both Thailand and South Korea showed signs of recovering, while the Indonesian economy's fate seemed to be tied up with political developments that were still uncertain.

1990–1999

The I.M.F. help, if it is granted, is likely to carry with it a range of belt-tightening requirements for the Thais—including reining in lending, allowing foreign banks greater access and, most important, cutting back Government spending. Some economists predicted that a recession could follow.

In Washington, a spokesman for the I.M.F. said it had dispatched about half a dozen officials, who arrived in Bangkok over the weekend, but that no determination on assistance had been made. Analysts, and bankers at the Union Bank of Switzerland, have estimated that Thailand will need as much as $20 billion in credits.

In a sense, a measure of economic hubris has overtaken Southeast Asia, and the face of the region has reflected it. Old cities have been transformed into stretches of mirrored towers, new centers of commerce and finance. Roads are clogged with the sclerosis of growing wealth, private cars and motorcycles. Airports, once genteel single-runway, cozy-terminal affairs, are woefully inadequate and vast new airports are either muddy construction sites or still on the drawing boards.

Growth seemed unstoppable. Investment from the United States and Europe surged, as did the appetites of the industrial nations for the products churned out of factories across the region, from semiconductors to running shoes, silk to tires.

Now, the euphoria has dissipated as the global currency traders have decided that some of the shine on Asian economies glittered over growing patches of rust. A spreading pattern of current-account deficits, wild overspending on property that sent prices in many countries spiraling upward, and a yearlong slowdown in exports convinced many traders that the region's currencies, beginning with the Thai baht, were worth a lot less than they were being traded for.

The swiftness with which devaluations have swept the region suggested that underlying problems had been ignored in the charge into economic growth. At the Asian Development Bank in Manila, Vishvanath V. Desai, the chief economist, perceives several broad problems that have eaten into the region's economies, problems that he says are correctable but that will inhibit any rapid return to the heydays of recent years. He lists them as follows:

¶ The steady appreciation of the United States dollar, to which many regional currencies have been linked. By making exports expensive abroad, this has undermined the competitiveness of these economies.

¶ A failure by many countries to invest in basic facilities and services, and in the development of banking systems and financial regulation. Such failures were compounded by a lag in investment in education, skills training and language competence, particularly in English.

¶ A growing tendency of wages to begin outpacing productivity gains.

¶ In some countries, a splurging on major building and infrastructure projects without regard for their necessity or the way in which they would be financed.

"These elements have been accumulating for some time," Mr. Desai said. "Some kind of cleansing I hope will take place now." [July 29, 1997]

2 Get Nobel for a Formula at the Heart of Options Trading

By PETER PASSELL

Two North American scholars won the Nobel Memorial Prize in Economic Science yesterday for work that enables investors to price accurately their bets on the future, a breakthrough that has helped power the explosive growth in financial markets since the 1970's and plays a profound role in the economics of everyday life.

Robert C. Merton of the Harvard Business School and Myron S. Scholes, a Canadian-born professor emeritus at the Stanford Business School, will share the $1 million award for helping devise a mathematical formula that provided the answer to a simple but seemingly insurmountable problem confronting Wall Street: how to measure the worth of an option.

Their solution helped lay the basis of today's vast global options marketplace, where the trading affects everyone with a stake in the financial markets, from employees who receive stock options as part of their pay to mutual fund investors who use options to hedge interest-rate risk.

An option is a type of investment that allows, but does not require, an investor to buy an asset, like stocks or bonds or wheat or pork bellies, at a prearranged price during a preset period of time.

Until 1973, when Mr. Merton and Mr. Scholes published their analysis, it was extremely difficult to assess all the variables that could affect the price of an option. Their work overcame that difficulty, which had limited the growth of the options markets.

"Such rapid and widespread application of a theoretical result was new to economics," the prize committee wrote. "Nowadays, thousands of traders and investors use the formula every day"—making it easy for businesses and individuals to hedge risks in the incredibly complex world of modern finance.

The announcement of the Nobel in economics, which has been awarded annually by the Bank of Sweden since 1969, excites the academic community, but usually ignites little genuine enthusiasm on Wall Street. Not so this year. "I'm thrilled," said William Brodsky, chairman of the Chicago Board Options Exchange, which owes a large part of its growth to the Nobel winners. "This Nobel not only recognizes Merton and Scholes's accomplishments, it underscores the importance of options in the world of finance."

The analysis the two worked out has been successfully applied not only to pricing options but also to numerous other "derivative" securities, so named because their value is determined by fluctuations in the value of other assets.

Using derivatives is now a common way to redistribute the risks of doing business. Although in recent years derivatives have been associated with some financial disasters—they played a role in the bankruptcy of Orange County, Calif., and the demise of Barings, Britain's oldest investment bank—derivatives are widely regarded as beneficial.

Farmers, for example, use derivatives when they sell crops on the futures markets even before the planting has been finished. By locking in a price, they protect themselves if prices fall, although they also give up the chance of a windfall if prices surge.

But what is the real worth of, say, an option to buy 100 shares of Intel at $105 each before next April or the right to borrow 400 million French francs at 9 percent by next Tuesday? By the early 1960's, a handful of economists had both an interest in the puzzle and the advanced mathematical tools to solve it.

"We knew the answer was there, and that someone was going to find it," recalled Paul Samuelson, an economist at M.I.T. who later won a Nobel for work in other areas of economics.

The breakthrough came from three researchers, each under the age of 30—and one not even an economist. Fischer Black, a mathematician with Arthur D. Little

Derivatives have been around for centuries—stock options, for instance, were being traded in Holland in the 17th century—but they became far more complicated and widely traded in the final quarter of the 20th century. That was largely the result of work by three economists, Fischer Black, Myron S. Scholes and Robert C. Merton, who together developed the first model for pricing options.

In 1997, Merton and Scholes shared the Nobel prize in economics for their work. (Black would no doubt have been included but for the fact he had died in 1995 and Nobel prizes are not awarded posthumously.) The Times celebrated their accomplishments when the award was announced.

In 1993, Merton and Scholes had joined with John Meriwether, a former vice chairman of Salomon Brothers, to form a hedge fund called Long-Term Capital Management. The fund used computers and pricing models to calculate the normal relationship between the prices of different securities, buying one and selling another when the relationship diverged from the normal range. If all went as expected, the trade would be profitable when markets returned to normal. Those bets could be made most easily using derivatives. Investors, mostly institutions, eagerly signed up despite the high fees being charged by the managers, who got 2 percent of the assets each year, plus 25 percent of the profits.

In 1998, financial markets were shaken by a series of events, most notably Russia's default on a large part of its debt, and there was a brief but strong flight to the safety of such assets as United States Treasury bonds. That panic devastated Long-Term Capital.

At a meeting arranged by the Federal Reserve Bank of New York, the rest of Wall Street agreed to bail out the fund, fearing that its collapse would lead to a dumping of securities that could bankrupt other funds and perhaps even some investment banks. The concept of "too-big-to-fail," which in 1984 had led to the rescue of Continental Illinois Bank, had been extended to hedge funds.

Eventually, markets stabilized, and the rescuers of Long-Term Capital got their money back with some profits. But the original investors suffered large losses in 1998 that were only partly recovered.

1990–1999

consultants in Boston, discovered that an acquaintance, Mr. Scholes, then a professor of finance at M.I.T., was also fascinated by the question of options value. They enlisted the help of an assistant to Professor Samuelson at M.I.T., Mr. Merton, who is the son of the famous Columbia University sociologist Robert K. Merton. Together they devised a mathematical formula, known as the Black-Scholes model, that took into account a variety of variables.

Mr. Black and Mr. Scholes had considerable difficulty finding a publisher. Their paper languished for three years before the prestigious Journal of Political Economy printed it in 1973. Mr. Merton walked an easier path, but only because he was a friend of the editor of the new Bell Journal of Economics. "Finance just wasn't part of the economics mainstream," Mr. Merton recalled in an interview yesterday.

The Chicago Board Options Exchange, the first devoted to options trading, opened just as the Black-Scholes theory was published. Although complicated, the computation involved could be easily—and virtually instantly—done on the pocket calculators that were just becoming popular.

Soon traders were valuing options on the floor of the exchange, punching half a dozen numbers into electronic calculators hard-wired with the formula. This not only meant quicker and more accurate pricing, it also increased the volume of options markets and reduced the cost of using options. Mr. Black and Mr. Scholes became so highly regarded at the exchange that when they visited, traders would give them a standing ovation.

Thanks to extensions suggested by Mr. Merton, uses for the formula have been found in virtually every nook and cranny of finance.

Mr. Merton, who earned his Ph.D. from M.I.T in 1970, taught there until 1988, when he moved to the Harvard Business School. The Nobel caps a long career in helping to transform corporate finance from a backwater to the hot zone of economics. "Bob Merton is the Isaac Newton of his field," Mr. Samuelson said.

In 1973, Mr. Scholes went back to teach at the University of Chicago Business School, where he had earned his Ph.D. In 1983 he moved on to the Stanford Business School, where he taught until retirement in 1996. That was hardly the end of his career, though. He and Mr. Merton are principals in Long-Term Capital Management, the immensely successful multibillion-dollar private investment fund formed by John Meriwether when he broke with his partners at Salomon Brothers.

"These guys can do finance both ways: high theory, or down and dirty," Stephen Ross, an economist at the Yale School of Management, said of the new Nobel recipients.

And Peter L. Bernstein, a consultant to institutional investors and a historian of the securities industry, said yesterday, "All I can say is: What took the Nobel committee so long?"

Mr. Merton said he had no particular plans for the $500,000 that he will receive at a ceremony on Dec. 10.

"It's all been a blast," he said. "My only regret is that Fischer Black isn't here to share the prize." Mr. Black, a partner in Goldman, Sachs and a former president of the American Economic Association, died in 1995 at the age of 57.   [Oct. 15, 1997]

FAULT LINES OF RISK APPEAR AS MARKET HERO STUMBLES

By DIANA B. HENRIQUES

Wall Street, often hard-nosed and cynical, was utterly dazzled by John W. Meriwether. He was viewed as a bond trader with a Midas touch, a mathematician of genius who found gold nuggets in markets where others saw only sand.

In the giddy 1980's, he presided over a team of bond traders who generated immense profits for Salomon Brothers with arcane strategies that were dubbed "rocket science." But in a world of sharp tongues and sharper elbows, Mr. Meriwether was softly self-possessed, inspiring confidence among equals and hero-worship among underlings. A brush with scandal, as the supervisor of a trader caught manipulating bids on Treasury securities in 1991, did little to tarnish his gleaming reputation. When he left the firm in February 1994, some of his best traders and two Nobel-laureate economists followed him into a celebrated exile in Greenwich, Conn.

There, with fishing breaks when the bluefish were running, Mr. Meriwether and his partners operated Long-Term Capital Management L.P., a largely unregulated investment pool for the wealthy known as a hedge fund. By early 1998, Mr. Meriwether's team had invested $90 billion, most of it borrowed from Wall Street bankers so confident of Mr. Meriwether's skills that a few had even sunk some of their personal wealth into his new fund.

And it was there, last week, that the glittering Meriwether image toppled from its Wall Street pedestal and shattered. A hastily assembled consortium of international banks and brokerage houses took possession of the faltering firm and pumped in $3.65 billion to prevent a disorderly collapse that could have panicked the credit markets and sent shock waves from small-town real estate offices to the halls of Government in Brazil. If the fund had been forced to liquidate its entire portfolio, its sales could have undermined the value of financial contracts worth as much as $1.25 trillion.

How one man, utterly unknown beyond his rarefied world, became such a potent source of instability in one of the deepest, richest markets in the world reveals how Wall Street can be seduced by outsized success and the trappings of genius. And while the last-minute rescue grew out of an emergency warning system that provides some comfort to the nation's financial markets, the march to the precipice reveals how little regulators, investors and even traders themselves understand the fault lines of risk buried in today's global financial landscape.

"It is too early to give the definitive answer to what the lessons are, but clearly firms have got to look at their exposure and leverage, and at what margins of safety they have in these transactions," said Peter Bakstansky, senior vice president of the Federal Reserve Bank of New York, which provided the framework for the rescue. "And they must have a better sense of the risk analysis being done by their borrowers."

A top Wall Street executive briefed on the negotiations last week said he was clear about the lesson for his own firm: "We will never let our exposure to one counterparty get to these levels again—never. He had gotten too big for the market. Everybody gave him too much money."

In a world where the concept of too much money is met with blank stares, John Meriwether was able to borrow heavily from more than a dozen financial institutions, each of which was largely unaware of how much he had borrowed from the others. Hedge funds are private partnerships that are not required to disclose their trading strategies, and that can take money only from institutions and wealthy individuals, on the theory that these sophisticated investors understand the above-average risks involved.

Mr. Meriwether's hedge fund was even more secretive than most, to prevent rivals from copying its strategy or from anticipating its next move. In essence, the fund placed bets that tiny deviations in the traditional relationships between the prices of various securities would eventually return to normal.

John W. Meriwether, hedge fund guru.
ASSOCIATED PRESS

For example, the interest rate on corporate bonds is usually about one percentage point higher than on comparable Treasury bonds, reflecting the greater risk of lending to companies. If the spread widened to more than one percentage point, the Meriwether team could bet with confidence that the relationship would ultimately revert to normal. Myron S. Scholes and Robert C. Merton, who shared a Nobel prize in economics, helped program powerful computers to recognize countless similar profit opportunities.

The profit on each of these trades was so small that the Meriwether fund had to make its money on volume. As one Salomon Brothers veteran described it, the fund was like a roulette player betting on red and doubling up its bets each time the wheel stopped on black. "A gambler with $1,000 will probably lose," he said. "A gambler with $1 billion will wind up owning the casino, because it is a mathematical certainty that red will come up eventually—but you have to have enough chips to stay at the table until that happens."

One way the fund accumulated its chips was by borrowing at least $20 for each $1 in capital.

At the end of 1997, Mr. Meriwether had so many chips that he was giving some back. Investors who had joined the fund after February 1994 were handed $2.82 for every $1 they had invested, and were told very politely to go away. Original investors from outside the firm—who considered themselves the lucky ones—took out their profits but kept their original stakes in the fund. After all, the fund had posted profits of 43 percent in 1995 and 41 percent in 1996.

The first gust of the approaching storm came in June. The fund was down 10 percent, its worst monthly loss ever. Early August was even worse. As the Russian financial markets and other emerging markets grew increasingly treacherous, investors sought the safety of Treasury securities, pushing up Treasury prices while most other bond prices fell. Unfortunately, this pattern was the opposite of the Meriwether team's bets, and its paper losses grew.

Around Aug. 15, Mr. Meriwether warned his investors and trading partners about the grim results. But with roughly $3.7 billion left in capital, the partners were still confident they could weather the storm, and many left on vacation.

Then came Friday, Aug. 21–a terrible day for the bond market as skittish buyers, dumping corporate bonds to buy Treasury bonds, sent Treasury rates to a 20-year low. Long-Term Capital's general partners rushed back to their Greenwich offices, working through the weekend and the following week to review their positions, which had dropped 40 percent that month.

They approached new investors. But when the stock market plummeted on Aug. 31, any hope for new money evaporated.

On Sept. 2, Mr. Meriwether invited existing investors to put in more money to help the fund stay the course. Again, there were some talks, but no cash.

Around this time, one key element of the Wall Street warning system was activated: Mr. Meriwether's clearing broker, the Bear Stearns Companies, intensified its scrutiny of the fund.

Another part of the warning system was tripped, too. The Federal Reserve Bank of New York, which monitors the key commercial banks that serve the Wall Street community, was questioning how much Mr. Meriwether owed to institutions under its supervision.

On Friday, Sept. 18, what had been a deeply worrisome problem became a full-blown crisis. The triggering event is still shrouded in official silence, but several people with sideline seats say that Mr. Meriwether, the celebrated bond trader, was blindsided by an unraveling stock investment. As the prices of Ciena and Tellabs shares fell following the collapse of their merger, Long-Term Capital had to provide additional collateral to brokers who had lent it money to buy those shares. Federal regulations on such transactions leave no room to wiggle.

In any case, the $3.7 billion in capital that Long-Term Capital had in mid-August had dwindled by more than two-thirds. It had become clear to several top Wall Street executives that Mr. Meriwether needed fresh money or his firm would fail.

"And if this firm had to liquidate in distress, the ramifications for the global marketplace would be very negative," one senior Wall Street executive said. How negative? "No one felt they could even quantify it. That's one of the things that made it so scary."

No one knew exactly the magnitude of the fund's liabilities, not even Bear Stearns, in part because the fund used complex financial contracts, known as derivatives, whose value was difficult to assess.

Though early reports have credited the Fed with pulling together–some say forcing–the bailout, it seems to have begun on Sunday afternoon, when Jon S. Corzine, a senior partner at Goldman, Sachs & Company, talked with Peter R. Fisher, an executive vice president of the New York Fed who was monitoring the crisis in Greenwich, and with top executives at Merrill Lynch, UBS of Switzerland and J. P. Morgan. Some of the firms had lent money to the fund, while others were trading partners or investors.

Those calls helped knit together a group to solve the crisis: Mr. Corzine; David H. Komansky, chairman of Merrill Lynch & Company, and Herbert M. Allison Jr., Merrill's president; David Solo from UBS A.G. and Douglas A. Warner 3d, chairman of J. P. Morgan & Company.

At 7:30 on Tuesday morning, the core group decided to gather on neutral ground in a private dining room that Mr. Fisher made available at the New York Fed's headquarters a few blocks from Wall Street. At the same time, teams from the investment banks were dispatched to Greenwich "to look at the situation," one top-level Wall Street executive said. That examination made it clear that the fund would not be able to cover its obligations if it were forced to hurriedly liquidate its positions.

At 7 P.M., sleek black limousines again converged on the Fed's headquarters. This time, the core group had invited six other banks and brokerage houses, including Morgan Stanley Dean Witter and the Travelers Group.

While the Fed officials encouraged the group to come together, how pivotal a role the Fed played in the rescue effort is the subject of considerable disagreement among the participants in the drama.

"The Fed just provided the forum," one senior Wall Street executive said. Some of the bankers, however, have complained privately that regulators were in fact pressuring them to rescue the fund.

The negotiations were difficult, but the executives finally agreed they had no alternative but to give Mr. Meriwether more money.

At 10 A.M. Wednesday, senior officers of 16 banks and brokerage firms assembled in a Fed conference room. They waited for more than a half hour for William J. McDonough, the president of the New York Fed, who had just returned from London. At 10:40, he came in to explain that Mr. Corzine of Goldman, Sachs might have found a buyer to come to Long-Term Capital's rescue.

"Everyone in the room knew" that the potential buyer was the celebrated investor Warren E. Buffett, said one senior executive who was briefed on the meeting. Mr. Buffett had stepped in to rescue Salomon Brothers in 1991, after the bond trading scandal that prompted Mr. Meriwether's departure, and his involvement would have injected instant confidence into the marketplace. When Mr. McDonough suggested a recess until 1 P.M., the executives left the Fed, no doubt with their fingers crossed.

When they returned, however, the Fed president announced that the potential buyer had balked. Mr. Komansky of Merrill Lynch then challenged the group: How much additional money would each firm contribute to keep the fund alive and forestall the crisis of confidence that its collapse could produce?

There were angry arguments and resentful speeches. Each executive knew that if his firm seized its collateral from Long-Term Capital and fled, only a few of them would reach the exit before the roof fell in. Nevertheless, collective action was difficult for such natural competitors, even with the Fed's brooding oversight.

In the end, 14 firms committed $100 million to $350 million each. That they could do so on such short notice is one happy result of the long, fat years in the capital markets that preceded these last anxious months. That the rescue effort was organized so smoothly suggests, too, that a strong habit of informal cooperation and close consultation has been forged in past crises.

At most, the deal bought the fund some breathing room in which their bets may, just possibly, ripen into the extraordinary profits that tempted them into this risky territory in the first place. But the cost was high. The rescue was essentially an informal, high-speed bankruptcy reorganization that turned Long-Term Capital's creditors into its new owners, who will oversee every aspect of the restructured firm's existence.

At the end of the week, Mr. Meriwether and his partners retained a sliver of equity in the firm that they built on genius and panache. Their 180 employees–most of whom had invested each year's bonuses in the fund–were left with little more than uncertain jobs.

But regulators and others are left pondering how a small band of traders could threaten the confidence that knits together the world's financial markets.

[Sept. 27, 1998]

Share of Wealth in Stock Holdings Hits 50-Year High

By EDWARD WYATT

After three years of rapidly rising stock prices, American households have more of their assets invested in the stock market than at any time in the last 50 years—and perhaps ever.

Even that most prized possession, the home, has fallen behind stocks for the first time in three decades.

An analysis by The New York Times of data compiled by the Federal Reserve shows that stock investments made up 28 percent of American household wealth—a measure that includes houses, cars and other tangible assets as well as financial assets. The figures are for the end of September, the most recent period available. And stocks accounted for 43 percent of financial assets, which include bank accounts, mutual funds and securities.

Both those stock allocation numbers have more than doubled since 1990, when the latest run of the bull market began.

The implications of this profound growth in stock exposure are many. The size of their paychecks aside, many Americans are feeling richer as the value of their stock holdings rises.

But with so much in stocks, a sharp market decline could seriously erode the financial well-being of Americans, even if their money is largely tied up in long-term retirement plans. In years past, the biggest asset of most Americans was the home. Where skyrocketing real estate prices once provided reassurance to the middle class, soaring stock portfolios now do. And stock prices are subject to much wider short-term swings than home values.

The extra wealth from stock portfolios has also encouraged Americans to spend more and save less. The Commerce Department reported last week that the rate of saving fell last year to 3.8 percent of disposable income, the lowest level in 58 years and less than half its postwar peak of 9.5 percent, set in 1974.

What Americans do set aside for saving, they increasingly allocate to stocks, rather than to more conservative investments. That heightened allotment accounts for about a third of the increase in stocks' share of wealth, with the other two-thirds coming from the rise in share prices.

The increased shift into stocks comes as stocks have been gaining 30 percent annually the last three years. "It's been jammed down their throats that they have to put their money in equities if they want anything left for retirement," said Melissa R. Brown, a stock market analyst at Prudential Securities.

But if stocks fail to continue to provide such large returns, Americans might find their assumptions about saving for retirement or college expenses fundamentally altered. Historically, gains on stocks have averaged 8 percent a year.

Concerns about how investors with bulging equity portfolios will react to a steep or prolonged downturn in stock prices have plagued Wall Street for several years. To allay fears of a panic, Wall Street analysts have often said that the average American's exposure to stocks is no greater than it was 30 years ago. But that estimate does not take into account many investment products that are gaining in popularity.

The long bull market has given few clues about what individuals will do. Last October, a sharp decline in stock prices caused many individual investors to pour new money into stocks. In contrast, institutional investors were heavy sellers.

Still, the last time Americans had their faith in stocks truly tested was the stock market crash of 1987. Then, stocks accounted for only 13 percent of household assets—half as much as today—and Americans had more money in their savings and checking accounts than in stocks.

"Individuals certainly are taking more risk today than they were taking five years

---

The stock market's advance during the 1990's seemed to be relentless, and a generation of investors came to see declines as buying opportunities. From 1989 through 1999, the Dow Jones industrial average hit record highs in every year. That was 11 in a row, obliterating the old record of six consecutive years, set from 1924 through 1929.

Not even the 1950's and 1960's—the last golden age for the stock market—had been as consistently good. From 1954 through 1966, the Dow had posted records in 11 of 13 years. Starting in 1982, the index set records in 15 of 17 years, the exceptions being 1984 and 1988.

As the good stock market news continued, bearish voices were gradually discredited, and more and more of the public's money was put into stocks, either through mutual funds, which gained in popularity as never before, or directly.

In 1998, The Times reported that the public had a greater percentage of its assets invested in the stock market than at any time on record.

The following year, the Metropolitan Diary column—a collection of whimsical anecdotes about life in New York—carried an item illustrating how pervasive interest in the market had become.

1990–1999

METROPOLITAN DIARY

By ENID NEMY

Sign of the times: Fred Ehrman was walking along 55th Street recently when he noticed four burly constuction workers sitting on the sidewalk, eating their breakfast and deep in conversation. An attractive woman passed in front of them but none of the men looked her way. As Mr. Ehrman passed by the men, he overheard the following exchange:

First worker: "So what happened last week?"

Second worker: "Telephone and the Internets had big drops but I made up that decline with my cyclicals and financials."

Mr. Ehrman's postscript: "I found myself ironically nostalgic for those old leering whistles."   [May 17, 1999]

ago," said Scott L. Lummer, chief investment officer of 401(k) Forum Inc., which sells investment advice on line. "A lot of that is for good reasons.

"But there is a growing set of the populace that looks at the last three years of returns and says, 'The market goes up 30 percent a year.' I'm not sure those people really understand the risks involved in stocks. They may have a lot more money in equities than they should."

How much is enough depends on who is talking. Wall Street professionals usually put the ideal portion of stocks at about 60 percent of one's financial assets. Some individuals go much further.

Don Matsanoff, a 36-year-old commercial real estate agent in Columbus, Ohio, believes he did not have enough money invested in stocks at the beginning of the 1990's. Less than half of his financial assets were in equities. By the end of last year, Mr. Matsanoff had raised that portion to more than 80 percent.

"With the returns I've seen in the market over the past few years, I'm putting a considerable percentage of the income I'm making at work back into the market," he said. "I'm confident that it will continue to grow."

With mutual fund managers commanding sports-star salaries and investment

shows on the airwaves, the man on the street may accept the news about rapid growth in stock ownership without flinching. But some of Wall Street's leading gurus have insisted that stock investments have not reached a new peak.

For example, Abby Joseph Cohen, the stock market strategist at Goldman, Sachs and one of the leading bulls on Wall Street, has noted that Americans have been increasing their stock investments in recent years as inflation has waned and as baby boomers save more for retirement. But, she says, the percentage of their financial assets in stocks "remains well below the levels of the late 1960's."

She and other Wall Street analysts have reached such conclusions by focusing only on holdings of individual stocks and stocks through mutual funds. Other categories of stock ownership, however, have grown steeply. At the end of 1996, employee-controlled plans accounted for half of the $3 trillion in corporate pension plans, according to the Federal Reserve, up from a quarter of the total when the 1980's began.

In those plans, the employee, rather than a professional pension fund manager, decides how to invest—in stocks, bonds or other assets. The same is true for variable annuities, which essentially combine the tax deferral of an insurance policy with a mutual fund, and other types of variable life insurance products, with returns based on market performance. Sales of those products have skyrocketed in recent years.

The analysis by The Times shows that when all indirect stock holdings are included, stocks account for 43 percent of household financial assets, up from 39 percent in 1968, and 28 percent of total household assets, up from 26 percent in 1968.

The numbers are higher than at any time since the end of World War II. But because the Fed data extend only to 1945, comparisons with earlier periods are difficult.

[Feb. 11, 1998]

Gates, on Capitol Hill, Presents Case for an Unfettered Microsoft

By STEVE LOHR

WASHINGTON, March 3—In his first testimony before Congress, William H. Gates, the chairman of the Microsoft Corporation, delivered a spirited defense of his company's business practices today and portrayed Microsoft as the standard-bearer of the nation's high-technology economy.

In listing his industry's achievements, Mr. Gates boasted that software makers had created more than two million American jobs, had contributed $100 billion to the economy last year and had generated technological change at an awesome rate.

Mr. Gates, who at age 42 is the nation's wealthiest person, stopped just short of reformulating the famous declaration of Charles E. Wilson, the president of General Motors, who told Congress in the 1950's, "For years I thought what was good for our country was good for General Motors and vice versa."

Yet at a time when Microsoft is defending itself against both an antitrust suit by the Justice Department and a rising chorus of criticism that it is abusing its considerable power in the marketplace, Mr. Gates minced no words about where he believed the real threat to the information age lay.

"Will the United States continue its breathtaking technological advances?" Mr. Gates asked members of the Senate Judiciary Committee. "I believe the answer is yes—if innovation is not restricted by government."

He made his comments in a four-hour hearing convened to explore, in the words of Senator Orrin G. Hatch, the committee's chairman, "how market power works in the software industry and whether Microsoft is abusing its market power."

Mr. Gates was one of six computer industry figures to address the committee on that issue today.

He was joined by two of his allies in the industry, a venture capitalist and two of his company's fiercest competitors, who warned the Senators that Microsoft's appetite knew no limits and was smothering competition in the software industry.

Senator Hatch, a Utah Republican, said Congress had no present plans for new antitrust legislation tailored to high-technology industries. The current antitrust laws date back a century to the era of the rail trusts, which led to the passage of the Sherman Antitrust Act of 1890.

In the hearing, Senator Hatch noted there is "nothing inherently wrong with one company having monopoly power. The issue is whether the company uses that power to enhance and expand its monopoly position."

Senator Hatch observed that monopolists are subject to closer antitrust scrutiny than other companies and they have to be more careful in their business practices. After the hearing he characterized Microsoft as a monopoly and said the company "will have to learn to live by the rules that govern monopolies."

The Justice Department sued Microsoft last October, contending that the company was violating a 1995 consent decree with the Government by forcing makers of personal computers to load Microsoft's Explorer program for browsing the Internet's World Wide Web as a condition of licensing its Windows operating system, which is the industry standard.

Microsoft asserts that Explorer is not a separate product but an "integrated feature" of Windows—and thus an allowable improvement to the operating system under the consent decree. In December, a Federal judge issued a temporary injunction ordering Microsoft to offer PC makers the choice of taking Windows without Explorer. Microsoft is appealing that order.

The Government is also considering bringing a broader antitrust case against Microsoft under the Sherman Act, Justice Department officials have said.

By 1998, Bill Gates had become the richest man in America, a man both hailed and reviled. His company, Microsoft, dominated the rapidly growing personal computer business and had already lost one limited antitrust case. That verdict would be overturned on appeal, but the Justice Department was considering filing new charges.

It was in that environment that Microsoft's founder and chairman first testified before Congress. To Gates, it was obvious that he was running a company that had done great good for America and the world. To his opponents, he ran a company that smacked of a monopoly that beat up on competitors, notably Netscape, the pioneer in Internet access, and that needed to be restrained by the law.

Gates ran into plenty of hostility, with senators talking about predatory pricing and monopolistic practices. When he was through, he told reporters, "I enjoyed this opportunity." As he left, he encountered a crowd of high school students, who broke into cheers.

1990–1999

William H. Gates, before Congress in 1998.

REUTERS

The fundamental antitrust issue before the Justice Department and Congress is whether Microsoft is using its dominant position in operating system software, where Windows controls 85 percent of the market, to gain an upper hand in new markets unfairly. Markets that Microsoft has entered in the last two years include not just Web browser software but also emerging areas of on-line commerce, from selling airline tickets and books to producing entertainment programming and publishing magazines on the Internet.

The two Microsoft rivals who joined Mr. Gates in the hearing room were James L. Barksdale, the president of the Netscape Communications Corporation, which makes the leading browser, Navigator, and Scott McNealy, the chairman of Sun Microsystems Inc., which is sparring with Microsoft over changes that Mr. Gates's company made to Sun's Java programming language.

Two other speakers, invited as Microsoft's allies, were Michael S. Dell, the chairman of the Dell Computer Corporation, and Douglas Burgum, chairman of Great Plains Software Inc. The sixth speaker was Stewart Alsop, a venture capitalist and columnist for Fortune magazine.

The testimony from the software executives was at times filled with technical jargon and acronyms, talk of beta software, HTML, Java OS, client-server, API's and vaporware. But the pro- and anti-Microsoft sides struck broad themes that have a certain resonance in Washington.

Mr. Gates's position—a now-familiar ode to the industry that he personifies—has a Reaganesque ring: It is morning in high-tech America. "I am proud to be part of an industry that has revolutionized the world in only 25 years," Mr. Gates said. "The computer software industry has produced more new products and services at affordable prices, created more economic opportunity and empowered more people than any other industry at any other time in history."

His opponents espoused a digital-age variant on the Vietnam-era domino theory: If some limits are not soon placed on Microsoft's relentless expansion into new markets, the company's spreading monopoly will trample rivals—not with superior products but with sheer market muscle. Competition and innovation, they say, will be stifled as a result.

Even so, Microsoft's competitors went to great pains to distance their stance from old-fashioned protectionism.

"Despite how some have painted the picture, the issue is not about one company versus another, or a personal battle between one C.E.O. and another," Mr. McNealy of Sun Microsystems said. "The issue is about protecting consumer choice in the marketplace. It is about protecting innovation. And it is about enforcing the laws of the land."

Netscape, Microsoft's main rival in Web browsers, still has more than 55 percent of the market, though its share has fallen rapidly in the face of Microsoft's aggressive marketing and improved browser design.

One practice that was questioned was Microsoft's contracts with some 40 Internet service providers, which prohibited them from promoting competing browsers.

[March 4, 1998]

In Largest Deal Ever, Citicorp Plans Merger With Travelers Group

By TIMOTHY L. O'BRIEN and JOSEPH B. TREASTER

Two of America's largest companies, Citicorp and Travelers Group Inc., agreed yesterday to a merger that would create the world's largest financial-services concern. Not since the freewheeling pre-Depression era would so many different financial businesses be corralled under one roof in this country.

The transaction was valued at $70 billion in stock when it was announced, making it the largest merger in history. Both companies' stock prices soared on the news, adding another $14 billion to the value of the transaction by the end of the day.

The deal is remarkable not only for its size but for its brashness as well. While banks like Citicorp and insurance and brokerage firms like Travelers have made substantial inroads into one another's businesses, there are still ample regulatory restrictions on how actively banks can sell products like insurance.

Just last week, a bill seeking to end laws dating back as far as the Depression that separate commercial and investment banking and limit the types of financial products that banks can offer was withdrawn in the House of Representatives. This proposed merger challenges regulators and lawmakers to either end these restrictions, scuttle the deal or force the merged company to cut back on what it offers the customer.

Whatever the outcome, the deal promises to ignite an intense legislative battle in Washington over the shape and future of financial services in America. It is also expected to speed the pace of merger activity across the financial landscape.

Competitors in Europe and Asia already have the ability to offer an array of banking and insurance products under one corporate umbrella. Now American companies are aggressively pushing for the same rights, in this case under the bright red umbrella that Travelers uses as its logo.

Travelers and Citicorp are betting that their profits and competitiveness would be enhanced by offering one-stop shopping for a broad range of services, from savings and checking accounts, credit cards, mortgages, stock and bond underwriting, homeowners, auto and life insurance, asset management, mergers and acquisitions advice, commercial loans, and derivative securities and foreign exchange trading.

Citicorp's chief executive, John S. Reed, and Travelers' chief executive, Sanford I. Weill, would jointly run the new company, to be called Citigroup Inc. "Frankly, we're probably talking about a restructuring of the financial services industry," Mr. Reed said of the agreement.

But it is not quite that simple. The transaction would have to negotiate a maze of regulations governing the banking industry that were put in place precisely to prevent the creation of the type of company Travelers and Citicorp now aim to put together. Those laws were enacted in response to public concerns about unfettered financial power and the economic consequences when such giants collapse.

Assuming that legal barriers are overcome—Mr. Reed and Mr. Weill said they believed that Federal Reserve officials were kindly disposed toward the transaction but regulators at the Comptroller of the Currency still have to weigh in—there are other sizable hurdles the merged company would face. Chief among those is the challenge of running a global company that would have revenues of about $50 billion, assets of $700 billion and a market capitalization of more than $140 billion.

The new company would vault ahead of other global financial giants, including Bank of Tokyo-Mitsubishi Ltd. and Deutsche Bank A.G., both of which already offer the menu of financial products that Citicorp and Travelers are trying to put together. The size of the deal would easily eclipse the largest merger agreement to date, Worldcom's bid to acquire MCI Communications for $37 billion.

The merger of Citicorp and Travelers "creates a big firm but they still have to do

It was the largest merger ever, but the real significance of the deal that formed Citigroup in 1998 was that it showed just how far the Depression-era rules on financial services had been eroded. The company, formed by the merger of Citicorp and Travelers Group, was in virtually every type of financial business conceivable, from insurance to banking to stock underwriting. Fearful that such interlocked companies could both abuse customers and create a crisis if one or the other part got into financial trouble, Congress had separated the businesses by law in the Glass-Steagall Act passed in 1933.

By 1998, regulators had carved loophole after loophole in that law. Companies that owned banks could also own brokerage houses, as long as the firms were not too large relative to the bank. That meant that Salomon Smith Barney, one of the largest brokerages in the country, could become a sister company to Citibank. But there was still a ban against banks merging with companies that underwrote property and casualty insurance, although the merged company could get a temporary waiver. In merging, Citicorp and Travelers were betting that Congress would act before that waiver expired. If not, they might have to sell part of the company.

1990–1999

THE HISTORY

By KENNETH N. GILPIN

They are two of the most venerable names in American capitalism, but Citicorp and Travelers Group have taken decidedly different paths to the pinnacle of the financial services business.

Citicorp first opened its doors at 52 Wall Street as the City Bank of New York on Sept. 14, 1812, only months after the War of 1812 had begun. It has had only one significant merger in its 186-year history, when it joined forces with the First National Bank in 1955.

If Citicorp, today the nation's second-largest bank holding company behind Chase Manhattan, is a byproduct of nearly two centuries of American and world economic history, Travelers is the work-in-progress of Sanford I. Weill, the Wall Street executive who since 1986 has transformed a string of ailing financial companies into powerhouses.

Since its creation, Citicorp has profited from booms and has been the leader among American banks in overseas expansion. In 1929 it became the first bank to open a personal loan department.

But the bank is no stranger to adversity. Citicorp has endured market panics, two World Wars, the Depression and, more recently, two financial events that nearly brought the franchise to its knees: the Latin American debt crisis and a mountain of bad loans in commercial real estate.

At its nadir in the early 1990's, Citicorp stock could be bought for $8.50. The shares closed at $142.875 last Friday, before soaring $37.625 yesterday, to $180.50.

Before December 1993, when the current Travelers took shape through his acquisition of the insurer by that name, Mr. Weill was the chairman of a decidedly less august-sounding enterprise, the Primerica Corporation. Primerica then consisted of the Commercial Credit Corporation, an ailing consumer-loan business Mr. Weill had bought in 1986 from the Control Data Corporation, and Smith Barney, Harris Upham & Company, the investment bank.

The Travelers, as it was then known, was founded in 1864 by J. G. Batterson, a Connecticut businessman, and wrote its first insurance policy in a Hartford post office. In 1897, the Travelers sold the first automobile policy. In 1919, it issued the first air travel policy, to President Woodrow Wilson.   [April 7, 1998]

something with what they've got," said Peter Davis, a financial services consultant with Booz Allen & Hamilton. "The challenge is managing a financial service conglomerate, adding on new retail distribution and expanding investment banking internationally."

The transaction would also combine two companies with very different cultures and chief executives. Although Citicorp is much more aggressive than some of its peers, it still tends to fit the profile of a cautious buttoned-down bank. Travelers, by contrast, is marked by the entrepreneurial style of its chief executive.

As recently as the early 1990's, Citicorp, currently the nation's second-largest bank after the Chase Manhattan Corporation, was teetering on the brink of insolvency as piles of bad real estate and Latin American loans threatened to swamp the company.

Citicorp, and other big banks caught in the same perilous position, pulled through the crisis largely because of a generous interest-rate environment engineered by the Federal Reserve chairman, Alan Greenspan. Mr. Greenspan kept interest rates unusually low, allowing banks to borrow money cheaply and lend at higher rates while they worked to get rid of bad loans.

Citicorp eventually recovered and by the mid-1990's it had emerged as one of the most competitive and profitable banks in the country. The 59-year-old Mr. Reed, as able a corporate survivor as there is among prominent chief executives, managed to keep the bank's board in his corner by never permitting a strong No. 2 to stay very long at Citicorp.

Under Mr. Reed's direction, Citicorp in recent years has emphasized its global consumer business, which includes such things as credit cards and savings accounts, while decreasing the bank's involvement in domestic wholesale businesses like corporate lending. Overseas, however, Citicorp still focuses its energies on corporate lending, because the bank has a competitive advantage in many emerging markets. In 1997, Citicorp had profits of $3.6 billion on revenue of $23.3 billion

For Mr. Weill, a dapper, thick-set executive who, at 65, keeps in shape riding a knobby-tired bicycle through the woods of his weekend home in upstate New York, the deal capped nearly 40 years of scrappy, Wall Street deal-making. He has built a huge personal fortune, but he has talked for years not only of making money but also of building a company with worldwide impact. He took a step in that direction last September with the purchase of Salomon Brothers for $9 billion.

Sanford I. Weill, left, chairman of Travelers, and John S. Reed, chairman of Citicorp.

Last year, with Salomon under its wing for the final quarter, Travelers reported net income of $3.1 billion on $27.1 billion in revenues.

More than half of Travelers' revenue comes from consumer finance, individual investments, investment banking and bond underwriting and trading. It sells life insurance and annuities through two subsidiaries, including Primerica Financial Services, which specializes in term or basic insurance without investment features. Travelers is the sixth-largest property and casualty insurer in the country, selling auto, homeowners and commercial coverage, with $8.6 billion in premiums last year.

Although analysts have been concerned about Citicorp's continued exposure to economic turmoil in Southeast Asia, Mr. Weill was briefed on the bank's prospects there and said he was not concerned that he was taking on any undue risk by merging with the company. Indeed, he said Citicorp's broad international presence, almost unmatched among American banks, was attractive to Travelers, which has been looking for ways to expand abroad. As for Travelers, it offers Citicorp a way to build on its securities and insurance offerings.

Investors appeared to share the executives' favorable assessment; the stock of Citicorp soared yesterday, rising $37.625 to close at $180.50. Travelers stock rose $11.3125, to $73.

With its suggestion that regulatory barriers might be forced down, yesterday's transaction resounded like a starter's pistol to some analysts, signaling the beginning of a great race for the country's insurance companies.

The prospective merger partners proved to be politically astute, quietly lobbying banking regulators and government officials for their tacit support before they announced the deal. This included a conversation by Mr. Weill and Mr. Reed with President Clinton on Sunday night to brief him on the transaction. And Mr. Weill and Mr. Reed kept their negotiations largely between themselves, helping to keep the transaction a secret until yesterday's announcement. No investment bankers were retained.

Big job cuts are not expected to be part of the merger, although there will undoubtedly be a serious winnowing of senior management ranks at the combined company. The transaction will be effected through a merger of Citicorp into Travelers, and Travelers plans to apply to the Federal Reserve to become a bank holding company.

Under the Bank Holding Company Act, enacted in the 1950's, all existing businesses, including insurance, can be retained and operated by the combined company for two years, a period that can then be extended by the Federal Reserve for three additional one-year periods. Citicorp and Travelers said they plan to reassess their options once that five-year dispensation ends, but in the meantime they will undoubtedly push hard to change existing laws.

Congress has so far been unable to overhaul the Glass-Steagall Act, the 1933 law separating commercial and investment banking, but bank regulators have moved independently over the last decade to erode the act's limitations. [April 7, 1998]

1990–1999

Deal Is Concluded on Netscape Sale to America Online

The Internet had been around for years, used largely by scientists and engineers, before it suddenly blossomed into the most important technological tool of the age. More and more people began buying items, trading stocks and accessing information over the Internet, and the stocks of companies that had virtually anything to do with the Internet became very hot in the late 1990's.

In 1995, The Times reported on the rapid growth of the Internet, and in 1998 it reported on the merger of America Online, the largest Internet access company, with Netscape, the company that had pioneered the software that made the Internet accessible to most computer users. They hoped that the combination would enable them to become the premier Internet company in the next century. To many, the merger looked like a defensive strategy by two companies worried about being eclipsed by the power of Microsoft.

By STEVE LOHR and JOHN MARKOFF

Envisioning a networked world in which the Internet is a limitless marketplace of information, entertainment, products and services, America Online Inc. laid out the details of an agreement, formally announced yesterday, to buy the Netscape Communications Corporation for $4.2 billion.

By moving quickly toward what both companies have recently come to see as the inevitable convergence of technology and media, America Online hopes that it will secure a solid lead in a battle already joined by giants like the Microsoft Corporation and the International Business Machines Corporation to transform the greater part of cyberspace into a vast virtual mall.

Part of that vision rests on an alliance with Sun Microsystems that America Online negotiated as part of the deal. Sun not only brings a cyber-savvy sales force to the effort but, even more important, a strong technology partner in developing Netscape's industrial-strength software for running Internet sites.

Sun is indeed a technology heavyweight. It owns the Java programming language, which is specially designed for Internet applications, and Solaris, which is among the most popular commercial operating systems for the powerful computers that big corporations use to serve up Internet services like the World Wide Web, E-mail and retail transactions. It also manufactures a highly respected line of powerful computers based on its own microprocessor chips.

But for America Online—and for the big Internet players against which it will compete—the real potential gold mine lies farther down the road, perhaps five years away, when people will venture on line for information or shopping not only from personal computers but also from inexpensive Internet appliances costing $200 each, pagers, cell phones and television set-top boxes.

Today, being wired remains a comparatively elitist activity—an estimated 25 percent of American households had access to the Internet last year, and 5 percent of households bought merchandise on line. But the executives at America Online and Netscape hope that their deal will accelerate the timetable for the day when the Net is ubiquitous.

"A new generation of Internet devices to be able to deliver our service anywhere is a key part of what this deal is about in the long run," said Stephen M. Case, the 40-year-old chairman of America Online.

For the present, however, the idea is to make America Online, the nation's leading on-line service, the standard way to get onto the Internet, the executives explained. Netscape, the Internet pioneer, is a crucial part of that effort, they said.

There is, to be sure, no assurance that this vision will prove accurate or, even if it does, that the America Online-Netscape combination will lead the way.

Still, it helped bring America Online and Netscape together. And the ability of the companies' executives to sell that vision to Netscape's whiz-kid programmers in particular will determine whether the merger succeeds.

Netscape's headquarters in Mountain View, Calif., will likely become a prime target for Silicon Valley headhunters. As is the case with any software company, Netscape's key asset is its talented programmers, many of whom may be reluctant to work for America Online, which they see as a middle-brow service catering to the on-line newcomers they derisively call "newbies."

"But these people want to change the world, and we've got to be clear that joining with America Online, along with the Sun component, really is a bigger opportunity for us," said Marc Andreessen, the 26-year-old co-founder of Netscape who led a team of young programmers from the supercomputing center at the University of Illinois to Silicon Valley to start the company in 1994.

Stephen M. Case, chairman of America Online.

"This ought to be the pre-eminent Internet company over the next decade," Mr. Andreessen declared, speaking from a cell phone on a street corner in Palo Alto, Calif.

Netscape, populated with computing sophisticates, and America Online, known as an Internet on-ramp for the technologically challenged, seem a corporate odd couple. But the two companies, its executives said, have been evolving toward each other for more than a year.

In a telephone interview from America Online's headquarters in Dulles, Va., Mr. Case described Netscape as an enterprise that had "morphed itself" from a dependency on sales of its software for browsing the Web—and "in Microsoft's cross-hairs"—into a reliance on advertising and other revenues from its popular Netcenter Web site and from selling Internet software to corporations.

The Netscape transformation was largely a reaction to Microsoft's competitive assault on its browser business—a central element in the Government's antitrust suit against Microsoft, which bundled its browser into its industry-standard Windows operating system, and also gave the browser away free.

After suffering a large loss last year and laying off workers early this year, Netscape announced that it would also distribute its browser free. It seems to have stabilized its business. Netscape announced yesterday that it earned $2.7 million on revenues of $162 million in its fourth fiscal quarter, ended in September.

Yet America Online has also changed in the last couple of years. Moving well beyond an on-line service for beginners, it now has an Internet chat service and runs its own all-in-one site on the Web, which includes E-mail, Internet searching, news, entertainment and on-line shopping.

"America Online has really changed from a closed on-line service for novice users to an Internet media and technology company with a diverse set of brands," Mr. Andreessen said. "These two companies have been moving in the same direction, and the fit is a good one."

The alliance with Sun is a related but separate agreement in which America Online agrees to purchase computer systems and services from Sun over the next three years worth $500 million at list price. From Sun, America Online will receive more than $350 million in licensing, marketing and advertising fees over the next three years as well as "significant minimum revenue commitments," a statement said.

The arrangement with Sun was crucial to calm Netscape's corporate software customers, from Citibank to Chrysler, concerned with entrusting a software business to America Online. Sun's sales force of 7,000 will now sell Netscape software, a big increase over Netscape's 700 people.

Still, it remains to be seen how well the arrangement with Sun will work. The appeal of Netscape's software for many corporate customers is that it works with many different computer operating systems, including Microsoft's Windows and Sun's Solaris. Whether Sun's sales force will favor versions tailored for its own operating system is an issue, analysts say.

"The danger in this deal is that America Online could completely fumble the software side of the Netscape business, and the big beneficiary would be Microsoft," said George F. Colony, president of Forrester Research Inc., a research firm.

[Nov. 25, 1998]

Marc Andreessen, co-founder of Netscape.

1990–1999

IF MEDIUM IS THE MESSAGE, THE MESSAGE IS THE WEB

By JOHN MARKOFF

SAN FRANCISCO, Nov. 19—The Associated Press was formed in the mid-19th century when a group of newspapers decided to invest jointly in a newfangled medium—the telegraph—to speed the collection and dissemination of information.

Last week, A.P. announced that it would adopt a newer-fangled medium—the World Wide Web—to begin distributing its articles and photographs over the global Internet. It was simply the latest, but perhaps most historically significant, move yet by an old-line media organization into the World Wide Web, the Internet multimedia information-retrieval system that appears on the verge of becoming a mass medium itself.

If the medium is the message, then the message these days is the World Wide Web.

In short order the Web, which three years ago was little more than a research tool for physicists and computer hobbyists, has flourished. It is being embraced by media concerns, consumer-product companies and businesses of various stripes that are creating thousands of so-called Web sites each month, with the number of computers playing host to one or more of these sites already exceeding 100,000.

Conservative estimates place the number of people who have used the Web in the millions, and it is not hard to find more breathless estimates in the tens of millions.

Capable of letting people use computers to send and receive text, sound, still images and video clips, the Web incorporates elements of the various print and electronic media that have preceded it. And yet, the Web is poised not to replace its predecessors but to take a place alongside them as a social, cultural and economic force in its own right.

Its complementary role is already evident: many radio stations and all the major television networks have Web sites promoting their programs and stars. Newspapers, including The New York Times, are devising cyberspace editions.

And few movies anymore are released without a promotional Web site, including "Goldeneye," the James Bond film that opened this weekend at theaters everywhere and on the Web at the address http://www.mgmua.com/bond. The site offers the movie's theme song performed by Tina Turner, more than a dozen video clips from the film and illustrated biographies of the cast members.

Prime-time television commercials by Toyota and other advertisers now routinely include a Web address. And Procter & Gamble, whose advertising has long helped underwrite the mass media, has even staked out prime Web real estate by reserving addresses that include flu.com and toiletpaper.com.

"We are poised on the edge of a new medium," Clay Felker, director of the magazine program at the University of California at Berkeley's graduate journalism school, said. "And it's going to change the nature of how we acquire information."

As with each mass medium that has arrived before it, the Web has reached this threshold through a confluence of a key technology, a ready audience and a stream of corporate backers willing to bet that profitable businesses can be built on it. But few experts are willing to declare that the Web has taken its place in the mass media pantheon because the profitable business formulas have yet to be found.

Newspapers and magazines make money by selling individual copies, subscriptions and advertising space. Radio and television stations sell air time to those with money and a message. Movie theaters sell tickets. But on the Web so far, despite seed-money by adventurous advertisers and some tentative efforts to charge for access to sites or services, there is no certainty that this

Tim Berners-Lee, Web mastermind.

ASSOCIATED PRESS

medium will achieve the critical mass that capitalism demands of its mass media.

"How do you make a business out of the World Wide Web?" asked Norman Pearlstine, editor in chief of Time Inc., which has an experimental Web site called Pathfinder that offers selected contents from the company's magazines (http://www.pathfinder.com). But because ad revenue alone is not carrying the freight, Time Inc. will begin testing ways to charge visitors to its site.

And yet, the technological prerequisites are firmly in place. The Web is an outgrowth of the Internet, which began as an academic research experiment in the late 1960's. For more than two decades the Internet remained largely inaccessible, used mainly by computer scientists and Pentagon researchers, university scholars and students.

Like the Internet, the Web began as a tool to let scientists easily and quickly share information. Conceived in the late 1980's by Tim Berners-Lee, who was then a software designer at CERN, the Swiss physics research center, the basic Web technology was first put to use in 1990.

The big breakthrough came in 1992, when student researchers at the National Center for Supercomputing Applications in Illinois created Mosaic, a simple software tool called a Web browser. Mosaic permitted access to information anywhere on the World Wide Web by letting the user point and click a computer mouse on highlighted words or images on the screen. The browser, which became available in commercial versions like Netscape Communications' Navigator, not only made Web sites easily accessible, it prompted businesses, organizations and even individuals to create new Web sites by the thousands.

Thus did the Web quickly become a standard and accepted way for the growing millions of the computer-literate to communicate and to entertain and inform themselves. And unlike each previous mass medium, the Web does not require its audience to be merely passive recipients of information.

One consequence of this democratization is that the Web can be a remarkably anarchic forum compared with the old-style mass media. "Think of this as television colliding with the telephone party line," said Paul Saffo, a computer industry consultant at the Institute for the Future, a Menlo Park, Calif., research firm. "In terms of social consequences, the Web is a great experiment. It's going to deliver us community with a vengeance—and we may find we don't want it." [Nov. 20, 1995]

Primer on Euro: From Birth to Growth as Unifying Force

By EDMUND L. ANDREWS

STRASBOURG, France, Dec. 29—This border city in Alsace-Lorraine has been French and then German and now French again, depending on who won the last war. But today it is a placid outpost in a more unified Europe: a home for the European Parliament, and a mecca for cross-border shoppers.

So it is not surprising that the European single currency, the euro, arrived here well before its official introduction this Friday. At the Cora supermarket, everything from bananas to televisions has been priced in euros (as well as in French francs) for months. At upscale restaurants like Roma, euro-pricing on menus is a fashion must.

And residents like Michel Raymond, who shops for Grand Marnier in France but for port wine in Germany, are opening euro checking accounts right after the New Year. "It will make things simpler for everybody," said Mr. Raymond, a retired French businessman. "Some things are cheaper here and others are cheaper on the German side. This will make the payments easier."

After decades of dreams, diplomacy and delays, the euro is suddenly real. On Thursday 11 European countries are to lock their exchange rates to the euro, now worth about $1.17, and cede to the new European Central Bank the power to set interest rates and monetary policy.

On the street it may look as if little has happened. But currency conversion represents the most important step in Europe's long quest for political unity. In getting to this point, the 11 euro nations for the first time have adopted a common economic policy that has reined in public spending, reduced debt and tamed inflation.

This achievement has seriously altered the political debate; indeed, governments in Germany, France and Italy have fallen in large part because of the spending cutbacks required to create the euro. Business strategy has been transformed, and more residents and visitors are thinking of Europe as a single place instead of a jigsaw of nationalities and a hodge-podge of currencies and laws.

Today's German marks, French francs, Italian lire and eight other currencies may be used for three and a half years more. (Euro notes and coins arrive on Jan. 1, 2002.) Local currencies are to be removed from circulation by July 1, 2002.

European stock and bond trades will be denominated entirely in euros, starting on Monday. All transactions between banks, which is frequently how Europeans pay their bills, will be in euros, even within the same country. Bank customers can write checks in euros, and many credit-card purchases will be calculated in euros. Euro travelers checks are coming.

Though Americans are largely bystanders, the euro will affect them, too.

At the start of 1999, 11 Western European countries embarked on the experiment of achieving monetary union without political union. They adopted the euro as a common currency, with rules that said that once a country joined the monetary union, it was in it for good.

In so doing, the countries gave up control of their own monetary policy to a European Central Bank. And they gave up the possibility of allowing any single currency to depreciate against the others—a relatively painless method of adjustment when an economy needs to reduce export prices to regain competitiveness.

In return, they got the certainty of assured exchange rates, meaning that a company in France could sign a contract with one in Italy with no more worry over currency risk than would be faced by a Massachusetts company dealing with one from Mississippi. And, some supporters of the euro hoped, the new system created a situation that would force countries to compete for companies as American states do, with tax breaks and other incentives that would reduce the costs of doing business.

As the euro was about to make its debut, The Times reviewed Europe's rationale in taking the step.

1990–1999

The euro: A bid for monetary union.

Travelers will be spared the necessity of changing dollars into different currencies, and currency risks will be reduced for money managers. That alone is expected to yield substantial savings.

The idea of a single currency dates back to the 1950's, when postwar diplomats like Jean Monnet, president of a precursor to the European Union, sketched out sweeping visions for economic and political unification. The idea was that the more each nation relied on the others for economic and political security, the more reluctant they would be to send their armies into battle.

But the real impetus came with the fall of the Berlin wall in 1989. The prospect of a reunited German power-house alarmed many Western European governments, and Francois Mitterrand, then the President of France, pressed his German counterpart, Helmut Kohl: France would support the reunification if Mr. Kohl would commit his Government to replacing the mark with a single currency administered by an independent central bank.

"After reunification, a lot of the neighbors around Germany were afraid that it might become politically and economically too strong," said Peter Wolf-Koppen, who oversees euro projects at Commerzbank in Frankfurt. "They first tried to make a political union, but they failed. A monetary union was the best they could do."

Mr. Kohl quickly became the euro's strongest champion, driven in part by memories of World War II.

"I have often been told that the euro was a techno-cratic idea, invented by finance ministers," remarked Christian Noyer, vice president of the European Central Bank. "That is clearly not the case. They had the simple idea that the money, the currency that people use every day, was a way to foster integration."

Two years after the fall of the wall, in the Dutch city of Maastricht, European leaders reached a basic accord, with a strongly German imprint. Countries would have to meet strict limits on deficits and would have to bring inflation down to Germany's level, about 3 percent.

But the Bundesbank, the influential German central bank, would take a back seat to an independent European Central Bank, which would focus on fighting inflation.

The euro's proponents argue that it will make Europe more efficient and competitive because pricing differences will stand out. Trade will be enhanced because foreign-exchange risks will be minimal. (Europe abolished most tariffs and other trade restrictions six years ago.)

But more important, supporters predict that the greater attention to prices will force cost-cutting by manufacturers. And while that may contribute to Europe's high unemployment, it may also initiate much-needed changes in costly regulations that hinder competitiveness today.

"This can work like a reform program for Europe, and be very good for the competitiveness of Europe," said Jurgen Stark, vice president of the Bundesbank. "On the one hand it is a great political challenge. But on the other it is a great opportunity for Europe to combine sound monetary and fiscal policy with more flexibility."

[Dec. 30, 1998]

Fight of the (Next) Century

CONVERGING TECHNOLOGIES PUT SONY AND MICROSOFT ON A COLLISION COURSE

By JOHN MARKOFF

SAN JOSE, Calif.—A battle for control of the future of computing is looming between the personal computer industry and consumer electronics manufacturers.

Its roots can be found in meetings like one held here in July 1995, shortly after Nobuyuki Idei became chief executive of the Sony Corporation. Briefing Mr. Idei on the importance of the Internet, Peter Sealey, a Sony consultant, noted that the year before, the dollar volume of PC sales had surpassed that of television sales in the United States for the first time.

"He stopped the meeting and challenged my data," Mr. Sealey recalled. "I think it was a shock to him that this had happened."

But if Mr. Idei's education about the rapidly expanding world of personal computing was abrupt, Sony's conversion to a digital products strategy has been complete.

For decades the world's pre-eminent consumer electronics maker, Sony has now realized that its core business is being profoundly transformed by digital electronics, in ways that pose both opportunities and threats.

In a huge strategic shift for a company that long relied on the elegance of its industrial design and the prestige of its brand name, Sony has come to recognize, its executives say, that a new era is arriving in which clever software, above all else, will determine whether products from televisions to telephones will succeed or fail in the marketplace.

That sets the stage for a grand confrontation. On one side are Sony and its peers in the consumer electronics business. On the other is the personal computer industry.

The Microsoft Corporation and the Intel Corporation, the twin engines of the PC world, are eagerly looking for new markets in which to expand. Beginning with the cable set-top box in the living room—a box they believe will bring the power of the Internet to tens of millions of TV viewers who do not now use computers—they have a vast range of Windows-based products on the drawing board, including toys, phones, even computers for the car that will do everything from read aloud your E-mail to help you with navigation.

Microsoft's strategy is to re-create the powerful business model of the personal computer industry in consumer electronics.

At the center would be Windows CE, a scaled-down version of the Windows desktop software that is now familiar mostly in palm-size computers, where it has been slow to win converts. It would be the foundation for tens of thousands of vibrant software applications and an intensely competitive market of hardware makers all vying to compete on price and performance.

Moreover, the PC itself would control an ever-expanding world of "smart" peripherals—TV's, audio systems, telephones, kitchen appliances and other electronic gadgets.

"This isn't the post-PC era; it's the PC-plus era," said Craig Mundie, Microsoft's senior vice president for consumer strategy. "The PC may be simpler to use in the future, but it will still broker lots of home services and control other smart appliances."

That vision presents a potentially grim future for Sony's $38 billion consumer electronics business. As a global standard setter, Sony has enjoyed high margins and big market shares. But the "PC-ization" of consumer electronics would most likely mean a world of increasing uniformity and low margins, like those that computer makers have experienced.

Sony's view of the digital future is far more decentralized. Its product designers sniff that the PC is the obsolete "mainframe" of the home. Instead, they envision

As the 21st century came into view, it seemed clear that computer technology was going to revolutionize a host of consumer products. But that raised the question of who would dominate that process: the companies that always made the consumer products in question, or the computer technology companies, which in practice meant Microsoft.

In 1999, The Times looked at the coming battle between Microsoft and the preeminent consumer electronics company, Sony. It was a curious battle, in which the two companies had announced a strategic alliance but were in fact developing very different strategies in hopes of dominating a market that both expected to expand dramatically in the new century.

1990–1999

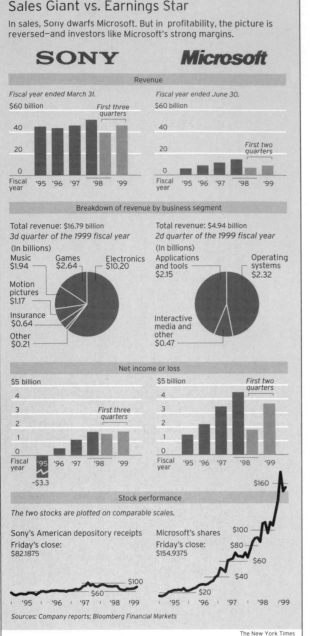

Sales Giant vs. Earnings Star

In sales, Sony dwarfs Microsoft. But in profitability, the picture is reversed—and investors like Microsoft's strong margins.

SONY · Microsoft

Revenue

Fiscal year ended March 31.
$60 billion — First three quarters
Fiscal year '95 '96 '97 '98 '99

Fiscal year ended June 30.
$60 billion — First two quarters
Fiscal year '95 '96 '97 '98 '99

Breakdown of revenue by business segment

Total revenue: $16.79 billion
3d quarter of the 1999 fiscal year
(In billions)
Music $1.94
Games $2.64
Electronics $10.20
Motion pictures $1.17
Insurance $0.64
Other $0.21

Total revenue: $4.94 billion
2d quarter of the 1999 fiscal year
(In billions)
Applications and tools $2.15
Operating systems $2.32
Interactive media and other $0.47

Net income or loss

$5 billion
Fiscal year '95 '96 '97 '98 '99 — First three quarters
-$3.3

$5 billion
Fiscal year '95 '96 '97 '98 '99 — First two quarters

Stock performance

The two stocks are plotted on comparable scales.

Sony's American depository receipts
Friday's close: $82.1875
$100 $60

Microsoft's shares
Friday's close: $154.9375
$160 $100 $80 $60 $40 $20

'95 '96 '97 '98 '99

Sources: Company reports; Bloomberg Financial Markets

The New York Times

---

homes in which dozens, even hundreds, of smart appliances are seamlessly interconnected, perhaps without a PC involved at all.

"Microsoft is going to have to change their business model to be effective in the world of consumer electronics," said Mario Tokoro, the computer scientist who is president of Sony's Information Technology Laboratories and a top adviser to Mr. Idei on computing and networking issues.

The system envisioned by Sony would let the consumer control a digital videocassette recorder from the television set, or vice versa—or control them both from a cellular phone. In recent demonstrations, the company has shown an integrated audio and video system tied together by I-Link, a high-speed digital connection to the cable box.

It will allow people to watch movies on demand, pause a live basketball game in mid-jump shot to go to the kitchen for a sandwich—then watch the rest of the game on delay—or transmit a home video to a friend on the other side of the country.

Moreover, the new Playstation II, introduced last week and scheduled to arrive in the United States next year, would connect to the network, serving as a digital versatile disk, or DVD, player, and perhaps even as a cable set-top box.

The collision of these competing visions has resulted in what one Sony executive calls a "strategic dance." Publicly, Sony has announced ambitious strategic alliances with Microsoft in the last two years to design consumer electronics products; quietly, it has been reshaping itself into what is likely to soon become Microsoft's most dangerous competitor.

"The relationship is fearful and respectful and wary," said Mr. Sealey, the consultant to Sony.

One measure of Sony's commitment to a digital future is that by the end of next year, it plans to employ an equal number of software and hardware engineers, according to Akikazu Takeuchi, president of Sony's Platform Software Development Center, which has recently built software laboratories in Japan, Europe and the United States.

The outlines of Sony's new software-centric strategy are already clear at the company's vast development and marketing center here in Silicon Valley.

A fast-growing group of software programmers are putting the finishing touches on a new operating system called Aperios, which is intended to control digital TV's, cellular phones, even robot "pets" that Sony plans to introduce later this year.

Aperios and Windows CE will face off for the first time later this year, too, as cable companies decide which operating system they will use in a new generation of set-top boxes that will bring interactive television to millions of homes.

Indeed, the introduction of the new cable boxes will be the first round in the struggle for dominance over the next generation of computing. And for Sony, its role as a leader in consumer electronics, an industry it virtually invented, is at stake.

Conventional wisdom in Silicon Valley has long been that for all its excellence in hardware design, Japan, for cultural reasons, has habitually lagged behind in software development, which benefits from free-spirited individualism.

Yet Sony's computer researchers defy the stereotypes. Regular visitors say the company's computer laboratory in Tokyo could easily be mistaken for one in San Jose or Santa Clara, right down to the comfortable beanbag chairs. And Mr. Tokoro, who heads the labs, is not only a well-respected researcher but also the acknowledged architect of the company's ambitious software strategy.

"It was one of the first Japanese labs that was an American-style lab, with open doors and no hierarchy," said David J. Farber, a professor of computer science at the University of Pennsylvania. "The young researchers there are happy to argue with Mario, which is unheard of in that culture."

Still, the arrival of Aperios will put Sony's commitment to computer software to the test. Moreover, the company has occasionally chased down technological blind alleys, most famously in the case of the Betamax. And until last year, when it re-entered the PC market with innovative, ultrathin laptops, it had failed consistently in personal computers and work stations.

Still, executives say Sony has made the important leap of recognizing that the very nature of its business has changed. "To Sony's credit, we now realize that our competitor is no longer Toshiba or Panasonic, but it's Microsoft and Dell," said one executive in the company's United States personal computer business, who spoke on the condition of anonymity.

And Sony has hard-won experience with the business model it is counting on for success in the software world.

The template is the company's conquest of the video-game business. In a bruising battle with Tokyo, Olaf Olafsson, then president of Sony's Interactive Entertainment division, persuaded the company to look for profits in software and licensing, and to sell the game hardware at cost.

The fight ultimately led Mr. Olafsson to resign in 1996. But the Sony Playstation became—and remains—a runaway hit in both the United States and Japan. Sony Computer, which is largely the Playstation business, provided 26.5 percent of Sony's operating profits in the first half of the current fiscal year.

Increasingly, Sony executives—like others in the consumer electronics industry—have come to realize that Microsoft covets markets that are not part of the traditional personal computer business. It already sells toys and games, and it is developing a growing array of smart consumer electronic gadgets.

Sony also recognizes the risk of relying on Microsoft to set software standards for the dawning age of digital consumer electronics. The broad agreements between Mr. Idei and William H. Gates, Microsoft's chief executive, to cooperate on a new generation of information appliances have so far gone nowhere.

"This is a love-and-hate relationship," Mr. Tokoro said. "Each of us has our own territory. But the computer people need consumer electronics markets to grow, and by cooperating with us they want to expand into our territory."

Microsoft executives, of course, have a comeback.

"Sony has been recognizing, begrudgingly, that the microprocessor is going to find its way into the traditional lines of business," said Mr. Mundie of Microsoft. "But the PC will remain an important launching pad for them."

[March 7, 1999]

Index

Page numbers of illustrations appear in italics.
An index of bylined writers follows this one.

A

ABC (American Broadcasting Company), 116, 259
African-Americans in business, 208–10, *208*
Air-conditioning industry, 8, 139, 158–59, *158*
Airplane and airline industry, 8, 11, 83, 264
    computerization of, 161
    deregulation of fares, 207
    jumbo jets, 187–88, *187*
    Lindbergh's solo flight, 112
    supersonic, 187
    trans-Atlantic commercial flights, 83, 112–13, *112*
    war effort, *114*
Alaskan oil, *168*, 193–94
Allied Stores, 4
American Can Company, 77
American Express Company, 204, 205
American Sugar Refining Company, 66
American Telephone & Telegraph Company (A.T.&T.) and Bell Labs
    bond yields, 1970's, 236
    breakup and Baby Bells, 262–64, *263*
    talking movies and, 71
    television and, 68–71
    transistor, 128
American Tobacco Company, 38, 65
America Online (AOL), 312–13, *312*
Amtrak, 211
Andreessen, Marc, 312–13, *313*
Antitrust. *See* Federal Government.
Antitrust Act (Sherman Antitrust Act), 11
    Microsoft, 307
    Northern Securities, 12, 20–21
    Standard Oil, 38–40
    U. S. Steel, 61, 65–66, *66*
Apple Computer Inc., 2, 265–66, 268, 269
Asia. *See also* Japan; Korea, South; Thailand.
    economic crisis, 1990's, 285, 299–300, 311
    Foreign Corrupt Practices Act and, 238–40
    stock market crash, 295
Automobile industry, 11, 35, 51. *See also*

Chrysler Corporation; Ford Motor Company; General Motors Corporation.
American Motors, 164, 165, 167
Dodge brothers, 78
imports, 139, 164, *164*, 167, 245, 298
small cars, 139, 164–67, *167*, 207, 231, 248
stock offerings, 156–57
stock speculation, 1920's, 78
strike and slowdown, Lordstown, 219–21, *220*
strike, sit-down, 103–6, *104, 105*
Studebaker-Packard, 164, 165
tax cut, 217
war effort, 119–22, *121, 122*
Avery, Sewell, 139, 153–54, *154*, 155, *155*
Avon Products, 191–92, *191*, 235

B

Bache Halsey Stuart Shields, 249, 50
Baer, George F., 15, 16
Bakers' Union No. 164, 23
Baltimore & Ohio Railroad, 39
Bank Holding Company Act, 311
Bank of America, 204
Banks, 11. *See also* Federal Reserve System; Glass-Steagall Banking Reform Act.
    Asian, 299–300
    ban on specific mergers, 309
    Citicorp-Travelers Group merger, 309–11
    competition, 236
    credit card industry, 204–5, *204*
    credit, unhealthy expansion of, 241, 243
    deposit guarantee, 48, 49, 83, 90, 278
    downsizing, 294
    European Central Bank, 315, 316
    global giants, 309
    holiday declared, 1933, 86–87, *87*
    Mexico-Latin American debt crisis, 245, 257–58, *257*
    Morgan, J. P., and, 41–44
    Panic of 1901 and, 14

Panic of 1907 and, 30–31
    reforms, 87, 88, 89, 90, 91
    savings and loan failures, 276–78
    stock market crash, 1929, 77, 81
    "too-big-to-fail" concept, 301
Barksdale, James L., 308
Baseball
    antitrust case, reserve system and Curt Flood, 222–23
    free agents, 207, 222, 224
    Turner, Ted, and, 260
Bell, Alexander Graham, 70
Bell Laboratories. *See* American Telephone & Telegraph Company.
Berners-Lee, Tim, 314
Bethlehem Steel, 181, 182, 183, 185, 186
Biotech industry, 251–53, *252*
Birdseye, Clarence, 61
Black, Eli M., 238, *240*
Black, Fischer, 301–2
Black-Scholes model, 302
Block, Joseph L., 181–82, *181*, 184, 185
Blough, Roger M., 177–79, *179*, 184, 185, 186
Blumenthal, W. Michael, 241, 242
Boeing, 112, *114*, 187–88, *187*
Boesky, Ivan, 286, 287–88
Bolton, Samuel, Jr., 14
Borden Inc., 279, 281
Brady Building, New York City, *10*
Bretton Woods, x, 7, 115, 125–26, *125*, 207, 218
Brown, Charles L., *263*
Buffett, Warren E., 304
Burns, Arthur F., 216
Bush, George, 257

C

Camdessus, Michel, *299*
Campeau, Robert, 4
Carrier Corporation, 158, 159
Carrier, Willis H., 8, 158
Carson, Rachel, 175–76, *175*
Carter, Jimmy, 207, 231, 233–34, *233*, 241, 242, 246
Case, Stephen M., 312–13, *312*
CBS (Columbia Broadcasting System)

cable, 259
downsizing, 294
radio, 67, 116–18, *116*
Records, 282–83
television, 144
Cetus Corporation, 252
Chakrabarty, Ananda M., 251, *252*
Chanel, Gabrielle (Coco), 8, 72–74, *73*
Chase National Bank, 94–96
Chevron Corporation, 279
Chicago, Burlington & Quincy
    Railroad, 12
Chicago Board Options Exchange, 301,
    302
Chrysler Corporation, 157
    bailout, 245, 246–48, *248*
    merger with Daimler-Benz, 246
    small cars, 164–67
CIT Financial Corporation, 195, 197
Citicorp, 310
    -Travelers Group merger, 309–11,
    310
Civil rights movement, 169, 208
Clifford, Clark, 184–86, *184*
Clinton, Bill, 285, 291, 311
Clocks, and radio competition, 68
CNN, 259–61, *261*, 289
Coal
    industry, Great Depression, 86, 89,
    92–93
    strike, 15–16, *16*
Coca-Cola Company, 270–71, *270*, 282
Columbia Pictures Entertainment Inc.,
    282–83
Communism in America, 134
Computer industry, 245. *See also* Apple;
    I.B.M.; Microsoft.
    antitrust case, Microsoft, 1, 265,
    307–8
    boom, 1980's, *244*, 245, 265–69
    business use, 139, 160–61, *161*, 169
    consumer electronics industry and,
    283, 317–19
    early (Eniac), 115, 127–29, *128*
    PC sales surpass televisions, 317
Conglomerates. *See* Corporate takeovers
    and mergers.
Conrail, 211
Consumer electronics, 282–83, 317–19.
Continental Illinois Bank, 301
Corporate takeovers and mergers,
    195–99, *195, 196, 199. See also*
    specific corporations.
    AOL-Netscape, 312–13, *312, 313*

Citicorp-Travelers Group merger,
    309–11, *310*
    leveraged buyout, RJR Nabisco,
    279–81, *279, 281*
    proxy battles, 147–48, 153–54
    raiders, 286
Cravath, Paul D., 62, 64
Credit cards, 204–5, *204*
Currency
    Act of 1913, 48–50
    Asian crisis, 1990's, 285, 299–300
    "Big Mac" index, 190
    Bretton Woods and dollar stability,
    115, 125–26, *125*, 207, 218
    dollar devalued, 86, 97, 207, 216–18
    euro, 315–16, *315*
    floating exchange rates, 125, 216, 218
    gold-dollar link severed, 216–18
    gold payment stopped, 86, 97–98

D

Daimler Chrysler, 246
Dell Computer Corporation, 308
Dell, Michael S., 308
Derivatives, 301–2, 304
Dirks, Raymond L., 227–30, *229*
Disney, Walt, 99–102, *99, 101*
Disneyland, 102
Donaldson, Lufkin & Jenrette, Inc.
    (D.L.J.), 202–3
Douglas Aircraft, 112, 187, 188
Douglas, William O., 94
Downsizing. *See* Economy, U.S.;
    Employment.
Drexel Burnham Lambert, 286, 287, 288
Du Pont (E. I. du Pont de Nemours &
    Company), 110–11, 252

E

Eastman, George, 131
"Economic Consequences of the Peace,
    The" (Keynes), 62–64
Economy, U.S.
    bank holiday declared, 86–87, *87*
    Bretton Woods and dollar stability,
    115, 125–26, *125*, 207, 216
    budget deficits, 256
    business booms, 139, 169
    dollar devalued, 86, 97, 207, 216–18
    downsizing of labor, 1990's, 245, 248,
    285, 292–94, *293*
    farming, 61

    foreign loans, 59, *See also* Deriva-
    tives; Mexico-Latin American
    debt crisis
    glossary of terms, 255
    gold-dollar link severed, 216–18
    gold payment stopped, 86, 97–98
    Great Depression, 61, *82, 83*, 84, 88–91
    inflation, 115, 123, 169, 177, 179, 207,
    216–18, 235, 241–43, 245, 254–56,
    275, 285
    interest rates, 235–37, 241–43, 245,
    254–56, 257, 275, 276, 277, 285
    manufacturing, 61
    Panic of 1901, 11, 12, 14
    Panic of 1907, 11, 30–31
    recession, 1970's–80's, 235, 241, 245,
    254–56
    savings and loan failures, 1980's,
    276–78
    stock market crash, 1929, 77–81, *78,*
    79, 80, 273
    stock market crash, 1987, 245, 272–75,
    274, 305
    "supply-side," 256
    tariffs on imports reduced, 45–46
    Thrift Stamps and Liberty Bonds, 59
    unemployment, 254, 285
    wage and price controls, 123–24,
    216–18, 254
    World War I and prosperity, 56–59
Education, business, 32–33, *33*, 200–201,
    210
Eisenhower, Dwight D., 139
Electrical equipment industry, price-
    fixing, 170–72, *172*
Elevators, 10, 11, 24, 25, *25*, 26
Employment. *See also* Great Depression;
    Labor.
    cuts in corporate work force
    (downsizing), 245, 248, 285,
    292–94, *293*
    Japan, 295–98
Environmental regulations, 175
Equitable Life Assurance Society build-
    ing, New York City, 24, 26, 41
Equity Funding Corporation of
    America, 227–30, *229*
Erie Railroad, 16, 39
Euro. *See* Currency; Europe.
Europe. *See also specific countries;* World
    War I; World War II.
    currency (euro), 315–16, *315*
    Foreign Corrupt Practices Act and,
    238–40

Europe *(cont.)*
  loans extended to, 59
  post-World War II rebuilding, 139
  Treaty of Versailles and German
    reparations, x, 61, 62–64
  Union, 315–16
European Central Bank, 315, 316

F

Farmers, 61
  drought of 1930's (dust bowl), 83
  Federal programs, 83, 86, 90
Federal Communications Commission
  (F.C.C.), 116–18, 264
Federal Government. *See also* Federal
  Reserve System.
  antitrust activities, 11, 12, 20–21,
    38–40, 41–44, 61, 65–66, 170–172,
    265, 307–8
  bank deposits guaranteed and bank-
    ing reforms, 83, 86, 87, 88, 89, 90, 91
  Brady bonds, 257
  Chrysler bailout, 245, 246–48, *248*
  Currency Act of 1913, 48–49
  deregulation of business, 207, 231,
    233–34, *234*, 276
  dollar devalued, 97
  Environmental Protection Agency, 175
  Foreign Corrupt Practices Act, 238
  gold payments suspended, 86, 97–98
  income tax instituted, 35, 46–47
  labor union regulation, 115, 132–34,
    132, 150
  "lemon" socialism, 245
  meat inspection bill, 27–28
  Mexico-Latin American debt crisis,
    245, 257–58, *257*
  minimum wage established, 83
  National Labor Relations Board
    (N.L.R.B.), 132–34
  National Recovery Administration
    (N.R.A.), and New Deal, 86,
    88–91, 92–93
  price-fixing charges by, 169, 170–72
  Resolution Trust Corporation (sav-
    ings and loan bailout), 276–78
  S.E.C. established, 94–96, 107
  Social Security Act, 83
  tariff bill passed, 45–46
  wage-price freeze, 1940's, 123–24;
    1970's, 216–18, 254
Federal Home Loan Bank Board, 276–78
Federal Reserve System, x, 5, 11, 30,

48–50, 55. *See also* Burns, Arthur
  F.; Greenspan, Alan; Miller, G.
  William; Volcker, Paul A.
  anti-inflation monetary strategy, 207,
    241–43, 245, 254–56, 277
  Bank Holding Company Act, 311
  banking reform and, 86–87, 90, 91
  creation of, 11, 30, 48–50, 55
  deregulation of ceiling on bank
    interest, 277–78
  Citicorp-Travelers Group merger,
    309–11, *310*
  hedge fund bailout, 301, 303–4
  stock crash of 1929 and, 77
  stock crash of 1987 and, 273
  success of, 1990's, 285
  "too-big-to-fail" concept, 301
Federal Trade Commission, anti-Joe
  Camel, 291
Federated Department Stores, 4
Flint, Michigan, 103, 106
Flood, Curt, 222–223, *222*
Food industry. *See also* Borden Inc.;
  Kraft Foods; Nabisco.
  frozen products, 61
  McDonald's, 169, 189–90, *189*
  meat inspection bill, 27–28, *28*
Ford, Edsel B., 53, 119, 157
Ford, Gerald, 207
Ford, Henry, 4, 35, 51–54, 119–20, 156, *156*,
  157. *See also* Ford Motor Company.
Ford, Henry, II, 156, *156*
Ford Motor Company
  assembly lines, Highland Park,
    Michigan, *34, 53*
  Ford's Model T, 51
  profit sharing, 35, 51–54
  public stock offering, 156–57
  small cars, 164–67, *167*
  wages, 35, 51, 54, 122
  war effort, 119–22, *121, 122*
  workday, 35, 51
Foreign Corrupt Practices Act, 238
France, 62–64, 75–76. *See also* Europe.
Franklin Simon Company, 204, 205

G

Galbraith, John Kenneth, 273
Gasoline shortages, 1970's, *206*, 207, 231,
  234
Gates, William H., ix, 1, 2, 3, 265,
  266–69, *267*, 307–8, *307*, 319
Genentech Corporation, 253

General Electric Company (G.E.), 144,
  145, 157, 161, 170–72, 209
General Motors Corporation (G.M.),
  61, 139, 157, 307
  small cars, 164–67, *167*, 248
  strikes against, 103–6, *104, 105*, 219,
    220
Genex Corporation, 251
Germany. *See also* Europe.
  Bundesbank, 316
  depreciation of currency, 75–76, *75,
    76*
  economy, 1980's, 273, 275
  European Union, 315–16
  Treaty of Versailles and reparations,
    x, 61, 62–64
  World War I, *56*, 58
Gibson Greeting Cards, 4
Glass, Carter, 48–50, *50*
Glass-Steagall Banking Reform Act, 88,
  89, 91, 309, 311
Goizueta, Roberto C., 270–71
Gold
  -dollar link severed, 216–18
  market and prices, 245, 249, 285
  payment-clause suspended, 86, 97–98
  standard, 97
Goldberg, Arthur J., 178–79, 184, 186
Goldman, Sachs & Company, ix, 304, 306
Grayson, Paul, 3, 269
Great Depression, 61, *82*, 83, *84*, 88–91,
  207, 273, 276, 292, 309
Great Northern Railroad, 12, 20–21
Greenspan, Alan, 285, 310
GTE Sprint, 263
Gulf Oil Company, 238, 279

H

Harding, Warren, 67
Harriman, Edward H., 2, 3, 12, 13, *14*
Harvard University, Graduate School of
  Business Administration, 32–33,
  32, 33, 200–201
Hedge funds, 301, 303–4
Heller, Walter, 178, 179, 180, 181, 182, 184
Hill, James J., 2, 12, 13
Hitler, Adolf, 75, 83
Hoover, Herbert, 67, 68–70, *69*, 83,
  84–85, 207
Housing, *138*, 158–59, 209, 254, 276
Hula-Hoop, 162–63, *162, 163*
Hunt, Nelson Bunker and W. Herbert,
  and silver market, 249–50, *249*

I

Iacocca, Lee A., 246–48, *248*
I.B.M. (International Business Machines Corporation), 8, 129, 160–161, 208, 209, 245, 265–69, 283
Idei, Nobuyuki, 317–19
Income tax, 35, 46–47
Inland Steel Corporation, 181, 182, 184, 185, 186
Insurance industry
    Citicorp-Travelers Group merger, 309–11, *310*
    scandal, 227–30, *229*
Interest rates, 235–37, 241–43, 245, 254–256, 257, 275, 276, 277, 285
International Monetary Fund (I.M.F), 125, 218, 243, 299–300, *299*
International Telephone and Telegraph Company (I.T.T.), 195–97, 240
Internet, 8, 262, *284*, 307–8, 317–19. *See also* Microsoft.
    AOL-Netscape merger, 312–13
    World Wide Web (WWW), 314
Interstate commerce, 11, 17–19, 39
Iran, 173, *234*
Iraq, 173–74, 232, 255
Isolationism, 58, 115
Israel, oil embargo and, 231–32, 255

J

Japan. 282, 295–98. *See also* Sony.
    cars, 164, 245, 298
    competition with American companies, 135, 137, 143, 317–19
    decline in economy, 1990's, 8, 275, 285, 295–98
    employment and downsizing, 295–98
    lifetime job, 298
    mergers and buyouts of American companies, 282–83
    post–World War II rebuilding, 139
    stock market, 245, 282, 295, 296, *296*
Japan Tobacco, 281
Jobs, Steven P., 2, 265–66, *265*, 269
Johnson, F. Ross, 279, 280
Johnson, John H., 208, 210
Johnson, Lyndon B., 169, 254
Jones & Laughlin, 181, 185, 195
"Jungle, The" (Sinclair), 27, 28–29, *28*

K

Kaiser Steel, 181, 182, 186
Keating, Charles H., Jr., 276, 278
Kennedy, John F., 6, 94, 169, 177–86, *178*
Kennedy, Joseph P., 94, 177, 178, 182–83
Kennedy, Robert F., *179*, 184, 185
Keynes, John Maynard, 61, 62–64, *63*, 125–26, *125*
Khashoggi, Adnan M., 239
Kohlberg, Kravis, Roberts & Company, 4, 279–81, *279*
Korea, South
    consumer electronics industry, 283
    economic recovery, 299
Kraft Foods, 281
Kravis, Henry R., 279–81, *279*
Kroc, Ray, 189–90
Kuwait, 173–74, 231–2

L

Labor. *See also specific labor unions.*
    A.F.L.-C.I.O. merger, 150–52, *150*, *151*
    auto slowdown and strike, Lordstown, 1970's, 219–21, *220*
    auto strike, sit-down, 103–6, *104*, *105*
    baseball, reserve system, 222–24, *222*, *224*
    coal strike, 15–16, *16*
    Committee for Industrial Organization, 103
    Congress of Industrial Organizations (C.I.O.), 103, 150–52
    downsizing and, 245, 248, 285, 292–94, *293*
    minimum wage, 83
    rail strike, 115
    regulation of, 115, 132–34, *132*, *133*, 150
    steel strike, 140–42, *142*
    steel wage offer, and Kennedy, 177–86
    Supreme Court strikes down limiting workday, 11, 22–23
    sweatshops, 35, 36
    Triangle Waist Company fire, 35, 36–37, *36*
    wages, 16, 33, 35, 51, 52, 54, 103, 121, 219
    women and, 121, *121*
    working hours, 22–23, 35, 51, 90
Land, Edwin H., 130–31, *130*
Landrum-Griffin Act, 150
Leveraged buyout, 279
Levittown, New York, *138*
Levittown, Pennsylvania, 158
Lewis, John L., 103, 105
Life magazine demise, 225–26, *226*
Lincoln Savings and Loan, 276, 278
Ling, James J., 195, 198–99, *199*
Ling-Temco-Vought (LTV), 195, 196–97, 198–99, *199*
Lochner's bakery, Utica, New York, 22–23, *23*
Long-Term Capital Management fund, 301, 303–4
Lottery ticket suit (*Champion v. Ames*), 17–19

M

Marconi, Guglielmo, *118*
McColough, C. Peter, 137
McDonald's Corporation, 169, 189–90, *189*
MCI Communications Corporation, 262–63, *264*
McNally, Dave, 222, 224, *224*
McNealy, Scott, 308
Meany, George, 150, 151, *151*
Meat inspection bill, 27–28, *28*, *29*
Meatpacking industry, 27–29, *28*, *29*
Media. *See also* Radio; Television.
    African-American owned, 210
    Life magazine demise, 225–26, *226*
    World Wide Web (WWW), 314
Meriwether, John W., 303–4, *303*
Merrill Lynch, Pierce, Fenner & Smith, ix, 250, 304
Merton, Robert C., 301–2, *303*
Messersmith, Andy, 222, 224, *224*
Metropolitan Life tower, New York City, 24–26, *25*
Mexico-Latin American debt crisis, 245, 257–58, *257*
Mickey Mouse, 99–102, *99*
Micrografx, 3, 269
Microsoft Corporation, 1, 6, 8, 245, 265, 266–69, *267*, *307*, 312. *See also* Gates, William H.
    antitrust suit, 307–8
    Sony and, 317–19
Milken, Michael, 9, 286–88, *288*
Miller, G. William, 241, 242
Mobil Oil Corporation, 231, 234
Montgomery Ward & Co., 139, 153–55, *155*
Morgan, J. P., ix, 1, 2, 11, 12, *12*, 16, 20, 21, 30–31, 35, 41–44, *42*, 48, 65

Morgan, J. P., & Co., 13, 30, 31, 41, 107, 304
Morgan, Junius, 2
Morgan Stanley, ix, 237
Morita, Akio, 282–83, *282*
Movies
    Columbia Pictures buyout, 282–83
    Disney and, 99–102, *99, 101*
    talking, 61, 67, 71
Mutual funds, 6, 305–306

N
Nabisco, 279, 281, *281*
Nader, Ralph, 164
National Recovery Administration
    (N.R.A.), 86, 88–91, 92–93
NBC (National Broadcasting Company)
    cable television, 259
    color television, 144–146
    radio, 67, 116–18, *116, 118*, 144
Netscape Communications, 307–8,
    312–13, *312, 313*, 314, *314*
New York Central Railroad, 3, 39, 139,
    147–48, *147*, 149, *149*, 211
New York City
    Great Depression in, *82*
    skyscrapers, *10*, 24–26, *25*
    Stock Exchange, *30*, 55, 57, *60*, 80, 94,
        95–96, 107–9, *109*, 202–3, *203*,
        214–15, 235, 236, 272
    Triangle Waist Company fire, 35,
        36–37, *36*
Nixon, Richard M., 125, 207, 212, 213,
    216–18, *218*, 235, 254
Nobel Prize in Economic Science,
    301–2
Northern Pacific Railroad, 2, 3, 11, 12, 13,
    13, 14, 20–21, *21*
Noyes, Alexander D., 5, 77, 78
Nylon, 83, 110–11, *110*

O
Oil industry, 207
    Alaska field near Prudhoe Bay, *168*,
        169, 193–94
    deregulation, 207, 231, 233–34, *234*
    embargo, 231–32, 235, 255
    gas shortages, 1970's, *206*, 207, 231,
        234
    Great Depression, 86, 92–93
    Organization of Petroleum
        Exporting Countries (OPEC),
        169, 173–74, *174*, 231–32, 255

Persian Gulf War, 285
    price hikes, 207, 216, 233–34, 257
    profits, 231
    Texas, price decline, 276
Organization of Petroleum Exporting
    Companies (OPEC). *See* Oil
    industry.
Otis elevators, 25, *25*

P
Paley, William, 116–18, *116*
Pan American Airways, 112–13, *112*, 161,
    187–88, *187*
Panic of 1901, 11, 12, 14
Panic of 1907, 11, 30–31
Penn Central Railroad, 211–13, *213*
Pennsylvania coal strike, 15–16, *16*
Pennsylvania Railroad, 39, 149
Persian Gulf War, 285
Pesticides industry, 175–76
Philip Morris, 281, 289–90
Photocopying, 115, 135–36
Photography
    Eastman Kodak, 130, 131
    instant cameras (Land camera or
        Polaroid), 8, 115, 130–31, *130*
    Sony digital, 283
Polaroid Corporation, 130, 235, 236
Price-fixing, 169, 170–72, *172*
Proxy battles, 147–48, 153–54

R
Radio, 35, 61, 67–68, *67*
    clock trade hurt by, 68
    first stations, 67
    microwave, 264
    monopoly in broadcasting broken,
        116–18, *116, 118*
    smallest, 143
    transistors, 115, 128, 143
Railroads. *See also specific railroads.*
    coal and, 15, 16
    computerization, 160–61
    decline of, 139, 149, 211–13, *213*
    Federal regulation, 90
    government ownership, 211
    oil companies and, 39
    proxy battles, 147–48, 149, *149*
    strike, 115
    trusts and mergers, 11, 12, 13, *13*, 14,
        14, 20–21, *21*, 43–44
    World War I, 58

RCA (Radio Corporation of America),
    4, 143, 144–46, *144*, 160
Reading Railroad (Philadelphia &
    Reading), 15, 16, 44
Reagan, Ronald, 256, *257*, 278
Reed, John S., 309–11, *310*
Renault, 167
Resolution Trust Corporation (savings
    and loan bailout), 276–78
Reuther, Walter P., 150, 151
RJR Nabisco, 4, 279–81
R. J. Reynolds, 281, 289–91
    Joe Camel advertising halt, 289, 291,
        291
Rockefeller, John D., ix, 11, 35, 38, 39, *39*
Roosevelt, Franklin D., 11, 83, 86, 87,
    88–91, *89*, 92–93, 96, 103, 123–24,
    155
Roosevelt, Theodore, 11, 15, 20, *21*, 28, 35
Russia, post-Soviet breakup, financial
    woes, 303

S
Sales, door-to-door, 191–92, *191*
Salomon Brothers, 280, 301, 303–4, 310
Salomon Smith Barney, 309
Samuelson, Paul, 301–2
Sarnoff, David, 116–18, *118*, 144, 146
    predictions for technology, 146
Saudi Arabia, 173, 231–32
Savings and loan failures, 276–78
Scholes, Myron S., 301–2, 303
Sculley, John, 265
Sears, Roebuck, & Company, 139, 153
Securities and Exchange Commission
    (S.E.C.), 94–96, 107, 238, 250
    crash of 1987 and, 274
    insider trading, Dirks, 227, 229, 230
    insider trading, Milken and Boesky,
        286–88, *288*
    outlaws fixed commissions, 207,
        214–15
Shearson Lehman Hutton, 280
Shell Oil Company, 252
"Silent Spring" (Carson), 175–76
Silver market/prices, 245, 249–50
Simon, William, 4
Sinclair, Upton, 27, 28, *28*
Singer Building, New York City, *10*,
    24, 25
Skyscrapers, *10*, 11, 24–26, *25*
Sloan, Alfred P., 103
Smoot-Hawley Tariff Act, x, 83, 84–85

Social Security Act, 83
Solomon, David, 287
"Snow White and the Seven Dwarfs"
    (movie), 99, 101, *101*, 102
Sony Corporation, 8, 143, *282*
    Columbia Pictures and CBS Records
        acquisitions, 282–83
    consumer electronics industry, 283
    DVD player, 318
    Microsoft competition, 317–19
    Playstation, 318
    Walkman, 283
Soviet Union (U.S.S.R), 125, 173–74, 285
Standard Oil Company, ix, 11, 35, 38–40,
    39, 252
Steel industry, *59*
    antitrust case, 61, 65–66, *66*
    federal seizure of mills, 139, 140–42,
        142
    Kennedy confrontation with, 177–86
Stock market
    Apple Computer, 265
    Avon Products, 191, 235
    bear market, 1970's, 207, 235–37
    brokerage firms go public, 169,
        202–3
    broker competition, 214–15, 237
    bull market, 1920's, 61, 77, 78–79
    bull market, 1950's, 139, 235
    bull market, 1960's, 202–3, *203*, 235
    bull market, 1980's, 272–75
    bull market, 1990's, 285, 296, 305–6
    conglomerates, 195–99
    crash, 1929, *60*, 77–81, *78, 79, 80*,
        235, 273
    crash, 1987, 245, 272–75, *274*, 305
    derivatives, 301–2, 304
    Dow Jones Industrials, 77, 83, 195,
        207, 235, *237*, 245, 272, 275, 305
    Equity Funding Corp. scandal,
        227–30
    fixed trading fees outlawed, 207,
        214–15
    Ford Motor Company, 156–57
    hedge funds, 301, 303–4
    I.B.M., 265
    insider trading, Dirks, 227, 229,
        230
    insider trading, Milken and Boesky,
        286–88, *288*
    Japanese, 245, 282, 295–97, *296*
    McDonald's Corporation, 189
    Microsoft Corporation, 265
    New York Central Railroad, 147

New York Stock Exchange, *30*, 55,
    57, *60*, 94, 107, 202–3, *203*, 214–15,
    236, 272
"nifty fifty," 235
Northern Pacific "corner," 12, 13
Panic of 1901, 11, 12, 13, 14
Panic of 1907, 11, 30–31
Penn Central, 211, 213
Polaroid Corporation, 235
public investment in, 285, 305–6
RJR Nabisco, 281
S.E.C. *See* Securities and Exchange
    Commission.
selling short, 12, 42, 94, 95
"Silver Thursday," 249–50
Wednesday closings of exchange,
    169, 202–3
Whitney scandal, 107–9, *109*
World War I and, 55–57
Sun Microsystems, 283, 308, 312
Supreme Court decisions
    antitrust case, baseball, 222–23
    antitrust case, Northern Securities,
        20–21
    antitrust case, Standard Oil, 38–40
    antitrust case, U. S. Steel, 61, 65–66,
        66
    biotech patents, 251, 252, *252*
    federal seizure of steel mills
        (*Youngstown Co. v. Sawyer*),
        140–42
    gold payments stopped (*Norman v.
        the Baltimore & Ohio Railroad*),
        86, 97–98
    insider trading and Dirks, 227, 229,
        230
    interstate commerce (lottery suit,
        Champion v. Ames), 11, 17–19
    labor law (*Lochner* v. *State of New
        York*), 11, 22, 23, *23*
Sylvania, 144

T
Taft, William Howard, 35, 40, *49*
Taft-Hartley Act, 115, 132–34, *132*,
    150
Taxes
    cut, 1960's, 169
    cut, 1970's, 216–18
    import, 218
    income, 35, 45, 46–47
    levies on industry, 91
    repeal on automobile, 217–18

Taylor, Frederick W., 32, *32*
Teamsters Union, 150, 153
Telephone and telecommunications
    industry, 70, 262–64
Television, 61, 67, 68–71, *69*, 83, 144–46,
    144
    cable industry, 259–61
    PC's surpass purchase of, 317
    VCR's, 8, 283
Tennessee Valley Authority (T.V.A.), 90
Textile industry, 93
    nylon and synthetic fiber, 110–11,
        110
Thailand, 299–300, *299*
Time Inc., 225–26, 314
Time Warner, 259
Tobacco industry, 279, 281, 289–91. *See
    also specific companies.*
    Joe Camel advertising, 289, 291, *291*
Tobin, James, 178, 180
Trade and tariffs, x, 45–46, 83, 84–85
Transistors, 115, 128, 143, 264
Travelers Group Inc., 309–11
Treaty of Versailles and German
    reparations, x, 61, 62–64
Triangle Waist Company fire, 35, 36–37,
    36
Truman, Harry S., 132, 139, 140–42, 151
Turner, Ted, 259–61, *261*

U
Underwood-Simmons Tariff bill, x,
    45–46
Union Pacific Railroad, 12, 57
United Automobile Workers, 219–21,
    220, 246, 247
United Brands Company, 238, *240*
United Mine Workers, 15, 16
United Nations, 125–26
United States Steel Corporation
    (U.S. Steel), 1, *59*, 61, 65–66, *66*,
    77, 169, 177–86
United Steelworkers of America,
    140–42, *142*
"Unsafe at Any Speed" (Nader), 164
Untermyer, Samuel, 41–44, *44*

V
Venezuela, 173–74
Vietnam War, 169, 254
Volcker, Paul A., 207, 241–43, *241*, 274
Volkswagen, *164, 167*

W

Wall Street. *See* New York Stock Exchange; Stock Market.
Warner Brothers, 67, 71
Weill, Sanford I., 309–11, *310*
Western Electric Company, 67, 68, 71
Westinghouse Electric Company, 170–72, *172*
Whitney, Richard, 107–9, *109*
Wiggin, Albert H., 94–95, *94*
Willow Run bomber plant, 119–22
Willys-Overland Motors, *122*

Wilson, Charles E., 139, 307
Wilson, Woodrow, 35, 45, *45*, 47, 48–49, *49*, 64
Wolfson, Louis E., 153–54, *154*
Women
    appointed to NY Central board, 148
    fashion, 72–74, 110, 111
    management positions, 200–201
    World War II and, 119, 122, *121*
World Bank, 125–26, *125*
World War I, 35, 55, 56, *56*, 57
World War II, 115

industry's war effort, 119–22, *121*, *122*
    wage and price controls, 123–24
World Wide Web (WWW), 314
Wozniak, Stephen, 2

X

Xerography. *See* Photocopying.
Xerox Corporation, 135, *135*, *137*, 195

Y

Young, Robert R., 3, 147–48, *147*

Byline Index

Andrews, Edmund L., 315
Barclay, Hartley W., 135
Barmash, Isadore, 191, 204, 205
Bedingfield, Robert E., 147, 153, 187
Bender, Marylin, 200, 208
Bennett, Robert A., 257
Bradley, John A., 158
Brown, Cyril, 75
Carmical, J. H., 173
Carroll, Wallace, 177
Catledge, Turner, 92
Charlton, Linda, 211
Clines, Francis X., 288
Cohen, Roger, 210
Cole, Robert J., 214, 227
Cowan, Edward, 231
Crowther, Bosley, 102
Dale, Edwin L., Jr., 218
De Maria, Lawrence J., 272
Dougherty, Philip H., 226
Durso, Joseph, 224
Eichenwald, Kurt, 286
Elliott, Stuart, 291
Freeman, William M., 162
Gargan, Edward A., 299
Gelman, Eric, 273
Gilpin, Kenneth N., 270, 310
Gould, Jack, 143, 144
Greenhouse, Linda, 230
Hazen, Charles Downer, 62

Henriques, Diana B., 303
Hilts, Philip J., 289
Holusha, John, 248
Ingraham, Joseph C., 166
Jensen, Michael C., 238
Jones, Brendan M., 159
Kennedy, T. R., Jr., 127
Kleinfield, N. R., 292
Koppett, Leonard, 222
Krock, Arthur, 97
Laurence, William L., 130
Lee, John M., 175
Lewis, Anthony, 170
Loftus, Joseph A., 140
Lohr, Steve, 249, 307, 312
Markoff, John, 312, 314, 317
Miller, Judith, 242, 246
Morgenson, Gretchen, 275
Nagle, James J., 189
Nash, Nathaniel C., 276, 278
Naughton, James M., 216
Nemy, Enid, 72, 305
Norris, Floyd, 190, 281
Noyes, Alexander D., 78
O'Brien, Timothy L., 309
Ostrolenk, Bernhard, 90
Oulahan, Richard V., 84
Pace, Eric, 225
Parisi, Anthony J., 251
Passell, Peter, 301

Pollack, Andrew, 137, 262, 266
Porter, Russell, 106, 125
Raskin, A. H., 150, 156
Rattner, Steven, 241
Reston, James, 182, 185
Robards, Terry, 202
Robbins, L. H., 99
Rutter, Richard, 164
Salmans, Sandra, 259
Salpukas, Agis, 219
Sanger, David E., 265, 282
Segal, Harvey H., 195
Shalett, Sidney M., 119
Shenon, Philip, 278
Silk, Leonard, 254, 255
Smith, William D., 193
Stark, Louis, 103, 134
Sterngold, James, 279
Strom, Stephanie, 298
Treaster, Joseph B., 309
Tolchin, Martin, 233
Tomasson, Robert E., 234
Trussell, C. P., 123
Uchitelle, Louis, 292
Vartan, Vartanig G., 235
White, William S., 132
Wright, Robert A., 188
WuDunn, Sheryl, 295
Wyatt, Edward, 305
Zipser, Alfred R., 160